THE REALM OF CRIMINAL LAW

The Realm of Criminal Law

R A DUFF

OXFORD
UNIVERSITY PRESS

OXFORD
UNIVERSITY PRESS

Great Clarendon Street, Oxford, OX2 6DP,
United Kingdom

Oxford University Press is a department of the University of Oxford.
It furthers the University's objective of excellence in research, scholarship,
and education by publishing worldwide. Oxford is a registered trade mark of
Oxford University Press in the UK and in certain other countries

First Edition published in 2018

Published in the United States of America by Oxford University Press
198 Madison Avenue, New York, NY 10016, United States of America

British Library Cataloguing in Publication Data
Data available

Library of Congress Control Number: 2018936196

ISBN 978–0–19–957019–5

Acknowledgements

This book is the final (long overdue) formal outcome of a project on *Criminalization*, funded by the Arts and Humanities Research Council (AHRC),[1] on which Lindsay Farmer, Sandra Marshall, Massimo Renzo, Victor Tadros, and I along with two PhD students (Andrew Cornford and Christine Kelly) spent four fruitful years. We contracted with Oxford University Press to publish a series of seven volumes: four edited collections from the workshops and the conference organized during the project, and three monographs written by members of the project. The four volumes and two of the monographs have been published;[2] this is the third monograph.

I have incurred a large number of debts during the book's long gestation period—more than I can hope to acknowledge explicitly here. I am grateful to the AHRC for the grant that made our project, and thus this book, possible. I am grateful to all those who took part in the project's various meetings, workshops, and conference, for a series of fascinating and fruitful conversations from which I learned a lot. I am grateful to the audiences and participants at a number of conference papers, seminars, and lectures (which the fallibility of my memory and my record-keeping prevents me from listing here) that I gave while I was or should have been writing the book for many helpful comments. I am grateful to the institutions with which I have been associated during the last ten years, since I began thinking about the book: to the University of Stirling Philosophy Department, which has provided a stimulating, supportive, friendly philosophical environment during all my time there; the University of Minnesota's Law School, where I gained much from interactions with a set of always interesting and interested faculty; and the University of Edinburgh's Law School, where I have enjoyed seminars and discussions with friendly and welcoming colleagues. I am especially grateful to the Israel Institute for Advanced Studies in Jerusalem, where I wrote most of a draft of the book while taking part in a collaborative project on *The Legitimization of Modern Criminal Law*. The Institute provides a wonderful intellectual environment in which to work, think, and talk—for which thanks are due to all its staff, and especially to its director, Michal Linial; and I was able to have long conversations with a splendid group of scholars—Vincent Chiao, Leora Dahan-Katz, Talia Fisher, Miri Gur-Arye, Alon Harel, Tatjana Hörnle, Doug Husak, Sandra Marshall, Jonathan Simon, and Ekow Yankah. Alon Harel also kindly organized a workshop, under the aegis of the *Jerusalem Review of Legal Studies*, at which a late draft of the book was discussed: I'm grateful to my commentators at that workshop—Miri Gur-Arye, Re'em Segev, Shachar Eldar, and Vincent Chiao.

A very special debt is owed to my collaborators on the *Criminalization* project, and to the three (Lindsay Farmer, Sandra Marshall, and Victor Tadros) with whom I worked on our previous project, *The Trial on Trial*. Apart from the fun we had working together on these projects, I have learned an enormous amount from them—although they might well add, when they read this book, that I have clearly not learned enough

[1] AHRC Grant No. 128737.

[2] *The Boundaries of the Criminal Law* (2010), *The Structures of the Criminal Law* (2011), *The Constitution of the Criminal Law* (2013), *Criminalization: The Political Morality of the Criminal Law* (2014); and L Farmer, *Making the Modern Criminal Law: Criminalization and Civil Order* (2016), V Tadros, *Wrongs and Crimes* (2017).

from them; while the book might have been better if I had paid more attention to some of their suggestions, it would have been very much worse without them.

I have drawn (sometimes heavily, sometimes lightly) on several previously published papers and book chapters (full details are given in the Bibliography)—'Relational Reasons and the Criminal Law'; 'Towards a Modest Legal Moralism'; 'Criminal Responsibility and the Emotions'; 'Legal Moralism and Public Wrongs'; and 'Discretion and Accountability in a Democratic Criminal Law'.

Also three papers co-authored with Sandra Marshall—'"Abstract Endangerment", Two Harm Principles, and Two Routes to Criminalisation'; 'Civic Punishment'; and 'Criminalizing Hate'.

I am grateful to the publishers of these journals and books for permission to use this material.

I am also grateful to Eve Ryle-Hodges and her colleagues at Oxford University Press for their help, and their patience, during the process of completing and publishing this book.

Finally, I should record (again) my largest debt to Sandra Marshall. As noted above, she was formally co-author of three papers from which I have drawn in parts of this book, but her contribution to the book goes far beyond that: apart from reading a penultimate draft, and so saving me from at least some of my errors and unclarities, she has discussed every aspect of the book with me over the years, and has been a constant source of stimulation, inspiration, sound advice, and moral support. I truly don't know what I would have done without her, but do know that (among other things) I would not have written this book: from which it follows, of course, that she must share in whatever discredit, as well as whatever credit, flows from it.

RAD

Contents

Introduction

A Theory of Criminalization?

In 2000, Andrew Ashworth asked whether English criminal law is a lost cause.[1] His question was provoked by the 'unprincipled and chaotic construction of the criminal law' in England in recent years; and his answer was that whilst the criminal law was indeed in practice, 'from the point of view of principle', a lost cause, it was still worth trying to 'identify a principled core of criminal law'.[2] Such a pessimistic view of our contemporary criminal law is shared by many in both Britain and the United States:[3] it is sometimes expressed by saying that we face a crisis of 'over-criminalization' (but I will say a bit more later about the scope of this 'we').

To say that we face a crisis of over-criminalization is to say that the scope of our criminal law is too wide: we criminalize too many types of conduct that should not be criminal.[4] One version of this criticism is that we are creating too many criminal offences, but it might not be best, or fully, expressed in those terms. For, first, it is surprisingly hard to determine just how many new offences are created each year, or how significantly the rate of crime-creation has increased in recent decades.[5] Second, at least some new offences seem to be created for very good reasons: for just two instances, the creation of the new, distinct offences of 'stalking',[6] and of 'revenge porn',[7] were intended to bring within the explicit, condemnatory scope of the criminal law kinds of conduct that surely deserve to be marked and treated as criminal. Third, over-criminalization can result not from the creation of too many offences, but from the over-broad definition of offences that are intended to deal with a properly criminalizable mischief: in trying to make sure that the statute leaves no gaps through which wrongdoers can escape, and that it can be more easily enforced, the legislature produces an over-broad specification of the kind of conduct that is to count as

[1] A J Ashworth, 'Is the Criminal Law a Lost Cause?'.

[2] 'Is the Criminal Law a Lost Cause?', 225, 253.

[3] For two American examples, see D Husak, *Overcriminalization: The Limits of the Criminal Law*, ch. 1; W Stuntz, *The Collapse of American Criminal Justice*. But for a rather more optimistic view, see D K Brown, 'Democracy and Decriminalization'.

[4] In talking of 'conduct' here I do not mean to beg any questions about the proper objects of criminalization—for instance by assuming that only 'acts' may properly be criminalized: 'conduct' should be treated here simply as a placeholder for whatever can be criminalized, whether or not it involves what we might normally count as a kind of 'conduct'.

[5] See especially J Chalmers and F Leverick, 'Tracking the Creation of Criminal Offences', and 'Quantifying Criminalization'; J Chalmers, '"Frenzied Law Making": Overcriminalization by Numbers'; J Chalmers, F Leverick, and A Shaw, 'Is Formal Criminalisation Really on the Rise? Evidence from the 1950s'. See also Husak, *Overcriminalization*, 8–11.

[6] Protection of Freedom Act 2012, ss 111–12, amending Protection from Harassment Act 1997.

[7] Criminal Justice and Courts Act 2015, s. 33; Abusive Behaviour and Sexual Harm (Scotland) Act 2016, s. 2.

criminal;[8] or it makes liability strict, thus failing to require the kind of culpability that could warrant criminal conviction.[9]

Despite the difficulty of formulating the charge of over-criminalization precisely, it does seem hard to resist the argument that our laws define as criminal too many types of conduct that should not be criminalized. This matters for a variety of familiar reasons, apart from the very substantial costs involved in administering such an expansive criminal law: two reasons can be noted here. First, such over-criminalization exposes too many people to the prospect of prosecution, conviction, and punishment for conduct that does not merit such a response: a response that can be destructively oppressive, given the character of our penal institutions,[10] and that can bring in its train a host of other damaging effects—the 'collateral consequences' of criminal convictions and criminal records.[11] Second, since it would be impossible, given the sheer quantity of conduct that satisfies the formal definition of some criminal offence, to detect and prosecute even the majority of criminal offences, such an over-broad criminal law gives a wide (and inadequately accountable) discretion to police and prosecutors in deciding what (and whom) to investigate and prosecute, enormous power to prosecutors to 'bargain' (or coerce) guilty pleas to enable the criminal process to function at all,[12] and a potentially oppressive weapon to police to control or coerce by wielding the threat of prosecution.

There is, however, from a normative theorist's point of view, a deeper problem with our contemporary practices and policies of criminalization, which underlies their tendency to excess. It concerns not the sheer quantity of criminalization, but the quality of the decision processes that lead to the creation of new crimes: the problem is not (or not only) that we criminalize too many types of conduct that should not be criminal, or have created a criminal law so expansive that we cannot enforce it with tolerable justice and efficiency, but that our criminalization decisions have become (were they ever not?) unprincipled. This is the point of Ashworth's reference to the 'unprincipled and chaotic construction of the criminal law',[13] and William Stuntz's comment that 'American criminal law's historical development has borne no relation to any plausible normative theory, unless "more" counts as a normative theory'.[14] The challenge then will be not so much to try directly to reduce the scope of the criminal law, but to work to develop a more principled criminal law. One way to do this is to try to develop a normative theory of criminalization—a theory that will provide principles by which criminalization decisions should be structured and guided. It is quite likely that this would result in a criminal law that was in various ways more modest in its scope than the law we now have: whilst we might see principled reason to criminalize some types of conduct that are not now criminal, we would also probably see principled reason to decriminalize more types of conduct that are now criminal. (A more principled approach should also result in a criminal law, and a set of institutions of criminal justice,

[8] For a striking example, see Offensive Behaviour at Football and Threatening Communications (Scotland) Act 2012 (now repealed). For a related phenomenon, see D Husak, 'Drug Proscriptions as Proxy Crimes'.

[9] See Ashworth, 'Is the Criminal Law a Lost Cause?', 227–8; A J Ashworth and M Blake, 'The Presumption of Innocence in English Criminal Law'.

[10] See Husak, *Overcriminalization*, ch. 1. It is worth noting that this applies not just to the more serious kinds of crime that typically attract sentences of imprisonment, but also to the wide range of lower-level offences that make up the bulk of criminal courts' business: see A Natapoff, 'Misdemeanors'.

[11] See M Love et al, *Collateral Consequences of Criminal Convictions: Law, Policy and Practice.*

[12] See Husak, *Overcriminalization*, 22–4, and further references there.

[13] 'Is the Criminal Law a Lost Cause?', 225.

[14] W Stuntz, 'The Pathological Politics of Criminal Law', 508.

that bear less harshly and less destructively on those who are accused or convicted of crimes.) We should not assume in advance, however, that this would be so: for the aim is not to achieve a narrower criminal law as such, but to achieve a criminal law that is more firmly grounded in, and guided by, a set of appropriate principles. We might not hope, realistically, that legislators and others involved in the creation and administration of criminal law could be persuaded to consider and adopt such a theory; but we might hope that it could provide a helpful structure, and foundation, for the critical examination of our current law, and for arguments aimed at its reform.

It was in the hope of developing such a theory that we embarked on the *Criminalization* project from which this book has emerged: our declared (and naïve) 'first objective' was 'to develop a normative theory of criminalization: an account of the principles and values that should guide decisions about what to criminalize and about how to define offences'.[15] We did not develop such a theory, although we did—we believe—achieve the more modest objective of 'working towards an overarching, theoretically informed, normative perspective' on 'the proper scope and structure of criminal law'.[16] Nor will this book offer such a theory—if that would involve providing a coherent set of substantive principles from which we could then derive substantive criteria by which to determine which kinds of conduct should, or should not, be criminalized. It will offer a 'master principle' of criminalization, which specifies what could give us good reason in principle to criminalize a type of conduct; but that principle will be a thin, formal principle that leaves most of the substantive work still to be done. It will also offer a theory of criminalization, as part of a theory of criminal law: an account, that is, of the proper role of criminal law in a democratic polity, and on that basis an account of how such a polity should set about deciding what kinds of conduct to criminalize. For reasons that should become apparent during the course of the book, however, the theory will not include the kind of substantive principle of criminalization that we might have hoped to establish.

Before saying a little more about the structure and contents of the book, and the kind of theory that it offers, I should say something brief about method.

Philosophers who seek to develop normative theories of criminal law are often accused of failing to take historical contingencies seriously enough. They offer, critics object, theories of 'criminal law' as if they were theorizing, from a position of Olympian detachment, about a practice or institution of an abstract kind, lacking historical and geographical location. They fail to attend to the implications of the fact that what they are theorizing is an actual practice or institution, or more precisely a diverse range of practices and institutions, located within wider sets of legal and social practices and institutions, and formed by complex historical contingencies: if we are to understand criminal law (which will always inevitably be to understand the criminal laws of particular societies), the role it plays or the aims it can serve, we must understand its historical development and its current sociological actuality.[17] Philosophical theorists

[15] This was how we described our aims in our original application for Arts and Humanities Research Council funding; for further details on the project (conducted by Lindsay Farmer, Sandra Marshall, Massimo Renzo, and Victor Tadros), see the Acknowledgements for this book, and R A Duff et al, 'Introduction: Towards a Theory of Criminalization'.

[16] Through the four edited volumes and three monographs that have emerged from the project (for details see the Acknowledgements), as well as the meetings and workshops that we organized.

[17] For different versions of this kind of critique, see N Lacey, 'In Search of the Responsible Subject: History, Philosophy and the Social Sciences in Criminal Law Theory', 'Historicising Criminalisation: Conceptual and Empirical Issues', and *In Search of Criminal Responsibility: Ideas, Interests, and Institutions*; A W Norrie, *Crime, Reason and History: A Critical Introduction to Criminal Law*; L Farmer, 'Criminal Wrongs in Historical Perspective', and *Making the Modern Criminal Law: Criminalization and Civil Order*.

also too often fail to attend, such critics argue, to the implications of the fact that normative theorizing itself cannot but be located within a particular historical context, and thus within some particular, contingent, tradition of thought. Such critics do not aim to preclude normative theorizing about criminal law, although there are questions to ask about what kind of normative theorizing they leave room for:[18] but they insist that theorists need to recognize both the political and intellectual context from within which they theorize, and the contingent and historically conditioned character of that which they theorize.

I will not try to engage here with this critique of some kinds of philosophical theorizing, or with the larger question of what kinds of normative theorizing are possible, or fruitful, in this context,[19] but should explain the kind of theory that I hope to develop. In this as in other normative contexts, we begin to theorize not from 'nowhere',[20] but from where we happen to be: from within a particular, contingent, intellectual and political context, together with an ill-defined but limited 'we' as our interlocutors—a 'we' with whom we share enough in the way of concepts and understandings to be able to engage in the theorizing conversation. We begin to theorize not with nothing (not with a *tabula rasa* on which we can then inscribe brand new institutions and practices), but with what we have: with a contingent, historically formed, set of practices and institutions—in the present case, with the practices and institutions that make up 'our' criminal law. The beginnings of our theorizing are thus local or parochial. But that is not to say that we cannot hope to transcend those local beginnings, to engage with a wider 'we', with interlocutors from different traditions and different starting points, with whom we find that we can converse and from whom we can learn; that we cannot aspire to take a broader view—if not 'from nowhere', then at least from a perspective broader than that from which we began. Nor is it to say that we must take for granted as an unchangeable given the particular institutions and practices with which we begin. First, we can hope to engage in a process of 'rational reconstruction' of those institutions and practices:[21] to excavate, or (re-)construct, the goals and values by which they purport to be structured; to construct on that basis a theoretical account of what 'our' criminal law claims to aspire to be, and in the light of that account to critically evaluate our existing practices, by way of an 'immanent critique'. Second, since our criminal law is part not only of a whole legal system, but of the political structure of a polity, we can extend our rationally reconstructive enterprise to theorize the criminal law in terms of its role in that larger context, and in the light of political values that we can discern in or reconstruct from that political structure—already a somewhat Herculean enterprise.[22] Third, we can reach beyond these localized practices and values, to engage with others with which we find that conversation is possible. We can recognize that other systems of criminal law differ from ours; that even central features of our own practice are contingent rather than necessary (something that awareness of the historical contingency of our practices should already have brought home to us): we can thus be led

[18] See C Kennedy, 'Immanence and Transcendence: History's Role in Normative Legal Theory'; also A W Norrie, 'Criminal Law and Ethics: Beyond Normative Assertion and its Critique'. For a good example of historically informed normative theorizing about the functions of criminal law, see V Chiao, *Criminal Law in the Age of the Administrative State*.

[19] See R A Duff, 'Theorizing Criminal Law'.

[20] See famously T Nagel, *The View from Nowhere*; also B Williams, *Descartes: The Project of Pure Enquiry*.

[21] See D N MacCormick, 'Reconstruction after Deconstruction: A Response to CLS'; below, Chapter 1 at n. 7.

[22] See R M Dworkin, *Law's Empire*, esp chs 7–10.

to imagine ways of changing, and improving, our own practices. We can and must also engage with political theory: in what kind of polity, structured by what values, can or should we aspire to live; what kind of criminal law, serving what kinds of goal, would be appropriate to such a polity?

Thus whilst we must start from where we are, we can and must transcend that very local starting point to engage in wider conversation with wider sets of interlocutors, and to theorize our existing institutions and practices in the light of wider theoretical understandings—in the end, as we will see in more detail later, in the light of political theory. One question I cannot pursue here concerns the ideal end points of such theorizing. Can we hope that, from such local starting points, we can work towards a universal theory of criminal law: a theory not of the precise institutional forms that criminal law must take in any polity, since those must depend on local contingencies, but at least of the basic structure and aims of criminal law, of the values and principles by which criminal law should be structured, at all times and all places? Can we hope to work towards a universal political theory, of the kind on which a universal account of criminal law must depend: a theory of how any polity should be structured, of the values that any polity should pursue? Or should we only aspire, more modestly but still ambitiously, to work towards an account of the role that criminal law should play, and the values, goals and principles that should structure it, in a more particular kind of polity, and towards a political theory that would make normative sense (at least to us) of such a polity—towards, that is, an account of a kind of polity, and a kind of criminal law, in and with which we (as the kind of human beings we are) could plausibly aspire to live?[23]

(This way of putting the matter might seem to beg the question: to 'beg the institution',[24] by assuming that a plausible political theory will justify criminal law—that the kind of polity in which we could plausibly aspire to live will include a system of criminal law. This would be to illegitimately rule out in advance any argument that what we should really seek to do is not to maintain or reform our criminal law, but to replace it by other more constructive, less destructively oppressive, ways of governing ourselves and dealing with each other: but such arguments must be addressed, not ignored.[25] In what follows I will try to justify, rather than simply assume, criminal law as an important element in a polity's structures of governance, by showing how it is distinctively suited to serve certain important ends.)

I will not comment here on the viability of aspirations to a universalist theory of criminal law (though I have grave doubts about them): my aims are more modest, and thus in a sense more parochial. I will offer a conception of criminal law as a distinctive kind of institution: a conception that is grounded, via a kind of rational reconstruction, in what I take to be central aspects of 'our' Anglo-American systems of criminal law; that I believe is also recognizable in other legal systems, notably those of other contemporary western democracies; but that I do not claim to be an account of what criminal law must be at all times or places. I will also offer an account of the kind of polity in which criminal law, as thus conceived, can play an important and

[23] And, perhaps (though this is not something I will tackle here), an account of certain minimal normative constraints or demands that any human polity ought to respect—for instance those that formal declarations of human rights aim to capture.

[24] See M M Mackenzie, *Plato on Punishment*, 41 (talking about justificatory theories of punishment).

[25] 'Abolitionism' is more familiar in relation to criminal punishment than to criminal law as such: but radical abolitionist theorists can be read as advocating, in the end, the abolition of the whole apparatus of criminal law in favour of practices of conflict resolution and repair. See e.g. N Christie, 'Conflicts as Property'; L Hulsman, 'Critical Criminology and the Concept of Crime'.

valuable role: that account draws on republican political theory, but it is not offered as a would-be universalist account of the form that any polity ought to take—only as an account of a kind of polity to which we can plausibly aspire. Theorists with universalist ambitions might reject such an approach as unduly parochial, and as not enabling the kind of foundational theorizing about what criminal law ought to be, and the kind of fundamental critique of our existing laws, that an adequately grounded normative theory of criminal law requires. My response to that kind of criticism consists in the remainder of this book, which will show how far we can get, how deep we can dig, and how fruitfully critical a perspective we can attain, from such local beginnings—how far the initially parochial can become, if not universal, at least not *merely* parochial.

These rather gestural remarks about method should become less obscure as I explain the structure of the book and the way in which I will build a normative account of criminal law—the task to which I must now turn.

Chapter 1 develops a conception of criminal law as a distinctive kind of legal institution, since a normative theory of criminal law must begin with some account of that which is to be theorized. This account is not meant to provide an analysis of 'the concept of criminal law'—of, for instance, the necessary and sufficient conditions for anything to count as a system of criminal law; nor is it meant to be a normatively neutral analysis that leaves entirely open the question of why criminal law might be important or valuable. Rather, it aims to identify, by a rationally reconstructive approach, what I take to be the normatively most salient dimensions of systems of criminal law like our own—dimensions, that is, not so much of the criminal law as it operates in its imperfect empirical actuality, but of the criminal law as it is supposed to be in terms of its own forms and self-presentation. On this conception the central dimensions of criminal law are the substantive law, which consists in a set not of 'prohibitions', but of declarative definitions of those 'public' wrongs that are to be formally marked in this way; the criminal process and the criminal trial, through which those accused of committing such wrongs are called formally to answer to those accusations, and to answer for those wrongs if their guilt is proved; and criminal punishment—though I resist the common idea that criminal punishment is what gives the criminal law its primary or essential purpose. I also discuss the processes of criminalization; the distinction between formal and substantive criminalization (between the law 'in the books' and the law 'in action'); and the discretion that the inevitable gaps between the law in the books and the law in action leave to officials, and to lay citizens, in determining what kinds of conduct are actually to be treated as criminal.

Chapter 2 provides a preliminary discussion of 'legal moralism'. In arguing that criminal law is concerned with wrongs, I commit myself to some version of legal moralism—to the claim that the wrongfulness of a type of conduct is essentially relevant to the legitimacy of its criminalization. This chapter draws some initial distinctions between different types of legal moralism, especially between 'negative' and 'positive' legal moralisms; it defends negative legal moralism (according to which we may not criminalize conduct that is not wrongful prior to its criminalization) against some recent criticisms; and it shows why some form of positive legal moralism, according to which the wrongfulness of a type of conduct gives us positive reason to criminalize it, is attractive. It goes on, however, to criticize the most familiar form of positive legal moralism, according to which we have good reason to criminalize *every* kind of morally wrongful conduct,[26] as being implausibly over-ambitious in relation to both the scope

[26] Michael Moore is the most prominent proponent of this species of legal moralism: see M S Moore, *Placing Blame: A Theory of Criminal Law*, 'A Tale of Two Theories'.

and the jurisdictional reach of the criminal law; and to argue that we should prefer a more modest version of positive legal moralism according to which criminal law is properly concerned only with 'public' wrongs. The idea of a public wrong will need to be explained with some care (an explanation that will be fleshed out in the following chapters). It receives an initial explanation in this chapter through a discussion of the way in which a profession might set about drawing up a code of professional ethics—a code that defines various types of 'professional misconduct': I will argue that we can draw a useful analogy between codes of professional ethics, as concerned with kinds of wrongdoing that fall within a particular kind of practice (the practice of medicine, for instance), and criminal law, as concerned with kinds of wrongdoing that fall within or bear on the distinctive practice of civic life—of living together as members of a polity.

Chapter 3 then begins the task of explaining that distinctive kind of practice of civic life, by looking first at the identity of those who participate in it—at what it is to be a member of such a practice. It argues that just as medical practitioners are the primary addressees (and owners) of a code of medical ethics, citizens are the primary addressees (and owners) of the criminal law. This argument requires a discussion of the normative basis on which the ambit and jurisdiction of domestic systems of criminal law can be properly determined, in particular of the rationale of the Territoriality Principle, which formally grounds ambit and jurisdiction in territory rather than citizenship (and of the various exceptions and qualifications to that principle). It also requires an account of citizenship, as membership of a distinctive kind of political, civic practice, and of the terms in which the criminal law should address the citizens whose law it is supposed to be. This inevitably leads into a discussion of the status of those who are not (at least not formally) citizens of the polity by whose laws they are nonetheless bound, and protected, whilst they are within its territory; of how the criminal law ought to address (and how their fellow citizens ought to address) those who dissent from the law's content, or deny its authority; and of the by now notorious distinction that Günther Jakobs has drawn between 'criminal law for citizens' (*Bürgerstrafrecht*) and 'criminal law for enemies' (*Feindstrafrecht*).[27]

Chapter 4 offers an initial account of the kind of practice in which citizens are engaged, as citizens: the 'public realm' that constitutes their life together as citizens—a realm that, in non-totalitarian polities, occupies only a limited part of their lives. This is the realm in which criminal law operates, as a species of public law. The concept of 'civil order' is central to an understanding of this public realm: a polity's civil order consists in the normative ordering of its civic life—of its existence as a polity. That normative ordering is structured by the set of goals and values through which a polity constitutes itself (its members constitute themselves) as a political community: it can be partly defined by a written constitution, a formal statement of the fundamental goals towards which the polity's collective activities are to be oriented, and of the values by which those activities are to be governed; but it is also implicit in the polity's institutions of government, and in its citizens' shared understandings of their civic life. Such a conception of civil order, as the ordering of the polity's public realm, depends on a normative distinction between the 'public' and the 'private': we need therefore to attend to the different distinctions between 'public' and 'private' that can be drawn, and to the ways in which such distinctions are often controversial. We also need to attend to the preconditions of civil order: what kinds of agreement, what kinds of shared understanding, among the citizens are necessary if civil order is to be possible; what can

[27] See e.g. G Jakobs, '*Bürgerstrafrecht und Feindstrafrecht*'; D Ohana, 'Günther Jakobs's *Feindstrafrecht*: A Dispassionate Account'.

those who share such understandings say to those who do not? But given a viable conception of a polity's civil order, and thus of its public realm, we can make better sense of the idea of a 'public wrong', as a kind of wrong that falls within that public realm, and that violates that civil order: such wrongs are the business of the polity's criminal law.

Chapter 5 puts some more substantial flesh on the relatively formal account of civil order provided in Chapter 4, by sketching the central aspects of the civil order of a particular kind of polity—a liberal republic of free and equal citizens: it draws on the republican tradition of political thought to portray the kind of polity in which, I suggest, we can plausibly aspire to live (the kind of polity that we can plausibly aspire to create). We can then see in more detail the role that criminal law, as a distinctive legal practice of the kind described in Chapter 1, can play in such a polity, as both helping to sustain, and partly constituting, its civil order. For once we understand the idea of a public wrong, as a wrong that violates or threatens an aspect of civil order, we can see how criminal law is an appropriate way of marking and responding to such wrongs. Its central role is to provide formal declarations of some of the central norms of that civil order, as norms that define what kinds of conduct citizens are entitled to expect from each other (and from the polity); and to provide the process through which those who are accused of violating these norms can be called to formal, public account. (The fact that criminal law is concerned with only some, not all, of the norms of civil order reminds us that criminal law is not the only kind of law that deals with public wrongs, and that not all public wrongs should be defined as legal wrongs—a point that will reappear in Chapter 7.) To say that the criminal law's central role is to declare such norms and provide for those who violate them to be called to public account is to deny that criminal punishment is the primary purpose of criminal law: but given the salience of punishment in our existing systems of criminal law (and its often harshly oppressive character), I must clearly say something about the role that punishment could play in the criminal law of a liberal republic.

Chapter 6 returns, at last, to the issue of criminalization, in particular to the question of whether a normative theory of criminalization should offer some kind of 'master principle' (or set of master principles) by which criminalization deliberations could be guided. Different kinds of would-be master principle are distinguished (positive from negative, responsive from preventive, pro tanto from categorical, thick from thin); some familiar principles (notably the 'harm principle', or more precisely the harm principles) are critically discussed. The upshot of this discussion is that a master principle needs to be positive rather than purely negative, and pro tanto rather than categorical; and that even a primarily responsive master principle will have a preventive dimension. Furthermore, the only plausible kind of master principle will be very thin: it will not provide substantive criteria for criminalization, but will instead provide formal criteria that leave most of the substantive normative work in deciding what kinds of conduct are to be criminalized still to be done. This is true of the master principle that emerges from the preceding chapters of this book: we have good reason to criminalize a type of conduct if and only if it constitutes a public wrong;[28] and it constitutes a public wrong if and only if it violates the polity's civil order. This master principle is extremely thin, since it leaves the normative questions of how the polity's civil order is to be constituted, and of what kinds of conduct should be taken to violate that order, still to be decided (decided through the kind

[28] The most a master principle can plausibly offer is an account of what gives us good reason to criminalize, not of what we should criminalize all things considered.

of public deliberation by which a democratic republic should form its criminal law); but we should not expect to be able to identify a master principle that is both thick and plausible; and the thin principle suggested here can still be fruitful in identifying the kinds of argument that must be offered for or against the criminalization of a type of conduct, and the kinds of consideration that are relevant (or irrelevant) to criminalization decisions.

Chapter 7 then seeks to make good on that claim for a 'public wrongs' master principle, but only after a further essential qualification. Criminalization is just one among a range of possible responses to public wrongs, distinguished from other responses by its concentration on the wrongfulness of the criminalized conduct and the need to call perpetrators to public, censorial (and penal) account: in asking whether we have good reason to criminalize a type of conduct, we must therefore ask whether we have good reason to criminalize it *rather than* to respond in some other way; and a master principle of criminalization must help us to see how we can make that kind of 'rather than' decision. To illustrate the work that a 'public wrongs' principle can do, I then briefly discuss examples of three kinds of criminal offence. First, I discuss examples of '*mala in se*', which consist in conduct that is held to be wrongful prior to its legal regulation. These are in one way the most straightforward kinds of offence to understand and to justify, but are in two respects less straightforward than is often supposed: for the criminalization process is a process not simply of trying to capture a pre-existing moral wrong, but rather of constructing a civic conception of the relevant wrong as a public wrong; and, partly for this reason, the standard distinction between '*mala in se*' and '*mala prohibita*' (the latter being understood to consist in conduct that might be wrongful only because it is legally prohibited), whilst still important, is less clear-cut than many think it is (or should be). Second, I discuss different types of '*malum prohibitum*', involving different ways in which violations of pre-criminal regulations can constitute criminalizable wrongs: the distinction between regulation and criminalization is important here, and we must notice the different ways in which regulatory violations can be wrongful—and can be wrongful even when the conduct itself does not cause the kind of mischief at which the law is aimed. Third, I discuss some examples of 'pre-emptive' offences, which criminalize conduct that does not itself involve the kind of mischief at which the law is ultimately aimed, but that is in some way preparatory to, or increases the (perhaps still remote) risk of, that mischief: one of the ways in which the criminal law has been expanding, especially in relation to terrorism, has been in the creation of wider kinds of pre-emptive offence; it is therefore important to see how far such offences can be justified—and how their creation can be subjected to principled constraint.

As should be evident from these chapter outlines, this book does not (despite its length) offer anything like a complete theory of criminal law or of criminalization: it offers an outline, or skeleton, of such a theory, but leaves much more work to be done to put substantive flesh on those bones; my hope is that it at least makes clear what kind of further work is required, and how we should embark on it. Four more particular gaps in the book's scope should also be noted here: these topics are omitted not because they are not important, but because their inclusion would have made the book (even more) unmanageably long.

First, the book focuses almost entirely on domestic criminal law; it says very little about transnational and international criminal law, despite their significance not only in their own right, but in their ever-increasing impact on domestic criminal law. I think (or hope) that we can still discuss the domestic law of a nation state as a set of institutions that are relatively autonomous in relation to the realms of transnational and international law, although a full account of domestic law must in the end attend to its relationship to those wider realms of law.[29]

Second, in discussing the role of criminal law in the life and governance of a polity, I say nothing about policing, although this is clearly an important dimension of criminal law: one of the functions of a system of criminal law is to authorize and regulate the activities of the police in investigating and preventing crime.[30] There is certainly a need for more sustained normative theorizing about the proper role and operations of the police; but that task cannot be pursued here.[31]

Third, in discussing both perpetrators and victims of crime, I focus entirely on individual human beings; I say nothing about corporations either as criminal agents or as victims. Again, this is not because a complete theory of criminal law would not need to include an account of the ways in which criminal law can deal with corporations,[32] but because I do not have the space to tackle that large set of issues in this book.

Fourth, I say very little about the internal structure of the substantive criminal law: about just how offences should be defined, in particular what kinds of *mens rea* or fault element should be required; about how different factors that bear on liability should be allocated as between offences and defences; or about how fine grained or coarse grained our offence definitions should be. Such matters as these clearly bear on the general question of criminalization. In particular, the scope of offences, just what range of conduct they criminalize, depends significantly on how precisely or vaguely they are defined, and what kind of fault (if any) they require;[33] insofar as criminal law has a communicative dimension (as I will argue it does) the form of its offence definitions will also matter for reasons of fair labelling.[34] However, this is one more range of issues that, for reasons of space, I will not try to tackle directly in this book.

Having explained what I aim to do in this book, and noted some of the things that I will not try to, I must now turn to the actual doing of what I aim to do.

[29] But see below, Chapter 3, sections 1 and 2, for some sketchy remarks on the relationship between domestic and international criminal law.

[30] Though the responsibilities and activities of the police stretch well beyond the prevention and investigation of crime; see e.g. E J Miller, 'A Fair Cop and a Fair Trial'.

[31] See J Kleinig, *The Ethics of Policing*; A Sanders et al, *Criminal Justice*; A J Ashworth and M Redmayne, *The Criminal Process*, chs 1–6; I Loader, 'In Search of Civic Policing: Recasting the "Peelian" Principles'; C Nathan, 'Principles of Policing and Principles of Punishment'.

[32] See C Wells, *Corporations and Criminal Liability*; M D Dubber and S Stern (eds), 'Symposium: Corporate Personhood and Criminal Liability'.

[33] See at nn 8 and 9 above.

[34] See J Chalmers and F Leverick, 'Fair Labelling in Criminal Law'.

1

Criminal Law

1. Analytical Theory and Rational Reconstruction

A normative theory of criminalization—an account of the principles by which deliberations about what to criminalize should be guided—must depend on an account of what criminal law is for. What purposes should it serve; what is its proper role in the life of a political community? An account of what criminal law is for must depend on an account of what criminal law is: what are its distinguishing features as a particular kind of law? This suggests that, before we embark on the normative or 'censorial' exercise of theorizing about what criminal law ought to be, we must first engage in the analytical or 'expository' exercise of determining what criminal law is.[1] However, both the character of that analytical exercise, and the distinction between the analytical and the normative, are problematic.

The analytical exercise is an exercise in conceptual analysis. It thus cannot consist simply in an empirical or sociological description of the existing institutions and practices of criminal law; it must rather seek to pick out the characteristics of those institutions and practices in virtue of which they count as institutions and practices of criminal law. Given that those institutions and practices are local, that they vary from country to country, and that they have developed through complicated and variegated histories, one question that must arise is whether we should aspire to a universal analysis of 'criminal law' as such—one that can tell us what counts as criminal law at all times and all places; or should we aspire only to a more local, more parochial account, which tells us only about *our* criminal law (whatever the scope of that 'our' might turn out to be)?[2] In line with my modest ambitions, as sketched above,[3] I will be content to provide only a relatively local analysis, of what we can recognize as criminal law, leaving aside both the question of just how expansive that 'we' might turn out to be, and the question of whether it would be possible to develop the analysis into one that could claim universality.

Another question concerns the relationship between the descriptive, the analytical, and the normative. If we begin with a set of empirically accurate descriptions of our existing institutions and practices (those that are normally described as institutions and practices of criminal law), we might come to think that they resist any coherent analysis; and that insofar as they are susceptible to analytical understanding, they resist any favourable normative theorizing. For what we find is not so much a coherently functioning criminal justice *system*, but rather a complicated and messy collection of parts which reflect the diverse and often conflicting historical forces that produced them;

[1] On analytical as against normative criminal law theory, see D Husak, *Philosophy of Criminal Law*, 20–26; for 'expository' as against 'censorial' jurisprudence, see J Bentham, *An Introduction to the Principles of Morals and Legislation*, ch. 19.

[2] Compare J Raz, 'Can There Be a Theory of Law?' on whether theories of 'the nature of law' can be 'universal', or only 'parochial'; Bentham (n. 1 above) on 'local' as against 'universal' jurisprudence (given the diversity of laws, in both content and form, expository jurisprudence can claim universal application only if it confines its attention to 'terminology' or 'the import of words').

[3] See above, Introduction at nn 19–25.

and insofar as we can provide coherent accounts of how they operate, they will often be accounts of various kinds of coercion, oppression, or exclusion for which justificatory normative theorizing seems impossible. We can, for instance, describe the ways in which large numbers of disadvantaged and vulnerable people are processed through a system that cannot claim to treat them justly or with consideration, and from which they cannot but be alienated;[4] we can suggest sociological accounts of the interests or goals that such practices actually serve.[5] But we should not then expect to be able to develop a normative justification for criminal law as thus conceived, or to identify the purposes that it should serve; the most we can say is that if that is what criminal law is, we should strive to abolish it.

An analytical account of criminal law that is to provide a basis for normative theorizing, and leave open the possibility of offering a normative account of the goals that criminal law should serve, must therefore be selective, and normatively informed. It must be selective, since it must pick out features of our existing institutions that are relevant to their identity as institutions of *criminal law*; and it must be normatively informed, because any such selection will reflect the theorist's understanding of which features matter as potential materials for normative theory.

One approach to this selective analytical enterprise is to strip criminal law down to its bare essentials. For instance, Chiao argues that criminal law is 'a generically coercive rule-enforcing institution' (distinguished from other such institutions by the harshness of the sanctions that it imposes), whose justifying function is to 'contribute[] to making social cooperation under the rule of law possible'.[6] This minimalist account portrays criminal law as one among other kinds of technique for ensuring compliance with rules, whose justification depends on its instrumental efficacy in serving a valuable end ('social cooperation under the rule of law'), and its consistency with whatever other normative constraints we should set on the means to be used in our pursuit of that end. The point to note here, however, is that it is not (and is not intended to be) a neutral account of what criminal law is: it selects one aspect of criminal law as central, and that selection reflects a normative conception of the kind of purpose that could justify such an institution.

My approach will be different, and analytically more ambitious. I will pay more attention to features of the practices, and the language, of criminal law, to provide a 'rational reconstruction' of criminal law as a distinctive kind of institution dealing in distinctive kinds of normative claim, and apt to play a distinctive role in the legal order of a political community. This will be a matter of rational reconstruction, rather than of simple description, since it will involve both a selection of the features on which to focus, and an interpretation of those features in the light of the ends or values that they can—I will suggest—be taken to reflect.[7] It will be an exercise in conceptual analysis

[4] For a few recent examples describing American criminal justice (where the problems are more vividly extreme than in Britain) in such terms, see M Alexander, *The New Jim Crow: Mass Incarceration in the Age of Colorblindness*; W Stuntz, *The Collapse of American Criminal Justice*; A Lerman and V Weaver, *Arresting Citizenship: The Democratic Consequences of American Crime Control*; I Kohler-Hausmann, 'Managerial Justice and Mass Misdemeanors'.

[5] For just two famous examples, see M Feeley, *The Process is the Punishment: Handling Cases in a Lower Criminal Court*; and J Simon, *Governing Through Crime: How the War on Crime Transformed American Democracy and Created a Culture of Fear*.

[6] V Chiao, 'What is the Criminal Law For?', at 139 (see also 144, 159). For more detail see his *Criminal Law in the Age of the Administrative State*: a crucial constraint is that the use of criminal law to enforce the rules of our public institutions must be consistent with the principles that make those institutions valuable.

[7] See D N MacCormick, 'Reconstruction after Deconstruction: A Response to CLS'.

insofar as I will be claiming that anything that we are to count as a system of criminal law must display at least some of the features that I will highlight (although, for reasons that will emerge in what follows, it might not display them all, and the ways in which they are displayed or instantiated can differ quite radically between different systems); but my purpose here is not so much to establish a set of conceptually necessary features of criminal law, as to describe a distinctive kind of institution—one that we can recognize as a system of criminal law—whose proper role in a political community we can then usefully discuss.[8]

In the remainder of this chapter I will therefore offer a partial rational reconstruction of what I will argue are the three main dimensions of a system of criminal law—of the kind of criminal law with which we are familiar. I will not be assuming that a political community *must* have such an institution, or that it must be justifiable; for that would be to beg the institution.[9] But I aim to describe a kind of institution of which we can then plausibly ask whether, why, and how it should figure in the governing structure of a political community.

One final caution is needed, however. I will be arguing that we can spell out an appropriate role for criminal law in a contemporary, liberal political community; and I will be operating with a conception of criminal law, to be developed in this chapter, grounded in a process of rational reconstruction that begins with the kinds of criminal law with which we are familiar—with 'our' criminal law. This will not, however, amount to a justification of our criminal law as it actually exists and actually operates: it will not, that is, aim to provide a comforting justification of the status quo. A process of rational reconstruction is a process of idealization: it reconstructs what the practice or institution in question must, in terms of the values intrinsic to it, aspire to be. It is entirely likely, then, that the result of the reconstruction will differ in more or less radical ways from the practice or institution as it actually exists, in the way that ideals typically differ from actuality: it provides, not a description of that actuality, but a standard against which the actual must be judged—and will no doubt be found to be more or less seriously wanting. The kind of justification of criminal law that I will offer is therefore a justification of criminal law as it ought to be, not of criminal law as it actually is—but in terms of values that can be discerned within, or excavated from, criminal law as it actually is. If that justification, and the ideal of criminal law that it portrays, is plausible, the question then will be whether, and how, we can work to bring the actual closer to the ideal—to turn our criminal law into what it ought to aspire to be.

2. Crime, Process, and Punishment

Systems of criminal law typically have three dimensions. First, the substantive criminal law defines a range of criminal offences: it specifies the kinds of conduct that will count as criminal, the conditions given which a person counts as committing a crime, and the defences by which one who commits a crime can avoid conviction. Central

[8] This approach also enables us to describe various features, including some salient features, of our existing practices of criminal law not just as conceptually inessential aspects of those practices as practices of criminal law, but as pathologies—as ways in which those practices are defective or misdirected, distorted, or perverted, in terms of the values and purposes that are internal to the kind of practice they purport, or are supposed, to be. Hence the aptness of the title of W Stuntz, 'The Pathological Politics of Criminal Law'; see also R A Duff, 'Perversions and Subversions of Criminal Law'.

[9] See above, Introduction at n. 24.

to the substantive criminal law are the offence definitions themselves, and it is worth noting the different terms in which these may be expressed in different systems. The American Model Penal Code, for instance, declares that 'a person is guilty of', or 'commits' a specified (type of) offence, 'if . . .'. English statutes typically say that a person is, or 'shall be', 'guilty of an offence', or of a specified offence, if. . . . In the German Criminal Code, by contrast, offence definitions declare that 'Whoever [acts in the way specified] shall be liable to' a specified type of punishment; similarly, the French Penal Code's offence specifications are set in terms of what types of conduct render a person liable to what types of punishment.

These modes of offence definition are worth noting because they do not sit happily with the common idea that the substantive criminal law consists essentially in 'prohibitions'—that the criminal law 'prohibits' certain types of conduct, on pain of conviction and punishment if one does what is prohibited. If one imagines the kind of sovereign described by classical legal positivism, whose law consists in 'commands' issued to a subject population, one might indeed talk of such a sovereign's criminal law as a set of prohibitions. The same is true if we see the substantive criminal law as consisting in 'rules', insofar as those rules are taken to be addressed to citizens rather than to courts:[10] for rules are (like prohibitions) to be obeyed or disobeyed, and when what they require is that those to whom they apply refrain from certain types of conduct, we might describe them as prohibiting such conduct. Thus Robinson's *Draft Code of Conduct*, which is addressed to citizens, is set in terms of what 'you may not' do.[11] Now I have argued elsewhere that we should not see the substantive criminal law in this way,[12] and will draw on this argument later; for the moment, we need note only that it is not clear in what terms we should describe the substantive criminal law's offence definitions—as prohibitions, as declarations of what constitutes a crime, or as creating liability relations. I return to this issue in section 3, where I will also discuss the kinds of regulation, related to but not properly part of the criminal law, that are more accurately described as prohibiting (or prescribing) certain kinds of conduct.

The second dimension of criminal law is procedural: it provides for the procedures through which actual or suspected or alleged commissions of what the substantive law defines as crimes are to be formally dealt with. Some of these procedures concern the prevention, detection, and investigation of (alleged) crimes: they govern the powers and activities of the police, and of any other officials who have roles to play in investigating crime. These dimensions of criminal law or criminal justice are enormously important, and deserve more careful theoretical attention than they have often received from criminal law theorists,[13] but they will not receive that attention here. My focus will rather be on the processes that follow from the completed investigation of alleged crime, when an alleged perpetrator has been identified. The most salient and familiar of these processes (in the literature of criminal law, if not in the actual world) is the criminal trial, in which a person is formally charged with a crime, and the court before which he is accused must return a verdict as to whether or not he is (provably) guilty of that crime: if the accused person does not formally admit his guilt, the trial will involve an examination of the evidence; if (as is increasingly common in some jurisdictions) the accused person formally admits his guilt, the verdict then follows more

[10] See e.g. M Dan-Cohen, 'Decision Rules and Conduct Rules: On Acoustic Separation in Criminal Law'; P Alldridge, 'Rules for Courts and Rules for Citizens'.

[11] P H Robinson, *Structure and Function in Criminal Law*, Appendix A.

[12] See R A Duff, 'Relational Reasons and the Criminal Law', 181–3; and at nn 46–8, 50–2 below.

[13] See above, Introduction at nn 30–1.

or less directly from that formal admission. What is less clear is how we should theorize this process (and how we should theorize the kinds of plea bargaining that have in some systems more or less completely replaced the trial, as a substantive process of determining guilt). This is the topic of sections 4 and 5.

The third dimension of criminal law is penal: those who are found to have committed crimes thereby become liable to penal sanctions.[14] One question is how much we should build into our initial, analytical, specification of this dimension of criminal law: should we look for some way of distinguishing criminal punishment, properly speaking, from the kinds of 'penalty' that might be imposed by a wide range of legal or extra-legal bodies?[15] Or should we take it that criminal punishment is a type of penalty, distinguished from others only by the body that imposes it; or, perhaps, by its often greater harshness, for instance in that it can consist in imprisonment or even death?

Another question is whether punishment is a necessary or essential feature of criminal law. We can imagine a system that defines a range of 'crimes', and provides a trial process through which those accused of committing such crimes are found 'Guilty' or 'Not Guilty', but that does not make any provision for the punishment of those who are convicted: perhaps it provides for avowedly therapeutic measures to be imposed if judged to be necessary, or for some 'restorative justice' process that is avowedly non-punitive. If we accept (which might be arguable) that such measures are not 'punishments' properly speaking, must we also accept that such a system would not be a system of *criminal* law, properly speaking?[16] Some theorists do suggest that punishment is at least a definitionally essential dimension, and perhaps even the primary internal purpose, of criminal law. Thus Husak argues that '[a] law simply is not criminal unless persons who break it become subject to state punishment',[17] whilst Moore argues that the function of criminal law is to secure the deserved punishment of wrongdoers,[18] and Chiao notes that '[p]erhaps it goes without saying that the criminal law and its associated institutions ... are institutions that we have set up to punish people'.[19] In similar vein, some suggest that it is punishment that makes criminal law distinctively problematic.[20] Now it would not be fruitful to spend time on the definitional question of whether a system of law without punishment could strictly count as a system of *criminal* law; and it is certainly true that when a system of criminal law imposes punishments, especially when those punishments are as harsh and destructive as those that our criminal courts often impose, they must loom large in any normative theorizing about criminal law. I will discuss this dimension of criminal law in section 6, but will argue that we should not let criminal punishment dominate our discussion of what criminal law is, or ought to be: its other two dimensions have meanings, and can serve significant purposes, that do not depend on punishment.[21]

[14] I leave aside for the time being the fact that penal sanctions can be imposed without a trial (although typically they require a formal admission of guilt): for English law see A J Ashworth and M Redmayne, *The Criminal Process*, ch. 6; see also P Duff, 'The Prosecutor Fine'; and below, Chapter 7 at n. 30.

[15] See e.g. J Feinberg, 'The Expressive Function of Punishment', 96–8, on the difference between 'punishments' and 'penalties' (the former, but not the latter, have 'reprobative' meaning).

[16] We might note that, in German, criminal law (*Strafrecht*) does seem to entail punishment (*Strafe*).

[17] D N Husak, *Overcriminalization: The Limits of the Criminal Law*, 78.

[18] M S Moore, *Placing Blame: A Theory of Criminal Law*, ch. 1.

[19] Chiao, 'What is the Criminal Law For?', 137: Chiao does not himself favour a focus on 'punishment', given its moralistic connotations, but in arguing (see at n. 6 above) that criminal law should be understood as a 'coercive rule-enforcing institution', he makes its sanctions essential to its purpose.

[20] See e.g. Husak, *Overcriminalization*.

[21] We must also bear in mind that conviction for a criminal offence can render one liable to a range of further, 'collateral consequences'—often onerous burdens, including deportation, subjection to

Finally, something must be said about criminalization—about what it is to criminalize a type of conduct: as we will see in section 7, this is not as simple a matter as it might seem. To criminalize a type of conduct is to bring it within the reach of the criminal law; but just what kinds of process, with what kinds of result, does that involve?

An analytical account of what criminal law is should therefore have something to say about what crime is; about the criminal process; about punishment; and about criminalization. We will see just how much we can usefully say, in analytical terms, in the following sections.

3. Crime

Glanville Williams famously argued that the only accurate way to define 'crime' is in terms of its legal implications: '[a] crime then becomes an act that is capable of being followed by criminal proceedings, having one of the types of outcome (punishment etc.) known to follow these proceedings'.[22] It is no doubt true that we cannot provide a substantive definition of crime, in terms of the kinds of conduct that do or could count as criminal. It is also true, I will argue, that we should understand the idea of crime partly in such procedural terms: to criminalize some type of conduct is, in crucial part, to make its perpetrators liable to a criminal process, and that is indeed an essential part of the reason for criminalizing it. However, we can say a little more than Williams allows—albeit in formal rather than substantive terms.

We can make progress by considering the distinction that some legal systems draw (whether formally or informally) between criminal law and other modes of non-criminal regulation: in the latter kind of case, breaches of the regulations attract penalties, but the breach is not defined as a crime, and the penalty is not defined as a punishment. Thus in Germany the 1968 Regulatory Offences Act transferred various categories of offence (including many road traffic offences) from the criminal law (*Strafrecht*) to a regulatory regime (*Ordnungswidrigkeitenrecht*): what had been crimes (*Straftaten*) became regulatory infractions (*Ordnungswidrigkeiten*), and financial sanctions that had been fines (*Geldstrafen*) now became administrative penalties (*Geldbussen*).[23] Even when no such distinction is formally drawn, courts and theorists often distinguish 'real' crimes from 'quasi-crimes' or (mere) 'regulatory offences'.[24] The English Law Commission has also recommended that more use should be made, in

continued supervision or detention, or exclusion from various normal civic entitlements, but that do not formally count as part of the punishment (but see the US Supreme Court's discussion of deportation in *Padilla v Kentucky* 559 US 356 (2010)): see M Love et al, *Collateral Consequences of Criminal Convictions: Law, Policy and Practice*; Z Hoskins, *Beyond Punishment? A Normative Account of Collateral Restrictions on Offenders*, and 'Criminalization and the Collateral Consequences of Conviction'.

[22] G Williams, 'The Definition of Crime', 123. See G H Gordon, *The Criminal Law of Scotland* (3rd edn), vol. 1, 7: the 'criminal law is probably, therefore, sufficiently defined as that branch of the law which deals with those acts, attempts and omissions of which the state may take cognisance by prosecution in the criminal courts'.

[23] *Gesetz über Ordnungswidrigkeiten* (1968; consolidated in 1975). For a useful introductory (and critical) discussion, see T Weigend, 'The Legal and Practical Problems Posed by the Difference between Criminal Law and Administrative Penal Law'; see also C Steiker, 'Punishment and Procedure: Punishment Theory and the Criminal-Civil Procedural Divide'; M D Dubber and T Hörnle, *Criminal Law: A Comparative Approach*, 96–7.

[24] See the judicial dicta cited in A P Simester, 'Is Strict Liability Always Wrong?', 23–4.

'regulatory' contexts, of 'civil penalties' and other kinds of non-criminal measure, rather than resorting too quickly to the creation of new criminal offences.[25]

What is the difference between a crime and a regulatory infraction; between criminalizing a type of conduct and subjecting it to a regime of non-criminal regulation? The immediate material effect of each kind of provision might be rather similar: an official determines that a person has engaged in conduct to which the law attaches a certain sanction, such as a monetary payment, and imposes that sanction. It is true that further consequences may follow when the conduct has been defined as *criminal*: crimes might attract harsher sanctions (notably imprisonment) than can be imposed on regulatory infractions; a person who is convicted of a crime acquires a criminal record, and may face a range of further 'collateral consequences'.[26] Perhaps then the difference between crimes and regulatory infractions should be understood simply in terms of the severity of the legal consequences that can follow: we should count as crimes those kinds of conduct that can render us liable to particularly harsh penalties,[27] or to the further consequences connected to a criminal record.

This kind of account fits with the approach of the European Court of Human Rights in its interpretation of Article 6 of the European Convention on Human Rights, which guarantees a set of procedural rights and protections (grounded in the idea of 'a fair trial') to '[e]veryone charged with a criminal offence': could those 'charged' with an *Ordnungswidrigkeit* (or with violating a similar type of regulation in other jurisdictions) be denied such rights, on the grounds that they are not charged with a *criminal* offence? The Court held that, although the transfer of a type of conduct from *Strafrecht* to *Ordnungswidrigkeitenrecht* involved formal 'decriminalization', this was not enough to make Article 6 inapplicable: that would depend on such substantive factors as the nature of the offence or violation and the severity of the penalty that could be imposed.[28] On one reading, this is to define 'criminal offence' in terms of the severity of the sanctions (or other legal consequences) that can attach to a violation: the protections guaranteed by Article 6 must be available to those who face severe legal sanctions, but need not be provided to those who face only such relatively modest sanctions as a *Geldbuss*.[29]

This does not, however, provide a plausible account of what distinguishes criminal offences from other kinds of regulatory violation, or criminal law from other kinds of regulation. Those who argue (as many do argue) that we should eliminate all or most of the collateral consequences of criminal convictions or criminal records,[30] or that we should radically reduce the severity of the sentences that may be imposed on those convicted of criminal offences (including removing imprisonment as a possible

[25] Law Commission, *Criminal Liability in Regulatory Contexts*: 'regulatory contexts' are those contexts 'in which a Government department or agency has (by law) been given the task of developing and enforcing standards of conduct in a specialised area of activity' (para. 1.9).

[26] See n. 21 above. As the example of prosecutor fines (see n. 14 above) shows, criminal sanctions do not always involve either a formal conviction or a criminal record; but that might show only that what is formally classed as a crime should sometimes be understood as a 'quasi-crime'—as in substance a regulatory infraction.

[27] Compare Chiao's suggestion (see at n. 6 above) that what distinguishes criminal law from other modes of legal regulation is the harshness of the sanctions it can impose.

[28] See *Engel v Netherlands* (1979–80) 1 EHRR 647; *Öztürk v Germany* (1984) 6 EHRR 409; *Garryfallou AEBE v Greece* [1997] ECHR 18996/91; *Lauko v Slovakia* (2001) 33 EHRR 40.

[29] Compare A J Ashworth and L Zedner, 'Preventive Orders: A Problem of Under-criminalization?': one reason for bringing certain kinds of 'preventive' order within the criminal law is to provide better protection for those who are to be subjected to them.

[30] See e.g. Hoskins, *Beyond Punishment?*; J B Jacobs, *The Eternal Criminal Record*.

punishment for many offences),[31] are not arguing that we should take many existing criminal offences out of the criminal law, and transfer them to a regime of non-criminal regulation: they are arguing for a criminal law that is less harsh, less damaging, in its impact on those who commit crimes. We can agree with the plausible claim that the harsher the impact of a legal measure on those who become liable to it, the greater the procedural protections that the law should afford them; but this is tangential to the distinction between criminal law and other kinds of regulatory regime.

The Law Commission suggests a better approach to distinguishing criminal law from other modes of non-criminal regulation: 'What sets criminal laws apart from civil penalties (and from other non-criminal steps that a regulator may take to deter or encourage conduct), is that either the intention or one of the important effects of criminal conviction is to create significant stigma.'[32] The idea that criminal convictions typically involve 'stigma', in intention or in fact, is a common one, and points towards a central distinctive feature of criminal law; but it does not capture that feature accurately.

Stigma is, as the Commission implies, an *effect* of criminal conviction, and it marks those who are stigmatized (for it is people, not actions, that are stigmatized) in a way that is likely to make a significant, deleterious, difference to their social standing and relationships: to be stigmatized is to be marked as other—as someone to be treated with suspicion or hostility. It is true that this is in fact often the effect of a criminal conviction—and many think it an entirely appropriate effect of conviction for many kinds of offence; but we would do better to leave open the question of what effect a criminal conviction should have on offenders' standing or relations with their fellow citizens. Someone who argues that we should try to reduce, if not to eliminate, the stigmatic consequences of criminal conviction need not be arguing that we should turn such convictions into findings that the person violated a non-criminal regulation: she could instead be arguing about what impact a criminal conviction should have, or be intended to have. To identify this distinctive feature of criminal law and criminal convictions more precisely, we should think not about stigma, but about the meaning of a criminal conviction, which is what underpins its (typically) stigmatic effect: about the censure or condemnation that a conviction involves.

A finding that a person committed a regulatory violation and is thus liable to a penalty might or might not imply, or lead others to believe, that her conduct merits censure, or that she merits blame for engaging in it; but a criminal conviction is essentially censorious.[33] That is why the Law Commission recommended that: 'The criminal law should only be employed to deal with wrongdoers who deserve the stigma associated with criminal conviction because they have engaged in seriously reprehensible conduct. It should not be used as the primary means of promoting regulatory objectives.' Criminalization would be justified only if imprisonment (for a first offence) or an unlimited fine might be warranted given the 'seriousness of wrongdoing in issue, and its consequences'.[34] This is to say that criminal law should be concerned with culpable

[31] E.g. A J Ashworth, *What if Imprisonment were Abolished for Property Offences?*; P Ramsay, 'A Democratic Theory of Imprisonment'.

[32] Law Commission, *Criminal Liability in Regulatory Contexts*, para. 3.8.

[33] Thus in German law an *Ordnungswidrigkeit* is an unlawful action ('*rechtswidrige Handlung*'), but it need not involve the kind of guilt or fault ('*Schuld*') that a crime must involve; and its commission might, but need not always, be censurable ('*vorwerfbare*'). See *Gesetz über Ordnungswidrigkeiten* s. 1; Weigend, 'The Legal and Practical Problems Posed by the Difference between Criminal Law and Administrative Penal Law', 71–2.

[34] Law Commission, *Criminal Liability in Regulatory Contexts*, paras 1.28–29.

wrongdoing: not merely with the violation of legal regulations, but with moral wrongdoing that merits condemnation or censure.[35]

The Law Commission's proposal might be read as suggesting, in line with its reference to 'significant stigma' as a mark of a criminal conviction, that the difference between crimes and mere regulatory violations lies in the degree of seriousness of the wrong committed: both involve 'reprehensible conduct' that merits some degree of 'stigma'; but we should reserve the criminal law for those more *seriously* reprehensible types of conduct that deserve *significant* stigma. We would do better, however, to draw a more categorical distinction than that: stigma, or censure as we should rather say, is essential to a criminal conviction in the sense that the very meaning of a conviction would be undermined if a court added that the convicted defendant had done nothing wrong and was wholly non-culpable, whereas this would not be true of a finding that someone had committed a regulatory violation. That is why people may talk of 'quasi-crimes':[36] these are offences that are formally part of the criminal law, but that cannot plausibly be seen or described as censure-worthy wrongs. That is why the language of criminal statutes and codes is often close to ordinary extra-legal moral language: although the criminal law's definitions of such crimes as murder, rape, theft and so on will diverge to various degrees from (in part because they need to be more precise than) our extra-legal moral concepts, the law's conceptions are recognizable as versions of those extra-legal concepts. That is why theorists often include some notion of censure in their analytical accounts of criminal punishment:[37] a key difference between punishment and other kinds of burdensome imposition that might have very similar material forms and impacts, including civil penalties, is that punishment is intended to communicate or to express censure. That is why we should object so strongly to convictions of those who are innocent of crime; or to statutes that impose strict criminal liability, understood as liability without fault;[38] or to statutes criminalizing conduct that cannot plausibly be portrayed as wrong: the reason is not (only) that people are then subjected to the prospect of material burdens that they had no fair opportunity to avoid,[39] but that they are unjustly portrayed and censured as wrongdoers, or that their conduct is unjustly portrayed and condemned as wrong.

This is not the place for a discussion of whether we should maintain a distinct, non-criminal, system of regulatory infractions, or indeed of whether, if we are to have such a system, it should penalize only wrongful, or only culpably wrongful, conduct, and what the meaning and effects of such penalties should be; I will return to such questions later.[40] The point to note here is simply that censurable wrongfulness is integral to criminal law in a way that it is not integral to a system of non-criminal regulation. If such a system penalized conduct that was not, and was not even alleged to be or portrayed as being, wrongful, it might be objectionable (if we think that such systems should respect a 'wrongfulness constraint'):[41] but its identification as a system of non-criminal regulation leaves open the question of whether it should respect such a

[35] For a different argument to a similar conclusion, see Husak, *Overcriminalization*, 72–7; see also A P Simester and A von Hirsch, *Crimes, Harms and Wrongs: On the Principles of Criminalization*, 10–14, 20–30.

[36] See at n. 24 above.

[37] See at n. 15 above; A von Hirsch, *Censure and Sanctions*, ch. 2.

[38] See e.g. D N Husak, 'Strict Liability, Justice, and Proportionality'.

[39] Compare H L A Hart, 'Legal Responsibility and Excuses'.

[40] See generally J Horder, 'Bureaucratic "Criminal" Law: Too Much of a Bad Thing?'; also Law Commission, *Criminal Liability in Regulatory Contexts*; and see below, Chapter 7, section 2(d).

[41] On the 'wrongfulness constraint' on criminal law, see Husak, *Overcriminalization*, 73–6; and below, Chapter 2, sections 3 and 4.

constraint. By contrast, a system of criminal law that criminalizes conduct that is not wrongful is, necessarily, to that degree defective or mistaken precisely as a system of criminal law; one that criminalizes conduct that is not even alleged to be or portrayed as being wrongful is, necessarily, a perversion of criminal law.[42] That is why it is always a sound objection to a proposed or existing criminal offence that the conduct it criminalizes is not wrongful: such an objection cannot be dismissed as irrelevant, but must be answered by showing how the conduct really is wrongful.

We can distinguish a weak from a strong version of this point. The strong version holds that absence of wrongfulness is necessarily a *conclusive* objection to a proposed or existing criminal offence: one who would justify the creation or retention of the offence can coherently do so only by arguing that the conduct criminalized *is* wrongful. The weak version holds that the absence of wrongfulness is necessarily a *relevant* objection to a proposed or existing criminal offence; but it allows that the creation of the offence might nonetheless be justifiable, for the sake of some other important consideration. I will have more to say about this distinction when I come to discuss legal moralism (in Chapter 2), but we will see shortly that which of these versions is more plausible depends in part on how we understand the idea of criminalization. If the enactment of a statute that formally defines a certain type of conduct as criminal constitutes the criminalization of that type of conduct, only the weak version of the claim is plausible: for reasons to be discussed later, we cannot plausibly insist that statutory offence definitions *must* capture only wrongful conduct. But if we understand criminalization in a broader sense, to include the ways in which officials interpret and apply criminal statutes, the stronger version becomes more plausible.[43]

I am not suggesting that our existing practices of criminal justice fit this picture: it is hard to maintain that our existing laws define and treat as criminal only kinds of conduct that are, or are honestly claimed to be, censurably wrong. That is not, however, an objection to the claims made here about the connection between criminal law and wrongdoing; it is rather a mark of the way in which our existing practices are defective precisely as practices of criminal law. I have not yet argued that, or why, we should maintain a system of criminal law; that argument will come later. But *if* we are to maintain such a system, it should criminalize only censurably wrongful conduct.

The claim that part of what is distinctive about criminal law is that it portrays the conduct that it criminalizes as wrongful might seem, on the one hand, so familiar as to be hardly worth arguing at such length; or, on the other hand, manifestly false. The latter charge would be backed by suggesting that the claim seems plausible only if we focus (as so many theorists still focus) on the most familiar and uncontroversial kinds of so-called *mala in se*: crimes consisting in conduct that is (uncontroversially) wrongful independently of its criminalization. Once we attend instead to that wide range of offences (by far the majority of offences defined by the criminal law and dealt with by its courts) that are classed as *mala prohibita*, since they consist in conduct that might well not be wrongful prior to its legal regulation, it becomes far less plausible, since so many such offences look more like technical rule violations than real moral wrongs. I will have more to say later about *mala prohibita*, and about the distinction between *mala in se* and *mala prohibita*:[44] for the moment, I will briefly note three points for further discussion.

[42] See n. 8 above; and V Tadros, 'Rethinking the Presumption of Innocence'.

[43] See below, section 7 and Chapter 2, section 4.

[44] A distinction that I assume here, and will defend later against objections like Bentham's: see J Bentham, *A Comment on the Commentaries*, iii, 63, on this 'acute distinction ... which being so shrewd, and sounding so pretty, and being in Latin, has no sort of occasion to have any meaning to it'.

First, the defining feature of *mala prohibita* is that the criminalized conduct is not, or might not be, pre-legally wrongful—wrongful, that is, prior to its legal prohibition: such conduct is not, we might say, prohibited because it is wrongful; it is wrongful because it is prohibited. This is not to say, however, that it is wrongful because it is criminalized: rather, it is prohibited by a pre- or non-criminal regulation; what is then criminalized is the violation of that regulation, on the grounds that such violations are wrongful. We will need to discuss later the grounds on which such violations may be argued to be wrongful, since we cannot just assume that they are; but this shows how a criminal law focused on wrongfulness can have room for *mala prohibita*.[45]

Second, this structure of criminalization is displayed in many statutes, which first lay down sets of regulations, and then define criminal offences that consist in breaking those regulations. For example, the Health and Safety at Work etc. Act 1974 defines certain general duties relating to health and safety for employers, employees, and manufacturers (ss. 2–7), and provides (s. 15) for the creation of 'regulations' to serve any of the Act's 'general purposes'; s. 33 then declares that '[i]t is an offence for a person ... to fail to discharge a duty to which he is subject by virtue of sections 2 to 7 [or] to contravene any health and safety regulations'. The Vehicle Excise and Registration Act 1994 enacts, in Parts I and II, requirements concerning the registration and licensing of motor vehicles; Part III then defines a range of offences that consist in failing to obey those requirements. This helps to explain my claim that the criminal law does not prohibit the conduct it defines as criminal.[46] The regulations whose violation is criminalized do indeed prohibit:[47] but it would be very odd to say that the criminal law—those sections of the Acts that enact criminal offences—'prohibits' the violation of those regulations, since those regulations already 'prohibit' the conduct that is then criminalized; it would be at best otiose, and at worst nonsensical, for the law to prohibit a failure to obey its prohibitions. Instead, we can see the criminalizing sections of these Acts as declaring that failures to obey such regulations constitute criminal wrongs, which render the person criminally liable.[48]

Third, it might well turn out that many of our existing criminal laws, in particular many of those that create *mala prohibita*, criminalize conduct that is not even claimed to be wrongful: not only is it not claimed to be pre-legally wrongful—that is a defining feature of *mala prohibita*; it is not even claimed to be wrongful in virtue of its character as the violation of a regulation. That is only to say, however, that those existing criminal laws are radically defective as criminal laws: either we should not sanction such conduct at all; or, if it is to be sanctioned, this should be done through a system of non-criminal regulation.

As to the charge of over-familiarity, I would be very happy if the claim that the criminal law is essentially concerned with wrongdoing was uncontroversial. However, first, the precise nature of that concern with wrongdoing is not yet clear, and will need to be explained; second, the claim (once clarified) is not uncontroversial, and will need to be further defended. That explanation and defence will be provided in Chapter 2; all I have tried to do so far is to show it to be plausible that a concern with wrongdoing is

[45] See further below, Chapter 2 at nn 53–5, and Chapter 7, section 5.

[46] See at nn 10–12 above.

[47] For the sake of simplicity of expression, we can recast positive prescriptions or requirements as prohibitions: a requirement to ϕ (to take specified safety measures, or to license one's car, ...) is a prohibition on not ϕing.

[48] Which is to say that the distinctive character of criminal law lies in part in the criminal process: the substantive criminal law defines the conditions under which we will be subject to the criminal process. See sections 3 and 4 below.

an essential feature of the substantive criminal law—that the offence definitions that comprise the criminal law's 'special part' consist in purportedly authoritative declarations of the range of wrongs whose perpetrators will be liable to criminal prosecution.

It matters, of course, that these definitions are (purportedly) authoritative. The criminal law does not just offer normative guidance: it claims the authority to define these wrongs, as wrongs that render us liable to prosecution. I will need to clarify the nature and grounds of that claimed authority later: this will involve discussing the kind of authority that the law must claim, and the reach of that authority;[49] and the ways in which citizens may relate to it (this will require us to examine the political grounding of criminal law in the governmental structures of a polity). All we need note here is that the criminal law's authority is not plausibly portrayed as the authority to prohibit the conduct that it defines as criminal. We have just seen that this is implausible in the case of *mala prohibita*, but it is also implausible in the case of *mala in se*.

To say that the criminal law prohibits the kinds of conduct that it defines as criminal is to say that it demands our obedience to these prohibitions (obedience is what prohibitions seek), which is also to say that it offers us new normative reasons for refraining from those kinds of conduct. That is what authoritative prohibitions purport to do: whatever reasons we may have had for Φ-ing, the prohibition gives us new, perhaps peremptory or exclusionary, reason not to Φ; we are to refrain from Φ-ing from respect for that authority. But that is not what the criminal law typically says to us in its definitions of such *mala in se* as murder, rape, criminal damage, and the like: it would be a strange message to a potential attacker to say that, whatever reasons he might have had to commit his attack in the absence of the criminal law, respect for the law should restrain him. The law rather presupposes that we already had ample, normally conclusive,[50] moral reasons to refrain from such wrongs—reasons to which it does not purport to add.[51] Its definitions of such wrongs as crimes constitute not prohibitions but declarations: declarations not that these are wrongs (it presupposes that), but that these wrongs are criminal wrongs—which is to say that they are wrongs of which the polity, through its laws, properly takes such formal, public notice, and whose perpetrators will therefore be liable to prosecution and punishment.[52]

It is true that the substantive criminal law can be seen as offering us new, prudential reasons for refraining from what it defines as crimes. The prospect of conviction and punishment might deter from crime those who are not, or not sufficiently, motivated by the pre-criminal reasons for refraining from such wrongdoing that the law presupposes; and if we think that deterrence has any proper role among the aims of a system of criminal law, we will take it that part of the point of the substantive criminal law is to provide citizens whose moral motivation is inadequate with supplementary prudential reasons for what would indeed count as obedience to its prohibitions: 'refrain from Φ-ing or else' is a sanction-backed prohibition on Φ-ing. This does not, however, undermine my argument that the primary purpose of the substantive criminal law is

[49] In other words, the 'ambit' and 'jurisdiction' of the criminal law: see further below, Chapter 3, section 1.

[50] Only normally conclusive, because through its specifications of general defences the criminal law recognizes that we can exceptionally have good reason to commit a *malum in se*.

[51] This is oversimplified: the law does sometimes offer new normative reasons, concerning the respect we should have for the law, to those who dissent from its definitions of criminal wrongs: see below, Chapter 3, sections 3 and 4.

[52] That is why the modes of offence definition noted at the start of section 2 are appropriate. They do not take the form of prohibitions: instead, they declare either that the specified type of conduct constitutes an offence (which is to say that it renders the agent liable to the criminal process), or that it renders the agent liable to a specified kind of punishment.

declaratory rather than prohibitory, and that it does not offer us new normative reasons for refraining from the conduct it defines as criminal. First, the prudential reasons offered by the law in its deterrent mode are not normative reasons: the criminal law does not tell us that we ought to refrain from what it defines as crimes in order to avoid punishment; rather, it offers such reasons as reasons that might in fact motivate those who are not sufficiently moved by the normative reasons on which it rests. Second, the legitimacy of deterrence depends on there already being sufficient, non-deterrent, normative reasons for us not to do what the law seeks to deter us from doing: if the criminal law is to have more normative authority than the gunman who coerces us to act as he wishes, what it seeks to deter us from must be something that we anyway, independently of its deterrent threats, have good normative reason not to do. A legitimately deterrent criminal law does not say to us simply 'refrain from Φ-ing, or else': it reminds us first that we ought not to Φ, and then adds a supplementary deterrent reason to motivate those unmoved by that (pre-criminal and non-deterrent) 'ought'.

These claims, about the way in which the substantive criminal law is concerned with (pre-criminal) wrongs, and about its declaratory rather than prohibitory character, will be explained and defended in the following chapters; but they are not yet sufficient to distinguish criminal law from other kinds of law that may also deal, and deal essentially, with wrongs. In particular, on some accounts of tort law, it is also essentially concerned with wrongs.

This is not true on all accounts: according to Lord Bingham, for instance, 'the primary role of the law of tort is to provide monetary compensation for those who have suffered material damage rather than to vindicate the rights of those who have not'.[53] On this view, tort law is concerned with harm and who pays for it. It might aim to allocate the cost of harms that have been caused away from those who innocently suffered them to those who are properly held responsible for causing them, and such allocations might depend on a finding of some kind of fault or wrongdoing. But such findings are not the focus of tort law in the way that wrongdoing is the focus of criminal law: they concern the conditions given which a plaintiff can secure a verdict against, and damages from, a defendant, but are not the focus of that verdict or of the law that warrants it. On other accounts, however, the distinctive function of tort law is precisely to deal with certain kinds of wrong—for instance to provide 'civil recourse' for those who have been wronged in certain ways;[54] this view sits comfortably with the fact that someone who has been the victim of a crime can in principle bring a tort suit against the perpetrator.[55] We need not try to adjudicate between such conflicting accounts of the nature and aims of tort law here;[56] but we need to address the question of how criminal law differs from tort law, if both deal or can deal with wrongs.

It might be tempting to follow Blackstone here, and say that while tort law deals with private wrongs, criminal law deals with public wrongs: while civil wrongs violate 'the civil rights which belong to individuals, considered merely as individuals', crimes 'are breach and violation of the public rights and duties, due to the whole community,

[53] *Watkins v Secretary of State for the Home Department* [2006] 2 AC 395 [9].

[54] See especially B Zipursky, 'Rights, Wrongs, and Recourse in the Law of Torts'; J Goldberg and B Zipursky, 'Torts as Wrongs', and *Torts*. See also *Ashley v Chief Constable of Sussex Police* [2008] 1 AC 962 (see n. 72 below).

[55] And in some jurisdictions victims can attach a civil case to the criminal prosecution: see e.g. the German Code of Criminal Procedure (*Strafprozessordnung*) §§ 403–6; and the Swedish provisions described in C Lernestedt, 'Victim and Society: Sharing Wrongs, but in which Roles?'.

[56] See generally J Oberdiek (ed.), *Philosophical Foundations of the Law of Torts*; M Dyson (ed.), *Unravelling Tort and Crime*.

considered as community, in its social aggregate capacity'.[57] Now I will argue later that we should understand crimes as public wrongs, but we will need to get clear about the particular sense in which they are 'public', and about the meaning of 'public' and 'private' in this context: both crimes and torts are 'public' wrongs in the sense that they are recognized as wrongs by the law, which is a public institution, and are dealt with through a public legal process.[58]

We can start to get clearer about the sense in which crimes are 'public' wrongs, and thus also about the difference between crimes and torts, by turning from the substantive criminal law to the second dimension of criminal law—the criminal process. What distinguishes crimes from torts is that they render the wrongdoer liable to a distinctive kind of legal process: this is the truth in Williams' suggestion, quoted at the start of this section, that '[a] crime then becomes an act that is capable of being followed by criminal proceedings'.[59]

4. The Criminal Process

When a type of conduct is defined as criminal, this gives the police new powers, preventive and investigatory: powers that they do not have in relation to non-criminal or extra-legal wrongs. They can take steps to prevent the commission of a crime, including the arrest of someone who is thought to be about to commit a crime; and they play a central role in the investigation of alleged crimes—a role that brings a range of powers to examine, to search, to question, and to detain: they do not have such powers in relation to alleged torts, or in relation to extra-legal wrongs. I will not discuss these powers here,[60] but will focus on the salient procedural differences between criminal and tort cases as they progress towards a hearing in court—although that progress can, as we will see, often be halted or diverted. By attending to these differences, we will be able to get clearer about the nature of crime, as distinct from other kinds of wrongdoing.

The procedural difference between torts and crimes is grounded in the fact that a tort case is brought (typically) by an individual plaintiff, whereas a criminal case is (typically) not. In a tort case an individual who claims to have suffered some relevant harm or wrong at another's hands sues that other person, seeking a remedy (different accounts of tort law give different accounts of the nature of that remedy—payment for the harm caused, or recourse for the wrong done). In a criminal case there might well be an individual victim or victims, a person who has been robbed or assaulted or defrauded or otherwise wronged in a way recognized by the criminal law; but it is not typically the victim who brings the case. In England, for instance, the case is investigated by the police, who pass it to a prosecutor if there is sufficient evidence of a crime and a perpetrator; the prosecutor then decides whether and on what charge to prosecute the alleged perpetrator; and when (if) the case comes to court it is listed not as '*Plaintiff v Defendant*', as a tort case is listed, but (in England, which still retains such visible marks of an undemocratic history) as '*Regina v Defendant*', or (in countries whose legal symbols are more democratic) as '*People v Defendant*', or '*State v Defendant*', or '*Commonwealth v Defendant*'.[61]

57 Sir William Blackstone, *Commentaries on the Laws of England*, Bk IV, ch. 1, p. 5.

58 See A Y K Lee, 'Public Wrongs and the Criminal Law'.

59 Williams, 'The Definition of Crime', 123; see at n. 22 above.

60 But see e.g. the range of powers defined in the Police and Criminal Evidence Act 1984.

61 Here again localism (or parochialism) appears, since what I say applies accurately only to certain 'adversarial' systems of criminal law, and in different systems different officials play different roles in

The contrast drawn in the previous paragraph is in various ways oversimplified. Tort cases are not always brought by and against individual plaintiffs and defendants: the parties might, for instance, be corporations, or even governments. Criminal cases are not always brought by 'the state', since they can be brought by regulatory agencies.[62] More significantly, alleged victims of crime can in some jurisdictions bring private prosecutions, and occasionally do so—although in England the Director of Public Prosecutions (DPP) has the power to take over a private prosecution and then discontinue it.[63] In some countries, the alleged victim can act as prosecutor or co-prosecutor for some kinds of offence: German law makes provision for *Privatkläger* and *Nebenkläger*,[64] and French law makes provision for instituting or joining a criminal prosecution as a '*partie civile*'.[65] In other jurisdictions prosecutions for certain kinds of offence can be brought only at the request, or only with the consent, of the alleged victim;[66] in some the alleged victim, or other interested parties, can demand an independent review of a prosecutor's decision not to proceed, or take the matter to court for judicial review.[67]

These are some of the ways in which the initially clear distinction between civil and criminal processes can be blurred. Other kinds of blurring concern what follows from a verdict against the defendant. A civil court can, for instance, award 'punitive damages', which go to the victim, but are meant to punish the defendant for the malicious or wilful wrongness of the tort he committed—thus blurring the distinction between tort damages and criminal punishment.[68] On the other side, criminal courts can make compensation orders against convicted defendants, requiring them to pay compensation to their victims.[69] We will need to ask later whether we have good reason to blur (if not to collapse) the distinction between torts and crimes in such ways; for the moment, however, since our interest is in analytical rather than in normative questions, we can leave such complications aside, to focus on the salient differences between the paradigmatic ways in which crimes and torts are dealt with. We can note five such differences.

the investigation and prosecution of crimes. However, I hope that some version of the aims and values of the criminal process that I identify in this section will also be discernible in systems whose processes differ significantly.

[62] The English Law Commission noted that in England and Wales over sixty national regulators have the power to make criminal laws and to prosecute breaches of them, as do 486 local authorities and various trading standards authorities (*Criminal Liability in Regulatory Contexts*, para 1.21; examples are given in paras 1.22–24).

[63] See Prosecution of Offences Act 1985, s. 6; http://www.cps.gov.uk/legal/p_to_r/private_prosecutions/#an01. Some non-governmental organizations, such as the Royal Society for the Prevention of Cruelty to Animals, can also bring 'private' prosecutions. In Scotland, by contrast, private prosecutions are harder to bring (and thus rarer): the would-be prosecutor must apply to the High Court of Justiciary for a 'bill of criminal letters', and the Lord Advocate can oppose the application: see *X v Sweeney* 1982 JC 70 for a rare successful application; and *Stewart v Payne, McQuade v Clarke* 2017 JC 155, for failed attempts to bring private prosecutions against drivers who had caused death.

[64] *Strafprozessordnung* §§ 374–402.

[65] See J R Spencer, 'Civil Liability for Crimes'.

[66] Compare the German category of *Antragsdelikte* (e.g. *Strafgesetzbuch* §§ 123, 185–94, 248b); Polish Criminal Code §§ 160.3, 161, 190 (thanks to Krzysztof Szczucki for information about Polish law). See also R Stevens, 'Private Rights and Public Wrongs', suggesting that when conduct is criminalized only because it constitutes an 'interpersonal wrong', it should be up to the victim whether a prosecution is brought.

[67] For the English provisions for independent review, see Crown Prosecution Service, *Victims' Right to Review Scheme*; for judicial review, see *R v Metropolitan Police Commissioner ex parte Blackburn (No.1)* [1969] 2 QB 118; *R (B) v DPP* [2009] 1 WLR 2072.

[68] See A Sebok, 'Normative Theories of Punitive Damages'.

[69] For English provisions, see Powers of Criminal Courts (Sentencing) Act 2000, ss 130–3.

First, a civil case is controlled by the plaintiff. She decides whether to sue, whether to pursue the case, or to settle it if a settlement is offered, whether to enforce any judgment in her favour. The burdens (both material and psychological) of bringing the case also fall on her. By contrast, a criminal case is controlled by criminal justice officials: the police decide whether to investigate the matter; a prosecutor decides whether and with what to charge the alleged wrongdoer, and negotiates any bargain that will avert a trial; the sentence is enforced by officials. Victims might have de facto influence on the process: the police might become aware of the crime only if the victim reports it; they or the prosecutor might not pursue it if the victim asks them not to. But the victim has no formal standing to demand that the perpetrator be, or not be, prosecuted.[70]

Second, both criminal and civil cases might aim to determine responsibility for some harm that occurred, in order to determine liability to a legal consequence; in both, the question whether the harm was caused by the defendant's conduct is central to that determination of responsibility. But the determination of criminal liability depends on culpability in ways that the determination of civil liability does not. A defendant's civil liability might be established by proving that his conduct fell below an objective standard of reasonable care, but more is needed for a criminal conviction—in English law, often, that he was at least reckless as to the risk of harm. A range of defences is also available in criminal cases that are unavailable in civil cases. I might avoid both criminal and civil liability by showing that the plaintiff consented to my action,[71] or that I was defending myself against her unlawful attack: but it would not avail me in the civil court, as it would in the criminal court, to show that I acted under duress, even if the court agreed that this rendered my action excusable, or that I acted on the unreasonably mistaken belief that I was defending myself against unlawful attack,[72] or that I was so mentally disordered that I was not criminally responsible for my actions.[73] Indeed, I might still be civilly liable even if the court found that my action was justified by necessity.[74] I could also mitigate my civil liability, but not my criminal liability, by showing that the plaintiff's negligence contributed to the damage.

Third, the liability imposed by a civil court that finds for the plaintiff is, typically, a liability to pay damages; in simple cases, the amount of damages is determined by the cost of repairing the harm for which the defendant is held responsible. If it costs £1,000 to rebuild my neighbour's garage after I destroyed it by my careless bonfire-lighting, and to restore, as far as is possible, the *status quo ante*, that is what the court will award, regardless of my means and of the extent of my culpability: it will matter

[70] This can be a particularly problematic issue in cases of domestic violence: see M M Dempsey, *Prosecuting Domestic Violence: A Philosophical Analysis*.

[71] But not always in the case of criminal law: see e.g. (and notoriously) *Brown* [1994] 1 AC 212. On defences in tort law generally, see J Goudkamp, *Tort Law Defences*.

[72] See *Ashley v Chief Constable of Sussex Police* [2008] 1 AC 962, for an illustration of the complexities in the relationship between criminal and civil wrongs. An unarmed man was shot and killed during a bungled police raid; the policeman who shot him was acquitted at his criminal trial for murder, because there was no evidence to rebut his claim that he acted in self-defence—that he believed he was under attack, and used force that was reasonable given that belief; but the court held that the victim's family could still bring a tort suit for assault and battery, on the grounds that whilst in criminal law an unreasonable mistaken belief that I am being attacked suffices for a defence of self-defence, in tort law such a mistaken belief must at least be reasonable if it is to ground a defence (and the court was tempted by the view that the belief must actually be true). See further below, Chapter 7 at nn 37–8.

[73] Nor would 'unfitness to plead' bar a civil trial. See Goudkamp, *Tort Law Defences*, 101–3 (and 166–84, 186–90 for arguments that insanity should, whilst 'unfitness to plead' should not, bar tort liability); see further at nn 104–5 below.

[74] See *Vincent v Lake Erie Transportation Co.*, 109 Minn 456, 124 NW 221 (1910).

neither whether I am rich or poor, nor whether my conduct was only modestly negligent or more seriously reckless. Liability imposed by a criminal court, by contrast, is a liability to be punished, and in systems that take culpability and proportionality seriously the severity of that punishment is determined not by the cost of repairing whatever harm was caused, but by the seriousness of the offence—orthodoxly understood as a function of the culpability of the agent and the seriousness of the harm caused. If the punishment is a fine, it is appropriate to proportion its cash value to the offender's means, since the fine's penal severity depends not on its absolute amount, but on what proportion of the defendant's resources it takes.[75]

Fourth, in both cases a full trial might be avoided by pre-trial negotiation: a civil case might be settled before it comes to trial; a criminal case might be (indeed in Britain and the US usually is) decided by a guilty plea, which itself often results from pre-trial bargaining, or be disposed of by a police caution or a 'prosecutor fine',[76] or be informally diverted from the criminal process. However, settlements in civil cases often explicitly exclude any admission of liability, whereas a criminal plea bargain still requires the defendant formally to plead guilty in court, and cautions similarly require an admission of guilt.[77]

Fifth, we can insure ourselves against civil liability but not against criminal liability.[78] If I and the person I harm are insured, our insurers might seek to settle without going to trial; but whether the case is settled pre-trial or by a verdict for the plaintiff, the money will be paid by my insurers, not by me. The affair will not cost me nothing: apart from the burdens of filling out an insurance form and, perhaps, having to appear in court, I might find that my insurance premiums have increased, or find it harder to obtain insurance, or have to pay the first £N of the award; but I will not have to pay the £1,000 that the court awards her. But if I am convicted in the criminal court, I must undertake or undergo the punishment: I cannot expect my insurers to pay the fine (though the law cannot prevent someone else paying it).

These differentiating features help to put some (largely procedural) flesh on the idea that the criminal law is concerned with public wrongs: with wrongs rather than just with harms, and with wrongs that are in some sense public rather than private. Its concern with wrongs is shown in the role played by considerations of culpability, in assigning liability and in determining sanctions: for if wrongdoing is the object of attention, and we are to treat those who commit the wrongs as responsible agents, we must attend to their culpability. It is also a feature of wrongdoing that the seriousness of the wrong, or the culpability of its agent, is not mitigated (in the way that tortious liability is mitigated) by the fact that the victim's negligence was a contributory factor: it might be careless, even reckless to walk through an area of town in which muggings are frequent: but that does not mitigate the guilt of the mugger who attacks me, or render his attack less serious.[79] If wrongdoing is the focus we can also see why a pre-trial settlement without any admission of wrongdoing or liability should not be acceptable, since it precisely fails to address the core issue. Finally, it is a defining feature of punishment that it must be intended to burden the person being punished (hence the bar on

[75] Hence the attractions of a system of 'unit fines' or 'day fines': see e.g. S T Hillsman, 'Fines and Day Fines'.

[76] See n. 14 above.

[77] That is not true, however, of prosecutor fines. See Duff, 'The Prosecutor Fine', at 574.

[78] In which context it is significant that insurance policies will not usually provide cover for punitive damages.

[79] There is of course more to be said about this: see e.g. V Bergelson, *Victims' Rights and Victims' Wrongs: Comparative Liability in Criminal Law*.

insurance against criminal sanctions);[80] if we ask what could justify the imposition of something that is not just foreseeably, but deliberately burdensome, a familiar answer is that the person must have rendered himself liable to this by his own wrongdoing.

As to the public character of criminal wrongs, this is shown (it partly consists) in the way in which the case is brought and controlled by public officials, in the name of the polity; and in the fact that what results from a verdict against the defendant is punishment rather than a payment or reparation to the victim. It is a controversial question in penal theory whether or in what ways the victims of crime should have a role in the determination of offenders' sentences,[81] or should be seen as in any way beneficiaries of their punishment, and it is a familiar criticism of our current institutions of criminal trials and punishments that they turn our attention away from the victims and their needs,[82] but this is not the place to engage with that controversy: for present purposes, we need only say that what marks out criminal law from other kinds of law, notably tort law, is that it is concerned with wrongs that are in this sense public—that the law's formal response to them is in the hands and under the control of officials rather than the victim.[83] This might suggest that what makes crimes 'public' wrongs is not that they are wrongs that are criminalized because they are 'public', but that they are wrongs that count as 'public' because they are criminalized—they are made 'public' by being criminalized. There is, as we will see, some partial truth in this.

The criminal process is thus a distinctively public process: but can we say any more than this about its distinctive character and aims, about how it differs from other kinds of legal process, without altogether abandoning the analytical for the normative?

The 'criminal process', broadly understood, extends from the initial police investigation of an alleged crime to the final conviction and sentencing (or of course the acquittal) of the person alleged to have committed it. In one sense, the focus of all the pre-trial stages of that process is on the criminal trial. In investigating crime, the police are trying not merely to establish whether a crime was committed and who committed it, but to establish whether there is, and to collect, evidence that can then be used to convict an offender in court. Similarly, a prosecuting official is concerned to establish whether there is sufficient evidence that a person committed a crime that could be used to secure a conviction in court. It might then be tempting to say that the trial is the natural or normal culmination of the criminal process—that if, for whatever reason, a trial does not take place (although there is sufficient evidence against a suspected offender), the criminal process is incomplete. It is true that police and prosecutors may divert people from the criminal process and the criminal trial in various ways: by not pursuing a case at all; by diverting alleged offenders to a non-criminal disposal—for instance, towards a 'restorative justice' process, or, for those with mental health problems, to psychiatric help; or by diverting them from a criminal trial by a pre-trial criminal disposal such as a caution or a prosecutor fine.[84] Some such diversions are ways of not treating the conduct in question as criminal: although it fits the formal definition

[80] On burdensomeness as a feature of punishment, see at nn 123–5 below.

[81] See the debates about the proper role, if any, of Victim Impact Statements in the sentencing process: see e.g. A J Ashworth, 'Victim Impact Statements and Sentencing'; E Erez, 'Who's Afraid of the Big Bad Victim? Victim Impact Statements as Victim Empowerment and Enhancement of Justice'.

[82] See N Christie, 'Conflicts as Property'; also M D Dubber, *Victims in the War on Crime*.

[83] And we could say that Christie's objection to the way in which the criminal law 'steals' the 'conflicts' in which crime consists from those to whom they properly belong is precisely an objection to criminal law as public law.

[84] See n. 14 above; R Allen, 'Alternatives to Prosecution'; C Hoyle and R Young, 'Restorative Justice: Assessing the Prospects and Pitfalls'.

of an offence, and comes to the attention of the police or prosecutor because it is an offence, they do not treat it as a crime, but rather as perhaps a 'conflict' that can be better dealt with informally, or as evidence of the person's need for psychiatric help. Other kinds of diversion, such as formal cautions and prosecutor fines, still treat the conduct as criminal, but treat it as not being seriously criminal enough to warrant going to court. However, the assumed primacy of the criminal trial, as the 'natural' or presumed culmination of the criminal process, is shown in the way in which such provisions are standardly described as 'alternatives' to, or 'diversions' from, the criminal process of prosecution and trial.

We should not, however, take this to give the trial, or indeed prosecution, *normative* priority over such other ways of dealing with alleged crimes: we should not, that is, assume that when there is sufficient evidence that someone committed a crime, that person should be prosecuted and brought to trial *unless* there is some strong reason not to do so. That would be to presume a 'legality principle', according to which a prosecutor must prosecute if there is sufficient evidence of guilt—although that 'must' is in practice far from absolute, since even systems that officially subscribe to the principle recognize a range of grounds on which prosecutors may decide not to prosecute.[85] By contrast, an 'opportunity principle' leaves more open the question of whether a prosecution should proceed: it is for the prosecutor to decide whether or not to prosecute, without any presumption in favour of prosecution.[86]

Such a principle is especially (although not only) evident in regulatory contexts. Regulations dealing with taxation, health and safety at work, environmental protection, and many other kinds of activity are often backed by criminal laws that make it an offence to violate a regulation: but the officials responsible for applying and enforcing such regulatory regimes often use criminal prosecution only as a last resort, when other methods of securing compliance or of dealing with non-compliance have failed; they decide how to respond, that is, not just without a presumption that they should prosecute unless …, but with a presumption that they should *not* prosecute unless other methods have failed.[87] Thus, for example, someone who is found to have evaded her taxes could face criminal prosecution, but might instead be offered an arrangement under which she pays the tax owed, plus a further substantial penalty payment, and avoids criminal prosecution or liability. This is, indeed, the most common way of dealing with tax evasion: in 2010–11 there were fewer than 500 criminal convictions for tax evasion, whereas 2,000 people were put into a 'Managing Deliberate Defaulters' programme without prosecution,[88] and others were dealt with through 'cost effective Civil Investigation of Fraud (CIF) procedures'.[89] (Some of these ways of avoiding prosecution still depend on the possibility of prosecution: regulators can prosecute any who fail to cooperate with their non-criminal measures, and the prospect of prosecution

[85] See e.g. P Asp, 'The Prosecutor in Swedish Law', 153–8; A Perrodet, 'The Public Prosecutor'; S Boyne, 'German Prosecutors and the Rechtsstaat'.

[86] See e.g. H van de Bunt and J-L van Gelder, 'The Dutch Prosecution Service', 123–5; also the English Crown Prosecution Service, *Code for Crown Prosecutors*; and at nn 161–5 below.

[87] See, e.g. I Ayres and J Braithwaite, *Responsive Regulation: Transcending the Deregulation Debate*; K Hawkins, *Law as Last Resort: Prosecution Decision-Making in a Regulatory Agency*.

[88] See HM Revenue and Customs, *Closing in on Tax Evasion*, 8.

[89] See e.g. HM Revenue and Customs, *HMRC Code of Practice* 9, on the CIF process; also *HMRC Criminal Investigation Policy*, on the considerations that guide HMRC decisions about whether to use the CIF process or a criminal prosecution: prosecutions are 'reserved for cases where HMRC needs to send a strong deterrent message or where the conduct involved is such that only a criminal sanction is appropriate'.

provides a strong incentive to cooperate.[90]) There is plenty of room for normative argument about the principles that *should* guide prosecutorial practice in different contexts: but our initial account of the criminal process should not beg such normative questions by building in a presumption that strong evidence of the commission of a crime should normally lead to prosecution and trial.

It is also worth noting here one further way in which the official collection of evidence (even of potentially conclusive evidence) of criminal conduct might not (directly) lead to prosecution or a criminal trial. One form that 'preventive justice' measures can take is the making of a distinctive kind of preventive order: given evidence that a person has been engaged or is engaged in a specified kind of criminal activity, an official can apply to a court for an order imposing restrictions on that person's conduct or movements—restrictions whose aim is to prevent his future engagement in such conduct. Such orders are civil, not criminal measures, formally speaking, and the process through which they are made is formally a civil, not a criminal process; but a breach of the order is then a criminal offence for which the person can be prosecuted. The Anti-social Behaviour Order (ASBO), now defunct,[91] is perhaps the best known example of this kind of measure; but our contemporary law contains many others.[92] This is a use of criminal law that we will need to discuss later: for the moment, we need note only that this is another way in which the official response to alleged or suspected offenders might not involve prosecution and trial (at least in the first instance).[93]

In various ways, then, the criminal process of investigation, evidence gathering, and charge preparation or consideration might not lead to a criminal trial, or to any formal finding of guilt or innocence; and even if it is correct to talk of them as involving diversions from or alternatives to prosecution and trial, we should not presume that prosecution and trial have normative priority as ways of responding to or dealing with alleged crimes. Nonetheless, the trial does mark a kind of culmination of the criminal process: an analytical account of criminal law must include it, and a normative theory of criminal law must include an account of the trial's proper role.

5. The Criminal Trial

I will focus here on criminal trials in 'adversarial' systems of criminal law: I hope that much the same structuring aims and values can be embodied in more 'inquisitorial'

[90] This feature of many regulatory regimes is formalized in the provisions for 'deferred prosecution agreements': see Serious Fraud Office, 'Deferred Prosecution Agreements'; D N Husak, 'Social Engineering as an Infringement of the Presumption of Innocence: The Case of Corporate Criminality'; R A Shiner and H Ho, 'Deferred Prosecution Agreements and the Presumption of Innocence'.

[91] Crime and Disorder Act 1998, ss 1–4 (see Anti-Social Behaviour, Crime and Policing Act 2014, Part II, for the 'Criminal Behaviour Orders' that replaced ASBOs). The literature on ASBOs is voluminous, but see especially P Ramsay, *The Insecurity State: Vulnerable Autonomy and the Right to Security in the Criminal Law*; A J Ashworth and L Zedner, *Preventive Justice*, ch. 4; A Cornford, 'Criminalising Anti-Social Behaviour'.

[92] See Ashworth and Zedner, *Preventive Justice*. Compare too the courts' power to bind someone over to keep the peace—a power that goes back to the Justices of the Peace Act 1361, but is now governed primarily by Justices of the Peace Act 1968, s. 1(7), and Magistrates' Courts Act 1980, s. 115: see the Crown Prosecution Service, *Binding Over Orders*; J Sprack, *A Practical Approach to Criminal Procedure*, 25.43–25.46.

[93] Although ASBOs and similar orders are often sought because there is insufficient admissible evidence to secure a conviction, they can be sought despite the (potential) availability of sufficient evidence.

criminal processes, but that is not a topic I can pursue here.[94] I will also focus initially on contested trials, in which a defendant is charged with an offence, and enters a plea of 'Not Guilty', so that the prosecution must then try to prove his guilt. It is of course a familiar (notorious) fact that the vast majority of trials in both Britain and the United States are uncontested, since the defendant pleads 'Guilty' in response to the charge at the outset of the proceedings—often as the result of a plea-bargain, or in the well-grounded expectation that they will receive a substantial discount on their sentence in return for a guilty plea.[95] I will have more to say about guilty pleas and plea bargains later, but for the moment will focus on the contested trial that a guilty plea averts.

On one common view, the purpose of the criminal trial is strictly instrumental: it serves the punitive aims of the state or polity by identifying those who are to be liable to punishment. Put in such simple terms, a system that encourages guilty pleas is clearly an efficient way of serving the trial's purpose: for guilty pleas identify those who are to be convicted and thus rendered liable to criminal punishment more speedily and cheaply than do contested trials. But the purpose of the trial is, of course, not supposed to be simply to identify, in some way or other, individuals to be punished: it is supposed to be to connect crime to punishment by identifying those who are liable to punishment *because they have committed an offence*; in which case, and especially given the danger that encouragement can become coercion, we would need to worry about whether guilty pleas are likely to be accurate—more accurate than are convictions following a contested trial.[96] So the purpose of the trial, or at least 'a primary function', is then 'accurate decision-making':[97] it should convict the guilty, and acquit the innocent; and, on a purely instrumental view, it should do this in order thereby to render the guilty formally liable to punishment (and to spare the innocent from the threat of mistaken punishment).

Of course, many features of our existing criminal process, especially in adversarial systems, seem ill-suited to this purpose. Quite apart from the stringent demand that the defendant must be acquitted if the prosecution cannot prove her guilt 'beyond reasonable doubt', many procedural rules, in particular those allowing or requiring the exclusion of certain kinds of evidence, cannot be plausibly justified as truth-serving: evidence that was illegally acquired, for instance, may be excluded even if it would contribute significantly to proof of a defendant's guilt.[98] Defendants are allowed to remain silent, rather than being required to give evidence, although their evidence could contribute significantly to the determination of their guilt or non-guilt.[99] Such

[94] On the 'adversarial'/'inquisitorial' distinction, see classically M Damaška, 'Evidentiary Barriers to Conviction and Two Models of Criminal Procedure'; *The Faces of Justice and State Authority: A Comparative Approach to the Legal Process*. On the extent to which the two models are still in practice distinct, see e.g. E Luna and M Wade (eds), *The Prosecutor in Transnational Perspective*, Section III; S Summers, *Fair Trials: The European Criminal Procedural Tradition and the European Court of Human Rights*.

[95] The English figures for guilty pleas vary between magistrates' courts (over 90% of convictions follow guilty pleas) and crown courts (over 70%): see Ashworth and Redmayne, *The Criminal Process*, 293–5; for US figures, see the Hindelang Criminal Justice Research Center's *Sourcebook of Criminal Justice Statistics*. On the discount for guilty pleas in England, see Ashworth and Redmayne, *The Criminal Process*, 312–17; and Crown Prosecution Service, *Reduction in Sentence for a Guilty Plea*.

[96] On the danger that innocent defendants might decide or feel compelled to enter guilty pleas, see e.g. J S Rakoff, 'Why Innocent People Plead Guilty'; R L Lippke, *The Ethics of Plea Bargaining*, 60–1, 82–4, 212–15; A W Alschuler, 'A Nearly Perfect System for Convicting the Innocent'.

[97] Ashworth and Redmayne, *The Criminal Process*, 321.

[98] See further P Roberts and A Zuckerman, *Criminal Evidence*, esp. chs. 1–4, 9, 11.

[99] See Roberts and Zuckerman, *Criminal Evidence*, ch. 13; and for useful recent discussions, see J Jackson, 'Re-Conceptualizing the Right of Silence as an Effective Fair Trial Standard'; H Quirk, 'The Right of Silence in England and Wales: Sacred Cow, Sacrificial Lamb or Trojan Horse?'.

features of the trial process can be readily explained, from an instrumentalist perspective, as side-constraints on the pursuit of truth: side-constraints that aim to ensure that the trial is fair, that the defendant's rights are respected, and that we subject defendants to the burdens of punishment only if we are sure of their guilt. It might now be said that the trial has two purposes: 'accurately to determine whether or not a person has committed a particular criminal offence and to do so fairly'.[100]

A related view of the trial somewhat inverts the relationship suggested above between truth-finding and the protection of defendants. The main point of the trial, on this view, is to protect us against the potentially oppressive power of the state: rather than allowing officials to determine for themselves, by whatever means and with whatever certainty they see fit, whether this person committed a crime and is therefore liable to punishment, we create this elaborate apparatus of the trial through which the allegation of criminal wrongdoing (an allegation that the criminal justice officials might be too ready to believe, or not willing to subject to suitably probing verification) is put to the test—and put to the test (in theory) publicly, so that justice can be seen to be done.[101] This kind of view is expressed in the United States Supreme Court's declaration that '[t]he purpose of the jury trial ... is to prevent oppression by the Government'.[102] 'A criminal trial is in part a search for truth. But it is also a system designed to protect "freedom" by insuring that no one is criminally punished unless the State has first succeeded in the admittedly difficult task of convincing a jury that the defendant is guilty.'[103]

What the Court said here about jury trials might be said about the criminal trial more generally as it is structured in democracies that purport to respect the rule of law: it respects citizens' dignity by protecting them from oppression by the state. The criminal trial's structure, the rules by which it is organized, reflect this aim just as much as they do the aim of truth finding. For the pursuit of that aim, and of the state's other controlling goals, is constrained by the demand that citizens be protected from oppression, and that their dignity be respected; that constraint helps to determine the internal structure of the trial. What this account shares with the instrumental account sketched above is a view of the trial as essentially concerned with the determination of punishment: what the trial protects us from is unjustified or over-hasty punishment.

Given the harshness of so many of the punishments imposed in our existing systems, such a focus on punishment as the salient outcome of the criminal trial is natural; but it might distort, since it ignores aspects of the trial that point towards a different picture of its purposes, one that gives the trial an intrinsic, rather than instrumental, significance as a response to alleged crimes. We can start to discern the contours of that alternative picture by considering two features of our trial system that do not fit easily into an instrumental account.

First, a defendant who is at the time when he is to appear for trial so mentally disordered that he cannot understand or respond to the charge against him, or advise his lawyer, or take part in the proceedings with any grasp of what is going on, may be found 'unfit to plead', in which case his trial is barred:[104] even if he was sane and competent at the time of the (alleged) offence, he cannot now be tried. It is true that

[100] Ashworth and Redmayne, *The Criminal Process*, 23.

[101] See R A Duff et al, *The Trial on Trial (3): Towards a Normative Theory of the Criminal Trial*, 94–6.

[102] *Williams v Florida* 399 US 78 (1970) at 100 (Mr Justice White).

[103] *Williams v Florida* 399 US 78 (1970) at 113 (Mr Justice Black).

[104] See Criminal Procedure (Insanity) Act 1964 s. 4 (as amended); Sprack, *A Practical Approach to Criminal Procedure*, 240–1; R A Duff, *Trials and Punishments*, 29–35, 119–23.

it will often be hard to determine the guilt of a defendant who can take no part in the trial: perhaps he would be able to offer an alibi, or give an explanation of his conduct that at least creates a doubt about his guilt. But this is not always true, and provision could be made for cases in which it is true by allowing the trial to proceed while warning the jury to consider whether the defendant's inability to give evidence creates a reasonable doubt about his guilt. Furthermore, the defendant's unfitness to plead does not bar every kind of inquiry into whether he is guilty: for whilst an unfit defendant cannot be tried, an inquiry is still held, the kind of evidence that would have figured in at a trial is led and examined, and the jury must determine 'whether they are satisfied ... that he did the act or made the omission charged against him as the offence'. If they are satisfied, he is not convicted: the jury 'make[s] a finding that the accused did the act or made the omission charged against him as the offence'; the court then makes a hospital order, or a guardianship order or a supervision and treatment order, or discharges the defendant.[105] These provisions for unfitness to plead seem to suggest a concern for something more, or other, than accurate fact-finding: we should not put an unfit defendant on trial even if his guilt could be proved beyond reasonable doubt; for there would be something grotesque about trying a person who cannot understand what is going on—whereas there is nothing grotesque about holding an inquiry into whether he committed a crime.

Second, it is seen as important that the defendant be present at his trial, and enter a plea, of 'Guilty' or 'Not Guilty', at the start of the trial. He has not only a right, but an obligation to be present at his trial, and can be arrested and brought to the court if he fails to appear:[106] a judge does have discretion to allow a trial to proceed in the defendant's absence, in particular if he is absent because he has absconded; but that discretion must 'be exercised with great caution'.[107] He is also expected to enter a plea, thus recognizing the court's authority to try him—although pleas are no longer coerced by the '*peine forte et dure*' from those who are unwilling to plead;[108] that is why those who wish to deny the authority of the court or the legitimacy of their trial might refuse to enter a plea.

Why should such things (the defendant's fitness to plead, his presence at the trial and formal, albeit minimal, participation in it by entering a plea) matter? There is an alternative conception of the criminal trial that explains this more plausibly than can an instrumental account. On this view, the trial is a process of calling to account.[109] A defendant who is accused of committing a criminal wrong is called to answer that charge through the criminal court. She is called to answer *to* the charge, by pleading 'Guilty' or 'Not Guilty'. If she pleads 'Guilty' she admits her culpable responsibility, and answers for the wrong that she thus admits. If she pleads 'Not Guilty', and the prosecution cannot prove the offence, she has nothing to answer for; she is acquitted. But if the prosecution proves that she committed the offence, she is called to answer *for* that commission. She might answer by offering a defence, which will, if successful, lead

[105] Criminal Procedure (Insanity) Act 1964, ss 4A–5A (inserted by Criminal Procedure (Insanity and Unfitness to Plead) Act 1991, ss 2–3). Note too that a defendant's incapacity at the time of trial is not a bar to a tort case: see n. 73 above.

[106] This is true in England of trials on indictment (see Bail Act 1976, s. 7), but not of summary trials (Magistrates' Courts Act 1980, ss 11–13).

[107] *R v Jones (Anthony)* [2003] 1 AC 1, para. 6 (Lord Bingham).

[108] See A Mckenzie, 'This Death Some Strong and Stout Hearted Man Doth Choose'. On pleading, see Sprack, *A Practical Approach to Criminal Procedure*, ch. 17.

[109] See Duff et al, *The Trial on Trial (3)*, on which see M Redmayne, 'Theorizing the Criminal Trial'. See also A Dzur, *Punishment, Participatory Democracy, and the Jury*.

to an acquittal. But if she offers no successful defence, she will be convicted—found guilty.

A conviction, on this view, is not merely a detached or factual finding that the defendant's conduct satisfied the law's definition of the crime with which she is charged, and did not satisfy the definition of any legally defined defence: it marks what must be a normative judgment by the 'fact-finder' that the defendant culpably committed the public wrong of which she was accused; it thus formally condemns her conduct as a wrong, and formally censures her, as the agent of that conduct, as a wrongdoer.[110] It is therefore crucial that the defendant be fit to plead: someone who is called to answer to a charge of wrongdoing must be capable of answering to it, or else her trial becomes a travesty. It also matters that the defendant be present, and answer to the charge: we should not force her to answer, since she should retain the freedom to express her dissent from the process, by refusing to play any active part in it;[111] but the trial seeks her participation.

Although I have focused here on the idea that the trial is a process through which someone accused of a crime is called or held to account, it is also a process through which the state, or the prosecutor as an official acting in the name of the state or the polity, is held to account. She must 'succeed[] in the admittedly difficult task of convincing a [court] that the defendant is guilty':[112] her accusation that the defendant committed the specified crime is put to the test; if the defendant challenges her accusation or her evidence, she must be able to respond to that challenge. As we will see later, such possibilities of challenging or contesting official conduct are important to the legitimacy of criminal law in a democratic polity.

I will have more to say later about the normative attractions of such a conception of criminal trials. My claim so far is not that this is how criminal trials *should* function; nor indeed am I (yet) rejecting a more instrumentalist normative view, according to which criminal trials should serve 'accurately to determine whether or not a person has committed a particular criminal offence and to do so fairly'.[113] My claim so far is only that if we aim to provide an analytical account of what criminal law is, by a rational reconstruction of our existing practices, we should recognize this as a possible function of criminal trials: for it enables us to explain features of our existing practices that instrumentalist accounts cannot so easily explain. Nor am I claiming that criminal trials as thus understood are a *necessary* feature of criminal law. It might be argued that anything that is to count as a system of criminal law must include not only a crime-defining substantive law, but a process through which authoritative determinations are made of the guilt or non-guilt of those accused of crimes, although I am not sure if even that is necessary: but I am not claiming that anything that is to count as a system of criminal law must include a formal trial process of calling to account. My claim is only that this is one form that criminal law can take, and that it is worth consideration as a possible element in a normative account of criminal law.

[110] This conception of the criminal trial thus depends on the conception of the substantive criminal law sketched in section 3 above: it presupposes that the criminal indictment charges the defendant with the commission of a (public) wrong. That is also why jury nullification, the acquittal of a defendant who has been clearly proved guilty in law, is significant (as well as problematic): it enables jurors to refuse to endorse the normative judgment on the defendant that the prosecution, and the law, ask them to make (see M Matravers, '"More Than Just Illogical": Truth and Jury Nullification'; Duff et al, *The Trial on Trial (3)*, 71–4).

[111] This provides part of the rationale for the right of silence: see Duff et al, *The Trial on Trial (3)*, 203–13.

[112] *Williams v Florida* 399 US 78 (1970) at 113; see at n. 103 above.

[113] Ashworth and Redmayne, *The Criminal Process*, 23; see at n. 100 above.

I should briefly discuss a further feature of our existing practices, which might seem to cast more doubt on a conception of the criminal trial as calling to account—but which in fact strengthens it. This is the pervasive practice of plea bargaining, by which so many cases are settled: for it might seem (and is often said) that this practice has become so central, and pragmatically essential, to the criminal process that we can no longer see the trial as concerned either with truth or with any genuine process of calling to account. The bargaining process between defence and prosecution (in which the defendant might well have little or no part to play) has become much more like the negotiations that might go on between the parties to a civil case, in which what matters is not any finding or admission of liability, but what compromises each party is ready to make in order to reach an agreement—though, as is often pointed out, the two sides in the negotiation are usually very far from equal.[114] Against this background, a plea-bargained plea of 'Guilty' can easily lose any meaning it is supposed to have as a formal admission or confession of guilt: it becomes simply a formal move in the game, signifying the defendant's acceptance of the terms of the bargain that was agreed between defence and prosecution. A *reductio ad absurdum* of this practice is found in the notorious *Alford* plea, when the US Supreme Court upheld the conviction of a defendant who said in the course of pleading 'Guilty': 'I'm not guilty but I plead guilty'—in order, he said, to avoid the threat of the death penalty if he went to trial.[115]

Now some 'realists' might argue that plea-bargaining is an inevitable, and indeed necessary, feature of a modern system of criminal law. If all, or even most, cases were contested, the only way to avoid the collapse of the machinery of criminal justice would be to increase its resources massively—which could be done only by a significant increase in taxation, or by shifting scarce resources from other areas of government spending. More generally, such a realist might say, we should recognize that, whatever the traditional rhetoric and formalities of the criminal trial might imply, the present reality is that the criminal process is a mechanism for processing large numbers of cases in as cost-effective way as we can manage, as part of a system that functions primarily to manage large populations of (alleged or actual) offenders.[116] From this point of view, the kind of theorizing in which I am engaged here is an exercise in philosophical fantasy: it amounts to the construction of castles in the air that might have their own charm, and that might be connected to features of the rhetorical superstructure of our criminal process, but that have no substantive connection either to what is actual or to what is practically feasible; such theorizing is thus useful neither as an exercise in reconstructive analysis, nor as normative theory that could speak to actual practice.

I do not deny the significant elements of truth in such a 'realist' picture, as a description of what our criminal law has come to be, and of the socio-political functions that it actually serves in its present forms; but I resist the suggestion that we should therefore simply accept this as the new reality of criminal law, and dismiss as relics of a now remote past (if they ever were more than rhetoric) the features to which I have

[114] See further Lippke, *The Ethics of Plea Bargaining*; Ashworth and Redmayne, *The Criminal Process*, 296–320; Duff et al, *The Trial on Trial (3)*, ch. 6.2.

[115] *North Carolina v Alford* 91 S Ct 160 (1970) (in fairness to the Court, it should be noted that one reason it gave for upholding Mr Alford's conviction was that there was strong evidence that he was actually guilty); see A D Redlich and A A Özdogru, 'Alford Pleas in the Age of Innocence'; also the disturbing case of Leroy Harris, reported in the *New York Times*, https://www.nytimes.com/2017/11/23/nyregion/rare-alford-plea-wrongful-conviction-rape-connecticut.html?ref=todayspaper&_r=0.

[116] Such realists might appeal to, for instance, M Feeley and J Simon, 'The New Penology: Notes on the Emerging Strategy of Corrections and its Implications', taking the developments that they identify as the template for an efficient contemporary system of criminal justice. See also Kohler-Hausmann, 'Managerial Justice and Mass Misdemeanors'.

been appealing. I think that it is still worth engaging in the type of rational reconstruction that I am pursuing in this chapter, to find out whether we can reconstruct a conception of criminal law that takes its rhetoric seriously; and then ask, as I will go on to ask in later chapters, whether this is a kind of institution that we could have good reason to create, or to try to recreate. I want therefore to keep in play a conception of the criminal trial as a formal calling to account, in which the defendant is expected to plead 'Guilty' only if this constitutes an honest admission of guilt; in later chapters I will explain why a democratic polity should maintain an institution of this kind. This is not to say that we should (ideally) ban plea bargaining or guilty pleas—although it might suggest that we should ban any process that is properly described as 'bargaining'; but it is to say that we must ask carefully just how guilty pleas, and inducements to make them, could properly figure in a process through which alleged wrongdoers are to be called to account.[117] Furthermore (this is why I suggested that our current plea-bargaining practices actually add force to this conception of the criminal trial), we should note how natural it is to describe a phenomenon like the *Alford* plea as a *reductio ad absurdum* of the practice, or to talk of the key aspects of such practices as 'pathologies':[118] they constitute corruptions of what the practice of criminal justice is, in terms of its own internal logic, supposed to be.

So much, for the moment, for the criminal process and the criminal trial as essential features of a system of criminal law. On the conception I have suggested here, the substantive criminal law serves to define a range of (public) wrongs as crimes; the procedural criminal law provide for the processes through which those who are alleged to have committed such wrongs are called to public account. But what of criminal punishment?

6. Criminal Punishment

I suggested earlier that we should not see punishment as the essential goal of the criminal process, and that it is unclear whether punishment is a necessary dimension of criminal law.[119] Nonetheless, systems of criminal law do typically impose punishments on those convicted of crimes: to criminalize a type of conduct is typically to render those who engage in it liable to punishment. Under many systems, those punishments can be extremely burdensome, depriving those subjected to them of many of the liberties and benefits that citizens normally enjoy, and subjecting them to harsh and damaging impositions; and, whether harsh or (relatively) mild, they raise distinctive questions of legitimacy and justification. I will not say much about punishment in this book—partly because I have said much about it elsewhere:[120] but an account of criminal law must say something about criminal punishment. An analytical account must

[117] I should note that if we emphasize, as I do here, the importance of pleading and of a guilty plea as an admission of guilt, we can still find room for those kinds of trial-avoiding disposals that require an admission of guilt by the defendant (and leave the option of going to trial open): but we should not so readily accept practices like that of 'prosecutor fines', or the negotiated disposal of cases of 'regulatory' crime, which involve no admission of guilt (see nn 14, 77, 87–90 above); they are too like practices of plea bargaining.

[118] See n. 8, and text at n. 115, above. See also Bibas, *The Machinery of Criminal Justice*, on the 'classic values' that have been lost (but could yet be retrieved) in our contemporary 'mechanized' criminal justice systems.

[119] See at nn 14–21 above.

[120] See R A Duff, *Punishment, Communication, and Community*; 'Responsibility, Restoration and Retribution'; R A Duff and S E Marshall, 'Civic Punishment'.

say something about it—even if we need not take a stand on whether a system without punishment should count as a system of *criminal* law. A normative theory must also say something about it: it must either show what role punishment can properly play, what ends it should serve, in a justifiable system of criminal law; or show that, and how, we could do without punishment.

As far as the analytical question is concerned, this is not the place (nor do I think it would be productive) to try to offer a precise definition, specifying the necessary and sufficient conditions for something to count as a (criminal) punishment.[121] We can say that punishment involves the imposition of something intended to be both burdensome and reprobative on a supposed offender for a supposed crime, by a person or body who claims the authority to do so. The cautionary use of 'supposed' and 'claims' points to the fact that punishment can be imposed on those who are in fact innocent of the alleged crime or whose conduct was not in fact criminal, or be imposed by one who in fact lacks the authority to do so. We need not deny that such impositions constitute punishments; but we must also recognize that they are defective precisely as punishments (even if they might be useful, or justified, on other grounds). Several points are worth noticing here.

First, what distinguishes punishments from taxes or 'penalties' is their typically reprobative nature.[122] Taxes might be imposed in order to discourage certain kinds of conduct, and penalties might be imposed to deter the penalized conduct (or to recoup some of the costs that it causes): but even if the primary purpose of punishment is deterrence, its imposition (the conviction and formal sentence that the offender receives in court, the administration of the punishment itself) typically also expresses the censure or condemnation that the crime is taken to warrant.

Second, punishment involves material exactions that are in themselves typically unwelcome: they deprive people of things they value (liberty, money, time); they require people to do things that they would not normally want to do or do voluntarily—undertake unpaid community labour, report to a probation officer regularly. What distinguishes punishment from other unwelcome impositions is that punishment is intended to ...: but to what? Some say that punishment must be intended to inflict pain or suffering:[123] but that suggests that what matters is pain or suffering as such, and thus invites the criticism that the state should not be in the business of trying to inflict pain or suffering,[124] which some penal theorists would reject as a distortion. Others argue that punishment must be intended to cause harm to the offender; adding, if they are careful, that what is intended must be 'prima facie' rather than 'all-things-considered' harm, to leave room for the possibility that punishment could be (intended to be) on balance beneficial to the offender.[125] But some theorists deny even this, since they deny that punishment must be intended to be (in itself) bad for the offender. Punishment, we should rather say, must be intended to be burdensome: for burdens can be accepted, even undertaken, willingly; they can be intended to be and be accepted as being beneficial—not merely on balance, as a price to be paid, but in and of themselves.

[121] See D Scheid, 'Note on Defining "Punishment"'; D Boonin, *The Problem of Punishment*, 3–28; M Zimmerman, *The Immorality of Punishment*, ch. 1.

[122] See at n. 15 above.

[123] See e.g. H L A Hart, 'Prolegomenon to the Principles of Punishment', 4: punishment 'must involve pain or other consequences normally considered unpleasant'.

[124] See N Christie, *Limits to Pain*, on 'pain-delivery'.

[125] See Boonin, *The Problem of Punishment*, 6–17; Zimmerman, *The Immorality of Punishment*, 3–10; N Hanna, 'Facing the Consequences', s. 2.

Third, one dimension of the on-going normative debates about punishment concerns the role that ideas of proportionality should play.[126] I will not engage in that discussion here, save to note that some notion of proportionality is essential to the very idea of punishment, since punishment must be *for* an offence. That is, there must be some supposedly justificatory relationship between a punishment and a crime for which it is supposedly imposed; the punishment must therefore be portrayed as a warranted response to *that* crime. This might rule out, as accounts of *punishment*, any accounts that suggested that the only considerations that should guide decisions about what to do to or with those found to have committed crimes should be future oriented, concerning for instance what will efficiently prevent future crimes. That is not to rule them out as accounts of how offenders should be treated—only as accounts of punishment.[127]

Fourth, punishment is on any account essentially relational. No one is simply punished; one is punished *for* an (alleged) offence. Standard definitions of punishment also make it relational in a further way: one is punished *by* some person or body; indeed, at least in the case of criminal punishment, it must be imposed by some person or body who is legally authorized to punish.[128] One question, which we need not pursue here, concerns the possibility of 'natural' punishment: if a wrongdoer suffers some significant loss or injury as a consequence of her wrongdoing, can the suggestion that that constitutes a (natural) punishment for her wrong be understood as more than a mere metaphor?[129] The more relevant question for present purposes concerns the nature of the relation between punishment and punisher: is the punisher's identity, and their authority or their standing to punish this person for this wrong, integral to the justification of the punishment as a punishment; or is the connection more contingent than that? Although a version of this question arises in any context of punishment, legal or extra-legal, we can focus here on its significance in the context of criminal punishment.

On some accounts, the question of whether some intentionally burdensome and reprobative imposition on an offender can serve the proper ends of criminal punishment if the imposer lacks the legal authority to punish is a contingent one. For if the justifying aim of a system of criminal punishment is, for instance, to deter future crime by imposing punitive burdens on offenders, or to incapacitate potential offenders, or to ensure that offenders suffer what they deserve to suffer, it is a further, contingent question whether such deterrent, incapacitative, or retributive burdens are best imposed by a state institution, or in some other way: a vigilante group could in principle achieve the goals that criminal punishment is intended to serve. Thus Moore thinks that the proper aim of criminal punishment (indeed, of the criminal law) is to inflict the suffering that wrongdoers deserve. That suffering could in principle be inflicted by anyone: but in practice we ought to reserve its infliction to a state system of criminal punishment, because the state is better placed than are private individuals to determine whether a person did culpably commit a wrong, how serious the wrong was, and what degree of penal suffering would be proportionate to it; and a system of state punishment is better placed to reduce the 'danger[] to virtue' that the infliction of punishment involves.[130] Thus if an offender who has avoided trial and conviction is subjected

[126] See e.g. A von Hirsch and A J Ashworth, *Proportionate Sentencing*.

[127] Compare Hart, 'Prolegomenon to the Principles of Punishment', 5, on the 'definitional stop'.

[128] See e.g. Hart, 'Prolegomenon to the Principles of Punishment', 5; Boonin, *The Problem of Punishment*, 23–4; Zimmerman, *The Immorality of Punishment*, 18–19.

[129] See P Winch, 'Ethical Reward and Punishment'.

[130] See M S Moore, 'A Tale of Two Theories', 42.

by a vigilante group to a kind of burden materially comparable to that which a court would have imposed as his criminal punishment, it seems that, for Moore, punitive justice has been achieved: we might not call what is done to him criminal punishment, and we might criticize the vigilantes for thus 'taking the law into their own hands'; but the offender has received his penal deserts. I will argue later that this kind of view is mistaken: if we are to make normative sense of a system of criminal punishment, we must understand it in more fully relational terms—not simply as a practice that serves to achieve independently identifiable ends, but as one that is constituted by, and whose value is to be found in, the civic relationship between punisher and punished. What the vigilantes do to the offender cannot have the meaning that it would need to have if it was to constitute his penal deserts: for the meaning, and thus the justification, of punishment depends on the standing of those who impose it—on their relationship to the wrongdoer, as well as on the relationship between the punishment and the wrong for which it is imposed.[131] For the moment, however, we need simply note that there is this question about the ways in which punishment (or criminal punishment) is essentially relational, and how deep that relationality goes.

So much, for the time being, for criminal punishment as a dimension of criminal law. I have not tried, and will not try, to show that it is not a necessary feature of criminal law; nor have I yet tried to show that it is not the, or a, primary purpose of criminal law. However, the account that I have given of substantive criminal law and of the criminal trial in the previous three sections has, I hope, provided some of the material for the argument I will develop later—that even if a system of criminal law must (analytically and/or normatively) include a system of criminal punishment, we should not see punishment as the primary purpose of such a system.

7. Criminalization

The final matter to be covered in this initial account of criminal law is criminalization: what is it to criminalize a type of conduct? In one way, an answer has already been provided by giving an account of the substantive criminal law, the criminal process, and criminal punishment: for to criminalize a type of conduct, we can say, is precisely to define it as a crime in the substantive criminal law, thus to render those alleged to have engaged in it liable to be prosecuted and tried, and to render those convicted of it liable to criminal punishment. However, more needs to be said about the process, or more precisely the processes, of criminalization—the processes through which conduct comes to be defined and treated as criminal.

Theorists sometimes talk as if criminalization consists simply in an authoritative legislative act: to criminalize a type of conduct is to enact a law that defines that conduct as criminal, or that 'prohibits' it on pain of sanction.[132] A normative theory of criminalization would then have to be a theory of the principles and aims that should guide legislatures in making such decisions. Even if we take this view, we must recognize that the formal enactment of criminal offences need not be the work of a national legislature, since other governmental bodies (national regulators, local authorities, trading standards authorities) may also have that power:[133] we might wonder whether such

[131] See Duff, 'Relational Reasons and the Criminal Law', 199–205; A Harel, *Why Law Matters*, ch. 3.

[132] See e.g. Simester and von Hirsch, *Crimes, Harms and Wrongs*, 3, and 6 on 'the act of criminalization'.

[133] See Law Commission, *Criminal Liability in Regulatory Contexts*, para 1.21 (see n. 62 above); also J Horder, *Ashworth's Principles of Criminal Law*, 60–1, on criminalization via secondary legislation.

power to enact criminal offences should be so widely distributed,[134] but we cannot take it for granted that it should not be. (We must also recognize the increasingly significant impact of international and transnational bodies on law-making within a polity: even when criminalization involves a national legislature, it might flow from the directives of a supra-national body.[135] As I noted in the Introduction, however, I will focus on domestic criminal law as made by and within national polities.)

However, we cannot identify criminalization with the legislative enactment of criminal laws: in some systems such legislation is not necessary for criminalization; and it is arguable that, once we distinguish 'formal' from 'substantive' criminalization, criminalization 'in the books' from criminalization 'in action',[136] we will also realize that legislation is not sufficient for substantive criminalization—and that substantive criminalization is what matters for normative theory.

Legislation is not necessary for criminalization in jurisdictions that retain some elements of common law offence definitions: in such jurisdictions courts can declare a given type of conduct to be criminal without having to cite any statutory provision that defines it as criminal—although they will need to appeal to past decisions and to the doctrines drawn from them to justify such declarations.[137] To discuss common law criminalization as a possible dimension of a normative theory of criminal law would lead us into the debates about codification,[138] and whether criminal law that is not firmly grounded in statutory law (if not in a single criminal code) can satisfy such normative requirements as democratic legitimacy, accessibility, consistency, and certainty. For the sake of simplicity, however, and since the relevant points can be made in relation to statute-based systems, I will avoid those debates, and talk only about statute-based systems—systems in which legislation is a necessary condition of criminalization in the sense that a type of conduct can be legitimately described and treated as criminal only if there exists a statutory offence definition within whose scope it can be shown to fall. Even in such systems, however, legislation is not a sufficient condition of criminalization, either in the books or in action.

First, even in such systems judges play an important role in determining the precise scope and meaning of the substantive criminal law.[139] This is most obviously the case in systems that operate under a constitution, and have a constitutional court that can not only declare statutes to be unconstitutional, but can thereby nullify them, so

[134] The Law Commission (*Criminal Liability in Regulatory Contexts*, paras 3.144ff) proposed that criminalization should require primary legislation.

[135] See, for instance, the European Union's developing powers, in relation to both procedural and substantive criminal law: V Mitsilegas, *EU Criminal Law after Lisbon: Rights, Trust and the Transformation of Justice in Europe*.

[136] See N Lacey, 'Historicising Criminalisation: Conceptual and Empirical Issues', 942–7; also Horder, *Ashworth's Principles of Criminal Law*, 4–10.

[137] Compare *Khaliq v H M Advocate* 1984 SLT 137, *Ulhaq v H M Advocate* 1991 SLT 614, in which the Scottish High Court held that selling 'containers of solvents and gas lighter fuel' to people who, the shopkeeper knew, would use them to sniff glue constituted an offence ('causing real injury to the person'). The 'question whether it was any longer within the power of the High Court to declare that certain conduct constitutes a new crime, i.e. one hitherto unknown to our law', did not arise, the Court held, since 'what is libelled here is not a new crime but merely a modern example of conduct which our law has for long regarded as criminal' (184 SLT 137, at 141–2; Lord Emslie). On the Court's 'declaratory power', see P Ferguson and C McDiarmid, *Scots Criminal Law: A Critical Analysis*, 123–5; C Kennedy, 'Declaring Crimes'.

[138] See e.g. A T H Smith, 'Codification of the Criminal Law—Part 1: The Case for a Code'; G De Búrca and S Gardner, 'The Codification of the Criminal Law'; J Lavery, 'Codification of the Criminal Law: An Attainable Ideal?'.

[139] I will, again for simplicity's sake, focus on their role in determining offence definitions; they also, of course, play an important role in determining the scope of defences.

that they cease to be (never were) valid law: for in such systems, a type of conduct is criminalized only if it is defined as criminal by a statute that survives, or is not subjected to, scrutiny by a constitutional court.[140] Even in systems without any effective constitutional scrutiny of the criminal law, however, judges play an important role. It might be firmly declared that law must be made by the legislature, and that the responsibility of courts is to apply the law that is thus made—not to change the law, or make new law: but it must be obvious that such declarations have more to do with political rhetoric than with adjudicative reality, for the simple and familiar reason that no statute can be self-interpreting. Courts have to interpret the meaning, and thus the precise scope, of a statute; and in doing so (even if we insist that they are in some sense 'discovering' rather than 'creating' the law) they can criminalize, or decriminalize, types of conduct by determining that they fall, or do not fall, within the statutory definition of the offence. Sometimes that role is explicitly recognized, even welcomed. Dubber, for instance, has suggested that the offence definitions and other norms specified in the German Criminal Code are 'incomplete by design': the Code is intended to be made more determinate, the actual scope of the criminal law is to be determined, by others—at one time, Dubber suggests, by 'professor-scientists' on whose works the courts would rely;[141] more recently by the courts themselves. But whether the judges' law-determining responsibility falls on them only in 'hard cases', or more generally (and whether we see that role as the Herculean role of seeking 'the right answer' in some law-transcending sense,[142] or as that of trying to arrive at the best, or at least an acceptable, decision), they play a crucial role in determining which kinds of conduct are actually treated as criminal by the legal system.

Two examples from English law, one of criminalization and one of decriminalization, will illustrate this point.

First, in 1992 the House of Lords held that a man who forced sexual intercourse on his wife without her consent was guilty of rape.[143] It had, the Law Lords agreed, been the (common) law that 'by their mutual matrimonial consent and contract the wife hath given up herself in this kind unto her husband which she cannot retract',[144] though that doctrine had been gradually cabined by a growing number of judicially crafted exceptions. 'The common law is, however, capable of evolving in the light of changing social, economic and cultural developments';[145] the Law Lords accepted the Court of Appeal's view that

> There comes a time when the changes are so great that it is no longer enough to create further exceptions restricting the effect of the proposition, a time when the proposition itself requires examination to see whether its terms are in accord with what is generally regarded today as acceptable behaviour. . . . It seems to us that where the common law rule no longer even remotely represents what is the true position of a wife in present day society, the duty of the court is to take steps to alter the rule if it can legitimately do so in the light of any relevant Parliamentary enactment.[146]

[140] See the examples discussed in Dubber and Hörnle, *Criminal Law: A Comparative Approach*, ch. 3.

[141] M D Dubber, 'The Promise of German Criminal Law', at 1054. This suggestion is borne out by the ratio of commentary to statutory text (and the brevity of that text) in standard editions of the German *Strafgesetzbuch*.

[142] See, classically, R M Dworkin, *Law's Empire*.

[143] *R v R* [1992] 1 AC 599: see Law Commission, *Rape within Marriage; CR v UK* (1996) 21 EHRR 363; and see further below, Chapter 2 at nn 68–76.

[144] Sir Matthew Hale, *History of the Pleas of the Crown*, vol. 1, ch. 58, p. 629; quoted in *R v R*, at 615.

[145] [1992] 1 AC 599, 616 (Lord Keith).

[146] [1992] 1 AC 599, at 610 (Lord Lane CJ).

Thus far, it might seem that the Court was simply exercising its familiar power to develop the common law: but statutory law was also in play, since s. 1 of the Sexual Offences (Amendment) Act 1976 defined rape as requiring 'unlawful sexual intercourse', and the defence argued that this gave statutory force to the 'marital exemption' (since 'unlawful' must mean 'illicit', i.e. extra-marital). The Court rejected this argument, and held that 'unlawful' in the Act was 'mere surplusage'.[147] In response to the objection that this 'goes beyond the legitimate bounds of judge-made law and trespasses on the province of Parliament[, since] the abolition of a rule of such long standing, despite its emasculation by later decisions, is a task for the legislature and not the courts',[148] the Law Lords accepted the Court of Appeal's argument that '[t]his is not the creation of a new offence, it is the removal of a common law fiction which has become anachronistic and offensive and we consider that it is our duty having reached that conclusion to act upon it'.[149] English appeal court judges are thus sometimes willing to expand the scope of the criminal law, so long as this can be argued not to conflict with the evident will of the legislature; what is also striking is that this decision provoked no outcry, from politicians, lawyers, or theorists.

Second, courts are also willing to narrow the scope of the criminal law, for instance by re-defining some crucial element in the offence definition. A familiar example is the definition of 'recklessness' in such statutes as the Criminal Damage Act 1971.[150] The House of Lords had notoriously held in *Caldwell* that, at least in the context of offences such as criminal damage, 'recklessness' did not require an actual awareness that one's conduct might cause harm: it was sufficient that the defendant's action created 'an obvious risk' of the relevant kind of harm, and that he 'either ha[d] not given any thought to the possibility of there being any such risk or ha[d] recognised that there was some risk involved and ha[d] nonetheless gone on to do it'.[151] The Court of Appeal had then held (reluctantly) that this also required the conviction of a girl of 14, although the risk would not have been obvious to her even if she had thought about it, since the question was whether the risk would have been obvious to a 'reasonably prudent person', not whether it would have been obvious to the particular defendant.[152] However, in 2003, the House of Lords 'departed from' *Caldwell*, to hold that recklessness in this context did require an actual awareness of risk: there was 'a compelling need to correct [*Caldwell*'s] misinterpretation since it was apt to cause injustice and offended a jury's sense of fairness'.[153] This was a narrowing of the post-*Caldwell* law, since it narrowed the definition of the offence by narrowing the definition of 'recklessness': it was greeted, not with protests that it was not for the courts thus to change the scope of the criminal law, but with general relief that the mistaken extension of the law created by *Caldwell* had now been corrected. Here again, then, English courts (especially what is now the Supreme Court) claim, without challenge, the power to change the substantive law.

I am not here concerned to defend the English courts' practice or to discuss the proper extent of such judicial power. My point here is only that if to criminalize a type

[147] [1992] 1 AC 599, at 623 (Lord Keith). [148] [1992] 1 AC 599, at 610 (Lord Lane).

[149] [1992] 1 AC 599, at 611 (Lord Lane); see at 623 (Lord Keith).

[150] Under s. 1 of the Act, recklessness is sufficient *mens rea* both for the basic offence of damaging property (s. 1(1)), and for the aggravated offence of damaging property intending or being reckless as to the endangerment of another's life (s. 1(2)). In the continuing absence of a statutory definition of 'recklessness', the courts were still developing the common law: but their decisions helped to determine the scope of the statutory offence.

[151] *Caldwell* [1982] AC 341, at 354 (Lord Diplock). This arguably extended the scope of the criminal law, since earlier cases had insisted on awareness of risk (see e.g. *Stephenson* [1979] QB 695).

[152] *Elliott v C (a minor)* [1983] 1 WLR 939. [153] *R v G* [2004] 1 AC 1034.

of conduct is to render those who engage in it liable to conviction and punishment, courts as well as legislatures are in fact agents of criminalization: they help to determine the meaning (and thus sometimes to extend or to constrict the scope) of the substantive criminal law. As we will see later, it is also inevitable that courts will have some such power: so the question we must ask is not whether they should have it, but what its scope should be and how (if at all) it can be rendered accountable. A theory of criminalization must therefore have something to say not just about legislatures, but about the courts, and how they should go about their criminalization tasks. (It is also worth noting, since it fits with the argument of section 3 that criminal law is concerned with wrongs, that in both the cases noted here the courts were concerned with issues of wrongfulness and culpability: a man who forces sexual intercourse on his wife without her consent commits, the court argued, the wrong of rape, since it would be 'offensive' to maintain the 'fiction' that in getting married she gave her irrevocable consent; and it would be an 'injustice' to treat as guilty of criminal damage a young person who would not have realized the risk that she was creating even had she thought about the matter.)

We have been concerned so far with formal types of criminalization, criminalization 'in the books': appellate decisions, as well as enacted statutes, constitute authoritative, formal modes of criminalization (or decriminalization). Even if this exhausts the realm of formal criminalization, however, there remains an extensive realm of substantive, or 'in action', criminalization in which there are many other agents of criminalization than legislatures and courts: other agents whose decisions help to determine whether a type of conduct is treated as criminal—whether those who engage in such conduct are actually thereby rendered liable to criminal prosecution, conviction, and punishment. We must be careful to distinguish different phenomena (though the distinctions will not be sharp): sometimes we should talk merely of failures to enforce criminal laws that are certainly in force; sometimes of decisions, in individual cases or as making policy for a certain type of case, not to enforce criminal laws that are in force; and sometimes of policy decisions not to prosecute certain types of conduct that can plausibly be described as decisions to decriminalize types of conduct that are still formally criminal. But even if we should talk of (substantive, 'in action') decriminalization only in the last kind of case (and I will argue that we should talk of it in at least that kind of case), a normative theory of criminal law and criminalization must also have something to say about the other kinds of case: for if we cannot say (and we will see why we cannot) that we should strive to prosecute every crime, we must say something about how decisions about when and what to prosecute should be made.

Consider, for instance, the policy decisions made by inspectorates who enforce tax laws, or health and safety laws.[154] Many types of conduct that fit the formal definition of a crime might be dealt with, as a matter of policy, by methods other than prosecution—perhaps by negotiated arrangements that aim to secure future compliance (and to pay for past non-compliance). Should we say that such policies, if well entrenched, amount to policies of substantive decriminalization, because those who engage in such conduct will not (and can know that they will not) in fact face prosecution and punishment? On the one hand, we might say that their conduct is still criminal, substantively as well as formally. The point here is not that the regulatory agency has the power to intervene in relation to such conduct only because it is criminal: for that power depends not on the criminal character of the conduct, but on the fact that it violates a regulation that the agency is tasked to enforce.[155] The point is, rather, that

[154] See at nn 87–90 above.

[155] On the distinction between pre-criminal regulations, and the criminalization of breaches of such regulations, see at nn 45–8 above.

the prospect (actual as well as formal) of criminal prosecution remains in the picture, as a 'last resort', and thus as an incentive for compliance with the arrangements. On the other hand, if the policy is so well entrenched in shared understandings of the agency's *modus operandi* that someone who was prosecuted without being given a chance to enter into such a negotiated arrangement would have reason to complain, we might argue that what is substantively criminalized is not now the original breach of the regulation by itself: what is substantively criminalized is such breach on condition that the violator refuses or fails to enter into and carry through a suitable arrangement. We need not decide this issue here (it is probably undecidable except by stipulation): the point to note is simply that what matters normatively about criminalization is not just what criminal rules are formally enacted by an authorized law-making body, but how those rules are applied in practice. What must be justified, to justify criminalizing a certain type of conduct, is not just the enactment of a statute defining that conduct as criminal, but such an enactment as justifying and being prone to produce certain consequences. Of course, if we could say that once a criminal offence has been formally enacted, then all those involved in applying or enforcing the law must treat any conduct satisfying the definition of that offence as criminal, the gap between criminalization in the books and criminalization in action would have little normative significance: we would simply have to note that gap as marking one of the many ways in which human beings fail to act as they ought to act. But if we accept, as I will argue later that we ought to accept, that there *should* (for reasons both internal and external to criminal law) be a substantial gap between formal criminalization in the books and substantive criminalization in action, we will see that a normative theory of criminalization must address it.

That normative argument will develop later in the book: we need now to take note of some of the other practices of criminalization in action that a complete theory would need to address.

Consider first the police as agents of criminalization. We have noted some ways in which the police might divert conduct that is formally criminal from the criminal process: some involve not treating it as criminal, but as, for instance, a 'conflict', or a symptom of the need for psychiatric treatment.[156] But police forces will also, more radically, fail to respond at all to some kinds of formally criminal conduct; which could be said, if it becomes an entrenched policy on which citizens can then rely, to amount to substantive decriminalization. Of course the mere fact that a police force decides to focus its (always limited) resources in a particular direction, knowing that this will leave many crimes that could have been detected undetected and unprosecuted, should not lead us to say that those types of criminal conduct have been substantively decriminalized. If a mobile speed camera is sited in this place rather than that, speeding elsewhere that is therefore not detected is not thereby rendered non-criminal; if burglaries involving goods below a certain value are not investigated, they are not thereby decriminalized. Similarly, a police decision not to continue investigation of a particular case, or not to take further action in relation to a particular criminal act, does not amount to decriminalizing the conduct in question. In such cases the police decide (for good or bad reasons) not to try to enforce what is still substantively the criminal law: those who commit the offences that are not investigated are still liable to prosecution; they would have no grounds for complaint if, against their empirically well-founded expectations and against the ordinary pattern of police practice, their conduct was investigated and

[156] See at n. 84 above.

they were prosecuted (unless they could show that the decision to pursue them was vindictive or discriminatory).[157]

Suppose, however, that a local police force adopts, and announces or allows to be known, a policy of not making arrests or bringing charges for a particular kind of offence: perhaps a policy of not arresting, prosecuting, or reporting those found in possession of small amounts of a certain prohibited drug. It might then be argued that such possession has, within that force's area, been decriminalized: it has not been legalized—if, for instance, those small amounts of the prohibited drug are liable to be confiscated, such possession has not been legalized; but it has in effect been decriminalized.[158] It might be objected that this is to confuse 'rules for citizens' with rules, if not 'for courts', then more generally 'for officials':[159] the rules for citizens, as declared in the criminal law's offence definitions, tell the citizens that they must not have such drugs in their possession (even in the area covered by this police force); but as an informal qualification to the rules for officials, the police force decides not to pursue breaches of that rule for citizens. This *might* be the best way to describe the situation, at least if the policy is informal and not well-established: but if the policy becomes so entrenched and well-known that there would be reason to complain of injustice if the police suddenly began to enforce the law in the books again,[160] it might be better to say that such drug possession has been effectively decriminalized in that area.

Prosecutors also have an important role to play in determining what is (treated as) criminal, though just what that role might be varies between different systems.[161] According to the official rhetoric of some civil law systems, for instance, prosecutors are bound by a 'Legality Principle', which requires them to prosecute whenever they have sufficient evidence, whilst prosecutors in common law systems operate instead under an 'Opportunity Principle' that gives them discretion as to whether or not to prosecute even when they have sufficient evidence to make a conviction likely.[162] This distinction has been gradually eroded,[163]

[157] See e.g. W LaFave et al, *Criminal Procedure*, ch. 13.4–5.

[158] See e.g. M Evans, 'Police are "Turning a Blind Eye" to Cannabis across the Country, Experts Claim'; also the story of the Obama administration's dealings with the possession of medical marijuana, as told in S S Taylor, *Marijuana Policy and Presidential Leadership: How to Avoid a Federal-State Train Wreck*. (In relation to the power to substantively (de)criminalize, it matters of course *who* decides the policy.)

[159] See at n. 10 above. This suggestion might be reinforced by appeal to 'acoustic separation': such policies are not addressed, and perhaps should not be made known, to the public (see Dan-Cohen, 'Decision Rules and Conduct Rules'). For persuasive criticism, see R Singer, 'On Classism and Dissonance in the Criminal Law: A Reply to Professor Dan-Cohen'.

[160] Or could such complaints be justified only if it could first be shown that the conduct had been decriminalized? I am inclined to think that what would justify the complaints would be the publicly known entrenchment of the policy, together perhaps with the fact that it was grounded partly in consideration of the character and (lack of) seriousness of the conduct in question, creating a reasonable expectation of continued non-enforcement.

[161] See generally M Tonry (ed.), *Prosecutors and Politics: A Comparative Perspective*; J Ross and S Thaman (eds), *Research Handbook on Comparative Criminal Procedure*; M Langer and D Sklansky (eds), *Prosecutors and Democracy: A Cross-National Study*.

[162] For a very useful survey, see D Kyprianou, *The Role of the Cyprus Attorney General's Office in Prosecutions: Rhetoric, Ideology and Practice*, ch. 2.3; see also Perrodet, 'The Public Prosecutor'. See above, at nn 85–6, and at nn 154–5 on regulatory agencies as prosecutors; I focus here on public prosecutors.

[163] See e.g. M Damaška, 'The Reality of Prosecutorial Discretion: Comments on a German Monograph'; §§ 153–5 of the German *Strafprozessorfnung*; M Bohlander, *Principles of German Criminal Procedure*, 25–7; A Sanders and R Young, 'The Rule of Law, Due Process and Pre-Trial Criminal Justice'.

but I will focus on English prosecutors, who avowedly follow an Opportunity Principle.[164]

English prosecutors must apply two tests in deciding whether to prosecute: an 'evidential' test and a 'public interest' test.[165] The evidential test is passed only if the prosecutor is 'satisfied that there is sufficient evidence to provide a realistic prospect of conviction'. The satisfaction of this test creates a presumption in favour of prosecution, but that presumption is defeasible: the prosecutor should not proceed if it is not in 'the public interest' to do so. I will have more to say later about how we should interpret each of these tests: my point here is only that the public interest test explicitly gives the prosecutor discretion about whether to treat as criminal—that is, to pursue through the criminal process—conduct that can be proved to satisfy the formal definition of an offence. Once again, if a prosecutor simply decides in an individual case not to prosecute a person whose guilt she could prove, we would not naturally talk of 'decriminalization': matters are different, however, if prosecutors adopt policies of not prosecuting in certain kinds of case, and especially if those policies are made by or for the prosecution service as a whole.

Sometimes, the prosecutorial role in (de)criminalization is made explicit, as something that the legislature expects and openly mandates. So when the British government introduced what became the Sexual Offences Act 2003, critics pointed out that ss 9 and 13 criminalized consensual sexual activity between young people aged fifteen—which, they thought, was absurd. A minister reassured these critics that that was not the Bill's 'intention', and would not be its 'effect': 'we shall be able to trust the Crown Prosecution Service (CPS) to ensure that that intention is followed'.[166] The government was asking Parliament to enact a statute whose offence definitions were avowedly over-broad, defining as criminal types of conduct that there was no intention to treat as criminal; and to rely on prosecutors to use their discretion to put that intention into effect. Suppose that two fifteen-year-olds engage in 'sexual touching', thus satisfying the definition of the offence of 'sexual activity with a child'. The matter comes to the attention of the police, who (perhaps from moralistic enthusiasm) send the case to the CPS; the prosecutor, in line with the government's expressed intention, decides not to prosecute. If this is a matter of CPS policy, as it must be, given the government's (and by implication the legislature's) clear intention, we should say that such sexual activity is criminal in the books, but is not (really) criminal: it was formally criminalized, but is not substantively criminalized, or has been substantively decriminalized.[167]

I am not here concerned to evaluate this legislative strategy of enacting offences defined in terms that are admittedly too wide, and relying on prosecutors to use their discretion to apply the law only to its 'real' targets. Critics might argue that it is a

[164] 'Opportunity Principle' might be a misleading label, if taken to imply that evidence of guilt provides simply an opportunity to prosecute; the principle is rather that prosecution should proceed only if it is 'opportune'.

[165] See CPS, *Code for Crown Prosecutors*, s. 4; Ashworth and Redmayne, *The Criminal Process*, 194–214.

[166] Hansard vol. 409, 15 July 2003, col. 248; Paul Goggins, a Home Office Minister. But see A P Simester et al, *Simester and Sullivan's Criminal Law*, 496–8, on the extent to which the CPS showed this trust to be misplaced.

[167] It is arguable that non-prosecution in such a case should be grounded not in the 'public interest' test, but in the 'evidential' test: the prosecutor should decide, not that though there is sufficient evidence of a (genuine) crime, 'public interest' factors external to the criminal law militate against prosecution, but that there is no evidence that a real crime (conduct involving the mischief at which the law is aimed) has been committed. See J Rogers, 'The Role of the Public Prosecutor in Applying and Developing the Substantive Criminal Law'.

recipe for sloppy legislation: to which the answer will be that while legislatures should do their best to define offences precisely, if they are to avoid enacting offences that are too narrowly defined effectively to address the mischief at which the law is aimed, they must sometimes enact offences that are on their face too broad or vague, and rely on the discretion of those who are to apply the law. The point here, however, is simply to note that this is another way in which parties other than the legislature are involved in the process of substantive criminalization.

Sometimes a policy-led exercise of prosecutorial discretion is not thus explicitly sanctioned by the legislature—which might raise worries about its democratic legitimacy.

It is a crime under English law to assist a suicide—though prosecutions require the consent of the DPP.[168] In a number of publicized cases, people helped their loved ones travel to the Swiss Dignitas clinic, to secure the kind of assisted death that was legally unavailable in Britain: such assistance clearly satisfied the statutory definition of the crime, but in no case did the DPP approve a prosecution. This was, however, a matter of *ex post* discretion: those contemplating such assistance had to hope that the DPP would exercise his discretion not to prosecute them. Unhappy with this situation, Debbie Purdy asked the DPP to tell her what factors would be taken into account in a decision about whether to prosecute a case of assisting suicide, so that she and her husband could know in advance whether he would be prosecuted if he helped her travel to the Dignitas clinic as her multiple sclerosis worsened. When the DPP refused to do this, she went to court, and the House of Lords backed her: the DPP had 'a duty to clarify his position', and must 'promulgate an offence-specific policy identifying the facts and circumstances which he would take into account in deciding' whether to prosecute.[169]

The DPP accordingly published a *Policy*: it did not, he insisted, 'decriminalise the offence of encouraging or assisting suicide' or give any assurance of immunity from prosecution to anyone who encouraged or assisted another's suicide (para. 6); but it listed sixteen 'public interest factors tending in favour of prosecution', and six 'tending against prosecution' (paras 43, 45).[170] This certainly enables those contemplating assisting to another's suicide to predict whether they will face prosecution: those who, acting from compassion and without any prospect of material gain, provide modest help to others who are intent on suicide can be confident that they will not face prosecution—and would have reason to protest if they were prosecuted.

What is less clear, however, is how the grounds for not prosecuting should be interpreted. Is non-prosecution an exercise of mercy towards those who commit such a crime in such difficult circumstances, and who are no doubt still afflicted by grief for the loved one whom they helped? In that case the conduct is still treated as a crime, but the demands of mercy divert the prosecutor from pursuing the criminal process.[171] Or does it mark a recognition of compassion as an excuse: that compassion, in such circumstances, can have a compelling effect that negates or mitigates culpability?[172] Or

[168] Suicide Act 1961, s. 2.

[169] *R (Purdy) v Director of Public Prosecutions* [2009] 3 WLR 403. In a previous case, the courts had backed the DPP's refusal to guarantee non-prosecution (*R (Pretty) v Director of Public Prosecutions* [2002] 1 AC 800).

[170] Crown Prosecution Service, *Policy for Prosecutors in Respect of Cases of Encouraging or Assisting Suicide*. See J Rogers, 'Prosecutorial Policies, Prosecutorial Systems and the Purdy Litigation'; P Lewis, 'Informal Legal Change on Assisted Suicide: The Policy for Prosecutors'; C O'Sullivan, 'Mens Rea, Motive and Assisted Suicide: Does the DPP'S Policy Go Too Far?'.

[171] This raises various questions about the meaning of mercy and its relationship to criminal justice, but they need not distract us here: see R A Duff, 'Mercy'.

[172] See R A Duff, 'Criminal Responsibility and the Emotions'.

is it an application of a '*De Minimis*' test: although such assistance satisfies the formal definition of the crime, it does not cause or constitute the kind of mischief against which the law is aimed?[173] That third reading, on which this kind of assistance is portrayed as not being (really) criminal, might seem implausible: but it is suggested by some of the Law Lords' remarks in *Purdy*, which implied that the reason for requiring the DPP to publish the policy was to enable law-abiding citizens to work out what they may legitimately do.[174] Although the published policy was formally a policy for prosecutors, it was thus not, in the court's eyes, a policy addressed only to prosecutors; it was to help citizens guide their own conduct.[175]

On this reading, the case of assisted suicide would be like that of youthful sexual activity and the Sexual Offences Act 2003, but with the crucial difference that in this case the DPP lacks any explicit parliamentary approval or acceptance of such a policy; indeed parliament has regularly refused to decriminalize assistance to suicide.[176] Once we turn to avowedly normative theorizing, we will therefore need to ask whether or how it can be appropriate for prosecutors to have such a decriminalizing discretion in a democratic polity's system of criminal law; but for the moment, the point is simply to note that in some systems they do in fact have such discretion. It is true that they do not have a matching discretion to *criminalize*: they can prosecute only if there is some existing (typically statutory) crime under which they can bring the case. But if they have a large enough range of crimes that they could charge, they also then have considerable discretion as to what they will charge: this leads into some serious worries about the plea bargaining process, and the kind of power that prosecutors (especially in the US) might have to 'induce' guilty pleas by threatening a raft of serious charges—but we need not pursue this issue at the moment.[177]

One final category of agents of criminalization should be mentioned: ordinary citizens, who will sometimes be able to choose whether to have conduct treated as criminal. Sometimes, of course, criminal or prima facie criminal conduct comes directly to the notice of the police—it is not up to lay citizens (as victims, witnesses, or perpetrators of the crime) to report it or to decide not to report it to the police. Even then they may have some de facto power to affect whether the conduct is fully treated as criminal—that is, whether its agent is prosecuted for it. If a crime victim tells the police that he does not want the case to be pursued, neither police nor prosecutor might be formally bound to accede to his request:[178] but they might nonetheless accede to it either from regard for his wishes or from concern that the case would not succeed without his cooperation.[179] If a victim or a witness refuses to give the police

[173] See the American Model Penal Code, § 2.12; and below Chapter 2 at nn 57–9.

[174] See e.g. [2009] 3 WLR 403 at paras 40 (Lord Hope), 59 (Lady Hale), 83–6 (Lord Brown). Similar remarks can be found in the later case of *Nicklinson v Ministry of Justice* [2015] AC 657, concerning the position of health care professionals who might assist a suicide—although in both cases the court was also at pains to insist that it was not for the DPP, or for the court, to change the law on assisted suicide.

[175] See at nn 10, 159 above on 'rules for citizens' and 'rules for courts' (or for officials).

[176] Most recently when the House of Commons rejected the Assisted Dying (No. 2) Bill in September 2015, by a majority of 212. Contrast the Scottish case of *Ross v Lord Advocate* [2016] CSIH 12, in which the Court of Session refused a similar request to require the Lord Advocate to publish guidelines—but partly on the grounds that the law in Scotland was entirely clear, and that the kind of assistance involved in such cases as *Pretty* and *Purdy* was not criminal under Scots law (which has no distinct offence of assisting suicide).

[177] See Husak, *Overcriminalization*, 21–4; and at nn 96, 114–18 above.

[178] But see at n. 66 above.

[179] The English *Code for Crown Prosecutors* requires prosecutors to 'take into account the views expressed by the victim about the impact that the offence has had' and 'to consider if a prosecution is likely to have an adverse effect on the victim's physical or mental health', but it makes clear that 'the

the information that would help them to identify the offender, or refuses to give relevant evidence in court, he can make it impossible for the case to proceed (although he might also then face criminal liability himself).[180] If the crime does not come to the direct notice of the police, victims and witnesses might then have more of a choice about whether to treat it as criminal—should they report it or not? This might seem to be nothing more than a choice about whether to report what is still a crime, even if they do not report it; and it might in some jurisdictions expose them to criminal liability for failing to report a crime, or for 'misprision of felony' (at least if the crime is serious), if they fail to report it.[181] However, it could amount to a more interesting reconceptualization of the conduct in question: instead of seeing it, and responding to it, as a crime, within the conceptual and practical framework of criminal law, those directly involved in the matter see it and respond to it as, perhaps, a 'trouble', or 'conflict', that they need to resolve among themselves.[182] Private citizens do not, of course, have the power to decriminalize types of conduct: but they do sometimes have the power to bring it about that instances of formally criminal conduct are, or are not, actually treated as criminal.

There is of course plenty of room for normative argument about whether or when we should in such ways refrain from treating what is (at least formally) criminal conduct as criminal; there are obvious objections to doing so, especially in the case of seriously victimizing crimes.[183] But my aim in this chapter has not been to argue for a particular normative position on such matters: it has been to point up various features of criminal law as a set of institutional practices that play a significant role in the life of a polity—features that a normative theory of criminalization must address. One such feature is the part that lay citizens can play in determining whether conduct that is formally criminal is in fact treated in action as criminal, and their power to ensure that it is not treated as criminal. We might not call this is a way of 'decriminalizing' the conduct; indeed, the culprit might sometimes still be liable to a criminal response of prosecution and punishment—not just formally, given the law in the books, but substantively, should the police have, and be disposed to use, the power to intervene. But it is a way of removing conduct from the ambit of the criminal law, which should reinforce one of the central points of this section: even when we have in place a criminal law that formally criminalizes a particular type of conduct, and have or could probably acquire conclusive proof that someone engaged in that conduct, there are choices to be made—by private citizens as well as by the officials of the system—about whether to treat that conduct as criminal by bringing it into the ambit of the criminal process. Such choices might not count as choices about whether to (de)criminalize; but a normative theory of criminalization, if it is to be (as it should) a theory about how criminal law should function as an institution, must have something to say about who should have such choices and how they should be made.

CPS does not act for victims or their families ..., and prosecutors must form an overall view of the public interest' (para. 4.12).

[180] E.g. for contempt of court if he refuses to give evidence.

[181] The offence of misprision of felony was abolished in England by the Criminal Law Act 1967, s. 1 (but a range of more particular offences of failing to report, dealing with particular kinds of crime or people in positions of particular authority, remain). See M Gur-Arye, 'A Failure to Prevent Crime—Should it be Criminal?'.

[182] See Christie, 'Conflicts as Property'; L Hulsman, 'Critical Criminology and the Concept of Crime'; and above, Introduction at n. 25.

[183] As when the police would describe domestic violence as a 'domestic' matter into which they should not (or would not) intervene, leaving it to the people concerned to sort it out for themselves.

8. Conclusion: A Conception of Criminal Law

In this chapter I have sketched the three central dimensions of a system of criminal law: the substantive criminal law, which purports to authoritatively define a set of 'public' wrongs; the criminal process, culminating in the criminal trial, as the process through which those suspected of committing such wrongs are investigated and may be prosecuted—a process that is plausibly understood as one of calling alleged offenders to public account; and criminal punishment, which should be understood (and must therefore be justified, if it can be justified) as an intentionally burdensome and reprobative imposition for an alleged crime—which leaves open the question of whether the meaning and justification of punishment must depend not only on the relationship between the punishment and the offence for which it is imposed, but also on the relationship between the punisher and the punished. Also crucial to the character and functioning (and thus to the justification) of criminal law, however, are the processes of criminalization: the formal and informal processes through which types of conduct are defined (formally or substantively) as criminal, and through which perpetrators of those types of conduct are rendered liable (formally or substantively) to prosecution and punishment; and the agents who have (formal or informal) roles to play in such processes. One analytical question about such processes is which of them should count strictly as processes of criminalization; but I suggested that we should not expect a clear answer to that question, and that it is anyway not an important one for a normative theorist. What is important for a normative theorist is that her theory be able to address these aspects of the criminal law as a functioning institution: for if we are to ask what kinds of conduct should be criminalized, or to identify the principles and values that should guide criminalization decisions, we must attend not only to the formal processes of criminalization in the books, but also to the processes through which formally criminalized conduct comes to be brought substantively within the ambit of the criminal process.

In sketching this conception of criminal law, I have attempted not to prejudge the normative questions about the proper role and scope of the criminal law that are to be discussed in the rest of this book. I have tried to sketch the central features of a distinctive kind of legal institution, in order then to ask what kind of role (if any) such an institution should play in a polity; but I have not assumed either that a polity should maintain such an institution, or that it should play a particular role. It is true that this conception does not purport to be a neutral description of the actual operations of our existing institutions of criminal law: it is the product of an exercise in rational reconstruction, and that reconstruction has aimed to describe an institution that is at least a plausible candidate for normative justification. But I have not assumed either that such a justification will be available, or that it will take a particular form: that will be argued later.

Nor indeed have I intended to rule out radically revisionary theories of criminal law, which might argue that we should reconceptualize criminal law to fit more coherently with a favoured normative theory. If someone argues, for instance, that we should see criminal law as just one amongst other kinds of regulation, distinguishable from others primarily by the harshness of the sanctions that it imposes,[184] I might say that this is not a conception of criminal law; but he might reasonably reply that what he is advocating is a radical reconceptualizing of criminal law—one that excises

[184] See e.g. Chiao, 'What is the Criminal Law For?'.

the normatively unhelpful accretions of our existing conceptions. It does not matter whether such a theorist is better seen as arguing that we should replace the criminal law by a different, non-criminal, institution of sanction-backed regulations; or as arguing that we should reconceptualize criminal law in this way. In either case, his argument must be met in substantive terms, as an argument about the kinds of institution we should have: it cannot be disposed of by the 'definitional stop' of saying 'But that's not criminal law'.[185]

The route I will take towards a normative account of the proper role of criminal law should become clearer in the following chapter, which discusses legal moralism. In saying that criminal law is concerned with wrongs, I locate myself in the legal moralist camp: by exploring the kinds of view that might be classed as versions of legal moralism, and by distinguishing my account from others, I will be able to clarify the sense in which criminal law is concerned with 'public' wrongs, and thus also show what needs to be done to explain and justify such a concern.

[185] See n. 127 above.

2

Legal Moralism and Public Wrongs

1. Principles of Criminalization?

In Chapter 1, I outlined an account of criminal law as a distinctive legal institution, involving distinctive practices of criminalization, of investigation and adjudication, and of punishment. The ultimate aim of this book is to work towards a theory of criminalization: an account, that is, if not directly of what we should criminalize, of how we should go about deciding what to criminalize, and of the proper starting points and structure of deliberations about criminalization. We might expect such an account to articulate principles of criminalization: a principle, or set of principles, by reference to which we can determine what we may or must, or may or must not, criminalize; or by reference to which we should at least determine what can or cannot count as a good reason to criminalize. I will discuss the character and role of such principles in detail later, although I will say something about one family of principles in this chapter: the main point to notice here, however, is that in working towards a theory of criminalization we should not *begin* by trying to identify principles of criminalization.

That is just where some theorists of criminalization do begin. Thus by page 10 of the first volume of his monumental *Moral Limits of the Criminal Law*, Feinberg already starts to discuss 'Commonly Proposed Liberty-Limiting Principles', and goes on to identify and define ten such principles, which he discusses in the rest of the four-volume work.[1] Principles of criminalization are not, however, self-standing principles, independent of any political context; they cannot be generated by moral reasoning from first principles. They are principles concerning the operation of a particular kind of legal institution that exists as part of a political structure: we can therefore develop them only on the basis of an account of the proper role of such an institution within such a structure. A theory of criminalization must be grounded in an account of the role of criminal law as part of the institutional structure of a polity; and such an account must itself be grounded in an account of the nature and aims of a polity—in political theory.

One aim of this chapter is to show why this is the proper approach for normative theorists to take to the question of criminalization. I will begin, however, by discussing one familiar family of principles of criminalization—principles that can be classed as versions of 'legal moralism'. One reason for doing this is that my account of criminal law in Chapter 1 clearly commits me to some version of legal moralism, since it portrayed criminal law as being essentially concerned with moral wrongdoing: it will therefore be helpful to make clear what I am, and what I am not, committed to. Another reason is that by showing the deficiencies in some other versions of legal moralism, I will be able to show what route we must take towards an adequate normative theory of criminal law, and why that route should begin with political philosophy. In the course of this discussion I will also draw some distinctions between the different

[1] J Feinberg, *Harm to Others*: the ten principles are initially defined at 26–7. See also A P Simester and A von Hirsch, *Crimes, Harms and Wrongs: On the Principles of Criminalization*.

forms that legal moralism can take—distinctions that will be important when we come to discuss other proposed principles of criminalization later.[2]

The label 'legal moralism' picks out a family of views about the proper aims and scope of the criminal law, according to which the justification for criminalizing a given type of conduct depends on the moral wrongfulness of that type of conduct: but that dependence can be of quite different kinds, and the relevant notion of wrongfulness can also differ.

2. Legal Moralism (1): Critical v Positivist

The first distinction we should draw, in order to set aside a kind of view that is sometimes classed as a species of legal moralism, but that is perhaps better understood as a distinctive kind of (morality-dependent) harm principle, is between what we can call (following Hart) a 'critical' and a 'positivist' legal moralism.[3] A critically moralist legislator or theorist (or interested citizen) who is wondering whether we have good reason to criminalize Φ-ing will ask whether Φ-ing is wrong in the appropriate way:[4] if her judgment is that Φ-ing is not thus wrong, she will conclude that we do not have reason to criminalize it—even if it is widely thought to be morally wrong by members of the society in question. By contrast, a positivist legal moralist will ask whether Φ-ing is thought to be wrong by members of this society—whether the prevailing social morality condemns it as wrongful: her view on whether we have reason to criminalize Φ-ing will depend not on her judgment of whether it is wrong, but on how it figures in that social morality—on, for instance, how strongly it is felt to be seriously wrong.

This distinction can be illustrated by contrasting two of the most famous English disputes about 'legal moralism' in the nineteenth and twentieth centuries.

The first of these disputes was between Stephen and Mill. In response to Mill's assertion of the harm principle, according to which the only legitimate reason for any kind of state or social coercion, including the use of criminal law, was to prevent harm to others,[5] Stephen insisted that the criminal law was properly used to punish moral wrongdoing:

> These acts have in fact been forbidden and subjected to punishment not only because they are dangerous to society, and so ought to be prevented, but also for the sake of gratifying the feeling of hatred—call it revenge, resentment, or what you will—which the contemplation of such conduct excites in healthily constituted minds. It will follow that criminal law is in the nature of a persecution of the grosser forms of vice.[6]

Although Stephen thought that criminal law should aim to 'gratify' ('in a regular public and legal manner') the feelings of members of the society, it should do so only by punishing conduct that is indeed immoral (and seriously so). That makes him a

[2] See below, Chapter 6; also J Edwards, 'Master Principles of Criminalisation'.

[3] See H L A Hart, *Law, Liberty, and Morality*, 17–20 on the distinction between 'critical' and 'positive' morality.

[4] The reason for the qualifying 'in the appropriate way' will become clear later in this chapter: see section 6 below.

[5] J S Mill, *On Liberty*, ch. 1, para. 9: see further below, Chapter 6, section 3; B Harcourt, 'Mill's On Liberty and the Modern "Harm to Others" Principle'.

[6] J F Stephen, *Liberty, Equality, Fraternity*, 162; on which see M O DeGirolami, 'James Fitzjames Stephen: The Punishment Jurist'.

'critical' legal moralist, who is interested in the justifying relationship between the real immorality of a type of conduct and its criminalization.

The second of these disputes, a century later, was between Devlin and Hart. The Wolfenden Committee had argued that 'there must remain a realm of private morality and immorality which is, in brief and crude terms, not the law's business' and that it 'is not the duty of the law to concern itself with immorality as such'.[7] Devlin responded that 'it is not possible to set theoretical limits on the power of the State to legislate against immorality', or to 'define inflexibly areas of morality into which the law is in no circumstances to be allowed to enter':[8] a society must have the right to protect itself by enforcing the shared morality that is essential to its survival. Now Hart, in his critique of Devlin's arguments, puts Devlin and Stephen on the same side: for both are concerned with the use of criminal law against conduct that violates the 'positive' morality of the society whose law it is—though Stephen can be said to hold an 'extreme', and Devlin only a 'moderate' version of the thesis that criminal law may be used to enforce that shared morality.[9] But this is a misreading of Stephen. Stephen did hold that one 'cannot punish anything which public opinion ... does not strenuously and unequivocally condemn';[10] a necessary condition of criminalization was that the conduct to be criminalized be immoral in the eyes of public opinion. But that was not a sufficient condition, since the conduct must also *be* immoral. That distinguishes him from Devlin, and makes him a critical legal moralist (even if he was not quick to criticize his society's prevailing morality), whereas Devlin was a positivist legal moralist. What Devlin meant by 'the enforcement of morals' was enforcement of 'the common morality': 'the morality which the law enforces must be popular morality'.[11] His concern was with a society's survival—something that depends, he argued, on the preservation of a shared morality, and is threatened if that morality is undermined. We cannot say a priori that there are kinds of perceived immorality whose tolerated indulgence would not threaten to undermine that morality: we therefore cannot say, a priori, that there are spheres of 'private' immorality that are, in principle, not the law's business. Devlin was not applying a principle of critical legal moralism, according to which what matters is whether a type of conduct *is* wrongful; he was applying an idiosyncratic harm principle, according to which the salient harm to be prevented was the collapse of the shared social morality and the disastrous social effects of such a collapse. He was, in that sense, a 'positivist' legal moralist: the morality that was to be enforced was the positive morality of the society in question.

I will not discuss Devlin's views further here:[12] my aim has been simply to distinguish these two kinds of 'legal moralism', and to make clear that my concern in what follows will be with critical legal moralism—with views according to which the focus, or ground, of criminalization should be actual rather than merely perceived wrongdoing. In a democracy in which decisions about criminalization are made on the basis of public deliberation, those decisions will reflect the prevailing morality of

[7] Sir John Wolfenden, *Report of the Committee on Homosexual Offences and Prostitution*), paras 61, 257.

[8] P Devlin, *The Enforcement of Morals*, 12–13.

[9] Hart, *Law, Liberty, and Morality*, 16–17, 48–51.

[10] Stephen, *Liberty, Equality, Fraternity*, 173–4.

[11] See *The Enforcement of Morals*, viii, x; also J Feinberg, *Harmless Wrongdoing*, 8, on 'impure legal moralism'.

[12] For a useful recent discussion of the Devlin–Hart debate, see M Renzo (ed.), '"Law, Liberty, and Morality": Fifty Years On'; see also G Dworkin, 'Devlin Was Right: Law and the Enforcement of Morality'.

the society: but if those engaged in the deliberation engage as critical legal moralists, they will not think it enough to point out that a type of conduct is in fact regarded as seriously wrong by most citizens; they will need to argue that it is *rightly* so regarded.

3. Legal Moralism (2): Positive v Negative

A second crucial distinction is between 'negative' and 'positive' versions of legal moralism. Negative legal moralists hold that wrongdoing (the wrongness of the conduct to be criminalized) is a necessary condition of justified criminalization, but not that it gives us any positive reason to criminalize. We must not criminalize conduct unless it is wrongful; but our positive reasons for criminalizing it may lie elsewhere—for instance in the fact that it causes or threatens harm to others. By contrast, a positive legal moralist holds that the wrongfulness of a type of conduct gives us positive reason to criminalize it: not necessarily a conclusive reason, since we might find stronger countervailing reasons against criminalization; but at least a good reason.[13] This distinction parallels that between negative and positive versions of retributivism in penal theory. For positive retributivists the justifying aim of a penal system is to impose deserved punishment: that wrongdoers deserve punishment gives us a good, if not conclusive, reason to institute a system of criminal law to impose such punishments on them. Negative retributivists, by contrast, hold that the positive aims of a penal system may lie in something other than retributive desert—for instance in the achievement of some consequential benefits. Retributive desert operates as a side-constraint on our pursuit of those justifying aims, a constraint expressed in the principle that we must not (knowingly) punish the innocent: thus guilt provides no positive reason in favour of punishment, but innocence constitutes a conclusive reason against it.[14]

For a negative legal moralist, we can say, the wrongfulness of a type of conduct is merely an 'enabling' condition or reason: it opens the way for positive reasons in favour of criminalization (for instance that criminalizing this type of conduct will prevent harm) to come into play. Were the conduct not wrongful, harm prevention could not give us positive reason to criminalize it; but if it is wrongful, we can then see harm prevention as a good reason to criminalize it. The fact that a type of conduct is not wrongful does not count as a reason against criminalizing it, which must be weighed against whatever reasons there might be for criminalizing it—not even as a reason against criminalization that will always outweigh any reasons for it. Rather, if a type of conduct is not wrongful we may not even consider criminalizing it, or consider anything as a reason to criminalize it.[15] For a positive legal moralist, by contrast, the wrongfulness of a type of conduct itself constitutes a positive reason to criminalize it.

Some version of negative legal moralism is obviously connected to my claim, in the previous chapter, that the criminal law deals with wrongs. It does not flow directly from that claim, since it adds to the conceptual claim, that the criminal law portrays the conduct that it criminalizes as wrongful, a normative claim that the criminal law should be used honestly—that criminalizers should use it only against conduct that

[13] Further distinctions will need to be drawn later within positive legal moralism: see below, Chapter 6, sections 3 and 4.

[14] On 'negative' and 'positive' retributivism, see D Dolinko, 'Some Thoughts about Retributivism', 539–43. Compare L Alexander and K Ferzan, *Crime and Culpability: A Theory of Criminal Law*, 7–10, on 'weak', 'moderate', and 'strong' retributivism.

[15] For the distinction between (positive) reasons and enabling conditions, see J Dancy, *Ethics Without Principles*, ch. 3; but see further section 4 below.

they believe to be wrongful. We should note too that the normative claim is better expressed in hypothetical terms: *if* we are going to maintain a system of criminal law, then we should use it honestly, to criminalize only wrongful conduct. That gives us no reason to maintain such a system, with its distinctive focus on wrongdoing—in preference, for instance, to a sanction-backed regime of regulations that does not purport to be concerned with wrongdoing: negative legal moralism, as it stands, has nothing to say about that latter possibility.

Some version of negative legal moralism is widely accepted, even by theorists who may not call themselves 'legal moralists'. Thus, for just three recent instances, Feinberg's version of the harm principle includes a negative legal moralist constraint on criminalization: 'harm', he argues, should be understood as wrongful harm; thus 'only setbacks of interests that are wrongs ... are to count as harms in the appropriate sense',[16] and only such setbacks of interests are the criminal law's concern. Similarly, one of the 'internal constraints' on criminalization that Husak identifies is 'the wrongfulness constraint', that '[p]enal liability may not be imposed unless the defendant's conduct is (in some sense) wrongful'.[17] So too, Simester and von Hirsch argue for a 'Necessity Thesis' about the relation of wrongfulness to criminalization: '[t]hat Φing is wrong is necessary to justify its criminalisation'.[18]

Positive legal moralism, by contrast, is far less commonly accepted, and is often viewed with suspicion, if not with horror, by liberal critics who see it as a disturbing throwback to the kind of oppressive moralism expressed in Stephen's notorious remark that 'criminal law is in the nature of a persecution of the grosser forms of vice'.[19] But a contemporary version of positive legal moralism is found in Moore's claim that the function of the criminal law is 'to attain retributive justice', by punishing 'all and only those who are morally culpable in the doing of some morally wrongful action':[20] the only good reason for criminalizing a type of conduct is that it is morally wrong, and therefore deserves the punishment that criminal law provides. Moore's version of legal moralism thus sets a 'positive constraint' on criminalization:[21] not only is the wrongfulness of a type of conduct a good reason to criminalize it, so as to ensure that its perpetrators receive the punishment they deserve; it is the *only* good reason that we could have to criminalize it.[22] By contrast, when Feinberg identifies (without endorsing) 'Legal Moralism (in the usual narrow sense)', he gives it a permissive reading: '[i]t can be morally legitimate to prohibit conduct on the ground that it is inherently immoral, even though it causes neither harm nor offense to the actor or to others'.[23]

Moore's is an exclusive legal moralism; what Feinberg identifies is a non-exclusive version of legal moralism, which allows that there might be other good reasons to criminalize. An exclusive legal moralism combines positive and negative principles: we have good reason to criminalize morally wrongful conduct and no good reason to

[16] Feinberg, *Harm to Others*, 36.

[17] D N Husak, *Overcriminalization: The Limits of the Criminal Law*, 72.

[18] Simester and von Hirsch, *Crimes, Harms, and Wrongs: On the Principles of Criminalization*, 22, 20. See also A Cornford, 'Rethinking the Wrongness Constraint on Criminalisation', n. 1, for further references.

[19] Stephen, *Liberty, Equality, Fraternity*, 162; see at n. 6 above.

[20] M S Moore, *Placing Blame: A Theory of the Criminal Law*, 33–5.

[21] On 'positive constraints', see J Edwards, 'Harm Principles', 257.

[22] See also M S Moore, 'A Tale of Two Theories', 32. A more familiar version of a positive constraint is Mill's Harm Principle: '*the only purpose* for which power can rightfully be exercised over any member of a civilised community against his will is to prevent harm to others' (*On Liberty*, ch. 1, para. 9; emphasis added).

[23] Feinberg, *Harm to Others*, 27.

criminalize non-wrongful conduct. By contrast, an inclusive legal moralism renders the negative and positive principles logically independent of each other: to say, as negative legal moralists say, that the absence of wrongfulness categorically precludes criminalization is not to say that the presence of wrongfulness is any kind of reason for criminalization; and to say, as inclusive positive legal moralists say, that the wrongfulness of a given type of conduct is always a reason in favour of criminalizing it is not to deny that there could also be good reason to criminalize types of non-wrongful conduct. Typically, however, positive legal moralists also accept, implicitly or explicitly, negative legal moralism: we have good reason to criminalize wrongful conduct, and may not criminalize non-wrongful conduct.

I will argue in later chapters for a version of positive legal moralism (but one quite different from Moore's), and I will need to say more about the content of, and the grounds for, a plausible version of positive legal moralism: about the kinds of wrong that we have reason to criminalize, about the character and strength of those reasons (and about what other reasons we might have for or against criminalization), and about why criminalization should be an appropriate way of responding to certain kinds of wrongdoing. All we need notice here is, first, that while Moore's legal moralism is ambitious in scope, since on his view we have good reason to criminalize *every* kind of moral wrongdoing, other versions of positive legal moralism are more modest, arguing that only some kinds of wrongdoing are candidates for criminalization; I will argue for a modest version. Second, while Moore grounds his legal moralism in the demands of retributive justice, this is not the only possible or plausible foundation for a positive legal moralism: as we will see, our reasons to maintain a system of criminal law that criminalizes wrongful conduct need not have to do with the infliction of retributive punishment on those who engage in such conduct.

I will also rely on negative legal moralism: if we are to maintain a system of criminal law that defines and censures certain kinds of conduct as wrong, we must use it honestly; we behave unjustly, and impermissibly, if we define and treat as criminal conduct that is not, or that we do not take to be, wrongful. However, before I rely on it, I should do a little more to clarify its meaning, and (in the following section) to defend it against some recent attacks.

Two clarifications are necessary here. One concerns the connection between criminalization and punishment, and whether a negative legal moralist's concern is really with punishment rather than with criminalization as such. On some accounts, what is basically wrong is the punishment of those who have done no wrong:[24] to criminalize non-wrongful conduct (to violate the negative legal moralist's constraint) is wrong because (and perhaps only because) it makes people liable to what would be unjust punishment. However, it is not only the prospect of unjust punishment that gives negative legal moralism its normative force. If to criminalize conduct is to portray it as wrong, this is to declare that those who engage in such conduct merit censure as wrongdoers: if the conduct is not wrongful, to criminalize it is to make a morally mistaken declaration; if the criminalizer does not even believe it to be wrongful, to criminalize it is to lie.[25]

[24] See e.g. Husak, *Overcriminalization*, 78 ('The state should not create crimes that will subject offenders to punishment without good reason to believe that the punishment to which such persons will become subject would be justified'); Moore, 'A Tale of Two Theories', 32 ('the legal moralist theory of criminal legislation—that all and only morally wrongful behaviors should be criminalized—can be seen to follow from a retributivist theory of punishment'). See further J Edwards, 'Criminalization without Punishment'; and above, Chapter 1, section 6.

[25] On the difference between these two kinds of defect in criminalization (error and dishonesty) see V Tadros, 'Rethinking the Presumption of Innocence', at 197–200.

Second, if, as the negative legal moralist insists, we may criminalize conduct only if it is wrongful, is that to say that it must be wrongful independently of its criminalization—that if we are to criminalize it, it must *already* be wrongful? It might seem obvious that this is how we should interpret negative legal moralism: for if wrongfulness is to be a constraint on criminalization, it must surely be prior to criminalization, or else criminalizers could, as it were, bootstrap the legitimacy of their activity; if they could make conduct wrongful by criminalizing it, they could easily satisfy the negative legal moralist's principle by the act of criminalization, which would deprive the principle of any substantive force. But matters might not be that simple, since some have argued that sometimes 'the very act of criminalization plays a constitutive role in marking conduct out as wrongful'.[26] Following Tadros, we can now distinguish the 'Strong Wrongness Constraint', that '[i]t is permissible to criminalize some conduct only if that conduct is wrong independently of its being criminalized', from the 'Weak Wrongness Constraint', that '[i]t is permissible to criminalize some conduct only if that conduct is wrong either independently of its being criminalized or as a result of its being criminalized'.[27] Of course, if the claim that we can make conduct wrong by criminalizing it was the claim that the mere act of criminalizing a type of conduct suffices to make it wrong, the Weak Wrongness Constraint would not constrain the scope of the criminal law; the claim must instead be that what can make conduct wrongful is its criminalization for good reason—and we will need then to know what counts as a good reason. I will not pursue that line of thought here, since I will argue that we should follow the simpler and more demanding version of negative legal moralism: we may legitimately criminalize a type of conduct only if it is wrongful independently of its criminalization. In the following section, I will therefore argue that negative legal moralists should not appeal to a Weak Wrongness Constraint as an alternative to a Strong Wrongness Constraint; and then offer an initial defence of a Strong Wrongness Constraint—although that defence will need to be filled out later, when I discuss in more detail some of the kinds of example to which critics of the Constraint appeal.

4. In Defence of Negative Legal Moralism

What distinguishes a Weak from a Strong Wrongness Constraint is that the latter is satisfied only if the conduct to be criminalized is wrongful prior to its criminalization, whereas the former is also satisfied if the conduct becomes wrongful as a result of being criminalized. But how could criminalizing a type of conduct that is not (yet) wrongful render it wrongful? This possibility will seem especially puzzling if we understand substantive criminal law, as I have argued we should understand it,[28] not as prohibiting the kinds of conduct that it defines as criminal, but as declaring them to be wrongs of which the polity takes such formal, public notice, whose perpetrators will therefore be liable to prosecution and punishment. For how could even a formal, and purportedly authoritative, declaration that a type of conduct is wrongful render it wrongful? Surely to declare something to be the case must be to declare it to be the case independently of that declaration; if wrongfulness is a necessary condition of permissible

[26] Simester and von Hirsch, *Crimes, Harms, and Wrongs*, 20; see also 72.

[27] V Tadros, 'Wrongness and Criminalization'. In this paper Tadros rejects the Strong Wrongness Constraint, but 'suspect[s] that the Weak Wrongness Constraint is a valid principle' (172): later, however, he also rejects the Weak Wrongness Constraint; see text at nn 39 and 40 below.

[28] See above, Chapter 1, section 2.

criminalization, that condition must surely be satisfied in advance of the criminalization that it is meant to render permissible.

Perhaps, however, that is too quick. Tadros offers an example that is meant to show how we can render a type of conduct wrongful by criminalizing it (I adapt the example slightly). Suppose that we are concerned about the harm caused by the misuse of knives, and realize that we could efficiently reduce such harm by bringing it about that people do not (generally) carry knives in public. Mere exhortations not to carry knives will be ineffective, because too many of those who might misuse knives will not be dissuaded; and others, who might have been willing to forswear knives, will see reason to continue to carry them for self-protection—and will commit no wrong in continuing to carry them for that reason. For the sake of more effective dissuasion, we might therefore enact a legal regulation, prohibiting the carrying of knives in public (whilst allowing some exceptions for those who have good reason to carry a knife).[29] But we will also realize that a mere regulation, even if backed by an administrative sanction, will be inadequately effective: too many people will still carry knives; and it will then still be morally permissible for others to carry knives as a self-defensive precaution. The only way to secure a large enough reduction in knife-carrying, we realize, is to criminalize it: for only the distinctive condemnation provided by a criminal conviction, and the distinctively condemnatory punishments that follow it, will dissuade enough people from carrying knives. Now, Tadros argues, once knife-carrying is criminalized, and people are therefore generally not carrying knives, individuals lose the moral permission to carry one for self-defence: the threat of a knife attack from someone else is sufficiently reduced, and does not now warrant such a defensive measure. We can then say that, once knife-carrying is criminalized, it becomes morally wrong. But it was not wrongful prior to its criminalization: for before it was criminalized, before its prevalence was thus reduced, it was morally permissible to carry a knife as a necessary measure of self-defence. This is therefore, Tadros argues, a case in which we might be justified in criminalizing a type of conduct, as an efficient way of reducing harm, but in which the conduct to be criminalized is not wrongful prior to its criminalization.[30]

This example is unpersuasive as an argument for a Weak, rather than a Strong, Wrongness Constraint, but in a revealing way. First, it reminds us of the importance of the distinction drawn earlier between regulation and criminalization:[31] we cannot render conduct wrongful merely by criminalizing it, but we can render it wrongful by enacting a regulation that prohibits it. In the absence of any legal regulation, carrying a knife in public might or might not be wrongful: it is wrong to carry one with the intention of using it to attack people or their property, or in a way that creates a serious and unjustifiable risk of harm; but merely carrying one might not be wrong, even if it is not a self-defensive measure. Once the regulation is enacted, however, it is arguably wrong to violate the regulation—to carry a knife in public other than for a reason recognized as a good reason in the regulation. It is only arguably wrong, since I am not appealing to a general duty to obey the law whatever it might require of us:[32] as we will see later, although citizens of a decent polity will respect its laws, their respect will be questioning and critical; they will ask for a justification of a regulation before they recognize

[29] Compare e.g. Criminal Justice Act 1988, s. 139.

[30] Tadros, 'Wrongness and Criminalization', 169–72; see also Tadros, *The Ends of Harm: The Moral Foundations of Criminal Law*, 323–5.

[31] See above, Chapter 1 at nn 45–8.

[32] For useful overviews of the ongoing debates about a duty to obey the law, see W Edmundson, 'The Duty to Obey the Law'; R Dagger and D Lefkowitz, 'Political Obligation'.

an obligation to obey it.[33] But we can suggest reasons why citizens ought generally to obey such a regulation, and would therefore do wrong in violating it. Perhaps we can see it as specifying what counts as safe conduct in relation to knife carrying, and thus as creating a more determinate standard of care than previously obtained. Or perhaps the regulation can claim Razian authority:[34] citizens should recognize that they are more likely to comply with the reasons that apply to them (to carry knives only when they have good reason to do so) by obeying the regulation than by deciding for themselves when to carry a knife. Enacting a regulation can, in these and other ways,[35] make a normative difference: it can make wrongful conduct that was not already wrongful. It would therefore be consistent with the Strong Wrongness Constraint to criminalize breaches of the regulation, so long as they are wrongful *qua* breaches of a regulation that ought to be obeyed. Such conduct is not wrongful independently of its legal regulation; but it is wrongful independently of and prior to its criminalization—which is what is required by the Strong Wrongness Constraint.

However, Tadros argues, so long as the regulation is not widely enough obeyed, there will be many instances of knife-carrying that it does not render wrongful: for many people will still have good self-defensive reason to carry knives. But once we criminalize breaches of this regulation, thus more effectively reducing the incidence of knife-carrying, many instances of knife-carrying that were not previously wrongful become wrongful: for they can no longer be justified as self-defensive carryings. That, he thinks, is how the Strong Wrongness Constraint is undermined, but a Weak Wrongness Constraint survives. However, the example does not undermine the Strong Wrongness Constraint. It is true in one way that conduct that was not previously wrongful will be wrongful once (and because) knife-carrying is criminalized: if Jones carried a knife as he did his weekly shopping before knife-carrying was criminalized he did not act wrongly, since carrying it was a permissibly self-defensive action; but once knife-carrying is criminalized, and its incidence has (presumably thanks to effective enforcement) been reduced, he would act wrongly in carrying a knife on his weekly shop, since this would no longer be a necessary self-defensive action. What is criminalized, however, is not 'carrying a knife on one's weekly shop', but 'carrying a knife when this is not necessary for self-defence'; and that latter conduct was not made wrongful by its criminalization, since it was already wrongful prior to its criminalization. Once we identify the appropriate action description, the description that picks out the legally relevant features of the conduct in question, we can see that criminalization still—as the Strong Wrongness Constraint requires—presupposes the wrongfulness of the criminalized conduct; it does not make that conduct wrong.

The enactment of the criminal law defining knife-carrying in public as an offence does play a causal role in the historical process through which the moral status of Jones's carrying a knife on his weekly shop changes from permissible to wrong: not because that enactment can by itself turn a permissible action into a wrongful action, but because its effective enforcement changes the circumstances in which Jones acts, in such a way that carrying a knife on his weekly shop is no longer necessary as a self-defensive measure. But this is not a problem for advocates of the Strong Wrongness Constraint. They do not deny that criminalization can have effects such that types of conduct that would not previously have fitted the law's definition of an offence now do fit it—so long as they now fit it not because the definition has changed, but because

[33] See further below, Chapter 5 at nn 142–3, Chapter 7 text following n. 158.
[34] See e.g. J Raz, 'Authority, Law, and Morality'.
[35] See further below, Chapter 7, section 5.

the law's enactment (and enforcement) make a relevant difference to the conduct's material context. All that they deny, and can still deny, is that criminalization can by itself, in virtue simply of its authoritative character as law, render previously non-wrongful conduct wrongful.[36]

I will argue later that in one particular kind of case we need to appeal to something related to a Weak Wrongness Constraint. When the criminal law addresses a visitor who does not share the values that it embodies, or a dissident who rejects those values, it will sometimes properly say to them that they ought to refrain from the criminalized conduct because it is criminalized; even if they reasonably regard such conduct as non-wrongful prior to its criminalization, they ought to recognize it as wrongful because it was criminalized through a legitimate democratic process. As a supporter of the criminalization of fox hunting, I would argue that we were right to criminalize it, because it is morally wrong.[37] However, in talking to an opponent of that law, I might argue that even if she still believes (in my view mistakenly, but not unreasonably) that fox hunting is morally permissible, she ought now to refrain from it out of respect for the democratic process from which the law emerged. Even in this kind of case, however, the legislature must respect a Strong Wrongness Constraint: if we are to justify criminalizing such conduct we must argue that it is wrongful prior to its criminalization; only if its criminalization can be thus justified, as the Strong Wrongness Constraint requires, can we claim that even those who deny its pre-criminal wrongness ought to refrain from it, and act wrongly if they engage in it, once it is criminalized. I will discuss this kind of case later:[38] my argument here is that, apart from its secondary role in such cases, the Weak Wrongness Constraint adds nothing substantial to the Strong Wrongness Constraint: we cannot render conduct wrongful by criminalizing it; so any plausible Wrongness Constraint must be Strong.

But is a Strong Wrongness Constraint plausible? As I have portrayed it, it sets a categorical constraint on the criminalization of non-wrongful conduct. But surely, it might be objected, we can imagine contexts in which we could justifiably criminalize conduct that is not wrongful. One such situation, analogous to those in which other purportedly strict categorical principles are put to the test, might be one in which we could avert catastrophe only by criminalizing some morally innocent type of conduct: but surely, the critic will argue, that the heavens would otherwise fall must be a good enough reason to commit what might be a relatively modest injustice. Tadros offers such an example. Suppose that a powerful country offers essential aid to an impoverished country, on condition that it criminalizes the possession of a particular recreational drug—a drug that the country's citizens would otherwise see no reason to criminalize, since it is harmless and in their eyes morally quite unproblematic. Suppose too that the aid is made conditional upon the effective enforcement of that criminalization: if people continue to use the drug, some must be punished. Tadros argues that the poorer country might be justified in criminalizing possession of the drug; but its possession is not wrongful, and is not made wrongful by being criminalized.[39]

36 A similar argument can deal with Tadros' example of the spy who ought to refrain from leaking a piece of information if, but only if, everyone else who has the information refrains from leaking it ('Wrongness and Criminalization', 168).

37 See Hunting Act 2004.

38 See further Chapter 3, section 4 below. We may note that in this kind of case it is appropriate to talk of obeying the criminal law—although I have argued that obedience is not what the criminal law normally or paradigmatically seeks (see above, Chapter 1 at nn 10–12, 45–52).

39 V Tadros, *Wrongs and Crimes*, 98–101: this is part of a larger argument that 'liability to punishment' is neither necessary not sufficient for criminalization.

There are two ways in which a legal moralist might respond to this example (if she accepts, plausibly, that it might be right for a country to give in to such coercion). One is to argue that, once we distinguish regulation from criminalization, we can see that the country has good reason to enact a non-criminal regulation prohibiting possession of the drug, and that once the regulation is in place citizens ought to obey it: not because disobedience would threaten the continuation of aid (since the aid is contingent on the effective criminalization of the drug, which is achieved if those who use it are punished), but because by using the drug they put their state in a dilemma. Either the state must punish them, although they have done nothing wrong; or it must endanger receipt of the aid, thus endangering citizens. But citizens ought not to act in ways that put their states in a dilemma: therefore they ought to obey the regulation (if obedience is not unreasonably burdensome); therefore they act wrongly in violating it, and such violations can be legitimately criminalized. There is something unsatisfactory about this argument, however: it seems to hold drug-using citizens responsible for the dilemma, rather than the powerful state that made its aid thus conditional; and if criminalization can be thus justified, the dilemma anyway disappears.

A better argument, which recognizes the oddity of this example (that what grounds the case for criminalization is that it is done under duress), is that what is required here, of both state and citizens, is a kind of pretence. The state must pretend that the use of this drug is wrong, in a way that properly concerns the law: it must act *as if* such use is a public wrong, and enact a law that purports to criminalize it. Citizens now have a duty to go along with the pretence, since they can see this to be necessary to protect themselves against the collective harm that the threatened loss of aid would entail. Going along with the pretence could involve not using the drug—behaving *as if* its use has been properly criminalized, and thus *as if* they had good reason, prior to its criminalization, not to use it. In that case, any who used the drug could be justly convicted and punished as having done wrong: the wrong would consist not in using the drug as such, but in failing to go along with a pretence with which they ought to have gone along. But going along with the pretence could, alternatively, be a matter of *either* not using the drug *or* accepting 'conviction' and 'punishment' if they do: this too involves acting as if the drug has been properly criminalized; users take part in the continuing pretence that they are criminal wrongdoers—a pretence that involves subjecting them to what all know is a charade of a trial, and a burden that only pretends to be a punishment. The burden will be materially real: but, first, it might be a burden that it was not unreasonable to expect citizens to accept (since they could avoid it by not using the drug); second, it does not involve the moral burden of being condemned as a wrongdoer, since it is evident to all that this is play acting.[40]

One could instead have argued that in such a case the polity does wrong its citizens, since it criminalizes and punishes, and thus authoritatively portrays as wrongful, conduct that it does not believe to be wrongful; but that, in an emergency of this kind, this is a wrong that, tragically, it must commit. But this is a less persuasive argument: partly because it ignores the point that, if the polity is a democracy, its citizens should be asked to consent to this measure—which, even if one can wrong oneself, makes a charge of wronging less plausible; and partly because it implies that this kind of external pressure constitutes a good reason to criminalize, whereas it is better to say that

[40] We might say something similar about Tadros' other example in this context: '[i]f the UK government fails to criminalize hopping, total world destruction will necessarily ensue' (*Wrongs and Crimes*, 98). But it is difficult to know what to say about fantastical (and radically under-described) examples of this kind.

it gives us reason to abandon or suspend our (normatively) normal way of thinking about criminalization, and to disrupt or pervert the appropriate kind of reasoning. In the same way, we can imagine a case in which an examiner feels compelled, in order to avert a threat of disastrous damage to her institution, to 'award' what she knows to be an unjustified (and thus unjust) grade: perhaps to 'fail' an essay that academically deserves to pass, because threatened with disastrous consequences by a malign outsider. That threat does not give her good reason to *fail* the piece of work—only reasons to do with the academic quality of the work are relevant to failing it; but it gives her reason to pretend to fail it—to act *as if* it is a failure.

However, negative legal moralism faces more powerful objections than this, aiming to show that we can sometimes justifiably criminalize conduct that is not wrongful either prior to or as a result of its criminalization—not merely in cases involving the kind of necessity or duress that Tadros imagines, but in the ordinary course of criminal legislation. Since these arguments will be relevant to my later discussions of reasons to criminalize, they are worth detailed attention here.

Cornford offers one such argument: what he calls 'the wrongness constraint' ('that conduct may be criminalised only if it is wrongful') is indeed plausible, but only when it is understood in a 'presumptive' sense: it is presumptively impermissible to criminalize non-wrongful conduct, but that presumption can be, and sometimes is, defeated.[41] One way in which it can be defeated, he suggests, is that given the fallibility of any criminal process, criminalizing a type of conduct will inevitably render liable to condemnation, punishment, and coercion (the effects that render the criminalization of non-wrongful conduct presumptively impermissible) some who did not in fact engage in that type of conduct: they will be found guilty by a procedurally fair trial, although they were in fact innocent. If we criminalize at all, we will therefore inevitably criminalize some non-wrongful conduct: we will facilitate the legal condemnation, punishment, and coercion of some who did not in fact commit the relevant kind of wrong.[42] The law in the books does not, it is true, define their conduct as criminal: but the law in action criminalizes them; it treats them as criminals by rendering them liable to conviction and punishment.

The problem with this argument is that it is not clear what has been supposedly criminalized when an innocent person is convicted. It cannot be her actual conduct, since all we know (all that is relevant) is that she did not commit the offence charged; but it would be odd to say that what is criminalized is the non-commission of the offence charged. This undercuts the argument: for the wrongness constraint is violated only if non-wrongful conduct is criminalized; but in mistakenly convicting an actually innocent person the law and the court do not treat her actually innocent conduct as criminal; rather, they mistakenly ascribe actually wrongful conduct to her. So these are not cases in which conduct is justifiably criminalized although it is not wrongful; we can still maintain the wrongness constraint as categorical, rather than only presumptive.[43]

[41] 'Rethinking the Wrongness Constraint'. Compare Tadros' discussion of a 'broad prohibition' on gun ownership (*Wrongs and Crimes*, ch. 17) criminalizing some non-wrongful gun possession: see below, Chapter 7 at nn 197–211.

[42] 'Rethinking the Wrongness Constraint', s. IV.A.

[43] Cornford's argument is reminiscent of an argument against retributivist objections to strictly consequentialist theories of punishment. Retributivists often object that strict consequentialists are committed to sanctioning the punishment of the innocent; to which the critic responds that, since any human system of criminal punishment will inevitably sometimes, mistakenly, convict and punish an innocent person, retributivists must either argue that we should punish no one, or sanction such punishments of the innocent—in which case they cannot bring that objection against consequentialist

Cornford offers another, and stronger, argument that the wrongness constraint is defeasible, by appeal to the justifiability of some 'over-inclusive crimes': crimes whose definitions capture not only the kind of conduct that constitutes the target wrong, but a wider class of conduct, some of which is not, and is not even thought by the legislature to be, wrongful.[44] His example is that of sexual activity with a child.[45] The wrongful conduct, which is the law's real target, is that of exploitative sexual activity by adults with children who are not mature enough to make rational decisions in sexual matters: but the legislature has good reasons (to do with the determinacy and clarity of the law, its preventive efficacy, and the value of avoiding the 'secondary victimisation' that would ensue if 'victims' had to appear in court to give evidence of their vulnerability) to define the offence simply in terms of the age of people involved—although knowing that this will criminalize some conduct that does not involve the relevant mischief. Furthermore, the benefits of such over-inclusive legislation would be lost if the law allowed a 'no wrongness' defence that would cover such innocuous conduct.

It might be argued that even if Cornford can show that a legislature could have good enough reason to criminalize types of conduct that are not wrongful in advance of their criminalization, thus refuting the Strong Wrongness Constraint, the Weak Wrongness Constraint survives: for once this law is in place, people have an obligation to obey it, and so do wrong in disobeying it, even if their conduct would not have been wrongful absent such a law. But, Cornford argues,[46] this is not so: no plausible account of our obligations to obey the law, or to obey justified laws, can show that it would always be wrong to break this law. Two teenagers engaging in consensual sexual activity might know full well that each is rationally competent to decide on such matters, and might not violate any of the values that could underpin an obligation to obey this law: they thus commit no wrong; but it is still permissible, Cornford argues, to criminalize their conduct, for the reasons sketched above. Legislatures should be reluctant to criminalize non-wrongful conduct, since the presumptive wrongness constraint is a powerful one; but they can sometimes have good enough reason to do so.

Edwards offers an analogous argument to the same conclusion.[47] His primary target is 'the punishment thesis'—that 'Φing is permissibly criminalized only if Φing satisfies the necessary conditions of permissible state punishment *once criminalized*';[48] but his argument against that thesis depends in part on an argument that we can have good reason to criminalize some types of conduct, tokens of which might not be wrongful either independently of being criminalized or as a result of their being criminalized. His example (one of many that could be given from the wide range of such offences) concerns pharmaceutical safety, and the best way to avoid manufacturers using unsafe ingredients or processes. Given the dangers and difficulties of letting manufacturers decide for themselves what is or is not safe, by criminalizing only the use of 'unsafe'

accounts (see e.g. M Bagaric, *Punishment and Sentencing: A Rational Approach*, ch. 5.3). The obvious, though not uncontroversial, answer to that argument involves an appeal to the distinction between intending to punish (deliberately punishing) known innocents, and maintaining a system that we know will sometimes mistakenly, i.e. against our intentions, punish actual innocents. I cannot discuss the soundness of such a response here, but if it is sound, an analogous response could also be made to Cornford (though he argues ('Rethinking the Wrongness Constraint', s. IV.A) that it is unsound): what is categorically precluded is the intentional, not the mistaken and contra-intentional, criminalization of non-wrongful conduct.

44 'Rethinking the Wrongness Constraint', s. IV.B.

45 See Sexual Offences Act 2003, s. 9.

46 'Rethinking the Wrongness Constraint', s. V.

47 Edwards, 'Criminalization without Punishment'.

48 'Criminalization without Punishment', 73; see at n. 24 above.

ingredients or processes, we might have reason instead to criminalize the 'use of any ingredient or process found on an authoritative list';[49] and although we know that there are some manufacturers who are sufficiently expert and careful to make safe use of some items on the list, we might also have good reason not to enable them to gain legal exemption, or to offer a defence of 'safe expertise'. However, he argues, a manufacturer who knows that she can safely use an item on the list does not act wrongfully even once her conduct is criminalized. It seems to follow that both the Weak Wrongness Constraint, and therefore the Strong Wrongness Constraint, must be rejected.

(Edwards also argues that although the conduct of such reliably expert manufacturers, in using ingredients that are on the list, might be permissibly criminalized, it does not follow that they are permissibly punished for that conduct. That is why, he claims, the punishment thesis is false: we may permissibly criminalize conduct that we could not permissibly punish. This point will be important shortly.)

Husak offers a similar line of argument, but to an opposite conclusion.[50] Criminal laws that define *mala prohibita* (like the law that Edwards imagines) criminalize types of conduct some—perhaps many—of whose tokens are probably not wrongful: they criminalize general types of conduct, for the sake of preventing some kind of harm; but we know that there will be cases in which a competent agent knows full well that she can engage in the criminalized type of conduct without causing, or creating any unreasonable risk of causing, the harm in question. We enact speed limits for road traffic, and drink-driving regulations that prohibit driving with more than a certain proportion of alcohol in one's blood, and enforce these through the criminal law, because this is a more efficient way to promote road safety, and to reduce the harms caused by accidents, than only making it an offence to drive dangerously or when impaired through drink.[51] We must also know that there are competent drivers who know that they could on occasion violate these regulations without creating any unreasonable risk of an accident, but we do not exempt them from the regulations, or allow them a defence to a criminal charge of speeding or drink-driving: for, we suppose, to allow such exemptions or defences would undermine the law's deterrent efficacy. Such drivers, however, surely do no wrong in violating the regulations when they know that they can safely do so. Edwards and Cornford might take this as further proof of the falsity of both the Strong and the Weak Wrongness Constraints: we have good reason to criminalize their conduct, although it is not wrong. Husak, however, takes it to cast doubt on the justifiability of such laws: for, he insists, we can permissibly criminalize conduct only if it is wrongful in a way that makes those who engage in it deserving of punishment;[52] but such drivers' conduct is not thus wrongful.

The distinction between regulation and criminalization is again relevant here: for in the kinds of example offered by Cornford, Edwards, and Husak what is criminalized can be understood as the violation of a legal regulation. This is explicit in Edwards' example, since in drawing up and enacting the 'authoritative list' of ingredients and processes that are not to be used, the regulator or legislature is in effect creating a regulation prohibiting the use of any items on that list; what is criminalized is a breach of that regulation—the use of an unauthorized, prohibited, ingredient or process. In Cornford's example the distinction is not explicit: for s. 9 of the Sexual Offences Act

[49] 'Criminalization without Punishment', 76.

[50] D Husak, '*Malum Prohibitum* and Retributivism'; see also *Overcriminalization*, 103–19; and *Ignorance of Law: A Philosophical Analysis*, ch. 4C.

[51] See e.g. Road Traffic Regulation Act 1984, s. 89; Road Traffic Act 1988, s. 5.

[52] See at nn 17 and 24 above.

seems directly to criminalize sexual activity with a person under the specified age (sixteen)—not to criminalize violating a regulation that prohibits such activity. However, we can understand the normative logic of this kind of provision by seeing it as combining the two analytically distinct stages of regulation and criminalization: its structure is analogous to that of speeding laws, which make it a criminal offence to break a speed limit that is defined in a separate regulation.[53]

So here is the shape of the argument that Cornford and Edwards offer. We have good reason, to do with the efficient prevention of various kinds of harm or wrong, to enact regulations of the kinds they describe. We also have good reason to make such regulations over-broad, in that they prohibit some conduct that will not in fact bring about or threaten to bring about the mischief at which they are aimed: they do not allow exceptions or exemptions for those who know that their conduct is safe (for the competent and conscientious manufacturer who knows that she can safely use an item on the proscribed list; for adults who know that their under-age sexual partners are fully competent to decide on such matters for themselves). Once the regulations are in place, it will then normally be wrong to violate them—even if one thinks one can do so safely. There will be different reasons for this: we might appeal, in different contexts, to the dangers of relying on one's own fallible judgment; to a claim that to violate the regulation is to be a free rider; to the claims of solidarity with one's fellows in obeying regulations that serve our common good (and that do not impose unreasonable burdens on us).[54] If it is wrong to violate the regulations, it is permissible, consistently with the Strong Wrongness Constraint, to criminalize breaches of the regulations. However, on the one hand, there will (we know) be some who commit no wrong in violating the regulations, since they know that they can violate them safely—without causing or threatening the mischief at which they are aimed, or violating any of the other values that might underpin an obligation to obey the regulations. But, on the other hand, we cannot afford not to formally criminalize their conduct along with that of those who violate the regulations without any such good reason. If the criminal law is not to undermine the regulations, or the values that justified making the regulations strict, it must be as strict as they are: its offence definitions must capture the conduct even of those who know that they could safely break the regulations; it cannot allow them a formal defence. In that case, however (unless we can appeal, as I do not, to some general obligation to obey the law) there will be people who commit the criminal offence, without what the law recognizes as a defence, but who do not act wrongfully in doing so: not because the law that defines the crime is badly drafted, or unjustifiably over-broad or strict; but because although we have good enough reason to formulate both the regulation and the criminal law in those over-broad, over-strict terms, some citizens will also sometimes have good enough reason to violate the regulation and to commit the offence. Their conduct will thus be morally permissible, but the law cannot afford to recognize that permissibility by defining their conduct as legally permissible (whether by means of a narrower offence definition, or by allowing them a formal defence).

[53] Thus s. 84 of the Road Traffic Regulation Act authorizes the making of 'orders' that 'prohibit' driving 'at a speed exceeding that specified in the order'; under s. 89 of the Act it is then an offence to drive 'at a speed exceeding a limit imposed by or under any enactment to which this section applies'. See also Chapter 1 at nn 45–8 above.

[54] See variously S P Green, 'Why it's a Crime to Tear the Tag off a Mattress: Over-Criminalization and the Moral Content of Regulatory Offenses'; R A Duff, *Answering for Crime*, 89–93, 166–74; R A Duff and S E Marshall, '"Abstract Endangerment", Two Harm Principles, and Two Routes to Criminalisation'; and at nn 34–5 above.

There is more to be said about the justifications for creating such regulations; about whether, when, and why it is wrongful to violate them; about whether and why the criminal law cannot be so formulated as to exempt from liability those who can safely break them. I will return to these issues later, when I discuss the role that various types of *malum prohibitum* can play in criminal law, since the examples to which Cornford and Edwards appeal are types of *malum prohibitum*.[55] For the moment, however, all I want to argue is that even if the negative legal moralist admits all that they claim about the examples they discuss, she can still preserve the Strong Wrongness Constraint: she can, that is, agree that there will be cases in which someone breaches a justified regulation whose breach the law formally, and justifiably, defines as a criminal offence, and for which he can claim no legally recognized defence, but commits no wrong in doing so; but still insist that we must not criminalize conduct that is not wrongful prior to its criminalization.

She admits that we can be justified in formally criminalizing such non-wrongful conduct—in defining it as criminal in the books; but not that we are justified in substantively criminalizing it—in criminalizing it in action.[56] Suppose that a legislature enacts a strict regulation of the type that Edwards and Cornford describe, and formally criminalizes breaches of it; suppose too that the statute allows no exemption or defence to agents who know that they can break the regulation safely. That does not suffice to make such an agent even formally liable to criminal conviction: for the polity's criminal code could include a '*De Minimis*' provision:

> The Court shall dismiss a prosecution if, having regard to the nature of the conduct charged to constitute an offense and the nature of the attendant circumstances, it finds that the defendant's conduct ... did not actually cause or threaten the harm or evil sought to be prevented by the law defining the offense or did so only to an extent too trivial to warrant the condemnation of conviction.[57]

If there are cases in which an agent violates a regulation, knowing that in doing so she is causing or threatening neither 'the harm or evil sought to be prevented' by the regulation itself, nor 'the harm or evil sought to be prevented' by the law that criminalizes breaches of the regulation,[58] these will be cases in which, if she is prosecuted, the court should dismiss the prosecution.

Suppose, however, that the polity's criminal code includes no such general provision, so that this person's conduct is therefore formally criminal. But suppose too that the prosecution service, or the inspectorate charged with administering the regulations and dealing with breaches of them, itself adopts a '*De Minimis*' principle: it will not prosecute, or take any further action, in cases in which it is satisfied that the person's conduct 'did not actually cause or threaten the harm or evil sought to be prevented by

[55] See further below Chapter 7, section 5. It might seem odd to describe the offence of 'sexual activity with a child' (Sexual Offences Act 2003, s. 9) as '*malum prohibitum*': I will justify (and qualify) that description later.

[56] On this distinction and its importance, see above, Chapter 1, section 7.

[57] Model Penal Code § 2.12. I say 'provision' rather than 'defence' because there are questions, which we cannot pursue here, about whether we should interpret the provision as defining a 'defence': see D N Husak, 'The *De Minimis* "Defense"'; M B Valentine, 'Defense Categories and the (Category-Defying) De Minimis Defense'. My own view is that it is a bar to trial, rather than a defence: the conduct alleged is not criminal. See also A Roberts, 'Dismissals as Justice', on the judicial power to dismiss cases 'for the furtherance of justice'—which implies a prosecutorial power to discontinue cases on the same grounds.

[58] That is, her conduct, *qua* breach of the regulation, is not wrongful in one of the ways mentioned above.

the law'—by the regulation or by the law that criminalizes breaches of the regulation. Suppose too that this principled policy is known to those concerned; it might even figure in a published statement of guidelines.[59] Those affected by the regulation can then know that such breaches will not be treated as criminal—will not be criminalized in action: the Strong Wrongness Constraint, as a constraint on substantive criminalization, is then still satisfied.

What I have sketched here is a familiar criminalization technique: a legislature enacts what it knows to be an over-broad criminal statute, and relies on prosecutors (and other enforcement officials) to use their discretion not to prosecute in cases in which a person's 'conduct … did not actually cause or threaten the harm or evil sought to be prevented by the law'.[60] Such a technique is, of course, far from unproblematic. It might encourage legislatures to be sloppy, rather than trying to define offences as precisely as possible, so that they capture, as far as is practicable, all and only the types of conduct that 'cause or threaten the harm or evil sought to be prevented'. It might make it harder for those who are affected by the law 'to understand its scope and foresee the consequences of [their] actions so that [they] can regulate [their] conduct without breaking the law'.[61] It accords considerable discretion to prosecutors and other enforcement officials: we must ask how their exercise of that discretion can be made accountable, and how citizens who will be affected by its exercise can be enabled to rely on its proper use. We might indeed decide in the end that the *De Minimis* principle should be given a more formal, more manifestly assured, status—for instance by following the Model Penal Code and making it a principle that is binding on courts (and thus more reassuring for citizens, and more certain to be applied by prosecutors); or by giving it statutory form as a principle that prosecutors and other officials must apply, and providing legal recourse for any who think that their prosecution violates it. We need not resolve such issues here: the point is that this is how we can consistently both assert a Strong Wrongness Constraint, that we must not criminalize conduct that is not already wrongful, and yet argue that we can sometimes justifiably enact criminal statutes that formally criminalize some conduct that is not wrongful. We make room for this possibility, thus rendering negative legal moralism more plausible, by seeing criminalization as something done not merely by formal legislation, but by the operation of the criminal justice system as a whole. The Strong Wrongness Constraint, like any principle of criminalization, should guide all the system's officials; to see whether it is respected we must look at the system as a whole—at enforcement as well as at legislation.

Both Cornford and Edwards recognize the possibility of this kind of argument. Cornford notes the possibility of arguing that the state should seek 'to avoid condemning and punishing' non-wrongful conduct that it formally defines as criminal, 'through policing and prosecutorial policies', and that this could preserve the wrongness constraint as a principle of 'substantive', if not 'formal', criminalization: his argument is only meant to show that 'the wrongness constraint is unsound as a principle of formal criminalisation'.[62] Edwards assumes the truth of the principle that 'it is permissible to punish B for Φing only if Φing is morally wrongful':[63] thus, it seems, while we might be justified in formally criminalizing conduct that is not wrongful, we cannot

[59] Compare the policy for dealing with cases of assisting suicide published by the Director of Public Prosecutions in England: see above, Chapter 1 at nn 168–75.

[60] See above, Chapter 1 at nn 166–7, for a case in which the technique was made explicit in the legislature.

[61] *R (Purdy) v DPP* [2009] 3 WLR 403, para. 40 (Lord Hope); see above, Chapter 1 at nn 169–75.

[62] 'Rethinking the Wrongness Constraint', n. 78.

[63] 'Criminalization without Punishment', 71.

be justified in punishing, or presumably in prosecuting, it; we should not substantively criminalize it. My argument has been, however, that if we are to understand the force and implications of a wrongness constraint, we must see it as setting a constraint on substantive criminalization. Of course it matters that we legislate carefully and conscientiously: we should be reluctant to enact criminal statutes that define as criminal conduct that is not wrongful. But even if, as Cornford and Edwards argue, we sometimes have good reason to enact such statutes, we can still avoid criminalizing (in the appropriate, substantive sense) non-wrongful conduct.

It might now be objected that this move, from formal to substantive criminalization, cannot help advocates of the Strong Wrongness Constraint. For a police or prosecutorial adoption of the kind of '*De Minimis*' policy suggested above must either be publicized, in a version sufficiently clear and precise to enable those whose conduct is affected by the regulation to work out whether they might face prosecution if they break it; or be kept secret, or published only in such general and vague terms as to leave those whose conduct is affected without any determinate guidance. In the former case, the situation would then not be substantively different from that in which the legislator provides a formal exemption or defence for those who know that they can safely break the regulation: if, as we are supposing, there are good reasons against providing any such formal exemption or defence, they also constitute good reasons against publishing such a policy. In the latter case, those reasons might not apply: in particular, we would not then need to worry that too many people will violate the regulation in the mistaken belief that they can do so safely, or in the hope that they will be able to persuade the police or the prosecutor that this might have been so. We will then face a different objection, however: that this kind of 'acoustic separation',[64] which conceals from the citizens the principles or policies that state officials will apply in their dealings with them, is unacceptable in a democratic state that is to show its citizens the respect that is due to them as responsible members of the polity.

We should certainly not rely on acoustic separation of this kind: as we will see later, this is not a way in which the criminal law should treat its citizens. What is unclear is how problematic the former possibility is. What the law (the law in action) says to those whose conduct is affected by the regulation is that they should obey the regulation ('should' as opposed to 'must'); and that if they are found to have broken it, even for what they take to be good reasons, they will avoid prosecution, conviction, and punishment (substantive criminalization) only if they can persuade the relevant official that those reasons were indeed good enough. This, we might hope, will make possible a more informal and more productive examination of doubtful cases, whilst providing what should still be a reasonably effective disincentive for those who are tempted to violate the regulation without good enough reason. The obvious worry about this approach (apart from the question of how we might make the discretion that the officials must now exercise appropriately accountable) is that it appears to place an informal burden of proof on those who think that they can violate the regulation safely: their breach of the regulation is taken to be wrongful, and thus to merit prosecution, unless they can persuade the official that it was not wrongful. However, if the regulation is well formulated, and if the burden of obedience it imposes (especially on those who could safely break it) is not unreasonable, as a burden that they are asked to accept for the sake of the common good that the

[64] See M Dan-Cohen, 'Decision Rules and Conduct Rules: On Acoustic Separation in Criminal Law'; above, Chapter 1, n. 159; also Cornford, 'Rethinking the Wrongness Constraint', n. 77.

regulation serves, perhaps it is legitimate to operate with such a presumption: we ought either to obey the regulation, or to make sure that we can show that our violation of it was not wrongful.

Whether and when this kind of approach—enacting a strict and over-inclusive regulation; criminalizing violations of the regulation without allowing a formal exemption or a defence to those who know that they could violate it safely; but leaving it to enforcement officials to apply a *De Minimis* principle to deal with such cases—could be legitimate depends on a range of factors, both normative and empirical. All I have tried to do here is show how a negative legal moralist can in this way allow that we might sometimes be justified in formally criminalizing some kinds of non-wrongful conduct, whilst still insisting on a Strong Wrongness Constraint as a necessary condition of permissible substantive criminalization. Whether and when we are thus justified is a question that we will only be able to answer later.

That completes my initial defence of negative legal moralism, and of the Strong Wrongness Constraint. Chiao argues that this kind of defence, appealing to a distinction between regulation and criminalization, saves negative legal moralism only by making it trivial. For what matters is whether the state acts justly in enacting a regulation and in enforcing it by a criminal sanction: if it does act justly in doing so, nothing is added to the justification of such a regulation, and such a sanction, by arguing that someone who breaches the regulation acts wrongly.[65] However, first, in enacting the regulation and in seeking to enforce obedience to it, the state must claim that the citizens ought to obey it: that is necessary if it is to address the citizens as responsible members of the polity, in terms of a law that claims to be their law.[66] That claim will need to be justified to them: not by appealing to some general duty to obey the law, but by showing how this regulation serves some aspect of the common good, in a way that does not impose an unreasonable burden on those who are required to obey it—that obedience is something that the citizens (even those who could safely breach the regulation) owe to each other for the sake of their common good; given such a justification, we can say that it is normally wrong to breach the regulation, and that breaching it can therefore warrant the censorial response that criminalization mobilizes. Second, we have seen that the Strong Wrongness Constraint can also do substantive work in guiding the decisions of those who enforce the law: it requires them not to prosecute one who did no wrong in breaching the regulation.

It is time now to take a first step towards positive legal moralism—and to note some of the problems that it raises.[67]

[65] V Chiao, *Criminal Law in the Age of the Administrative State*, ch. 5.5.

[66] See further below, Chapter 5, section 4, and Chapter 7, text following n. 158.

[67] See T S Petersen, 'New Legal Moralism: Some Strengths and Challenges'. I should note one further distinction here. I have been treating legal moralism (in both its negative and its positive forms) as a responsive principle: what makes it permissible, or gives us good reason, to criminalize a type of conduct is that it itself is wrongful; criminalization is a response to wrongful conduct. We might instead portray it as a preventive principle: what makes it permissible or gives us good reason to criminalize a type of conduct is that by doing so we can prevent future wrongdoing (see J Edwards, 'An Instrumental Legal Moralism'). The distinction between responsive and preventive principles is more familiar in the context of the harm principle(s), and will be discussed later (below, Chapter 6, section 3), when I will also defend my focus on a responsive form of legal moralism.

5. Towards a Positive Legal Moralism: Initial Attractions and Puzzles

According to negative legal moralists, the fact that a type of conduct is not morally wrongful precludes its criminalization, but the fact that it is morally wrongful gives us no positive reason to criminalize it; it just removes a barrier to criminalization. Positive legal moralists, by contrast, argue that wrongfulness provides a (if not the only) positive reason for criminalization. We will need to ask in more detail later just why wrongfulness should provide such a reason: but it will be useful here to show why some version of positive legal moralism might seem plausible—and to show why its more ambitious versions should seem implausible.

Consider again the criminalization of marital rape in English law.[68] It had been the common law doctrine that a man could not rape his wife, since 'by their mutual matrimonial consent and contract the wife hath given up herself in this kind unto her husband which she cannot retract'.[69] But the Law Lords now firmly held that 'in modern times any reasonable person must regard that conception as quite unacceptable'.[70] They recognized that, in removing the 'marital exemption', they were altering the (common) law; but 'where the common law rule no longer even remotely represents what is the true position of a wife in present day society, the duty of the court is to take steps to alter the rule if it can legitimately do so in the light of any relevant Parliamentary enactment'.[71] This is striking, because the decision seems to flout the principle of legality: a person should be criminally liable only for conduct that had at the time of its commission been formally declared to be criminal; criminal offences must not be created with retroactive effect.[72]

So why should the defendant not complain that he was unjustly convicted, since his conduct was not criminal at the time he committed it? He could admit that it constituted a serious moral wrong against his wife, for which he could be held morally answerable by her, and by others whose business it was. But it was not a wrong that the law had defined as criminal, therefore not one for which he could be called to account in a criminal court, therefore not one for which he could be justly subjected to criminal conviction and punishment. The court was not, it is true, creating a brand new crime: it was expanding the scope of an existing crime. But it was making criminal conduct that had not until then been criminal—or at least had not been formally declared to be criminal: if *R* had consulted his lawyer or the police, in advance, to check that his understanding of the prevailing law was correct, he would rightly have been told that he would be committing no crime if he forced sexual intercourse on his non-consenting wife.

The court's answer to such a complaint would presumably be that 'any reasonable person must regard [Hale's] conception as quite unacceptable':[73] but what does that amount to? The answer is not, presumably, that it was foreseeable by 'any reasonable person', that the courts would decide in this way. It is, rather, that such a view is, in the

[68] *R v R* [1992] 1 AC 599; see above, Chapter 1 at nn 143–9.

[69] Sir Matthew Hale, *History of the Pleas of the Crown* (1736), vol. 1, ch. 58, 629; quoted by Lord Keith in *R v R* [1992] 1 AC 599, 615.

[70] *R v R*, at 616 (Lord Keith).

[71] [1992] 1 AC 599, at 610 (Lord Lane CJ, giving the Court of Appeal's decision, endorsed by the Law Lords).

[72] Hence the full principle of legality: '*Nullum crimen, nulla poena sine praevia lege poenali*'.

[73] *R v R*, at 616 (Lord Keith); see at n. 70 above.

contemporary world, obviously unacceptable, morally and socially: so much so that no person with a minimally reasonable moral conception of the world could accept it. Since 'the common law rule no longer even remotely represents what is the true position of a wife in present day society', 'the law should declare that a rapist remains a rapist subject to the criminal law, irrespective of his relationship with his victim':[74] which can best be read as saying that a husband who forces sex on his wife commits a wrong of just the same kind as that committed by someone whom the criminal law already defines as a rapist, and should thus also be counted, in law, as a rapist. Furthermore, 'any reasonable person' would recognize that such a person's conduct is of this moral kind: if *R* recognized this, he in effect recognized that his conduct should count as criminal, and so cannot complain if the court does count it as criminal; if he failed to recognize this, he thereby showed himself to be not just ignorant of what the law in fact was, but culpably morally blind.[75]

What does this have to do with legal moralism? First, it obviously mattered to the court that *R*'s conduct was morally wrong. Second, however, its wrongfulness was not simply (as negative legal moralists would argue) a necessary condition for holding it to be criminal; it was, rather, the central positive reason for holding it to be criminal—which points in the direction of positive legal moralism. Third, however, what the court saw as reason to count it as criminal was not just that it was wrong in some way or other, but that it was wrong in the same way as that of an extra-marital rapist—that it involved the very same kind of wrong as that involved in what was already and uncontroversially criminal: this suggests (so far) only a very modest legal moralism. Fourth, it was clearly also important that the defendant could and should have realized this for himself: this connects to an idea that will be important in the following chapters, that of criminal law as a common law. A citizen is not meant to see the criminal law as a set of prohibitions, laid down by some authority for her to obey—as a set of requirements imposed on her by an external power: rather, she is to see the criminal law as expressing (or attempting to express) norms and values that she is asked to recognize and accept as her own (her own as a citizen); her conduct should be guided by those norms, as she can honestly and in good faith interpret them.[76]

The second aspect of *R v R* noted in the previous paragraph, that the conduct's wrongfulness provided a, if not the, central positive reason for criminalizing it, reflects a quite familiar feature of criminalization debates: public arguments that we should criminalize a type of conduct that is not currently criminal typically appeal to its supposed wrongfulness as a central reason for its criminalization. This is true, for instance, of recent debates about online harassment of various kinds, including 'revenge porn';

[74] *R v R*, at 610, 611 (Lord Lane, Court of Appeal). The 'true position of a wife in present day society' is thus not merely the position that she is, as a matter of sociological fact, recognized as having: it is the position that she is rightly recognized, by 'reasonable' (i.e. minimally decent) people, as having.

[75] I cannot discuss here the argument that 'moral blindness' could amount to a moral excuse, and should therefore also amount to a legal excuse (on which see Husak, *Ignorance of Law*). Nor can I discuss the suggestion that what a reasonable person would realize is not that Hale's view is normatively unacceptable, but rather that as a matter of fact it is at odds with the now prevailing social morality (although that might be suggested by some of the court's language): the court was clearly endorsing, and holding that any reasonable person would endorse, that morality (but compare *Ghosh* [1982] QB 1053 on dishonesty in theft).

[76] We might then say that, for the positive legal moralist, the criminal law's offence definitions (at least of *mala in se*) should, as far as possible, reflect the pre-legal wrongfulness of the conduct that is criminalized. As we will see later, however (Chapter 7, section 4), this would be an oversimplification: although the criminal law must be grounded in and draw on a pre-legal morality, its offence definitions also involve the *construction* of wrongs as public wrongs.

about hate crimes and hate speech; and about domestic abuse. It is true that advocates of criminalization typically appeal to the kinds of harm that such conduct causes, but it is also true that that harm is typically described in ways that make its wrongfulness central: the harm is the harm involved in being *victimized* in these particular ways by another's wrongful conduct.[77] It is precisely that wrongfulness, the fact that the conduct victimizes another person, that is taken to make criminalization appropriate.

Such examples do not of course show that we ought, as normative theorists, to accept some version of positive legal moralism. Nor indeed do they show that positive legal moralism holds exclusive sway in public debates about criminalization: they do not show either that people think that the wrongfulness of a given type of conduct is a sufficient condition for its criminalization—only that they see (certain kinds of) wrongfulness as a relevant or good reason; or that people see wrongfulness as the only principled reason for criminalization—that they would not see other considerations, unrelated to wrongfulness, as good reasons to criminalize. All these examples are supposed to show is that the central idea of positive legal moralism is not unfamiliar or strange: that it is worth taking seriously as a candidate principle of criminalization.

However, on the other hand, the central claim of some versions of positive legal moralism, once spelt out in more detail, does seem strange and implausible. For on an account like Moore's we have good reason to criminalize *every* kind of moral wrongdoing: the proper aim of criminal law is to 'serve retributive justice'; to do this, it 'must punish all and only those who are morally culpable in the doing of some morally wrongful action'.[78] Thus we have reason to criminalize, indeed it seems that we *must* criminalize, in order to secure their punishment, not only such wrongdoers as the marital rapist, the online troll who harasses a victim, and the domestic abuser, but also those who violate the moral obligations that bind us in our more intimate relationships: we should criminalize cheating on one's spouse or partner, betraying one's friend's confidence, letting one's colleagues down. These kinds of example must provoke an appeal to Wolfenden's slogan: they belong to 'a realm of private morality and immorality which is, in brief and crude terms, not the law's business'.[79]

Such examples of these are in one way, as we will see, unfair to Moore: he does not believe that we ought to criminalize these types of conduct. They serve here not to refute positive legal moralism, or his version of it, but simply to remind us that whilst a positive legal moralist claim that we ought to criminalize a particular type of conduct because it is wrong seems plausible in relation to some types of wrong, it seems quite implausible in relation to others. We thus need to draw a further distinction, between expansive and modest versions of positive legal moralism.

Moore's is a prime example of an expansive legal moralism: *every* kind of moral wrong is, in principle, deserving of criminalization. It is worth getting clear, however, both about the ways in which his legal moralism is expansive in principle, and about the ways in which it is limited in its final practical implications.

His legal moralism is expansive in two ways. It is expansive, first, as to the types of conduct that are in principle criminalizable. Culpable moral wrongdoing deserves retributive punishment, which it is the function of criminal law to inflict: as citizens we therefore have reason to argue for the criminalization of, and as legislators we have reason to criminalize, every type of moral wrongdoing.[80] This is not to say, Moore

[77] On how harms can involve wrongs see further Duff, *Answering for Crime*, 126–35.

[78] Moore, *Placing Blame*, 35.

[79] Wolfenden, *Report of the Committee on Homosexual Offences and Prostitution*, para. 61; see at n. 7 above.

[80] Moore, *Placing Blame*, ch. 1; see also M S Moore, 'Four Reflections on Law and Morality', 1540.

would insist, that we have good reason to criminalize every kind of conduct that people generally regard as morally defective, for two reasons. First, only moral wrong*doing*, conduct that violates a moral obligation, is deserving of punishment and thus in principle worthy of criminalization: other kinds of moral failing, such as lack of virtue, are not eligible.[81] Second, the scope of the morality of obligation is, in Moore's view, narrower than many (illiberal) people suppose: many kinds of conduct that an illiberal legal moralist might see reason to criminalize are not, Moore argues, even in principle criminalizable, because they are not morally wrong; this is true in particular of all kinds of fully consensual sexual conduct.[82] Nonetheless, on Moore's account we have good reason to criminalize every breach of a moral obligation, including the kinds of breach of intimate or collegial obligations noted above. Moore can also argue that while his positive legal moralist principle gives us good or *pro tanto* reason to criminalize (indeed, it seems to require us to criminalize) every kind of wrongdoing, we have in the end, all things considered, stronger reasons not to criminalize many kinds of wrong—reasons external rather than internal to legal moralism. We must attend, for instance, to the difficulty of proving the commission of some kinds of wrong, and the even greater difficulty of proving the culpability of their agents; to the radical intrusions into personal privacy that would be involved in trying to enforce laws criminalizing the more personal or intimate kinds of wrong, and other kinds of damage to lives and relationships that such enforcement would cause; and, above all, to the 'presumption of liberty', which always counts against criminalization.[83] That presumption is sometimes defeated by the demand that we ensure that wrongdoers receive the punishment they deserve; but it is often not defeated even when we are certain that a particular type of conduct is morally wrong and thus deserving of punishment. Thus the end result of a Moorean deliberation about the proper scope of the criminal law might be extensionally very similar to that favoured by his liberal opponents: what begins as a vastly expansive realm of potentially criminalizable conduct turns out in the end to be much more modest in scope.[84] The fact remains, however, that on Moore's account we have good reason to criminalize every kind of moral wrongdoing—even if that reason is quite often outweighed or defeated by reasons against criminalization: but it does seem very odd to say that we have any reason at all to criminalize my betrayal of my partner or my friend—or my failure to buy my round in the pub, which is surely a breach of the (modest but still real) obligations that partly define that type of social interaction.

Moore's legal moralism is also expansive, as are many other principles of criminalization, in a second way that is less often noticed: it is expansive as to the location, and perpetrators, of the wrongs we have reason to criminalize. If moral wrongdoing deserves punishment, it presumably deserves punishment wherever, by whomever, against whomever it is committed. So we all have reason to promote the imposition of such suffering on wrongdoers anywhere in the world, and thus reason as legislators

[81] See M S Moore, *Act and Crime: The Philosophy of Action and its Implications for the Criminal Law*, 44–59.

[82] See e.g. *Placing Blame*, 662; 'A Tale of Two Theories', 32; 'Four Reflections on Law and Morality', 1540–1.

[83] See Moore, *Placing Blame*, ch. 18; 'A Tale of Two Theories', 32–3; 'Liberty's Constraints on What Should be Made Criminal'. But see J D Thaysen, 'Infidelity and the Possibility of a Liberal Legal Moralism'.

[84] Indeed, in some respects a Moorean criminal law would be narrower than those favoured by many liberals: see the critique of 'hate crime' legislation in H Hurd and M S Moore, 'Punishing Hatred and Prejudice'; and below, Chapter 5 at nn 51–7, Chapter 7 at nn 119–23.

to bring all wrongdoers within the reach of our criminal law.[85] Those reasons are not restricted by geography or territory. The English legislature has reason to bring within the scope of English criminal law not just wrongs committed within England, but those committed anywhere in the world—to count as a crime under English law, triable in the English courts and punishable in its penal system, murder, rape, theft committed anywhere in the world, and indeed such wrongs as vandalizing property or drunken driving; to criminalize, and to seek to punish, criminal damage committed by a Turk on the streets of Istanbul. (Correlatively, of course, the Turkish legislature has reason to count as criminal under Turkish law the criminal damage committed by an English person on the streets of London.) Once again, Moore can point out that there are persuasive countervailing reasons against giving domestic criminal law such a global scope: reasons to do with the practicability and costs of trying to enforce such a globally ambitious criminal law and with the importance of respecting other states' sovereignty. He might also cite, as grist to his mill, the jurisdiction over 'crimes against humanity' that is claimed by international criminal tribunals and by national legal systems asserting 'universal jurisdiction',[86] even when this infringes the sovereignty of the state within which the crimes were committed: if wrongs are so grave that the demands of retributive justice become insistent, but the local legal system and its courts are unwilling or unable to meet those demands, other states or international bodies might be justified in intervening to ensure that retributive justice is done. However, we should be puzzled by the suggestion that the English legislature has any reason at all, however obviously and conclusively it is overridden or defeated, to define vandalism committed by a Pole in Krakow as a crime under English law.

The points made in the previous two paragraphs were not intended to amount to a refutation of Moore's version of legal moralism, any more than the points made earlier in this section were intended to amount to an argument in favour of positive legal moralism. They were no more than initial moves in what will be a long discussion, and were meant only to remind us of the intuitive plausibility of some version of positive legal moralism, whilst also highlighting the prima facie implausibility of the expansive version articulated by Moore.

The obvious way to resolve this tension between the intuitive plausibility of some version of positive legal moralism, and the prima facie implausibility of Moore's expansive version, would be to articulate a more modest legal moralism, according to which only certain kinds of wrong are even in principle candidates for criminalization: for a modest legal moralist, what gives us reason to criminalize a type of conduct is not simply that it is morally wrongful, but that it is an appropriate or relevant kind of wrong. The challenge then, of course, is to explain what counts as an appropriate or relevant kind of wrong: to see just what that challenge might involve, we can explore one traditional way of trying to meet it, by appealing to the idea of public wrongs.

6. 'Public' and 'Private' Wrongs

A Moorean legal moralism, its critics might argue, fails to recognize the importance of the distinction between 'public' and 'private' wrongs: whilst we do have reason to

[85] '[T]he world is better if it is morally better, and to the extent legislators can achieve that moral betterment through law, they should do so' (Moore, 'Four Reflections on Law and Morality', 1540).

[86] See L Reydams, *Universal Jurisdiction*; and below, Chapter 3, section 1.

criminalize every kind of public wrong, we can have no reason to criminalize merely private wrongs.

There are in fact, as we have already seen, two distinctions between 'public' and 'private' wrongs in play here.[87] There is the distinction within the realm of law between criminal wrongs and private wrongs such as torts—a distinction among those wrongs that are legally cognizable; and there is the distinction between those wrongs that are legally cognizable, that can ground a legal action of some kind, and those of which the law takes no cognizance—those that are in the law's eyes purely private.[88] An account of criminal law that appeals to the idea of public wrongs must be able to explain both these distinctions. The problem is that while we can easily provide a procedural account of these distinctions, that does not appear to give the modest legal moralist what she needs. On a proceduralist account, a wrong is public rather than purely private if it can ground some kind of legal action; and it is, within the realm of law, criminal rather than private if it can lead to a distinctively criminal process of prosecution, conviction, and punishment.[89] Now what legal moralists seem to offer, and what Moore certainly offers, is an account of the grounds on which we can decide whether a given type of conduct should be legally cognizable, and if so whether it should be cognizable as a crime: but a purely proceduralist account of the distinctions between 'public' and 'private' wrongs cannot provide that; it tells us what follows from deciding to treat a wrong as public rather than as private, but not what can ground that decision—which is what we need to know.

We will see in this section that an appeal to the idea of public wrongs cannot indeed by itself provide a substantive principle or criterion of criminalizability; but it does point the way towards a more plausible version of legal moralism. To see this, we can usefully return to Blackstone's classic formulation of the idea of crimes as public wrongs: whilst private wrongs infringe 'the civil rights which belong to individuals, considered merely as individuals', crimes 'are breach and violation of the public rights and duties, due to the whole community, ... in its social aggregate capacity.... [They] strike at the very being of society, which cannot possibly subsist, where actions of [that] sort are suffered to escape with impunity'.[90]

Blackstone's distinction was of the first kind noted above: a distinction within the law between public and private legal wrongs.[91] An equally famous appeal to the second kind of distinction, between wrongs that are and wrongs that are not legally cognizable, is found in the Wolfenden Committee's previously quoted declaration that 'there must remain a realm of private morality and immorality which is, in brief and crude terms, not the law's business'.[92]

Some more recent theorists have also appealed to a distinction between 'public' and 'private' wrongs to characterize the kinds of wrong with which the criminal law

[87] See above, Chapter 1 at nn 57–8.

[88] Thus adultery could be understood as a purely private wrong, of which the law takes no notice; or as a legally recognized private wrong, as when it is a ground for divorce; or as a public wrong, if it is criminalized.

[89] See the definitions of crime offered by Williams and Gordon (above, Chapter 1 at n. 22), and the distinction between a criminal and a civil process discussed above, Chapter 1, section 3.

[90] Sir William Blackstone, *Commentaries on the Laws of England*, Bk IV, ch. 1, p. 5.

[91] As Blackstone notes at the beginning of Book IV of the *Commentaries*.

[92] Wolfenden, *Report of the Committee on Homosexual Offences and Prostitution*, para. 61; see at n. 7 above. (Moore would certainly agree that consensual homosexual conduct in private is not, in principle, the criminal law's business; but that, he would say, is because it is not wrong at all.)

is properly concerned.[93] Moore objects that such appeals to an idea of public wrongs fail to offer any substantive, non-question-begging 'criterion for the public/private distinction' as 'a distinction that is supposed to mark the proper limits of criminal legislation'.[94] As we will now see, this objection is in one way well-founded; but that requires us to rethink, rather than abandon, the role that an idea of public wrongs can play in marking out the proper realm of the criminal law.

Blackstone seems to offer two possible criteria: first, a wrong is public if it violates a duty that is owed 'to the whole community', rather than to an individual; second, that it is public if it affects 'society' rather than only an individual victim, or 'strike[s] at the very being of society'.[95] But the first criterion gives us no substantive help: we must then ask which duties are owed 'to the whole community', and the obvious, but entirely unhelpful, answer is 'those whose violation is criminalizable'. The second criterion appears more substantial, if we read it as being concerned with the actual or likely consequences of the wrong in question for the society as a whole: but—apart from the problem of determining just what kinds of consequence will then be relevant—we should resist the idea that what makes such central *mala in se* as murder, rape, and other attacks on the person criminalizable is not their impact on their individual victims, but their impact on or implications for the wider society; I agree with Moore that we should criminalize such wrongs precisely because of the wrong they do to their individual victims. That still leaves us, however, without any substantive criterion for 'public wrongs'. Nor will it help, Moore argues, to talk in vague terms of the shared values by which a community defines itself: communities 'can and do share values ... about all kinds of human behaviour, incest between adults as much as murder, picking one's nose in public as much as theft', and 'regard these shared values as constitutive of their being moral communities'.[96] So appeals to the idea of 'public' wrongs are either empty, if 'public' just means, in effect, 'in principle criminalizable', or vulnerable to the (often misguided) moralizing of different communities: they do not help us to set determinate limits to the scope of the criminal law, or provide clear guidelines about what we can have good reason to criminalize.

On three points Moore is right. First, the idea of a 'public' wrong cannot provide a plausible, substantive criterion of criminalizability. Nor should it be intended to do so; it is in this context a formal rather than a substantive idea, just as 'moral wrong' is a formal rather than a substantive idea. We might agree, that is, that the criminal law should be concerned with 'moral wrongs', or with 'public wrongs', although we

[93] See e.g. S E Marshall and R A Duff, 'Criminalization and Sharing Wrongs', and 'Public and Private Wrongs'; G Lamond, 'What is a Crime?'; Husak, *Overcriminalization*, 135–9; R A Duff, 'Towards a Modest Legal Moralism'.

[94] 'Liberty's Constraints on What Should be Made Criminal', 199; and see 'A Tale of Two Theories', 40–41. See also J Edwards and A P Simester, 'What's Public About Crime?', at 108: '[i]f the idea of a public wrong is to help us make progress with the limits of the criminal law, ... it must be understood in a way that allows public wrongfulness to figure as a premise in arguments about what there is reason to criminalise'; on some accounts of that idea, however, 'to say that Φing is a public wrong is to announce the conclusion of an argument rather than one of its premises'. (I will attend to some of the other criticisms that Edwards and Simester make later: see below, Chapter 4 at nn 126–37, Chapter 5, section 7.)

[95] See also C Allen, 'The Nature of a Crime', 233–4: 'Crime is crime because it consists in wrongdoing which directly and in serious degree threatens the security or well-being of society, and because it is not safe to leave it redressable only by compensation of the party injured'. For cognate ideas, see e.g. L C Becker, 'Criminal Attempts and the Theory of the Law of Crimes' (causing 'social volatility' as the hallmark of crime); and S Dimock, 'Retributivism and Trust' (crime as undermining the kind of trust on which a society depends).

[96] 'Liberty's Constraints on What Should be Made Criminal', 199.

disagree on the substantive question of what kinds of conduct constitute moral wrongs, or public wrongs; once we agree on the formal point, we must move to a more substantive discussion of the content that these formal notions should be given. Someone who believes that sodomy should be criminalized might agree with Moore that the proper aim of criminal law is, formally, to achieve retributive justice, by punishing all and only culpable moral wrongdoers; but they differ in their substantive views of the content of morality.

Second, different political communities might therefore agree that criminal law is concerned only with public wrongs, but give different contents to their criminal laws, reflecting different conceptions of what counts as a public matter, and as a public wrong. A political community that criminalizes sodomy gives force both to its conception of morality (according to which sodomy is a moral wrong), and to its conception of the public realm and what falls within it (according to which sexual relationships are a public matter). Moore would have to recognize that such a polity is faithfully applying a legal moralist principle, in criminalizing (only) what its members take to be moral wrongdoing—although he would disagree with them about what they should count as moral wrongdoing. Similarly, I would have to recognize that they are faithfully reflecting their own understanding of what counts as a public rather than a private matter: I would also disagree with them about whether sodomy is a moral wrong, but that disagreement is irrelevant here; my prior disagreement would be about whether they should define the public realm in this illiberal way, to make consensual sexual relations a public matter.[97]

Third, if we take as our starting point the whole (wide, variegated) realm of moral wrongs, and then ask how within that realm we can distinguish 'public' from 'private' wrongs, we will be hard put to provide any plausible, non-vacuous answer, unless we accept Moore's approach, and argue that we should count as 'private' those wrongs which, despite their immorality, we ought not to criminalize because to do so would be to intrude unacceptably on the liberty or privacy of those concerned. To take that approach would be (as the 'despite' in the previous sentence makes clear) to accept Moore's version of legal moralism: we have good reason to criminalize every kind of moral wrongdoing, but stronger countervailing reasons not to criminalize many of them; and when those reasons concern the regard we should have for individual liberty or privacy, we might call the wrongs that are thus exempted from criminalization 'private' wrongs.

Is this then to agree with Moore that his is the only viable form of legal moralism; and thus that if we reject Moorean legal moralism (maybe because we find its implications, noted above, implausible) we must reject positive legal moralism as such? Not yet: for there is an alternative—a different form of positive legal moralism, which does not have those implications, but which avoids the problems noted above. The key to recognizing this alternative is to see that we must start the discussion in a different place: not with wrongs, but with the idea of the public.

The distinction between the 'public' and the 'private' cannot, I have agreed, provide us with a substantive criterion by which we can distinguish within the wide realm

[97] This need not reflect the kind of moral relativism that Moore rejects; it does not preclude the claim that there is a truth of the matter about the content of morality. The point is simply that to say that criminal law is concerned with moral wrongs, or with public wrongs, is to specify the kind of question we must ask in determining what we have reason to criminalize, but is not yet to answer that question. See further below, Chapter 4 at nn 81–3.

of moral wrongs those that are in principle criminalizable from those that are not. Indeed, it would be more accurate to say that to count a wrong as 'public' is precisely to assert the conclusion that it is, in principle, the law's business—rather than a substantive ground or criterion for that conclusion.[98] Similarly, to claim that a wrong is 'private' is to assert the conclusion that it is in principle 'not the law's business'; it does not provide a substantive reason in support of that conclusion. But that—the whole wide realm of moral wrongs—should not be our starting point, either as theorists thinking about the proper scope of the criminal law, or as would-be legislators thinking about what we should criminalize. To take that as our starting point would invite the familiar criticism that legal moralists advocate a kind of state-controlled moralistic witch-hunt. To the question 'What should we criminalize?', the legal moralist seems to answer 'Moral wrongdoing': whether that answer is an expansive 'In principle, all moral wrongdoing', or a modest 'These kinds of wrongdoing', it seems to urge legislators to seek out moral wrongdoing (of the appropriate kinds) to ensure that it is then criminalized and punished. That might be how some legal moralists see the criminal law's task: to ensure that moral wrongdoers suffer the retributive pains that they deserve (as Moore urges), or that the 'grosser forms of vice' are persecuted, in order to gratify the justified 'feeling of hatred ... which the contemplation of such conduct excites in healthily constituted minds' (as Stephen thought).[99] But it is not the only or the best way to make sense of legal moralism: legal moralism need not be 'moralistic' in a pejorative sense.[100]

To put the point crudely, if we are to develop a plausibly modest version of legal moralism, and understand the role that criminal law should play in a decent republic, we must indeed focus on the idea of 'public wrongs', but our starting point should be the 'public' rather than 'wrongs': we should begin, that is, by thinking not about wrongs, but about the public realm—the realm in which public wrongs are identified. Rather than starting with the whole realm of moral wrongs as our canvas, and then asking which of them should be the criminal law's business, we must think about the criminal law's business, as a distinctive kind of legal institution; and to do that we must think about the polity's business (its *res publica*), since the criminal law's proper business must be to contribute, in some distinctive way, to the polity's business. In thinking about the polity's business, we will arrive at a conception of the public realm, as the realm in which that business is conducted; and—or so I will argue—as we think about how the polity might organize matters in that public realm we will see reason to maintain a system of criminal law as an appropriate way of marking and responding to wrongs that figure within that realm. The 'public' wrongs that are, in principle, the business of the criminal law thus will not need to be distinguished, within the whole realm of wrongs, from 'private' wrongs: they will come to our attention already marked as public wrongs, since they will come to our attention as we think about matters that are already understood as belonging in the public realm.

We can begin to see the force and implications of this point by looking first not at criminal law and the polity's business, but at what I will suggest is an aptly analogous enterprise: at how a profession might develop its code of ethics.

98 See Edwards and Simester, 'What's Public About Crime?', 108 (n. 94 above).

99 Stephen, *Liberty, Equality, Fraternity*, 162.

100 See e.g. C Taylor, *Moralism: A Study of a Vice*; A Archer, 'The Problem with Moralism'.

7. Starting with the Public: Professional Ethics

Suppose that members of a profession decide to rethink the structures and processes through which they govern their affairs; or that those engaged in a particular kind of practice (public relations, for instance) decide to constitute themselves as a profession, and set about constructing a system of governance for the profession; or that a new university is created, and a committee is appointed to consider how it should be organized and run. We can expect that, in each such case, part of the new or revised structure of governance will be a code of ethics or a disciplinary code, along with procedures through which that code is to be enforced and applied (indeed, those who seek public respectability for their practice might seek to define themselves as a profession partly by creating a code of ethics). The code will define kinds of wrongdoing that those who are bound by the code (members of the profession or the university) ought to eschew, and that amount to professional *mis*conduct if committed; and it will provide for a process through which charges of misconduct are to be adjudicated, and suitable sanctions imposed on those against whom they are proved.

(We should note here, but then put aside, one disanalogy between some professional codes and the criminal law. A professional code might cover not only matters of ethical (mis)conduct, but also matters of competence: thus the General Medical Council (GMC)'s guidance on Good Medical Practice for doctors, which specifies what is required of them as doctors, includes 'You must be competent in all aspects of your work, including management, research and teaching' as its first requirement;[101] and a doctor's 'fitness to practise' can be judged to be impaired on the basis of 'adverse physical or mental health' as well as of 'misconduct'.[102] Matters of competence involve ethical requirements—to keep one's skills and knowledge up to date, for instance, to undertake suitable training, to 'recognise and work within the limits of [one's] competence':[103] but whilst we should try to maintain a reasonably firm distinction between the criminal law, as dealing with wrongdoing, and various kinds of non-criminal process or institution to which we subject those who are non-culpably incompetent to take part in civic life with the freedoms to which citizens are normally entitled,[104] a professional body might be less concerned to draw such a distinction. We need not ask here whether they should be more scrupulous; we can limit our attention, for present purposes, to the procedures through which professional codes define and deal with what are clearly matters of professional *ethics*.)

The bodies that draw up codes of professional ethics operate under the aegis of the law: their constitutions and procedures may require legal approval; some of the regulations they administer might be laid down by law;[105] there might be scope for appeals to a court by those who think that they have been wrongfully treated. But, whilst they might count as 'public' rather than as purely 'private' bodies, in the sense that members of the polity have a proper interest in their operations, they are not part of the polity's institutional apparatus of self-governance: they have substantial autonomy to

[101] General Medical Council, *Good Medical Practice*, para. 7.

[102] See Medical Act 1983 (as amended), s. 35C; also General Medical Council (Fitness to Practise) Rules (2004, No. 2608; http://www.gmc-uk.org/consolidated_version_of_FTP_Rules.dec2015.pdf_64002624.pdf).

[103] *Good Medical Practice*, para. 14; and see paras 7–13.

[104] Though these distinctions are not in fact always clear or sharp—another issue I cannot pursue here.

[105] See e.g. Medical Act 1983, Solicitors Act 1974, and the charters by which universities are governed.

determine their own structures and operations—and codes of ethics. (It is important to bear in mind, however, that what they produce are not 'codes of ethics' as such, but codes of 'professional ethics'—codes governing professional conduct.)

Two things should be evident about the logical (if not the chronological) ordering of such a profession's deliberations about a code of ethics. First, a code of ethics will not be the first item of business as they work out the profession's governing structures and practices; indeed, it *could* not be their first item of business. Second, when they do come to discuss the proper content and scope of their code of ethics, they will not begin with the whole realm of moral wrongdoing, and of moral wrongdoers, as their potential canvas.

The code of ethics cannot be the first matter for decision because it is a code of *professional* ethics, which defines good and bad, right and wrong, professional conduct: to know what should fall within the code's scope, its drafters will need first to work out what falls within the realm of professional conduct. An answer to this question will partly depend on what other regulations are drawn up to govern the profession, since professional misconduct often consists in violating such regulations. However, the creation of such a system of governance itself depends on something prior: on a conception of what the practice or profession that is to be regulated *is*. The code's drafters will need first to consider what it is to be a lawyer, or a doctor, or a university: what kinds of aim and value define the practice, what sorts of activity fall within its scope? To answer these questions they might be able to consult a constitution or a charter, or a mission statement, if there is one; or they might need to (re)construct answers from what has hitherto been implicit in the practices of those involved in the profession, rather than explicit in any document. Their answers will specify what we can call the *res publica* (the public affair) of that profession: the goal-related activities and relationships that constitute the shared business of those within the profession; the goods at which those activities and relationships are aimed. This will also be to define the roles of those within the practice—the role of doctor, or of lawyer, or of professor (and thus also the correlative roles of patient, client, and student). An account of these roles is an essential prerequisite for the formulation of a code of ethics—although the code might also provide a more precise determination of the roles: for the roles will be constituted by the sets of duties, responsibilities, and rights that those who take on (or find themselves in) the roles are to have—the duties, responsibilities, and rights whose violation will constitute professional misconduct; they will make clear how members of the profession should behave towards their patients, clients, or students, and towards each other. But such specifications must depend on an understanding of the profession's *res publica*—of what, given its aims, falls within its scope: for roles are defined, the sets of duties, responsibilities, and rights that constitute them are determined, by the ways in which the role-bearer is to contribute to that *res publica* and to the achievement of those aims.[106]

The deliberations that will lead to the creation of a code of professional ethics must therefore begin with an understanding of the *res publica*, the proper concerns and aims, of the practice in question. Given such an understanding, members of the profession will be able to consider what kinds of institutional structure, and what kinds of regulation, will best serve its ends. What will also emerge, as a by-product of this process of self-constitution, is a set of ethical expectations and norms, to do with the ways in which the profession's defining goals and values, and the institutional structures that

[106] Those with Wittgensteinian inclinations might talk here of practices or of forms of life; see also A Harel, 'The Triadic Relational Structure of Responsibility: A Defence', on 'units of responsibility'.

serve those goals and values, will figure in the lives of its members: how they should treat each other, and treat those with whom they have professional dealings.

These expectations and norms are by-products in the sense that their formulation is not the primary aim of the process of constructing the profession: rather, in structuring the profession, as a practice that exists to serve some identifiable good, its members will also inevitably develop views about how they should conduct themselves in relation to that good—views, that is, about how they should play their roles as members of the profession. But they might also see reason to formulate those norms and expectations in a code of professional ethics—a code that will specify more clearly what is expected of members of the profession, by way of professional conduct, and thus also what will count as professional *mis*conduct. The point of such a code will be partly to make clear, to members of the profession and to others, what is expected of members: but it will also probably need to go beyond the mere declaration of norms and expectations, to provide for some appropriate response to violations of those norms and expectations. This is not a logically necessary feature of a code of professional ethics: a profession might think it enough to declare its guiding norms and values in a code, whilst leaving violations of those norms to be dealt with informally by its members. But it must make clear—to its members and to others—that it does take its norms seriously, and ensure (as part of what is involved in taking them seriously) that they are respected; and the obvious way to do that is to provide for a formal response to alleged violations of the code—a formal process through which alleged violations can be adjudicated and, if proved, sanctioned. The procedure might be analogous to that of a criminal trial, in that the person accused of misconduct will be called to a hearing to answer the accusation; and if she is found 'guilty', she will then face a sanction. Those sanctions might include requirements to undertake reparative actions, if those are possible; or a fine; or an analogue of probation, which requires the person to work for a time under special supervision, and might limit what she can do; or expulsion—temporary or permanent exclusion from the profession: doctors can be struck off the medical register, lawyers can be disbarred, professors can be sacked.[107]

We can now see why the drafters of the code will not begin with the whole realm of moral wrongdoing, and of moral wrongdoers, as their canvas (the second evident point signalled four paragraphs ago). When they begin to deliberate about what kinds of conduct they should define as professional misconduct, and what range of agents the code should bind, they will not think that they have good reason to include every kind of moral wrongdoing in the code, or to claim for the code authority over all moral agents, before seeing better reason to limit its scope and authority;[108] nor will they think that they must find some criterion by which they can distinguish, within the realm of moral wrongdoing, those kinds of wrong that are the code's business, from those that are not.[109] For they will already know that they are concerned (only) with professional misconduct—that is, with wrongdoing committed within the realm of the profession and its practice; and they will already know that the code is to be binding only on those engaged in or with the profession. That is to say, when they begin their task, they already have an idea of what counts, for their purposes, as the 'public' realm (the *res publica*) of this profession, of who belongs in that realm, and of the kinds of conduct (professional conduct) that are their business. Thus those whose responsibility

[107] See, for just one example, the provisions laid down in General Medical Council, *Professional Conduct and Discipline: Fitness to Practise*, ss 9–22 (disciplinary procedures), 23–8 (sanctions).

[108] Compare the two ways in which Moore's legal moralism is (over-)expansive, at nn 80–6 above.

[109] Compare the discussion of how to distinguish 'public' from 'private' wrongs in section 6 above.

it is to draw up the code of professional ethics for medicine, for instance, already know that their concern is with conduct that belongs within the practice of medicine: with the conduct of medical practitioners as it bears on their roles, responsibilities, and duties as medical practitioners. They will have no interest in conduct—right, wrong, morally indifferent—that falls outside the practice of medicine, or in aspects of medical practitioners' lives that do not have to do with their medical responsibilities (or with the activities of those who have nothing to do with the medical profession): such conduct, those aspects of the lives of medical practitioners, count as 'private' in relation to the medical profession.

This distinction between the 'public' and the 'private' realms is normative and context-relative. It is normative in that the question of whether something is a public or a private matter is the question whether it is something that *properly* concerns a specifiable 'public', something in which they have a *legitimate* interest; it is context-dependent in that both the identity of that public, and the scope of its legitimate interests, depend on the practice or form of life in which the distinction is being drawn. Thus a doctor's treatment of her patient counts as 'public' in the context of her medical life, but as 'private' in the context of her membership of a golf club. It is something in which her fellow doctors properly take an interest, and something for which (if it involves mistreatment) she may be called to account by her fellow doctors or by a professional disciplinary committee: but fellow members of her golf club have no such interest in it, and no standing to call her to account; if they sought to do so, she would not have to explain, or justify, or excuse her treatment to them—she could simply tell them that it is not their business. (Her unsporting behaviour on the golf course, by contrast, is a public matter in the context of the golf club, but private in the context of her medical life.) So too, her religious beliefs count as private in relation to her medical life, in that her colleagues have no right, as colleagues, to inquire into them or call her to account for them—unless and until they impinge on her conduct as a doctor; in the context of her church, by contrast, they are public matters, in which her priest or fellow members of the church may properly take an interest.

I am using 'public' here in an admittedly slightly unusual way: members of a profession (or of a golf club) would not usually describe the matters that are their business as 'public' matters. But the (normative and context-relative) distinction that I am drawing between the 'public' and the 'private' is not unusual or unfamiliar, and it is often marked by saying that something is, or is not, a 'private' matter—which is to also say, in my terms, that it is not, or is, a 'public' matter. The distinction, we could say, is a way of marking out different normative spaces. Any practice defines a distinctive normative space—a space that is structured by its defining goals and values, occupied by its distinctive activities, and peopled by its practitioners: what falls within that space is, relative to that practice, a 'public' matter, which properly concerns its members; what falls outside that space is, relative to that practice, a 'private' matter, which is not their business.[110]

There will, clearly, be plenty of room for argument about the various matters that bear on the formulation of a code of professional ethics. There might be arguments about how the defining goals and values of the profession should be understood, and about who is to count as a member of the profession, and thus to be bound by its

[110] It is important to be clear, however, that the normative space is not a physical space: what happens in 'private' physical space (for instance rape or assault in the home) can be normatively 'public', as a criminal matter. As we will see later (Chapter 4, section 4 below) this distinction will need to be complicated in the context of a polity.

code. We need not discuss these kinds of argument here: of more relevance here is the distinction between two other kinds of argument that might arise: one is about what should count as *mis*conduct; the other, logically prior, argument is about what should count as *professional* conduct.

For instance, the code drafters might have very different, conflicting views about the ethics of sexual relationships—about, for instance, the importance of sexual fidelity, about what kinds of consensual sexual conduct are or are not morally appropriate: but they will need to discuss and try to resolve such differences only if they have first determined that doctors' sexual conduct is a professional matter—that it falls within or bears essentially on their behaviour as doctors. They might (indeed, we should hope that they would) decide that doctors' sexual conduct should not generally fall within the scope of their professional lives unless it bears directly on their patients' health and well-being:[111] in which case the code will concern itself only with sexual relationships between doctors and their patients,[112] and with such relationships only as they do or might affect the patient's well-being; the code drafters will not need to discuss or resolve their differences about sexual conduct in general. They will need to decide what should count as 'misconduct' in sexual relationships with patients: should the code declare that *any* such relationship constitutes professional misconduct, given the dangers of exploitation, of breach and loss of trust, and other kinds of damage that such relationships involve; or should it try to specify which kinds of sexual relationship are professionally (in)appropriate?[113] (Similarly, universities need to decide whether to define any sexual relations between staff members and students as professional misconduct, or only certain kinds of sexual relationship or certain kinds of sexual conduct.) Even in this context, however, they will not need to engage in a general debate about what kinds of sexual conduct are morally appropriate or inappropriate: they will need to discuss a different question—what kinds of sexual conduct or relationship are inconsistent with, or damaging to, the relationship between doctors and their patients? A doctor accused of professional misconduct on grounds of his sexual conduct might thus, under a properly drafted code of medical ethics, have two possible responses to the accusation. He might be able to show that the other person was not a patient (or a former patient, or member of a patient's family), in which case he does not have to answer for or justify his behaviour to this medical disciplinary tribunal. Or, if he admits that the tribunal has standing to call him to account (because the other person was a patient), he might be able to argue that the relationship, and his conduct within it, did not involve the kind of mischief at which the code's provisions are aimed. My concern here is not with the substantive question of what should count as falling within the realm of 'professional conduct', or of how misconduct should be defined in that realm. It is simply to distinguish the two different questions that the code's drafters must ask and answer: first, what counts as professional conduct; and second, what counts as professional misconduct—misconduct within a person's professional life?

There is of course fertile ground for disagreement about the scope of 'professional conduct', once we move beyond its obvious core. Thus British universities used to

[111] Or unless, the General Medical Council would add, it involves criminal conduct: for any criminal conviction 'may lead to disciplinary proceedings even if the offence is not directly connected with the doctor's profession' (General Medical Council, *Professional Conduct and Discipline*, para. 3; see Medical Act 1983, s. 35C(2)(c)).

[112] The drafters will also need to decide whether the code should attend to sexual relationships with former as well as with current patients, and with members of a patient's family: see General Medical Council, *Professional Conduct and Discipline*, paras 47–8.

[113] See General Medical Council, *Professional Conduct and Discipline*, paras 47–8, 68–75.

include a 'gross moral turpitude' clause in their disciplinary codes, and many now have a clause covering conduct that 'brings the university into disrepute', which can be used to treat as disciplinary offences conduct that falls well outside the scope of professional academic activities as narrowly conceived. Under the GMC's code, professional misconduct includes any conduct 'derogatory to the reputation of the profession': the 'public reputation of the medical profession requires that every member should observe proper standards of personal behaviour, not only in professional activities but at all times'.[114] Critics of such provisions will argue (surely with some reason) that they involve over-extensive definitions of professional misconduct: not because the conduct that can then be treated as professional misconduct is morally unproblematic (is not misconduct), but because it should not count as professional conduct. To justify bringing a type of conduct within the scope of a code of professional ethics, it is not sufficient to argue that it is morally wrong; it must first be shown that it is a type of professional conduct—conduct that falls within or bears on the person's professional role. Thus the GMC justifies the inclusion of 'personal relationships between doctors and patients' within the code of practice by pointing out that such 'emotional and sexual relationships' can 'disrupt the patient's family life or otherwise damage the maintenance of trust between doctors and patients';[115] and by including conduct 'derogatory to the reputation of the profession' it claims that the 'public reputation of the medical profession' is an important aspect of its *res publica* (it bears on the trust that patients must be able to have in their doctors). Such justifications might or might not be persuasive; but some such justification must be provided if conduct is to be brought within the reach of the code. Before a profession can decide whether a certain type of conduct constitutes professional misconduct, it must decide whether it constitutes professional conduct at all: whether, that is, it is something done in the course of the person's profession,[116] or something that could implicate her 'fitness to practise' that profession.[117]

Similar points could be made about any kind of association or practice whose members see their enterprise as having an ethical dimension. They will operate with some formal or informal understanding of what kinds of conduct belong to the practice, and will on that basis have some formal or informal understanding of what should count as *mis*conduct that is the business of the practice's members; and they may find that they disagree not just about what kinds of conduct are ethically acceptable or unacceptable, but about what kinds of conduct are their business. For one more instance, should a person's membership of an extremist political party that advocates racist policies be enough by itself to warrant her dismissal from a teaching post; or should she face dismissal only if it can be shown that her political beliefs influenced her conduct towards her pupils and colleagues in inappropriate ways? To justify the former view it is not enough to argue that the party's political views are morally repellent: it must also be argued that they are in some way relevant to a teacher's role—that one who holds those

[114] *Professional Conduct and Discipline*, para. 49: misuse of drugs or alcohol, 'dishonest behaviour', and 'indecent or violent behaviour' might 'occasion disciplinary proceedings', as can any criminal conviction (see n. 111 above).

[115] *Professional Conduct and Discipline*, para. 68; see also para. 48.

[116] See *Professional Conduct and Discipline*, paras 6–7: what is now called 'serious professional misconduct' used to be defined as 'infamous conduct in a professional respect': something done 'by a medical man in the pursuit of his profession ... which will be reasonably regarded as disgraceful or dishonourable by his professional brethren of good repute and competency' (quoting Lord Justice Lopes in 1894).

[117] The idea of a doctor's 'fitness to practise' is central to *Professional Conduct and Discipline*, and it is clear that 'fitness' covers both technical and ethical competence.

views cannot at the same time be committed to the values and attitudes that we properly expect of teachers.[118]

I should make clear what I am and am not arguing: in particular, I am not arguing that fellow members of a person's profession should just ignore the serious moral wrongs that he commits if they do not bear on his professional conduct. Suppose that I come to know about some egregious moral wrong committed by an academic colleague—perhaps a wrong that is also criminal: he has left his partner in a cruelly damaging way, or committed a fraud against the polity (evading his taxes) or a corporation. Suppose too that the wrong has no direct impact on or implication for his academic conduct: he still behaves properly towards students and colleagues; he is still honest in his teaching and research. Suppose too that I and my university rightly do not share the extensive definition of academic misconduct that includes some version of 'gross moral turpitude'. In that case, I have no reason to respond to, to take any notice of, his conduct *as an academic colleague*: no reason to call him to account for it in our professional dealings, or to table it for discussion at a departmental meeting, or to report it to the university authorities as a disciplinary matter. It is not a matter of academic conduct, and therefore cannot be a case of academic misconduct: which is to say that it is not my business as his academic colleague. But that is not to say that it is not my business *tout court*. If I am not just a colleague, but a friend, it might be my business; if his conduct is criminal, it is (as we will see later) my business as a citizen, and I might have reason not just to call him to account for it myself, but to report it to the appropriate authorities; some would also argue that his wrongdoing is my business as a moral agent—as a fellow member of the moral community—so that I have reason to call him to account simply as a fellow moral agent.[119] Even if his conduct is my business in one of these ways, however, that does not make it my business as his colleague, or bring him within reach of the university's disciplinary code.

The central point here can also be expressed in terms of answerability. The code of medical ethics defines the wrongs for which doctors will be held responsible: wrongs for which they will be called to answer by and before a Medical Practitioners Tribunal.[120] In enacting that code, the GMC asserts its authority both to define such wrongs, and to call to formal account those alleged to have committed them. Now responsibility, understood as a matter of answerability, is essentially relational. It involves not just a dyadic relationship (I am responsible for *X*), but a triadic relationship: I am responsible for *X* to *S*, and I am responsible as *Φ*—in virtue of satisfying some normatively laden description that makes me responsible for *X* to *S*.[121] Thus Jones might be answerable to a Medical Practitioners Tribunal (acting by the authority of the GMC, in the name and on behalf of the medical profession as a whole) for her misconduct. But she is answerable only *as* a doctor who falls under the authority of the GMC: if she is not a doctor, or not a doctor within the ambit of the GMC's authority, she is not answerable to this body. And she is answerable only *for* a kind of wrongdoing that is defined as professional misconduct, that is, as falling within or impinging on her activities as a doctor. She is answerable to others for other kinds of wrong that she commits: she is answerable for her marital misconduct as a wife to her husband and to other family

[118] See e.g. https://www.theguardian.com/education/2010/nov/02/bnp-members-barred-teaching.

[119] Compare T M Scanlon, *Moral Dimensions: Permissibility, Meaning, Blame*, 139–40: 'the moral relationship' that grounds the legitimacy of moral blame is a matter of the 'mutual concern that, ideally, we all have toward other rational beings'. But see below, Chapter 3, text at nn 44–5.

[120] On these tribunals and their remit, see General Medical Council (Fitness to Practise) Rules (n. 102 above).

[121] See further Duff, *Answering for Crime*, ch. 1.2; also 'In Response', 353–61.

members or friends; answerable for her betrayals of friendship as a friend to her friends; and so on. But she is not answerable for these wrongs as a doctor to her profession.[122]

I suggested above that a useful analogy can be drawn between the criminal law and a code of professional ethics: the role of the criminal law in the life of a political community is analogous to the role of a code of ethics in the lives of the members of a profession; the task of drawing up a criminal code is analogous to that of drawing up a code of professional ethics. I will defend this suggestion and explore some of its implications in the following chapters, but should first give a clearer indication of what the analogy will amount to, and comment briefly on the relationship between codes of professional ethics and the criminal law.[123]

8. Professional Ethics and the Criminal Law

A code of medical ethics deals with what should count as right and wrong conduct within the distinctive practice of medicine; it defines as professional misconduct, and provides for a formal response to, conduct that violates the norms of the practice—norms that reflect its defining goals. A doctor, as a member of that practice, is then answerable to fellow members of the practice for her conduct as a doctor—for conduct in which she engages as a doctor, or that bears directly on her medical activities. In order to determine the proper content and ambit of the code of ethics, its drafters must therefore begin with a conception of the practice of medicine: a conception of its defining goals and values, of the kinds of conduct that fall within it, and of the range of people who belong to it:[124] they must, that is, begin with a conception of the contents and reach of what is to count as the 'public' realm of medical practice. Their concern will then be with what kinds of conduct within that realm should be defined as professional wrongs; they will have no interest in types of conduct that fall outside that realm, types of conduct that are not in this sense 'public'—public, that is, in the context of the practice of medicine.

Analogously, I will argue, criminal law can be seen (with qualifications) as a code of civic ethics, dealing with what is to count as civically right or wrong conduct within the distinctive practice of civic life—the enterprise of living together as a political community: it defines as criminal, and provides a formal public response to, conduct that violates the norms of that civic enterprise. The defendant in a criminal court is, paradigmatically, called to answer as a citizen (as a member of that civic practice) to her fellow citizens, for her alleged commission of a civic wrong. The criminal law deals with conduct that is 'public' in that it falls within or bears directly on the civic enterprise (the polity's public realm), and so properly concerns the polity's members: it has no interest in conduct that falls outside that realm. That is why I said at the end of section 6 that if we are to determine what should count as a public wrong, we must

[122] As a matter of 'positive' medical ethics, she is answerable for anything that the code defines as professional misconduct; 'critically', she should be answerable only for what should be defined as professional misconduct.

[123] Another useful comparison, although I cannot pursue it here, would be between criminal law, codes of ethics for professions, and military law as enforced through a system of courts martial: see e.g. Army Act 2006.

[124] This raises issues that I cannot pursue here about who should count as members of the practice, and particularly about the status and role of patients, since medical personnel should surely be answerable not just to each other, but to their (actual and potential) patients: see the GMC's provisions for lay membership of tribunals (http://www.gmc-uk.org/concerns/hearings_and_decisions/medical_practitioners_tribunals.asp).

begin not with wrongs, but with the public: we must first develop a conception of the scope and structure of the public realm of the polity (and of who belongs to it); only then can we see what role the criminal law can play, as a way of dealing with wrongs committed within that realm. To develop such a conception of the public realm, however, we must articulate a conception of the polity whose public realm it is: just as those drafting a code of medical ethics must first have a conception of what medicine is as a distinctive practice, so those who are to draft a polity's laws, including its criminal laws, must first have an idea of what the polity is, as a distinctive kind of practice—of its proper goals and goods, of what it is to live together as a political community.

As for the relationship between codes of professional ethics and the criminal law, there is at least some extensional overlap between them: some kinds of professional misconduct also fit the law's definitions of criminal offences. If a doctor steals from a patient, that might not constitute professional misconduct in itself; perhaps it was a matter of chance that the person from whom he stole turned out to be his patient.[125] But if he takes advantage of their professional relationship to steal from her, that constitutes both professional misconduct and a crime: he is liable to face both a criminal charge of theft in a criminal court, and an accusation of professional misconduct before a Medical Practitioners Tribunal. This might seem to create a problem of double jeopardy: is he now being subjected to two 'prosecutions', two punishments, for the same wrong? Double jeopardy would certainly be an issue if the criminal court and the medical tribunal were engaged in the same enterprise—for instance in the enterprise of punishing moral wrongdoing: he would then be facing two punishments for the same instance of wrongdoing. But these tribunals are not engaged in the same enterprise, or concerned with the same wrong. The medical tribunal is concerned with the doctor's professional conduct as a doctor: with the way in which his conduct towards his patient violated his professional responsibilities, the duty that he owed to the patient as his patient, thus casting doubt on his 'fitness to practise' as a doctor. The criminal court, by contrast, is concerned with his conduct as a member of the polity, with his violation of his civic responsibilities as a citizen. Although it is under one description (for instance, 'stealing £1,000 from Ms Howarth') the same conduct that brings him before the criminal court and the Medical Practitioners Tribunal, that conduct constitutes two distinct wrongs, each of which concerns a different 'public' to whom he is answerable.

(It might be suggested that a further crucial difference between the two processes is that only one is concerned with punishment; if what really matters about double jeopardy is that it exposes the accused person to being punished twice for the same offence, we therefore need not worry about it in this context. For while a criminal court's concern in sentencing an offender is backward-looking, to determine an appropriate punishment for his past wrongdoing, a medical tribunal's concern in determining sanctions is forward-looking: it must ask whether, or under what kinds of condition, the doctor can be trusted to behave properly towards his patients and colleagues in the future.[126] It is not clear, however, how far a medical tribunal's concern should be purely forward-looking, or how far it is or should also be concerned to decide what kind of sanction would constitute an appropriate response to the doctor's misconduct; and it can be argued that sentencers in criminal courts should be concerned not merely (if at

[125] I leave aside here the question of whether a criminal conviction for theft should by itself be enough to put in doubt his 'fitness to practise' as a doctor: see n. 111 above.

[126] See General Medical Council, *Professional Conduct and Discipline*, paras 23–30, and at n. 107 above.

all) to find a retributively appropriate sentence, but (also) to find a sentence that will help reduce the chances of future offending by the defendant. I cannot pursue these issues further here.)

I have been talking as if crimes and professional misconduct are entirely separate: the wrong for which the person is held liable is different in each case, as must also therefore be the focus of each tribunal before which the doctor appears. But that is an over-simplification, for at least two reasons. First, although the theft of which the doctor is liable to be convicted is defined in terms that make no reference to the doctor–patient relationship (unlike the professional misconduct for which he faces the medical tribunal), when the judge comes to decide his sentence, in the light of a judgment about the character and seriousness of the theft, the fact that he took advantage of his patient's trust might well figure as an aggravating factor. Second, the law defines some crimes in terms that explicitly involve professional misconduct. To give just two recent examples, s. 20(1) of the Criminal Justice and Courts Act 2015 makes it an offence for a 'care worker' to 'ill-treat or wilfully to neglect' someone in their care,[127] and s. 26 makes it an offence for a police officer to exercise 'the powers and privileges of a constable improperly'.[128] These are both clearly cases of professional misconduct; but rather than simply leaving it to the relevant professional body to deal with them as disciplinary matters, the criminal law takes them up as criminal offences.[129]

The rationale for such measures is obvious enough. Such professions as medicine, policing, banking, and other financial services (not to mention the law), are not self-contained enterprises that directly affect only their professional members: they deal with 'the public', with lay citizens who rely on them for their professional services; and given the powers and competences of the professionals, and the contexts in which they exercise those powers and competences, they can clearly have significant impacts on the interests and well-being of those who rely on them. That is why the professions' self-regulation may be legally regulated,[130] and why the criminal law can sometimes properly take an interest in professional misconduct. What is also worth noting in this context is the kind of understanding (explicit or tacit) that might obtain between the criminal law and a profession about the appropriate division of labour in dealing with wrongs that could be treated as either professional or criminal (or both).[131] Here is one example.

Abortion is a crime in England, unless two medical practitioners make a good faith judgment that one of various specified conditions (concerning the risk that a continued pregnancy would pose to the health of the woman or her family) is satisfied.[132] Those conditions do not include the parents' preferences as to the foetus' gender: that

[127] A 'care worker' is defined (s. 20(3)) as someone who is paid to provide health or social care.

[128] Such powers and privileges are exercised 'improperly' if they are exercised 'for the purpose of achieving a benefit' for the officer, or 'a benefit or a detriment' for someone else, and 'a reasonable person would not expect the power or privilege to be exercised for the purpose of achieving that benefit or detriment'. Other examples can be found e.g. in laws regulating financial services.

[129] Other connections between criminal law and professional codes or norms include, first, the way in which the criminal law can be used to back a profession's authority by making it an offence to practise the profession without a licence, or to claim falsely to have a licence (see e.g. Solicitors Act 1974, ss 20–1; Medical Act 1983, s. 49); and second, the way in which professional standards of care and competence may be relevant in determining whether a defendant's conduct was 'grossly negligent' (see *Adomako* [1995] 1 AC 171).

[130] See at n. 105 above.

[131] This connects to the earlier discussion of criminalization (above, Chapter 1, section 7): the fact that a type of conduct fits the formal, statutory definition of a criminal offence does not determine that it will or should be treated *as* a crime.

[132] See Abortion Act 1967, s. 1.

they would prefer a child of one gender cannot count in law as a good reason to abort a foetus of a different gender.[133] A newspaper claimed to have proof that two doctors were offering sex-selective abortions. After a police investigation, the Crown Prosecution Service (CPS) decided not to prosecute them: there was 'sufficient evidence to provide a realistic prospect of conviction', but it would not be in 'the public interest' to proceed with the case.[134] According to the Director of Public Prosecutions (DPP), explaining this decision:

> one highly relevant factor ... is that the responsible professional body, in this case the General Medical Council, is already involved and has the power to remove doctors from the medical register. Taking into account the need for professional judgement which deals firmly with wrongdoing, while not deterring other doctors from carrying out legitimate and medically justified abortions, we have concluded that these specific cases would be better dealt with by the GMC rather than by prosecution.[135]

It is true that '[t]he evidence in this case was finely balanced':[136] there was room for doubt about whether a court would convict, and the CPS officials might have thought that, given different standards of proof applied by the different bodies,[137] there was more chance of a 'conviction' before a Medical Practitioners Tribunal, which also has the authority to impose severe sanctions (removal from the medical register). But the reference to 'the need for professional judgement' suggests a further consideration: although the question is whether these doctors were guilty of wrongdoing, the wrongdoing would have consisted in the improper exercise of their professional judgement, which is a matter better judged by fellow professionals.

There are in principle two ways of reading this kind of decision. On one reading, it marks a judgment that although these doctors' alleged actions fitted the law's definition of a crime, they are better understood as instances of potential professional *rather than* criminal conduct, and so as 'internal' matters for the profession rather than (in the law's eyes) public matters of concern to the polity as a whole. On the other reading, this division of labour is more a matter of delegation than of separation: sex-selective abortion is still a matter of proper public concern, as a public wrong; but it is sometimes more efficiently dealt with by the relevant professional body, which can now be seen to be acting on behalf of the polity, and in effect at the request of the criminal law. The latter reading seems more plausible in this case: the DPP was delegating the matter to the GMC, rather than recognizing that it was an internal matter of professional ethics; and there is clearly room for argument about whether and when such delegation is justified. But we might sometimes think it proper for a profession to decide to treat as an internal matter something that formally fits the definition of a crime; in such cases, the former reading might be more plausible.

Suppose that a university professor applies for a promotion or a prize that would bring her a financial advantage—a salary increase, a monetary award; but she does so on the basis of work that was plagiarized. This arguably constitutes an offence of

[133] Unless, perhaps, the child's gender would seriously affect the mother's health: see British Medical Association, *The Law and Ethics of Abortion*, para. 2.1.5.

[134] See Crown Prosecution Service, *Code for Crown Prosecutors*, para. 4.1–12; above, Chapter 1 at n. 165.

[135] See http://www.cps.gov.uk/news/latest_news/cps_statement_abortion_related_case/.

[136] Ibid.

[137] On the GMC's standard of proof see General Medical Council, *To Consider: Introduction of the Civil Standard of Proof*; on its implications for double jeopardy, see Doctors Defence Service—UK, 'Double Jeopardy? GMC "Prosecutes" Doctors Acquitted of Crimes'. I cannot pursue here the question of whether professional bodies are right to operate with a lower standard of proof.

attempted fraud under English law: she 'dishonestly makes a false representation' (that the work was her own work), and 'intends, by making the representation ... to make a gain'.[138] However, it might well be dealt with by the university's internal disciplinary process, leading to dismissal or some less drastic professional sanction, rather than being referred to the police as a criminal offence. This seems appropriate, since what is most salient about this wrongdoing is not the prospective financial gain, but the plagiarism as a serious breach of academic values—the values by which the university defines itself as an academic institution. More generally, then, in deciding whether a particular kind of wrong that fits the definition both of a crime and of professional misconduct in the wrongdoer's own profession should be treated as a crime, or as professional misconduct, we must ask whether its criminal or its professional character is the more salient.

There are thus some interesting questions to be asked about the relationship between codes of professional ethics and the criminal law; but they are not my main concern here. My aim has been to discuss codes of professional ethics as providing an illuminating analogy to criminal law. It is to that analogy that we must now turn.

9. Criminal Law and Practice-Relative Reasons

Those who draw up a code of medical practice will be, in a sense, medical moralists: that is, whilst their code might deal with various non-ethical matters, such as competence to practise,[139] it will also deal with moral wrongdoing—with ethical misconduct or moral wrongdoing within the practice of medicine.[140] The same is true of other professional codes: that is why they can be described as codes of professional ethics. Those drawing up a medical code will not, however, be medical moralists in the way that Moore is a legal moralist: for whereas on Moore's view every kind of moral wrongdoing is, in principle, the criminal law's business, wherever and by whomever it is committed,[141] the drafters of a code of medical ethics will not think that every kind of moral wrongdoing is even in principle their business. First, they will be concerned only with wrongs committed within the realm of medical practice—within the practice's *res publica*; and although, as we have seen, there is room for argument about the boundaries of that realm,[142] it clearly does not include every kind of moral misconduct, since it does not include every kind of conduct. Second, they will be concerned only with wrongs committed by those involved in that practice, not with wrongs committed by non-members.[143] The drafters might each believe, in reflective moments, that the world would be 'morally better', and thus 'better', if all wrongdoers underwent the retributive suffering that they deserved; but they would not then ask

[138] Fraud Act 2006, s. 2(1). It is true that she probably makes no explicit representation, in her application, that the work is her own; any such explicit representation would have been made (if at all) when she submitted the work for publication: but a 'representation may be express or implied' (s. 2(4)); and she surely implies that the work is her own by listing it in her CV.

[139] See at nn 101–4 above.

[140] We need not concern ourselves here with questions about the relationship between the ethical and the moral, or between 'ethics' and 'morality' (see B Williams, *Ethics and the Limits of Philosophy*, especially chs 1, 10). The sphere of the ethical might be wider than that of the moral, and is certainly wider than that of moral obligation or duty; but a code of ethics will include moral requirements.

[141] See at nn 78–86 above.

[142] See above, at nn 111–17.

[143] Indeed, if they are drawing up a code for a national body, such as the GMC, their remit will not extend, even in principle, to everyone involved in the practice of medicine anywhere in the world. But compare World Medical Association, *International Code of Medical Ethics*.

whether they could 'achieve that moral betterment through' the code they are drafting, or whether they have reason to define every kind of moral wrongdoing as 'professional misconduct'.[144] They *might*, if they take a retributivist view, think that part of their task is to ensure that *medical* wrongdoing, wrongdoing within the practice of medicine, is suitably punished—though it is not clear whether retribution, as thus understood, is a plausible aim for a code of medical ethics; but they could not plausibly think that they have an interest, as drafters of this code, in wrongdoing that falls outside the realm of medical practice; such conduct is 'in brief and crude terms, not [their] business'.[145] They will have some idea of how the practice of medicine makes 'the world ... better', since they will have a conception of the distinctive goods at which the practice of medicine aims:[146] but their concern is limited, *ab initio*, to (mis)conduct that falls within that practice.

To say that the drafters of a code of medical ethics are 'medical moralists' is thus to say that they are concerned with moral wrongdoing that falls within the sphere of medical practice; it is not to say that they are or should be concerned to bring all moral wrongdoing into the sphere of medicine, or into the scope of their code. Moore's legal moralism, however, is of that latter kind: for he wants to bring all moral wrongdoing (in principle) into the sphere of the law, and thus (in principle) within the scope of the criminal law. The more modest legal moralism that I espouse, by contrast, is of the former kind: it holds that the criminal law is properly concerned with, and only with, moral wrongdoing that already falls within the public realm to which the criminal law belongs and which it helps to regulate. That is why in explaining the idea of public wrongs, we must begin not with wrongs, but with the public.[147] Those drafting a code of professional ethics must first have an idea of what the profession is—of its proper aims, its proper sphere of activity, what kinds of conduct belong to it; similarly, those drafting a polity's criminal code first need some idea of what the polity is—of its *res publica*.

Suppose we are members of a committee whose task is to draft, not a code of professional ethics, or a set of constitutional arrangements for a club or an academic institution, but a set of laws for a polity: we are to assist, as Founding Parents, in the constitution of a new polity, or in the reconstitution of an existing polity. We will probably (perhaps inevitably) come to think that the polity's governing institutions should include a system of criminal law, a practice that defines a set of public wrongs and provides an appropriate formal response to them: but even that much cannot be assumed in advance; argument will be needed (and will be provided in the following chapters) to show why our institutions should, or must, include a practice of this kind. However, just as the drafting of the code of professional ethics could not be the first item of business for those working out a profession's governing structures and practices,[148] the drafting of a criminal code could not be the first item of business for the Founding Parents: to come to see both that a criminal code is needed, and what its scope should be, they first need a conception of the polity whose code it will be. That conception will be a conception of a particular kind of practice—of its proper aims, its

[144] See Moore, 'Four Reflections on Law and Morality', 1540: 'the world is better if it is morally better, and to the extent legislators can achieve that moral betterment through law, they should do so'; see at n. 85 above.

[145] Wolfenden, *Report of the Committee on Homosexual Offences and Prostitution*, para. 61; see at n. 7 above.

[146] Compare Aristotle, *Nicomachean Ethics*, I.1; also A MacIntyre, *After Virtue: A Study in Moral Theory*, ch. 14, on 'practices'.

[147] See the end of section 6 above.

[148] See text preceding n. 106 above.

defining values, its scope, and its membership: it will, that is, be or reflect a political theory. Only on the basis of such a theory will they be able to see why a polity needs a practice of criminal law (why such a practice is necessary if it is to achieve its distinctive ends in ways that are consistent with its defining values), and what form that practice should take (how it can help to achieve those ends in ways that are consistent with those values).

I also suggested above that when the drafters of a profession's governing institutions come to discuss the content and scope of their code of ethics, they will not, and could not plausibly, begin with the whole realm of moral wrongdoing and of moral wrongdoers as their potential canvas.[149] Now the same is not straightforwardly true of the Founding Parents: they could, when they come to draft the criminal code, begin in a Moorean spirit by seeing every kind of moral wrong, wherever and by whomever it is committed, as a candidate for criminalization. Once we see how they could begin in this way, however, we will also see how implausible it is that they should do so—and how inconsistent with the liberal values that Moore espouses. They could take this view of the potential scope of their criminal law only if they thought that one of the polity's goals should be the attainment of retributive justice, by securing the punishment of 'all and only those who are morally culpable in the doing of some morally wrongful action':[150] but why should they take that view of the polity's goals?

Perhaps they believe that the world is 'morally better' if culpable wrongdoers are punished as they deserve; that the world is 'better' if that 'moral betterment' is achieved; that a polity has the power to assist the achievement of that betterment by creating a system of criminal law that criminalizes moral wrongdoing; and that they therefore have reason to create (or even 'should' create) such a system.[151] Now that form of thought, which moves directly from recognizing some good, and realizing that I could so act as to make its actualization more likely, to the conclusion that I have reason so to act, is familiar—at least amongst philosophers. Dempsey, for instance, asserts the 'normal correspondence thesis'—that 'if a person can realize a value through her action, then normally she will have a reason so to act as to realize that value'.[152] In similar vein, Gardner espouses an 'agent-neutralist' view of reasons for action according to which all reasons are 'impersonal in respect of attention': if a value (for instance, for Mooreans, that of retributive justice) is a source of reasons for action (actions that would help towards its realization), such reasons give every rational agent reason to act, if she can, so as to assist in realizing that value.[153] Just what a particular agent thus has reason to do depends on how (if at all) she can assist the value's realization, as well as on other reasons that apply to her; who, if anyone, should have what duties or responsibilities in relation to the actualization of that value will also depend on considerations about 'the efficient use of rational energy'—on who is best placed efficiently to actualize the value.[154] But in principle, it seems, any rational agent has reason to act to realize a value: for instance, we 'all have one and the same reason (the fact that the wrong is

[149] See text following n. 107 above. [150] Moore, *Placing Blame*, 35.

[151] See Moore, 'Four Reflections on Law and Morality', 1540; see at nn 85, 143–4 above.

[152] M M Dempsey, *Prosecuting Domestic Violence: A Philosophical Analysis*, 83. Dempsey is talking about how prosecutors should understand their role, and the reasons for action that apply to them. She argues later that, as a conceptual matter, there might be some values that a prosecutor, given her specific bureaucratic role, *cannot* realize (87–91): but the only value that seems to be thus ruled out is retribution. See further at nn 157–8 below.

[153] J Gardner, 'Complicity and Causality', 62–3; see also Gardner, 'Relations of Responsibility', 89–91.

[154] Gardner, 'Reply to Critics', 277–8.

a wrong) to avoid the commission of any wrong by anyone'.[155] It is true, Gardner argues, that considerations concerning 'the efficient use of rational energy' can generate 'agent-neutral reasons for people to reason and react agent-relatively over a range of cases':[156] for instance, although we 'all have one and the same reason ... to avoid the commission of any wrong by anyone', I will normally make more efficient use of my rational energies if I focus my practical attention on wrongs that might be committed by me or by those close to me, *as if* only they give me reasons to act—as if only they are my business. But the ultimate, non-derivative reasons for action that should ground my practical deliberations and my actions are impersonal and agent-neutral. What should matter to me, ultimately, is not that I refrain from committing wrongs myself, or that I do not assist (or that I hinder) the commission of wrongs by those to whom I am personally connected (*my* friends, or members of *my* family or of *my* department, or citizens of *my* country) but that fewer wrongs are committed in the world: I should focus on these narrower categories of wrongdoing or wrongdoer only if and because that is how I can contribute most efficiently to that ultimate goal.

In similar vein, Dempsey argues that we must distinguish 'a full philosophical account of the reasons that actually do bear on the justifiability of [the] conduct' of legislators in deciding what to criminalize, from an account of 'the range of considerations [they should] take into account' in their deliberations: 'it is possible', she therefore argues, that '(1) it is true we have good reason to criminalize any and all wrongdoing *and* (2) legislators should not bear that truth in mind when acting qua legislators'.[157] The distinction between a 'full philosophical account' and an account of how legislators or other criminal justice officials should reason is related to another distinction she draws, between 'having a *reason* to ϕ and ϕ-ing being one's *business*'. It might be true, on a philosophical account, that legislators have reason to criminalize 'any and all wrongdoing', since doing so could, for instance, serve the value of retributive justice. But when we come to specify the legislature's institutional role, we will see good reason not to make 'any and all wrongdoing' their business: for a range of factors, including 'epistemic and efficiency considerations', militate against allowing legislators to think in such expansive terms about all kinds of wrongdoing as candidates for criminalization.[158]

If we accept this view of reasons for action, the two ways in which Moore's version of legal moralism appears over-expansive are less troubling.[159] For while a Moorean national legislature would, in principle, have reason to criminalize the commission of any moral wrong, by anyone, anywhere in the world, it would quickly recognize that the most efficient way for it to serve the goal of retributive justice would be to focus its criminalizing efforts on wrongs committed within the national boundaries of the polity whose legislature it is—within the territory over which that polity exercises effective authority. It would also soon recognize that its deliberations about what to criminalize within those boundaries should be limited by principles that reflect the constraints set by such values as liberty and privacy.

Indeed, Moorean Founding Parents, in deciding on the proper powers and responsibilities of the legislature, might see good reason to set limits on the kinds of wrongdoing

155 'Reply to Critics', 277. See also 'Relations of Responsibility', 89: 'all reasons are ultimately the same reasons for everyone'. See also, more generally, J Gardner and T Macklem, 'Reasons'.

156 'Complicity and Causality', 65.

157 M M Dempsey, 'Public Wrongs and the "Criminal Law's Business": When Victims Won't Share', 256.

158 'Public Wrongs and the "Criminal Law's Business"', 257.

159 See at nn 80–6 above.

that the legislature should view as being even in principle its business. The Founding Parents might themselves start from 'a full philosophical account of the reasons that actually do bear on the justifiability' of the legislature's decisions about criminalization.[160] If they are Mooreans they will therefore see good reason for the polity to assist in the enterprise of ensuring that culpable wrongdoers are punished: for we 'all have one and the same reason', grounded in the universal, impersonal, agent-neutral value of retributive justice, to ensure that they are punished;[161] and a polity is, given its powers, well placed to assist that end. They will therefore see good reason to create a system of criminal law, whose function will be to inflict retribution on culpable wrongdoers; they will see reason to criminalize all types of wrongdoing and wrongdoer (since all deserve punishment); and they will therefore see reason so to define the role and responsibilities of legislators that they will see all kinds of wrongdoing as candidates for criminalization. However, as they think about the other values relevant to the legislature's activity, and about 'epistemic and efficiency considerations', they will realize both that there will be *good enough* reason to criminalize only some kinds of wrongdoing, and that the legislature will be more likely to make rationally justified decisions if they see only certain kinds of wrong as even in principle candidates for criminalization. The legislature should therefore be required to deliberate *as if* it could have no legitimate authority over wrongs committed beyond the polity's borders,[162] and should be bound by constitutional constraints that cabin the criminal law within the boundaries set by such values as liberty and privacy.[163] Thus if we attend to the ultimate, basic reasons that should determine a legislature's criminalization decisions, a Moorean legal moralism might look over-expansive: but, a Moorean might reply, that is because we imagine the legislature actually deliberating in such an expansive way; whereas in fact, if the Founding Parents have done their job well, the legislature will take a much more modest, much less expansive, view of the potential scope of the criminal law.

The upshot of this line of argument, if it is sound, is that my worries about the apparently over-expansive character of a Moorean legal moralism were misplaced, for two reasons. First, if the attainment of retributive justice is a good, then it surely is a source of reasons for anyone who can contribute to its attainment: for how can I think that something is a good, yet deny that I have any reason to act so as to protect it or bring it about? Second, however, once we distinguish the two levels or contexts of practical reasoning that Gardner and Dempsey distinguish, we will see that this does not require legislatures, or others actually involved in criminalization decisions, to consider as a practical option the criminalization of all kinds of moral wrongdoing anywhere in the world: for they will sensibly operate with a more limited view of what is their business. What made Moorean legal moralism seem over-expansive was the thought of a legislature or criminal policy-maker seriously considering the criminalization of such (obviously 'private') wrongs as betraying a marital partner or a friend, or of robberies

[160] Dempsey, 'Public Wrongs and the "Criminal Law's Business"', 256; see at n. 156 above.

[161] Gardner, 'Reply to Critics', 277; see at n. 154 above.

[162] Although it might sometimes need to decide whether to claim universal jurisdiction over certain types of extra-territorial wrong (see at n. 86 above). I leave aside here the possibility that the Founding Parents might define jurisdiction (partly) in terms of citizenship rather than only of territory, so that wrongs committed by or against the polity's citizens anywhere in the world come within the reach of its criminal law: see M Hirst, *Jurisdiction and the Ambit of the Criminal Law*, 49–52; and below, Chapter 3 at nn 14, 77–8.

[163] See e.g. *Roe v Wade* 410 US 113 (1973), on privacy in relation to abortion; see further below, Chapter 4 at nn 85–92.

committed in distant countries: but on this more sophisticated account, legislatures and policy-makers would not consider these as options.

Some deep questions arise here about the nature of practical reason, and our place as agents in the various normative worlds in which we find ourselves.[164] For Gardner and Dempsey, all values speak to every agent as an agent: to recognize something as a (dis)value is to recognize it as a reason for action, and as a good reason if I am well-placed to act in a way that might realize that value or avert that disvalue. In that sense any value is everyone's business. Now I agree that values speak to us all, in that they invite appropriate responses from us all, but that is not to say that they all speak to us all *as agents*: sometimes the appropriate response to a value is a respect or recognition with no practical implications (other than that I should not interfere with it)—not because I am not well-placed to help realize it, but because it is not connected to me as an agent. The site of my agency (as of anyone's agency) is not the whole world; my agency is grounded in the more limited, particular forms of life in which I function, and in which I find my reasons for action. Those reasons are, indeed, sometimes agent-neutral: the desperate suffering of any human being gives any other human being reason to act, in virtue simply of their fellow humanity. But, 'agent-relativists' will insist, that is not true of all reasons—not even of all moral reasons.[165] That Jane promised Joe to meet him for a drink certainly gives her reason to act—to meet him; it gives some others (Joe, their friends) reason to act—to encourage her to keep her promise, perhaps to help her overcome any difficulties: but even if I, a stranger, know about the promise and could make it more likely that Jane keeps it, I might quite rightly think that it is none of my business; by which I would mean not, as Dempsey suggests, that although I have reason to intervene it is not my business to do so,[166] but that I have no reason, because I have no standing, to intervene.

However, we need not pursue the debate about agent-neutral and agent-relative reasons here, because there are two more particular reasons to be suspicious of this sophisticated version of an expansive, Moorean legal moralism. First, we must ask why the Founding Parents would take the attainment of retributive justice as one of the polity's proper aims.[167] Second, it is still true on this account that legislators have good reason to criminalize every type of moral wrongdoing, wherever and by whomever it is committed—even if the reasons not to criminalize many types of wrongdoing, or to set geographical limits on the reach of the polity's criminal law, are such that legislators should not normally even think in such terms: but that should still strike us as an implausible view of the reasons that legislators have.

As to the Founding Parents, if they started by trying to think about all the goods in the world, with a view to deciding which of them the polity could efficiently help to actualize, it is not clear how they could work towards such a decision; nor is it clear why they should include retributive justice in the list of goods to be pursued, so as to justify the creation of a system of criminal law through which to pursue it. They

[164] For a useful survey and discussion of these questions see M Ridge, 'Reasons for Action: Agent-Neutral vs. Agent-Relative'.

[165] And it seems clearly false of other kinds of reason. I might think, truly, that *A*'s taste in literature is atrocious, and that he should read other authors; or that the interior design of his home is an aesthetic abomination, and that the world would be better were it radically changed. I can make such judgements, and be appalled by what I see; if *A* asks my advice, or I have standing in the matter (as his friend, partner, or decorator), I have reason to encourage him to change his ways. But if I lack such standing, I have no reason to intervene.

[166] Dempsey, 'Public Wrongs and the "Criminal Law's Business"', 257; see at nn 157–8 above.

[167] We are still assuming, for the sake of argument, that retributive justice is a genuine good.

should of course recognize justice, retributive and distributive, as a constraint on their planning: they should not design a polity that would perpetrate *injustice.* But why should they make the attainment of retributive justice a positive aim—especially given how expensive its pursuit will be? If they found themselves with a system of criminal law, and if they accepted a Moorean account of criminal law as a functional kind,[168] they would have to take retributive justice as an aim: but if they are to act as proper Founding Parents, they cannot take the existence of criminal law for granted; they must justify its creation and maintenance. I do not claim that no such justification is possible—I will indeed offer one later. Nor do I (yet) claim that justification could not be in terms of Moorean retributivism—though the justification I will offer will be very different, and I hope I have said enough to render a Moorean account less plausible. My claim is so far only that we will need a justification, in terms of the polity's appropriate aims. That justification will need to be grounded in a political theory of the polity, which must include an account of the distinctive goods that the polity should pursue and protect (just as a theory of medical practice must include an account of its distinctive goods); only then will we able to see whether and why those distinctive goods should include that of Moorean retributive justice.

As to the reasons that legislators have to criminalize, we should again look separately at the geographical scope of the criminal law, and at the kinds of conduct that we could have reason to criminalize. We can bring out the significance of the question of geographical scope by looking briefly at extradition. If I commit a theft in Chile while visiting there from Scotland, and return home, the Chilean authorities might seek my extradition; if the conditions that our extradition statute specifies are met, I am liable to be arrested by the Scottish police and extradited by order of a Scottish court.[169] I am not, however, liable to be tried for the theft in a Scottish court, or to be convicted and sentenced under Scots criminal law: for what I did in Chile is not a crime under Scots law, even if (leaving location aside) it fits Scots law's definition of an offence. This is true even if it would be feasible for a Scottish court to decide the case—for instance, if the victim and necessary witnesses happened now to be in Scotland: the Scottish court has the authority to order my extradition, but not to try me. Now on a Moorean account, or any account that takes the aim of criminal law to consist in serving impersonal values that generate agent-neutral reasons for action, such jurisdictional arrangements as these simply reflect decisions about efficiency (and respect for state sovereignty). A Scottish court could in principle do retributive justice in cases like mine, and in rare cases it might be able to do so more efficiently than could a Chilean court: but our rules of criminal law and criminal procedure reflect the fact that it is almost always more efficient for crimes to be dealt with in and by the polity in which they are committed. Extradition from Scotland to Chile and trial in Scotland would both be attempts to serve the same end—for a Moorean, retributive justice; but the former will almost always be the more efficient way to serve that end. On the opposing view for which I will argue, the end cannot be specified in such agent-neutral terms: it is that the wrongdoer be called to account by those whose distinctive business his wrong is—by, that is, the Chilean polity. *That* is not an end that Scottish criminal courts can hope to achieve; the best they can do is assist the Chilean courts to achieve it, by extraditing me.

[168] Moore, *Placing Blame*, 33; see at n. 20 above.

[169] See UN Model Treaty on Extradition (http://www.un.org/documents/ga/res/45/a45r116.htm); Extradition Act 2003.

Gardner might reply that in recognizing that the Scottish court has reason thus to assist the Chilean court, and that there is therefore reason for Scots law to enable this, I am conceding his point. Even if it is true that only the Chilean court has reason to prosecute, convict, and punish me (just as, analogously, only I have reason to keep a promise I made, since no one else can keep it), this shows only that that reason is 'personal in respect of conformity'. But in allowing that the Scottish criminal justice system (and, by implication, that of any polity) has reason to assist the Chilean courts in this way, I am implicitly agreeing that that reason is 'impersonal in respect of attention', in the sense that it generates reasons for everyone to act, if they can, in ways that will assist the attainment of that end; and his claim that all reasons are ultimately agent-neutral is the claim that they are agent-neutral or impersonal at least 'in respect of attention'.[170] This is not a battle that I need to fight here—although I would say that what (ultimately) guides the Scottish court, or guides the legislature in enacting an Extradition Act, is not so much a recognition of some impersonal good, as a relational recognition of the character and demands of cooperation within what aspires to be a community of nations. All I am pointing out here is that we can give an account of the proper aims of criminal law that portrays the good to be achieved as essentially relational; in which case a polity can have *no* reason to define as criminal, and to bring within the scope of its criminal law, wrongs committed anywhere in the world (although it can have reason to assist other polities in bringing to justice those who violate their criminal laws).[171] Beccaria's comment is still apt here:

> There are also who think, that an act of cruelty committed, for example, at Constantinople may be punished at Paris; for this abstracted reason, that he who offends humanity, should have enemies in all mankind, and be the object of universal execration; as if judges were to be the knights-errant of human nature in general, rather than guardians of particular conventions between men.[172]

One might quarrel with 'conventions', and we will need to discuss the suggestion that those who commit certain egregious wrongs (such as those properly classed as 'crimes against humanity') do indeed 'offend[] humanity' and must answer to 'humanity';[173] but the spirit of the comment is sound: it is not the job of domestic criminal law to pursue wrongdoers throughout the world.

This point is connected to the conception of the criminal trial that I sketched earlier.[174] If the criminal trial is a process through which accused persons are called to answer, we must ask to whom they are answerable, and by whom they are called to answer. For answering is essentially relational: I cannot just answer, nor can I just answer for Φ; I answer for Φ to someone who has the standing to call me to answer. As we will see, a criminal defendant is paradigmatically called to answer by and to her fellow citizens: the good at which the criminal process aims is not an impersonal or non-relational good, such as the identification of criminal wrongdoers, or that

[170] Gardner, 'Complicity and Causality', 62–3; see at nn 153–6 above.

[171] I will then need to say something about crimes over which Scots law might claim 'universal jurisdiction' (see at n. 86 above), and crimes that fall within the scope of an '*aut dedere aut judicare*' convention requiring the state in which the alleged perpetrator is found to either extradite him or prosecute him (see e.g. *Hague Convention for the Suppression of Unlawful Seizure of Aircraft*, Art. 7; also M C Bassiouni and E M Wise, *Aut Dedere Aut Judicare: The Duty to Extradite or Prosecute in International Law*): see below, Chapter 3, sections 1 and 2.

[172] C Beccaria, *An Essay on Crimes and Punishments*, 134.

[173] See Rome Statute of the International Criminal Court, Preamble and Art. 7; and below, Chapter 3 at nn 47–62.

[174] See above, Chapter 1, section 5; and at nn 120–2 above, on responsibility.

wrongdoers are held to account; it is that they are called and held to account *by the appropriate body*—by their own polity. Something similar is true, I will argue, of punishment: punishment is analogously relational, in that its meaning and justification involve not merely the imposition of an appropriate penal burden on an offender for an offence, but the imposition of such a burden by an authorized person or body. I am not just punished, or just punished for an offence: I am punished by *A*, and we cannot understand, or justify, my punishment as a punishment without understanding that relationship between the punisher and the punished.[175]

As for the kinds of conduct that we have reason to criminalize, Moorean Founding Parents will begin by regarding every type of moral wrongdoing as in principle apt for criminalization (something they have good reason to criminalize), even if they then see stronger reasons not only not to criminalize some kinds of wrongdoing, but also to constrain the scope of the legislature's deliberations about criminalization—for instance through constitutional constraints protecting liberty and privacy. But why should they, on what basis could they, start from that position?

One way to do so would be to begin from a totalitarian, rather than a liberal, conception of the polity and its *res publica*: a conception according to which the polity has a proper interest in every aspect of its citizens' lives. The Founding Parents might then see reason to withdraw from some areas of citizens' lives, for the sake of such values as privacy and liberty: but this requires a deliberative balancing of considerations for and against interference; how should they weigh the importance of attaining retributive justice, for instance, against the value of privacy or of liberty? But, a liberal critic will object, to engage in such weighing is already to go too far. If I am told that my betrayal of a friend gives the polity reason to punish me, and thus gives its legislature reason to criminalize such wrongs; but that (luckily for me) the countervailing reasons against criminalization are so powerful that a legislature should not even be allowed to consider it as an option: I might reply that no such weighing is appropriate, since such relations between friends are not the polity's business. Analogously, I might know that I could make money by selling salacious gossip about my famous friend to the popular press: if I see this as a reason to sell the gossip I have already gone wrong (and betrayed our friendship), even if I then recognize that the reasons against selling the gossip are much stronger than the reasons for doing so. Similarly, in weighing the reasons for and against criminalizing the wrong I do to my friend, the Founding Parents already go wrong by seeing the relationship of which that wrong is part as any of its business—as something to which it has reason to attend, as part of 'a full philosophical account of the reasons that actually do bear on the justifiability' of its decisions.[176] Some wrongs that I could commit against a friend are of course criminalizable: if I defraud, or assault, my friend, I cannot claim that this is not the criminal law's business (though what counts as fraud or assault may be conditioned by the nature of our friendship). But that is because such actions transcend the (private) realm of friendship: they violate the bonds not just of friendship, but of citizenship, or humanity.

Moore would, no doubt, reject such a totalitarian conception of the polity, but he should then qualify his legal moralism: for if legislators have good reason to criminalize every kind of moral wrongdoing, every aspect of the citizens' lives is in principle their business—which is what his critic denies. A liberal polity, as we will see, begins with a conception of a limited public sphere: a sphere that excludes, as not the polity's business, broad spheres of 'private' life and conduct. Wrongs committed within those

[175] See Duff, 'Relational Reasons and the Criminal Law', 204–6.

[176] Dempsey, 'Public Wrongs and the "Criminal Law's Business"', 256; see at n. 157 above.

private spheres are not criminalizable: not because, though there is good reason to criminalize them, there is better reason not to do so; but because those spheres are not the polity's business.[177] Moore's constraints on criminalization therefore appear too late, as constraints on criminal law. If they appear only when we consider what to criminalize, they were presumably not operative earlier, when the Founding Parents were considering the scope and contents of the polity's *res publica*: had they been operative at that earlier stage, they would not be necessary now. But had they been operative earlier, they would not have been constraints on *criminalization*, concerned with which kinds of wrong the polity should take an interest in: they would have been constraints on the realms of conduct, on the aspects of citizens' lives, in which the polity could properly take any interest. If some type of wrong, such as the betrayal of a friend's confidence, falls within a realm of private conduct, what bars its criminalization is not that, although it is wrong, it should be treated as a private wrong, but that it does not fall to be judged as either right or wrong by the polity at all.

(Moore has responded to an earlier version of this criticism by arguing that 'public wrongs do need to be wrongs too, in Duff's mind as well as my own. In which case wrongness as such is a reason for prohibition for Duff as much as for me'.[178] But this does not follow: partly because Moore's first sentence seems to be a statement of negative legal moralism, whereas the second is a statement of positive legal moralism—and therefore a *non sequitur*; partly because I deny that 'wrongness as such' is a reason to criminalize, if 'wrongness as such' means the fact, by itself, that a type of conduct is wrong. Wrongness is, on my account, a reason for criminalization—but only if it is committed within the public realm; that is where Moore and I differ.)

The force and implications of these remarks should become clearer in the following chapters. I have been arguing so far, in the final sections of this chapter, for three main claims.

First, any useful discussion about what should be criminalized, or about the goals, principles, and values that should guide deliberations about criminalization, must be grounded in political theory, in that it must be grounded in an account of the polity and its *res publica*. To say that the criminal law is concerned with 'public wrongs' is to gesture towards this point, since it is to say that the criminal law is concerned with wrongs that belong within the public realm; so we must work out an account of that public realm, of what it includes, before we can think about which kinds of wrong are criminalizable. This should also reinforce the general point that we must not consider the criminal law in isolation: it is a part of the whole apparatus of law, which is itself part of the institutional structure of the polity; to work out what the criminal law's scope should be, we must work out what role it can properly play within that institutional structure—which again requires us to think about the *res publica* of which that is the institutional structure.

Second, an account of the *res publica* of a polity (as of any practice) will also be an account of the kinds of agent-relative (practice-relative) reasons for action that apply to its members, and that will therefore underpin and guide its laws. As a parent, I have a distinctive reason to care for my child: I have that reason in virtue of my role within

[177] Dempsey might now accuse me of ignoring the distinction between 'having a *reason* to ϕ and ϕ-ing being one's *business*' (see at nn 157–8 above). But that distinction is puzzling: to say that I have reason to ϕ must surely be to say that ϕ-ing could, indeed should, figure in my practical reasoning at some point, even if only when I seek 'a full philosophical account' of the reasons that bear on my conduct; which is to say that it is my business.

[178] M S Moore, 'Responses and Appreciations', 354.

a distinctive human practice—the family; I do not have that reason to care for others' children, nor do others have that reason to care for my child.[179] Doctors have distinctive reasons to behave in certain ways towards their patients and their colleagues, and a code of medical practice reflects those reasons: such reasons are practice-relative in the sense that they flow from the goals and values that define the practice of medicine, and apply to doctors in virtue of their membership of, their role within, that practice. Something similar is true, as we will see later, of a polity and its members. Their membership of the polity gives them distinctive reasons to act, and react, in certain ways towards each other—reasons that flow from the goals and values that define their polity as a distinctive practice; reasons that they do not have in relation to those outside the polity, and that others do not have in relation to them. Their laws will be grounded in those reasons, and it is those kinds of reason that should guide the Founding Parents' deliberations.[180]

Third, once we consider the criminal law in its larger institutional and political context, we can see why an expansive, Moorean legal moralism is implausible as a theory that liberals might espouse: for it implies that every kind of moral wrongdoing, and so almost every kind of human conduct (on the plausible assumption that almost every kind of human conduct admits of moral misconduct or wrongdoing), is in principle the law's business; whereas a liberal account of the polity's *res publica* would draw a firm distinction between those areas of conduct that are, and those that are not, 'public'. Now some theorists think that once we reject Moorean moralism, and insist on the 'public' character of criminal law as part of the institutional apparatus of the polity, we must reject legal moralism altogether, in favour of a 'public law' conception.[181] I will argue that we should instead espouse a more modest legal moralism of public wrongs.

Those drafting a code of medical ethics need a conception of the practice of medicine. There are two dimensions to that conception: a conception of the practice's distinctive activities, goals, and values; and a conception of its membership—of who counts as a participant in the practice. Analogously, the Founding Parents of a polity's constitution must begin with a conception of the polity as a distinctive practice. This requires a conception of the distinctive activities, goals, and values of this practice; and a conception of its membership—of who counts as a member of the polity, bound by its laws. In the next chapter I will take up the latter question, of membership.

[179] Which is not to deny that I might have other reasons to assist others' children, and that others might have other reasons to assist mine: but these will not be the same kinds of reason, or reasons to offer the same kind of care.

[180] Is this to say that members of a polity have practice-relative reasons not to behave towards each other in ways that the law defines as criminal (not to assault or steal from each other, for instance): reasons that they do not have in relation to non-members? As we will see (below, Chapter 3, section 3) that does not follow: we have the same reason not to assault or steal from anyone; the practice-relative reasons that we have as members of a polity concern a range of distinctive civic responsibilities, including a responsibility to respond appropriately to certain kinds of wrong (and see above, Chapter 1 at nn 49–52, and below, Chapter 6, section 6).

[181] See below, Chapter 4, section 2.

3

Citizenship and the Criminal Law

I argued in the previous chapter that we can draw a useful analogy between the criminal law and codes of professional ethics: it is time now to start making good on that suggestion.

The central task of those who are to draft a code of professional ethics is to define what is to count as professional misconduct. If they are to do that, they need to work out what is to count as professional conduct—conduct that falls within the profession, conduct engaged in by members of the profession as members: for professional misconduct is misconduct in the course of one's professional conduct. If they are to do that, they need to have some idea of what the profession, the practice whose code this is to be, is: what kinds of activity fall within it, what are its defining goals and values, who are its members? Only then can they understand what the profession is, as a distinctive kind of practice; only then can they start to decide what should count as professional *mis*conduct—conduct that violates those aims and values. Thus the drafters of a code of medical ethics must begin with a conception of the practice of medicine: of the distinctive ends or goods at which this practice aims; of who should count as a member of the practice; of what kinds of conduct count as (professionally) 'medical'. The code will be binding on a limited range of people, and on a limited dimension of their lives: it will be binding on medical practitioners, but not on those who have no part in the practice of medicine; it will be binding on medical practitioners as far as their professional lives are concerned, but not in relation to the non-professional, 'private' (as far as the profession is concerned), aspects of their lives and conduct.

The code will also make provision for dealing with violations. A familiar way to do that is to create a tribunal, such as a Medical Practitioners Tribunal,[1] to hear cases of alleged misconduct: professionals accused of misconduct are thus called to answer to the accusation, and to answer for their misconduct if that accusation is proved; they are called to answer by and to the fellow members of the profession, whose business their alleged misconduct is. When Jones is charged with professional misconduct before a Medical Practitioners Tribunal, she is called to answer as a doctor, to her profession and those engaged in it, for an alleged violation of the code of ethics that governs their collective medical activities—that governs that particular realm of their lives. But she is not answerable before this Tribunal for other aspects of her conduct, however wrong they might be, that are not connected to her medical activities; nor is anyone unconnected to the medical profession answerable before this Tribunal for any misconduct in which they might have engaged.[2]

[1] See above, Chapter 2 at n. 120.

[2] As we saw above (Chapter 2, section 7), there is plenty of room for argument and doubt not just about the proper aims and values of the profession, but about who should be treated as belonging to it (as bound by its code), and about which kinds of conduct should count as 'professional', or as bearing on the person's professional life. As we will see, versions of these kinds of question, as well as questions about who should have the standing to call misconducting members to account, also arise in relation to the criminal law.

To make good on the analogy that I have suggested, I must show that questions analogous to those that face the drafters of a professional code of ethics face those who would draft a criminal code, and begin to offer answers to those questions. I will start with the question of who should be taken to belong to the relevant practice: to whom, that is, is the criminal law addressed; whom does it bind, or claim to bind; and, if we can see the criminal trial as a process of calling alleged wrongdoers to answer,[3] by and to whom are those accused of crimes called to answer?

1. Ambit, Jurisdiction, and Territory

I have argued elsewhere that we are, paradigmatically, criminally responsible as citizens to our fellow citizens. The citizens of a polity are the primary addressees of its criminal law: our criminal law speaks, paradigmatically, to us as citizens of the polity whose law it is (and speaks in our collective voice); it is, paradigmatically, as citizens that we are bound by the criminal law; a defendant in a criminal court appears, paradigmatically, as a citizen who must answer to his fellow citizens.[4] Since this argument will be important in what follows, I should briefly rehearse, but also expand, it here.

We are, it is natural to say, both bound and protected by the criminal law, and answerable in the criminal courts for criminal wrongs that we are accused of committing. However, that way of speaking is elliptical: for it does not explicitly tell us *which* criminal law binds and protects us, or *which* courts have the authority to call us to answer. As I go about my daily business in my home city of Edinburgh, I am bound and protected by the criminal law of Scotland: if I commit a crime I am liable to be arrested by the Scottish police, and brought to trial in a Scottish court; if I am the victim of a crime, I will look for help from the Scottish criminal justice system, and will be entitled to protest if none is forthcoming. I am not in the same way bound or protected by Polish criminal law, or answerable in the Polish criminal courts, in relation to my Edinburgh life: even if what I do, or what is done to me, in Edinburgh fits the definition of, for example, theft in the Polish criminal code, it is not a crime under (a violation of) Polish criminal law—it does not fall within the ambit of Polish criminal law; nor am I, or the person who stole from me, triable in a Polish criminal court—it does not fall within the jurisdiction of the Polish courts.[5] Similarly, a theft committed in Warsaw is not a crime under Scots criminal law (even if it fits the definition of theft in Scots law); nor is its perpetrator triable in a Scottish criminal court—not even if, by chance, both perpetrator and victim happen to come to Scotland, and the perpetrator goes to the police to confess what he has done.

Ambit and jurisdiction are typically defined in territorial terms: in the simple, normatively central, case, crimes committed within the territorial boundaries of Scotland fall within the ambit of Scots criminal law, and under the jurisdiction of Scottish courts; crimes committed outside those boundaries do not.[6] A normative theory of

[3] See above, Chapter 1, section 5.

[4] See R A Duff, *Answering for Crime*, ch. 2; also 'Responsibility, Citizenship and Criminal Law'; 'Relational Reasons and the Criminal Law'. The reasons for the qualifying 'paradigmatically' will become clear shortly.

[5] On 'ambit' and 'jurisdiction' (or 'venue', as it is sometimes called), see M Hirst, *Jurisdiction and the Ambit of the Criminal Law*, ch. 1; L Farmer, 'Territorial Jurisdiction and Criminalization', 230–1.

[6] Thus apart from certain ('exceptional') statutory exceptions, 'the whole body of the criminal law of England deals only with acts committed in England' (*Cox v Army Council* [1963] AC 48, at 67; Viscount Simonds).

criminal law must be able to explain (or give reasons for rejecting) this feature of domestic systems of criminal law; it must also be able to say something—rationally reconstructive, justificatory, or critical—about the various determinations and qualifications of, and exceptions to, this 'Territoriality Principle'.

Some of these determinations and qualifications have to do with what counts as commission within the territory of a polity or a state, and need not long detain us here. Thus the Law Lords were once exercised by this question: if I post a letter in England to a person in Germany seeking to blackmail her, am I guilty of blackmail ('mak[ing] an[] unwarranted demand with menaces') under s. 21(1) of the English Theft Act 1968, because in posting the letter I made the demand; or should we say that the demand was not made until the letter reached its recipient in Germany, so that the blackmail was not committed in England?[7] Such questions, which have become more frequent as technological developments have made more kinds of action at a distance possible, might be answered by provisions in the general part of a criminal code,[8] which might also bring within the ambit of domestic criminal law conduct committed abroad that attacks or threatens 'domestic legal interests',[9] or 'bears a reasonable relation to a legitimate interest' of the state.[10] Other determinations or qualifications have to do with what is to count as the polity's territory: thus, for instance, crimes committed aboard British ships on the high seas,[11] or aboard British aircraft in flight anywhere in the world,[12] fall within the ambit of English criminal law, and the jurisdiction of English courts: which is to say, in effect, that British ships and aircraft are treated as (*as if* they were) British territory.[13] These kinds of provision highlight the point that territory is not in this context a matter of mere geography: it is a political-legal matter, of how the polity is to define itself as a form of human life. Humans are embodied beings, who live in geographical space; polities must, therefore, be grounded in geographically determinable spaces (spaces that constitute their homes), which are determined by political processes and arrangements.

Other qualifications or exceptions to the Territoriality Principle make citizenship rather than territory the basis of ambit and jurisdiction. This might be a matter of general principle, included in the general part of a polity's criminal law. Thus German criminal law, for instance, operates with both a principle of 'nationality', under which the conduct of German citizens anywhere in the world falls within the ambit of German criminal law; and a principle of 'passive personality', under which its criminal law covers crimes committed anywhere against German citizens: a British citizen who robs a German citizen in London is therefore guilty of robbery under German law, and is in theory triable in a German court for the crime, as is a German citizen who robs a

[7] See *Treacy v DPP* [1971] AC 537.

[8] See e.g. §§ 3–7 of the German *Strafgesetzbuch*; and § 1.03 of the American Model Penal Code.

[9] *Strafgesetzbuch* § 5, which goes on to specify the '*inländische Rechtsgüter*' thus protected.

[10] Model Penal Code § 1.03(1)(f). Recent cases of people whose extradition the US sought for hacking into American computer systems from England have highlighted some of the problems here: see, for instance, http://www.guardian.co.uk/world/2012/oct/16/gary-mckinnon-not-extradited-may?INTCMP=SRCH (Gary McKinnon), http://www.bailii.org/ew/cases/EWHC/Admin/2018/172.html (Lauri Love). See more generally I Cameron, *The Protective Principle of International Criminal Jurisdiction*.

[11] See Hirst, *Jurisdiction and the Ambit of the Criminal Law*, 4–5, 12–14; Merchant Shipping Act 1995, s. 279. For useful discussion of two nineteenth-century cases, see Farmer, 'Territorial Jurisdiction and Criminalization', 225–8.

[12] See Hirst, *Jurisdiction and the Ambit of the Criminal Law*, 12; Civil Aviation Act 1982, s. 92.

[13] See e.g. Offences at Sea Act 1799, s. 1: offences committed 'upon the high seas' are to be treated 'as if they had been committed upon the shore'. See Farmer, 'Territorial Jurisdiction and Criminalization', on the use of 'fictions'.

Frenchman in Paris.[14] Or it might be done in a more piecemeal way: for instance, a murder committed by a British citizen anywhere in the world counts as murder in English criminal law, and is triable in an English court;[15] the same is true of any of the list of sexual offences specified in Schedule 2 of the Sex Offenders Act 1997.[16]

Other exceptions to the Territoriality Principle concern universal jurisdiction, when a state's criminal law covers, and its courts have jurisdiction over, certain types of crime committed by anyone (citizen or not) against anyone (citizen or not) anywhere in the world. This can be a result of signing an international convention that includes an '*aut dedere aut judicare*' ('extradite or prosecute') clause. For instance, under the UN Torture Convention, each signatory must 'ensure that all acts of torture are offences under its criminal law' and must 'take such measures as may be necessary to establish its jurisdiction' over such offences when they are committed 'in any territory under its jurisdiction', or committed by or against one of its nationals (in the latter case, if the signatory 'considers it appropriate'), or 'in cases where the alleged offender is present in any territory under its jurisdiction and it does not extradite him'.[17] Thus, in English law, a 'public official or person acting in an official capacity, whatever his nationality, commits the offence of torture if in the United Kingdom or elsewhere he intentionally inflicts severe pain or suffering on another in the performance or purported performance of his official duties'.[18] Similarly, Article 7 of the 1970 Hague Convention for the Suppression of Unlawful Seizure of Aircraft requires that a signatory 'in the territory of which the alleged offender is found shall, if it does not extradite him, be obliged, without exception whatsoever and whether or not the offense was committed in its territory, to submit the case to its competent authorities for the purpose of prosecution'.[19]

In these cases, a state extends the ambit and jurisdiction of its domestic criminal law to capture crimes committed abroad, by and against non-citizens: it is not a matter of allocating jurisdiction to an international tribunal, such as the International Criminal Court (ICC), on the basis of international criminal law;[20] but the extensions are mandated by international conventions to which the state is a signatory.[21] A state might also, however, assert universal jurisdiction over a type of crime even without any such international mandate: for instance, Belgium extends the ambit and jurisdiction of its criminal law to cover a range of crimes committed outside Belgium by Belgian citizens

[14] German *Strafgesetzbuch*, § 7.1–2: the conduct must be criminal 'at the locality of its commission' (unless that locality 'is not subject to any criminal jurisdiction'); see also e.g. the French *Code Pénal*, art. 113.6–7, and (for the passive personality principle in US federal law) USC 18 § 2.332.

[15] Offences Against the Person Act 1861, s. 9; D Ormerod and K Laird, *Smith and Hogan's Criminal Law*, 558.

[16] Sex Offenders Act 1997, s. 7. The Act distinguishes ambit from jurisdiction: the conduct counts as an offence under English law whoever commits it, so long as it 'constituted an offence under the law in force' in the place where it was committed (s. 7(1); ambit); but it is triable in English courts only if it is committed by someone who was at the time, or has since become, a British citizen or resident (s. 7(2); jurisdiction).

[17] UN Convention against Torture and other Cruel, Inhuman or Degrading Treatment or Punishment (1984), arts 4–5.

[18] Criminal Justice Act 1988, s. 134(1); *R v Bow Street Metropolitan Stipendiary Magistrate ex parte Pinochet Ugarte* [2000] 1 AC 147.

[19] For other conventions that include such a provision, see M Cherif Bassiouni and E M Wise, *Aut Dedere Aut Judicare: The Duty to Extradite or Prosecute in International Law*; they list twenty-four types of 'international offence' that are covered by such conventions (p. 7).

[20] See Rome Statute of the International Criminal Court (1998).

[21] See also, for more general domestic provisions of this kind, § 6(9) of the German *Strafgesetzbuch*, art. 23.4(g) of the Spanish *Ley Orgánica del Poder Judicial*: see L Reydams, *Universal Jurisdiction*, 142, 183.

or by foreigners who are then found in Belgium; and although some of these crimes are covered by international conventions, others are not.[22]

Finally, we should note the provisions that exist for extradition between states: if a Scotsman commits a crime in France, and then goes home, he can be arrested in Scotland under a European Arrest Warrant issued in France, and sent to France for trial;[23] or if he commits a crime outside Europe, but in a country with which there is an extradition treaty, he can be arrested by Scottish police and extradited by order of a Scottish court.[24] An important point to note here is that unless the case falls under an '*aut dedere aut judicare*' convention, Scottish courts lack jurisdiction to try the alleged perpetrator for the crime; and even if the extradition treaty includes, typically, a 'dual criminality' requirement,[25] this means only that the conduct must be such that it *would have* been criminal under Scots law had it been committed in Scotland, which is not to say that it must *be* criminal under Scots law.[26]

So what could a normative theorist say about this range of principles and provisions? What normative sense can we make of the Territoriality Principle as the most common basic principle of ambit and jurisdiction—and of these various qualifications and exceptions to it? (A complete normative account will also need to have something to say about the jurisdiction of international criminal tribunals, such as the ICC, and the ambit of the international criminal law that such tribunals apply: this topic will inevitably figure in what follows, but my main focus will be on domestic criminal law.)

An obvious answer to this question appeals to pragmatic considerations and to a principle of state sovereignty. On this view, normative theorizing about the criminal law must begin, not with the kinds of local, geographically limited concern that the Territoriality Principle makes salient, but (like all foundational theorizing) with certain universal and agent-neutral values or demands: for instance with the demand of justice that moral wrongdoers suffer the retributive punishment they deserve; or with the need to prevent harm, or wrongful harm; or with the value of civic peace and the need to protect it. Such demands and values provide reasons for action for all rational agents, to do what they can to assist the satisfaction of such demands or the protection of such values;[27] those reasons apply to us both individually, and collectively as states or polities. Criminal law, as one type of institutionalized collective action, can help to meet such demands, to protect such values, and to serve such ends; and in a world that is still a world of nation states, who maintain an increasingly limited but still substantial

[22] *Loi contenant des dispositions en vue de la répression de la traite des êtres humains et de pornographie enfantine* (Act for the Suppression of Trade in Humans and of Child Pornography): see Reydams, *Universal Jurisdiction*, 103–4; see also § 6 of the German *Strafgesetzbuch* (Reydams, *Universal Jurisdiction*, 183), and Reydams, *Universal Jurisdiction*, 11–16 on the historic debate about whether states can legitimately claim such jurisdiction without an explicit mandate under international law or international conventions.

[23] See European Commission, *European Arrest Warrant*; also N Schallmoser, 'The European Arrest Warrant and Fundamental Rights'; S Alegre and M Leaf, 'Mutual Recognition in European Judicial Cooperation: A Step Too Far Too Soon?'. Compare too the ways in which American states help each other to retrieve fugitive suspects (often through the federal offence of 'unlawful flight to avoid prosecution'; Fugitive Felon Act, 18 USC § 1073).

[24] See UN Model Treaty on Extradition; also European Convention on Extradition; Extradition Act 2003; M C Bassiouni, *International Extradition: United States Law and Practice*; and above, Chapter 2 at nn 169–71.

[25] See e.g. Extradition Act 2003, ss 64–5, 137–8.

[26] But see e.g. German *Strafgesetzbuch*, § 7(2)2, for a unilateral version of '*aut dedere aut judicare*'.

[27] See e.g. J Gardner, 'Relations of Responsibility'; M M Dempsey, 'Public Wrongs and the "Criminal Law's Business": When Victims Won't Share'; above, Chapter 2, section 9.

degree of sovereignty over their own territories and their own affairs, this gives every nation state reason to create and maintain a system of criminal law.

On such a view, every state has reason to create and maintain a system of criminal law that is universal in its ambit and its jurisdiction. Wrongful conduct deserves punishment wherever it is committed; wrongful harms and threats to civic peace need to be prevented wherever they occur. If a nation state is to serve the ends of retributive justice, harm prevention, or the maintenance of civic peace, it thus has reason to criminalize (to define as criminal, to give its courts jurisdiction over) wrongful, wrongfully harmful, or peace-threatening conduct anywhere in the world, by and against whomever it is committed. That is not to say, however, that every state has *conclusive* reason to claim, or to exercise, such universal jurisdiction. As with any kind of demand or good, we must ask how it can be most efficiently satisfied or realized, and how we can efficiently assist its satisfaction or realization.[28] In a world of nation states, the answer will be that the demands or goods related to criminal law are, usually, most efficiently satisfied or realized if effective nation states are left to deal with wrongs committed within their own territories: they should determine, that is, what kinds of conduct to criminalize within their territories, and should have jurisdiction over such crimes. This doctrine also respects the value of state sovereignty, which constrains the extent to which states may interfere in others' 'internal' affairs: states should generally have the power to make and apply their criminal law, as they should have the power to deal with other internal matters, free from interference by other states.[29] Other states can, however, assist in the realization of the proper ends of the criminal law by, inter alia, being prepared to arrest alleged offenders found within their territory, and to extradite them to the states where they allegedly offended.

Thus if we now ask why the ambit and jurisdiction of English criminal law should not extend to cover crimes committed by and against anyone anywhere, why an assault committed by a Pole on a fellow Pole in Warsaw should not count under English law as a criminal assault triable in an English court, the answer will be that there is no reason of fundamental principle why it should not—and some reason of fundamental principle why it should. But so long as Poland is itself a functioning nation state that can deal effectively with such matters, it should have the right, and the responsibility, to do so, for reasons that have to do both with the efficient division of labour between nation states and with a proper respect for state sovereignty. It might sound strange to suggest that English criminal law should encompass Polish assaults: but that is just because it is so obvious that English legislators ought, in their practical deliberations, to take a more limited, local view, since that is normally how they can best serve the values that matter. What should ultimately guide their conduct, what ultimately justifies it, are such agent-neutral (state-neutral) reasons as the pursuit of retributive justice, or the prevention of harm or the protection of civic peace: but such agent-neutral reasons give them good reason 'to reason and react agent-relatively over a range of cases';[30] they should usually attend only to wrongs, or wrongful harms, or threats to civic peace, that occur within their territories—the lands over which they exercise legitimate power.

[28] Compare J Gardner, 'Complicity and Causality', 85, on 'the efficient use of rational energy'.

[29] Other states, we might say, should recognize that although they do have reason to criminalize, and to claim jurisdiction over, the relevant kinds of conduct wherever, and by and against whomever, they are committed, it is not their business to criminalize or to claim jurisdiction over such conduct when it is committed outside their territory: see Dempsey, 'Public Wrongs and the "Criminal Law's Business"', 256–7; above, Chapter 2 at nn 157–8.

[30] Gardner, 'Complicity and Causality', 65; see above, Chapter 2 at n. 156.

This kind of account can explain why the Territoriality Principle should generally determine ambit and jurisdiction: states generally have good enough reason to criminalize relevant types of wrongful or harmful conduct committed within their own territory—whether by and against their own citizens or by or against non-citizens who happen to be within their territory; but they do not generally have good enough reason to criminalize conduct committed outside their territory. It can also explain why states should generally be willing to extradite alleged offenders to the state in whose territory they alleged offended, since that is generally the more efficient way of dealing with the alleged crime; but they can properly impose a 'dual criminality' requirement,[31] to ensure that what the other state will prosecute and punish the alleged offender for is indeed something that from the perspective of the agent-neutral values that should structure the criminal law merits criminalization. It can also explain at least some exceptions to the Territoriality Principle. For instance, some crimes covered by '*aut dedere aut judicare*' conventions typically have a trans-national character, and thus are not best treated as the local business of a particular state.[32] In other cases, it could be argued that it is (agent-neutrally) of great importance to prosecute some egregiously serious kinds of wrong, but that the states in whose territories they are committed might be unable or unwilling to prosecute them effectively. Such wrongs might be brought within the jurisdiction of an international criminal tribunal, such as the ICC,[33] or be covered by international conventions that include '*aut dedere aut judicare*' provisions,[34] or by unilateral assertions of universal jurisdiction by other states.[35] The justification in each case is that, given the seriousness of the mischief that needs to be addressed and the danger that the state with territorial jurisdiction will be unable or unwilling to address it effectively, states should be ready to cede jurisdiction to other states or to international bodies; if they are unwilling to do so, other states or international bodies might be justified in 'piercing' their sovereignty.[36]

This kind of account might struggle to make normative sense of the principles of nationality or passive personality under which states claim jurisdiction over crimes committed by or against their own citizens outside their territory:[37] such crimes are surely in general most efficiently dealt with by the state in whose territory they are committed; and it is not clear why, on this account, states should take a special interest in the extra-territorial actions or sufferings of those who are their citizens. But whether this kind of account is offered as a normative theory of jurisdiction, or as a rational reconstruction of our existing institutional structures, it can reject such provisions as mistakes—as deviations from the principles that make best sense of our practices.[38]

[31] See at n. 25 above.

[32] See e.g. the 1970 Hague Convention for the Suppression of Unlawful Seizure of Aircraft (at n. 19 above).

[33] See Rome Statute of the International Criminal Court, Preamble: the signatories affirm 'that the most serious crimes of concern to the international community as a whole must not go unpunished', and their determination 'to put an end to impunity for the perpetrators of these crimes and thus to contribute to the prevention of such crimes'; but note that, consistently with the argument sketched here for the primacy of a Territoriality Principle, the ICC respects a principle of 'complementarity', according to which the ICC can claim a case only if the state with initial jurisdiction is 'unwilling or unable' to investigate it properly or prosecute it (Art. 17).

[34] See e.g. the UN Convention against Torture and other Cruel, Inhuman or Degrading Treatment or Punishment (1984); nn 17–18 above.

[35] See at n. 22 above.

[36] See C Wellman, 'Piercing Sovereignty'; A Altman and C Wellman, *A Liberal Theory of International Justice*, ch. 4.

[37] See at nn. 14–16 above.

[38] Compare A Chehtman, 'The Extraterritorial Scope of the Right to Punish'; *The Philosophical Foundations of Extraterritorial Punishment*, esp. chs 2–3: Chehtman justifies a version of the

This kind of account rests on an essentially instrumental conception of criminal law, and of its provisions concerning both ambit and jurisdiction: the justifying purposes of the criminal law lie in the ways in which it can contribute to the realization of certain impersonal values, and the arrangements made for the ambit and jurisdiction of particular systems of criminal law should depend on how those contributions can be most efficiently made (but also bearing in mind the significant, though not absolute, value of state sovereignty). I will not directly engage here with a general critique of instrumental conceptions of law,[39] or rehash my discussion of agent-neutral and agent-(or practice-)relative reasons in Chapter 2, section 9; I will instead suggest that this kind of account cannot do justice to significant aspects of criminal law as a distinctive type of legal institution—aspects that we can highlight by asking about the law's voice, and about *whose* law the criminal law of a particular polity is (or should be).

2. The Law's Voice

The criminal law, I suggested in Chapter 1, should be seen as a communicative enterprise: in its substantive dimension, it declares certain kinds of conduct to constitute public wrongs—to be wrongs that merit a formal public response; in its procedural dimension, it provides the process through which those accused of committing such wrongs are called to formal public account. If this is right, we need to ask various questions about the law's voice. In what, or in whose, voice does the criminal law speak, and to whom? By whom, to whom, are defendants in criminal trials called to answer, and by what right? An instrumental account of the kind sketched above seems to offer no answer to the first question, unless it is that the law speaks in the voice of the impersonal ends or values that it serves. Its answer to the second question must be that the law is addressed to anyone who can hear it, but (insofar as the Territoriality Principle obtains) especially to those within the territory of the state whose law it is. It is unclear how it can answer the third question, perhaps because that question will seem unimportant within this instrumental perspective. But we can find more fruitful answers to these questions by thinking about the relationship between law and the political community whose law it is.

This is also to say that we need to look beyond the state if we are to understand the voice and authority of the criminal law. In one sense, of course, criminal law is, like all domestic law, the creation of the state: only given the institutional structure that a state provides can criminal law exist. But to say that the voice of the criminal law is the voice of the state would be to elevate the state into something more (and more disturbing) than an institutional apparatus of governance—into a sovereign standing above and apart from the people who are to be governed. That might all too often be the political reality—that we, as citizen-subjects, find ourselves under the power of a state apparatus over which we have very limited control collectively (and none individually): but if we are thinking normatively about what ought to be, we should rather see the state as the set of institutional mechanisms through which a political community arranges

Territoriality Principle in terms of the interest that individuals living within the territory of a state (permanently or temporarily, and whether or not they are citizens) have in the effective enforcement of a system of criminal law within that territory; and while extra-territorial jurisdiction over what are properly defined as international crimes can, he argues, be justified, the principles of nationality and of passive personality cannot.

[39] See especially A Harel, *Why Law Matters*.

its self-governance; and we should, I will suggest, then understand the criminal law as claiming to speak in the voice of the members of that political community—of its citizens.

We can best see the force of this point by thinking again about the criminal trial as a process of calling to account.[40] For we must ask not merely who is called to account (alleged offenders), but by whom they are called; and an answer to that question must specify a community by and to which (by and to whose members) they are accountable—a linguistic and normative community to which the one who is called either belongs (in a paradigm case) or is suitably related (in non-paradigm cases). Calling to account requires a linguistic and normative community because when *A* calls *B* to account, the intelligibility (and thus the legitimacy) of that calling depends on *B* being able to understand and respond: it makes no sense to call someone to answer if she cannot do so.[41] The calling and answering must therefore be conducted in a language that is, if not *B*'s first language, accessible to her, either directly through her own linguistic grasp or through an interpreter; and the values by reference to which *B* is called to account, which she is accused of violating, must be accessible to her as values that are, or that she could make, her own. We call *B* to account for doing something that, we claim, she should not have done, for acting as she had good reason not to act; but we can say that *B* ought to have *Φ*-ed, or had good reason to *Φ*, only if that reason to *Φ* was within *B*'s conceptual and motivational grasp.[42] In calling *B* to account we also seek some response from her—an answer that might involve a denial that she acted as we allege, or that she violated the values to which we appeal; or a reasoned rejection of those values; or an explanation of her action which admits that she acted against the reasons that we cite, but justifies or excuses her action; or an admission that she acted wrongly, and an apologetic explanation of her conduct. But whatever kind of answer she is to give, she will be able to give it only if she can understand the charge to which it is to be an answer: only if she can understand, that is, not merely whatever factual claims we make about what she did, but also the values to which our accusation appeals, and recognize those values as conceivable sources of reasons for action.

So too, when the substantive criminal law defines certain kinds of wrong as public wrongs, it must speak, or claim to speak, in the voice of a linguistic and normative community whose law it is, and whose values it thus declares; and it must speak to an audience who can be expected to understand those declarations as grounded in what could be reasons for action—reasons for them to act. In defining theft, for instance, as a crime, the law defines it as a wrong—something that its addressees have normally conclusive reason not to do, for which they will be liable to be called to public account if they do it; but they can have such reasons only if they can understand the (supposed) wrongness of theft, and the law that declares its wrongness.

Furthermore, only given such a linguistic and normative community can those who would call a person to account legitimately claim the standing to do so. To call people to account is to claim (at least by implication) that the conduct for which we call them to account is our business. It is not enough to show that what they did was wrong, or something that they had good reason not to do; we must also be able to show that it

[40] See above, Chapter 1, section 5; also Chapter 2 at nn 120–2.

[41] That is why it is so important that a defendant in a criminal trial be fit to plead—capable of understanding and answering to the charge: see above, Chapter 1 at nn 104–5.

[42] There is more to be said about the sense in which the reasons that we take *B* to have must be within her reach: for useful surveys see M Alvarez, 'Reasons for Action: Justification, Motivation, Explanation'; S Finlay and M Schroeder, 'Reasons for Action: Internal vs. External'; and see below, Chapter 4 at nn 134–5.

is a wrong that properly concerns us—a wrong for which they must answer to us. But it can concern us only if there is some appropriate normative relationship between us and the agent—a relationship that might be deepened (or destroyed) by the calling (and answering), but that cannot be created *ex nihilo* by the calling. Such normative relationships can exist only within normative communities or practices: we might be related as friends, or as members of a family or clan, or as colleagues in a profession or workplace, or as fellow participants in a sport; in each case the relationship presupposes a practice within which, and only within which, it can make sense. As we saw in the previous chapter,[43] I am answerable for my conduct to fellow members of a practice within which that conduct belongs—but not to strangers who play no part in the practice (and not for conduct that is 'private' in relation to the practice). I must answer to my fellow players for my sporting misconduct in the game we are playing, and perhaps to the game's governing body: but an outsider has no standing to call me to account for that misconduct; nor do my fellow players have standing, *qua* fellow players, to call me to account for misconduct that falls outside the game.[44]

What then is the normative community, the practice, that domestic criminal law presupposes: what is the community, the practice, within which alleged criminal wrongdoers can be called to account? It might be argued that the answer to this question is obvious: even if I am right that the criminal law is a communicative enterprise that depends on a normative community whose law it is, and to which those who are called to account belong, such a community is readily found. For the criminal law is concerned with moral wrongdoing, and moral wrongdoing is the business of every moral agent, since all are members of the moral community. So the language in which the criminal law should speak is the language of morals—a language intelligible and accessible to all moral agents; it can thus, in principle, be addressed to all moral agents; and any moral agent can, in principle, be called to account under any system of criminal law for wrongs that thus properly concern all her fellow moral agents. As we have seen, there are good reasons, both practical and principled, why a particular polity's law should claim only a more limited ambit and jurisdiction—why it should generally bring within its ambit only wrongs committed within its territory, and why it should generally claim the right to call to account only those who commit such wrongs: but in doing so it is still speaking in the voice and on behalf of the universal moral community, by whose values all moral agents are bound and to which all are answerable.

There is room for argument about whether all moral wrongs are, even in principle, the business of all moral agents: if I regularly fail to buy my round for the friends with whom I drink every week, I must admit that I am answerable to them for this breach of the values that define our shared activity (a breach that constitutes a moral wrong, albeit a relatively minor one); but I, and they, might insist that it is no business of a passing stranger. But even if that is true of such relatively minor moral wrongs, it is surely not true of the more serious or egregious wrongs with which the criminal law typically deals: if I see, or become aware of, a murder, a rape, a violent assault, or a fraud, I surely cannot say with a clear conscience that it is none of my moral business, and literally or metaphorically pass on by. There might in fact be nothing I can do about it, either to prevent it or to respond to it—nothing I can directly do myself,

[43] See above, Chapter 2, section 9.

[44] With games and sporting ethics, as with medicine and medical ethics (see above, Chapter 2, section 8), there will be some overlap between sporting misconduct and crime: some kinds of sporting misconduct are also criminal; and there might be room for discussion about whether a piece of misconduct should be dealt with as (and only as) sporting misconduct, or (also) as a crime.

nothing I can do to assist others in preventing or responding to it: but it surely gives me good reason, as a moral agent, to act if I am able to do so. Such moral wrongs are the business of all of us; it is for such wrongs that the criminal law should hold us to account in the name, ultimately, of the moral community to which we all belong.

Some would, in a Kantian spirit, take this moral community to be the community of rational agents.[45] Others would ground our fellowship in our humanity rather than in our rationality,[46] in which case we could connect this line of thought about domestic criminal law to a familiar way of talking about international criminal law. On this view I am, in principle, answerable for my criminal wrongdoing to humanity, to all my fellow human beings, although for the reasons noted above it is usually more efficient for that task of calling to account to be delegated, as it were, from 'humanity' to local states which can perform it through their domestic systems of criminal law. However, when local states fail to discharge this responsibility (a responsibility that they owe to humanity itself), and if the crimes are egregious, other states or international bodies can properly step in, on behalf of humanity, to hold the wrongdoers to account. Thus the founding statute of the ICC talks of 'atrocities that deeply shock the conscience of humanity', and 'the most serious crimes of concern to the international community as a whole'.[47] Such crimes, when committed within the territory of a nation state (as is often true of 'crimes against humanity'), might be most efficiently dealt with by that state's domestic courts: hence the principle of complementarity, under which a case is 'inadmissible' if it 'is being investigated or prosecuted by a State which has jurisdiction over it'. But when that local state 'is unwilling or unable genuinely to carry out the investigation or prosecution', the ICC can take the case.[48]

Now the idea of 'humanity' as a community to which such egregious wrongdoers should be called to answer, because their wrongs are the business of all of us in virtue simply of our shared humanity, is indeed attractive, at least rhetorically: what is less clear is whether it can provide a substantive grounding either for the authority of such international criminal tribunals as the ICC, or for systems of domestic criminal law.

A first and obvious point is that domestic systems of criminal law do not deal only with the kinds of egregious wrong that fall within the jurisdiction of the ICC, in relation to which talk of 'shocking the conscience of humanity' has its rhetorical force. Even if it makes sense to say that a murderer or torturer is answerable to 'humanity' for his crime, it is less plausible to say that I am answerable to humanity for my theft of an iPhone, or for falsifying my tax return. Renzo has argued that we can deal with this point by accepting an expansive but still limited conception of 'crimes against humanity', as crimes that violate their victims' humanity: for such crimes, the offender is in principle answerable to all of humanity, although often, especially when the crime is committed by a private individual, the offender can be called to answer by the domestic courts of his nation state. Other crimes, however, do not violate their victims' humanity, but only the civic duties that the offender owes to his fellow citizens: for such crimes, the offender is only answerable locally, to his fellow citizens.[49] For the

[45] Compare T M Scanlon, *Moral Dimensions: Permissibility, Meaning, Blame*, 139–40; see above, Chapter 2, n. 119.

[46] See e.g. R Gaita, *Good and Evil: An Absolute Conception*, ch. 3.

[47] Rome Statute of the International Criminal Court, Preamble. Compare Bassiouni, *International Extradition*, 39–40, on the idea of a '*civitas maxima*', as a community that embraces all human beings, and whose public order is threatened by crime.

[48] Rome Statute, art. 17.1(a): see art. 1 for complementarity, art. 7 for the definition of 'crimes against humanity'.

[49] M Renzo, 'Responsibility and Answerability in the Criminal Law'.

reasons given in the following paragraphs, however, I do not think that we can be held criminally (as distinct from morally) answerable to 'humanity' for any wrongs, however serious.

Second, appeals to a community of humanity might be not only rhetorically powerful; they might also express an aspiration to build a genuine (although so far no more than nascent) moral community of human beings, united by a shared recognition of, and concern for, each other as fellows. They cannot, however, be appeals to humanity as even a nascent political community, to which perpetrators and their victims, and all of us, belong as individuals, since there is no such community:[50] but what criminal law and criminal trials require is political community. Criminal law is not simply the moral law, nor is a legislature simply an agent of the moral law: for law is a political institution; a legislature must therefore see itself as acting in the name of, and the laws it enacts must claim to speak in the voice of, a political community. In a world of nation states, the only plausible candidate for that political community is the local polity, whose legislature it is. If the legislature is to determine the proper aims and scope of the criminal law that it is to enact, it must therefore have some conception of the character and aims of the polity whose legislature it is—some conception of its *res publica*:[51] but we have not yet been given any reason to think that its *res publica* should include not only wrongs committed in its own territory, or by or against its own members, but also wrongs committed anywhere by and against anyone; nor any reason why it should claim the standing to call the perpetrators of all such wrongs to account. This is not yet to say that no such reasons could be given, since we have yet to explore the kinds of account that might be offered of a polity's *res publica*: but it is to say that the political community within and to which domestic criminal law can be said to hold defendants to account must be the local polity whose law it is; and that if that local polity is to be seen as somehow acting in the name and on behalf of some larger political community, we need an account of what that larger community is, of which kinds of wrong fall within its *res publica*, and of what the relationship is between that larger political community and the local polity.

Sometimes such a larger political community might be identifiable. The United States, as a federal system, might seem to be an example, and it is true that the criminal laws and courts of the individual states are bound and constrained by the requirements of the (federal) constitution. This is not, however, the kind of example we need, since the two systems of criminal law, state and federal, are still separate: within the constraints set by the constitution, states make their own criminal law, which does not purport to be, or to reflect, 'American' law; the state courts act and speak in the name not of 'America', but of the individual state whose courts they are. Thus while federal criminal cases are indeed listed as '*United States of America v D*', state criminal cases are listed as '*State v D*', or '*People v D*', or '*Commonwealth v D*': the defendant is called to answer not by and to the United States, but by and to the local polity. European criminal law is a better example, since Article 83 of the Treaty on the Functioning of the European Union authorizes the European Parliament and Council to pass directives that 'establish minimum rules concerning the definition of criminal offences and sanctions' either in relation to 'particularly serious crime with a cross-border dimension' (s. 1), or when 'the approximation of criminal laws and regulations of the Member States proves essential to ensure the effective implementation of a Union policy' (s. 2): the national legislature of a member state might be seen as acting, in relation to

[50] See D Luban, 'A Theory of Crimes against Humanity', 124–41.

[51] See above, Chapter 2, section 9.

these kinds of directive, in the name or on behalf not simply of the member state, but of the European Union as a larger political community of which it is part.[52] We can indeed (some of us hopefully, some of us pessimistically) see the European Union as a gradually developing political community; we might then say that, at least in relation to crimes in which the European Parliament and Council take such an interest, the domestic courts are calling alleged perpetrators to answer not just to their local polity, but to the European polity, in whose name and on whose behalf the courts now act. But there is no such political community, even in nascent form, that includes all human beings as its members. I can identify myself as a Scottish, a British, and a European citizen; I can see Europe as a polity to which I belong as an individual member.[53] I can also intelligibly see myself as a member of a moral community of humanity—but not as an individual member of a political community of 'humanity'.

It is also worth asking whether, even for those 'atrocities that deeply shock the conscience of humanity', or 'the most serious crimes of concern to the international community as a whole',[54] we should see a body like the ICC as the ideal body to call the perpetrators to account. If we are to take seriously the rhetoric of 'humanity', we must suppose that it is—or would be if it could be seen to be a genuinely international, impartial tribunal: for as an explicitly international court, it could claim to speak directly for 'humanity' or the 'international community'. From this point of view, the principle of complementarity is in essence a pragmatic principle:[55] it will usually be more efficient for the nation state within whose national jurisdiction the crime against humanity was committed to prosecute it; that state is then speaking and acting not for its own polity, but for humanity. On the other hand, however, this does not seem to do justice to the claim that when the perpetrators can be tried locally, that is in principle a more appropriate way of responding to their crimes. It would have been appropriate for Augusto Pinochet to have been brought to trial in Chile for his crimes against Chilean victims (against, we might say, the Chilean people),[56] and for Bosco Ntaganda to be brought to trial in the Democratic Republic of the Congo,[57] had those states been able and willing to bring them to a fair trial: not because the ICC cannot truly be seen to be acting, impartially, in the name of humanity,[58] but because they should ideally be called to account in and by their own polities, for alleged crimes committed against those polities and their fellow citizens. From this point of view, the principle of complementarity marks a recognition of the principled priority of national jurisdiction: to bring a case to the ICC is not to make it evident that the defendant is being called to

[52] See generally V Mitsilegas, *EU Criminal Law After Lisbon: Rights, Trust and the Transformation of Justice in Europe*; also E Baker, 'A Case of "Nested Enforcement": Article 83(2) TFEU, Compliance and the Area of Freedom, Security and Justice Post-Lisbon'.

[53] Although at the time of writing it seems that I will not be able to count myself as, formally, a European citizen after March 2019.

[54] Rome Statute of the International Criminal Court, Preamble; see at n. 47 above.

[55] And, perhaps, more consistent with respect for state sovereignty: see at n. 29 above; A Cassese et al, *Cassese's International Criminal Law*, 298 (and ch. 16 generally); F Jessberger, 'International v. National Prosecution of International Crimes'. It will be clear from even a glance at these materials that my discussion of the principle is a sketchy exercise in rational reconstruction.

[56] See *R v Bow Street Metropolitan Stipendiary Magistrate ex p Pinochet Ugarte* [2000] 1 AC 147; there were indeed moves to indict and try Pinochet in Chile before his death.

[57] *The Prosecutor v Bosco Ntaganda* ICC-01/04-02/06.

[58] See L Sadat, 'The International Criminal Court', 151–3. See also the critique of the ICC by African countries: M du Plessis et al, *Africa and the International Criminal Court*; O Boycott, 'Rising Nationalism Leaves International Criminal Court at Risk'.

answer to humanity; it is to try to make up for the failure of the local state to do its duty—but in the recognition that the making up cannot but fall short.[59]

How then should we explain the (claimed) standing of such tribunals as the ICC: in whose name can they claim to speak? That is not my primary concern here—my focus is on domestic criminal law; but a plausible answer might be developed if we think of a community composed not of individual human beings, but of nations.[60] When the ICC calls a defendant to answer to a charge of committing a crime against humanity, it is speaking in the name of this community of nations, on behalf of the citizens of the nation in which the crime was committed, citizens whose own state apparatus has failed them by its unwillingness or inability to prosecute the crime. The crime should properly be prosecuted within the polity in which it was committed, by its own criminal courts: the perpetrator should be called to answer to, and by, the political community against whose members he committed the crime. If this is not done, and especially if the crime is committed 'as part of a widespread or systematic attack directed against [a] civilian population',[61] the state has not just failed in its duty to protect its citizens against such crimes and to call their perpetrators to account: it has rendered itself complicit in those crimes, and sets itself against the polity whose institutional embodiment it is supposed to be.[62]

This also helps to make clear the normative foundations of extradition, which should be seen as a matter of cooperative relations between the members of the community of nations.[63] A theft committed by an English visitor to Brazil is not a crime under English criminal law, even if its elements match the English definition of theft: it falls outside the ambit of English law. English courts thus lack the jurisdiction to try her when she returns home: for her theft is not the (direct) business of English criminal law, nor is she answerable for it to her fellow English citizens. But the British polity recognizes that other polities have, as Britain has, a legitimate interest in calling to account those who commit crimes in their territory, and that this interest is more effectively served if polities are willing to help each other in this enterprise: that is why it is willing to sign extradition treaties with other polities, and so to extradite the alleged thief to Brazil under its extradition treaty with Brazil.[64] Her theft thus becomes, indirectly, the business of the British polity, once a request for extradition is made: but only because it is the direct business of the Brazilian polity, which seeks Britain's assistance in the matter. When the alleged thief appears for an extradition hearing in an English court, she is not being called to answer to the charge of theft, or to answer for

59 By way of partial analogy, consider how children whose parents are unable or unwilling to care for them may be taken into care by a local authority: ideally, the children would receive *parental* care; but when that is not possible, they must be cared for by others. The analogy is only partial, since foster parents can become, in both normative and social terms, real parents; but it illustrates the point that on this conception international criminal tribunals are a second-best solution.

60 A community of nations, or of polities, rather than of states (contrast Bassiouni and Wise, *Aut Dedere Aut Judicare*, 31–6), since political community is constituted by a nation or polity, of which the state is (or should be) the institutional manifestation and mechanism.

61 A defining feature of crimes against humanity: see Rome Statute, Article 7(1).

62 Compare R Gaita, 'Literature, Genocide and the Philosophy of International Law', 139, on humanity as 'a constituency [not] of moral agents, nor of human beings, but of human beings as citizens in the plurality of nations that comprise the community of nations'. See also H Grotius, *De Jure Belli ac Pacis*, Book II, ch. XXI, §§ III–IV: Bassiouni cites Grotius for the idea of a '*civitas maxima*' (see n. 47 above); but it is clear that Grotius was concerned with relations between nations. We can give a similar account of claims to universal jurisdiction by individual nation states: see above, at nn 17–22.

63 See at nn 23–6 above.

64 Extradition Treaty between the Government of the United Kingdom of Great Britain and Northern Ireland and the Government of the Federative Republic of Brazil, 1995.

the theft—that is not the English court's business: the question is whether the English court should in this way assist the Brazilian polity in its effort to call her to account. That assistance is, quite properly, not unconditional or unquestioning: it must not be given if, for instance, the alleged conduct would not 'constitute an offence under the law of the relevant part of the United Kingdom',[65] or if the person to be extradited would face capital punishment.[66] But that is because, in general, if we are asked either individually or collectively to assist another in some enterprise, our assistance should not be given blindly: we should be ready to cooperate in this way only if we can see the end that the other is pursuing as at least a reasonable one (which is not to say that it must be one that we share).

I have been arguing that the community by and to which those who commit crimes under a domestic system of criminal law are called to account, the community in whose name domestic criminal law speaks, cannot plausibly be seen as 'humanity'. If it could be seen as humanity, it would follow that the French legislature has some reason to criminalize thefts committed not just in France, but anywhere in the world, and to make them triable in a French court: probably not, for the reasons noted above, a good enough reason, but still some reason to do so, on behalf and in the name of humanity. However, it is not plausibly the job of domestic criminal law or of its courts to pursue wrongdoers throughout the world;[67] nor is it plausible to say that the reason why we choose not to criminalize crimes committed abroad by foreigners against foreigners is that we see the merits of a division of labour between nation states. French law is silent about, claims no authority over, Turkish thefts: not because France recognizes that such thefts can be dealt with more efficiently by the Turkish legal system, nor because France tolerates such thefts or thinks them less serious than thefts committed in France, but because France has no standing to judge them or respond to them.

But what does 'France' mean here? Since criminal law is part of the political structure of a polity, the reference must be to France not simply as a geographically defined territory, nor just as a state in the sense of a certain institutional structure of law and governance, but as a polity (of which the French state is or should be the institutional mechanism): as a political community whose law French criminal law is, by and to which alleged offenders against that law are called to account. To say that French criminal law is the French polity's law is to say that it is in the voice of that polity that French criminal law speaks, about wrongs which it recognizes as and declares to be public wrongs, whose perpetrators it will call to public account.[68] That is not yet to say that French criminal law is also addressed only *to* members of that polity; nor indeed is it so addressed, since we have already seen that it claims to bind and protect everyone who is within French territory, whether French or foreign. However, it is plausible to claim that its primary or paradigmatic addressees are indeed the members of the French polity. For, as I noted above, we are paradigmatically held to account as members of a normative community by the members of that community; and the relevant community here must be the French polity (I will comment in the following section on how domestic criminal law can also address those who are not members of the polity).

[65] Extradition Act 2003, s. 137(3)(b)—the 'dual criminality' requirement; see at n. 25 above.

[66] See e.g. art. 7 of the Extradition Treaty between the UK and the USA, 2003.

[67] See C Beccaria, *An Essay on Crimes and Punishments*, 134 (quoted above, Chapter 2 at n. 172).

[68] Which is not to say that the French polity's voice, as expressed in its laws, is always its own independent voice. Some of a polity's domestic criminal laws flow from transnational conventions by which it is bound (see at nn 17–21, 52 above). Nonetheless, French criminal law speaks, directly, in the voice of the French polity.

The conclusion of this section should be unsurprising: that the voice of a domestic system of criminal law is the voice not of humanity, or of a universal moral community, but of the polity whose law it is; that is the voice in which the polity defines what it will count as public wrongs, and in which it calls alleged perpetrators of such wrongs to public account. It is thus essentially a local voice, addressing a local audience: it does not seek to address the whole world, or claim the authority to define what should count as public wrongs anywhere in the world, and to call those who commit any such wrongs, anywhere in the world, to account. Its primary addressees are its own members, and its primary focus is on wrongs committed by them within the polity. But who or what are these members; what is it to be a member of a polity?

(It might be objected that in thus focusing on the domestic criminal law of nation states, and on the members of such states as the law's primary addressees, I am begging the question against cosmopolitanism as a normative political ideal: I am assuming, without argument, not merely the de facto existence of nation states and their domestic criminal laws, but the normative adequacy of such a structure, rather than engaging with the suggestion that we should aspire to a genuinely cosmopolitan political community within which we could all recognize and address each other as civic fellows.[69] My own normative inclination is to give the idea of nationhood, or the nation state, a more foundational status than radical cosmopolitans allow,[70] but I will not try to defend that here: one cannot fight every battle at once. I will assume that a normative theory of criminal law for our contemporary world must be in large part a theory of domestic criminal law: of the criminal law of nation states which, whilst in many ways interdependent, retain a significant degree of national autonomy, particularly in relation to criminal law. Those laws are sometimes influenced, their content is sometimes determined, by the requirements of transnational and international commitments: but we can still properly talk of the criminal law of France as something distinct both from the law of Germany and from international (or indeed European) criminal law; and we can ask what role a nation's criminal law should play in its civic life.)

3. Citizens, Non-citizens, and the Criminal Law

An obvious answer to the question 'What is it to be a member of a polity?' is that it is to be a citizen: that is indeed true, so long as we do not build too much into the concept of citizenship, and recognize how the laws of a polity can also bind some non-citizens.

We must not (at this stage) build too much into the concept of citizenship because, if we are to say something general about the relationship between criminal law and political community, we must remember that not all political communities are democracies, and that non-democratic polities have criminal laws that claim authority over their members: if membership is identified with citizenship, citizenship must be able to take the form of, for instance, being subjects of a monarch who claims our obedience. In a monarchy, the law (including the criminal law) is the monarch's law; the peace that the criminal law protects is 'the king's peace';[71] and those accused of committing criminal offences may be called to answer by and to the monarch—hence the English naming of criminal cases as '*Regina v D*'. Nonetheless, a monarch's law must also claim to be the polity's common law, in the sense that it must claim to express the polity's

[69] For a useful survey of cosmopolitan ideas, see P Kleingeld and E Brown, 'Cosmopolitanism'.
[70] See e.g. D Miller, *On Nationality*, and *National Responsibility and Global Justice*.
[71] On the King's peace, see e.g. F Pollock, 'The King's Peace'; M Dubber, 'Paradigms of Penal Law'.

shared values, even if the monarch claims the authority to define those values;[72] it must claim to serve not (not merely) the monarch's good, but the polity's 'common good', even if the monarch claims the authority to define that good.[73] However, since my aim is to work towards a plausible normative conception of criminal law, and since one fairly minimal, but essential, desideratum of such a conception is that it be a conception of criminal law as part of a democratic polity, I will take citizenship to be a matter of democratic membership, as suggested by the familiar rhetorical distinction between 'citizens' and 'subjects':[74] the peace that criminal law might aim to preserve is then the people's peace, not the king's peace;[75] and those accused of criminal wrongdoing are then called to answer by and to the polity—the 'People' or the 'Commonwealth'—rather than the monarch.[76] The criminal law then is (or aspires to be) a common law in the sense that it is a law that citizens make for themselves and make (or should make) their own. On this view, the voice of the criminal law is the (collective) voice of the citizens—a voice in which they talk, as it were, to themselves in terms of the shared values that define them as a polity.

(An account of the criminal law's ambit and jurisdiction based on citizenship can make good sense of the principles of 'nationality' and 'passive personality', which bring within the ambit of a polity's criminal law and the jurisdiction of its criminal courts crimes committed by, or against, its citizens abroad.[77] For if the criminal law is our law as citizens, protecting and binding us as citizens, one could argue that that binding and protection should follow us wherever we go: that a German citizen should be as bound, and protected, by German criminal law when she travels to Poland as she is when at home in Germany. If she commits in Poland what German law defines as a crime, her conduct should be criminal under German law, and she should be answerable for it in a German court; if she become the victim of a crime in Poland, although German law and its officers were powerless to prevent that, her attacker should be triable in a German court. For as a citizen she is, to her fellow German citizens, one of 'us'; and we could believe that what is done by, or to, one of us is our business, just as much as what is done in our civic home. This is not to *recommend* such principles: we could instead argue either that, although we have some reason to extend the ambit and jurisdiction of our criminal law in one or both of these two ways, we should defer to the polity in which the crimes are committed, and leave the matter to their criminal law; or that wrongs committed by, or to, our fellow citizens are properly our business only when they are committed within our civic home. My point is only that if we ground ambit and jurisdiction in citizenship rather than in territory, we can at least make sense of these doctrines.[78])

[72] On this conception of the common law, see G Postema, *Bentham and the Common Law Tradition*, chs 1–2. The idea of the law of a political community as its common law can be given a more democratic meaning: see e.g. R M Cotterrell, *Law's Community*, ch. 11, on the 'community' as against the 'imperium' model of law; see also J Waldron, *Law and Disagreement*, 56–60, on '*lex terrae*'.

[73] See further R A Duff, *Trials and Punishments*, ch. 3.

[74] Which is why it seemed natural for a new Canadian citizen to express her objection to having to swear allegiance to the queen by saying 'I prefer to be a citizen, not a subject' (Lorraine Harriral, as quoted in *The Guardian*, http://www.theguardian.com/world/2016/mar/31/naturalized-canadians-recant-oath-to-queen-royal-monarchy).

[75] See further below, Chapter 4 at nn 30–6, on civil order and civil peace.

[76] As criminal cases are named in e.g. New York ('*People v D*') and Massachusetts ('*Commonwealth v D*'). In other states (e.g. Washington) it is the 'State' by and to whom defendants are called to account: for the reasons noted above, it is clearer to talk of the people or the commonwealth.

[77] See at n. 14 above.

[78] I leave aside here some of the complications that arise about citizenship even if we attend only to formal, legal membership. For example, according to my passport, I am a citizen of the European

The following chapters will begin to develop a conception of criminal law as a criminal law for citizens: some initial clarification can be provided in the remainder of this chapter, by looking at three apparent problems for such a focus on citizenship. An account of the criminal law as the common law of a polity of citizens, expressing the values that they share, might fit—a critic will argue—a limited, closed, homogeneous polity whose territory contains only citizens, all of whom avow as their own the values that the law expresses: but that is a very long way from the kinds of society in which we now live, whose criminal laws we are to theorize—so far away as to amount not to an ideal model of criminal law as it ought to be, but to a philosopher's fantasy that cannot help us understand what criminal law could or should be for us.[79]

For first, in contemporary western societies domestic criminal law does not have to deal only with citizens. Very many of those who suffer or commit offences, many of those who look to our criminal justice institutions for help or who appear in our criminal courts, are not citizens: they might live in the country, but not as citizens, or be temporary visitors. A criminal law for citizens cannot, it seems, be *their* criminal law: how then can it address them, and how can they hear it?

Second, such societies are also characterized, not by a rich set of shared political values to which all their citizens are committed, but rather by deep disagreements on matters of value, and by deep cultural differences that preclude the normative homogeneity on which this conception seems to make criminal law depend. If a legitimate criminal law must be able to claim to express the community-defining values in which all the polity's citizens share, we cannot realistically aspire to a legitimate criminal law. Or, to put the point the other, and more plausible, way round, if we are to develop a normative theory of criminal law that is appropriate for societies like our own, we cannot appeal to this conception of criminal law as a polity's common law: for there is, usually, no such single polity. A contemporary criminal law, it might seem, must therefore be a criminal law for a society that does not constitute a unitary polity.

Third, to the extent that our contemporary criminal law does speak in the voice of a unitary polity, whose shared values it embodies, it often speaks a language of exclusion—an exclusion that it also enacts. The citizens in whose voice the criminal law speaks, and whom it protects, are the 'law-abiding citizens': but such a law then also excludes, and defines as enemies or outsiders, those who are not 'law-abiding'. A 'criminal law for citizens' (*Bürgerstrafrecht*) can generate, all too easily, a criminal law for enemies (*Feindstrafrecht*),[80] and treat as enemies those who will not or cannot conform.

In this and the following two sections I will try to defuse this objection. In this section I will say a little more about the idea of citizenship,[81] and about how a polity can address those who are not citizens without excluding or demeaning them. In section 4, I will discuss the problems of dissent and difference: how can the criminal law claim to express 'our' shared values as a polity, when the facts of disagreement and difference

Union and of the United Kingdom of Great Britain and Northern Ireland; when asked for my nationality on official forms, I might put 'British'; but when it comes to criminal law I am (when at home in Edinburgh) within the ambit and under the jurisdiction not of British, or United Kingdom, criminal law (there is no such thing), but of Scots criminal law (some of which was enacted by the United Kingdom parliament in Westminster); and if asked less formally for my nationality, I might reply 'Scottish' (whilst silently humming 'Flower of Scotland').

[79] For just one recent criticism of this kind, see J Edwards and A P Simester, 'What's Public About Crime?', 118–21, 129–31.

[80] See G Jakobs, 'Bürgerstrafrecht und Feindstrafrecht'; and section 5 below.

[81] For a classic discussion of dimensions of citizenship (distinguishing 'civil', 'political', and 'social' citizenship), see T H Marshall, *Citizenship and Social Class*.

seem to undermine the existence, or possibility, of any such communal 'we'? In section 5, I will address the problem of 'enemy criminal law', and show how a civilized polity's criminal law can be properly inclusive, even or especially in its dealings with those who commit criminal offences. I will in these discussions go well beyond any normatively neutral analysis of the concept of citizenship: I will be sketching a conception of citizenship, in relation to criminal law, that is informed by substantive political values, and that can apply only to certain kinds of polity. A fuller explanation, and partial defence, of this conception will need to wait on the account of a liberal republican polity that the following two chapters will sketch: for that will be an account of the kind of polity whose criminal law could plausibly deal with its citizens in the ways, and address them in the tones, that I suggest here. But it is worth providing this initial sketch here, partly to ward off initial objections to focusing in this way on citizenship, and partly to make clearer what kind of normative account of a polity will be needed: in what kind of polity, structured by what kinds of value, could the criminal law operate in this way?

The criminal law's (indeed, the law's) primary addressees are, I have suggested, the citizens of the polity whose law it is. In a democracy, it should therefore be, or aspire to be, the common law of the citizens: they should be able to recognize it as 'our' law—as a law that expresses their shared civic values, a law through which they speak, collectively, to themselves and each other. When the law defines wounding, or criminal damage, or tax evasion, as criminal, citizens are not supposed to hear this as a prohibition issued to them (imposed on them) by a sovereign distinct from the citizenry: they are supposed to hear it as a declaration that this wrong (which they should be able to recognize as a wrong independently of the criminal law, in terms of shared values in which the law itself is grounded) is a public wrong that merits collective condemnation and a public, formal calling to account for any who commit it.[82]

However, to say that the criminal law is 'our' law is also to say that it is not 'your' law: if English law belongs, as 'our' law, to English citizens, it does not belong to French citizens; it is not their law. Similarly, to talk about citizens as the primary addressees (and owners) of the law of a polity might seem to exclude non-citizens from its benefits and burdens. While citizenship is in one way an inclusionary concept (citizens are included within the scope of the criminal law's demands and protections), it is at the same time (and inevitably?) exclusionary: absent a polity to which all human beings belong, the identification of members of one group as citizens is also the identification of members of all other groups as non-citizens. This conceptual point would not be a source of difficulty if polities were isolated from each other, so that citizens of each polity lived only and always in that polity: but that is, of course, far from the truth. Within the territory of any modern polity there will be a large number of non-citizens: people who are in the territory as, for instance, tourists, or short-term business visitors; or who entered for a longer period as workers, or to join family members; or who have made their lives and homes in the polity, although they have not been granted, or perhaps have not sought, citizenship; or who have entered as refugees, as asylum seekers, or as would-be immigrants (legally or non-legally). Such non-citizens are still bound by the polity's criminal law in that, first, the law's ambit usually covers all conduct within the polity's territory; and, second, those who commit crimes within

[82] See above, Chapter 1, section 2. Note that in criminalizing tax evasion, the law is criminalizing the violation of a prior legal regulation: the wrong involved is still pre-criminal, but is not pre-legal; see above, Chapter 1 at nn 44–8. Note too that such declarations, unlike prohibitions, invite the kind of critical engagement, and disagreement, that characterize a democracy; see further Chapter 5 at nn 31, 141–3 below.

that territory are liable to be put on trial in its criminal courts. There are, of course, formal and informal exceptions to these generalizations: formally, some crimes can only be committed by citizens, or by others who are in some sense members of the polity;[83] and informally, the police might use their discretion, in dealing with minor offences committed by visitors, to send them home rather than having them prosecuted. However, the key point is that non-citizens who are within the polity's territory are, typically, bound by its criminal law—and should also be protected by it in that they should be able both to expect official help in preventing crimes against them, and to expect that if they do become victims of crime the polity will pursue the case, and the perpetrator, as assiduously as it would in the case of a citizen.

This might seem to argue in favour of grounding the criminal law's ambit and jurisdiction in a Territoriality Principle: surely the law should treat everyone within a polity's territory equally. So if I insist that the criminal law's primary addressees, and owners, are the polity's citizens, this invites the objection that I am, if not actually encouraging, at least opening the way to a worrying kind of discrimination that favours citizens over non-citizens. Citizens receive the full benefits of the law's protection, including the due process and human rights protections enjoyed by those facing criminal charges:[84] but non-citizens, it might seem, cannot claim the same assured right to such protections; they must depend on the grace and good will of the citizens whose law it is.[85]

This kind of objection leads into a number of issues that I cannot discuss here. First, we need to examine not just the idea of citizenship, but the conditions for becoming, or being, a citizen—in particular, how generous a polity should be towards those who wish to become citizens, since the more welcoming a polity is to new citizens, the fewer there will be who must live under laws that are not theirs. Second, we should distinguish the formal, legal status of citizen from a more substantive normative status: many who are not legally citizens are substantively members of the community, who have made their lives there and *should* be recognized formally as citizens.[86] I might, Zedner suggests, deal with this point by talking of 'denizens' rather than 'citizens':[87] but I prefer to retain the idea of citizenship, and argue for an inclusionary rather than an exclusionary conception of what it is to be a citizen, and of how people should be able to become citizens—full members of the polity in which they make, or seek to make, their lives.

[83] So William Joyce ('Lord Haw-Haw'), an American citizen, was held to be guilty of treason under English law only because at the time of his wartime broadcasts from Nazi Germany he held a British passport, and thus 'enjoy[ed] the protection of the Crown' (see *Joyce v DPP* [1946] AC 347); see also 18 USC § 2381—only someone 'owing allegiance to the United States' can commit treason under American federal law.

[84] See e.g. Article 6 of the European Convention on Human Rights.

[85] For such worries, see especially L Zedner, 'Security, the State, and the Citizen: The Changing Architecture of Crime Control', and 'Is the Criminal Law only for Citizens? A Problem at the Borders of Punishment'.

[86] This point is vividly illustrated by the number of people deported from the United States each year following a criminal conviction who are not legally citizens, but have lived in the country for a long time—sometimes since childhood: they are sent to what is legally their 'home', but are in substance being expelled from their home to what is now a foreign land. For a tragic example see the case of Rosa Ortega (https://www.theguardian.com/us-news/2017/feb/21/rosa-ortega-voter-fraud-texas-mexico-trump), who was brought from Mexico to Texas as a baby, had a green card that entitled her to permanent residence but not to vote, and (not realizing this) voted in several elections: aged 37, she was convicted of voter fraud and sentenced to eight years in prison—and faces deportation to Mexico at the end of her sentence. (See also J Stumpf, 'The Crimmigration Crisis: Immigrants, Crime, and Sovereign Power'; Pew Trust, *What Crimes are Eligible for Deportation?*).

[87] 'Is the Criminal Law only for Citizens?', at 53.

Third, there will still be many who find themselves, temporarily, within the jurisdiction of a polity's laws, without being either formally or substantively citizens. We can understand their normative position by seeing them as guests—visitors to whom the polity and its members owe duties of hospitality, and who owe the polity and its members the respect and concern that guests owe their hosts. It might seem that the idea of hospitality cannot give such non-citizens the kind of secure status that they should have—that it is too fragile, too reliant on the hosts' good will, to protect them against exclusion or denigration:[88] but, although it is all too true that polities can be unwelcoming to strangers, and discriminate against them, this is far from inevitable; we can talk seriously of *duties* of hospitality that we owe to guests. A conception of hospitality has played a central role in recent discussions in political ethics,[89] but my aim here is more modest: I simply want to appeal to the familiar idea that we owe duties, characterizable as duties of hospitality, towards those whom we invite or admit to our homes.[90] Such an aspiration to political hospitality is expressed in the Preamble to Argentina's 1994 Constitution, which declares the constitution to be established in order to 'form a national union, guarantee justice, secure domestic peace, provide for the common defence, promote the general welfare and secure the blessings of liberty to ourselves, to our posterity, and to all men of the world who wish to dwell on Argentine soil'.[91]

There is much more to be said about what guests should be able to expect, about what can be expected of them, and about different kinds of 'guest'; a few comments must suffice here.

First, as to different kinds of 'guest', it might seem that 'guest' is an inappropriate label for at least many of the non-citizens who are within a polity's territory. Guests are invited; but while that is true of some non-citizen incomers, who might have been invited in to work, or encouraged to visit as tourists, others request, and are allowed, entry, or enter without formal permission.[92] I'll comment on illegal (or non-legal) entrants shortly, but the distinction between invited and allowed incomers seems insignificant in this context: both are formally admitted to the polity's territory, and thus count as (short- or long-term) guests of the polity.

Next, as to what guests should be able to expect, and what can be expected of them, we need not here discuss the general question of what access such guests should have, and on what terms or conditions, to a range of health, welfare, and educational services; or what part they should be able to play in the polity's public deliberations about its governance. All we need say here is that it seems obvious that they should be bound and protected, as citizens are bound and protected, by the polity's criminal law. But why should that be so obvious? A full answer to this question must depend on an account of the proper scope of criminal law, but an initial sketch can be given here.

[88] See e.g. Zedner, 'Is the Criminal Law only for Citizens?', at 46–7. For an interesting and useful discussion of some of the issues concerning the position of 'non-resident aliens', see A Walen, 'Constitutional Rights For Nonresident Aliens: A Doctrinal And Normative Argument', esp. at 80–98.

[89] See e.g. D Gauthier, 'Levinas and the Politics of Hospitality'; J Derrida, *Of Hospitality*; A Hoogenboom, 'In Search of a Rationale for the EU Citizenship Jurisprudence'; G Brown, 'The Laws of Hospitality, Asylum Seekers and Cosmopolitan Right: A Kantian Response to Jacques Derrida'.

[90] For a useful historical discussion, see G Baker, *Politicizing Ethics in International Relations: Cosmopolitanism as Hospitality*.

[91] English translation available through the International Constitutional Law website, at http://www.servat.unibe.ch/icl/info.html.

[92] Guests are also, of course, free to leave when they like (hence the obvious irony of saying that someone serving a prison term is a 'guest of Her Majesty'); but that dimension of guesthood need not concern us here, since we should be able to assume that a polity's guests are free to leave.

As to protection, we must remember that the criminal law does not *create* the wrongs that it condemns and punishes.[93] If it did create those wrongs, an emphasis on citizenship would indeed have worrying implications: it would imply that the central or paradigm version of a crime such as murder or rape would be its commission against a citizen, while the murder or rape of a non-citizen would only be counted as a criminal wrong by a kind of extension—as if it was not quite the same, or as serious a, wrong. But the law that defines such *mala in se* as criminal does not create their wrongfulness: rather, its point is to declare that these (pre-existing, pre-legal) wrongs are, when committed within the polity's jurisdiction, wrongs for which their perpetrators are liable to be called to answer by the polity through its criminal courts. The wrong committed by one who criminally attacks a visitor or a guest is just the same wrong—of murder, or rape, or assault—as it is if the victim is a citizen; what makes it the business of this polity's criminal law is that it is committed within the polity's territory—within its civic home. If we invite or allow someone into our home, any wrongs committed against them while they are there become our business: not because only then should we recognize them as wrongs (we do not deny that they are wrongs when committed elsewhere), but because only then are they our business as hosts. The location of the wrong, as being committed within the polity, bears not on its character as a wrong, but on whether the polity has the standing to define it as a wrong that is 'our' business, and to call its perpetrator to public account. Its location is a condition, rather than part of the object, of criminal liability:[94] what the perpetrator of an assault in England is tried and convicted for is not 'assaulting *V* in England', as if the location of the assault was part of the wrong; but 'assaulting *V*', given that (on condition that) the assault was committed in England.

Criminal wrongs committed within the polity are indeed its business, and our business as its citizens, whether they are committed by a citizen or by a non-citizen, which brings us to the way in which guests are bound, as well as protected, by the polity's criminal law: criminal wrongs they commit within the polity's territory would have been wrongs wherever they were committed;[95] they become our business, as wrongs whose perpetrators it is our right and responsibility to call to account, because they are committed within our civic home. It does not matter whether they are committed against a citizen, or against another visitor: the wrong is the same in either case; only jurisdiction depends on where it is committed. However, there are some complications here to do with the precise nature of the wrong committed by a visitor. Suppose that a visitor acts in a way that is in accordance with his own values, and is consistent with the criminal law of his own country, but that he knows is defined as criminal in this polity:[96] what should the criminal law, and the citizens, of this polity say to him?

(I put the question here as that of what 'we' should say to the visitor who commits a crime in our polity. This might seem infelicitous, as suggesting that 'we', readers of this book, are always the insiders who belong, and who wonder what to do with a problematic visitor—whereas we of course might be the visitors, wondering how to deal with, and how we will be dealt with by, the insiders. This is certainly a danger, to

[93] See at n. 82 above, and Chapter 1, section 2.

[94] On the distinction between objects and conditions, see Duff, *Answering for Crime*, ch. 4.3.

[95] This is true, at least, of straightforward *mala in se*, whose wrongfulness is (supposedly) pre-legal, but it is less obviously true of *mala prohibita* which presuppose a local regulation: see at n. 97 below.

[96] I assume knowledge of the law here to avoid entanglement with issues about ignorance of law (see D N Husak, *Ignorance of Law: A Philosophical Analysis*): but insofar as knowledge of the polity's laws is like knowledge of local conventions, a visitor's not unreasonable ignorance of the local law should be accepted as an excuse.

which philosophers who talk confidently about what 'we' should do or say are often insufficiently alert; but it is quite hard to avoid in this context, without convoluted circumlocutions.)

Sometimes, what is appropriate is a 'When in Rome' argument. We do not ask the visitor to sign on, as it were, to our laws or to the values they embody; we do not claim that he ought to recognize that his conduct was wrongful independently of our laws; all we say is that whilst he is our guest he should for that reason respect our local rules and obey them. This point applies most straightforwardly to *mala prohibita*: offences consisting in the breach of a local rule that is itself a matter of convention, when the wrong—whether committed by a citizen or by a visitor—is the breach of a justified local regulation.[97] But it also applies in a different way to cases in which we should recognize that there might be reasonable disagreement, or reasonable differences between different cultures (especially given different cultural backgrounds that may alter the meanings of actions), about values that inform our criminal law—for instance, about what counts as offensive conduct, or as dishonesty. We should sometimes recognize that a visitor does indeed care about dealing honestly with those with whom she is doing business, or about not engaging in publicly offensive behaviour; but that she comes from a culture with quite different understandings of what counts as honest dealing, or as offensive conduct—and that we should not condemn those understandings as unreasonable. We can still say to her that she ought to obey this polity's laws, and prosecute her for committing a criminal wrong if she does not. The wrong for which we now convict and censure her, however, is not the substantive wrong that the law claims to define (for which a citizen who commits that crime might be censured), but the wrong of failing to respect local conventions as she should. As we will see in section 4, although the substantive criminal law of a well-functioning polity does not paradigmatically seek obedience from its citizens,[98] citizens can have a duty to obey laws with whose content they reasonably disagree; visitors too ought to obey the local laws even when they do not share the normative conceptions that underpin those laws.

In other cases, however, the law (and we) should speak more robustly about the substantive wrong that the visitor has committed. If a wife-beater or 'honour' killer is visiting from a country where such conduct is morally and legally sanctioned, we should not say to him that he should respect our local conventions and obey our local laws whilst he is here; we should rather say that his conduct constitutes a public wrong for which we will call him to account if he commits it in our country. We do not call him to public legal account for that conduct if he commits it outside the ambit of our criminal law, since wife-beating or 'honour' killing committed abroad is not the business of our courts, and is not a crime under our law: but it is important to be clear that in saying that he is not, on that basis, guilty of a crime under our law, we are not saying that what he does is not wrong. Our law is silent on wife-beating committed abroad, not because it declares such conduct to be permissible, but because such conduct is not its business: the collective voice in which our law claims to speak, the voice of the citizens of the polity, is not a relativist voice that portrays the wrongness of wife-beating as conditional on local cultural norms; but it is a voice that recognizes the limits of its

[97] Even then, we might say that the reason why a visitor should obey the local regulation has to do with the respect they should have for local conventions, whereas the reason why citizens ought to obey has more to do with the concern they should have for the aspect of their common good that the regulation is intended to serve.

[98] And see above, Chapter 1 at nn 50–1. This of course leaves open the possibility that both citizens and visitors might act justifiably in disobeying an unjust law; in neither case should obedience be blind.

authority. What makes wife-beating a crime here but not abroad is not that it is wrong because, or only when, it is committed here, but that only then is it the business of our courts and of the law that they apply. As moral agents, we can comment on the morality of such conduct wherever it is committed: but what gives us the standing to pass legal judgment on it as criminal is that is committed within our polity.

Some difficult questions about the ways or the sense in which the moral character of actions may be 'relative' lurk in the background here,[99] and can complicate the task of deciding which of the two responses sketched above will be appropriate; but we cannot pursue these questions here. The criminal law's voice is not a relativist voice: it speaks of what is wrong, not of what is taken to be wrong within a particular perspective or framework; it condemns the conduct even of those who do not share the values it expresses (the 'honour' killer, the wife-beater). That is consistent with a recognition that there can be reasonable disagreements and reasonable differences within and between cultures—which is why a 'When in Rome' response to a visitor can be appropriate. All I have claimed here is that such a response is not always appropriate—that sometimes we, as the citizens whose law this is, should insist that the conduct that our law defines as criminal is wrong in a way that should be recognized as such by both citizens and visitors; I have not tried, and will not try here, to determine just when this is the more appropriate response.

My suggestions in the previous three paragraphs might seem inhospitable: if we are going to invite or allow guests into our civic home, surely we should be willing to make some allowances for their different cultural backgrounds—especially since some of those guests will have entered not as short- or long-term visitors who could just as easily have stayed at home, but as refugees or asylum seekers who had no safe home in which to stay. Part of the answer to this worry will be provided in the following chapter, when we discuss the nature of the political community into which visitors are invited, and the extent to which it can and should make room for cultural and normative diversity;[100] this will also cover refugees and asylum seekers insofar as what they seek is a home.[101] The other part of the answer lies in the discretion that both officials and lay citizens should exercise in applying the criminal law:[102] even when a visitor has committed what the law justifiably defines as a criminal, public wrong, it might be appropriate to regard that commission as 'understandable', and non-culpable—and so not to treat it as a prosecution-warranting crime (much will depend, of course, on the nature of the crime committed).

There is at least one other important difference between citizens and non-citizens when they commit crimes: non-citizens, unlike citizens, can be deported following conviction for a criminal offence.[103] In the case of short-term visitors, especially tourists, this might be reasonable: when a visitor misbehaves (badly) the host can properly ask him to leave, and push him out if he refuses (unless, of course, being forced to leave would expose him to serious harm). But such measures are also applied to long-term residents who have made their home in the polity without becoming citizens,[104] and we must ask how this could be justified. One answer might be the one suggested above: that those who have made their home in the polity should be treated as citizens, and thus should not be liable to deportation. Another answer is that if we are to

[99] For a useful survey of the relevant debates, see C Gowans, 'Moral Relativism'.

[100] See below, Chapter 4, section 6, Chapter 5, section 3.

[101] See at n. 86 above.

[102] See above, Chapter 1 at nn 156–82.

[103] For the provisions in English law, see Immigration Act 1971, s. 3(5)–(6).

[104] See n. 86 above.

consider deporting those who have homes elsewhere because they have been convicted of a criminal offence, that measure must be justified as part of their punishment. At present, it counts formally as an administrative measure separate from their punishment, but this seems unjustified: they are being expelled from the polity because they have committed a crime; how can that be justified other than as part of their punishment for that crime? If it is seen as a punishment, however, we must ask whether it is proportionate to the seriousness of the crime committed; and the answer must often be that it is not—in which case it is unjustified.[105]

I have not so far talked about the position of those who enter a polity illegally or non-legally. This leads into a complex set of issues, collected now under the label 'crimmigration'—the ways in which immigration law and criminal law have become intertwined to (as critics argue) the normative detriment of each mode of law.[106] Suppose that we have good reason not to operate with an 'open borders' policy: that a polity is entitled to set some conditions even on temporary entry, and to keep some people out.[107] Those who enter, having either been refused entry or not sought it, cannot count as 'guests', except in the sense that a trespasser is an 'unwelcome guest'; so does the account that I have sketched imply that they are not protected (and also not bound) by the criminal law of the polity into which they trespass? They are certainly still bound by it: they have entered the polity's home, and thereby subject themselves (like it or not) to its law.[108] They are also protected by it, because (as noted above) the nature and wrongness of the wrongs with which criminal law has to deal do not depend on the national identity or location of their victims; and because it is still our business to deal with, to respond to, such wrongs when they are committed in our territory. We are entitled to expel (i.e. to deport) such intruders (*if* we were entitled to deny them entry in the first place), unless that would expose them to the danger of serious harm; but whilst they are in the country they are fully entitled to the law's protection.

We might distinguish two kinds of unlawful entrant—trespassers and burglars. The trespasser simply seeks entry, and gains it unlawfully (i.e. without trying to obtain, or having failed to obtain, the necessary permission). The burglar, by contrast, gains unlawful entry with the intention of committing criminal wrongs within the polity:[109] obvious examples include those engaged in an 'ordinary' criminal enterprise, and those engaged in terrorist activity aimed against the polity. It is of course unlikely that the burglar will declare his criminal intentions as he enters or as soon as he is detected, but if some relevant conduct in execution of those intentions can be proved, he is liable to conviction for a relevant offence under the polity's laws: perhaps not for a criminal attempt, if his enterprise is in its early stages, but for a preparatory offence. However, his status is otherwise the same as that of any other trespasser.[110]

[105] See further Z Hoskins, *Beyond Punishment? A Normative Account of Collateral Restrictions on Offenders*, chs 2, 6; see also *Padilla v Kentucky* 559 US 356 (2010).

[106] See e.g. Stumpf, 'The Crimmigration Crisis'; D Sklansky, 'Crime, Immigration and Ad Hoc Instrumentalism'; A McLeod, 'The US Criminal-Immigration Convergence and Its Possible Undoing'.

[107] I do not assume that this supposition is uncontroversial: see S Benhabib, *The Rights of Others. Aliens, Citizens and Residents*; A Spena, 'A Just Criminalization of Irregular Immigration: Is It Possible?'; D Miller, *Strangers in our Midst: The Political Philosophy of Immigration*.

[108] This leaves open the question of how and in what ways a polity can legitimately criminalize unlawful entry, or conduct associated with it: see Spena, 'A Just Criminalization?', and 'Iniuria Migrandi: Criminalization of Immigrants and the Basic Principles of the Criminal Law'; A J Ashworth and L Zedner, *Preventive Justice*, ch. 10; A Aliverti, 'The Wrongs of Unlawful Immigration'.

[109] Compare Theft Act 1968, s. 9: 'A person is guilty of burglary if ... he enters any building or part of a building as a trespasser and with intent to commit' any of a specified set of offences therein.

[110] But see further at n. 170 below on the status of terrorists who define themselves as enemies of the polity.

I have been talking so far about non-citizens who find themselves in a polity's territory, and may find themselves at odds with its criminal laws, and with the values that those laws express. But citizens can also find themselves at odds with (what purports to be) 'their' criminal law, and with (what purport to be) the values of 'their' polity—perhaps so seriously at odds that they deny that it is their law: how should the law address them?

4. Dissenters and Recusants

There are two problems concerning dissent and disagreement in relation to the criminal law, only one of which is addressed in this chapter. One problem is whether we can, in contemporary societies that are characterized by deep-seated cultural and normative differences, identify such a thing as 'the polity' whose shared values its criminal law could aspire to express: I will discuss this problem in more detail in the following chapter.[111] The second problem, which is the focus of this section, arises if the first problem can be solved. Suppose, for the time being, that a polity is possible: that we can identify a set of public values that are sufficiently shared by the polity's members and recognized by them as 'our' values; and that the polity can therefore operate with a system of criminal law grounded in and expressing those values. Suppose too that it is a tolerably just polity, whose laws have a legitimate claim on its citizens' allegiance; that, in particular, its criminal laws are tolerably just, in their substance, their procedures, and their consequences (we are now in the realms of imagination, but I hope not of fantasy): what the law defines as criminal is indeed wrongful in the appropriate way; the criminal trial, and all other aspects of the criminal process, treat all those subjected to them justly; and the punishments imposed on those who are justly convicted are themselves proportionate and civilized. Suppose, finally, that part of what makes the substantive criminal law legitimate and just is the modesty of its scope: in particular that it implicitly recognizes the existence of reasonable normative disagreement among citizens on a range of issues and, as far as possible, avoids defining as criminal kinds of conduct about whose wrongful or public character there is reasonable disagreement. Nonetheless, the criminal law of such a polity will in all probability sometimes have to take a controversial moral stand. It must, for instance, declare either that all forms of euthanasia are criminal, or that some are not: it will in either case be at odds with the deeply held beliefs of some citizens, either by declaring to be wrongful conduct that they believe should be permitted, or by not defining as a public wrong conduct that they believe to be deeply wrong—for reasons given which it is a public wrong if it is wrong at all. So too, to take a less dramatic example, with fox hunting:[112] the law must either define it as a public wrong, as against the views of those who regard it as at least permissible, and perhaps even as a public good; or (if only through silence) imply that it does not constitute a public wrong, as against the views of those who argue that it involves a maltreatment of animals that should be seen as a public wrong.[113]

More generally, the criminal law of even a tolerably just polity will not be able to assume a complete normative consensus, as to its content and its procedures, among the

[111] See below, Chapter 4, section 5.

[112] See Hunting Act 2004, criminalizing (most) hunting of mammals with dogs.

[113] On some of the problems that normative dissent and difference create for liberal criminal law, see N Lacey, 'Community, Culture, and Criminalization'; Edwards and Simester, 'What's Public About Crime?', 118–21.

citizens whom it claims to bind. Some citizens might reject the authority of the polity and its governing structures altogether, on the basis either of anarchist objections to all political authority, or of a principled critique of this particular polity: they might therefore reject the authority of the criminal court in which they are brought to trial; they are not, they argue, answerable in or to this tribunal. Others might object to the substantive content of the criminal law, arguing either that the conduct that is criminalized is not wrong at all, or that it is not a public matter: someone who objects to the law that criminalizes his consensual sado-masochistic activities might argue either that such conduct is not wrongful (thus implicitly admitting that it could be the law's business); or that, whether or not it is wrong (a question he claims is irrelevant here), it is a private matter that is not the law's business.[114] What can the criminal law say, what can those citizens who accept the law say, to such dissenters? (It might be tempting to say that the question here is about what 'we' should say to such dissenters; but that would beg important questions about the identity and scope of that 'we'. To put the question in this way implies that 'we' are those whose values the law expresses, confronted by a 'they' who dissent; but of course 'we' could be the dissenters. We will do better to ask what the criminal law should say, in what terms, to those who dissent.)

I will not try to engage here in any depth or detail with the radical dissenter who rejects the authority of the polity completely. The law, the polity whose law it is, must be able to say to her that she ought to accept its authority (we will see shortly what that authority involves, in the case of criminal law), and that claim must be grounded in some general account of political authority and obligation. All I will say here is that I would appeal to a conception of 'associative' duties as a basis for the law's authority.[115] Such duties or obligations are not a matter of choice, not even of hypothetical choice of the kind to which contractualists and contractarians appeal. Rather, we find ourselves (whether through birth, or upbringing, or other kinds of chance) in various kinds of association, each with their own normative structure of rights and responsibilities; and though it might (and undoubtedly should) be possible to seek revisions to those structures or to leave the association,[116] while we belong to it we are stuck—stuck with it, stuck with our fellow members (associates), and stuck with the responsibilities assigned to us. That is not to say that we have to accept those responsibilities, since some associations have no justified claim on our allegiance: but allegiance is on this view a matter not of choosing, but of recognizing that I am (or am not) bound by these ties.

We can briefly consider here the people whom Edwards and Simester call 'recusants', who do not see themselves as part, as citizens, of the political community in whose territory they live, although they cannot or will not emigrate.[117] They are not rootless or homeless, but they do not find their associative home in this polity; they would therefore deny that they have the kinds of associative obligation to which I am appealing—not because they deny associative obligations as such (they might recognize many of those, arising from associations with which they do identify themselves), but because they deny or reject their membership of this association. In what terms

[114] See, notoriously, *R v Brown* [1994] 1 AC 212; and see further below, Chapter 4 at nn 93–7.

[115] See e.g. R Dworkin, *Law's Empire*, ch. 6; J Horton, 'In Defense of Associative Political Obligations', *Political Obligation*; D Miller, *National Responsibility and Global Justice*; J Seglow, *Defending Associative Obligations* (also Duff, *Punishment, Communication, and Community*, ch. 2); and see further below, Chapter 5 at nn 13–14.

[116] Compare *Universal Declaration of Human Rights*, art. 15(2): 'No one shall be ... denied the right to change his nationality'.

[117] See Edwards and Simester, 'What's Public About Crime?', 119–20, drawing partly on M Renzo, 'Associative Responsibilities and Political Obligation'.

could the polity and its citizens (those who do see themselves as citizens), and its criminal law, address them?

The polity and its citizens (who can still call themselves the recusants' fellow-citizens) need not take the recusants' denial of membership as dispositive—even if the recusants did not enter the polity voluntarily, and cannot realistically leave it: for it is a feature of associative obligations that they can be non-voluntarily incurred. I might deny that I have any moral responsibility, any duty, to assist a stranger whom I know to be in desperate need, or to help a brother whom I have not seen for thirty years: to which the reply might plausibly be that, whether I recognize it or not, whether I chose it or not, I do have such a responsibility, in virtue simply of the association that binds us together—that she is my fellow human being,[118] that he is my brother. Such claims can be, and are, disputed: but they are not undermined or refuted merely by the fact that those against whom they are made reject them. So too, the recusants' fellow citizens might insist that they do have obligations—civic, political obligations—towards the polity of which they are members, whether they like it or not, and towards their fellow citizens: insisting on such obligations cannot of course by itself make them real, but denying them cannot by itself make them unreal.[119]

The polity's criminal law will then also address recusants as citizens: but that is not to say that it will insist that they must see themselves as citizens. The associative obligations on which their fellow citizens insist are civic, political obligations, a failure to discharge which opens them to civic criticism: but not all civic obligations should be turned into legal obligations, and, as we will see in more detail later,[120] a liberal polity will see very good reason to leave many of them as nothing more than civic obligations. For just one instance, the (self-avowed) citizens of a liberal democracy will presumably recognize a responsibility to play a part in the democratic enterprise of self-governance, including (minimally) a duty to vote in elections; recusants will presumably deny any such responsibility or duty, and will be open to criticism from their fellows for failing to discharge it. But given the important role of individual freedom, and in particular freedom of thought and conscience, in a liberal polity, there is good reason not to create a sanction-backed legal duty to vote: recusants should be able, without legal sanction, to enact their rejection of this association by refraining from voting.

That is not to suggest that recusants should in general be exempt from the criminal law and its authority—any more than guests should be: but what the criminal law demands of them will be nothing more (or less) than it demands of guests—that they refrain from crime, and appear in court, if summoned to do so, when accused of criminal conduct. The recusant is addressed as a citizen, but remains free to see those demands as imposed on her by an alien association, and to respond to them as a guest in the polity, or as an unwilling victim of an oppressive power; she will face no legal sanction for doing so, since she will be in breach of no legal duty in doing so.

We will be able more clearly to understand a recusant's relationship to the criminal law, and the demands that the criminal law can make on her, by turning to the second, less radical, kind of dissent noted above: that of a citizen who does not deny her membership of the polity, or indeed the authority of the polity, but who objects to the substantive content of a particular criminal law (or set of criminal laws).

[118] See e.g. Gaita, *Good and Evil: An Absolute Conception*, ch. 3.

[119] I leave aside here the question of whether a liberal polity should make it possible for citizens to give up their citizenship without emigrating—to remain in the polity's territory as long-term guests.

[120] See at nn 139–47 below.

It might seem that if she is bound, as a matter of her associative obligations, to recognize the law's authority, nothing more needs to be said: that general obligation generates or includes an obligation to obey the law, which must include an obligation to obey the criminal law; even if she disagrees with its content, she ought to obey it.[121] There are two problems with this response. The first is that, as I argued earlier, the substantive criminal law does not consist in prohibitions that we are to *obey*:[122] rather, it claims to identify a set of pre-existing wrongs (kinds of conduct that are wrongful prior to and independently of their criminalization) as 'public' wrongs, whose perpetrators are liable to be called to public account through a criminal process. As we will see shortly, there are contexts in which the criminal law does demand our obedience: but that is not the way in which the substantive criminal law initially addresses us. The second problem is that, even when obedience is at stake, a recognition of authority, including recognition of the law's authority, need not entail an acceptance of an obligation simply to obey—to do *X* just because the authority requires or demands it. If the authoritative person or body is to treat those over whom she or it claims authority as responsible agents (as the criminal law ought to treat its citizens), they must be given reasons to explain and justify the demands that are made, and must be able to critically evaluate those reasons for themselves.[123] So what reasons can be given to the dissenting citizen, who denies that she ought to refrain from some conduct that the law defines as criminal?

The criminal law makes two kinds of claim on us: first that we refrain from conduct that it defines as criminal; and second that we be ready to answer for such conduct in a criminal court if we engage in it. The authority that the criminal law must claim is thus, first, the authority to define those wrongs as public wrongs; and second to call to formal account those who commit such wrongs.[124] I will discuss the second kind of claim shortly. As for the first kind of claim, the reasons that the criminal law must initially offer citizens concern the wrongness of the conduct in question: we ought to refrain from murder, rape, theft, and so on, not because the law prohibits such conduct (not 'because the law says so'), but because such conduct is wrong; to which the criminal law adds, in defining such conduct as criminal, that perpetrators are liable to be called to public account for it through the criminal process. This is true not only of such '*mala in se*' as murder and rape, which are wrongful prior to their legal regulation, but also of '*mala prohibita*', which involve conduct that is not wrongful prior to its legal regulation. As we saw earlier, such offences still consist in conduct that is supposedly wrongful prior to its *criminalization*:[125] it is wrong as breaching a legal regulation that citizens ought to obey; and whilst it is thus wrongful only because it is prohibited by the law, the law that prohibits it is not the criminal law.

121 Because, some would say, the law's authority makes it a source of 'content-independent' reasons for action—for obedience: see T Christiano, 'Authority'; for a useful critical discussion of the idea of content-independent reasons, see P Markwick, 'Law and Content-Independent Reasons'; in response, see N P Adams, 'In Defense of Content-Independence'.

122 See above, Chapter 1, section 3.

123 This is the proper response to philosophical anarchists who argue that to accept a political authority is thereby to surrender one's autonomy (see e.g. R P Wolff, *In Defense of Anarchism*): see W Edmundson, 'The Virtue of Law Abidance'.

124 From that second claim flow further claims to do with enabling the criminal process of calling such wrongdoers to account—claims, for instance, that we assist, or at least not hinder, the police as they investigate crimes; and that we be ready to answer, if necessary as defendants in a criminal court, warranted accusations of criminal wrongdoing, even if we know that we are innocent.

125 See above, Chapter 1 at nn 44–8.

The first, most obvious response to a dissenting citizen will therefore be a robust reminder or reassertion of the public wrongfulness of the conduct in question. If a man argues that husbands have the moral right to beat (or, as he might put it, 'chastise') their wives, and that such conduct should therefore not be criminal, the appropriate reply is to insist that such conduct is a serious wrong—and that he is wrong to deny this.[126] In such cases part of the point of criminal law is to declare authoritatively that this constitutes a public wrong, whose perpetrators will be called to public account. The law might also function as a deterrent, offering prudential reasons for what will then count as obedience to those who are not sufficiently motivated by its moral message, but its primary meaning is still declaratory: it does not claim that husbands ought to refrain from beating their wives out of respect for the law that prohibits such conduct; it rather defines such conduct as a wrong from which they already had conclusive reasons to refrain—reasons that the law presupposes and recognizes rather than creating.

The previous paragraph was in one way misleadingly over-simplified, since the criminal law cannot simply reproduce a pre-legal conception of the relevant wrong: it must provide a formal legal determination of the wrong;[127] and even if there is no dissent about the pre-legal wrongness of, for instance, rape, or wounding, the law's definitions of their scope and content as *criminal* wrongs are likely to diverge from the often ill-defined, vague, or inchoate pre-legal conceptions of them that citizens may have. Sometimes the law's statutory definition will be too broad, for pragmatic reasons, formally criminalizing conduct that legislators do not suppose to be wrong or intend to be prosecuted: in such cases police and prosecutors need to exercise their discretion to ensure that conduct that is not relevantly wrongful is not substantively criminalized.[128] In other cases, the law's definition of the offence will be narrower than the extra-legal conception of the relevant wrong; in yet other cases the difference will rather concern the precise labelling of and distinctions between wrongs—how, for instance, murder should be defined, and distinguished from other types of homicide.[129] I will say a little more about this kind of issue later,[130] but focus for present purposes on the simpler case in which the dissenter denies that the conduct that is criminalized is wrong. This case is simpler, but still not as simple as I have so far implied: sometimes, the robust 'You are wrong' response will not be appropriate.

That response will be less clearly appropriate in cases in which the law should recognize that the dissent is not unreasonable. It must still take a stand, since to remain silent is also to take a stand, and if the stand it takes (through an appropriate process of democratic deliberation) is that the conduct that many regard as a public wrong should not be criminal, what it says to dissenters need only be that, whilst they can disapprove of the conduct socially, and criticize it informally, they should not look to the criminal law to condemn it, or try forcibly to prevent it as they might legitimately try to prevent crime. But what can it say when the stand it takes is to criminalize conduct that the dissenters wrongly but not unreasonably (in the eyes of those whose values it represents) regard as morally permissible? Here perhaps the criminal law does offer us normative reasons for *obeying* its requirements. Rather than simply declaring that the dissenter's

[126] So too, if he argues that whether or not such conduct is wrong, it is a private (or 'domestic') matter into which the law should not interfere, the appropriate answer is that it is a public matter in the sense that it concerns his fellow citizens, who have the standing to call him to answer for it.

[127] See D N MacCormick, 'Reconstruction after Deconstruction: A Response to CLS', 548–9; and below, Chapter 7, section 4, on constructing criminal wrongs.

[128] See above, Chapter 1 at nn 156–82.

[129] On which see e.g. J Horder, *Homicide and the Politics of Law Reform*.

[130] See below, Chapter 7 at nn 98–110.

conduct is an incontrovertible public wrong from which she already had conclusive reason to refrain, and for which she can now be called to public account and censure, the law can speak in the terms in which it is often said that a liberal criminal law should address conscientious dissenters and civil disobedients: 'Until you can secure a change in the law through the democratic political process, you should respect the results of that process, and obey the law it produces even if you disagree with the content of that law'.[131] That, it can be said, is something that the dissenter owes to her fellow citizens as members of a democratic polity. What she now owes, however, is obedience. The claim is not, or not simply, that she already had conclusive reason to refrain from what the law now defines as a crime, since it is recognized that she does not accept that she has any such reason, and that she might not be unreasonable in that denial. The claim is rather that, even if she can see no sufficient pre-criminal reason to refrain, she ought to see the fact that the conduct has been criminalized, through a process of democratic deliberation, as a reason to obey the law that criminalizes it—to refrain from the conduct because it is criminal.[132]

My suggestion that we should distinguish these two ways in which the criminal law can and should speak to dissenters raises three further questions that I cannot pursue in detail here. First, how can we distinguish these two kinds of case? Why should we say, as seems plausible, that the law should speak in the former, unqualified way to a person who sees nothing wrong in beating his wife, or in defending his family's 'honour' by killing the daughter who dates a man from a different race or religion; but in the latter, more nuanced way to someone who argues that certain forms of requested euthanasia are morally justifiable and should be legal, or that fox hunting is a legitimate sport? How can we distinguish 'unreasonable' from 'not unreasonable' views?[133] One possibility might be to try to distinguish cases in which the dissenters can be seen as offering an interpretation of values that are shared as part of the polity's ever-evolving civic morality, from those in which their claims cannot be seen as an interpretation of that morality. Some hunters appeal to a moral conception of our relationships with other animals that takes animal cruelty seriously as a wrong, but portrays hunting as something that need not be cruel and that can be pursued without denying the hunted animal's moral significance. Proponents of some forms of 'voluntary' (or, to be more precise, requested) euthanasia can claim to be interpreting the central value (they might even say the sanctity) of human life. But no such argument can be made by the wife-beater or the 'honour' killer. Such a distinction is normatively laden: it does not provide a normatively neutral basis on which to distinguish the 'reasonable' from the 'unreasonable'. It also presupposes the possibility of identifying a set of values, whose meaning and implications might be contested, but that could be said to be 'our' values

[131] The normative force of this response depends, of course, on the extent to which the current law is the result of a genuinely democratic process, and the extent to which there is a continuing public political process through which dissenters can argue their case and be heard. I leave aside here the question of whether that public political process should include the courtroom itself: whether, that is, a dissenter should be able to argue in court her claim that the law is wrong, and secure an acquittal if she can persuade the court (the judge, the jury) of this—as happens in fact in some cases of 'jury nullification'. See below, Chapter 5 at nn 148–55.

[132] I must therefore qualify the 'Strong Wrongness Constraint' for which I argued in Chapter 2, section 4: the law must declare the criminalized conduct to be wrongful prior to its criminalization, but also declare that even someone who denies that pre-criminal wrongfulness ought to see reason to obey the law—a reason that must be independent of that pre-criminal wrongfulness, and depends on the conduct having been criminalized (see above, Chapter 2 at n. 38).

[133] There is clearly a connection here with the idea of reasonableness as it figures in discussions of 'public reason'; see further below, Chapter 4 at nn 134–5.

as a polity: I will discuss what this involves, and how it can be possible even in societies characterized by deep cultural and normative differences, in the following chapter. But it suggests a possible way of deciding the terms in which the criminal law should address dissenters.

Second, if the law should speak to some dissenters in the terms I have suggested, that should make some difference, if not to the label of the offence for which they are convicted, at least to their sentence: they should be censured now not as wrongdoers who committed an unarguably substantive public wrong, but rather as citizens who have shown a lack of proper respect for the democratic process by committing what they know that their fellow citizens have deemed to be a public wrong, after a process in which their dissenting voices were or could have been heard.

Third, the tones in which I have suggested the criminal law should speak to a reasonable dissenter might seem more appropriate in some cases, such as hunting, than in others, such as euthanasia. It seems legitimate to say to the fox hunter that he should, despite his sincere and not unreasonable belief that hunting should not be criminalized, refrain from it out of respect for the democratically enacted law that criminalized it; but could we honestly say something similar to someone who has come conscientiously to believe that she must provide her terminally ill loved one with the help that he has so earnestly requested to achieve the death that he wants? Can we respect her motives for such an action, and yet tell her that she should refrain out of respect for the criminal law: or should we recognize that respect for the law or the democratic process is not a reason that we could expect to outweigh, to cancel, or to exclude the reasons that motivate her to commit euthanasia? One crucial difference between her and the hunter is that she regards her action not merely as morally permissible, but as something that she must do, so that in saying that she should obey the law we ask her to act against her conscience; but the mismatch between what motivates her to commit euthanasia—the moral significance and depth of that motive—and the reasons we offer her to obey the law is also important. If this is right, perhaps in cases such as this (whatever should count as 'such as this') the criminal law cannot seek respectful obedience: it must either declare the action to be wrong, and its agent wrong to think it right; or provide a 'conscience clause' that allows an agent with conscientious objections to refraining from what the law defines as criminal to avoid conviction for acting in accordance with her conscience.[134]

I have been talking so far about how the criminal law should address a dissenter who argues that her conduct should not be defined as a public wrong, although I have deferred the question of whether she should be able to argue this case in court. But there will be other dissenters who do not seek to argue such a case in court—who will indeed refuse to argue it, or to engage with their trial at all, because they deny that the court has the authority or standing to try them.

As I noted above, one kind of authority that the criminal law claims is the authority to call a citizen to answer to a charge of wrongdoing, to determine through a trial whether she is responsible for the commission of the offence charged, and if she is held responsible, to determine whether (in the light of any defence she offers) she should be held liable for its culpable commission.[135] Although defendants retain a right of silence at their trial, they are still required to attend their trial, and to conduct themselves

[134] See D Lefkowitz, 'Should the Law Convict Those Who Act from Conviction? Reflections on a Demands-of-Conscience Criminal Defense'; also K Brownlee, *Conscience and Conviction: The Case for Civil Disobedience*.

[135] On the criminal trial as a calling to answer, see above, Chapter 1, section 5.

properly in court; they are expected (but are not now forced) to enter a plea:[136] by conforming to such requirements or expectations, the defendant shows her recognition of the court's authority to bring her to trial. But a defendant might, for any of a variety of principled reasons, want to make it clear that she does not accept that authority—that she is not, as she sees it, answerable for this alleged conduct before this court.

Now if we can properly insist that the defendant is bound by the law, we can say that she has a civic duty to accept, to recognize, the court's authority and to play her assigned role in the trial. Indeed, if the law is, as I have suggested it must aspire and claim to be, her law as a citizen, then she has a civic duty to assist its operations: in this context, to assist in the process through which she is called to answer to her fellows. She should be ready to answer to her fellow citizens, since she ought to take seriously her own standing as a responsible member of the polity, and ought to recognize their standing to call her to answer; she ought to be ready to play her part in this civic institution—the criminal trial—through which that answer is to be given. Indeed, we can say not just that she ought to appear for trial, enter a plea, and behave appropriately in court, but also that she ought (as a matter of civic duty) to enter an honest plea, and be ready to give evidence and undergo cross-examination at her trial. By an 'honest plea', I mean that she should plead 'Guilty' if she knows that she is guilty of the crime charged, and 'Not Guilty' if she knows that she is not guilty, or is unsure; but these claims need further explanation.[137]

As to entering honest pleas, it might be true that someone who pleads 'Not Guilty', knowing that he is guilty as charged, is not strictly lying to the court: he could instead, depending on how we should interpret the plea, be claiming merely that he is not *provably* guilty, or challenging the prosecution to prove his guilt. But a civic duty to be ready to answer for our public conduct in a criminal trial involves more than a duty not to lie: it involves a duty to play an active, and honest, role in the process; and that role must encompass admitting, confessing, one's guilt if one knows it—which is to plead 'Guilty'. It also therefore requires a readiness precisely to answer to the charge and for one's conduct, by giving evidence and answering questions.

The correlative duty to plead 'Not Guilty' if one knows that one is not guilty (or is not sure) might look odd: why would someone who knows he is innocent think of pleading 'Guilty'? One answer is that in a system that relies heavily on plea bargaining, and in which insisting on going to trial brings a risk of a much harsher sentence on conviction, it might be prudent for an innocent to accept a plea bargain, rather than face the danger of mistaken conviction.[138] But even without the pressure created by a system of plea bargaining, innocents might find it less burdensome to plead 'Guilty' and accept a modest punishment than to plead 'Not Guilty' and face a full trial (especially if the trial would be public). Even in a decent system of law, going to trial is a costly, burdensome process; a defendant might sometimes regard the cost of a false conviction as lower. Her civic duty is nonetheless, on the account sketched here, to plead 'Not Guilty'. As a citizen, she has a responsibility to assist, or at least not to hinder, the enterprise of criminal law: but that enterprise is perverted rather than served by the conviction of an innocent; in pleading 'Guilty', she would pervert the course of justice. Furthermore, given a conception of the criminal trial as a process through which alleged public wrongdoers are called to answer to their fellow citizens, innocent defendants have a role-related responsibility to appear in court to answer the

[136] See above, Chapter 1 at nn 106–8.

[137] See further R A Duff and S E Marshall, 'Civic Punishment', 40–5.

[138] See above, Chapter 1 at n. 96; also J Bowers, 'Punishing the Innocent'.

charges they face, and their answers should be honest: but a plea of 'Guilty' can only be a purported admission that I committed the crime, and cannot but be a lie if I know that I am not guilty.[139]

It might seem harsh to hold that innocent defendants have a duty to take on the burdens of facing a trial, even when they believe that their own interests would be better served by pleading 'Guilty'. However, first, civic duties can be burdensome. Second, the strength or even existence of such a duty will depend on the decency of the criminal justice system: on whether the burdens of trial are not unreasonable, whether appropriate efforts are made to avoid convicting innocents, whether the punishment that would follow conviction would be civilized. Third, to assert such a duty implies that the defendant has a right to receive the kind of support that she needs if she is to discharge her duty—support that must be provided, most obviously, through the institutions of the criminal law itself, including the provision of effective legal assistance. Finally, to assert a civic duty is not to say that it should be made a legal duty—that a defendant who pleads 'Guilty' knowing that she is innocent should be convicted of an offence (although as I noted above, she arguably commits the offence of perverting the course of justice; and if, for instance, she did it for money, to shield the person she knew to be guilty, a prosecution might be appropriate). This distinction between civic and legal duties is crucial for both guilty and innocent defendants.

Our civic duties or responsibilities belong with a conception of what it is to be a good (or at least not a bad) citizen.[140] Some might be formalized (and thus probably also altered and limited) into legal duties or responsibilities, some of which may be backed by the criminal law, so that failure to discharge them is a criminal offence: thus the civic responsibility to contribute to the financial resources that the polity needs is formalized into a legal duty to pay one's taxes; and a wilful failure to discharge that duty is then defined as a criminal offence. Others, however, are not given the formal force of law: they are nothing more (or less) than aspects of what we hope is a shared understanding of what it is to be a citizen, enforceable only by informal persuasion from our fellow citizens. If we have a civic duty to ϕ, we have reason to impose a legal duty to ϕ, since failure to discharge a civic duty is a public wrong that in principle merits formal public censure; but that reason might not be conclusive—and this is, for present purposes, especially true in the context of the criminal trial.

Defendants have a legal right to plead 'Not Guilty' even when they know they are guilty, in the sense that if they are convicted they cannot then face a further charge of, or extra punishment for, failing to plead 'Guilty'.[141] They have a legal right to refuse to enter a plea, in that although a plea of 'Not Guilty' will then be entered on their behalf,[142] they are neither forced to enter a plea themselves nor punished for not doing so. And they have a legal right to remain silent during the trial (a right not to give evidence, a right not to submit to questioning), in the sense that they will not be compelled to give evidence, or be punished for not doing so: until 1994, in England,

[139] See above, Chapter 1 at n. 115 on the 'Alford plea'.

[140] Compare R Dagger, *Playing Fair: Political Obligation and the Problems of Punishment*, 217, on citizenship as a 'public office'. The substantial existence of such civic responsibilities of course depends on the existence of a genuine political community; see further Chapter 4, section 6 below.

[141] Or should we say that systems which offer a substantial discount for guilty pleas, whether through a process of plea bargaining or through their principles of sentencing, do in effect impose a 'trial penalty', which amounts to an additional punishment for pleading 'Not Guilty' (on trial penalties, and how they can be distinguished from 'waiver rewards', see Lippke, *The Ethics of Plea Bargaining*, chs 1–2)? That is an objection both to our current practices of plea bargaining and to offering substantial discounts for pleading guilty: that it punishes the person who goes to trial.

[142] See Criminal Law Act 1967, s. 6(1)(c).

this was a rather stronger right, in that the court or jury was not supposed to draw adverse inferences from a defendant's silence in court; but since 1994, although it remains true that the defendant is not punishable (for contempt of court) if he refuses to give evidence or to answer questions, 'the court or jury ... may draw such inferences as appear proper' from such refusal.[143] Now on some views such rights as these are part of the fundamental normative structure of the criminal trial, as a process whose function is to protect citizens against the oppressive power of the state. That is not true on the account of the trial sketched in Chapter 1, since a process that calls a citizen to answer to his fellow citizens for his alleged wrongdoing must claim to lay on him a duty to answer—to take part, and to take part honestly, in the trial. But that is, so far, only a civic duty: something that is expected of him as a citizen, given the role played by the institution of the trial in the life of the polity (of his polity). We do then have reason to transform that civic duty (or some version of it) into a legal duty; but we also have familiar reasons not to do so.

Some of those reasons concern the inevitable imbalance of power between state and citizen, and the consequently unequal terms on which the defendant is likely to participate if she does so (or if she feels compelled to do so), but others concern the importance of allowing a dissenter to express her dissent. There is room for argument about whether defendants should be able to offer (should be formally heard if they want to offer) objections to the trial itself, or to the legitimacy of the court as a forum in which they ought to answer—just as there is room for argument about whether a defendant who wants to answer a charge by claiming that the particular law is unjust, or by offering a defence that she knows the law does not formally recognize, should be heard in the court. Minimally, however, and even though a refusal to participate cannot bar the trial, the defendant who rejects the court's authority or the trial's legitimacy should be allowed to express that rejection in a refusal to play any role in her trial. Her fellow citizens might still think, and say of and to her, that she ought to take part—that she is failing in her civic obligations if she refuses to take part (and insist that she is a citizen, who has those obligations, even if she disavows her membership of the polity): but those civic obligations should not be turned into sanction-backed legal obligations; a refusal to participate should not be made into a crime.[144]

We can now return briefly to the case of recusants, who deny their normative membership of the polity in which they live.[145] Their fellow citizens might criticize them for failing to recognize or acknowledge the associative civic obligations that they have as members of the polity whether they like it or not; but many of those obligations will not be legal obligations. The criminal law will still claim authority over them (as of course do other laws), as it does over others within the polity's territory. It does not claim the authority to impose binding prohibitions that make wrong conduct that was not already wrong:[146] but it does claim the authority to define the wrongs that are to count as public wrongs, and to call anyone accused of committing such wrongs to

[143] Criminal Justice and Public Order Act 1994, s. 35. See further R A Duff et al, *The Trial on Trial (3): Towards a Normative Theory of the Criminal Trial*, 208–11.

[144] See further Duff and Marshall, 'Civic Punishment', 39–45.

[145] See at nn 117–21 above.

[146] Though the non- or pre-criminal regulations, breaches of which constitute *mala prohibita*, do claim authority to make conduct wrong by prohibiting it; and whilst the reasons to obey some such regulations might not depend on associative obligations of the kind that the recusant denies, the reasons to obey others will depend on such obligations. We need not, for instance, appeal to associative obligations to explain the duty that anyone, citizen or not, has to obey local traffic regulations, insofar as they serve to safely coordinate the activities of drivers; but we do need to appeal to such obligations to explain why one should obey a summons to serve as a juror.

answer to that accusation. However, although in the eyes of the law, and of the polity, this authority over recusants depends on the associative obligations they have as citizens, the law does not demand (on pain of sanctions) that they accept this authority in those terms: it is still open to them, as far as the criminal law is concerned, to see themselves as (long-term) guests in the polity, or even as non-voluntary 'guests'; they should still be able (without fear of legal sanctions) to enact their denial of membership—for instance by refusing to participate in their trials (if prosecuted), or by declaring that they are obeying the law under protest.[147]

This section has been concerned with the tones and terms in which the criminal law should address the citizens whom it claims to bind, and how, in a decent society, the citizens should respond. It has assumed that even when we are charged with crimes, and prosecuted in a criminal court, we ought to be addressed and treated as citizens, and have responsibilities as citizens to play an appropriate part in the proceedings. However, there is a third problem for an account of criminal law that focuses on citizens as its primary addressees: it concerns the possibility that a law that binds us as citizens can also deprive us of our citizenship if we fail to show it the respect that it demands; or that a polity that sees itself and its members as bound by a criminal law that is 'our' law might exclude from citizenship those who fail to respect that law.

5. Citizens and Enemies?

Citizens can be legally deprived of their citizenship (so long, under human rights conventions, as this does not leave them stateless): thus the English Home Secretary can deprive someone of citizenship if she is 'satisfied that the person has done anything seriously prejudicial to the vital interests of the United Kingdom', unless doing so would render the person stateless.[148] This is, however, a limited provision, especially given that it can be applied only to people who have another polity that they can call their own, so that the loss of this citizenship will not leave them politically homeless. This is an important constraint, to which I will return shortly;[149] for the moment, however, we should look at some of the less complete, sometimes less formal, ways in which people can be deprived of their status as citizens.

Citizenship involves membership of a particular kind of association—a polity. Associations often make membership conditional on good conduct (or the absence of seriously bad conduct), and are often ready to expel members who misbehave, or fail to display the appropriate loyalty towards the association's values and practices. Something like this is also disturbingly true of prevalent attitudes in some contemporary societies towards those who commit crimes—attitudes expressed in such slogans as 'the war on crime', which easily becomes a war on criminals (for wars are fought against enemies, not against fellow citizens), or 'three strikes and you're out'—out from civic society, exiled for ever to the confines of the prison; in the frequent portrayal of serious offenders (or at least, those who commit the kinds of crime that 'we' do not commit) as monsters, or dangerous predators; in the visceral reaction of disgust

[147] Edwards and Simester bring in the figure of the recusant because, they argue, it causes problems for an account of crimes as public wrongs; I will discuss that aspect of their argument later.

[148] British Nationality Act 1981, s. 40; compare the much more limited provisions for natural-born US citizens in the Immigration and Nationality Act (8 USC 1481) § 349, which allows only 'voluntary' renunciation.

[149] See at nn 167–8 below.

displayed by some English politicians to the idea that serving prisoners might be allowed to vote—a paradigm exercise of citizenship.[150] We could also point to the ways in which criminal punishment and its collateral consequences, and more generally the practices of criminal law, serve in effect, if not by design, to deny or undermine the status as fellow citizens of those who are subjected to such measures (perhaps most dramatically, or most dramatically documented, in the United States).[151]

Behind the demonization of some kinds of offender, behind the inhuman treatment to which so many incarcerated offenders are subjected (demonization and treatment that seems to deny not just their civic but their human status) there lies a serious question, which is brought clearly into view by Jakobs' now notorious distinction between a criminal law for citizens (*Bürgerstrafrecht*) and a criminal law for enemies (*Feindstrafrecht*).[152] I do not mean to suggest that Jakobs would favour either modes of punishment such as 'supermax' prisons of the kind that shame some American states, or the haste with which some systems move to treat offenders as enemies: indeed, he insisted that although those who have shown themselves to be 'enemies' are to be 'depersonalized', that depersonalization should be partial and temporary, and it should be possible for 'enemies' to regain their status as 'citizens' given a suitable change of attitude.[153] But his characterization of 'enemies', and of the implications of being recognized as an 'enemy', highlight the questions that exclusions from citizenship raise. Enemies

> cast themselves as enemies and undermine the ability of the criminal law to command authority by carrying themselves in a manner which signals a fundamental lack of motivation to abide by its norms.... [An 'enemy' is] an actor whose behaviour suggests that he has durably deviated from the path of the law and that he can no longer provide a minimal guarantee that he will conduct himself as a law-abiding citizen.[154]

The question then is whether we should (or cannot but) operate with such a conception of the 'enemy', as someone who has in effect excluded himself from citizenship; and, if we should or must do so, what should follow for our understanding and treatment of such enemies.

The answer to the first question might seem obviously and necessarily 'Yes', for a variety of reasons. A polity is one kind of association, and we do not normally think that membership of an association (voluntary or not) must be wholly unconditional. Professions, clubs, unions, all have provisions for the expulsion of members who engage

[150] After the European Court of Human Rights held (*Hirst v UK (No 2)* 74025/01 (2005) ECHR 681) that the UK's blanket ban on voting for all convicted prisoners was a violation of their human rights, the Prime Minister said in Parliament that it made him 'physically ill even to contemplate having to give the vote to anyone who is in prison' (*Hansard* 3 November 2010, col. 921; David Cameron).

[151] For just a few recent documents, see e.g. M Alexander, *The New Jim Crow: Mass Incarceration in the Age of Colorblindness*; H Butler, 'Supermax Prisons: Another Chapter in the Constitutionality of the Incarceration Conundrum'; G Chin, 'The New Civil Death: Rethinking Punishment in the Era of Mass Conviction'; A Lerman and V Weaver, *Arresting Citizenship: The Democratic Consequences of American Crime Control.*

[152] G Jakobs, '*Kriminalisierung im Vorfeld einer Rechtsgutsverletzung*'; '*Bürgerstrafrecht und Feindstrafrecht*'. For useful discussions, see D Ohana, 'Günther Jakobs's *Feindstrafrecht*: A Dispassionate Account', and 'Trust, Distrust, and Reassurance: Diversion and Preventive Orders through the Prism of *Feindstrafrecht*'; C G-J Díez, 'Enemy Combatants Versus Enemy Criminal Law'; Zedner, 'Security, the State, and the Citizen'.

[153] See G Jakobs, *Staatliche Strafe: Bedeutung und Zweck*, 34–46; as reported by Ohana, 'Günther Jakobs's *Feindstrafrecht*', 356.

[154] Ohana, 'Günther Jakobs's *Feindstrafrecht*', 355, citing Jakobs, '*Selbstverständnis der Strafrechtswissenschaft vor den Herausforderungen der Gegenwart (Kommentar)*', 52.

in serious (and persistent) misconduct that is utterly at odds with the association's values and goals: why should polities be different? It is true that, on some views, our membership of more intimately personal kinds of association may be seen (at least in aspiration) as unconditional: 'She is still my daughter/mother/wife', I might think, however badly she has behaved.[155] But polities do not involve that kind of intimacy or that kind of depth. If, for instance, we take a contractualist or contractarian view, it is natural to think that a sufficiently flagrant and persistent violation of the basic terms of the contract must render it void—I can no longer claim to be a party to it or a beneficiary of it. If we instead see the polity in more communitarian terms, it seems natural to say that members can be legitimately expelled from this as from other kinds of community, if they persist in behaving in ways that are radically inconsistent with the community's defining values. Communities can be too quick to expel non-conforming members; but they surely have the right to expel serious and serial violators of their values. Contracts can be drawn in unfair terms; but contractors surely have the right to include clauses specifying kinds of conduct that nullify the contract. We should see citizenship as a right, not a privilege: but many rights can be forfeited;[156] why should the rights of citizenship not be forfeitable? If someone displays, through his persistent criminal conduct, an utter disregard for the polity's values and for his fellow citizens, why should we have to continue to treat him as a fellow citizen—especially if, as Jakobs argues, this threatens the (perceived) authority of the criminal law; and especially if he poses a serious threat of doing further serious harm to others?

So the familiar line of argument goes: but what follows from it? On some accounts, it looks as if such loss of citizenship must be total: the enemy is to be 'depersonalized';[157] the offender is owed no duties of justice; if his crimes are extreme (like those of 'contract killers, war criminals, tyrants, and certain terrorists') he ceases even to be a 'direct moral object' of benevolence.[158] There are resonances here of the ancient doctrine of 'civil death',[159] which in its most extreme form rendered the person an outlaw—someone outside the law's protection, who could be killed or otherwise mistreated with impunity. Blackstone argued, for instance, that since a pirate 'has renounced all the benefits of society and government, and has reduced himself afresh to the savage state of nature, by declaring war against all mankind, all mankind must declare war against him'.[160] The idea of outlawry is still part of the rhetoric of criminal law in some contexts: '[Terrorists] are *hostis humani generis*, enemies of all mankind and as such should be viewed as outlaws. Their acts should be treated as offences against the law of nations and every state can and should [bring] them to justice'.[161]

On other accounts, the loss (or suspension) of citizenship is only partial, and is better described not as a loss of citizenship, but as a suspension of some of the ordinary rights of citizenship (just what rights or claims are lost or suspended, on either radical

[155] Compare Stephen Blackpool's relationship to his wife in Charles Dickens' *Hard Times*.

[156] And some philosophical accounts of criminal punishment and its justification rest precisely on an argument that those who commit crimes thereby forfeit some, if not all, of their civic rights (of their standing as citizens). See e.g. A Goldman, 'Toward a New Theory of Punishment'; C Morris, 'Punishment and Loss of Moral Standing'; also C Wellman, 'The Rights Forfeiture Theory of Punishment'.

[157] See at n. 152 above.

[158] Morris, 'Punishment and Loss of Moral Standing', at 61, 72.

[159] See H Saunders, 'Civil Death—A New Look at an Ancient Doctrine'.

[160] Sir William Blackstone, *Commentaries on the Laws of England*, IV.5.iii, 71.

[161] Dr Peter Tomka, Permanent Representative of the Slovak Republic to the United Nations; statement to the United Nations General Assembly 56th Session, Agenda item No. 166: Measures to eliminate international terrorism (New York, October 2001).

or modest versions of the view, will depend on how we understand citizenship, and the rights of citizenship, in the first place).

Any determinate answer to the question of whether, and to what extent, those who commit crimes should be taken to have forfeited their standing and their rights as citizens must depend on a normative account of political community and of criminal law's role in it—which I have not yet offered. But we can make some progress towards seeing what kinds of answer are possible, with what kinds of implication, by starting at the extreme, and asking what kinds of political (or moral) status, if any, could be seen as inalienable, non-forfeitable. On some accounts the answer seems to be 'None': sufficiently terrible wrongdoing can make someone '*hostis humani generis*', turn him into an 'outlaw'; there are some wrongs that 'demand not only condemnation, but damnation in the full religious meaning of the word—that is, the doer not only puts himself outside the community of men; he also separates himself in a final way from a moral order that transcends the human community'.[162]

We can set against that kind of view the (challenging and demanding) suggestion that

> even such people are owed unconditional respect, meaning, not that they are deserving of esteem, but that they are owed a kind of respect which is not conditional upon what they have done and which cannot be forfeited. Some will say that even the most terrible evil-doers are owed this respect as human beings and that we owe it to them because we are human beings.[163]

I call this view challenging and demanding not because I suppose that it is usually difficult for us to recognize others as our fellow human beings to whom we owe respect (I hope that is not true), but because as an absolute and unconditional demand it is challenging when we contemplate (or, far more arduously, confront) those who perpetrate the most terrible crimes—most obviously, 'crimes against humanity'. It should not be so dramatically challenging in the ordinary context of domestic criminal law, but it is worth noting that the very institutions of international criminal law can be seen as accepting it. Consider the aims of the ICC: 'to put an end to impunity for the perpetrators' of 'the most serious crimes of concern to the international community as a whole', who 'must not go unpunished'.[164] But to prosecute such perpetrators, to bring them to justice, is precisely to treat them as fellow human beings, members of a normative community to which they must answer for what they have done; outlaws, by contrast, are just that—outside the reach and the protection of human law.

What follows from a recognition that those who persistently commit the most serious crimes are still, at the very least, human beings—our fellow human beings?[165] Certainly that they must not be 'depersonalized', or denied any claim on our human 'benevolence';[166] but also surely that they still retain their human rights—one of which, according to the Universal Declaration, is 'the right to a nationality'.[167] This is not the place for a detailed discussion of that right, of what it means or whether it is or should be absolute;[168] my point here is simply that nationality, having a polity to which one

[162] P L Berger, *A Rumour of Angels*, 87.

[163] R Gaita, *Good and Evil: An Absolute Conception*, 2.

[164] Rome Statute of the International Criminal Court, Preamble. For a fuller development of the point here, see R A Duff, 'Can We Punish the Perpetrators of Atrocities?'.

[165] See at n. 46 above. [166] See at nn 153, 158 above.

[167] *Universal Declaration of Human Rights* (http://www.un.org/en/universal-declaration-human-rights/), art. 15.

[168] We should note, however, that according to art. 15(2), 'No one shall be arbitrarily deprived of his nationality', which implies that a non-arbitrary deprivation is possible and could be consistent with human rights: see e.g. the very cautious language used in the Resolution on *Human Rights and Arbitrary Deprivation of Nationality* adopted by the Human Rights Council of the United Nations General Assembly in 2014, esp. paras 12–14, 16–17 (https://documents-dds-ny.un.org/doc/

belongs as a member, is recognized as a crucial human interest. For as social beings, we can find our good only within communities that enable us to understand our lives and pursue recognizable human goals; and in the world we have, political communities (nations) are an essential type of community. Being a national of some polity might not entail being a citizen of that polity; but if citizenship is the core case of full membership, this argues strongly against, even if it does not simply debar, a complete denial of citizenship to offenders, however serious their crimes. We should also note, first, that such offenders remain ours in the sense that we, as their fellow citizens, must retain responsibility for them: we cannot simply exile or deport them, unless another nation that will respect their rights and allow them membership is willing to take them. Second, those serving sentences in our prisons are typically still required to obey our laws, including the criminal law—which implies that they are still seen as members of the polity, who are bound by its laws: were they genuinely outsiders, non-members, the prison regime and the laws that it enforces would be and could claim to be nothing more than exercises of brute power, rather than authority. That might be how they are often (and reasonably) seen and understood by the people on whom they are enforced; but it is not what they should purport to be.

An adequate account of the status that offenders, and those serving sentences, should retain or attain must depend on a political theory of the polity and of membership of a polity. Nothing I have said so far shows that a polity cannot, or indeed that it should not, make full membership as a citizen conditional on the absence of (persistent) criminal behaviour—that it cannot, or should not, exclude at least from full citizenship those who persist in violating its laws. I will argue later that a decent polity will maintain an inclusionary, rather than an exclusionary, attitude towards those who commit even the most serious crimes—that it will address them, prosecute them, and convict and punish them, not as people who have forfeited their civic standing, but as citizens who are being held to account by their fellow citizens:[169] but I have not yet provided the basis for such an argument. I have tried so far to show only that an account of criminal law as the law of a polity *need not* be exclusionary: a polity can take an inclusionary attitude to citizens who violate its laws. Nor will I argue that membership of an inclusionary polity can *never* be lost or forfeited. The most plausible case for such forfeiture might be that of a 'home-grown' terrorist who defines himself as an enemy of the polity by attacking it.[170] We should note, however, that a country's enemies are not thereby outlaws: the avowed terrorist is still bound and protected by law; but by international law and the laws of war (suitably revised to cope with these new kinds of warfare), rather than by domestic criminal law.

Nor have I so far precluded either capital punishment or genuinely lifelong imprisonment as possible punishments for egregious crimes: all I have suggested is that

UNDOC/GEN/G10/127/96/pdf/G1012796.pdf?OpenElement). But even if that is so, the right to a nationality is a powerful one.

[169] Note that to call someone to account for his alleged wrongdoing is also to commit ourselves to attending to any answer he offers, and being ready to answer to him; accountability is reciprocal: see below, Chapter 5 at nn 148–55.

[170] We need not engage here with the debates about how 'terrorism' should be defined (on which see I Primoratz, 'Terrorism'); for present purposes it is enough to say that a terrorist 'engage[s] in violence against [civilians] in order to induce fear or terror in others, with the aim of destabilizing or degrading (or threatening to destabilize or degrade) an existing social order' (S Scheffler, 'Is Terrorism Distinctive?', 5–6). Note, however, that what I say could apply only to avowed terrorists who declare their active commitment to a terrorist cause (or whose commitment has been proved)—not to those who are only suspected or accused of involvement in terrorism.

if these are to be justified as punishments, they must be shown to be consistent with recognition of the person as a fellow member of the polity. I would indeed argue that, while someone who committed a terrible crime *could* accept or even seek his own death as a way of making moral reparation to (and thus of reconciling himself with) his fellow citizens, that is not something that we could ever justifiably impose on him,[171] and that we cannot justify sentences of 'life without possibility of parole'—LWOPs: even if presumptively lifelong sentences could be justified in certain extreme cases, the offender must be given the prospect of a way back, by persuading a court or a panel that he is fit to return to ordinary life.[172] This was recognized by Jakobs, when he argued that those who had defined themselves as 'enemies' must be given a chance to regain their status as citizens. It was recognized by Lord Judge CJ in the English House of Lords (now the Supreme Court). A sentence of 'Imprisonment for Public Protection', he insisted, 'does not require the abandonment of all hope for offenders on whom it is imposed. They are not consigned to penal oblivion. To the contrary, common humanity, if nothing else, must allow for the possibility of rehabilitation.'[173]

Such claims, however, go beyond anything I have argued so far. The most I can say so far is that in thinking about how we may punish offenders, we should begin by seeing them as citizens; ask how far what we impose on them or require of them could be consistent with that civic status—for instance, whether we can treat those serving prison terms as citizens in prison (rather than as people excluded from citizenship during their sentences); and then ask whether there are ways in which their citizenship might justifiably be qualified or suspended in light of their crimes.[174]

The last of these points might suggest that it is a mistake to treat 'citizenship', as I have been implicitly treating it, as a unitary, all or nothing, matter—as if one is either fully a citizen, or not a citizen: for surely citizenship is better seen as a package of rights and responsibilities, some of which can be removed or suspended without thereby making the person a non-citizen. That might, however, be a dangerous way to put the point, since it might encourage us to see some or all offenders as less than full citizens (which is not far from seeing them as second-class citizens). It would perhaps be better to insist (although this will need more normative argument than I have yet offered) that offenders remain full citizens, and ask what burdens or deprivations can properly be imposed on them, or required of them, consistently with still recognizing their citizenship; but I will be able to develop this argument only after saying much more about the kind of political theory of the polity and its members on which I will be relying.

That is the task to which I will turn in the following chapters. I should first, however, note one substantial objection to the analogy I have been relying on between the criminal law and professional codes of ethics.

171 See Duff, *Punishment, Communication, and Community*, 152–5.

172 On LWOPs, see C Ogletree and A Sarat (eds), *Life without Parole: America's New Death Penalty?*.

173 *R (on the application of Wells) v Parole Board for England and Wales* [2010] 1 AC 553, para. 105; see the European Court of Human Rights decision on the case, *James v UK* (2013) 56 EHRR 12. For Jakobs, see at n. 153 above.

174 See further Duff and Marshall, 'Civic Punishment'. The right to vote is clearly of symbolic importance here: see at n. 150 above. See M Tripkovic, *Punishment And Citizenship: A Theory Of Criminal Disenfranchisement*; also, for a nuanced argument that imprisonment should bring the loss of the right to vote (and that we should therefore drastically reduce the use of imprisonment as a punishment), P Ramsay, 'A Democratic Theory of Imprisonment'.

6. From Citizens to the Civic Realm

This chapter has been concerned with the question 'As what and to whom are we answerable under the criminal law?'. Someone who appears before a Medical Practitioners Tribunal appears as a doctor who is called to answer to her profession—to her fellow doctors (as well as to a wider audience of actual or potential patients). Someone who appears before a university disciplinary panel is called to answer as an academic (a professor, or researcher, or student) to her academic fellows. Someone who appears as a defendant in a criminal trial, I have argued in this chapter, is being called to answer (paradigmatically) as a citizen, to her fellow citizens. But *for what* is she being called to answer?

The charge is, as I argued in Chapter 1, a charge of wrongdoing, which is also true of the doctor or the academic; but what kind of wrongdoing? The formal answer is that in the case of doctors or academics the charge must be one of professional misconduct: a doctor must be accused of misconduct in his practice of medicine, a professor of misconduct in her academic activities. As we saw in Chapter 2, there is plenty of room for controversy about what falls within these categories; but at least we know what question we are asking when we ask what should fall within the remit of a Medical Practitioners Tribunal or of a university's disciplinary panel. We also know how to set about providing more determinate answers: we must begin with some account of the relevant practice (of medicine, of a university); we can then identify what counts as professional conduct and professional misconduct. But how can we begin to answer this question for the criminal law? Can we identify a practice of whose aims and purposes we could try to give an account, as we can for medicine or for a university?

It might seem that the analogy I have suggested between the criminal law and such practices as medical or university ethics codes and tribunals falls down here: indeed, that I have committed the kind of category mistake of which Aristotle can be rightly accused when he argues that there must be a distinctive human '*ergon*' ('characteristic activity')—

> Well, do the carpenter and the tanner have characteristic activities and actions, and a human being none? Has nature left him without a characteristic activity to perform? Or, as there seem to be characteristic activities of the eye, the hand, the foot, and generally of each part of the body, should one assume that a human being has some characteristic activity over and above all these?[175]

Aristotle can be accused of begging the question about whether there is some distinctive human good, determined by a distinctive activity which stands to 'human being' as 'carpentry' stands to 'carpenter' or 'seeing' stands to 'eye'. So too, I might be accused of begging a question in favour of the kind of answer I want, by assuming that there must be some distinctive kind of practice or activity that stands to criminal law as medicine stands to medical ethics: why should we assume anything like this?[176] Should we not rather say that whereas codes of medical or academic ethics govern particular practices (each having its own distinctive goals and goods), which constitute distinct and limited aspects of human life, criminal law has no such limited sphere of operation, and no such distinctive, substantive ends?

[175] Aristotle, *Nicomachean Ethics*, I.7, 1097b.
[176] And see Edwards and Simester, 'What's Public About Crime?', 130.

The criminal law, such a critic might argue, can be seen as helping to provide or sustain the conditions under which such particular practices as medicine and academic research and teaching can be pursued; it can be seen, more generally, as helping to provide or sustain the conditions under which a human social life can be lived at all. But it cannot plausibly be seen as belonging itself to a practice that has a distinctive set of substantive goals and goods: it rather functions to provide a necessary underpinning for such practices.[177] If we think of a theocracy, in which the entire life of the polity is understood as being directed towards the glory of a god, and guided by his divine commands, we could see the polity itself as a practice oriented towards a distinctive set of substantive goals and goods; but one key difference between a theocracy and any kind of liberal polity is precisely that a liberal polity eschews any such enforced unity of aims.

This chapter, and the two following chapters, constitute an extended response to this kind of objection: they aim to show that we can develop a plausible and attractive conception of political community, and in particular of a liberal republican community of free and equal citizens, within which criminal law (as the kind of institution described in Chapter 1) can play a role analogous to that played by professional codes of ethics. That role will be normatively more substantive, and more ambitious, than that of 'a generically coercive rule-enforcing institution', since the criminal law will, on this account, help to constitute as well as to sustain what we can call the 'civil order' of the polity as a distinctive kind of practice; my aim will be to persuade readers that we should, as a matter of idealizing normative theory, understand criminal law in these more ambitious terms.

As a first step towards that goal, I have argued in this chapter that we should see ourselves as being paradigmatically bound by the criminal law as citizens, and answerable under the criminal law to our fellow citizens, which is also to say that we are bound and answerable as members of a particular kind of community—a political community. That suggestion generates some of the questions that this chapter has addressed: how members of a political community can or should relate to non-members; how a polity can address members who dissent from its ruling values or practices; whether a polity can properly expel or exclude members who flout those values. But if we are to answer such questions, we must examine the nature of such a community more closely: what kind of community can political community be; in what kind of political community could criminal law address, and be heard by, the citizens in the ways described in this chapter? We can already say that although a political community *might* claim to be all-encompassing, so that no aspect of its members' lives falls outside its scope or its jurisdiction,[178] polities (and in particular liberal polities) are typically more modest in their claimed scope: just as they claim jurisdiction only over a limited territory and a limited range of people, so they claim jurisdiction only over limited dimensions of their members' lives—which is why the distinctions between the 'public' and the 'private' are crucial for liberal polities and their citizens. Neither medical nor academic communities (however we identify them) claim to be all-embracing or all-encompassing: they claim only a limited range of people as their members, and as being bound by their codes;

[177] See e.g. V Chiao, 'What is the Criminal Law For?' on criminal law as 'a generically coercive rule-enforcing institution' that 'contributes to making social cooperation under the rule of law possible'; above, Chapter 1 at n. 6.

[178] Which is one way to understand totalitarianism—in terms of 'the erasure of the difference between public and private life' (T Snyder, *On Tyranny: Twenty Lessons from the Twentieth Century*, 88, on Hannah Arendt).

and they claim to encompass, to make their business, only limited dimensions of the lives of those members—those dimensions that are implicated in the shared practice, the shared activities and concerns, by which the professional community is defined. The same is true, I will argue, of a political community, whose criminal law can then be seen as a code of civic ethics.

That is what I will try to show in the following chapters: for any political community (and we will need to attend to the conditions of existence for such a community), we will be able to identify its civic realm—its *res publica* as a polity; we will be able to discern the civil order by which that civic realm is structured; and we will be able then to see its criminal law as helping both to constitute and to sustain that civil order.

4

Civil Order and the Public Realm

1. Public Wrongs and the Public Realm

I argued in Chapter 2, in response to Moore's expansive version of legal moralism, that we should see the criminal law as being concerned not with moral wrongs as such, but with, and only with, 'public' wrongs.[1] The challenge then is to explain the distinction between 'public' and 'private' wrongs, and to show how it can help us in thinking about the proper scope of the criminal law—in the end, in our deliberations about what kinds of conduct we have good reason to criminalize. Moore objects that appeals to the idea of public wrongs fail to provide any substantive 'criterion for the public/private distinction' as 'a distinction that is supposed to mark the proper limits of criminal legislation',[2] and I agreed that the concept of public wrongs cannot serve this role, since it is a formal rather than a substantive concept. In particular, we cannot plausibly maintain that a wrong counts as 'public' if and only if it has some materially harmful impact on 'the public', as distinct from an individual victim: if I murder my aged great-aunt, who lives with me, my action must count as a criminalizable wrong on any plausible account of criminal law, and therefore as a public wrong on the view I am defending, whether or not it has any harmful effects beyond my house. Following Blackstone, we might say that crimes 'strike at the very being of society, which cannot possibly subsist, where actions of [that] sort are suffered to escape with impunity':[3] but this should not be taken to mean that 'the very being of society' will inevitably be undermined *as a consequence* either of the mere commission of such crimes, or of their unpunished commission. There is, we will see, a close relationship between the 'subsistence' of a polity and the effective criminalization of (the denial of 'impunity' for) certain kinds of wrong: but that relationship is internal, not causal or consequential, and the threat to subsistence is an implication of the failure to criminalize what we should criminalize, rather than an independently identifiable ground for criminalization. To say that a wrong is 'public' is not to specify some inherent characteristic, or consequential effect, of the wrong, in virtue of which we have reason to criminalize it: rather, it is to locate the wrong in the 'public' sphere or realm—in a particular normative space within which the question of criminalization can then arise; being 'public' is a feature not of the wrong itself, but of its normative location.

That is why I suggested, in Chapter 2, that if we are to understand the idea of public wrongs, or to determine what kinds of wrong should count as public, we must begin not with wrongs (of which we can then ask which are public), but with the public realm: once we have an account of what that realm is, of what kinds of conduct fall within it, we can say that wrongs which fall within that realm are public wrongs. I then illustrated this suggestion by looking at the way in which a profession might come

[1] See above, Chapter 2, section 6.

[2] M S Moore, 'Liberty's Constraints on What Should be Made Criminal', 199; see above, Chapter 2 at n. 94.

[3] Sir William Blackstone, *Commentaries on the Laws of England*, Bk IV, ch. 1, p. 5; see above, Chapter 2 at n. 90.

to draw up a code of professional ethics. It must begin with some conception of its *res publica*, of its distinctive business; this can then generate an account of its public realm—an account, that is, of which aspects of its members' lives and activities are to count as parts of their professional lives and thus as the business of their professional colleagues; professional wrongs, or professional misconduct, which can figure in the profession's code of ethics and be a matter for professional disciplinary measures, will then be wrongs committed within that public realm. So too, I suggested, if we are to identify the kinds of wrong that are to count as public in a political community, we must begin with an account of the *res publica* of that community (or of that particular kind of community). This was also one of the conclusions of Chapter 3. We are bound by and answerable under the criminal law (paradigmatically) as citizens—members of a political community: so if we are to determine the proper scope of the criminal law, we must understand its role in that kind of community, and what could constitute such a community's public realm. A totalitarian political community might claim to encompass every aspect of its members' lives; but a polity will typically be defined in more limited terms, as encompassing only some aspects of its members' lives and activities, analogously to the ways in which professions, and other kinds of community, claim only a limited scope. We therefore need to ask how a polity might define, and how we can identify, its public realm.

This might seem an unpromising approach to identifying a category of 'public' wrongs that are to be in principle criminalizable, since to talk in this way of the 'public' might seem to be to talk of a rather limited sphere of activity. We might think, for instance, of the 'public' life in which we engage when we take part in the polity's 'public' activities, including most obviously political activity; or of the official activities of those engaged in 'public' service, as politicians, or civil servants, or other kinds of official. Now there are criminal wrongs that can be committed in, and sometimes can only be committed in, these kinds of context: there are various kinds of electoral offence,[4] and distinctive offences of 'misconduct in public office';[5] there are also offences that consist in conduct that undermines a polity's public institutions—tax evasion and social security fraud are obvious examples. These form important parts of the criminal law: but it would not be plausible to suggest that wrongs must be 'public' in this sense if they are to be criminalizable, or that the public realm within which wrongs could be criminalizable consists in this kind of 'public' life. We might also think of the public realm as the realm of 'public order'—of public as opposed to private places and spaces, within which conduct can be 'orderly' or 'disorderly'. Here again, we find a plethora of familiar criminal offences: the whole raft of 'public order' offences;[6] offences such as failing to remedy a 'statutory nuisance',[7] and 'public nuisance' (consisting in conduct that 'endanger[s] the life, health, property or comfort of the public, or [obstructs] the public in the exercise or enjoyment of rights common to all Her Majesty's subjects'.[8] Offences like these are also important parts of the criminal law: but they are only part of the criminal law, and it would not be plausible to suggest that they exhaust its proper range.[9]

[4] See e.g. Crown Prosecution Service, *Election Offences*.

[5] See Law Commission, *Reforming Misconduct in Public Office*.

[6] See C Wells and O Quick, *Lacey, Wells and Quick Reconstructing Criminal Law: Text and Materials*, chs 4–7; also D Ormerod and K Laird, *Smith and Hogan's Criminal Law*, ch. 32.

[7] See Environmental Protection Act 1990, ss 79–82, 87–98.

[8] See Archbold, *Criminal Pleading, Evidence and Practice*, para. 31.40; also Law Commission, *Simplification of Criminal Law: Public Nuisance and Outraging Public Decency*.

[9] Also relevant here might be the traditional English idea of 'the king's [or queen's] peace', which Allen thought (optimistically) in 1953 had 'become the People's Peace, the sinews of a healthy social

If the public realm is the realm in which wrongs are public, and therefore at least in principle criminalizable, wrongs, it must be a realm in which such wrongs as murder, rape, assault occur—even when they are committed in a private space: for a system of criminal law must surely count such wrongs as criminal.[10] We therefore need to see whether we can give an account of the idea of the public, or the public realm, which allows us to count murder and rape as 'public' wrongs. The analogy between criminal law and codes of professional ethics, which I suggested in Chapter 2, section 6, implies that we should be able to do so: the public realm of a practice or community is its *res publica*, which can certainly encompass what is done in private places. The fact that a doctor misbehaved towards a patient in the 'privacy' of her home during a home visit, rather than under the public gaze of other patients in a waiting room, cannot negate a charge of professional misconduct: such conduct counts as 'public' in the context of the medical profession, since it occurs within the public realm of medical practice.

How then can we identify the *res publica*, and thus the public realm, of a polity? I will argue in what follows that we can do so by attending to the idea of civil order, as an order that criminal law helps both to constitute and to sustain; but we should first note two other accounts that make the notion of the 'public' central to an understanding of criminal law.

2. Criminal Law as Public Law

Some theorists, notably Malcolm Thorburn and Vincent Chiao, have been developing what they call a 'public law' conception of criminal law and criminal justice.[11]

Thorburn and Chiao resist what they portray as the unduly moralized conceptions of criminal law that they ascribe to theorists such as Moore and me: it should, they insist, be understood as a coercive institution of the state, serving the proper aims of the state—aims that do not essentially include making citizens moral, or responding punitively to their moral wrongdoing. The proper purpose of the state, on Thorburn's account, is to 'put in place a rightful context for our actions', so that we can 'interact with others in a way that is respectful of everyone's freedom'; a context 'within which we can be free and independent persons ... as we live together with others'.[12] That context is constituted by a range of state institutions, and sustained by criminal law as a coercive practice that serves to 'resist any attempt to supplant the law's rules with private preferences'.[13] What the state thus provides, and the criminal law enforces, is a set of jurisdictional provisions, defining what falls within each person's private jurisdiction (as a free and equal moral agent), and what rather falls within the jurisdiction of the state acting in our name and on our behalf. The criminal law is concerned 'with

life' (Sir Carleton Allen, *The Queen's Peace*, 183): but that is closer to the idea of civil order, which I will discuss later in this chapter; the queen's peace is the peace that, in theory, protects us all, in private as well as in public places.

[10] Or does this display a parochial assumption about the necessary scope, or core contents, of the criminal law? We will see later (Chapter 7, section 4) how an independently plausible theory of criminal law makes such wrongs obviously criminalizable.

[11] See M Thorburn, 'Criminal Law as Public Law', 24; V Chiao, 'What is the Criminal Law For?', 138; also Thorburn, 'Constitutionalism and the Limits of the Criminal Law'; 'Punishment and Public Authority'; Chiao, 'Two Conceptions of the Criminal Law', and *Criminal Law in the Age of the Administrative State*. See also S Garvey, 'Was Ellen Wronged?', on a 'political' as against a 'moral' model of criminal law.

[12] 'Constitutionalism and the Limits of the Criminal Law', 88, 97.

[13] 'Constitutionalism', 88.

the protection of jurisdiction, both public and private, rather than with the identification of moral wrongs';[14] what the state should therefore criminalize are 'efforts to undermine the whole system of equal freedom itself',[15] by exceeding one's own jurisdiction and invading that of the state. Chiao's focus is, rather, on the rule of law and the possibility of social life. Criminal law 'supports the possibility of the rule of law—a collective life under stable public institutions—by providing crucial support to shared attitudes of reciprocity'; it does this as 'a coercive rule-enforcing institution providing an assurance of general cooperation with legal rules'.[16] Criminal law might also serve other ends, but that is its 'one important function', which it can serve by threatening and imposing harsh sanctions on those who violate the rules.

There are important differences between Thorburn's and Chiao's views—about the nature of the order that criminal law serves to secure, about the way in which criminal law helps to secure that order, and thus also about the most significant features of the criminal law itself. What their views share, however, is an insistence on setting criminal law in the context of the state, and of the distinctive ends that the state should serve; a rejection of Moore's suggestion that the state should take the punishment of moral wrongdoing as a primary aim—not just because they reject Moore's particular brand of retributivism, but because they deny that the criminal law has any such primary concern with moral wrongdoing; and an argument that there is a distinctive kind of political order (a system of equal freedom as a context in which people can live together as free and equal moral agents; collective life under stable institutions) that the state should maintain and that criminal law can help to sustain. On this view,

> the criminal law is not an autonomous normative universe to be understood and justified in terms drawn from inter-personal morality. It is an integral component of society's basic structure, and should be understood and justified in those terms, regardless of whether it does or does not additionally punish moral wrongdoing as such.[17]

Thorburn and Chiao take Moore, Gardner, and me to be proponents of the kind of 'moralism' that they oppose—a moralism that portrays the criminal law as being concerned with moral wrongs identifiable independently of the law, and as an institution that is to be theorized as if it were independent of other legal institutions, in terms of its distinctive character as a response to such pre-legal wrongs. Moore does espouse that kind of moralism, as we saw in Chapter 2, and in earlier work I have portrayed criminal law in this way. However, I can now say that Thorburn and Chiao are right to insist (as I have been arguing in this book) that we must theorize criminal law as part of the institutional, legal structure of the state—a theorization that belongs to political philosophy rather than to moral philosophy, if we understand 'moral philosophy' as concerned with 'inter-personal morality' rather than with political structures. We must therefore theorize criminal law as part of the institutional structure of a political community: for a state is or should be the institutional mechanism through which a polity governs itself; its institutions must be theorized in terms of their contribution to the polity's existence and its good.[18]

[14] 'Criminal Law as Public Law', 31. [15] 'Constitutionalism', 100.

[16] 'What is the Criminal Law For?', 138, 139.

[17] Chiao, 'What is the Criminal Law For?', 139.

[18] On 'polity' and 'state', see R Dagger, *Playing Fair: Political Obligation and the Problems of Punishment*, Introduction, 9, on 'the body politic' as against 'the agency or agencies that are supposed to serve that body'. Dagger also talks of polity rather than community, because polities 'do not require the shared commitment to a conception of the good or the multi-faceted relationships that define communities, at least on a strict definition of "community"' (ibid., 10): for reasons that will

However, it does not follow from this that the criminal law is not essentially concerned with 'the identification of moral wrongs';[19] nor that its primary purpose could not be to 'punish moral wrongdoing as such',[20] even if 'punish[ing] moral wrongdoing as such' means the punishment of pre-legally identifiable moral wrongs, because they are wrongs—as Moore's retributivist legal moralism holds. We can imagine, even if we cannot admire, a political community that declares one of its foundational aims to be the imposition on culpable moral wrongdoers of the retributive suffering they deserve (not as its only aim, but as an intrinsic good it is committed to pursuing), and that for that reason maintains a distinctive practice of criminal law. Normative theorists of such a polity who advocate this conception of the criminal law will be offering a 'public law' conception of criminal law, which portrays it as part of the institutional structure of the polity, and grounds its aims in the aims of the polity whose law it is. It is not a conception that liberals will share, since they would dissent from any such view of a polity's proper aims: but it justifies criminal law as 'an integral component of society's basic structure', and insists that 'punish[ing] moral wrongdoing as such', far from being something that criminal law might 'additionally' do, is its central purpose. The objection to such a conception of criminal law is not that it mistakenly holds to a 'private right', rather than a 'public law', conception of the criminal law,[21] but that it is grounded in a substantive political theory about the proper aims of the polity that we should, for substantive normative reasons, reject.

Chiao would respond that the framers of a polity's constitution could indeed take retribution to be *a* purpose of criminal law—even 'a basic principle of their society's political morality'; but that the criminal law's 'most basic function' is 'stabilizing cooperation with public institutions', which it does as a 'generically coercive rule-enforcing institution'. That operation has 'functional priority' over other possible aims, such as retribution: the constitution makers could reasonably decide not to take retribution as an aim, but 'could not reasonably choose to pursue retributive justice while foregoing stable and effective public institutions'.[22] Now it is certainly true that we could maintain an institution of retributive punishment only as part of a wider (and stable) institutional structure, whose stability depends on 'an assurance of general cooperation with legal rules'; and that we could secure such an assurance through a 'generically coercive rule-enforcing institution' whose sanctions were not intended or understood as punishments for moral wrongdoing. But we could take the securing of such assurance, by such means, to be the basic or primary function of criminal law only if we should see criminal law simply as a 'generically coercive rule-enforcing institution'. Moore would deny this, since he argues that we should understand criminal law as a 'functional kind' whose function is precisely to inflict on moral wrongdoers the retribution they deserve.[23] I also deny this, since I argued in Chapter 1 that what distinguishes criminal law from other types of legal institution is its focus on moral wrongdoing: it defines a range of public wrongs, and provides the formal process through which those accused of committing such wrongs can be called to public account. On such accounts, even if criminal law also serves to enforce obedience to legal rules, that is

become clearer in this chapter, I will take polities to be, at least in aspiration, communities, though of a limited kind.

[19] Thorburn, 'Criminal Law as Public Law', 31.
[20] Chiao, 'What is the Criminal Law For?', 139.
[21] See Chiao, 'Two Conceptions of the Criminal Law', 19.
[22] 'What is the Criminal Law For?', 146.
[23] Moore, *Placing Blame*, 33–5; see above, Chapter 2 at nn 20–1.

not its distinctive function, since that function could be discharged by other kinds of coercive, sanctioning practice that did not focus on moral wrongdoing. If we then ask why a polity's constitution framers might include such a distinctive institution of criminal law as 'an integral component of society's basic structure', the answer could still, from within a public law conception of criminal law, be that they would or should do so because the attainment of retributive justice should be one of the polity's basic commitments; or that they should do so because the polity should be committed to recognizing, marking, and responding in this way to the kinds of wrong with which the criminal law deals.

I do not intend to defend a Moorean account of criminal law, or of retributive punishment as the primary purpose of criminal law. My point is only that a 'public law' conception of criminal law could still be a legal moralist's conception: even if legal moralists have too often failed to pay sufficient attention to criminal law's public character, as part of the institutional structure of the polity, they can recast their account as 'public legal moralism'. The question then will be whether they can justify their account in the appropriate terms: whether, that is, they can show not merely that it is good that moral wrongdoers be punished, or called to formal public account, or that this conduces to the moral betterment of the world; but that such a practice contributes to the proper aims of a decent polity. That is what I will try to do, for criminal law as portrayed in Chapter 1, in what follows. In doing so, I will also need to address Chiao's argument about the prime importance of securing 'an assurance of general cooperation with legal rules', by showing how criminal law as thus conceived does have a partly preventive, and (re-)assuring, purpose.[24]

Thorburn and Chiao ground their accounts of criminal law in what I will call (for reasons to be explained shortly) conceptions of a polity's civil order; accounts, that is, of a kind of political ordering (a system of equal freedom that enables people to live together as free and equal moral agents; collective life under stable institutions) that constitutes the essential framework of the polity. I will also sketch a conception of civil order, and of the role that criminal law can play in such an order, as partly constituting it and as helping to sustain it; on this conception the primary function of criminal law (as an important aspect of the civil order) is precisely to identify and to provide an appropriate response to certain kinds of moral wrong. Its function is not to identify or respond to 'moral wrongs as such'—to every moral wrong that can be identified and understood independently of the (criminal) law: it is concerned only with moral wrongs that are 'public' in the sense that they implicate the polity's civil order. But it is their moral wrongfulness, as kinds of conduct that should be in this way formally marked and condemned, and whose agents should be called to public account and formally censured, that makes criminal law appropriate to them.

Before I begin to explain this conception of civil order, I should attend to a further point of difference between me and Thorburn and Chiao: that they agree with Moore that criminal law is primarily concerned with punishment. 'Perhaps it goes without saying that the criminal law and its associated institutions ... are institutions that we have set up to punish people', says Chiao.[25] We must, Thorburn argues, 'recognize the

[24] Thorburn initially grounded his argument in a discussion of criminal law justifications ('Justification, Powers and Authority'); more recently (in 'Punishment and Public Authority'), he appeals to a conception of 'robust public authority', an authority both sustained and partly constituted by criminal punishment, analogous to the authority that parents have over their children. I cannot engage directly with his arguments here, but will offer an alternative conception of the polity, of the state, and of the relationship of a democratic polity to its citizens. On Thorburn's account of 'robust public authority', see Eldar, 'Criminal Law, Parental Authority, and the State'.

[25] Chiao, 'What is the Criminal Law For?', 137.

crucial role played by coercive punishment'; and he objects that my account, focused on defining wrongs and calling their perpetrators to account rather than on punishment, 'seems to take as its object an institution that is too different from the modern criminal justice system we know to be anything we could call a theory *of criminal justice*'.[26] It is not worth spending time on the question whether a system that defined a set of public wrongs, and provided a procedure through those who commit such wrongs were called to formal account and subjected to public censure, but that did not impose further punishments on such perpetrators,[27] would count as a system of criminal law;[28] I would just note two points here.

First, any normative theory of criminal law must have something to say about punishment, since it is such a salient, and normatively problematic, dimension of existing systems of criminal law: it must either explain how criminal punishment can be justified, what ends it should serve, and how it can be permissibly allocated and administered; or explain how a polity could, and why it should, operate without criminal punishment. I can indeed provide an account of how a system of criminal punishment (albeit one very different from our own) could be justified—an account that makes substantive criminal law and the criminal trial, as I portrayed them in Chapter 1, basic to its justification.[29] However, secondly, I will argue in what follows that we can provide a plausible role for a practice of 'criminal law' that defines offences and calls to public account those accused of committing them, without yet asking whether it should include a system of punishment, or a coercive system of rule-enforcement. Or (to put essentially the same point the other way round) if we begin with the idea that a polity will need 'a coercive rule-enforcing institution', we must ask why such an institution should take the form of a system of criminal law: a plausible answer (I will argue) will refer to the punishment-independent significance of a substantive criminal law that defines a set of public wrongs, and of a system of criminal trials that call to public account those accused of committing such wrongs; which is also to say that we should not see punishment as the (primary) internal end or purpose of the criminal law.

It is time now to move on to the account that I want to offer of civil order and the role of the criminal law within such an order. It has some resemblance to, and some significant differences from, the accounts that Thorburn and Chiao offer of the kind of political order that the state is to sustain, and of the role of criminal law within that order; but I will not try to identify all those resemblances and differences as my account proceeds.

3. Constituting a Polity's Civil Order

An opposition between a 'public law' conception of criminal law, or of law in general, and a conception of (criminal) law as concerned with 'morality', is not new: it can be found, for just one instance, in Ferguson's account of law in the eighteenth century—

[26] Thorburn, 'Constitutionalism', 96 (see also 'Punishment and Public Authority'); see above, Chapter 1, sections 5 and 6.

[27] Or did not impose the most normatively problematic types of punishment, which impose material burdens on offenders: on material as against symbolic punishments, see R A Duff, *Trials and Punishments*, 148–9, 240–2.

[28] Or, for that matter, on the question whether a 'coercive rule-enforcing institution' (Chiao, 'What is the Criminal Law For?', 139; see at n. 16 above) would as such constitute a system of criminal law, as distinct from a non-criminal system of regulatory enforcement. See above, Chapter 1 at n. 6.

[29] See above, Chapter 1 at n. 120.

We are not to expect that the laws of any country are to be framed as so many lessons of morality, to instruct the citizen how he may act the part of the virtuous man. Laws, whether civil or political, are expedients of policy … to secure the peace of society.[30]

Ferguson's reference to 'the peace of society' belongs to a tradition of thought that portrays law in general, and criminal law in particular, as functioning to secure and preserve 'civil peace';[31] that tradition is closely connected to one that focuses, as my account will focus, on the idea of 'civil order' rather than that of 'civil peace'.[32] The reasons for preferring 'civil order' to 'civil peace' should become clear in what follows: they have to do with the fact that 'order' connotes, more than 'peace' does, some idea of structure and organization. Whether we talk of 'order' or 'peace', however, we must bear in mind that what is involved is not simply the absence of overt conflict, or disorder.[33] Cruder versions of 'law and order' politics might suggest that 'order' is achieved simply by forceful repression: but that is not what is urged by theorists of civil order. The order that concerns them is a structured, normative order: it involves a stable arrangement of institutions and practices that allows people to know where they stand, where they should stand, and where they will stand. We might call it 'orderly', save for the connotations of regimentation that come with that adjective: a viable civil order might be a relaxed one in which spontaneity is widely valued; it might (perhaps must, if it is to be healthy) also be one that allows room for its own disruption and reform, in which even radical and vigorously activist dissent is itself part of the civil order that it seeks to change. In non- or anti-democratic polities, the civil order will be hierarchical: each class or caste will have its appropriate place in the hierarchy, and its members will know their place—their station and its duties.[34] In a democratic polity, there will be no such hierarchy, since a central structural value must be that of civic equality—at least as an aspiration, if very often not as achieved fact: that is why arguments that certain groups are suffering unjust discrimination, being treated as less than equal, are quite naturally expressed as arguments that they are not being treated as full citizens, since to be a citizen of a democracy is to be an equal member of the polity.

Civil order is at least in part legal order: that is to say, it is structured by law, and consists in important part in legally constituted institutions and legal practices. So our public institutions are central to our civil order, as are the laws by which we regulate our conduct. For that reason, we might distinguish 'civil' from 'social' order, on the grounds that what distinguishes civil order is 'the existence of legal institutions in the sense not only of the existence of norms of conduct but also as an apparatus of

[30] A Ferguson, *Principles of Moral and Political Science*, vol. II, 145, quoted by L Farmer, *Making the Modern Criminal Law: Criminalization and Civil Order*, 37; I am greatly indebted to Farmer's discussion of civil order.

[31] See D N MacCormick, *Institutions of Law: An Essay in Legal Theory*, esp. ch. 12: critically discussed in M Del Mar and Z Bankowski (eds), *Law as Institutional Normative Order* (see especially N Jareborg, 'A Comment on Personality and Corporate Crime', M Ulväng, 'Criminal Law and Civil Peace'); A E Bottoms, 'Civil Peace and Criminalization'.

[32] See especially Farmer, *Making the Modern Criminal Law.* Farmer draws on, though radically developing, ideas in M Oakeshott, 'On the Civil Condition'.

[33] We should remember the remark that Tacitus puts in the mouth of the Caledonian chieftain Calgacus, about the Romans' imperial behaviour: '*ubi solitudinem faciunt, pacem appellant*' (where they make a desert, they call it peace; *Agricola*, ch. XXX). See also Lord Byron, *Bride of Abydos*, Canto 2, stanza 2: 'He makes a solitude, and calls it—peace'). See Farmer, *Making the Modern Criminal Law*, 28: 'Civil order is more than order. It is order of a particular kind, which must be defined and secured through law as a central element of its civility'.

[34] Compare F H Bradley, 'My Station and its Duties'. Note, however, that even a non-democratic civil order could allow room for dissent, and for reform (though not for revolution) that would transform the hierarchy.

rule which can regulate social relations and settle disputes by adjudicating between norms'.[35]

This need not be read as an a priori claim that begs the question against all the different versions of anarchism, some of which might be read as arguing that we can have civil order without law.[36] It is, rather, a claim about civil order as it is found, and understood, in polities like our own; for us, as we are now collectively constituted, civil order is legal order. That is not to say, however, that civil order consists *only* in legal order. A polity's civil order includes a social order—a set of social practices and expectations that, although they exist and are sustained within the framework of law, are not themselves legal practices, and are not directly regulated by law.

We can start to put a little more flesh on the idea of civil order by turning to constitutions. As I noted in Chapter 2, professions and other kinds of institutional practice might have constitutions, or charters that function as constitutions, which define their *res publica*—what they are about, their defining goals and values, and the structures of rules and principles by which they will organize their activities.[37] To take just two examples, the Constitution of the World Health Organization ringingly declares, in its first article, that '[t]he objective of the World Health Organization ... shall be the attainment by all peoples of the highest possible level of health'; its further articles then specify the means by which it will pursue that objective.[38] Similarly, although with less universalist ambitions, the Charter of the University of Stirling declares that the 'University shall be a body for the purposes of teaching, examining and the promotion of research', and then goes on to specify the ways in which and the institutional structures through which those purposes are to be pursued.[39] More generally, associations of all kinds, whether they be sporting associations, or clubs, or charitable organizations, or professional bodies, typically have a constitution, either written or tacit: that is to say, they have, and might have written down in a formal constitutional document, a conception of what the association is for—of the aims and values that define it as this particular (kind of) association; of what its membership is (including, if relevant, provisions for how membership can be acquired and lost); and of the means through which it will pursue its defining goals and respect its defining values. The same is true of polities, as distinctive kinds of political association: the constitution of a polity defines, indeed constitutes, the central elements of its civil order.

I cannot illustrate this general claim by quoting from an English, British, or United Kingdom constitution, since there is no such document from which I could quote. I begin instead with the Polish constitution of 1997, since this provides a useful example of how a constitution defines central aspects of a polity's civil order. Its first article declares that the 'Republic of Poland shall be the common good of all its citizens'.[40]

[35] Farmer, *Making the Modern Criminal Law*, 41.

[36] See Farmer, *Making the Modern Criminal Law*, 28: it is 'an anthropological claim about human society'.

[37] See Chapter 2, section 7 above. We could say that the constitution of a practice or profession defines what is for its members '*cosa nostra*', our business or our affair—were it not for the unfortunate connotations of that phrase.

[38] See http://apps.who.int/gb/bd/PDF/bd48/basic-documents-48th-edition-en.pdf#page=7; the preamble says more about how 'health' is to be understood (as 'complete physical, mental and social well-being and not merely the absence of disease or infirmity'), and why it is of such importance.

[39] See http://www.stir.ac.uk/media/services/calendar/other/the-charter.pdf; the quoted passage is from s. 3.

[40] For an English translation of the Constitution, see http://www.sejm.gov.pl/prawo/konst/angielski/kon1.htm. For an illuminating discussion of the relationship between criminal law and the constitution, drawing especially on the Polish constitution, see K Szczucki, *Proconstitutional Interpretation of Criminal Law*.

Like the early articles of many constitutions, this might seem to be a matter more of high-flown rhetoric than of substantive content: but it actually brings out three important features of a civic constitution—of the constitution of a national polity.

First, it talks of '*the Republic of Poland*', which is also to talk (if we attend to the etymology of 'republic') of the public concern or public business—the *res publica*—of Poland.[41] A political community, like any kind of community, must be defined (it must define itself) in terms of some shared goals or activities that constitute its business. The *res publica* of medicine (of the medical profession, as a distinctive community) is, we might say, the promotion of health and the curing of sickness; and the *res publica* of a university, as an academic community, is the promotion of learning, the pursuit of knowledge, and the education of students. Such descriptions of the *res publica* of a community mark out the kinds of activity in which its members will be engaged, the goals that they will pursue, and the aspects of its members' lives with which it is concerned (and so too, by implication, the aspects with which it is *not* concerned). As a professor, I am engaged in academic research and teaching: these aspects of my life and my activities belong within the academic community to which I thus belong, and are of proper interest to other members of that community; I can expect to be subject to demands and rules concerning how I should conduct myself as an academic, perhaps to a code of professional ethics; and I can be held answerable by and to my academic colleagues for my conduct or misconduct in these matters. But other aspects of my life do not fall within the *res publica* of my profession: my conduct towards my family, my dealings with other people outside the university, are not part of my academic activity, and thus do not (should not) concern other members of my profession; if I mistreat my children, this is not a violation of my academic duties, nor something for which my university has the right to hold me to account.[42] Analogously, when a political community defines its *res publica*, it defines both which aspects of its citizens' lives and activities are its business, and (by implication) which are not: it defines the polity's public sphere, and thus also marks out a private sphere, into which the polity and its laws must not intrude.

Second, the *res publica* of Poland, as a political community, is '*the common good*'. This is, perhaps, something close to a conceptual truth, reminding us of Aquinas' remark that law is 'an ordinance of reason for the common good':[43] the business of a political community must surely, almost as a matter of definition, be the 'common good'; the substantive task is then to determine the scope and content of that common good. It is nonetheless important to note that what is taken for granted here is that the good in question is the common good: it must, that is, be the good of the whole community, not just of some part of it; it must be a good that is shared—a public good in which all can participate. Even a monarch who claims absolute, perhaps divinely ordained, authority must claim that her laws (her 'ordinances') serve not her personal good, or the good of her family or her allies, but the common good of the whole community that she claims the right to rule: otherwise, she might exert effective power, but cannot claim law-making authority. The 'common good' is, however, a formal notion, whose

[41] I am relying on the English translation of the Constitution, which is dangerous when focusing on the meaning and resonances of particular words; but I hope that what I say can be connected to the original, Polish text.

[42] There is, of course, plenty of room for argument about what does, or does not, fall within the *res publica* of a profession (see above, Chapter 2 at nn 110–18); but on any account *some* aspects of its members' lives fall outside it.

[43] Aquinas, *Summa Theologiae* Ia2ae90.4 ('*rationis ordinatio ad bonum commune*'). See also P Pettit, 'Law and Liberty', 53–8, on the connection between the common good and the public interest.

content is yet to be specified—and could be specified in terms of any of a wide range of values. In particular, 'the common good' of a polity need not be understood, any more than an individual's good need be understood, in terms of a conception of self-interest that sharply separates 'my', or 'our', interests or good from those of others, or from other values that may demand our allegiance.[44] A polity could coherently take it to be part of its common good to pursue retributive justice by securing the deserved punishment of moral wrongdoers: its common good, its members could believe, consists in part in serving the demands of justice. Similarly, when Article 1 of the Iranian constitution declares that '[t]he form of government of Iran is that of an Islamic Republic', and Article 2 declares that republic to be 'based on belief in ... the One God ..., His exclusive sovereignty and right to legislate, and the necessity of submission to His commands',[45] it is not denying that the *res publica* of Iran is the common good of its people: rather, it is declaring that common good to consist in submission to the commands of Allah. More generally, when constitutions declare, as they typically do, the foundational aims or values of the polity, they are specifying its common good.

Third, the good that constitutes the *res publica* of Poland is the common good of '*all its citizens*'. Here again, as with the idea of the common good itself, this could but need not amount to an assertion of a narrow notion of national self-interest—as when would-be presidents shout 'America First', meaning by this that the interests of America and American citizens are to be given preference, by the American government, over those of other nations and their citizens. But 'the common good of all its citizens' could be coherently interpreted in highly altruistic, or even in a way cosmopolitan, terms. For, first, 'its citizens' could be taken to include 'all people of the world who wish to dwell on [Polish] soil'.[46] Second, a charitable association, or a religious order, could define its *res publica* as consisting in service to the needs of others: so too, a polity *could*, as far as the logic of constitutions is concerned, define the common good of its citizens as consisting in their collective commitment to serving the needs or the good of their fellow human beings, and specify the rest of the polity's governing structures and organization in terms of what is needed to serve that end efficiently.[47] I do not suggest that this is either likely or plausible as a polity's constitutional conception of its citizens' common good—it is perhaps even less likely than it is for an individual to define her own good in such altruistic terms, and less plausible as a claim about how we should define ourselves as a polity. But what is both likely and plausible is that a polity should understand the common good of its citizens *partly* in terms of what they owe to others. Thus the Polish Constitution declares that 'all citizens of the Republic' recognize 'the need for cooperation with all countries for the good of the Human Family'.[48] We can also hope that the common good of the polity's citizens will

[44] Thus 'good' here is to be understood in terms of the Greek idea of *eudaimonia* or well-being: as a formal notion (see Aristotle, *Nicomachean Ethics* I.7, 1097b), whose content might then be specified in terms of the values to which we should devote our lives.

[45] An English translation of the Iranian Constitution is available at the International Constitutional Law website (along with translations of many other constitutions): http://www.servat.unibe.ch/icl/index.html.

[46] See the Preamble to the Argentinian Constitution, discussed above, Chapter 3 at n. 91.

[47] Thanks to Massimo Renzo for raising this point. So what counts formally as nationalism could be in substance a kind of cosmopolitanism: such a conception of our common good is nationalist in that it is about *our* good as a polity, how *we* are to live as citizens of it (not about how the whole world is to live); but it is cosmopolitan in substance in that we identify our civic good in terms of our contribution to the good of others.

[48] Polish Constitution, Preamble. That cooperation should include participation in the institutions of international and transnational criminal law: see above, Chapter 3, section 2.

be understood as including hospitality towards those who come into the polity either as guests or as would-be citizens.[49]

The Polish Constitution thus makes explicit in Article 1 what must be at least implicit in any constitution: it offers an initial, albeit formal rather than substantive, specification of the business (the *res publica*) of this political association—the common good of its members; and as it goes on in its later articles to give that formal specification a more substantive content, it begins to define what is to count as a good life for this polity and its members. More precisely, it begins to specify what is to count as a good *civic* life for its members, a good life for them in their role as citizens. It need not aim to specify or to secure every aspect of human good for the individuals who are citizens: the common good is the public good in which they are all to share, and whilst that common good should make it possible for them to pursue their individual conceptions of the good, it need not itself include those individual goods. I say 'need not' rather than 'does not' in order not to foreclose, as a matter of logic, the possibility of a more totalitarian constitution that aims to include the individual goods of its members within their common good as citizens. More commonly (and plausibly), however, a constitution will, by implication, distinguish the 'common good', which is the polity's concern *qua* political association, from the individual goods that its citizens will pursue within the shared structures of the polity; in polities that define themselves as liberal, that distinction will be an important one, and the sphere of the common (or public) good will be defined in part precisely so as to leave (and support) an extensive sphere of individual or private good.[50]

To say that '[t]he Republic of Poland shall be the common good of all its citizens' is thus to make what is one way a largely formal claim, whose substantive content is yet to be filled in—a task to be discharged in part by the rest of the Constitution; but it is also to provide a framework, a scaffolding, for the task of specifying a polity's *res publica*—which is also, as we will see, the task of defining or constituting its civil order.

The Polish Constitution goes on to fill out some of the framework laid down by Article 1. It identifies the general values, such as 'social justice' (art. 2) and the 'inviolable' 'dignity of the person' (art. 30), which are to be foundational to the polity's concerns; the 'freedoms and rights' that are to be respected and fostered, as well as the 'obligations' of citizenship (ch. 2)—including such familiar rights as freedom, equality, privacy, due process, and assembly; the various social institutions and practices, such as marriage (art. 18) and private ownership in a 'social market economy' (art. 20), through which individuals are to be enabled to pursue their own goods; and the institutions of law and government through which the polity is to govern itself and pursue its common good (such as the Sejm and the Senate, the President and the Council of Ministers, the judiciary, and the separation of powers between them; art. 10). These provisions help to specify the content of 'the common good', and the institutional

[49] See above, Chapter 3, section 3.

[50] Since I appealed earlier both to Aquinas and to Aristotle, I should note that we must therefore here dissent from Aristotle's conception of the role of 'political science' as 'the highest master science' whose 'end will include the ends of the [other sciences], and will therefore be the human good' (*Nicomachean Ethics*, I.2). We should also dissent from one aspect of Oakeshott's generally illuminating discussion of civil order—his argument that 'civil association', as the distinctive 'practice' in which citizens are engaged as '*cives*', is not 'an enterprise with a common purpose to pursue or a common interest to promote or protect'; '*respublica* does not define or even describe a common substantive purpose, interest, or "good"' ('On the Civil Condition', at 122, 147). In a liberal polity the 'common good' will certainly consist, in central and crucial part, in preserving the freedom to pursue a wide range of substantive 'private' goods, whose content is not specified; but it will also necessarily have substantive content of its own (see further below, Chapter 5, section 3).

means through which that good is to be pursued, fostered, and sustained; they also thus help to define, and their implementation helps to constitute, the civil order of Poland as a polity. As I noted above, the civil order is not simply a matter of the absence of conflict or disorder: it consists in a particular kind of structuring—an ordering—of the polity and its civic life. We can now see more clearly what formal elements a specification of a polity's civil order needs to include.

It will include, of course, the various governmental and public institutions through which the polity is to govern itself. The constitution need not itself specify all of these: it might specify the central institutions of governance and law, as the Polish Constitution does in Article 10: but other public institutions—such as those dealing with education, with health, with social welfare, with culture—will be created by governmental action. But the civil order does not consist, even in its formal, legal dimensions, only in these kinds of institutional structure: as the Polish Constitution makes clear, it also includes the substantive ends and values towards which the polity's life is to be oriented, and by which it is to be shaped; and the rights or freedoms that are to be respected both by the state (as the polity's institutional order) and by its members. Those ends, values, and rights are likely to be under-specified in the formal constitution: for instance, just how 'social justice', and the 'inviolable' 'dignity of the person', should be understood, and what they require or imply, will need to be worked out through the familiar processes of political argument, public deliberation, and judicial findings.[51] Similarly, the American Constitution begins by declaring that

> [w]e, the People of the United States, in Order to form a more perfect Union, establish Justice, insure domestic Tranquility, provide for the common defence, promote the general Welfare, and secure the Blessings of Liberty to ourselves and our Posterity, do ordain and establish this Constitution for the United States of America.[52]

The further clauses of, and later amendments to, the Constitution then attempt to specify in more substantive detail just how those ambitions are to be understood and pursued; and the extent to which that is an ongoing, indeed never-ending, task is evidenced by the activities of the Supreme Court, and by the amount of American legal scholarship that is focused on the Constitution.

A constitution will typically include both ends and constraints: it will specify goods that the polity and its governing organs must aim to advance and protect (these might be as general and vague as 'social justice' in the case of Poland, or 'the general welfare' in the case of the US); but it will also specify constraints, most obviously in the form of rights, that must be respected and that therefore set limits on the permissible scope of governmental action. More precisely, in some cases the relevant rights are explicitly rights against the state: this is true of many of the Amendments to the US

[51] For just one illuminating German example, see 115 *Entscheidungen des Bundesverfassungsgerichts* [BVerfGE] 118 (2006). According to Article 1(1) of the German Basic Law (*Grundgesetz*), 'Human dignity is inviolable. To respect and protect it is the duty of all state authority'; the Constitutional Court then had to decide whether a law authorizing the minister of defence to order the shooting down of a hijacked passenger plane if it was going to be used as a weapon (following 9/11) was constitutional; it held that it was unconstitutional, since shooting the plane down would violate the human dignity of the innocent passengers on board (for a useful account and discussion, see T Hörnle, 'Hijacked Airplanes: May They be Shot Down?').

[52] We could also of course look to the Declaration of Independence: its assertions of equality, of the rights to life, liberty, and the pursuit of happiness, and of the need to 'institute new Government, laying its foundation on such principles and organizing its powers in such form, as ... shall seem most likely to effect their Safety and Happiness', are also partial delineations of the *res publica* of the new polity.

Constitution,[53] and is likely to be a central feature of the constitution (written or unwritten) of any liberal polity, given a concern to protect citizens against the overweening power of the state. However, first, a constitution will also need to specify the kinds of goal or good that the polity, and so the state as its institutional manifestation, should pursue, however vague and general those specifications might be. Second, at least some of the rights that the constitution entrenches will be rights not (just) against the state, but against one's fellow citizens, individually or collectively—which will then lay on the state a responsibility not just to respect those rights by not violating them, but to protect them against violations by others.

This is clearly true, for just one instance, of human dignity: if it is 'inviolable', it must be a responsibility of 'all state authority' not just to respect it, but to protect it.[54] This point, and the connection between such values and the civil order, are neatly illustrated by the notorious case of 'dwarf-tossing': a French mayor's decision to prohibit dwarf-tossing in the town was upheld by the Conseil d'État, on the grounds that the municipal police had authority to 'take all measures to prevent a violation of public order, one of whose elements is respect for human dignity', and that this 'attraction' contravened 'respect for the dignity of the human person'.[55] A significant feature of this decision is that the relationship between respect for human dignity and 'public order' is portrayed as constitutive, not contingent or causal: what justifies a ban on activities that violate human dignity is not that they might cause some breach of public order, but that they themselves constitute such a breach, since they violate an important element of public order; thus a display of dwarf-tossing that passed off peacefully would still constitute a violation of public order. This shows that 'public order' is to be understood as 'civil order' as I have been portraying it, and that dignity is a crucial constituent of the French civil order, as it is for the German and Polish civil orders—it is something to be respected by state action, but also protected by state action against violation by other citizens.[56]

I have been talking so far about the formal, legal dimensions of a polity's civil order: about the institutions and legally ordained practices by which it formally governs itself, about the ends and values, and the constraints, that are constitutionally or legally specified. Legal structures of these kinds are central to the civil order of a modern polity; but whilst civil order (as I am using the idea) depends on law and the rule of law, it extends beyond the realm of legal institutions; it encompasses the informal, extra-legal practices and expectations by which our social lives as citizens are structured. A simple example of this dimension of civil order is the practice (or the absence of a practice) of queuing. Many societies have practices of queuing, typically

[53] Thus e.g. 'Congress shall make no law respecting an establishment of religion or prohibiting the free exercise thereof; or abridging the freedom of speech or of the press; or the right of the people peaceably to assemble, and to petition the Government for a redress of grievances' (First Amendment). This point is, as we will see, especially important when it comes to the delineation of the 'private' realm. When the US Supreme Court held that it was unconstitutional to criminalize abortions with the first trimester of pregnancy (*Roe v Wade* 410 US 113 (1973); see at nn 85–92 below), or to criminalize consensual homosexual conduct (*Lawrence v Texas* 539 US 558 (2003)), it took no formal view on the moral permissibility of such conduct: it appealed to the (qualified) right to privacy that it found in the Constitution (particularly in the Fourteenth Amendment), which set limits on the authority of the state to intervene in such matters.

[54] As Article 1(1) of the German *Grundgesetz* declares (see n. 51 above). Thus when Article 1(3) declares that '[t]he following basic rights are binding on legislature, executive, and judiciary as directly valid law', they must be taken to bind those authorities to protect as well as to respect them.

[55] Conseil d'État statuant au contentieux, n°143578, lecture du 27 octobre 1995; see also Conseil d'État statuant au contentieux, n°136727, lecture du 27 octobre 1995.

[56] See further below, Chapter 6 at nn 101–3, 130–1, Chapter 7 at nn 119–25.

governed by informal, often tacitly understood rules—rules about when and how queues should form, how they are ordered, when it is permissible to leave one's place in the queue without losing it, when (if ever) it is permissible to jump the queue, and so on. In societies that take queuing seriously, it might also sometimes be regulated a little more formally, as when government offices or other kinds of organization introduce ticketing systems for queues. Usually, however, the practice is informal: its rules are tacitly understood by those who are used to it, and are enforced, if at all, only by 'the moral coercion of public opinion',[57] rather than by law.

Queuing is just one example of a more general social conception of 'civility', which marks the informal dimension of civil order.[58] Civility is a matter of how we behave, and expect each other to behave, towards each other in our social dealings in public spaces—how we interact in our ordinary lives as citizens: the way we behave in the streets is a good example of this informal dimension of civil order—the prevailing conventions of courtesy, of making way (or not making way) for others, of assisting (or not assisting) those who ask for help or look as if they need it. There is of course rich scope here for cultural variance and mutual misunderstanding: conduct that is accepted as 'civil' at home might be perceived as—might indeed be—uncivil (uncouth, rude, uncivilized) if I behave thus in another country; and what I perceive as uncivilized or rude habits of public behaviour in another country might be better understood as entirely consistent with the local conceptions of civility and appropriate conduct.

Another central dimension of the civil order is trust. Not only does it enable people to know where they stand, and where they will stand, as a matter of fact; that much is true, after all, of a Hobbesian state of nature. It enables them to form and sustain normative expectations about how others will behave towards them—both negative, that they will not be subjected to random attack or violence, and positive (depending upon the nature of the polity) that they will receive help in certain kinds of situation.[59] Such trust is not, of course, unconditional or naïve even in a tolerably well-functioning polity: we know that we can be attacked or endangered by others, and that we cannot always count on finding or being offered help when we need it; we take precautions, both in our general conduct and when we know that we are in a situation in which trust, of the kind on which we usually rely, would be imprudent. But a certain level of trust is necessary for any kind of tolerable life: trust both in our civil institutions, that they will provide the support and protections that they are supposed to provide; and in our fellow citizens, that they will generally respect the basic norms of civic interaction—and not only because they are threatened with sanctions if they do not. This kind of trust is, as we will see in more detail later, sustained in part by the law: we can rely on each other because we can rely on the law.[60] However, it is not—it cannot be—purely a matter of law: civic or social trust must extend beyond what the law could directly guarantee; and even if we can rely on each other only because we can rely on the law, we can rely on the law only because we can generally rely on each other to respect it.

I have been sketching a formal account of the idea of civil order, as the order (institutional, legal, and informal) that constitutes a polity as a particular kind of practice or

[57] J S Mill, *On Liberty*, ch. 1, para. 9.

[58] See Farmer, *Making the Modern Criminal Law*, 55–9; also D Nance, 'Civility and the Burden of Proof'.

[59] See e.g. MacCormick, *Institutions of Law*, 208, 216; Bottoms, 'Civil Peace and Criminalization', 234–5, 238: also S Dimock, 'Retributivism and Trust'.

[60] See also Chiao's emphasis on 'an assurance of general cooperation with legal rules': 'What is the Criminal Law For?', 139; see at n. 17 above.

form of life, and that thus also constitutes its civic or public realm. I will need to say more shortly (in section 5) about the diversity of such orders, and about the conditions of their existence (section 6); I will then (in section 7) need to address the question of how criminal law can fit into such an order—though a full answer to that question will depend on a more substantive account of a particular type of civil order. First, however, I must say a little more about the distinctions between the 'public' and the 'private' that almost any polity must draw, and that will be drawn, explicitly or implicitly, in the account it gives of its civil order.

4. The Public and the Private

Although the idea of a 'civil order' might be reserved for political communities, we can find something analogous in every kind of practice. The account of such practices as medicine and education that I discussed in Chapter 2, section 6, the account of the practice's *res publica* that expresses its members' normative self-understanding of what they are (of what they are about) as doctors or as academics, is an account of their medical or their academic order: it is how they constitute themselves as this particular kind of practice, on the basis of their defining goals and values, and through the institutions by which their activities are governed; it is a self-constitution that might be specified in a formal constitution.

One important feature of such practices is, I argued, the distinctions that they draw between the 'public' and the 'private': between those matters that belong to the practice, and are therefore the business of its members, and those that do not. Various aspects of my life and my conduct belong to, or bear directly on, my role as a doctor, or a professor: they are matters in which my colleagues can properly take a professional interest, and for which they can call me to account. Other aspects, however, are in that context private: if challenged about them or called to account for them by my colleagues or by my professional body, I can properly reply that the matter is not their business. What should count as 'private' or as 'public' is sometimes contestable: but we can identify at least an uncontestable core of the public (for instance a doctor's medical treatment of her patients, a professor's academic writings); and contested cases will need to be argued out in terms of how the practice's *res publica* should be understood, and of how the kind of conduct in question does or does not bear on it.

What is true of these kinds of practice is also true of a polity, as a distinctive kind of civil or political practice. In any but the most extravagantly totalitarian polity, a distinction will be drawn between matters that are public and those that are private, in relation to the polity and its civic life: a distinction between those aspects of its citizens' lives that properly concern the polity and their fellow citizens, simply in virtue of their role as citizens, and those that do not. More precisely, *distinctions* will be drawn between the public and the private: for there will be different such distinctions, reflecting different modalities of public and private, and different civic contexts in which the distinctions are drawn.[61]

First, we should distinguish a formal or legal distinction between public and private, from an informal, social distinction. The polity's law (including its constitutional law) explicitly defines its formally public realm, in defining the goals, values, institutions, and practices that constitute its civil order: what belongs or pertains to that order

[61] There will also often be disagreement about where and how these distinctions are to be drawn: see section 5 below.

falls within the public realm. The law might also explicitly demarcate certain private realms, whose privacy is to be legally protected. Thus the Polish Constitution declares that Poland's economic system is grounded in a 'social market economy, based on the freedom of economic activity, private ownership';[62] and that everyone 'shall have the right to legal protection of his private and family life ... and to make decisions about his personal life'.[63] This is not to say that family life, or market activity, or what one does with one's own property, escapes all legal regulation: but it declares that within the limits set by the law (for instance the laws defining assault and other kinds of personal violence, or fraudulent contracting, as criminal), citizens may behave as they choose; they can expect the law not to interfere, and to protect them against interference from others. But the law and the constitution also implicitly mark out private spheres, by remaining silent: what is not declared to be part of the public realm is therefore part of the private realm, beyond the reach of the law. If the law is silent about, for instance, consensual sexual relations between competent adults, such activities are thereby implicitly defined as belonging, as far as the law is concerned, to the private realm.

Beyond the law, we also find informal distinctions between the public and the private: these are displayed, often without being articulated, in our responses or lack of response to how others behave, as well as in our responses to such responses.[64] In some communities, for instance, what I do (or do not do) with my garden is understood to be a public matter: not only is it appropriate for passers-by to inspect it and pass comment on it, but I may be challenged or called to account by others if I fail to keep it tidy and well groomed; nor is it appropriate for me to respond to such challengers by saying that it is not their business. In other communities, by contrast, this is seen as a private matter (so long as my gardening or lack of it does not materially impinge on others): others will not generally peer into my garden, and will certainly not be entitled to challenge me about it; I can properly respond to any such challenge not by defending my practice, but simply by saying that it is not their business. There might be no legal regulation of such matters: it might not be an offence, or a violation of a national or local regulation, to have an untidy, overgrown garden (unless it endangers others' health or safety); how I keep my garden will then be a legally private matter. But it might nonetheless be seen by members of the local community as a socially public matter, which is their business.

In discussing both legal and informal distinctions between public and private, we also need to distinguish positive from critical, or normative, accounts of those distinctions. We might note that as a matter of positive law, in a society that criminalizes sadomasochistic conduct even when it occurs between consenting adults 'in private', such conduct is a legally public matter; but we might go on to argue, normatively, that it should be defined as legally (and socially) private, so long as the participants are competent and consenting.[65] We might note that as a matter of the prevailing, positive, social norms in this neighbourhood, the colour one paints one's front door is seen as a public matter, in that neighbours regard it as their proper business to comment on it, and to object to what they see as an aesthetically displeasing choice of colour; but we might go on to argue, normatively, that this is an unduly intrusive conception of the

[62] Article 20.

[63] Article 47; see also Article 8 of the European Convention on Human Rights: 'Everyone has the right to respect for his private and family life, his home and his correspondence'. This of course leaves open, for interpretation on the basis of other aspects of the idea of civil order, which aspects of life are to count as parts of 'private life'.

[64] Compare H L A Hart, *The Concept of Law*, 55–60, on the existence of social rules.

[65] See *R v Brown* [1994] 1 AC 212; see at nn 93–7 below.

public sphere, and that such matters should count as private. In the end, my concern will be with a normative account of the public realm; but my concern here is with the role that distinctions between public and private play in a community's positive self-understanding and self-governance.[66]

Second, distinctions between the public and the private can be more or less local: just as they are drawn within professional practices, and are then relative to those practices, so they might be drawn within, and be relative to, civic communities that are more local than the polity. What is a public matter in the context of medical practice is the business of other members of that practice, but not thereby the business of people outside that practice; and what is private in the context of medical practice might be public in other contexts (the loud parties I hold are not the business of my fellow medical practitioners, so long as they do not affect my work, but are the business of my neighbours). Similarly, within a local community (a village, a neighbourhood, an apartment building) there might be a generally shared understanding both of what counts as a public matter and of how people should behave in such matters—as well as of what by contrast counts as a private matter that is not one's neighbours' business: perhaps, for instance, there is an understanding that people will clear the snow from the pavement outside their own house—an understanding that is informal rather than legal, but nonetheless normative, so that a failure to do so will attract what is understood to be justified criticism from one's neighbours (but not from outsiders—it is not their business); by contrast, how I conduct myself outside the neighbourhood is not the business of my neighbours *qua* members of this local community, although it might be their business as my colleagues (if it concerns my professional life) or as citizens (if it involves criminal activity).[67] Our concern here, however, is with the distinctions between the public and the private as they are drawn at the level of the polity: the distinctions between what does, and what does not, properly concern my fellow citizens simply in virtue of our shared citizenship.

Third, there are different modalities of publicity and privacy: some concern the various kinds of information that others are, or are not, entitled to acquire; some concern what count as proper, or improper, objects of attention; some concern what should be publicly supported, funded, or organized, and what should instead be left to private initiatives; and some—the most relevant to our present purposes—concern the kinds of intervention (if any) that are, or are not, appropriate. Thus my private information is information that should be within my control: it is up to me to decide who else (if anyone) should have access to it, and with whom (if anyone) to share it; others act wrongly if they acquire it or try to acquire it.[68] As for attention, this concerns both how we respond to each other in public spaces, and how we understand the idea of private space. In public spaces, we are of course visible and audible to each other: we cannot avoid seeing and hearing each other, and we must indeed be able to do so if we are to avoid collisions. But there will also be conventions of privacy concerning the kinds of attention that we may properly pay to each other: do we look passers-by in the eye, or avoid eye contact; do we look, with interest or admiration or disdain, at

[66] See further section 5 below.

[67] Evidently, there will be differences between and within communities on such matters (in some localities there will not even be an identifiable community of neighbours): other local communities will not, for instance, have such an expectation about snow clearing; and members of a community in which such an expectation is a local civic norm might dissent from it. I will comment later (in section 5) on the implications of such diversity and dissent in the context of the polity.

[68] The wrong might or might not be a legal wrong: here too we should distinguish legal from informal distinctions between public and private.

how others dress; do we listen to the conversations that are going on around us?[69] As to private spaces, there may also be conventions about how we attend, or do not attend, to them when they are visible (as well as about what counts as a private space): if the interiors of others' houses are visible through their uncurtained windows, is it appropriate for passers-by to gaze in at them; or is that improperly intrusive? (The difference between looking, or gazing, and merely seeing, is clearly important here.)[70]

We should focus here, however, on the modality of intervention—on the distinction between the 'public' in which others have in principle the standing to intervene, and the 'private' in which they have no right to intervene. Here again we must distinguish formal from informal, legal from extra-legal, distinctions. There is a distinction between what permits of official intervention, most obviously by the police, and what does not permit of such intervention, and a related distinction between matters in which others (officials or not) are legally permitted to intervene, and matters in which intervention is not legally sanctioned; and outside the law, there is a distinction between what we recognize, extra-legally, as a matter in which others have a right to intervene, and what we count as a private matter in which they have no such right. We must also distinguish different kinds of intervention. Given that our interest here is, ultimately, in the criminal law, we can focus on interventions that imply or express an adverse attitude to the conduct in question.

Outside the law, intervention might take the form of nothing more dramatic or intrusive than adverse comment addressed to the agent, or a calling to account for what she is doing: to claim that the matter is private is to say that others have no standing even to criticize or call to account. If I am sitting in a café eating a double burger and chips, a passing stranger might think that I am being imprudent with my health; but if she approaches me and challenges my behaviour, I might respond, not by answering for my conduct (by explaining, justifying, excusing it, or admitting its imprudence), but by saying that it is none of her business. I am answerable to some others for my dietary misconduct—my family, my doctor, perhaps my friends; but not to this stranger.[71] Extra-legal intervention can also take more forceful forms: I might stand in your way if you try to jump a queue, or push you back. Here we come within

[69] This question arises very evidently in relation to loud conversations on mobile phones on public transport: is it appropriate to listen, perhaps with fascinated interest, to the side of the conversation that it is hard not to hear; or should we try to close our ears to it, or turn our attention from it?

[70] It is worth noting too, in the contexts of both information and attention, that I might violate my own privacy, and invade the privacy of others, by revealing private information or by behaving in ways that attract attention to what should be private conduct. Compare A P Simester and A von Hirsch, *Crimes, Harms and Wrongs: On the Principles of Criminalization*, 98–106. What is to count as 'behaving in ways that attract attention to what should be private conduct' (as 'exhibitionism', or as 'flaunting') can of course itself be a difficult or contested normative issue. We might think, for instance, that if a couple hold hands and kiss in a public place, this should be recognized as 'private' behaviour—as something that warrants neither intervention nor the kind of attention that consists in gazing rather than simply seeing (matters would be different if they embarked on full sexual intercourse). Some would still, however, apply this only to heterosexual couples, and regard similar conduct by homosexual couples as public misconduct: see notoriously *Masterton v Holden* [1986] 3 All ER 39 in which a gay couple were convicted of 'insulting behaviour' (Metropolitan Police Act 1839, s. 54(13)) for kissing at a bus stop in a way that caused two passing heterosexual women to feel 'insulted' and 'threatened'. I do not aim here to justify such oppressive discrimination—it is unjustifiable: my point is simply to illustrate the normative complexity of the distinctions we draw between the public and the private.

[71] Matters might be different if her reason for challenging me had to do not with my health but, for instance, with the immorality of eating meat: we then need to ask whether moral wrongdoing as such, or this particular kind of (alleged) wrongdoing, is everyone's business; see above, Chapter 3, text between nn 44 and 45.

reach of legally cognizable interventions, since my pushing you might fit the formal definition of criminal battery, although it is highly unlikely that it will be treated as a criminal matter either by those involved or by the police should they be called;[72] and as the interventions become more forcible, as in cases of defence of self, or others, or property, we are firmly in the realm, if not of formally legal interventions (as by the police), at least of legally regulated interventions.[73]

As for legally sanctioned interventions, whether by officials or by others, the most obvious of these for our purposes fall within the realm of criminal law: they include provisions for police intervention to prevent or investigate crimes, for defensive or preventive interventions by private individuals, and of course for the arrest and trial of alleged offenders; to define a type of conduct as criminal is to define it as a public wrong in which other citizens and officials of the polity may properly (or indeed should) intervene in such ways. But there are other ways in which conduct can be made legally or formally public, and thus liable to legally sanctioned intervention: by, for instance being subjected to various kinds of regulatory regime, or by being brought within the reach of tort law.[74]

These distinctions between 'public' and 'private' matters cut across the distinctions (which are also normative distinctions) between public and private places and spaces. As we saw above, what is done 'in public' can still be a private matter, in that others have no right or standing to pay particular attention to it or to intervene in it. Correlatively, what is done 'in private' can still be a public matter, for instance in the obvious case of crimes committed within the 'privacy' of the home. Even in the days when domestic violence was often seen as a private matter into which the police should not intervene, what was taken to make it 'private' was not its spatial location behind the doors of the home, but its normative location within the institution of marriage; the gradual recognition of it as 'public' marked a development in our collective understanding of that institution.

The distinctions between 'public' and 'private' identified so far do not explicitly include a distinction between public and private wrongs. The reason is that that is not a fundamental or self-standing distinction: it is derivative from other distinctions between public and private. A 'public' wrong is a wrong committed in a public normative space, and a 'private' wrong is one committed in a private normative space: before we can decide which kinds of wrong are 'public', we must first have a conception (a normative and context-dependent conception) of what should count as a public realm. That is why an account of crimes as public wrongs must begin not with wrongs, but with the public; and since the relevant public realm for the criminal law is the public

[72] See Criminal Justice Act 1988, s. 39; Ormerod and Laird, *Smith and Hogan's Criminal Law*, 708, on battery as requiring only 'any unlawful touching'. And see above, Chapter 1, section 7 on what constitutes criminalization.

[73] Here as elsewhere there may be divergences between legal and extra-legal understandings both of what counts as 'private' and of what kinds of intervention are permissible. The former are illustrated by disagreement about domestic violence, against partners or children, given the (sadly continuing) survival of views about the rights of husbands to 'chastise' their wives and the rights of parents to 'chastise' their children. The latter are shown in the disagreements about what kind of force a householder may use against unlawful intruders, as in the case of Tony Martin (*Martin* [2003] QB 1; see e.g. https://www.theguardian.com/law/2011/oct/31/self-defence-law-legislation-pr).

[74] A nice example is provided by the case of the bed-and-breakfast owners who refused to let a gay couple take a double room, which was held to constitute unlawful discrimination (*Preddy v Bull* [2013] 1 WLR 3741): whilst it is up to me, as a private matter, whom I invite into my home as guests, once I begin to run a business offering bed and breakfast, my conduct comes within the public realm. See further at nn 99–101 below.

realm of the polity whose law it is, that is why we must begin with the idea of civil order: for a polity's civil order constitutes its public realm. We will see later how a conception of public wrongs, and of criminal law as an appropriate response to such wrongs, can emerge from such a conception of civil order.

I have not said much so far about the substantive content of the idea of civil order—or about the different contents it will be given in different polities; nor, therefore, have I said much about the substance of the distinctions between public and private that a polity can draw. My concern so far has been formal rather than substantive, to show what the distinctions amount to, and what role they play. I should again emphasize, however, that although I have been talking about what is actually counted as public or as private, my interest is ultimately normative, not descriptive. Criminal law, I will argue, should function to sustain a polity's civil order. It follows that, in one sense, a polity uses criminal law appropriately so long as it is using its criminal law to sustain its civil order, whatever that order might be; in the same sense, a government puts the institutions of governance to their proper use if it uses them to pursue what it takes to be the polity's common good. It does not follow, however, that we must accept as justified any criminal law that sustains the civil order of a particular polity: that we could, for instance, have no criticism to offer of laws that criminalize homosexual conduct, or forbid women to drive a car, or permit a husband to beat his wife, so long as they are the laws of a polity whose civil order, as it conceives it, is structured by a rigid heterosexual conception of permissible sexual conduct, or by a conception of women's place that precludes activities as autonomous as driving, or by a conception of marriage and of the status of women that gives husbands that kind of authority. I must agree that such polities are acting in accordance with their own defining values—with their own civic consciences; in the same way, I must agree that someone with abhorrent moral views acts in accordance with his conscience if he puts them into practice. That does not prevent me from criticizing him, or from criticizing the polity; but it does affect the form that such criticism should take.

One kind of criticism of a criminal law is internal to the polity whose law it is: we can argue that this law is inconsistent with the polity's own self-defining values, or that it does not serve to sustain its civil order as it conceives it. Another kind of criticism, however, is external: it admits that the law does sustain the civil order as it is currently conceived, but objects to that conception of the civil order. Perhaps a polity conceives consensual sexual relationships as a public matter, since its existing civil order is partly structured by a conception of appropriate sexual conduct: consistently with that (heterosexual, marriage-focused) conception, its criminal law might define homosexual conduct, or adultery, as a criminal offence.[75] But, its critics can argue, it ought not to conceive its civil order or structure its civic life in these terms; therefore it should not criminalize such conduct. Nothing I have said or will say precludes such criticism; indeed, it is a vital feature of any democratic, indeed any civilized, polity.

My comments in the previous paragraph were over-simplified, since they suggested that the would-be critic is confronted by a unitary, coherent and accepted conception of the polity's civil order, and then needs to find a position from which to criticize it. More commonly, however, she will be operating within a much messier conceptual and normative structure. For one thing, the formal civil order as constituted by the law might not be consistent with the informal, extra-legal civil order as constituted by

[75] See e.g. A Carroll and L Itaborahy, *State Sponsored Homophobia 2015: A World Survey of Laws*; J Sweeney, 'Undead Statutes: The Rise, Fall, and Continuing Use of Adultery and Fornication Criminal Laws'; and at nn 82–3 below.

the shared self-understanding of the polity's members: so a critic of the law might be able to argue on the basis of that extra-legal civil order—that the laws should reflect that civil order, but that this law fails to do so.[76] Furthermore, it is unlikely that the informal civil order (or indeed the formal civil order) of a contemporary polity will have the kind of monolithic uniformity that my comments have implied: we can expect to find differences and disagreements within the polity, among its members, about how they should understand their civic life. It is to the implications of such differences and disagreements, both between and within polities, that we must now attend.

5. Differences and Disagreements

Different polities have different civil orders, both formal and informal—that is an obvious fact about our world. Within a single polity, we can also expect to find differences: differences, perhaps, between the formal and the informal civil orders, if the law seeks to preserve or to construct an order that is no longer, or is not yet, the order in terms of which citizens understand their civic lives; and differences within the informal civil order, when different people or groups have different conceptions of what that order is, or what it should be. As far as the former kind of difference is concerned, the law might lag behind changes in extra-legal understandings of the civil order; or it might be taking a lead, seeking to change that extra-legal understanding and thus that extra-legal order.[77] This should remind us, if we need reminding, that neither the formal nor the informal civil order is fixed and unchanging, or unchangeable. Extra-legal conceptions of our civic life can change, as can our laws and institutions; constitutions can also change—either explicitly through formal constitutional amendments, or implicitly as interpretations of the values or rights in terms of which the formal, legal civil order is constituted change.[78]

Such differences, both within and between polities, might be, and be perceived as, nothing more than differences: we live thus, and you live thus. They might, however, constitute not just differences, but disagreements: we think that you are mistaken, misguided, or plain wrong to live as you do and to understand or structure your civil order in that way; and you think the same of us.[79] I will comment shortly on the implications of such disagreement within a polity, but should say something brief about disagreements between polities. There are familiar questions about the possibilities of normative critique of other political systems than our own:[80] more precisely, what room is there for what kinds of critique, drawing on what kinds of foundation, if we cannot argue either, as if from within, that the other polity is untrue to its own values, or that

[76] A kind of criticism with which the courts themselves can engage, as the court did in *R v R* [1992] 1 AC 599 in bringing intra-marital rape within the law of rape (see above, Chapter 1 at nn 143–9).

[77] The former possibility can be illustrated, again, by the criminalization of intra-marital rape; the latter by the introduction of the stricter drink-driving laws in England in 1967 (Road Safety Act 1967; see Bottoms, 'Civil Peace and Criminalization', 261–4).

[78] Which is to say that the idea that constitutional courts could or should do no more than discern the meaning that the constitution always had is a myth; but that is not a debate into which we need enter here.

[79] It is sometimes a real question whether we should see a difference as a disagreement, or merely as a difference. This is not the question of whether we should 'tolerate' others' divergent ways of life: for to tolerate something presupposes a judgment that it is in some way wrong, something to which we have reason to object; but to recognize that a difference is merely a difference is to recognize that we have no reason to object.

[80] And see above, Introduction at nn 19–25.

its conception of civil order is at odds with foundational values that we and they share? All I can say here is, first, that we can obviously regard other polities' civil orders as not merely different, but oppressive, or unjust, or in other ways objectionable; second, that we must also ask whether and how we can properly express such judgments to them, and attempt to change their minds; and third, and for present purposes most crucially, that a critique of their criminal laws cannot focus simply on their criminal law, but must attend to their conception of civil order, and to how their criminal law is connected to that conception. For if criminal law serves to sustain a polity's civil order, a critique of its criminal law must argue either, from within, that it fails to sustain its civil order as it is understood; or, from without, that its conception of civil order is misguided or wrong.

I can therefore reject Moore's objection that my account of crimes as public wrongs 'is in danger of returning us to the conventionalist and relativist ethics that made Devlin's brand of legal moralism so distasteful'.[81] Suppose we are talking about, or to the members of, a polity that criminalizes 'fornication':[82] as it defines its civil order, sexual relations belong to that order, and are properly conducted only within monogamous, heterosexual marriage; fornication thus violates the civil order, and is something into which the polity, through the formal apparatus of the criminal law, can legitimately intervene. On the account I am offering, we cannot fault the logic of this exercise in criminalization: this polity criminalizes what is, in terms of its existent, self-defined civil order, a public wrong. But Moore is similarly placed: he must agree that this polity is criminalizing what it takes to be a serious moral wrong—one serious enough to make it worth incurring the costs of criminalization to ensure that it is punished. That does not mean that either he or I must therefore agree that the polity is justified in this use of its criminal law, since we can each argue that it is unjustified: Moore can argue that they should not view consensual, adult non-marital sex as morally wrong;[83] I can argue that we need not, and should not, discuss the morality of consensual non-marital sex in this context, since it should not be included within the public sphere—that the polity should not define its civil order in this (illiberal) way. Neither of us might succeed in persuading its legislature that such conduct should not be criminalized: but the point here is that neither of us need refrain, on relativist grounds, from criticizing it.

This example illustrates a more general point, which also applies to disagreements within a polity about the scope and contents of its civil order: that if we disagree about whether a polity has good reason, even in principle,[84] to criminalize a type of conduct, we might be disagreeing either about whether it is a public matter at all, or about whether it is wrongful. The difference between these types of disagreement is important, since it affects the kinds of argument, and the kinds of consideration that will be (ir)relevant. A few recent controversies will clarify this point.

[81] M S Moore, 'Liberty's Constraints on What Should be Made Criminal', 199; see above, Chapter 2 at n. 97.

[82] For a useful account of the continuing history of fornication laws in the United States, see Sweeney, 'Undead Statutes': 'fornication' is sometimes defined simply as sex between unmarried people, but sometimes requires the sexual relationship to be 'open and notorious' or to involve (open) cohabitation. This is of course just one of a wealth of examples of laws that criminalize conduct on the basis of objectionable conceptions of both morality and civil order.

[83] See above, Chapter 2 at n. 82. On marriage, see further at nn 108–15 below.

[84] I say 'in principle' because there might also be disagreement about whether the reason is good enough, given the costs of criminalization and other values that might weigh against it.

Consider first debates about whether or under what conditions abortion should be criminal. These often focus on the morality of abortion, but there is a prior question, as the United States Supreme Court clearly recognized in its landmark decision in *Roe v Wade*.[85] It did not ground its decision on the kind of discussion of the morality of abortion found in moral debates outside the law—beyond the determination that a foetus does not count in law as a person, so that abortion is not homicide. Instead it appealed, on the one hand, to the (qualified) right to privacy that it found in the Constitution; and on the other hand, to the state's 'compelling interests' in protecting the health of the pregnant woman and in protecting potential life, which could qualify or limit that right. Each interest 'grows in substantiality as the woman approaches term and, at a point during pregnancy, each becomes "compelling"': the interest in protecting the woman's health becomes compelling 'at approximately the end of the first trimester' (since until then 'mortality in abortion may be less than mortality in normal childbirth'); the interest in protecting potential life becomes compelling once the foetus is viable. But before either interest becomes 'compelling', the state may not interfere: 'the attending physician, in consultation with his patient, is free to determine, without regulation by the State, that, in his medical judgment, the patient's pregnancy should be terminated. If that decision is reached, the judgment may be effectuated by an abortion free of interference by the State.'[86]

I am not concerned here with the soundness of the Court's arguments, or of its interpretation of the Constitution, but only with the character of its judgment about first trimester abortions. The Court does not engage in arguments about the morality of early abortion: it argues neither that such abortions are morally permissible, nor that later abortions are not. Rather, it argues that first trimester abortions are a private matter, to be decided by the woman and her doctor:[87] it is not for the polity to take a collective view on the permissibility of such abortions—a view that the state could then enforce. Furthermore, even after the first trimester the state may attend only to certain kinds of consideration (about the woman's health; and then after viability, about the preservation of potential life): only these constitute the kinds of 'compelling state interest' that could justify interference with the right. It follows that legislators wishing to propose legal limitations on the availability of abortion, or the criminalization of abortions committed outside those limits, are constrained both as to what they may propose, and as to the kinds of reason that they can offer to justify what they propose, if their legislation is not to be unconstitutional: they may not propose limits on first-trimester abortions, and must justify limits on later abortions by reference either to the woman's health or to the need to protect potential life—and argue that those considerations are weighty enough to justify limiting the woman's right of privacy.

The Court should not be read as holding that it is only after the first trimester that abortion could be argued to be morally wrong; or that these are the only kinds of consideration that can bear on the morality of abortion. Its determinations were political, not moral: by which I mean not that they were political rather than legal,[88] but that they concerned the scope and content of the public realm—the realm of the polity as a political community. As individuals, as believers in this or that religion, as members of families, citizens can discuss the morality of abortion as they see fit; as citizens,

[85] 410 US 113 (1973). [86] 410 US 113 (1973), at 162–3.

[87] I leave aside here the objections we might have to assigning this authoritative role to the doctor.

[88] And I do not intend to get involved in the (fruitless) debates about whether in general the US Supreme Court, or other constitutional courts, can be said to be making 'legal' *as distinct from* 'political' decisions.

however, who are engaged in determining the laws that are to govern their civic lives, they must (according to the Court) have nothing to say about first-trimester abortions, since they belong to the private realm; and what they have to say about later abortion must be set in terms of the woman's health or (after viability) the preservation of potential life, and the impact of such considerations on the right to privacy.[89]

Translated into the terms in which I have been talking, the Court's argument amounted to the claim that the American civil order, as defined in its Constitution, included the protection of the health of its citizens, and of viable human life; but it did not include the protection of non-viable human life. There was therefore no need to debate the morality of abortion in the first trimester: that was not an issue that properly concerned the state. Abortion during the first trimester could count as a public matter in one way: it could be argued that abortion services should be available through a publicly funded health service.[90] In terms of permissible state or public intervention, however, first trimester abortion must be recognized as a private matter.

(I might be accused of misrepresenting the Court's argument here. On an alternative reading, the Court allowed that all abortion is a public matter, since it bears on the woman's health and the protection of potential life, both of which are matters of proper state interest, as bearing on the civil order. However, we must weigh the right to privacy against these interests; and during the first trimester (or, in the case of potential life, before viability) those state interests are not strong enough to be 'compelling'—they cannot outweigh or qualify that right. My concern here is not with the constitutionally proper interpretation of this American decision: I need claim only that what I have sketched here is a coherent and plausible line of argument.)

A complication here concerns the distinction between formal and informal civil orders. The Supreme Court's decision concerned the formal civil order: abortion in the first trimester is not the business of the state, or of its officials acting in their official capacity. But could citizens still argue, consistently with that decision, that even early abortion is their informal business, because it bears on their extra-legal civil order? I think that they could not (unless they were arguing that the decision in *Roe v Wade* was wrong): for intervention, even of an informal social kind, would violate the woman's legally protected right to privacy.

There was of course nothing inevitable about the Court's determination of the boundaries of the public realm in this context: nothing inevitable either historically, in the context of the history of the American Constitution, or normatively, as a matter of how that realm could be plausibly or intelligibly defined. A more radical 'pro-choice' view is that the law should never interfere with or set limits on abortion (though it should of course regulate medical practice to protect patients): not because abortion is never morally wrong (for pro-choice advocates need not argue this) but because it is never the polity's business—a view that would need to depend on a denial that the foetus has any civic standing, or is the proper concern of the polity. A more radical 'anti-choice' view is that the law can legitimately interfere at any stage, for instance because from the moment of conception the 'unborn child' (as it would typically be described) has a claim on the attention and protection of the polity: this need not be

[89] Theorists of 'public reason' might say that the Court is here specifying the reasons by appeal to which citizens can seek to persuade each other in 'public' deliberation. We can describe the matter in those terms—so long as they are not taken to imply a commitment to the more ambitious claims of such theorists (see further at nn 134–5 below). All it means here is that this is how this polity, through its constitution, has defined its public realm.

[90] See at nn 68–74 above on the different modalities of public and private.

to say that all abortion should be prohibited, or that it should be allowed only under extreme circumstances (such as a serious threat to the woman's life), but only that the polity has the right to determine the conditions under which abortion is to be permissible, and to enforce that determination through the law. English law, which permits abortion under specified kinds of circumstance, takes such a view: abortions carried out by a doctor within the first twenty-four weeks of a pregnancy are not criminal so long as two doctors certify that this is necessary to avert risks to the woman's health, or that there is a 'substantial risk' that the child would 'be seriously handicapped'.[91] This makes abortion a public matter, as bearing on the civil order (which is thus so defined as to include the interests or standing of the foetus): early abortion must be justified if it is to be legal—rather than simply saying, as *Roe v Wade* allows those concerned to say, that it is not the law's business.[92]

This distinction, between questions of wrongfulness and questions about what belongs in the public realm as bearing on the polity's civil order, can also be neatly illustrated by the notorious English case of consensual sado-masochism.[93] The court held that sado-masochistic conduct was criminal if it caused actual bodily harm,[94] even if it was fully consensual and occurred in private. There are two different ways in which one can argue that the decision, or the law that it applied, was wrong—that such conduct should not be criminal; they reflect two different understandings of the significance of consent in this context. The first is to argue that this kind of conduct, so long as it is consensual, is not wrong: it is a permissible way of seeking mutual sexual pleasure, or of expressing mutual love and respect. This would be to accept that such conduct is the law's, and the polity's, business, as implicating an aspect of its civil order (most obviously, as causing physical injury and thus affecting the physical well-being of those involved): it must be justified if it is not to be liable to some kind of intervention; and the participants' consent is central to that justification. The other argument, however, gives consent a different role, as blocking the need for justification: on this view, the participants' consent transfers what would otherwise have been a public matter into the private realm; the participants need not now justify their sexual practices to their fellow citizens, since they are not their business. On this latter view, their fellow citizens can have any of a range of opinions about the morality of such sexual practices, and might think that such practices are immoral for any of a variety of reasons: but they have no reason either to criminalize them, or to intervene in other ways, since they must recognize that they are private. This was the view asserted by the Wolfenden Committee: 'there must remain a realm of private morality and immorality which is, in brief and crude terms, not the law's business'.[95]

[91] Abortion Act 1967, s. 1. The effect of this provision is to preclude what would otherwise have been criminal liability under the Infant Life (Preservation) Act, or s. 58 of the Offences Against the Person Act 1861: for the details (and complications) see Ormerod and Laird, *Smith and Hogan's Criminal Law*, 689–703.

[92] An issue worth noting here concerns the role of the requirement that the need for an abortion must be certified by two doctors: is that to be understood as part of what makes the abortion itself non-wrongful (or not wrongful in a way that concerns the law); or as prescribing the way in which someone performing an abortion must prove that it was non-wrongful? See further below, Chapter 7 at nn 135–6.

[93] *R v Brown* [1994] 1 AC 212; appealed, unsuccessfully, as *Laskey et al v UK* (1997) 24 EHRR 39. I ignore here some of the complicating factors, concerning the scope and competence of some of the participants' consent.

[94] Offences against the Person Act 1861, s. 47 (see also s. 20 on wounding).

[95] Sir John Wolfenden, *Report of the Committee on Homosexual Offences and Prostitution*, para. 61.

(Suppose, however, that someone argues that such conduct is wrong because it demeans or degrades all those who take part in it—that it violates their human dignity; and that the polity's constitution gives a central role to dignity, as do, for instance, both Poland's and Germany's?[96] Does this make it a public matter, since it implicates this central aspect of the polity's civil order? In that case, the principled argument against criminalizing such conduct would need to be a moral argument that it is consistent with a mutual respect for dignity among the participants. However, this kind of argument might still not be necessary. It would admittedly not be plausible to argue that consent forecloses any question about dignity, or that what one consents to cannot violate one's dignity—that just as *volenti non fit injuria*, so too *volenti non fit indignitas*: for one can surely violate one's own dignity; in which case consent cannot negate or preclude violation. But if the polity's constitution also makes right to privacy or 'private life' a central aspect of its civil order,[97] it might be argued that the participants' consent makes their mutual conduct an aspect of their private lives—and that this trumps any public concern with dignity.)

This distinction, between arguments about what is 'public' or 'private', and arguments about what is wrong or permissible, can also be illustrated by looking at debates about euthanasia and assisted suicide. One argument for decriminalizing them when they are competently requested is that under those conditions they are not wrongful; another is that if they are thus requested they are a private matter into which the state or the polity has no right to intervene. On the latter view, we need not believe them to be morally permissible or justified; we need believe only that it is not for us to intervene in what should be the 'private' choice of the person concerned. This need not be to say that the law can have no role here: given the dangers of 'consent' that is improperly induced or not fully competent, one could argue that assisting or causing another's death should be criminal unless there is a suitable guarantee (for instance, a signed statement by a qualified practitioner) that this was done at the person's competent request. That would, however, be quite different from the more usual kind of legalization, which attaches some substantive conditions, concerning the person's condition and prospects, to the permissibility of assisting their death: on that view assisted dying is the polity's business, even when it is done at the competent request of the person concerned; it is for us collectively, not for them, to determine when and whether it is justified.[98]

The distinction between arguments about what is public or private and arguments about what is morally permissible does not concern only the criminal law. Consider the case of the bed and breakfast owners who refused to let a double room to a gay

[96] See Article 30 of the Polish Constitution, and Article 1(1) of the German *Grundgesetz* (see nn. 51, 54–6 above).

[97] See e.g. European Convention on Human Rights, art. 8: 'Everyone has the right to respect for his private and family life' (also Polish Constitution, art. 47)—although 'interference ... with the exercise of this right', may be permissible if it is 'in accordance with the law' and is necessary for, inter alia, 'the prevention of disorder or crime, [or] for the protection of health or morals'.

[98] See the examples collected in Kennedy Institute of Ethics, 'Euthanasia Regulations Around the World'; also the Assisted Dying Bill (No. 2) 2015 in England. Recent English cases on assisted dying (see above, Chapter 1 at nn 168–76) were partly concerned with issues of 'privacy', since one question concerned the implications of the 'right to respect for [one's] private and family life' enshrined in ECHR, art. 8. The courts accepted that the criminalization of assisted dying constituted an 'interference' with that right, since 'the right of an individual to decide how and when to end his life ... is one aspect of the right to respect for private life' (*Haas v Switzerland* (2011) 53 EHRR 3, at [51]); but such interference could be justified under art. 8(2) as being 'necessary in a democratic society ... for the protection of health or morals, or for the protection of the rights and freedoms of others' (see *Conway* [2017] EWHC 2447).

couple.[99] The court held that running a bed and breakfast establishment brought them within the ambit of s. 81 of the Equality Act 2006, and of the Equality Act (Sexual Orientation) Regulations 2007. Under regulation 4(1), those providing 'goods, facilities or services' to the public must not discriminate against would-be customers on any of the specified grounds (including sexual orientation): this qualifies the 'general rule' that 'suppliers of goods and services' may 'pick and choose their customers'.[100] Had they been inviting people into their home, as a 'private' matter, they could have picked and chosen as they liked, and could have lawfully refused invitations on grounds of race, or religion, or sexual orientation:[101] but once they were engaged in the 'public' activity of providing 'goods, facilities or services' to 'the public', they lost that freedom of choice. To say that they could pick and choose as they liked in such private matters is not to say that it is morally unproblematic to discriminate among those who might seek entry to one's home on grounds of, for instance, their race or sexual orientation (consider here not just the invitations that I might issue to parties, but people who seek admission, for instance to use a toilet or a telephone): it is not to deny that I wrong the person concerned if I turn someone away on such grounds. It is, rather, to say that such conduct is not the law's business—and thus that it is not for the court, speaking in the voice of the law, to judge such conduct.

It might be argued that here again I am misreading the case, and that a Moorean reading is more plausible. I commit just the same wrong, it might be argued, if I turn someone away from my house on grounds of her race or sexual orientation, whether she is a would-be customer of my bed and breakfast business or a stranger asking to use my telephone; we have therefore just the same reason to make that a legally cognizable wrong. The reason why we should bring the former but not the latter kind of discrimination within the reach of the law (if we should) has to do not with the nature of the wrong, but with the seriousness of its impact (it is more harmful to be turned away as a customer), and with the weight of the considerations that may count against making the wrong justiciable (considerations most obviously of privacy and individual freedom). But this underplays the difference between the two kinds of case. Once I embark on providing 'goods, facilities or services' to the public, I take on a new and different role from that which I play simply as a householder deciding who to admit to my property: I bring my activities, and so also my house, into the public or civic realm. We could of course so define the public realm as to incorporate both kinds of conduct—thus, for better or worse, finally overturning the idea that my home is my castle; in this as in other contexts, the distinction between the public and the private is contestable and changeable: but in distinguishing the public and private realms as English law now does, we distinguish the two kinds of wrong—one civic or public, the other private—that the householder can commit in turning people away.

We can find plenty of other examples of ways in which polities can differ from each other or within themselves about what falls within the public realm as part of their

[99] *Preddy v Bull* [2013] 1 WLR 3741; see n. 74 above. The owners' policy was in fact not to let double rooms (as opposed to twin-bedded rooms) to unmarried couples, given their belief that all extra-marital sexual relations were sinful, and that in letting a double room to an unmarried couple they would be promoting sin. This was held to discriminate against the gay couple on the grounds of sexual orientation because, unlike a heterosexual couple, they could not satisfy the requirement to be married (this was before the legalization of gay marriage).

[100] [2013] 1 WLR 3741, at 3744 (Baroness Hale).

[101] And compare Regulation 6(1), which 'provided an exception from regulation 4 for people who take into their own home and treat as members of the family, children, elderly persons or persons requiring a special degree of care and attention' ([2013] 1 WLR 3741, at 3745–6; Baroness Hale).

civil order. Religion is one such example. Some polities are constitutionally secular: the French constitution declares, in its first article, that 'France is an indivisible, secular, democratic and social Republic'.[102] Citizens are still free to hold and practice their religious beliefs, as private matters outside the purview of the polity and the state; but if the Republic is secular, this can set limits on the display of religious beliefs and rituals in what are counted as 'public' contexts—for instance in state education.[103] Other polities are constitutionally religious: Article 1 of the Iranian constitution declares that '[t]he form of government of Iran is that of an Islamic Republic', and Article 2 that this republic is 'based on belief in . . . the One God'.[104] Within such a polity, religious belief and behaviour are public matters, as part of its *res publica*. Other polities fall between these two extremes. England, for instance, has an established church, twenty-six of whose bishops sit in its parliament's upper chamber as 'lords spiritual', and whose head is the sovereign; many of its public rituals have a religious dimension; and blasphemy against the Christian god was a criminal offence until 2008.[105] On the other hand, a person's religious beliefs are generally recognized to be a private matter, between her and her god (if any) and her fellow believers; and where once there was a legal requirement or social expectation to swear a religious oath, people may now 'affirm' instead, without formal or informal penalty.

Second, consider planning regulations of various kinds as they apply to private property—regulations concerning what may be built (or destroyed), to what kinds of design, even in what colours. At one, libertarian, extreme we would find no constraints on what a person does with her own land, unless what she does has a material impact on others' persons or property: she can build what she likes, in whatever style she likes; she can pull down her house and build another; the law cannot constrain her, and if challenged by others (her neighbours) about her choices and actions, she might reply that it is none of their business. Here again we can distinguish two kinds of response through which a person might seek to ward off critical challenges from others. One response is justificatory: the property owner justifies her actions in aesthetic, or economic, or ecological terms. The other response is a denial that she needs to answer to her neighbours on this matter: what she does on her property is her business, not theirs; she is not answerable to them for her choices. The latter response appeals to a distinction between the public and a private realm: what she does on her property is 'public' in the sense that it is visible to all (unless she builds a concealing hedge or wall); but it is a 'private' matter in the sense that, she argues, it is not for others to intervene, either by law or by informal social pressure. At the other end of the spectrum (in polities that recognize private property, including real estate), we may find a system of strict planning regulations: people need a formal licence to destroy or to build; there are strict controls on what may be built. Some such controls may be based on considerations of health and safety (the health and safety of the owners themselves, and of those to whom they will rent or sell what they build), or on environmental and ecological considerations, but some may be based on aesthetic or cultural grounds—to preserve historically interesting and aesthetically pleasing buildings from demolition, to prohibit the building of eyesores and buildings that clash with their surroundings.

[102] And see the *loi du 9 décembre 1905 concernant la séparation des Églises et de l'État*.

[103] This strict '*laïcité*' of the French *res publica* has generated some well known recent controversies, for instance over the law banning the wearing of religious symbols in public schools (*loi no 2004-228 du 15 mars 2004 encadrant, en application du principe de laïcité, le port de signes ou de tenues manifestant une appartenance religieuse dans les écoles, collèges et lycées publics*).

[104] See at n. 45 above.

[105] It was abolished by s. 79 of the Criminal Justice and Immigration Act 2008.

In between we might find polities in which there are few governmental planning regulations and restrictions, but there are informal social conventions, that give one's neighbours standing to comment on and to challenge what one does with one's own property: someone who neglects his garden might violate no formal law or local by-law, but might violate strong local conventions, and be told so quite forcefully; the state of his garden is not a private matter. These differences too are differences in how communities distinguish, formally or informally, between public and private matters.

Third, consider the ways in which contracts might be treated. The possibility of contracts is of course itself, in polities like our own, an important aspect of the *res publica*: the law, and the institutions that it structures, enable us to make not merely private agreements whose force and enforcement are matters only for the parties concerned, or socially recognized agreements which can be enforced only by 'the moral coercion of public opinion', but legally binding agreements that can be enforced by law.[106] Now on one view, whilst contracts belong to the public realm, to the *res publica*, in the sense that they are legally enforceable, their *content* is a private matter: contracting parties can contract to anything they wish, and can go to law to enforce their contract (unless the fulfilment of the contract would have some legally cognizable adverse effect on non-consenting third parties, or would in other ways involve a breach of law); that reflects a view of autonomy as an absolute value, so that the only constraints on contracts should be procedural—to do with voluntariness and deception. On another view the polity has a legitimate interest in the content of contracts, not only when their fulfilment might violate another law, but when it would be '*contra bonos mores*': '*bonos mores*' in this context has been usually interpreted as concerned with sex and gambling, to preclude the enforcement of gambling debts or of sexual contracts.[107] Here again we find different views about the scope of the public realm in relation to the private: about how far the content of contracts is a purely private matter, or is potentially public.

Finally, consider the ways in which marriage may be understood. We can again sketch two extremes. At one extreme, marriage is understood as an important part of the polity's civic life, and is strictly defined, for instance in monogamous and heterosexual terms.[108] It is central to the polity's shared social understanding of human relationships, as the proper form of life for citizens—all should aspire to marriage (and children); those who do not, or who aspire in vain, are liable to criticism or pity. It is given institutional form by the law, which both makes marriage possible as a legal relationship and governs its forms, its implications, and also its dissolution (by setting constraints on what can count as grounds for divorce or annulment). It is given positive support, not only in sermons and exhortations, but also, for instance, through various kinds of tax advantage. It might be protected by the criminal law—thus being defined as 'public' in a way that sanctions formal intervention by the state: 'deviant' marriages, such as bigamous or polygamous marriages, might be not just nullified, but criminalized, even when they involve no fraud or coercion between the parties

[106] Recall Hart's comments on the importance of 'power-conferring' rules in law—laws that confer power on the individual citizen to make such things as contracts and wills: Hart, *The Concept of Law*, 27–8. On 'the moral coercion of public opinion' see Mill, *On Liberty*, ch. 1, para. 9.

[107] For the modern law, see J Poole, *Textbook on Contract Law*, ch. 16.

[108] See e.g. Article 18 of the Polish Constitution: 'Marriage, being a union of a man and a woman, as well as the family, motherhood and parenthood, shall be placed under the protection and care of the Republic of Poland'.

involved;[109] marital wrongs such as adultery may be criminalized.[110] At the other extreme, marriage would have no such social or legal centrality. We could, for instance, envisage a system under which adults could make various kinds of legally binding cohabitation contract, without constraint on gender or number, or on the precise content of the contract (although there would be legal requirements concerning children and their care); churches or other organizations could conduct 'marriages' under their own rules, but such marriages would have no legal standing; and there would be no social expectation that people should enter into such formal relationships.[111] Britain falls (somewhat messily) between these extremes. Marriage is still publicly recognized and supported as a model relationship, if not now as the only model; though it is now recognized, both legally and socially, that marriage need not be heterosexual,[112] bigamous and polygamous forms of marriage remain criminal; civil partnerships are formally recognized as an alternative to marriage that brings many of its legal benefits—but are available only to same sex couples.[113] Adultery is still a legally cognizable wrong: but it is not a criminal wrong, since it is up to the injured party to bring it to law as grounds for divorce—or not to pursue it formally;[114] and it is thus possible for married couples themselves to decide, as a matter of private morality, whether in the context of their marriage adultery is a wrong, and if so how serious a wrong it is. Marriage is thus still in many ways a public matter, as part of the polity's civil order: but participation in the practice and adherence to its rules is now more a matter of private agreement than of formal public expectation, and the forms that participation in the practice can take are more diverse.[115]

The examples discussed in this section were intended to illustrate both the complexity of the various normative distinctions, formal and informal, that we draw between what is 'public' and what is 'private', and the ways in which polities or people may differ or disagree in their views about what is, or should be, a public matter—about the scope, content, and structure of their civil order. Such differences and disagreements are a familiar feature of modern societies—as are the changes in both legal definitions and social understandings of the public and private realms to which they can lead: as I noted at the beginning of this section, conceptions of the public realm can change, and can sometimes be changed through political action. Differences, disagreements, and changes of these kinds need not undermine the existence of a political

[109] For bigamy and polygamy, see e.g. Offences Against the Person Act 1861, s. 57; Model Penal Code § 230.1; German *Strafgesetzbuch* § 172. For a useful theoretical discussion of the criminalization of polygamy, see D N Husak, 'Polygamy: A Novel Test for a Theory of Criminalization'.

[110] See at nn 75, 82 above, on adultery and fornication.

[111] On possibilities for marriage (or its absence) in a polity, see E Brake (ed.), *After Marriage: Rethinking Marital Relationships*; C Chambers, *Against Marriage: An Egalitarian Defence of the Marriage-Free State*.

[112] See e.g. Marriage (Same Sex Couples) Act 2013.

[113] For whom marriage was at that time unavailable: see Civil Partnership Act 2004; see also *Steinfeld v Secretary of State for Education* [2017] HRLR 3.

[114] And adultery must be heterosexual (https://www.gov.uk/divorce/grounds-for-divorce); we must hope that this is a temporary quirk of English law.

[115] The introduction of same sex marriage also makes it possible for same sex relationships to become, optionally, 'public', rather than a purely 'private' matter: that is, a same sex couple now have a formal, legally recognized, way of publicly declaring and celebrating their relationship—*if* they wish to do so. Thus conduct that was once public, as constituting a criminal offence, became private in the first wave of liberal reform, exemplified by the Wolfenden Committee's argument (see at n. 95 above), and remains private as far as criminal law is concerned—it is not something into which the polity can legitimately intervene. In other ways, however, it has become a more (optionally) public matter, in the sense that such relationships are not now just ignored, or tolerated, but are publicly recognized, supported, and celebrated as ordinary forms of human love and commitment.

community, or the stability of its civil order: indeed, they are features of a flourishing democratic polity. However, we must turn now to a more radical objection to the kind of account I am developing of criminal law as connected to a polity's civil order—that in contemporary societies like our own we do not have, we cannot find, the kind of unified political communities on which that account depends. If some version of this objection is sound, an account like mine might still be attractive as a thought experiment—wouldn't it be nice if we had such communities: but it would offer a fantasy rather than an ideal towards which we could even aspire, and thus could not offer us a normative theory of criminal law.[116]

6. The Possibility of Civil Order?

In Chapter 3 I discussed the issue of individual dissent: what can 'we' (we who claim to speak in the polity's voice, on the basis of its shared values and its conception of its civil order) say to one who dissents from or does not share those values? But I have not yet addressed two more radical kinds of criticism of the account I am developing.

One criticism denies that we can find, in contemporary, conflictual societies like our own, the kind of civil order that my account requires. For even if we can identify a coherent formal legal order, a coherent structure of institutions and law,[117] we cannot find the kind of substantive civil order, structured by substantial values in terms of which the citizens can understand their shared lives, that is needed if a polity is to exist as a political community: all we have, after the failure of the 'Enlightenment Project', are the ruins of practices that perhaps once made sense and could give material form to a shared conception of a civic enterprise—mere 'simulacra' of morality and of political community.[118] I will not address such pessimism directly here, except to suggest, first, that it might reflect a 'disappointed metaphysical absolutism' of a kind analogous to that which Finnis diagnosed among proponents of 'critical legal studies'.[119] For if we begin with an implausibly (metaphysically) ambitious view of what could count as a rational foundation for a practice or a polity, and find that no such foundation is available, we may be led to a despairing denial of the rationality of any such practice—when what we should instead do is question our starting point.[120] We cannot, of course, rule out a priori the possibility that such pessimism is justified: we have no metaphysical or moral guarantee of the existence or survival of a political community; something that has the formal institutional structure of a community could indeed have become a hollow shell whose superstructure disguises what is in reality no more than an uneasy *modus vivendi*, or the exercise of coercive power by some over others. But we can still hope that we live in what is, or can become, a political community. Second, 'can become' in the previous sentence is important: it reminds us that community in general, and political community in particular, can be a matter of aspiration as much as

[116] See e.g. J Edwards and A P Simester, 'What's Public About Crime?', 130–1.

[117] Which some critics would deny: see for instance, in relation to criminal law, the arguments of proponents of 'critical legal studies' (e.g., most drastically, M Kelman, 'Interpretive Construction in the Substantive Criminal Law'; more moderately, A W Norrie, *Crime, Reason and History: A Critical Introduction to Criminal Law*; in response, D N MacCormick, 'Reconstruction after Deconstruction: A Response to CLS'; R A Duff, 'Principle and Contradiction in the Criminal Law: Motives and Criminal Liability').

[118] See A MacIntyre, *After Virtue*, chs 1–6; also A W Norrie, '"Simulacra of Morality"? Beyond the Ideal/Actual Antinomies of Criminal Justice'.

[119] J Finnis, 'On "The Critical Legal Studies Movement"', at 160.

[120] See above, Introduction, at nn 18–25.

of established fact; that what constitutes us as a community can consist partly in our shared aspiration to achieve the comity that community requires. Third, we should not be overly demanding in specifying the existence conditions for a political, or any other kind of, community, or the nature and extent of the agreement in values on which it depends. Any community, any 'form of life' (and political community is a form of life), requires 'not only agreement in definitions but also . . . in judgments':[121] but such agreement is quite consistent with wide and deep disagreement.[122] The agreement cannot, it is true, be *purely* procedural, about the procedures through which we are to try to resolve our differences or decide how to live together: for a procedure depends on some substantive conception of those who are to take part in it, and what they owe to each other.[123] But it can be substantially procedural, and thus consistent with wide and deep substantive disagreement.

Another, more challenging, criticism emerges from these points about agreement. It does not deny the existence of genuine normative community, whose members see themselves as engaged in a shared practice: the objection is not that there is no such community, but rather that there are too many. In our contemporary western societies, we find (and we are indeed urged by advocates of 'multiculturalism' to welcome and to embrace) a variety of different communities, which may be united internally by rich sets of shared values (moral, political, and religious), but which are divided from each other by deep gulfs across which no sufficiently substantial normative agreement can be found to ground a shared polity. A critic who makes this kind of claim can then offer us two ways in which we could understand the role of criminal law in the context of such deep cultural differences.

The more pessimistic account of how criminal law could function in societies characterized by such profound cultural diversity accepts that we may be able to connect the society's criminal law to some conception of 'civil order' and of the defining values of 'the polity': there might well be a political community whose shared values are expressed in the society's institutions and laws. But that is not, the pessimist will argue, a political community that includes all those who are supposed to belong to the polity and to be bound by its laws; it is, rather, a community of the (relatively) powerful or favoured, who can impose their shared values and understandings on the members of the other relatively disadvantaged communities within the jurisdiction that the polity claims.[124] The problem here is not (simply) that of whether the criminal law should recognize a 'cultural defence'—not even if we take it that such a defence would be justificatory rather than excusatory, permitting people to commit what the law defines as a crime if that is what their own culture's values prescribe (or permit);[125] it goes deeper than that. A 'cultural defence' implicitly accepts the overarching authority of the law

[121] L Wittgenstein, *Philosophical Investigations*, 242.

[122] Indeed, disagreement, as distinct from difference or mere mutual incomprehension, is possible only given some underlying level of agreement: if we are to disagree in the answers we give to certain normative questions, we must agree about what those questions are, as well as about what could count as possible answers to them.

[123] On proceduralism, see e.g. J Waldron, *Law and Disagreement*; D Archard, 'Political Reasonableness'.

[124] To say that they 'impose' their values on other communities is to say either that they cannot claim that these are values that the others should accept—the gulf between them is too deep for such a claim to be plausible; or that they make such a claim, but also make no honest effort to justify it.

[125] On the cultural defence see A D Renteln, *The Cultural Defense*; K Greenawalt, 'The Cultural Defense'; W Kymlicka et al (eds), *Criminal Law and Cultural Diversity*. For useful discussions of 'multi-culturalism', see P Kelly (ed.), *Multiculturalism Reconsidered: Culture and Equality and Its Critics*; W Kymlicka, *Multicultural Odysseys: Navigating the New International Politics of Diversity*.

under which it is to be brought: it accepts that the law is binding on members of the culture in question, and argues that it ought to make some accommodation for their distinctive values. The objection raised here, however, casts doubt on that authority: it is that members of minority or non-hegemonic cultural groups can reasonably believe that they are being subjected to, rather than included in, the dominant group's exercise of political power, and therefore have reason to deny that this is their law.

A more optimistic account of criminal law in profoundly diverse societies is that it 'can help make such societies possible', by 'set[ting] standards for co-operation that, rather than assuming consensus, accommodate *dissensus*': it can function not to 'help implement a moral consensus but, *inter alia*, [to] enable people to live harmoniously in its absence'.[126] Criminal law, on this view, does not need the underpinning of shared values, the shared conception of a civil order, that I have portrayed as necessary to a polity; a central part of its rationale in our contemporary societies is indeed to make social life possible in the absence of any such underpinning.

The more pessimistic view is certainly plausible in some cases: there are societies in which the ruling or dominant group cannot claim legitimate authority over the subjugated groups whom they claim to bind by their laws. An obvious, safely historical, example is that of apartheid South Africa. The law, including the criminal law, might have been the law of the white minority: a law they could recognize and accept as their own, as reflecting and protecting their values and their conception of civil order. But it was not a law that the members of the black majority could be expected to recognize or to own as *their* law—as a law that could plausibly claim to serve the common good of a political community of which they could see themselves (and see themselves as being seen by others) as members. We might still say that they were living under a system of law, and were prosecuted and punished under a criminal law: but we would also have to say that it was radically defective as a system of law, just insofar as it could not plausibly be portrayed as their law. It failed to be what law must claim to be;[127] and if that failure was radical enough, if the claims made for the law's authority over such an oppressed majority were hollow enough, we might say that it was not a system of law at all, but merely an exercise in coercive power dressed up as law. Analogously, if a university system is gradually transformed into a system that sells paying customers the kinds of training or expertise that they demand, critics might initially argue that it is failing as a system of university education, in terms of the goals and values internal to the idea of a university; if that failure becomes radical enough, they might then say that it is no longer a university system (in anything but name).

I will not pursue here the question of how far such a pessimistic view is also true of some of our own societies. It is obviously true that, in one sense, we do have systems of criminal law: we have all the institutional apparatus of law, including criminal law; and that apparatus continues to operate. But that does not rule out the possibility that its operations are pathological;[128] or that it effectively functions in relation to at least a significant proportion of the society as an exercise in oppressive power rather than the rule of law.[129] However, we should not be too quick to suppose, as both pessimists and (relative) optimists suppose, that we cannot find in contemporary western societies

[126] Edwards and Simester, 'What's Public About Crime?', 131 (emphasis in original).

[127] Compare Aquinas, *Summa Theologiae* 1a2ae90–97: he does not here make the claim often ascribed to natural law theorists that 'unjust law is not law', but says that law that radically fails to be what, in terms of its '*ratio*', it ought to be, is a 'perversion' or 'abuse' of law, or 'spoilt' law.

[128] See W Stuntz, 'The Pathological Politics of Criminal Law'.

[129] See e.g. the American literature cited above, Chapter 3, n. 151.

the kinds of shared value, or the collective engagement in a shared civic practice, that make political community possible, even across cultural groups with profoundly different values and beliefs. In particular, there are three mistakes we need to avoid in this context.

The first mistake is to exaggerate the kind and extent of agreement in values that is required for political community to be possible. A pluralist, liberal polity does not depend on its members sharing a rich, comprehensive conception of the good; part of its civil order is indeed to protect and support its members in their pursuit of their own very different conceptions of the good. It follows that, in such a polity, the political community of citizens is only one of the communities to which its members belong—and probably not be the most significant one; the shared practice of civic life is only one of the practices in which they are engaged—and is probably not the most important practice in their lives. Some agreement in values, substantive as well as procedural, is needed, as I noted above:[130] citizens must be ready to recognize each other as fellow participants in the enterprise of living together as a polity, though the civic life that they live together might be only a small part of their lives. But such agreement in values, and in mutual recognition as fellow citizens, is consistent with deep differences and disagreements in conceptions of the good.

Second, and relatedly, we should not exaggerate the difficulty of achieving such agreement, even in a society characterized by deep cultural differences and distances: we should not portray as unbridgeable gulfs what are in fact normative, cultural variations across which understanding, shared deliberation, and eventually agreement (on a limited but significant set of political issues) are possible, especially if those involved on each side of such discussion are willing to engage, and willing to accept a pluralist vision of the polity that allows maximum space for different cultures to pursue their own goals and their own visions of the good. We cannot *guarantee* such agreement, even between the dominant or majority voices of each group: we cannot be confident of finding a Rawlsian overlapping consensus,[131] or a Gaus-ian convergence on a set of principles or values that all sides can find at least acceptable.[132] But that is not to say that we cannot *hope* to achieve agreement, partly by finding connections between our diverse normative starting points. Edwards and Simester doubt whether 'the requisite moral consensus exists' in societies such as the USA or the UK, but argue that law, and in particular criminal law, can 'enable people to live harmoniously in its absence'.[133] However, if what the law enables is indeed 'harmonious' living, living together as something distinct from, and more than, mere co-existence without conflict, it requires some consensus about the character and conditions of such harmony—a consensus that is necessary not just for a criminal law, but for the whole apparatus of law and government. That is the kind of consensus that can establish a shared civil order, and that we can hope to achieve across deep differences between the various cultural groups that compose a liberal polity.

The third mistake is to suppose that where we cannot reach agreement, we (the majority or dominant group) can claim that the norms and values that structure our civil order are binding on those who dissent from them only if (as ambitious advocates of 'public reason' suppose) we can justify those norms and values 'by appeal to ideas

[130] See at nn 121–3 above.

[131] See e.g. J Rawls, 'The Idea of an Overlapping Consensus'.

[132] G Gaus, *The Order of Public Reason: A Theory of Freedom and Morality in a Diverse and Bounded World.*

[133] See at n. 126 above.

or arguments that those persons, at some level of idealization, endorse or accept'.[134] Some people believe, some groups share a collective belief, that it is right for girls to be subjected to (what we insist on calling) female genital mutilation, or for a husband to beat (or, as they might claim, 'chastise') his disobedient wife, or for a parent to kill a daughter who has 'dishonoured' her family by her choice of sexual partner, or for believers to kill someone who insults their god. The law, speaking in the civic voice of a liberal polity, will say that they are wrong to act on such beliefs, and will be held to criminal account if they do so, but this need not depend on a claim that they are already committed to values from which such conclusions about the wrongfulness of such conduct could be derived; we might recognize that to accept such normative conclusions would require a profound (but rationally possible) change in their beliefs and their conception of the world. Nor need the polity say only that, whatever their beliefs, they should respect the local conventions and refrain from conduct that 'we' regard as wrong: it can argue that they ought to recognize that conduct as (a public) wrong. That 'ought' must be supportable by appealing to reasons that the dissenters *could* recognize and accept as good (indeed conclusive) reasons, and there are familiar puzzles about the meaning of 'could' in such contexts: but whilst I could come to accept a reason only if that reason was in some sense accessible to me, within my rational grasp, that is not to say that I could come to accept it only if I already, 'at some level of idealization', accepted premises from which that reason follows.[135] If members of a dissenting group then object that the polity has no right to make such demands on them, since they do not recognize this polity as theirs or as having authority over them, the only answer (which is a perfectly adequate answer) is that they, and we, are stuck with each other as fellow members of this political association,[136] and that the associative duties that they, and we, thereby acquire are not to be voluntarily rejected. We can say that they have the right to leave, to emigrate to another polity—although we must also recognize that it might be hard or impossible to exercise that right, or to exercise it in a way that would mark an improvement in their eyes. We can also say (and had better make sure that it is true) that they can play a full part in the political deliberation by which the polity determines and develops its civil order, find a respectful hearing for their arguments in that deliberation, and try to persuade others that their views should prevail—or that they should be allowed to prevail within their own communities:[137] whilst we might regard their views as unreasonable (which is why we insist that they are wrong), we must still recognize them as full participants in the polity's public deliberations.

But, it might be argued, if the normative differences between us are sufficiently deep, if the disagreements are sufficiently intractable, should the dominant group not be ready to allow the dissenting group its own political autonomy: should it not, that is, either be allowed to secede, and to claim its status as an independent polity; or at least have significant powers devolved it, so that it can govern its own members as it and they see fit? This raises issues that we cannot pursue here: all I would say is that the kinds of example suggested above all involve conduct that (as we see it and insist that

[134] J Quong, 'Public Reason' (Quong provides a useful survey of the debates). For forceful critique of more ambitious conceptions of public reason, see D Enoch, 'The Disorder of Public Reason', 'Against Public Reason', 'Political Philosophy and Epistemology: The Case of Public Reason'.

[135] The controversy over 'internal' and 'external' reasons is obviously relevant here: what kind of connection must there be between a putative reason to Φ and my existing set of values for it to be true that I have reason to Φ, or that there is reason for me to Φ? See famously on either side of that debate B Williams, 'Internal and External Reasons', J McDowell, 'Might There Be External Reasons?'; also, to my mind persuasively, J Dancy, *Practical Reality*.

[136] See above, Chapter 3 at nn 115–16. [137] See Pettit, 'Law and Liberty', 51–8.

we are right to see it) seriously wrongs other people; to allow such a group to secede, or to devolve power over such matters to it, would be to betray or abandon those who would then be victimized; but we surely owe it to them, as fellow citizens (not to mention fellow human beings) not thus to abandon them.

Finally, it is worth emphasizing the point that a polity's civil order need not be a monolithic and unchangeable structure of values, norms, institutions, and ways of thought. It can be, and in flourishing liberal polities will be, a work in progress; it will accommodate very different views about individual goods, and about the common good; it will provide democratic structures within which such different views can be publicly debated and deliberated; its conception of its public realm and its common good will include such debate;[138] and it will be susceptible to change and development in the light of those debates. Political community of this kind might be as much a matter of aspiration as of established fact, and I do not mean to understate the extent to which in our existing societies we fall short of that aspirational ideal, or the significant political problems that we face in trying to work towards it (including that of persuading each other that it is an ideal towards which we should work); but we can still recognize it as an ideal towards which we can sensibly aspire.

7. Civil Order, Criminal Law, and Public Wrongs

I have so far been offering a rather formal account of civil order as the normative structure of a polity; indeed, I have emphasized that a civil order need not, as far as the logic of civil order is concerned, be a democratic order, and that different polities will ground their civil orders in very different conceptions of their ends, of their common good, of the values by which their members are to live together, and of the scopes of their public and their private realms. They will also (to connect the discussion in this chapter to the discussion of citizenship in the previous chapter) have different conceptions of citizenship: any conception of civil order will include some idea of whose order it is—an idea not just of what it is to be a citizen, but of how citizenship is acquired, of what it requires, and of whether and how it can be lost; polities will differ in how inclusionary or exclusionary, how modest or ambitious, their conceptions of citizenship are. In the following chapter I will offer an inclusionary conception of citizenship: but that will depend on a more substantive account of political community and civil order than I have so far tried to offer.

I have also so far said almost nothing about the relationship between a polity's criminal law and its civil order—beyond suggesting that criminal law can both sustain, and partly constitute, the civil order; nor can I say more here, on the basis of such a formal account of civil order. For the role that criminal law can play will depend on a more substantive conception both of criminal law and of civil order: how a polity conceives its criminal law will depend on how it conceives its civil order; and the role that such an institutional practice might play will depend on the kind of order in relation to which it is to play it.

If, for instance, we see criminal law as 'a coercive rule-enforcing institution', characterized by the harshness of the sanctions it threatens and imposes,[139] we will probably see it as playing an essentially instrumental role in sustaining a civil order that can be characterized independently of it—although that order must be such as to make

[138] Compare, classically, Mill on the value of freedom of speech in *On Liberty*.

[139] Chiao, 'What is the Criminal Law For?', 138–9; see at nn 16, 22 above.

normatively possible that kind of coercive relationship between the polity and its citizens. If instead we portray criminal law, as I portrayed it in Chapter 1, as an institutional practice that functions primarily to define and declare a set of public wrongs, and to call those accused of committing such wrongs to formal public account, we are relying on a particular conception of civil order, as an order that requires or makes room for this kind of legal practice. If, therefore, I am to give the conception of criminal law that I sketched in Chapter 1 a more adequate normative grounding, and show what role criminal law as thus conceived might play in a polity's civil order, I must progress from the formal to the more substantive, to begin to flesh out a substantive conception of a particular kind of civil order; that is the task of the following chapter.

This will also involve developing a more substantive account of the idea of public wrongs, as the kind of wrong that properly concern the criminal law. A public wrong, we might now say, is a wrong that violates or threatens the civil order. Indeed, something like this now seems to be a defining criterion of 'public wrong': since the public realm, as far as the polity is concerned, is constituted by its civil order, a wrong can count as public in the polity's eyes only if it in some way implicates that civil order. However, we cannot yet say anything more determinate than that 'something like this' is a defining criterion, since we do not yet have a clear enough idea of how public wrongs relate to civil order—whether, for instance, 'violate' and 'threaten' are appropriate verbs to describe that relationship. Nor, indeed, can we yet say whether threatening or violating the civil order is a sufficient, as well as a necessary, condition for being a public wrong: whether that is true depends on how we should understand the idea of threatening or violating civil order. An earthquake or other natural disaster, an attack by an enemy army, can certainly do substantial harm to a polity's institutions and operations; and though we might hope that a stable and secure polity will be able to resist and adapt to such emergencies, we must surely also admit both that there could be disasters (natural or manmade) that would destroy the civic institutions of even a stable and secure polity, and that less overwhelming disasters can still threaten civil order—even if the threat is resisted. Perhaps a *violation* of civil order, as something distinct from a contingent threat that might undermine or damage it as a consequence, requires wrongful action: an earthquake does not violate civil order, although it certainly disrupts ordinary civic life; nor does a direct enemy attack violate civil order, though it might be intended to disrupt the polity's functioning consequentially (as distinct from treason committed by a traitor, and from the covert work of fifth columnists, as well as from civil war, which clearly do violate civil order).[140] But we still need to ask what is to count as a 'violation' of civil order, and whether everything we are to count as a public wrong, or as being in principle criminalizable, must constitute a violation of the polity's civil order—or whether it is enough that the conduct in question somehow threatens the civil order without violating it. We will also need to ask whether the violation of civil order is what makes the conduct in question wrong; or is it rather what constitutes an already wrongful type of conduct as a public wrong?

These suggestions do not, of course, help to give the idea of public wrongs any substantive content: it is still a formal notion, which will be given substantive content only by spelling out a substantive conception of civil order. Nor, accordingly, does the idea of a public wrong yet offer us a substantive principle, or criterion, of criminalization: critics will still object that I have not provided a substantive, non-question-begging

[140] If the attack constitutes the crime of aggression (Rome Statute of the International Criminal Court, Art. 8 *bis*), it can be said to violate the civil order; but that order is the order of the 'community of nations'.

'criterion for the public/private distinction' as 'a distinction that is supposed to mark the proper limits of criminal legislation'.[141] But that is not what I have been trying to do. I have, rather, been trying to explain the relevant concept of the 'public' as marking a particular kind of normative space; and I have connected that concept to the idea of civil order, as the normative structure of a political community. To give the idea of a public wrong any substantive content, we must develop a more substantive conception of civil order: this will involve appealing to a normative political theory—to a normative conception of how a polity should define itself. That is the task to which I must now turn.

[141] M S Moore, 'Liberty's Constraints on What Should be Made Criminal', 199; see above, Chapter 2 at n. 94.

5

A Liberal Republic and its Criminal Law

1. Political Theory and Civil Order

In the previous chapter, I offered a rather formal account of the idea of civil order: a polity's civil order is that institutional, legal, and social ordering through which it defines, actualizes, and sustains its guiding goals and values. Civil orders can be, to different degrees, static or mutable, monolithic or pluralistic, coherent or conflicted; they are not always democratic; they can define larger or smaller (or simply different) realms of the 'private' that are not the business of the polity or the state; they can be structured by values and goals that others deplore. However, all must (if they are to count as civil orders at all) embody a conception of the polity's *res publica*, and of its members' common good. They must also include a conception of membership: of how membership of the polity is acquired, and whether and how it can be lost; of the standing (or the standings, in non-egalitarian polities) of members, and of their claims on each other and on the polity, as well as of the standing of non-members who find themselves in the polity's territory.[1]

I have said almost nothing yet about the relationship of criminal law to a polity's civil order, for good reason: whether a polity will have any role at all for a system of criminal law, and what that role could be, will depend on how criminal law is understood, and how the polity conceives its civil order. It is true that if we see criminal law simply as a technique for controlling human conduct (by, most obviously, the threat and imposition of sanctions), we will be able to see it as playing roughly the same role in different kinds of polity—so long as their conception of their civil order makes normatively possible that kind of coercive relationship between the polity and its members. But, first, we will still need to ask what kind(s) of 'control' are legitimate within the civil order of the polity. Is it, for instance, consistent with the values that structure that civil order to use coercive modes of incapacitation on those judged likely to cause harm, and could criminal punishment then be used as one such mode of incapacitation? Does the polity's understanding of the status of its members, and of their relationship to the state, make it legitimate to use criminal punishment as a deterrent? Second, if we instead see criminal law as I have suggested we should see it,[2] as a practice that defines a set of public wrongs and calls to formal public account those accused of committing such wrongs, we need to ask what kind of polity, with what kind of civil order, could have a role for an institution of that kind—and what that role could be.

That is the question that I will begin to answer in this chapter, which aims to put some flesh on the formal skeleton of an account of civil order and political community that I sketched in the previous chapter. This will also help to support the account of criminal law that I offered in Chapter 1, by showing how such an institution plays an important role in a plausible normative account of political community; and it will fill out, and support, the account of citizenship in relation to the criminal law that I sketched in Chapter 3, by characterizing a kind of polity in which citizenship could

[1] See above, Chapter 3, section 3. [2] See Chapter 1 above.

have that kind of significance. This should remind us, if we need reminding, of the way in which criminal law theory must depend on political theory. A normative theory of criminal law must be a theory of criminal law's role in or in relation to a polity's civil order, since criminal law is part of the institutional structure by which that civil order is constituted and sustained; so it requires a normative theory of civil order, which must be part of a political theory of the polity, of the state, and of the relationships between the polity and its citizens. This is not to say that each different political theory will generate a different account of the role of criminal law: it might well be that different theories converge on similar accounts of criminal law. But we can expect theories that differ quite radically from each other to generate different accounts of criminal law: consider, for instance, the accounts of criminal law that might be given by radically individualist libertarians who believe in a minimal state, by traditional communists, and by advocates of an Islamic state whose law would be sharia law. If we ask, however, what kinds of political theory could make what kinds of sense of systems of criminal law like those in contemporary western democracies, despite the many differences between them, we should not expect to find a single answer, since different theories will each be able to rationalize at least the central features of those systems;[3] one question then is whether there will be particular, controversial, cases in which the theory one holds will make a difference to one's view about what should be criminalized.

We are not short of accounts of (at least aspects of) criminal law grounded in political theory of various kinds.[4] I will not discuss or compare them here, save to note that whilst they attend in detail to questions about what should be criminalized and to the goals of criminal punishment, they tend to pay little or no attention to the criminal process or the criminal trial—which is, I will argue (in line with my comments on the criminal process in Chapter 1) a mistake. I will instead sketch a particular kind of political theory—a liberal communitarian republican theory—as a basis for a particular kind of conception of civil order, of criminal law, and of the role of the criminal law in such an order. I will not attempt to argue for such a theory, or to show it to be superior to others: I am not sure in the end what would count as such an argument, beyond a clear presentation of the theory and its implications, together with the implicit question 'Isn't this a normatively plausible picture of civic life?'. Nor indeed will I discuss the details of the kind of theory on which I will be relying: different proponents of this kind of theory will differ, sometimes deeply, about the substantive features of the civil order, about just what role a system of criminal law should play in relation to such an order, and about the types of conduct that should (even in principle) be criminalized; I will not engage in detail with (let alone try to settle) such differences here. My aim is, rather, as much illustrative as persuasive: that is, although I hope that the kind of

[3] Which is also to say that the Herculean endeavours of a Dworkinian theorist (or judge) will probably not come up with a single 'best fit' theory: see R M Dworkin, *Law's Empire*.

[4] For a small recent selection (and leaving aside works focused particularly on punishment), see e.g. S Besson and J L Martí (eds), *Legal Republicanism: National and International Perspectives*, Part IIB (essays by J L Martí, R Dagger, R Gargarella); R A Duff and S P Green (eds), *Philosophical Foundations of Criminal Law*, Part I (essays by M Thorburn, R Dagger, M Matravers, M Dubber, A Ristroph, R A Duff); V Tadros (ed.), *Symposium on Political Philosophy and Criminal Justice* (papers by S Garvey, M Matravers, A Haque, F Tanguay-Renaud, Y J Lee); R A Duff et al (eds), *Criminalization: The Political Morality of the Criminal Law* (essays by P Pettit, S Dimock, M S Moore); A Brudner, *Punishment and Freedom: A Liberal Theory of Penal Justice*; A Ripstein, *Force and Freedom: Kant's Legal and Political Philosophy*, esp. ch. 10; V Tadros, *Wrongs and Crimes*; J Kleinfeld, 'Reconstructivism: The Place of Criminal Law in Ethical Life'; also clearly relevant here are Thorburn's and Chiao's 'public law' accounts of criminal law (see above, Chapter 4, section 2).

theory I sketch will be persuasive, partly in virtue of the kind of conception of civil order and criminal law that it generates, I also aim to show the way in which we must proceed if we are to develop a viable normative theory of criminal law, and thus a viable normative account of criminalization; we must begin with civil order, and must therefore begin with a political theory that can generate an account of that order.

To say this is not to deny the possibility of developing a theory of the proper aims and scope of criminal law that will count as a kind of legal moralism: we must begin with political theory, and must theorize criminal law as a public institution (as 'public law'), but this does not preclude theorizing it as a public institution that is distinctively concerned with moral wrongdoing;[5] and as I indicated in Chapter 2, that is precisely what I will be doing. To emphasize the need to begin with political theory is, however, also to say that a viable version of legal moralism cannot begin with the moral: it must begin with an account of political community and civil order, and then show how, given such an account, a polity will have good reason to maintain an institution of criminal law that is especially concerned with moral wrongs that implicate that civil order—wrongs that are committed within the public realm constructed by that civil order.

The importance and implications of this point can again be briefly illustrated by *Roe v Wade* and the debate over the legal status of abortion.[6] If we ask whether, or under what conditions, the law should permit abortion, it might be tempting to embark straight away on a discussion of the morality of abortion—on the implicit assumption that we have good (although not necessarily conclusive) reason to criminalize abortion when and only when it is morally wrong: this indeed is the way that a Moorean retributivist would begin to tackle the question. Even if our answer to this first moral question is that abortion is sometimes morally wrong, there will then be further questions to be asked about whether we should, on balance and all things considered, criminalize it. What other values, for instance of liberty or of privacy, might such criminalization infringe? What further harms might it cause?[7] The point here, however, is that our starting point must, on this view, be with the morality of abortion. That was not, however, how the US Supreme Court grounded its decision. It began, rather, with the right to privacy enshrined in the Constitution, and asked whether or when the state had a 'compelling interest' that could justify qualifying or limiting that right; and it held that the relevant interests, in protecting women's health and in the protection of potential life, were not 'compelling' during the first trimester of pregnancy. Two points about this decision are relevant here.

First, the right to privacy marks out spheres of our lives that are not the polity's business—spheres that do not, that is, fall within the public realm; spheres that are not part of the civil order. Conduct falling within those spheres, including most obviously (in this context) what we do to our own bodies, might be moral or immoral, but the polity should take no public view on that: to say that it is a private matter is not to say that it is morally permissible or right; it is to say only that it is not our civic business.

Second, that right is not absolute: it can be limited or qualified in the light of a 'compelling interest' of the polity—which is to say that it can be limited when it impinges on some important aspect of the civil order. Then the polity can take an interest in, and seek to regulate what is done: but even then the interest it can take, and the grounds on which it can regulate, are constrained. It may not embark on an

[5] See above, Chapter 4, section 2.

[6] *Roe v Wade* 410 US 113 (1973); see above, Chapter 4 at nn 85–92.

[7] See above, Chapter 2 at nn 83–4.

unconstrained inquiry into the morality of the conduct in question, but must attend only to the considerations that bear on the 'compelling interest' that has been identified as being implicated. If we agree that the polity has a proper interest in the health of its members and in the protection of potential life, and that those interests can become 'compelling', powerful enough to warrant piercing the normal boundaries of privacy, we agree only that those interests can provide grounds for limiting abortion—not that, once the bounds of privacy are breached, a more general inquiry into the morality of abortion becomes legitimate.[8] As individuals, citizens (including judges deciding on the constitutionality of abortion laws) may have a range of moral views about abortion. As citizens, however (and so also as judges) they may attend only to the considerations that flow from the polity's 'compelling interests'—only, if the court in *Roe v Wade* was right, to the additional danger to the woman's health posed by abortion after the first trimester, and to the protection of the potential human life of a viable foetus.

The general point here is quite a simple one. If we are discussing the morality of a type of conduct, that is what we discuss, directly. Under what conditions, if any, is it morally permissible to seek or to perform an abortion? Under what conditions, if any, is it permissible to commit suicide, or to assist another's suicide, or to kill another at his or her request? If we are discussing what should be criminalized, however, the structure of our discussion must be more complicated. We must first ask, as a political question (as a question of political morality), whether this is a matter in which the polity has a proper interest; if so, what the nature and scope of that interest is; and, if it does have a proper interest, what kinds of factor are relevant to the decision about whether and how to intervene. This is not to say that there is then no room for argument about the moral rightness or wrongness of the type of conduct under discussion: there sometimes will be. But whether there is such room or not will depend on the prior question of whether the conduct falls within the public realm; and what room there is, and what kinds of argument may be adduced, will also depend on the prior question of what kinds of argument are relevant in this (public) context. For instance, according to advocates of a harm principle, the only relevant considerations concern the harmfulness of the conduct in question, or whether criminalizing it would prevent harm: this need not be because they think these are the only kinds of consideration that bear on the morality of any kind of conduct, but because, they insist, these are the only kind that are relevant to the public question of whether it should be criminalized (or subjected to some other kind of coercive interference). So too, someone who argues that it should not be a crime to attempt suicide, or to assist another's suicide at the person's competent request, need not argue that such conduct is not morally wrong; only that it does not fall within the public realm—and, accordingly, that its morality is not a matter for political debate or decision.

Thus I am not suggesting that arguments about criminalization can never appeal to the kinds of moral consideration that figure in moral arguments outside the law: indeed, in two ways they can. First, nothing I have said precludes the possibility that a polity will espouse some expansive version of legal moralism. It might, for instance, take the moral virtue of all its citizens to be part of its civic enterprise, part of the civil

[8] I leave aside here the plausible argument that the polity's interest in the health of the woman has implications rather different from its interest in the potential life of the foetus, and that the former interest could not properly lead, even in principle, to a legal ban on abortion—that if the polity is to respect its members' autonomy, the most it could properly do as far as the woman's health is concerned is to require that abortions, like any serious medical procedure, are carried out only on the basis of informed consent.

order that it aims to sustain; or it might take the retributive punishment of moral wrongdoing (at least when committed within its borders or by its citizens) as one of its aims.[9] In both cases, its decisions about what to criminalize would then depend on judgments about the extra-legal morality of the conduct in question. I have not ruled out such conceptions of a polity's *res publica*; all I have suggested so far is that when we realize that such versions of legal moralism depend on such conceptions of the *res publica*, we will realize how unattractive they must be to any liberal. But, secondly, even liberals who eschew such expansive versions of legal moralism should allow room for some kinds of moral argument in their deliberations about criminalization: sometimes, as we will see, a liberal criminal law will rightly address pre-legal moral wrongs, and its offence definitions will be grounded in an understanding of the character and contours of those wrongs. However, what room there is for moral arguments of this kind will depend on the prior political question of what falls within the polity's *res publica*, what bears on its civil order; which is to say that discussions of criminalization must always start, even if they do not finish, with the political.

I must now turn, finally, to the promised illustrative sketch of a conception of civil order—a conception grounded in a liberal communitarian species of republicanism.[10]

2. Political Community

My starting point is, in one sense, 'communitarian' rather than 'individualist';[11] but given the complexity of the debates between 'communitarians' and their opponents, and the increasing unclarity about the precise meanings of the various labels used in those debates,[12] this needs to be explained. I leave aside here, as being irrelevant for present purposes, metaphysical issues about individualism. Even if we accept a metaphysically communitarian argument to the effect that political theory cannot be grounded in a conception of atomic, isolated individuals who might then create, from nothing, social order by way of a contract (since a contract itself presupposes a normative community), individualists can still argue for a normative, as distinct from metaphysical, individualism. They can argue that we must each begin, in our normative deliberation if not in metaphysical reality, in isolation, and find reasons to enter into association with others: even if we do not begin metaphysically with isolated, asocial 'I's, each of us must begin our practical deliberation about political association as an 'I' who has detached myself from my existing political commitments; and we must each ask whether and on what terms this 'I' should associate herself or himself with these other people.[13]

For communitarians, by contrast, we begin our normative political or social deliberations not in isolation as detached individuals, but as a 'we'—as individuals who are already in association or solidarity with historically contingent groups of others, who should and can detach themselves from such associations only if given reason to do

[9] It could in principle espouse the more expansive, imperialist kind of legal moralism to which Moore's account seemed to open the way (see above, Chapter 2 at nn 85–6); but that would be even less plausible than this more localist type of moralism.

[10] In the following two sections I draw on R A Duff, *Punishment, Communication, and Community*, ch. 2.

[11] This is the appropriate distinction to draw, rather than one between 'communitarian' and 'liberal', since as we will see, communitarians (of the type that interests me) can be liberals.

[12] For useful introductions see D Bell, 'Communitarianism'; S Avineri and A de-Shalit (eds), *Communitarianism and Individualism*; S Mulhall and A Swift, *Liberals and Communitarians*.

[13] See M Matravers, *Justice and Punishment*, ch. 7; also C Taylor, 'Cross-Purposes: The Liberal-Communitarian Debate', on 'ontological' as distinct from 'advocacy' issues.

so: the question then is not how 'I' should live, or what associations 'I' should form, but how 'we' should live—how we should live together. I must ask that question for myself, and find an answer to it that I can accept: but the content of the question is set in the first person plural, not the first person singular.[14] This is not to deny that we must often ask what to do, how to live, in the first person singular: that is an essential feature of one dimension of moral thought, in which we must engage as individuals deliberating about the aims and structure of our personal lives. But we must also engage in moral thinking that is political or social rather than individual, about how we should live as members of the various groups or associations in which we find ourselves—which is to think about how these groups or associations should live as plural subjects; and that kind of thinking is not just about how 'I' am to live, but about how 'we' are to live together.

Who then constitutes this 'we'? Initially, the communities and associations in which we find ourselves: these form the given from which we must begin. This is not to say that we must just accept, as unchangeable givens, whatever such communities we are born or brought up into. We can, and sometimes must, question not only the particular values and practices of communities of which we are and remain members, but our very membership of a community: should I remain a member of this church, of this polity, of this union? But this is not a question that I must always raise, if my continued membership of a community is to be rationally justified; nor, if it is raised, must it always be answered in terms of my interests or values simply as an individual. Suppose I live in a family; or in a group of friends who came together not through our deliberate choices, but through the various unchosen contingencies of our lives: why is it rationally incumbent on me to detach myself in thought from my family or my friends, so as to ask, from the outside, whether I should remain in this community (as distinct from asking, from the inside, how we should lead our lives together)? Or, if I ask (or am asked) such a question, why should my reflective answer not just be 'But these people are my family/my friends'? That would express a recognition of a particular kind of fellowship with these others: I might not have chosen them, but we are now bound together. That fellowship need not be unconditional: it could happen that, for a variety of possible reasons, I come to realize that I should cut myself off from my family or my friends. In the absence of such reasons, however, I see myself as bound in fellowship with them, and understand my life, and my good, as bound up (at least in part) with theirs.

So too with citizenship of a polity. I can come to see myself as a member of this polity, I can come to see it as mine and its members as my fellow citizens, by being born into it and growing up in it: I did not choose to be English, or British, or American, and might not have chosen such fellow citizens had I been given the choice: but we are here together. Of course, we should look critically at the structures and practices of our polities: they are not given, as the unchangeable framework of our civic lives. Of course, I may be led, and sometimes I should be led, to question my membership of this polity: perhaps it is so corrupt that I ought to leave it (or perhaps I should stay and fight to change it). Of course, a polity's boundaries are not set in stone: I might come to see myself not as British, but as Scottish, and might join an ultimately successful campaign for independence; or to see myself as a member of an oppressed minority in an oppressive state, and to think that we (and here again I think of what 'we' should do) should strive to maintain as best we can our own distinct way of life. But nonetheless

[14] This is the way in which associative duties are grounded, and why one needs to be some kind of communitarian to recognize them; see above, Chapter 3 at nn 115–16.

I can, unless I am unlucky in my situation, recognize myself as a member of a political community.

This is not to say that for communitarians we must begin (metaphysically or morally) with communities *rather than* with individuals, as if individuals are subordinate to the communities to which they belong—which might imply that their interests could be readily sacrificed to the interests of the community. It is to say that we must begin with individuals in community: with individuals who already recognize themselves as living in community with others.[15]

To say that I *can* thus recognize myself as a member of a political community, and can see my good as partly bound up with the collective good of my fellow citizens, is not to say that this is inevitable. If I am unlucky, I might have been born into an oppressive or dysfunctional polity; I might come to recognize myself as an outsider, or as belonging to an oppressed group whose members cannot plausibly see themselves as citizens of this polity. Even if I am lucky, in that I am born and raised in a well-functioning polity that accords me all the benefits of citizenship, I might not identify myself normatively as a citizen: I might find my normative identity, and my good, in other of the communities and practices to which I belong.[16] All that I am claiming here, however, is first that a polity can exist as a political community, and sustain a system of law that its members can be expected to recognize as their common law, if but only if a sufficient number of its members do identify themselves as citizens. Second, citizenship, and the obligations that it brings, need not be a matter of voluntary choice: citizenship can be chosen, as when I choose to emigrate to a new country; but it can also, like other roles that bring associative obligations, be something that I acquire non-voluntarily, without choosing it. Third, however, membership of a political community does not *necessarily* bring associative obligations to respect its laws or to share in its aims: in an unjust or oppressive polity, those who support it will of course insist that all its members have such obligations; but their insistence can and should be rejected. (I leave aside here the question of whether members of such polities might have associative obligations to resist or to struggle for reform.)

Now communities can be oppressive in many ways. In particular (one of liberals' chief anxieties when 'community' is invoked), they can be over-ambitiously all-embracing, claiming every aspect of their members' lives: nothing is private, everything is everybody's business, and there is stringent pressure to conform in all one's activities to a detailed set of social norms. One model of such total community is a monastery or a nunnery; another is the kind of small village that is portrayed alternately as idyllic or as terrifying. Communities can also be exclusivist: they can be very reluctant to admit new members, and very quick to exclude or expel (physically or socially) those who

[15] There are deeper philosophical issues here. Some concern the conditions of individual thought and experience: I would appeal to the Wittgensteinian view that I can think, and identify myself as an individual, only within a linguistic and social community—that takes us back to the issue of metaphysical individualism. Others concern the nature of moral recognition. Individualists might say that we can recognize others as having moral claims on us by recognizing them as individuals who belong to a morally relevant category—as beings who can feel pleasure and pain, for instance (for Benthamites); or as rational beings (for Kantians). Communitarians might reply that what is foundational is not such a process of rational categorization, but a recognition of fellowship: I recognize the other as a fellow human being, or fellow creature, who has a claim on my attention and concern (see above, Chapter 3 at n. 118; also C Diamond, 'Eating Meat and Eating People'). Others appeal to solidarity (as recognition, as achievement) as a central idea here: for different versions of this see e.g. A Camus, *The Rebel*; R Rorty, *Contingency, Irony, and Solidarity*.

[16] See M Renzo, 'Associative Responsibilities and Political Obligation'; J Edwards and A P Simester, 'What's Public About Crime?', 119–20; above, Chapter 3 at n. 117.

refuse or fail to conform; such exclusivist tendencies are, as is often noted, a worryingly prominent feature of much contemporary penal rhetoric and practice, which exclude offenders from the 'law-abiding' community that is to be protected from them. These are not, however, features of communities as such, but of certain kinds of community; they belong, one might say, not to the nature of political community, but to its pathologies. Communities can be limited, and relatively undemanding; they can be open-armed; they can be slow to exclude or to expel. This point is more easily recognized once we remember that our political community is not the only, and is for most of us not the most significant, community to which we belong. I am a citizen, and lead parts of my life in the civic realm of the polity, but I am many other things as well—I have many other roles: I am also, and I also live as, a member of a family or of another kind of intimate, cohabiting partnership; I also hold a job, which involves membership of another kind of community; I am involved in other kinds of activity (hobbies, voluntary work, activism of various kinds) which involve membership of other communities.[17] Some of these communities are intimate, and might have little room for privacy: that is true of many families—though not a necessary feature of the family. Others are far less intimate or personal: they take up only a small part of the person's life, and leave many aspects (especially many of the deeper or more personal aspects) out of their public realm. Think, for instance, of a workplace in which there is a genuine normative community of fellow workers, who share a commitment to the ends that define their enterprise, and to each other as fellow members of the enterprise (I realize that might not be true of many workplaces), but in which there is also a shared sense of the community's boundaries: the co-workers do not associate with each other outside the workplace, and their interactions and conversations within the workplace, their interest in each other, focus only on the work itself.[18]

So to talk of a political community need not be to talk of a community that is oppressively stifling, or totalitarian, or exclusivist in its unwillingness to admit new members or its readiness to expel misbehaving members: it could be to talk, instead, of a liberal community—to which we must now turn.

3. A Liberal Republic

A political community could be a liberal community: that is why the often-drawn distinction between 'liberals' and 'communitarians' is seriously misleading. A political community could, that is, define its civil order in terms of liberal aims and values—though it would give those aims and values a significantly different reading than they receive from more individualist liberals.

It would be rash, given the diversity of views that might claim or be given the label 'liberal', to try to specify a set of distinctive 'liberal' values, but obvious candidates include such values as autonomy, freedom, and privacy (the last of these being understood as a matter, not so much of being able to keep information about oneself

[17] At least, I must hope that I belong to such other communities—else my life is likely to be sadly impoverished.

[18] That might seem an implausible, or inhuman, kind of community: surely, for instance, if a workmate suffered a serious illness, or bereavement, 'true' colleagues would express a sympathetic interest and help—and not merely because illness and bereavement can interfere with work. One reason for this is that they are also fellow human beings, with (we hope) human sympathy for each other's tragedies; another is that our communities can often spill out of their formal boundaries, so that colleagues can become friends.

'private', as of being left with an extensive sphere of 'private' life in which to pursue one's own conceptions of the good). Others might add dignity to this list—a slogan that has come to prominence in recent years, with the familiar danger that the idea is so stretched, to cover every matter that concerns us, that it loses determinate content;[19] others (drawing on Kantian themes) might posit sovereignty as the core value.[20] I will not try here to draw up an authoritative list, although I will have more to say later about some of these values. Nor will I engage with the familiar arguments about the relationship between the 'right' and the 'good'; about whether liberals can both insist that the state must be neutral as between different goods, and insist on such values as autonomy and privacy;[21] and about 'perfectionist' as against 'non-perfectionist' versions of liberalism.[22] But I should say something about the ways in which liberal communitarians can understand the central goods of a liberal polity—in particular such apparently individualist goods as autonomy, freedom, and privacy.

One familiar communitarian argument against individualist liberals is that they fail to notice the ways in which goods are 'socially constituted', and the way in which some important goods are communal or common, rather than purely individual, goods.[23] To which liberal individualists might reply that whilst we can recognize various ways in which goods are 'socially constituted', the goods thus constituted could still be the goods of individuals, and be good only because they are chosen and valued by those individuals; and that communal or common goods are goods precisely because they are important to the individuals who make up the community.

Such goods as autonomy and privacy are 'socially constituted' in the sense that they can be understood and pursued as goods only within a social context that gives them their meaning and significance. Thus autonomy,[24] understood as the possession and use of the capacity for rational thought and action (including thought about ends or goods, as well as instrumental thought about means), is not something that could be identified, valued, or achieved in asocial, 'rational agents': for that capacity is a capacity to participate in forms of social life and thought, which is acquired only through induction into such forms of life. That capacity for rational thought and action is necessary if we are to be genuinely the 'co-authors of our own narratives':[25] but we cannot claim or hope to be sole authors of those narratives; and co-authorship is a social activity, possible only within a social context which determines the forms it can take, and the value it can have. So too, privacy does not concern a realm of the 'private' that is given in advance of any particular social context; it rather concerns a sphere that is socially defined by a particular community.[26]

Liberal individualists need not deny that goods are in this sense socially constituted: goods that are thus constituted can still be individual goods. The more significant communitarian claim is that such goods should be understood as shared, communal, goods. This is not to say that they must be seen as collective goods *rather than* as individual goods: it is individuals who achieve (or are denied) these goods, and whose lives

[19] But see J Waldron, *Dignity, Rank, and Rights*.

[20] See e.g. A Ripstein, 'Beyond the Harm Principle'.

[21] On which see e.g. W Kymlicka, *Liberalism, Community and Culture*, especially chs 3 and 5.

[22] On perfectionist liberalism, see famously J Raz, *The Morality of Freedom*; G Sher, *Beyond Neutrality*.

[23] See generally Mulhall and Swift, *Liberals and Communitarians*, Part I.

[24] See generally G Dworkin, *The Theory and Practice of Autonomy*, Part I; Raz, *The Morality of Freedom*, 369–429; Sher, *Beyond Neutrality*, chs 2 and 3.

[25] A MacIntyre, *After Virtue*, ch. 15.

[26] See C Sypnowich, 'The Civility of Law: Between Public and Private'; and above, Chapter 4, section 4.

go well or badly depending on whether or not they achieve them; so too, in academic communities it is individual academics who achieve or fail to achieve the goods of knowledge and understanding. Nor is it to say that they *cannot* be seen in individualist terms: as an academic, I could see my intellectual achievements purely as my goods, contributing to my academic career; as a citizen, I could care for my autonomy and privacy as being of value to me independently of the extent to which others achieve such goods. But it is to say that to see these goods in such purely individualist terms is to fail to understand them as the community's defining goods, to fail to relate myself to them as a member of the community. As an academic, I should care about the extent to which *we* achieve the goods of knowledge, and see my advances not merely as mine, but as contributions to our common pursuit: that is what it is to be a member of an academic community. As a citizen of a liberal political community, I should care about the extent to which all citizens achieve the goods of autonomy and privacy, and value my own autonomy and privacy only insofar as others too can achieve those goods. This is not to say that I must subordinate my autonomy or privacy to a mysterious collective good; or that I can be properly called on to sacrifice my autonomy or privacy for the sake of the autonomy or privacy of others. It is rather to say that within a liberal polity my autonomy and privacy have value as those of a citizen living with other citizens as free and equal members of the polity—others who share an understanding both of the civic life that we lead together, and of the sphere of privacy within which we can pursue our different and more individual goods.[27]

A political community can thus be a polity whose members espouse genuinely liberal values, and aim to sustain each other not only in their collective life as citizens, but also and crucially in the maintenance of an extensive realm of privacy for every citizen, within which they can pursue the goals, the goods, the values by which they define their own lives. Those private spheres will still (generally) be spheres of community, since we generally find our goods in communities of various kinds (families, friendships, professions, hobbies, voluntary work, and so on); but those communities are distinct from the political community to which we belong as citizens. They are also communities in which we are more likely to establish more intimate personal relationships: for our civic relationship with our fellow citizens, simply as fellow citizens, is relatively formal, even distant; in a liberal polity that values privacy and a pluralism of goods, and that is sensitive to the fact that political community is generally unchosen, we are not expected to be friends with our fellow citizens.[28] A liberal communitarian will still, however, understand this relationship in different terms from those typically favoured by more fundamentally individualist liberals: I do not see my fellow citizens as individuals to whom I am bound by the terms of some imagined contract—a contract that I am to imagine myself having chosen to make; I see them precisely as fellows, bound together with me in a typically unchosen association.

The kind of political community that I envisage here can be called 'republican', as well as 'liberal'—a liberal republic. 'Republican' has now come to be used as a label for almost as wide a variety of political theories as has 'liberal',[29] and I will not offer a

[27] Compare R M Dworkin, *Taking Rights Seriously*, 262–3, on 'liberty as license' and 'liberty as independence'.

[28] Some republicans would, following Aristotle, portray the civic relationship as a (kind of) friendship (Aristotle, *Nicomachean Ethics*, Bk VIII; see S Schwarzenbach, 'On Civic Friendship'; S E Marshall, 'The Community of Friends'). Friendship is certainly a better model than the family, given the hierarchical and intimate character of the latter, but can still mislead.

[29] For a useful survey, see F Lovett, 'Republicanism'. See also S Besson and J L Martí, 'Law and Republicanism: Mapping the Issues'; R Dagger, 'Republicanism and the Foundations of Criminal Law'; E N Yankah, 'Republican Responsibility in Criminal Law'.

fully fledged 'republican' theory here; but I will draw on some of the central themes of contemporary republican theories.

A republican polity will, like any polity, function with a (more or less articulated) conception of its civil order, which will be structured by a shared understanding of its common good. The civil order of a liberal republican polity will be structured by the kinds of liberal value discussed above; given the liberal concern to leave citizens as expansive a private realm as possible, it will be modest in its scope and reach. It will consist in procedural, as well as substantive, values:[30] for an important part of the polity's good will be the way in which its members are able to take part in the kinds of collective deliberation that develop and revise the substantial dimensions of their conception of their common good. But it cannot be a purely procedural conception of civil order: partly because even a procedural conception requires some substantive conception of those who are to participate in the procedure, and how they are to see and treat each other; partly because if it is to remain a republican polity (though of course there is no a priori guarantee that it will), its substantive values must themselves be recognizable as versions of republicanism. It will include a suitable set of formal institutions of government: institutions through which law can be made and administered, through which public services can be provided, through which the citizens can debate matters of public concern and give effect to the outcomes of such debates, and (crucially) institutions through which government and its agencies can be challenged and held to account.[31] But, like any civil order,[32] it will also have a significant informal (extra-legal, non-governmental) dimension of shared social understandings and habits of conduct. I will not try to go into detail here about the range of institutions of governance that a liberal republic might maintain (I will discuss the role of criminal law in the following three sections), but should identify some of the fundamental ideas and values that can structure a liberal republic's civil order, and can ground a plausible ideal of political community.

One such fundamental idea is citizenship, as a matter of active, engaged membership of the polity, understood as a particular (and particularly important) kind of association. The active character of citizenship will not play a large role in what follows, but it belongs with the idea of a common law that I sketched earlier:[33] if the law, and in particular the criminal law, is our law, it should be a law that we play an active part in sustaining and enacting (not merely a law that we obey as subjects); more generally, if we are to govern ourselves, then we must be active in that enterprise of governance. This leaves open a range of familiar, and controversial, questions about what form that activity should take, in particular about how far, and in what ways, a republican polity should be a participatory democracy:[34] without engaging in this controversy, I will say a little later on about the proper role of citizens in determining the actual ('on the streets') scope of the criminal law.[35] Citizenship should also be understood in inclusionary terms: it should, that is, be relatively easy to gain, and hard to lose.

[30] See Besson and Martí, 'Law and Republicanism', 24–8.

[31] Hence the importance, in Pettit's republican theory, of the idea of a 'contestatory citizenry': see e.g. P Pettit, *Republicanism: A Theory of Freedom and Government*, 183–200; *On the People's Terms: A Republican Theory and Model of Democracy*, 215–18, 225–9.

[32] See above, Chapter 4 at nn 57–60.

[33] See above, Chapter 3 at nn 72, 82; see also R A Duff and S E Marshall, 'Civic Punishment'.

[34] Contrast e.g. A Dzur, *Punishment, Participatory Democracy, and the Jury*, and J L Martí, 'The Republican Democratization of Criminal Law and Justice', with H S Richardson, *Democratic Autonomy: Public Reasoning About the Ends of Policy*, and Pettit, *On the People's Terms*.

[35] See below, at nn 154–5, and Chapter7, section 3; and above, Chapter 1 at nn 177–82.

This inclusionary attitude is certainly not an essential feature of republicanism: republics can (like any political community) be reluctant to admit new members, and quick to expel members who violate their defining values and principles. I will not say more here about the willingness to admit (to welcome) new members,[36] but should say something about the reluctance to exclude or expel existing members, since this bears directly on the role and functioning of the criminal law. As has often been noted, criminal punishment, and criminal law more generally, often operate in radically exclusionary ways;[37] the question here is whether and why we should resist this kind of exclusion, if those subjected to it have violated the polity's central values. A polity is one kind of association, and associations generally have, and use, the right to expel members who seriously (and repeatedly) violate the rules of association; indeed, we could say that one who wilfully (and persistently) violates those rules thus displays his lack of commitment to the association, and in effect excludes himself: so why should this not apply to political associations? We may say that polities should be slower than other associations to exclude members, given the importance of civic membership to human flourishing;[38] but why should they not be entitled to expel persistent and serious wrongdoers? They cannot, now, physically exile or deport their citizens (unless they can find another home for them); but they can deprive them of civic standing, and subject them to internal 'exile' behind the walls of a prison. I have no knockdown argument against such a view—and have agreed that, in extreme cases, a temporary or even presumptively permanent deprivation of civic membership might be justified, so long as it leaves the excluded person a real way back;[39] nor am I sure what could constitute an argument against it, as distinct from a moral appeal for a more inclusionary conception of offenders and of our relationship to them (although even to put the matter in that way implies a distinction between 'them' and 'us', and ignores the fact that many of 'us' are offenders).

What could ground, or be expressed in, such an appeal is an idea(l) of solidarity with each other as (often radically) fallible and imperfect human beings who must live together if we are to flourish at all. For most of us, even in times of increased mobility, citizenship is not something that we acquire voluntarily: it is thrust on us in virtue of our birth; we find ourselves as members of this or that polity. But that unchosen membership is also essential to our wellbeing: the polity provides the structure within which we can pursue our own lives, and should provide the support that makes such pursuit possible; it can give us an important part of our identity. Furthermore, and crucially, a polity is not (it should not aspire to be) an elect society of saints: it is a polity of human beings, who are prone in all kinds of way to weakness and to vice, to wrongdoings both trivial and serious. To recognize another as a fellow citizen should thus not depend on judging that she is worthy of fellowship with 'us' (who assume ourselves to be virtuous); it should be a matter of recognizing a fellowship that we already share, for better or worse, as members of this polity. This does not require us to ignore, or to downplay, the often serious wrongs that we and others commit: we must take them seriously, as wrongs for which their perpetrators should be called to account by and to their fellows—which is precisely what the criminal process, through which alleged offenders are called to answer to the polity, should do.[40]

[36] But see above, Chapter 3 at nn 85–7.

[37] See above, Chapter 3, section 5.

[38] See above, Chapter 3 at nn 167–8 on 'the right to a nationality' (*Universal Declaration of Human Rights*, art. 15).

[39] See above, Chapter 3 at nn 171–4.

[40] See above, Chapter 1, sections 4–5; and below, at nn 90–5.

Another republican value is that of freedom, understood as 'non-domination': what matters for political freedom is not merely that I and my actions are in fact left free from the (arbitrary) interference of others, but that that freedom from interference is assured; that I am not open or vulnerable to arbitrary interference from others. What undermines freedom, in this sense, is not the fact of interference, but the very fact that others have the power to interfere (at will); what gives me freedom is that I am not thus vulnerable to others.[41] Pettit captures this idea of non-domination in a usefully vivid slogan, the 'eyeball test', which I want to appropriate but also to extend, as a test not just of republican freedom, but of civic recognition. As Pettit explains it, it is a one-way test of republican freedom as non-domination: free citizens 'can look others in the eye without reason for the fear or deference that a power of interference might inspire'.[42] But it should be a two-way test: republican citizens ought to be willing, as well as able, to look each other in the eye—to recognize each other as fellow participants in the civic enterprise. That is an essential feature of public discourse: we engage with others, with any other citizens who wish to engage, in discussing matters of civic significance; and to engage with others as participants we must be willing to look them in the eye—with a look not of threat or fear, but of recognition of fellowship. It might be objected here that the eyeball test reflects a particular, culturally biased, conception of how equal recognition is expressed: that an unwillingness or refusal to look or be looked in the eye might manifest a kind of modesty or decorum, or a particular conception of respect for privacy, rather than a denial of equal fellowship.[43] What matters, however, is that members of a republican polity must be ready and able to recognize each other as equals and as fellows. The social and material forms through which such recognition can be expressed will vary between different cultures: in those in which it is displayed in a willingness to look each other in the eye (and denied by a refusal to do so), the eyeball test is a useful democratic slogan; if in other cultures that is not a way of expressing a recognition of others as one's equal fellows, other slogans will be appropriate.

A third important principle (or slogan) of liberal republicanism is that of 'equal concern and respect'. The slogan is Dworkin's, who is concerned with what governments owe their citizens, rather than with what citizens owe each other: we need not, 'as individuals, treat our neighbor's children with the same concern as our own or treat everyone we meet with the same respect'; but a government must 'treat all those in its charge as equals, that is, as entitled to its equal concern and respect'.[44] It can also apply, however, to what citizens owe each other. In our lives as private individuals (as members of families, as friends) we do not owe equal concern or respect (in some senses of the terms) to everyone: what I owe to my children, to my friends, is different from and typically more than what I owe to other citizens. But in our mutual dealings as citizens, equal concern and respect is just what we owe each other; indeed, since the government must claim to act in our name, if this is what the government owes, we owe it too. To say that this is what we owe each other in our dealings as citizens is to say that it should guide our conduct in the public, civic realm: the realm in which we interact

[41] This kind of account has been developed in most careful detail by Pettit: see e.g. *Republicanism*, and *On the People's Terms*; for a useful summary, and further references, see Lovett, 'Republicanism', s. 1.2. For some interesting applications of the idea of non-domination to aspects of criminal law and criminalization, see A Harel, *Why Law Matters*. For a persuasive suggestion that republicans should replace Pettit's 'modally robust' conception of non-domination with a more modest notion of 'non-deference', see V Chiao, 'Discretion and Domination in Criminal Procedure: Reflections on Pettit'.

[42] *On the People's Terms*, 84.

[43] Thanks to Mathilde Cohen for pressing this kind of objection.

[44] R M Dworkin, *A Matter of Principle*, 190.

not as friends or as family members, but as citizens. Concern is especially a matter of welfare, although polities will take different views about what sorts of welfare ought to be provided publicly by the polity, or privately by individuals. Respect concerns such values as dignity and privacy. It is exemplified by, for instance, the way in which citizens engage in public debate—by their willingness to listen to each other as equal participants in the enterprise of self-governance; and also in the limits set on the ways in which citizens and the government may intrude into individuals' lives. That concern and respect are equal, because democratic citizens must recognize each other as equal participants in the civic enterprise. In their private lives, they may be partial, paying particular attention to friends, family, or other intimates: but when acting in the public realm as citizens, they must treat each other as equals.

It might be objected that such slogans as 'equal concern and respect' do not mark out a truly democratic conception of equal citizenship: 'equal concern and respect' are typically afforded, not to every member of the polity, but only to the members of socially advantaged groups. But this objection is misdirected. The slogan expresses an aspiration—one of which the actual social and political structures of contemporary democracies often fall far short: but the failure to accord equal concern and respect to all members of the polity (which is a failure to treat them as full members of the polity) marks a failure not of that democratic slogan, but of the polities that fail to live up to it. Theorists of criminal law cannot afford to ignore such failures, which can have significant implications for criminal justice—for the very possibility of criminal justice;[45] but our concern here is with the slogan as partly defining what a democratic polity should aspire to be(come).

A republican conception of the common good will also, we can expect, include a conception of civic virtue—of what makes for a good citizen.[46] To talk of concern, of respect, of recognizing fellowship, is also to talk of the emotions that republican citizens are disposed to feel: for to be concerned for others, to respect them as fellows, is to be disposed to feel a range of appropriate emotions, which will also motivate appropriate action. We can therefore talk about civic virtue, understood in Aristotelian terms, as a matter of being properly disposed in relation to our fellow citizens:[47] a disposition which includes patterns of appropriate emotion, as well as of attention, deliberation, and action. This is likely to raise liberal, or at least anti-perfectionist liberal, hackles, since they will protest that a liberal polity must remain neutral as to the good, whereas notions of virtue, civic or otherwise, precisely involve conceptions of the good.[48]

However, first, to say that a republican polity will have a conception of civic virtue, and will see the encouragement of such virtue as one of its proper aims, leaves open the questions of just how such virtue is to be understood, and what kind of efforts a polity should make to encourage it. We could provide an account of civic virtue in terms of a commitment to a familiar range of liberal values; and we could insist that whilst the polity's members should seek to encourage its development (especially in the young), it should not try to require or enforce it, let alone allow it (or rather its absence) to figure

[45] Hence the importance of debates about the possibility of doing criminal justice in radically unjust societies: see e.g. W Heffernan and J Kleinig (eds), *From Social Justice to Criminal Justice: Poverty and the Administration of Criminal Law*; A Ristroph, 'Conditions of Legitimate Punishment'; R A Duff, 'Discretion and Accountability in a Democratic Criminal Law', s. 5.

[46] See e.g. R Dagger, *Civic Virtues: Rights, Citizenship, and Republican Liberalism*; E N Yankah, 'Legal Vices and Civic Virtue: Vice Crimes, Republicanism and the Corruption of Lawfulness'.

[47] See Aristotle, *Nicomachean Ethics*, Book II.

[48] Perfectionist liberals may be less worried by talk of virtue, or by the suggestion that a liberal polity should seek to encourage the development of appropriately liberal virtues in its citizens.

in its criminal law as a ground of liability.[49] For, second, we must distinguish an ideal of civic virtue, as something to which citizens should aspire, from the idea of civic duty as what we owe each other and can demand of each other; what we can hope for from what we can require (and, within what is required, what is required by law from what is socially required as a civic duty). Virtue belongs to the former category: all that we can properly require, legally or socially, is appropriate conduct; that extensive area of privacy into which a liberal polity will not intrude, and will not allow the state to intrude, includes the realm of 'private' thoughts and feelings. We might aspire, and hope that our fellows aspire, to Aristotelian civic virtue, but our civic (and legal) duties are more modest: they do not concern how we think or feel about each other, so long as those thoughts and feelings are not displayed in the public realm; they concern how we behave towards each other in that realm.[50] This is not to say that a liberal republic can do nothing to foster civic virtue; only that the civic duties of its citizens, duties whose performance we can demand from each other on pain of public censure, fall well short of civic virtue.

That is not to say, however, that our duties consist only in certain kinds of 'behaviour' as understood reductively in terms of bodily movements and their effects. Our civic duties, like all duties, consist in actions, not mere movements; and an important dimension of actions is their meaning. The equality of concern and respect, the recognition, that we owe each other is a matter not merely of the material impact of our conduct, but of the attitudes that our actions manifest or enact: do we treat each other as fellow citizens; are our actions appropriate ways of actualizing equal concern and respect for our fellows?[51] However, our actions can enact appropriate attitudes even if we do not in fact feel the emotions appropriate to those attitudes: I can do my civic duty by treating another as a fellow, treating her with due concern and respect, although my feelings towards her are at odds with such attitudes. This is a familiar phenomenon in our personal lives: we must often grit our teeth (but not show that we are doing so) in order to do our duty despite our contrary emotions; I behave politely towards another, although I feel like insulting him.

In our more intimate dealings with each other, it matters whether we are merely enacting appropriate attitudes. If the best I can do with my partner, or my friends, is to enact attitudes without feeling the emotions intrinsic to them, there is something amiss with me, or with our relationship. It might be reasonable to ask me what I ('really') feel as I act appropriately, and to say that action without appropriate feeling is of little value.[52] In our public lives, however, the civic lives we lead with others who are not intimates, whilst we may hope that appropriate conduct flows from appropriate emotion, this is not something we should insist on or inquire into. This is true of our everyday dealings, and of the minimal civility we can expect of each other: if an American says 'Have a nice day', or a stranger says 'I'm sorry' when she bumps into me on the street, it would be impertinent (not pertinent, rude) to ask 'Do you mean that?'. It is also true of the rituals of civic life: of public funerals, of ceremonies

[49] For recent debate on this topic, see H H Lai and A Amaya (eds), *Law, Virtue and Justice*. Note too that on any plausible account civic virtue is only one kind of virtue: thus a polity committed to promoting civic virtue is not thereby committed to promoting virtue as such, or to 'making men moral' (compare R P George, *Making Men Moral: Civil Liberties and Public Morality*).

[50] Fuller's distinction between the 'morality of duty' and the 'morality of aspiration' is relevant here: see L Fuller, *The Morality of Law*, ch. 1.

[51] On actions as 'enacting' attitudes see A Kauppinen, 'Hate and Punishment' (although I would not follow all of Kauppinen's account; see R A Duff and S E Marshall, 'Criminalizing Hate', at n. 17).

[52] See M Midgley, 'The Objection to Systematic Humbug'.

to commemorate those killed in war or to praise those who have performed notable public service, and other ways in which a polity gives formal expression to its sense of itself. Officials and lay citizens have their roles in such rituals, and should play them with an appropriate demeanour, but it would be impertinent to ask whether they really feel the emotions appropriate to the attitudes they are enacting: what matters is the enactment.

There are attitudes—of equal concern and respect, of mutual recognition—that we ought to enact towards our fellow citizens. There are also attitudes that we ought not to enact: attitudes inconsistent with the equal concern and respect, with the recognition as fellows, that we owe each other. These include, for instance, 'hatred', as a distinctive civic vice. I will have more to say about hatred later, when we discuss the legitimacy of 'hate crimes';[53] but it is worth saying something about it here, as an illustration of the way in which even a resolutely liberal republic, which takes seriously the 'privacy' of thought and feeling, can take a proper interest in the enactment of certain attitudes. Theorists differ about how 'hatred' should be understood in this context,[54] and whether 'hate crime' is a useful label for the kinds of wrong discussed here; some liberal theorists also protest that hatred is an emotion, and is therefore not something that should concern a liberal republic's criminal law, which is properly concerned with actions, not with the emotions that might lie behind them.[55] We can, however, identify a kind of hatred, 'civic hatred', that should be of concern to the citizens of a liberal republic, as being inconsistent with their civic duty.

Many attitudes, although in some way aversive, are consistent with recognizing the other as a fellow. I might dislike someone, find him boring, disapprove of his morals or his taste in art, be irritated by him, or jealous of him. Such reactions might stand in the way of being his friend, or make me less inclined to accept his social invitations, but need not undermine my recognition or treatment of him as a fellow citizen. Hatred, however, as we can understand it in this context, is different, as involving a radical alienation or exclusion: to hate is to exclude from fellowship and recognition. I would like to destroy what I hate, or push it right away from me; it is something unworthy of my respect, concern, or attention; it has no place in my life. So too, what we hate collectively is something that we wish to exclude from our shared life: we might feel loathing or contempt for those whom we hate; we cannot accord them respect or concern.[56] We can behave appropriately towards those whom we hate: like other attitudes and emotions, hatred (even when powerfully felt) can be resisted or overcome. Hatred itself, however, is inconsistent with respect, concern, or recognized fellowship: it must be overcome if we are to behave as we should.

To hate a fellow citizen is thus already to lack civic virtue—even if I recognize that I should not hate, and behave as I should. If I enact that hatred in my conduct towards the other person, I violate my civic duty to her. For the enactment of this exclusionary and alienating attitude must involve conduct that is itself exclusionary and alienating.

[53] See below, Chapter 7 at nn 119–23.

[54] See, usefully, T Brudholm, 'Hatred as an Attitude'.

[55] See e.g. H Hurd, 'Why Liberals Should Hate "Hate Crime Legislation"'; H Hurd and M Moore, 'Punishing Hatred and Prejudice'. For useful critiques of this kind of argument, see e.g. M Al-Hakim, 'Making Room for Hate Crime Legislation in Liberal Societies'; D Kahan, 'Two Liberal Fallacies in the Hate Crimes Debate'.

[56] Compare attitudes to enemy soldiers in wartime: the rules of *jus in bello* enjoin us, on a plausible reading, to respect enemy soldiers as our fellows (even if we are trying to kill them); by contrast, to urge soldiers to hate the enemy is to urge them to abandon any such conception of the enemy as a fellow (soldier, or human being) to whom respect could be owed. See N Biggar, *In Defence of War*, ch. 2, on 'Love in War'.

If that conduct is verbal, its meaning is explicit: it says to the other person that she does not belong in the polity. We could also talk of a kind of defamation: the German Criminal Code defines 'Incitement to Hatred' as 'assault[ing] the human dignity of others by insulting, maliciously maligning or defaming segments of the population'.[57] Such an attitude can also be enacted in my non-verbal behaviour—in attacks that express or take their meaning from hatred of the other. If I act simply as an individual who hates another individual, nothing of civic moment might hang on my action. But if my conduct has a collective aspect, and is directed against members of an already vulnerable group, its character changes: if my hatred is enacted against a group identified by a characteristic that is more widely seen and treated as contemptible or hateful, as disqualifying members from proper citizenship, then its enactment becomes genuinely threatening. The point is not simply that, empirically, my conduct is more likely to hasten their exclusion: it is that such a context affects the meaning of my conduct—just as saying, however fiercely, 'I'll kill you' constitutes a more genuine threat if I say it while brandishing a knife than if I say it while brandishing a pea-shooter.

A liberal republic will be a republic of citizens who recognize each other in civic fellowship (the 'eyeball test'). They will treat each other in ways that are materially appropriate, in that they do not violate the rights or the private spheres of their fellows ('equal respect'), and provide the kinds of assistance or support that citizens should be able to expect from each other individually or collectively ('equal concern'). Their civic behaviour towards each other will enact appropriate civic attitudes, and will not enact inappropriate, uncivil attitudes of hatred or contempt. They will be ready to engage with each other in mutually respectful public deliberation about the polity's civic affairs, including deliberation (which might involve radical disagreement) about its civil order. They will not expect or seek intimacy with their fellow citizens simply in virtue of their citizenship: their relationships, *qua* citizens, will be to a degree formal or detached as compared to those between friends or other kinds of intimate, since they recognize the limited scope of the civic relationship, and the importance of those private realms into which one's fellow citizens cannot claim the standing—simply in virtue of that civic relationship—to inquire or interfere. More precisely, if such a republic is a republic of human beings, rather than of angels or saints, its members will share an aspiration to live in this way, an aspiration of which they will often fall more or less radically short; or they will recognize that they should share such an aspiration, even when they cannot bring themselves to share it; or they will be told by their fellows, with whom they are (voluntarily or non-voluntarily) associated, that they ought to share such an aspiration.[58] Our question now is: what role, if any, will such a republic have for a system of criminal law?

4. A Liberal Republic's Criminal Law: (1) Norm Declarations and Calling to Account

On some views of criminal law, it plays an autonomous role in a polity's civil order. Thus a Moorean polity, for instance, would take the 'moral betterment' of the world as one of its aims—as part of its common good; it would see the attainment of retributive justice, consisting in the punishment of those who culpably commit moral wrongs, as

[57] *Strafgesetzbuch* § 130(1); see also J Waldron, *The Harm in Hate Speech*, ch. 3 on 'group defamation' and T Hörnle, 'Criminalizing Behaviour to Protect Human Dignity', esp. 317–19.

[58] See above, at nn 13–14, and Chapter 3 at nn 115–16, on associative duties and the polity.

one way in which the world could be morally improved; and it would therefore see good reason to create and maintain a system of criminal law to serve that end.[59] I suggested in Chapter 2, however, that this is not a plausible aim for a liberal polity, and the discussion in this chapter should have reinforced that suggestion. Given such a polity's commitment to an extensive private realm for its citizens, it will not see all moral wrongdoing as being, even in principle, its business: its collective view of wrongful conduct that falls within that private realm will not be 'It's morally wrongful and so deserving of punishment, *but* for the sake of liberty (or privacy) we should refrain from criminalizing it'; but more simply 'It's not our business'—which is to say that it is not our business even to form a collective view on its moral character. Similarly, on Moore's account a polity would have some reason to create a criminal law that encompassed wrongs committed anywhere in the world (for their punishment would also conduce to the moral betterment of the world): but it seems implausible that a liberal polity would define its civil order and its public realm in such expansive (even imperialist) terms. However, this is not yet to rule out a retributivist account of criminal punishment, nor yet to deny that a liberal polity could create and maintain a system of distinctively criminal law in order to serve the goal of retribution: for its civil order, and its conception of its common good, will be structured by a concern for justice; so if justice demands that culpable wrongdoers be punished, the polity will therefore have reason to create an institution whose function will be to serve that end.

I will shortly offer a rather different account of why such a polity should maintain a system of criminal law, and will not pursue the arguments against a Moorean brand of retributivism here:[60] for our present purposes the point to note is that the scope of 'culpable wrongdoers', the range of wrongs and wrongdoers whose just punishment could be the polity's responsibility, must be determined through an account of the polity's civil order. If a type of wrongdoing falls within the polity's public realm, as defined by its conception of its civil order, its perpetrators do indeed—given a retributivist view of punishment—deserve criminal punishment at the polity's hands: but a liberal polity's public realm will be a limited realm, and many kinds of wrong and wrongdoer will fall outside its limits; in which case, even if it is still true from a detached, god's eye view, that they deserve punishment at someone's hands, they do not deserve punishment at the hands of this polity—they are not this polity's business.[61]

On other views, criminal law plays an essentially instrumental role in relation to the polity's civil order. It is 'an integral component of society's basic structure',[62] in the sense that it is part of the institutional structure of the polity, and is indeed (contingently) essential to its functioning; but insofar as it is understood simply as, for instance, 'a coercive rule-enforcing institution',[63] it plays a secondary, instrumental role in relation to the central features of that structure. We begin, that is, with a conception of the polity's public or civil order—for instance as 'a collective life under stable public institutions', a life that is informed by 'shared attitudes of reciprocity'.[64] That conception makes as yet no mention of criminal law: but we realize that if it is a human order, it is vulnerable to various kinds of threat, from those who fail, or refuse, to enact

[59] See above, Chapter 2 at n. 151; also Chapter 4, section 2.

[60] See above, Chapter 1, section 6; also R A Duff, 'Legal Moralism and Public Wrongs'.

[61] It is true that a liberal polity will recognize various obligations of a transnational or international kind, which might include obligations either to claim a universal jurisdiction over certain types of crime, or to assist in the enterprise of international criminal law: see above, Chapter 3, sections 1 and 2, on the questions that these kinds of supra-national criminal law raise.

[62] Chiao, 'What is the Criminal Law For?', 139; see above, Chapter 4, section 2.

[63] Ibid., 139. [64] Ibid., 138.

those necessary shared attitudes of reciprocity. We will therefore see a need, a role, for criminal law as a coercive institution, to deter rule-violations and thus 'provid[e] an assurance of general cooperation with legal rules'—an assurance that people need if they are to sustain the requisite 'shared attitudes of reciprocity'.[65] This need not be to deny that the criminal law can also serve other valuable roles, for instance 'condemning wrongs and vindicating rights'; but its primary role, its 'one important function', is that of coercive rule-enforcement.[66] (Thorburn's account of criminal law as public law is not, or not so clearly, instrumentalist: it functions to protect a normative order in which we can live together as 'free and independent persons', and serves to 'resist any attempt to supplant the law's rules with private preferences';[67] but its role is not simply deterrent or preventive, and it is partly constitutive of, not merely instrumental to, the state's 'robust public authority'.[68])

One merit of this kind of view is that it makes criminal law 'subsidiary'. The doctrine (or the slogan) of 'the subsidiarity of criminal law', and the related idea of 'the fragmentary character of criminal law', are familiar in German criminal law theory, and are often connected to the '*ultima ratio*' principle, that criminal law should be the polity's 'last resort'.[69] Criminal law plays, or should play, a 'subsidiary' role in that its role 'is merely to provide "subsidiary" protection for the interests that the law recognizes and protects'; and it is 'fragmentary' in that it 'protects only some *Rechtsgüter*, and its protection is sometimes selective rather than general'.[70] I will return to *Rechtsgüter* later, and will suggest that whilst the 'subsidiary' character of the criminal law is an aspect of its primary role, its 'fragmentary' character has more to do with how it should function in relation to other elements of civil order. That is to say, if we ask what gives us good reason to criminalize a type of conduct, the answer will reflect criminal law's subsidiary character, but not its fragmentary character: if the protection of *Rechtsgüter* is the criminal law's proper purpose, we have good reason to criminalize every kind of conduct that injures or threatens a *Rechtsgut*. But when we ask what we should criminalize all things considered, the answer will give criminal law a 'fragmentary' character: not every injury or threat to a *Rechtsgut* should be criminalized.[71]

However, I will argue, first, that we should not understand the relationship between criminal law and civil order in purely instrumental terms: for the criminal law of a liberal republic partly constitutes the civil order that it serves to protect. Second, the criminal law's primary purpose has to do, not with the coercive prevention of, or resistance to, kinds of conduct that threaten the civil order, but with the provision of an appropriate response to those kinds of moral wrong that constitute public wrongs. This argument will depend on, but also help to support, the account of criminal law I offered in Chapter 1, as an institution whose two central dimensions are its declarative definitions of sets of public wrongs, and the provision of a process through which those accused of committing such wrongs are called to formal public account. That account was offered not as a neutral analysis of 'criminal law' as such, but as a rational reconstruction of salient features of systems of criminal law like our own. Such a reconstruction gains plausibility if the institution that it reconstructs can be shown to

[65] Ibid., 138, 139. [66] Ibid., 138.

[67] M Thorburn, 'Constitutionalism and the Limits of the Criminal Law', 88, 97.

[68] See M Thorburn, 'Punishment and Public Authority'.

[69] For a useful English language discussion of these slogans, and the relationships between them, see N Jareborg, 'Criminalization as Last Resort (*Ultima Ratio*)'; see also D Husak, 'Applying *Ultima Ratio*: A Skeptical Assessment'.

[70] Jareborg, 'Criminalization as Last Resort', 532, 525.

[71] See further below, Chapter 7, section 2.

fit with a political theory that is itself normatively plausible, as a theory of the kind of polity in which the institution can function.

The starting point for this argument about the role of criminal law in a liberal republic is, as it is for other 'public law' theorists (or any plausible theory of criminal law), the recognition that in human life, where there is conduct there will also be misconduct. A polity's civil order is, as we have seen, structured by a range of values: it includes various ends that are to be pursued, as constituting the polity's common good (ends such as those avowed by the American constitution—'domestic tranquility', 'the common defence', 'the general Welfare', 'the Blessings of Liberty'); certain foundational values that ground the common good ('social justice', 'equal concern and respect'); certain rights that are to be respected ('privacy', 'dignity'); and various institutions that are necessary to the effective pursuit of those values. Those values make demands on members of the polity: as citizens, we should assist in the pursuit of those ends, respect those foundational values and guide our civic conduct by them, respect those rights, and recognize those institutions as authoritative.[72] Now were we a community of angels or of saints, we would have no need of criminal law: we would embrace those values wholeheartedly, and guide our actions by them. We would still need a set of institutions and rules to coordinate our conduct towards those goods that we are collectively pursuing; but we would not need to wonder what to do about violations of our values, or breaches of the institutional rules, since none would violate or breach them.[73] Even a community of not-quite-saints would have no need for criminal law: perhaps a not-quite-saint would occasionally slip from grace; but she would at once repent, confess, and remedy such slips. On the other hand, were we a collection of amoral psychopaths, who lacked any practical understanding of values as sources of reasons for action, we would have no capacity either for political community or for criminal law:[74] we would be unable to constitute ourselves as a polity, or to create or sustain a civil order, or to speak or hear the voice of the criminal law—a voice that speaks in terms of values and of wrongs. We might find a *modus vivendi*, but could not engage together in a shared project of civil life under the rule of law.

We are, however, neither saints nor psychopaths: we are human beings. We are able both to recognize and to respond to values; we are able to form normative relationships with others, and to constitute and sustain ourselves not merely as individuals or as aggregates of individuals, but as communities; we can recognize goals, goods, and rights as worthy of respect and support, and guide our conduct accordingly; we can recognize the legitimate claims on us of institutions that serve our common good, and accept their procedures and rules as authoritative. But we are also liable to fall far short of angelic or saintly perfection. We disagree, sometimes irresolubly, about the relevant matters of value. We are prone to do wrong—to obstruct others' pursuit of valuable goals, to violate others' rights or the goods and values that make a legitimate claim on us, and to breach the institutional regulations that we should obey. We are also prone

[72] Which is not to say that we should conform unquestioningly to their requirements: citizens of a liberal republic will respect its laws and its institutions, but that respect will be critical; see at nn 141–5 below.

[73] Or would not breach them knowingly or carelessly, while non-culpably inadvertent breaches would be at once recognized and remedied.

[74] I do not mean to engage here with the continuing controversies about the character of 'psychopathy' and about its implications for responsibility (see e.g. L Malatesti and J McMillan (eds), *Responsibility and Psychopathy*): all that I mean to claim here is that *if* there is a condition that involves an inability to comprehend (as a matter of practical reason) the realm of other-regarding thought and value, then a collection of people suffering that incapacity could neither form a community (moral or political), nor sustain a system of criminal law.

to deny that we have done wrong, even when we know that we have; we too often refuse to face, or to admit, our own wrong-doing. But we are not beyond redemption: we can, if not by our own often feeble efforts, then through the intervention of others who criticize us and call us to account, come to recognize our wrongs, and seek to make reparation (moral as well as material) for them. Furthermore, this capacity for responding to value matters to us: when we exercise it, we also realize (although we also quite often forget, when not exercising it) that the values to which we respond are important for us—that they matter to our lives, both individual and social.

A polity's civil order is thus vulnerable to (among other dangers) human wrongdoing. As we will see in more detail later, such wrongdoing can threaten civil order both instrumentally and intrinsically. An instrumental threat has some potential consequential impact on the functioning of the polity or its civil order: for instance, it might cause some disruption to 'the queen's peace', or undermine the operations of the polity's institutions. An intrinsic threat is damaging even if it has no such consequential impact: a murder or a rape, to take the obvious examples, violates the civil order simply in virtue of its commission, whatever further effects it may or may not have, and whether or not it is discovered; for it contradicts a basic condition of our civic lives, and of the individual's standing as a citizen.[75]

As members of a polity, we can therefore both, on our better days, recognize and respond to its defining values; and also recognize that we are on our worse days likely to violate them. Such violations will be as diverse in character as the values (the goals, goods, rights, and institutional processes and regulations) that are violated: many will be harmful, in some sense of that protean concept—perhaps all will be, if we interpret 'harm' in a broad enough sense;[76] but even if they are not harmful, they matter to us insofar as we are committed to those values. How then are we to deal with or respond to such violations? That is a question that any human polity must answer.

An obvious first answer is that we must seek to prevent them, or at least to minimize their occurrence. We should seek to prevent or reduce them not only for the sake of prevention itself, in order to protect the goods and values that would otherwise be violated, but also for the sake of the central value of security or assurance.[77] If we are to be able to pursue our lives in a political community, or to have any chance of attaining the goods (shared or private) that the polity aims to protect, it must not only be the case that there are relatively few attacks on or violations of the polity's defining values; we must also have some assurance that this is so—we need not only to be relatively safe from wrongdoing, but also to know that we are relatively safe. There are many ways in which a polity can try to prevent or reduce the commission of wrongs, or violations of its civil order. Some will involve responding (or threatening to respond) to such conduct in certain ways—ways intended, most obviously, to deter such conduct, or to render those who engage in it less able to repeat it, or so to modify their attitudes that they voluntarily refrain from repeating it (the familiar trio of deterrence,

[75] See at nn 111–13 below. This is not to say that the wrongness of murder or rape consists, in the polity's or in the law's eyes, in this violation of the civil order; rather, that it violates the civil order is what makes it the polity's business. See further at nn 107–8 below.

[76] By insisting, for instance, that we all have an interest in the maintenance of the goods and values that define our polity, which is set back by any violation of those goods or values: see further below, Chapter 6 at nn 148–50.

[77] See variously Pettit, *On the People's Terms*, on 'non-domination' (n. 41 above); Chiao, 'What is the Criminal Law For?', on the need for 'an assurance of general cooperation with legal rules'; P Ramsay, *The Insecurity State: Vulnerable Autonomy and the Right to Security in the Criminal Law*, on the fragility of our autonomy; L Zedner, *Security*, 14–19, on the two dimensions of security; and above, Chapter 4 at nn 59–60, on trust.

incapacitation, and reform). Other preventive methods involve pre-emption rather than reaction: they include education, public exhortation, and measures of 'situational prevention' to make the wrongful or order-violating conduct less attractive or less feasible,[78] as well as measures targeted at those thought likely to engage in such conduct. Other familiar modes of prevention include various kinds of 'therapy' or 'treatment', which respond to wrongful or order-violating conduct less as wrongful than as socially problematic; and, in some of its forms, 'restorative justice', which portrays the issue not as one of wrongful conduct but as of 'troubles' or 'conflicts', to be dealt with in restorative ways by those directly involved.[79]

We must bear in mind, however, that whatever preventive measures we put in place, we can be confident that they will not prevent *all* wrongful or order-violating conduct: the reason for this is not just that human procedures are always fallible, but also that the preventive measures that we use, whether *ex ante* or *ex post*, must be consistent with the polity's defining values.[80] This is especially true of pre-emptive measures that coerce or constrain citizens before they have been found to have engaged in the kind of conduct that we aim to prevent: even if it could be argued that those who engage in such conduct lose some of their rights against some kinds of coercive treatment by the polity,[81] those who have not engaged, or have not been found to have engaged, in such conduct must still be treated with the equal concern and respect that is due to all citizens. I will not discuss here the constraints that this will place on permissible methods of pre-emptive wrong-prevention;[82] the relevant point is that such constraints ensure that pre-emptive prevention will be far less than perfectly effective.

Now criminal law can be expected to play a preventive role. The most obvious way in which it can do this is through the threat and the imposition of punishment, especially insofar as we can see punishment as serving deterrent, incapacitative, or reformative purposes; but I will defer any discussion of punishment until section 6, in line with my suggestion in Chapter 1 that we should not regard punishment as the primary function of criminal law. I will focus initially on substantive criminal law, as defining a range of public wrongs; and the criminal process, as the process through which those alleged to have committed such wrongs are called to formal public account. If we consider criminal law as thus understood (criminal law without punishment) only in preventive terms, it will quite reasonably be seen as somewhat ineffective—far less effective, certainly, than other methods of preventing civil-order-violating conduct (including criminal law with punishment). However, first, as a mode of prevention it has the merit of being wholly consistent with, indeed thoroughly expressive of, the polity's defining values—which is partly why I said earlier that it is partly constitutive of the polity's civil order; second, its value does not consist primarily, or even significantly, in its preventive efficacy.

One function of the substantive criminal law is simply declarative (or expressive): the polity has reason to declare, in some suitably formal way, the norms that its

[78] On 'situational' prevention and its problems, see A von Hirsch et al (eds), *Ethical and Social Perspectives on Situational Crime Prevention* (we cannot yet talk here of 'situational crime prevention', since we have not yet found a role for criminal law).

[79] See e.g. N Christie, 'Conflicts as Property'; L Hulsman, 'Critical Criminology and the Concept of Crime'.

[80] Compare Chiao, *Criminal Law in the Age of the Administrative State*, ch. 2: the use of criminal law to enforce institutional rules must be 'consistent with the principles that make [those] institutions . . . worth supporting in the first place'.

[81] On rights-forfeiture theories of punishment see Chapter 3, n. 156 above; but see at nn 38–40 above on the importance of recognizing wrongdoers as citizens.

[82] But see below, Chapter 7, section 6, on pre-emptive criminal offences.

citizens have determined should guide their civic conduct—its public norms. This is not to espouse an 'expressive theory of law';[83] it is simply to make the more modest, and limited, claim that an institution can have good reasons to make a formal declaration of the norms that are to guide its members' conduct beyond the desire to ensure compliance with those norms by threatening sanctions against those who violate them. To say that it declares these norms is to deny, implicitly, that this is a matter of norm-*creation*: although it involves a process of developing precise determinations of norms that are extra-legally somewhat vague or indeterminate, and giving purportedly authoritative backing to norms that are extra-legally controversial, the enterprise is one of giving public, concrete form to norms that are already the polity's norms.[84] A polity will also, we have seen, have good reason to create various kinds of regulation that do create norms:[85] but these regulations are not part of the criminal law, and the criminalization of their violation can be justified (when it is justified) by appeal to a civic duty to obey the regulation—a duty that is not a creation of law. Among the reasons for such a public, formal declaration of norms are, for instance, to remind the citizens that these are indeed norms by which they should guide their civic conduct; to make clear that these are the polity's *public* norms, as distinct from whatever private norms citizens or groups of citizens might espouse outside the civic realm; to make clear—in cases of controversy, or doubt, or vagueness or unclarity—just what the norms are; and to make it explicit (and thus also to give fair warning) that these are norms whose breach will render perpetrators liable to a formal public response.

Even without the prospect of punishment, such formal declarations of what constitute public wrongs can have some preventive effects: they can remind us (if we need reminding) of how we should or should not conduct ourselves; and they can warn us that if we misconduct ourselves we will face the prospect of being prosecuted. Even without the prospect of punishment following a conviction, the prospect of prosecution can have a dissuasive effect, since prosecution itself is a burdensome business, and conviction is, for most people, unwelcome and unpleasant. I call this a 'dissuasive' rather than a 'deterrent' effect, because deterrence is normally taken to involve the provision of new, prudential reasons for action—reasons separate from those taken to justify the attempt to dissuade. What justifies our attempt to dissuade each other from, for instance, evading our taxes is the duty we suppose that we have to pay our taxes—a duty grounded in our civic responsibility to contribute financially to the common good. But if we seek to 'deter' tax evasion, what we will offer is not that reason (which we suppose has failed or might fail), but a prudential reason grounded in the unpleasant consequences that we attach to tax evasion. Now the prospect of trial and conviction is indeed, for many people, a deterrent in the sense that it is an unattractive prospect of something that will be painful, and harmful to one's interests: but for many (even most) of those many people it is not a matter of *pure* deterrence, since the pain and harm will be infused by the guilt and shame involved in the recognition that one has done wrong, and in being seen by one's fellows to have done wrong; someone who has no such concern for the propriety of her own actions, or for her standing with her

[83] On which see, critically, M Adler, 'Expressive Theories of Law: A Skeptical Overview'; for a response see E Anderson and R Pildes, 'Expressive Theories of Law: A General Restatement'.

[84] See above, Chapter 1 at nn 46–52; but see also below, Chapter 7, section 4, for an important qualification.

[85] See above, Chapter 1 at nn 45–8, Chapter 2, section 4, and below, Chapter 7, section 5.

fellows, will not find the prospect of prosecution and conviction unpleasant in the same way, or to the same degree.[86]

However, the initial way in which the substantive criminal law, in its declaratory mode, aims to dissuade us from wrongful conduct is a matter not of deterrence, but rather of reminding us of the good reasons that we already have to refrain from the conduct that it defines as criminal. For to declare a type of conduct to be wrong is to declare that it is conduct in which we ought not to engage—conduct that we have good, indeed normally conclusive, reason to eschew. If the law, and in particular the criminal law, is to address us as responsible citizens, it must at least initially address us in terms of those very reasons that should, it claims, guide our conduct, and that thus justify its attempts to guide our conduct;[87] indeed, if it is to be, as it should be, our common law, it must address us in our own collective voice, in terms of the values that are our shared values, by which we must therefore already be committed to guiding our conduct. Even if the law then also addresses us in terms that are at least partly prudential and deterrent (a question to be discussed later), it cannot begin in such terms: for to address us in purely deterrent terms is to address us, not as members of the normative community whose law it is, but as outsiders who cannot be, or are not, expected to share in the community's values; it is to alienate us from the law, and from ourselves as owners and agents of that law.[88]

A declarative criminal law is not (initially) a deterrent law; but it cannot plausibly be *merely* declarative: it cannot simply declare *ex ante* that certain kinds of conduct are wrong. For a polity (any community) that takes its action-guiding values seriously must also be ready to respond to violations of those values. Some reasons for responding are forward-looking: we aim to dissuade the perpetrator, and others, from future wrongdoing (this need not be a matter of deterrence—we can hope to dissuade by pointing out, emphatically, that what the person did was wrong). Indeed, insofar as the response includes condemnation of the wrong that was committed, it is necessarily forward-looking, since to condemn a past action is also to say that it should not be done, now or in future. But a simpler reason for responding has to do with what it is to take values seriously. To care about something is, inter alia, to be disposed to react appropriately to what impacts on it: if I care for my friend (if I am her friend), I am disposed to be gladdened by her success or good fortune, saddened by her failures or misfortune, and indignant at wrongs done to her—as well as saddened by wrongs that she commits; if I care about the pursuit of philosophical understanding, I will be gladdened by advances towards it (mine or another's), frustrated by my failures to make progress, and disposed to argue against what I take to be mistaken views.[89] So too, if we care, as citizens, for the values that we collectively profess (and to profess them is to profess to care for them), we cannot be indifferent to their violation; and though we can respond to such violations non-publicly, in how we think or feel, we

[86] Which is why this kind of 'deterrence' would be most effective on those who might be thought to need it least: those who are already to some degree (if inadequately) motivated to refrain from crime.

[87] See Duff, *Punishment, Communication, and Community*, 56–8, 80–2, on 'transparent persuasion'.

[88] For a differently formulated (and, I now think, overstated) version of this kind of objection see R A Duff, *Trials and Punishments*, 176–86.

[89] Our actual dispositions are rarely as pure as these remarks might imply: it is all too likely that I will be jealous of my friend's or my colleague's successes, concerned with the pursuit not so much of understanding as of *my* recognized success, and disposed to argue particularly against views that threaten mine or that I think I can gain attention by attacking. But these are some (depressingly familiar) pathologies of friendship or of philosophical commitment; my concern here is with the more ideal paradigms of which they are pathologies.

will also appropriately look for some suitable public response. Part of the motivation for such a response might be instrumental: we want to make it clear—to anyone who might doubt it—that we do take these values seriously; we want to avoid appearing or being seen to condone their violation. But such instrumental reasons depend on a non-instrumental and non-contingent connection between being committed to certain values and being disposed to respond to their violation: to be thus committed *is* to be thus disposed—which is why a lack of response is liable to be taken to reveal a lack of commitment to the value in question, or to amount to condoning its violation.

What might that response involve, in the case of criminal law? I have answered that question in what I said about the criminal process, and about the substantive criminal law as declaring that the wrongs it defines as criminal are wrongs for which the perpetrators will be liable to be held to formal public account; but we need to be clear about why such a calling to public account is an appropriate—and sometimes necessary—response to civic as to other kinds of wrongdoing.

The point can be most clearly developed in relation to victimizing wrongs. Our responses to a wrong need not, of course, respond to it *as a wrong*, and no doubt sometimes should not do so. This is one element of truth in 'abolitionist' versions of 'restorative justice' that urge us to see what are defined as crimes as 'conflicts' or as 'troubles' rather than as wrongs, and to focus our efforts on repairing the harm caused and suffered rather than on attaching blame and punishment to the (supposed) wrongdoer.[90] Although they are wrong to think that we can always separate the harm from the wrong, since sometimes the harm is partly constituted as the particular, serious kind of harm that it is by the wrong that wrought it;[91] and although, I will argue, if we are to take the wrongdoing as seriously as we should, we must sometimes make it salient in our response: it is true that sometimes the most sensible response to conduct that is indeed wrongful is to respond to it not as a wrong but as a (symptom of) a problem that needs to be resolved without attempting to assign culpable responsibility. Two bickering neighbours might have wronged each other in various ways; but if they are to find a way to live together in peace, or at least without conflict, they might be well advised to focus not on who wronged whom, but on how they can reconcile, or find some compromise between, their conflicting expectations and habits. Often, however, an appropriate response to a victimizing crime will make salient not just whatever harm the victim has suffered, but the wrong that was done to him: we owe him sympathy for that harm as our fellow, and attempts to help him repair or at least ameliorate it; but we also owe it to him to recognize and address that wrong.

For two reasons, we can most appropriately address the wrong by calling, or trying to call, to account the person(s) who committed it. First, it is plausible to think that part of what we owe the victims is to seek to call those who wronged them to account for those wrongs. It is a common complaint among crime victims that the police have not investigated 'their' crime with sufficient commitment, or that prosecutors do not bring charges against 'their' offender: that 'their' crimes have not been taken seriously enough. This is also a familiar motivation for civil suits in cases of alleged negligent killing: those who have lost loved ones in a train crash or a hospital, and who suspect that this was due to negligence by a rail company or its employees, or by doctors, might bring a civil case whose formal aim must be compensation, but whose real aim (so they argue) is to call to account those whose negligence caused their loss. What they

[90] See n. 79 above; also L Walgrave, 'Imposing Restoration Instead of Inflicting Pain'.

[91] See R A Duff, *Answering for Crime*, 127–8.

properly seek is not (just) compensation for whatever independently identifiable harm they suffered, but an accounting for the wrong that was done.[92]

Second, once we see what is properly involved in calling the wrongdoer to account, we can also see that this is something we collectively owe to those who commit, as well as to those who suffer, such wrongs. Granted, on one familiar but crude kind of retributive view, what victims properly demand is that those who wronged them should be made to suffer: this goes with the idea that what wrongdoers deserve is to suffer, and that the polity's first responsibility is to make sure that they suffer. Such a demand for suffering is admittedly one aspect both of public opinion and of many victims' responses to their crimes, and if we focus on that demand, it is indeed hard to see its satisfaction as something that we owe *to* those who are to be made to suffer: if that is what punishment is, the idea of a right to be punished is as absurd as its critics claim. However, this is not the only salient demand, nor is it the demand on which we should initially focus. We should instead focus on the demand that the wrongdoer be called or held to account for what he has done—that he answer for it. This is, I suspect, as powerfully felt a demand as the demand that he be made to suffer, as is shown most clearly in the case of international criminal trials: what matters, to many people, is not so much that those who perpetrated 'crimes against humanity' be punished (what punishment, we might ask, could fit such wrongs?), but that they be called to public account for what they have done. But to call someone to account is to address him as a responsible agent, and as a fellow member of a relevant normative community. I can be called to account only if I am a responsible agent who can be expected to answer for what he has done, and only by fellows who are themselves committed to the values for an alleged violation of which I am now called to account, and who participate in the particular form of life within which I am thus called. To call someone to account for an alleged wrong, however condemnatory that calling is, is therefore also to show him a certain kind of respect, even concern, as a fellow who is, along with us, bound and protected by the values to which that calling appeals.[93]

To say that we owe it to the wrongdoer to call him to account is to say that he has a right to be thus called, and therefore, if the calling takes the form of a criminal prosecution, a right to be prosecuted: but a right to be prosecuted might sound as strange as a 'right to be punished'. As with the supposed right to be punished, so too with the right to be prosecuted, we can distinguish a conditional from a categorical version of the right. The conditional right to be punished is the right that, *if* we are going to respond to a wrong in a way that impacts adversely or burdensomely on the perpetrator, we punish him *rather than* subjecting him to other kinds of adverse measure—to purely incapacitative detention, for instance, or to compulsory psychiatric treatment.[94] The conditional right to be prosecuted is analogously, the right that *if* we are going to respond to the wrong in a way that enacts or displays our condemnation of it, and that bears adversely on the perpetrator, we prosecute him rather than subjecting him to other kinds of adverse response—for instance to immediate ostracism or exclusion, or to punishment (which might be better described as lynching) without a trial. A categorical right to be punished would be a right to be punished if one has committed a wrong—a right to be punished even if the alternative is that nothing is done to one as a result of one's wrongdoing. Analogously, a categorical right to be prosecuted would be a right to be prosecuted even if the alternative was simply to have one's wrong ignored. I will not discuss the (supposed) right to be punished further here; but the right to be

[92] See above, Chapter 1 at nn 54–5. [93] See above, Chapter 3 at n. 164.

[94] Compare H Morris, 'Persons and Punishment'.

prosecuted can be argued to be a categorical, rather than a merely conditional right. For if to prosecute someone is to address her as a responsible member of the political community, as a participant in this form of civic life, it is an aspect of what we owe to each other as fellow citizens: the 'equal concern and respect' that we owe each other, the recognition of each other as fellow citizens, is displayed in, inter alia, our responses to the wrongs that we commit. Simply to fail to respond to another's wrong, when that other is a fellow citizen and the wrong a (non-trivial) civic wrong, is to imply that neither she nor her wrong is worthy of our attention or notice; but that is not how we should address our fellow citizens.[95]

It is important to be clear that on this account what we owe to victims and perpetrators is not (simply) to condemn the wrong or the wrongdoer. Condemnation does indeed express a concern for the victim, and for the values that wrong violated, and it at least implies a recognition of the wrongdoer as a responsible agent: but it does not by itself address him as a responsible fellow member of the normative community, because it does not require or invite him to *respond* to the charge of wrongdoing—to deny the charge, to defend himself, or to own his guilt. A polity that was quick to exclude wrongdoers might not invest much in a process that calls them to answer—beyond what was needed to make reasonably sure that they were guilty; but a polity that takes an inclusionary attitude to its members, and that still treats them as citizens even when they commit serious wrongs, will be committed to calling them to account for their civic wrongdoing.

Calling to account, as a way of treating each other as responsible agents, might not seem to require a formal criminal process. Advocates of restorative justice often also make responsibility salient in their accounts of how we should collectively respond to (what we see as) crimes, but they advocate informal processes of mediation rather than a formal process like the criminal trial. What is important, they argue, is to develop less formal structures and procedures through which responsibility can be discussed, negotiated, accepted, and discharged—through which people can take responsibility for their actions, and agree on how to discharge that responsibility through reparative actions.[96] They differ, however, over just what those structures and procedures should be, and sometimes fail to appreciate the significance of the distinctive kind of calling to account that the criminal law can provide.

One point that should be clear is that we must attend not just to harms, but to wrongs: what is at stake is not just determining (or negotiating) responsibility for some harm that was caused, but determining responsibility for a wrong that was done. Responsibility for harm can, typically, be discharged by repairing or paying for the harm, but we need to ask how responsibility for wrongs can be discharged, and what goes with accepting it. The point to notice here, however, is that a process that is to do justice to victims and to what they have suffered must aim not merely to call a harm-causer to account, or bring him to recognize his responsibility for that harm, but to call a wrongdoer to account for the wrong he has done.

Further important issues are raised by the emphasis that advocates of restorative justice often place on informal negotiation between the parties most directly involved

[95] A categorical right to be prosecuted or punished is not an absolute right: there might be good reasons not to prosecute, or punish, culpable wrongdoers (for instance to do with 'the public interest'; see above, Chapter 1 at n. 165), in which case non-prosecution or non-punishment does not violate their rights; see further Chapter 7, section 3 below.

[96] See generally G Johnstone, *Restorative Justice: Ideas, Values, Debates*; G Johnstone (ed.), *A Restorative Justice Reader*.

in the affair rather than a formal determination by a court. What matters, they argue, is that people should discuss their concerns, explain their actions and reactions, freely and openly. They should be able to come to accept their own responsibilities, and to recognize that the responsibility for a harm might not be properly allocated to just one person—that often it must be shared in nuanced ways that cannot be captured in the formal process of a criminal trial, which is focused on just one person, the defendant. These are certainly valuable features of the ways in which we can conduct our social lives, and even when a 'conflict' in which we find ourselves involves criminal conduct, we might do better to try to resolve our problems through such informal processes rather than by appealing to the formal (and coercive) apparatus of the criminal law. But such informal processes will not always be adequate.

First, they privatize the conflict, as something which properly concerns only those directly involved in it or close to it: but some kinds of wrong should be treated as public matters, which concern us all as citizens. I will have more to say later about what kinds of wrong these may be, and about how we should decide which wrongs are apt for criminal law and which should be left to a civil process; but all we need say so far is that if they are public wrongs, which violate our collective values, that gives us reason to look for a formal, public, collective response.

Second, wrongs that we should treat as public are typically wrongs that require categorical recognition and condemnation rather than those kinds of nuanced negotiation (and compromise) that a 'conflict'-oriented process is likely to involve. We should sometimes (perhaps more often than we are inclined to) ask versions of Christie's question, 'How wrong was the thief, how right was the victim?':[97] we will sometimes come to see that, having initially portrayed ourselves as innocent victims, we should accept some responsibility for what happened, in a way that reduces the responsibility of the person we portrayed as the perpetrator. Sometimes, however, that is not appropriate. One reason is that sometimes it is simply not plausible to argue that the victim was in any direct way even partly responsible for the wrong; and although if we delved more deeply into the conditions from which the wrong emerged, we might see reason to share a deeper kind of responsibility more broadly,[98] it is also important to our conception of ourselves and of each other as agents that we take full responsibility for our actions. But there is another reason. When what is at stake is who is to pay the cost of a harm that has been caused, a victim who was partly responsible for the harm should bear part of the cost; responsibility is thus shared, and is thereby reduced for each of the people concerned. Responsibility for wrongs, however, is not so readily reduced by being shared. The victim of a burglary, for instance, might have behaved carelessly in leaving her door unlocked; it might be appropriate for her to criticize herself, or even for a friend to criticize her imprudence. But whilst 'contributory negligence' can play a proper role in civil cases, since it warrants the conclusion that responsibility, and the cost of the harm, should be shared between plaintiff and defendant, no such conclusion is warranted in a case like this: it would be illegitimate for a criminal court to ask, 'How wrong was the burglar, how right was the victim?'. The burglar should not be heard to argue in mitigation that the victim's negligence was a contributory factor in the burglary, since her negligence does nothing to reduce the attacker's culpable responsibility. In this context, unlike that of liability to pay for harm, we cannot say

[97] Christie, 'Conflicts as Property', 8.

[98] Compare A Norrie, *Punishment, Responsibility, and Justice*, 220–1, on a 'relational theory of blame', according to which responsibility 'lies with individuals *and* with societies of which they are a part, so that, neither individualized nor denied, it is shared'.

that responsibility for the crime is shared: the burglar's action normatively constitutes a true *novus actus interveniens*, for which he alone should be held criminally responsible.[99] The attacks that constitute paradigmatically criminal *mala in se* are wrongs from which all citizens should be able to expect to be categorically safe; they are therefore to be categorically condemned rather than negotiated. That is why, for instance, it is right to prosecute domestic violence as a crime, rather than seeing it as a private matter to be negotiated between those directly involved, or as grounds for a civil suit. Such violence must be marked categorically as wrong—a kind of wrong in which we should collectively take an active interest as fellow citizens of both victim and perpetrator.[100]

A further aspect of informal procedures is worth noting: that it is harder to set limits on what is raised for critical discussion. What begins as a conflict between neighbours over some precise, limited issue can easily spread out, once the discussion begins, to bring in other aspects of their lives; if the aim is to restore their relationship, anything about the relationship that is problematic can be brought up. This is, of course, sometimes precisely what is needed, especially in a close-knit community, but it is worrying for those who are committed to an ideal of liberal political community that respects the boundaries of our personal lives. In such a polity we are related to, and deal with, the majority of our fellow citizens not, admittedly, as complete strangers (since we recognize them as fellows), but as people with whom our civic bonds are limited and relatively shallow. We share a civic life with them, but that life is only one dimension of our lives, and we should be able to keep much about the other dimensions of our lives private—shared only with members of the closer groups with whom we choose to live or find ourselves living in greater intimacy. When we commit wrongs that count as 'public', we must be willing to answer for them publicly, but even then the realms of private life and thought should be protected. The fact that I committed a wrong against a fellow citizen should not give my fellows the right to discuss every aspect of my life that bothers them. But that is just what can happen in an informal discussion of our 'conflict'.

I have suggested so far that a polity that takes civic wrongdoing—wrongdoing that impinges on its civil order—seriously, and whose members aspire to treat each other with due respect and concern as responsible citizens, will need to make provision for those who commit such wrongs to be called to account for them, but that it must also protect such wrongdoers against responses that intrude into what should be the private dimensions of their lives. More precisely, it will need to make provision for those who are accused of such civic wrongdoing to be called to answer such accusations, and to answer for those wrongs if the accusations are found to be true. For guilt is not typically evident from the start, without doubt or the need for further inquiry: we typically begin with suspicion or accusation, not with manifest and indubitable guilt. If we are

[99] I do not mean to suggest that the primary wrongdoer's responsibility can never be reduced by the victim's role in what happened (for an ambitious—I think over-ambitious—argument along these lines, see V Bergelson, *Victims' Rights and Victims' Wrongs: Comparative Liability in Criminal Law*): I do not, for instance, mean to rule out in advance the possibility that the partial defence of provocation can be rationalized by arguing that the victim shares responsibility for the attack that he provoked. All I am claiming here is that the paradigm cases of *mala in se* (the kinds of wrong that, as we will see, we have the simplest and strongest reason to criminalize) are cases in which responsibility cannot be thus shared.

[100] Compare R E Dobash and R P Dobash, *Women, Violence and Social Change*, ch. 7, on what the CHANGE programme requires; M M Dempsey, *Prosecuting Domestic Violence: A Philosophical Analysis*. I assume here that a liberal republic's criminal law will certainly define such wrongs as rape and domestic violence as crimes; we will see later (in Chapter 7, section 2) why this is so—why such wrongs are obvious violations of the civil order.

to call civic wrongdoers to account, we must first establish that they are indeed civic wrongdoers; and if we are to do that in a way that treats them as responsible citizens (as citizens who are able, and who should therefore be enabled, to answer for themselves), we should do it through a process that calls them to answer the accusation of civic wrongdoing, and protects them against unwarranted or over-hasty judgments of guilt. I have suggested that the kinds of informal process favoured by advocates of restorative justice might not be of this appropriate kind. We do, however, have an institution that, in the aspiration that its form and rhetoric imply, even if all too infrequently in its actual operations, is of that kind: the criminal trial, as described in Chapter 1. The trial is a process through which citizens are called by their fellows to answer charges of civic wrongdoing, and to answer for that wrongdoing if it is proved against them: it thus provides an appropriate response to what the polity defines as crimes. It constitutes the calling to account that civic wrongdoing requires—a calling that takes the wrongdoing seriously and addresses its agent as a responsible citizen. It is precisely focused on the wrongdoing, not just on the harm that might also have been caused, and focuses on that wrongdoing as a public rather than a private matter: the polity calls the alleged perpetrator to account for a wrong that concerns all citizens. However, it respects the bounds of private life: what is at issue is whether the defendant is guilty of the particular wrong specified in the indictment; only matters bearing directly on that issue are to figure in the trial.

There is much more to be said about the criminal trial, and the ways in which it must protect those whom it calls to answer; more too about how a polity should treat those who are accused of crimes, and those who are acquitted of crimes, as well as those who are convicted—the meaning of the presumption of innocence is clearly of central importance here.[101] All I have argued here is if we ask how a liberal republic of the kind sketched in this chapter could respond to (actual or alleged) civic wrongdoing, a plausible answer is that it could do so by maintaining a system of criminal law whose function is, first, to declare and define the range of wrongs that it counts as public wrongs—as wrongs that concern all its members in virtue of their shared membership; and, second, to provide a process through which those accused of committing such wrongs can be called to formal account—called to answer to the accusation, and to answer for the wrong if it is proved. I have not yet discussed criminal punishment, and the role that it might play—that will be a topic for section 6 of this chapter: I have so far been concerned only with a criminal process that culminates, if the accused person is proved guilty, in a formal conviction that censures him for his wrongdoing. Before turning to the question of what might follow a conviction, however, I should say something more about the relation of criminal law, as conceived here, to the polity's civil order.

5. A Liberal Republic's Criminal Law: (2) Criminal Law, Criminal Wrongs, and Civil Order

I have suggested that we should see criminal law not in simply instrumental terms as helping to sustain a civil order whose structural features can be identified independently of the criminal law that is to protect it, but as partly constitutive of the civil order

[101] See further R A Duff et al, *The Trial on Trial (3): Towards a Normative Theory of the Criminal Trial*; Duff, 'Who Must Presume Whom to be Innocent of What?'.

that it is also to sustain. We can now see why this is so—why the institution of criminal law as I have described it embodies values that determine, in important ways, the civic character of the polity of which it is part. A polity that maintains such an institution is, first, a polity that takes civic wrongdoing seriously: it is concerned not merely to prevent kinds of conduct that are in some way undesirable or harmful, but to mark out for formal censure certain kinds of wrongdoing. Second, it is a polity that takes agency and responsibility seriously, and insists on treating its members as responsible citizens: the criminal law addresses them as agents who can guide their own conduct by appropriate kinds of reason (reasons to which the law appeals in defining conduct as criminal, as well as the more prudential reasons that the law might offer insofar as it aims, as a second best, to deter); and it calls them to answer, as responsible agents, for their alleged wrongs, through the criminal trial. In maintaining such an institution, a polity thus constitutes itself and its civil order in a particular way, as one that is structured by these kinds of concern, and this kind of respect for its citizens—concerns and respect that must also figure in other aspects of its life.

We can now make more plausible sense of Blackstone's remark that crimes as public wrongs 'strike at the very being of society, which cannot possibly subsist, where actions of [that] sort are suffered to escape with impunity'.[102] This is not plausibly read as a claim about the consequences of unpunished crime, or as akin to Devlin's claim that the survival of a society's shared morality, and therefore of the society itself, is threatened if it allows conduct that is perceived as seriously immoral to go unpunished.[103] Whatever Blackstone himself might have meant by it, his claim is most plausibly read as concerning the implications, rather than the contingent consequences, of the kinds of wrong that should be criminalized; and as concerning the implications not merely of such wrongs themselves, but of failing to criminalize them, thus allowing their perpetrators 'to escape with impunity'. For in defining its civil order, a polity defines and presents itself as being committed to the values that structure that civil order: but to fail to respond to violations of those values is to undermine that self-definition, and so its own identity; for such failure is inconsistent with the normative commitment professed by that definition. What 'cannot possibly subsist' is the 'society' that is supposedly constituted by this civil order: for a society that fails to respond to violations of its purported civil order is not one that is truly constituted by (a commitment to) that order. As we can now see, a liberal republic will plausibly provide that response through a system of criminal law and criminal trials: that is how it takes civic wrongdoing seriously in a way that recognizes and treats the wrongdoers as responsible members of the polity.

On this view, when we ask whether and why a system of criminal law should figure as part of a polity's institutions of governance, our answer will not be set simply or primarily in terms of the criminal law's utility as an instrument for ensuring, and assuring, general conformity to the polity's other norms: it will be set primarily in terms of the need (a normative rather than purely pragmatic need) to take wrongdoing seriously by making it in this way formally salient, and the need to treat its members (the need that its members treat each other) as responsible agents. This is not to say that the criminal law's efficacy in reducing the incidence of certain kinds of conduct is not also important, although we need to be cautious in making claims about what criminal law can achieve by way not of crime-reduction (we could reduce 'crime' simply

[102] Sir William Blackstone, *Commentaries on the Laws of England*, Bk IV, ch. 1, p. 5; see above, Chapter 2 at nn 90–5, Chapter 4 at n. 3.

[103] P Devlin, *The Enforcement of Morals*; see above, Chapter 2, section 2.

by decriminalizing various types of conduct), but of reducing the incidence of disvalued types of conduct. The point here is not simply the by now familiar point that conformity to the law is not easily secured by a system of pure deterrence: that people are more likely to refrain from crime when they see the criminal law and its claims as legitimate.[104] It is also that, in the case of criminal law and of the *mala in se* that it defines, the law does not primarily seek or rely on *obedience*: it depends on the fact that people generally refrain from such conduct not because the law prohibits it, but because they anyway see it to be wrong.[105] It also matters, not simply that the law has some preventive efficacy, but how that 'prevention' is achieved, or what kind of prevention it is: that it is a mode of prevention consistent with (or even expressive of) a due recognition of the citizens' status as responsible agents. Nonetheless, if we thought that the existence and operations of a system of criminal law did *nothing* to reduce the incidence of the kinds of conduct it defines as criminal, we would have good reason to look for other ways of dealing with such conduct (given the costs that criminal law involves): even those who insist that the primary significance of criminal law does not lie in its efficiency as a means to further ends ought to recognize that its effects are relevant to its justification, since certain kinds of effect (inefficacy, or significant consequential harm) would undermine its justification. I defer discussion of this issue until section 6.

Another matter requiring comment here concerns the relationship between violations of civil order and criminalization. If we say that criminal law functions to sustain civil order, we might seem to be committed to the view that what justifies the criminalization of a type of conduct is precisely that it somehow violates the civil order; and that the criminal-wrong-making feature of the conduct, the feature on which the criminal law focuses, must therefore be its implications for or its impact on civil order. This will provoke a familiar objection: that such an account of the grounds of criminalization distorts the normative picture. If we ask why rape is criminalizably wrong, or what a rapist is properly convicted of, the right answer is surely not that his conduct violates the civil order, since that distracts our and the law's attention away from the victim of the rape: the rapist should be convicted for the wrong that he has done to this victim; his conduct should be criminalized because it is wrongful in that victim-oriented way.[106]

To meet this objection, and to show how a system of criminal law whose primary role is the preservation of civil order can respond without distortion to such victimizing wrongs as rape, we should recall the distinction between objects and conditions of liability.[107] The object of liability is that for which the person is held liable—convicted and censured; it is the intentional focus of the criminal law and the criminal trial. There are also typically conditions of liability: conditions that must be satisfied if a person is to be held liable, but that are not part of what he is to be held liable for. I am criminally liable in an English court for committing rape only if I committed it in England, and not if I committed it in France; but that is not to say that what I am held liable for is 'rape in England', as if committing it in this particular country is a dimension of the wrong for which I am to be condemned. The location of my crime in England is a condition of my liability for it in English courts, since it is what brings

[104] See, classically, T Tyler, *Why People Obey the Law*; also Chiao, *Criminal Law in the Age of the Administrative State*, ch. 7.5.

[105] See above, at nn 87–8.

[106] This is an analogue of what Dagger calls the 'irrelevance objection' to 'fair play' theories of punishment: see R Dagger, *Playing Fair: Political Obligation and the Problems of Punishment*, 191–4; also Edwards and Simester, 'What's Public About Crime?', 114–18.

[107] See Duff, *Answering for Crime*, ch. 4.3; above, Chapter 3 at n. 94.

it within the ambit of English criminal law and the jurisdiction of its courts: but it is not part of the object of my liability, of what I am held liable for; the criminalizably wrongful character of my act is unaffected by that aspect of its location.

What then of the violation of (or the threat to) civil order that is on this account a necessary condition of criminalization? To say that the criminal defendant is convicted *for* his violation of civil order does invite the objection noted above; but that is not what we should say. Rather, the wrong for which he is convicted is, in the case of victimizing crimes such as rape, the wrong that is done to the individual victim: but a legal condition of his being properly convicted is that that wrong constitutes a crime under English law (if he is in England); and a normative condition of its being criminalizable by English law is that it threatens or violates the civil order of England. That is not what makes rape, or this rape, wrong; nor would its wrongful character differ if it was committed somewhere else: but that is what makes it the business of, brings it properly within the ambit of, English criminal law, and thus within the jurisdiction of English courts. It is the collective business of English citizens as citizens of that polity, whereas the rape committed in France is not their civic business.[108]

Three further points might clarify this matter. The first is that what violates or threatens civil order might, as we have seen, not just be the conduct that is to be criminalized, but also a failure to criminalize it. If a commitment to taking civic wrongs seriously, and therefore to responding to them appropriately, is part of our civil order (part of how we define ourselves as a polity), we ought to create and sustain institutions that will fulfil that commitment; and the criminal law is just such an institution. But then to fail to criminalize a wrong that is our business, a wrong that threatens or violates the civil order, is also itself to violate that civil order. However, to say that we therefore criminalize such wrongs *in order to* sustain the civil order would be misleading, as implying that the primary reason for criminalization is consequentialist: to achieve the positive effects on civil order that flow from criminalization, or to avert the adverse effects on civil order that flow from a failure to criminalize. Such effects will indeed often be relevant. Insofar as the criminal law does have wrong-preventive effects, criminalization will reduce the incidence of wrongs that violate or threaten civil order—and also of retaliatory, vigilante, or pre-emptively defensive violence by citizens; it can provide citizens with some assurance that they will not be victimized, and that if they are victimized the law will intervene on their behalf. Consideration of such effects as these are often relevant to decisions about what we should, all things considered, criminalize: for such decisions must attend to the costs of criminalization, as well as to possible alternatives to criminalization;[109] the consequential benefits of criminalization are then relevant considerations, to set against its costs. This is not to say, however, that such considerations are relevant, let alone that they are the only or primarily relevant kinds of consideration, to our initial decision that we have good reason to criminalize a type of conduct: what initially gives us such reason is simply the fact that this conduct is our business and is wrongful.

Analogously, an academic institution might realize that to fail to respond to plagiarism, by condemning it and calling plagiarisers to account, might harm the

[108] Compare Thorburn, 'Constitutionalism and the Limits of the Criminal Law', 102: 'The wrong of rape—and of murder, assault, etc—is precisely the objectification of one person by another, but that objectification is of concern to the state because it is the state's job to ensure the survival of the system that makes it possible for us all to interact on terms that preserve the status of us all as free and equal moral agents'.

[109] See in more detail Chapter 7, section 2 below.

academic enterprise, by giving the impression that the institution does not care about such things; such prospective harm is then a consideration that might reasonably figure in its deliberations about how, all things considered, it should respond to plagiarism, including decisions about what resources to devote to detecting and prosecuting it: but what initially gives the institution reason to take such formal, censorial note of plagiarism is not that this is a good way to protect the institution against future harms, but that plagiarism is a serious academic wrong. Analogously again, it is no doubt true that helping a friend in need might, consequentially, strengthen or reinforce the friendship, while failing to help might do consequential harm to the friendship; it is also true that attention to such considerations might help to overcome an initial disinclination to help (if I am weak-willed, or if helping would be costly): but if the friendship is a genuine one, what initially gives me reason to help is the very fact that she is my friend and needs my help. To see that my friend needs my help is to see that I have good reason to help; that is an implication of friendship. To recognize that plagiarism is an academic wrong is to see that as an academic institution we have good reason to respond to it, by defining it as a breach of our code of ethics or discipline; that is an implication of commitment to the academic enterprise. Similarly, if as members of a polity we recognize a type of conduct as a civic wrong, we thereby recognize that we have reason to respond to it by criminalizing it: for if it is a civic wrong, it is our collective business, as implicating some aspect of our civil order; if it is thus a wrong that is our business, it is a wrong to which we have reason to respond; and, as we have seen, criminalization is an appropriate response to such wrongdoing. We could say that we respond in this way, by criminalizing the conduct, because not to do so would be to violate our civil order; a university could be said to define plagiarism as an academic wrong because to fail to do so would undermine its academic integrity; I could be said to help my friend because not to do so would violate or undermine our friendship.[110] But such violation or undermining is not a consequence of such failures; it is intrinsic to them—it is what they are.

The second point concerns the ways in which conduct can violate or threaten civil order. One way in which conduct can threaten civil order is via its consequential impact on our shared social life.[111] It might, for instance, cause anxiety or insecurity in other people, by making them afraid for their own safety; it might provoke retaliatory or defensive violence from others; it might have a deleterious effect on the functioning of the institutions through which the polity governs itself and orders its affairs. But just as the criminal law can, as we saw above, be partly constitutive of a particular kind of civil order, so that its relationship to civil order is internal rather than (only) instrumental, so wrongs can violate civil order in a (de)constitutive, rather than an instrumental, way. A 'perfect' murder or fraud that remains undetected might have no consequential impact on a polity's civic or social life: *ex hypothesi*, it cannot breed insecurity, anxiety, 'social volatility', or loss of trust.[112] Such consequential impact, however, is necessary neither to the object nor as a condition of legitimate criminalization: the wrong that we criminalize need not involve any such consequential harm; nor is it a normatively necessary condition of criminalizing a particular type of conduct that it has or might have such effects. A murder or fraud violates civil order, even if it remains undetected,

[110] Even that might be misleading: in the simple case what motivates me to help my friend (my reason for helping) is that she, my friend, needs my help. See further at n. 138 below.

[111] See above, Chapter 4 at nn 4–9.

[112] See L C Becker, 'Criminal Attempts and the Theory of the Law of Crimes'; S Dimock, 'Retributivism and Trust'; above, Chapter 2 at n. 95.

because it is itself inconsistent with (indeed, it is an attack on) one of the central values by which that order is structured—one of the values essential to the polity's civic life. We will, it is true, realize that we have good reason to treat the agent's conduct as criminal only if we discover that it did constitute murder or fraud—only if the crime turns out not to have been a 'perfect' crime: but that discovery does not turn the conduct into a violation of civil order, by making it likely that it will have that kind of harmful consequential impact; what we discover is that the agent's conduct was already, before it was discovered, a violation of civil order.[113]

The third point concerns jurisdiction again—what makes a crime our business. I noted earlier that an account of the criminal law's authority that makes citizenship foundational (as mine does) can explain why its jurisdiction should be defined in primarily territorial terms, and how it is also binding on non-citizens who find themselves within the polity's territory: the fact that a wrong is committed within our territory does not make a difference to the character or seriousness of the wrong, but does make it our business, since it is committed in our home—if not by or against one of us, then by or against a guest.[114] We can now put a little more substantive flesh on that point. A wrong committed in Paris does not violate or threaten the civil order of England; but the same kind of wrong committed in London does violate or threaten the civil order of England, since a polity's civil order is, like the polity itself, geographically located.[115] It might seem that I cannot now make sense of the claims to universal jurisdiction that national courts can make:[116] how can a crime, however serious, committed in Chile, against Chilean citizens, by Chilean officials, bear on the civil order of Spain, in such a way as to warrant an alleged perpetrator's arrest in England and extradition to Spain for trial in a Spanish court?[117]

The answer to this question depends on how we should understand international criminal law in general, and in particular on how we answer the question: in whose name can a Spanish court claim the standing to bring Augusto Pinochet to trial for his alleged crimes in Chile? If we say that the Spanish court acts in the name of 'humanity', or of 'the community of nations', or of the Chilean people whose own government and courts have let them down,[118] we seem to turn away from the civil order of Spain—which would also seem to undermine any claim that the criminal law of a polity must be focused on that polity's civil order, and point us back towards the kind of non-relational account of criminal law, as serving the universal ends of justice, that I rejected in Chapter 3. If I reply that a polity's conception of its own civic realm, of its common good, and thus of its civil order, should include the proper discharge of its duties and responsibilities towards other polities and towards people outside its

[113] Compare J Gardner and S Shute, 'The Wrongness of Rape', 215–17. A 'pure' rape, they argue, with no harmful consequences, is still properly defined as criminal: but the reason for this concerns the consequential efficacy of criminalization in reducing the incidence of harmful rapes—and their further harmful consequences. On my account, by contrast, whether or not a rape has adverse further effects on its victim or on others, it violates the civil order; and that by itself gives us good reason to criminalize it—to define it, and to respond to it (if it is in the end detected) as a public wrong.

[114] See above, Chapter 3 at nn 94–5.

[115] This does not rule out the principles of nationality or of passive personality (see above, Chapter 3 at nn 14, 77–8): a polity could define its civil order to encompass its citizens wherever they are. Again, I do not advocate these principles (which could amount to a kind of imperialism—a polity lays claim to wrongs committed in another polity's civic home); I merely note the sense they can still make.

[116] See above, Chapter 3 at n. 22.

[117] See *R v Bow Street Metropolitan Stipendiary Magistrate ex p Pinochet Ugarte* [2000] 1 AC 147; above, Chapter 3 at nn 18, 56.

[118] See above, Chapter 3, at nn 60–2.

borders,[119] the polity's boundaries seem to be in danger of dissolving: why should we not now say that the polity's basic aim must be that of doing good, or pursuing justice; and that the (primarily territorial) limits that it generally sets on the ambit and jurisdiction of its criminal laws reflect a pragmatic recognition that that is how it can usually best serve that impersonal, universal aim?

We need not, however, be driven back down that path. Associations of many kinds, and their members, can recognize that they have duties towards others outside the association: the goods at which the association aims, the 'common good' of its members as members of this association, can be understood partly in terms of those duties, whose satisfaction will sometimes take priority over their associational self-interest as more narrowly understood. But this does not undermine the claim that the life and activities of the association (whether it is a profession, or a club, or a polity) must be structured by a conception of *its* distinctive order or *res publica*, of its distinctive good as a particular kind of association—and of the distinctive good of its members as members of the association: in the case of a polity, that conception is a conception of its civil order.

6. A Liberal Republic's Criminal Law: (3) Criminal Punishment and Civil Order

I have so far carefully (some might say disingenuously) avoided talking about the role that a system of criminal punishment might play in relation to a polity's civil order: this lack must now be remedied, for two reasons. The first is that, whether or not criminal punishment is a defining or necessary feature of criminal law,[120] it is a ubiquitous feature of our systems of criminal law: an account of the role of criminal law in a liberal republic must therefore either explain why and how such a republic could do without criminal punishment, or include an account of the role of criminal punishment in such a republic. The second reason is that even if we accept that criminal law, in its substantive and procedural modes, can serve the valuable ends of declaring a polity's core values and calling to formal public account those who violate them, we might suspect that this is inadequate as a justification for the institution of criminal law. It might seem inadequate partly because it is not clear that those ends are important enough to justify the manifold costs involved in creating and maintaining such an institution (given that we can go some way towards achieving them, especially the declarative aim, by less formal and less expensive mechanisms); and partly because a polity consisting of human beings who are aware of their own fallibility might well think it more important to find effective methods of reducing the incidence of the kinds of wrong with which criminal law has to deal.[121] Taken together, these objections suggest that if we are to justify such an institution, we must include criminal law's penal dimension, which attaches punishments to the convictions that emerge from the criminal process: without that dimension, it would not be effective enough in preventing crime either to serve the polity's essential aims or to justify its costs. Those of a more retributivist persuasion will have different reasons for regarding a system of 'criminal' law that ended with wrongdoers' formal conviction and made no provision for their punishment as

[119] See above, Chapter 4 at nn 46–9. [120] See above, Chapter 1 at nn 14–21.

[121] See e.g. Chiao, 'What is the Criminal Law For?', 145–8. See also V Tadros, *The Ends of Harm: The Moral Foundations of Criminal Law*, ch. 5, for an analogous critique of a purely communicative account of criminal punishment; M Thorburn, 'Constitutionalism and the Limits of the Criminal Law', 96.

inadequate—that it would fail to satisfy the demands of justice: for, they will insist, wrongdoers deserve not merely conviction (and the censure that conviction involves), but the material burden of punishment; otherwise the system fails to take their wrongdoing seriously enough, or to respond adequately to it.

For reasons given earlier, I will not spend long discussing criminal punishment here.[122] It is hard to assess the first complaint about a system of criminal law without punishment—that its value would be insufficient to justify its costs: this is partly because it is not clear just what those costs would be, once we take punishment out of the picture; but also because it is not clear just how important it would be to call public wrongdoers to public account if this could not lead to criminal punishment. We can explore this issue a little further by looking at the idea of impunity, and the suggestion that a key purpose of criminal law is to prevent wrongdoers from enjoying impunity for their wrongdoing. This was one avowed aim of the creation of the International Criminal Court: its founding statute declared the determination of the states parties 'to put an end to impunity for the perpetrators of these crimes and thus to contribute to the prevention of such crimes'.[123] Gross has also argued that criminal punishment can be justified only if we 'know with certainty that crime without punishment—impunity—would be, or would produce, an intolerable state of affairs';[124] which suggests that the avoidance of impunity is the primary justifying aim of a system of criminal punishment. This does point towards an important truth about the goals of criminal law; but not in quite the way that Gross supposes.

First, both Gross and the Rome Statute talk of impunity for 'crimes'—thus presupposing the existence of a criminal law, violators of which are not to be allowed impunity: but our question here concerns the very creation or maintenance of criminal law; the relevant notion of impunity must therefore be that of impunity for the commission of wrongs that can be identified as such prior to and independently of a criminal law—which is not to say that they must be identifiable as wrongs pre-institutionally, or independently of a civil order, or even pre-legally.[125] Should it be an important responsibility for a political community (or, in the case of international criminal law, a community of nations) to try to ensure that those who commit certain kinds of wrong do not commit them with impunity; and, if so, does this require the creation of a system of criminal law that includes punishment?

Second, both Gross and the Rome Statute connect impunity to freedom from punishment. In the Rome Statute, shortly before the passage on impunity quoted above, the states parties affirm that 'the most serious crimes of concern to the international community as a whole must not go unpunished'; and although Gross talks of people being 'allowed to commit a crime without being called to account', and of 'hollow formalities leading to acquittal', as instances of impunity,[126] his concern is clearly with the need for (and thus the justification of) punishment as the means by which impunity is avoided. Now it is true that both the etymology of 'impunity', and its common usage, suggest that it involves guaranteed or tolerated freedom, if not from punishment strictly speaking, at least from the materially burdensome or painful consequences that might have been expected to follow from the commission of the wrong. It is also true

[122] See above Chapter 1 at n. 120.

[123] Rome Statute of the International Criminal Court, Preamble.

[124] H Gross, *Crime and Punishment: A Concise Moral Critique*, 2.

[125] See above, Chapter 1 at nn 44–5, on '*mala prohibita*' as wrongs that are pre-criminal, but not pre-legal.

[126] Gross, *Crime and Punishment*, 2.

that, if we have a system of criminal law that attaches punishment or the threat of punishment to conviction for a crime, then someone who is convicted but is allowed to avoid punishment (for no good reason) might be said to have secured a measure of impunity. But if our concern is with why we should create a system of criminal law in the first place, and with a pre-legal notion of impunity for wrongs that are not already threatened with punishment, we can use 'impunity' in a wider sense that is not so closely tied to punishment. We naturally say, in the context of egregious extra-legal moral wrongdoing, that the wrongdoer should not be allowed to 'get away with it'; but we need not mean that she should be made to suffer some kind of formal or informal punishment. We might mean in part that insofar as she profited from the wrong, she should be deprived of her ill-gotten gains; but also that she should be called to account for her wrong by her fellows, who should not condone her wrongdoing by their silence. If a wrongdoer is held to account within the relevant normative community by its members, she does not enjoy impunity, even if she is not punished. So too, a system of law that provided for alleged offenders to be called to account through something like a criminal trial, and to be formally convicted and so censured if proved to be guilty, would not be a system that allowed offenders impunity, even if it made no provision for punishment to follow conviction: they would not be allowed to 'get away', or 'get away scot free', with their crimes.[127]

Third, Gross focuses primarily on the disastrous effects of impunity: although he at first talks of being sure that impunity '*would be*, or would produce, an intolerable state of affairs', he then focuses on the 'intolerable state of affairs' that would be produced. Similarly, the Rome Statute talks as if the main point of 'put[ting] an end to impunity for the perpetrators of these crimes' is 'to contribute to the prevention of such crimes'. It would be absurd to deny that consequences matter to the justification, the design, and the operations of a system of criminal law: but it would be wrong to conclude that *only* the consequences matter, or to deny that sometimes what makes consequences significant is that they flow from the satisfaction, or frustration, of expectations whose legitimacy cannot be explained in consequential terms.

As to the former point, I have argued in this chapter that the enterprise of calling those who commit public wrongs to formal public account has a significant value that does not depend on its beneficial effects. As to the latter point, it is true that if criminal law serves a partly deterrent purpose, some of its relevant effects (the change in the level of wrongdoing compared to what it would otherwise have been) can be identified independently of anyone's normative expectations: but insofar as the problematic consequences of impunity would flow from how people reacted to what they perceived as impunity, they depend on those people's normative expectations; people would react thus because they had a normative expectation that wrongdoers would be called to account—an expectation that was now frustrated. Further, what gives such consequences their normative force, as reasons to create a system of criminal law to prevent impunity, is that such expectations are reasonable. It is only because citizens reasonably expect their polity to respond to civic wrongdoing in a certain way that their likely reactions to a failure to do so count as they do—as reasons to satisfy those expectations; if such expectations were quite unreasonable, they would still give the

[127] It might be argued that both an informal extra-legal calling to account, with the criticism that it involves, and a criminal trial, with the formal censure that conviction brings, constitute punishment: something intentionally burdensome imposed on a wrongdoer for his wrongdoing. I would not deny this; but my point here is that the avoidance of impunity need not involve the threat or the fact of punishment as something going beyond formal or informal censure.

polity reason to do something about them, but it would not be obvious that what it should do is satisfy them. That members of the polity would react adversely to a failure (as they would see it) to attach punishment to crime, that they would see this as an unacceptable kind of 'impunity', does not yet justify the creation of a system of criminal punishment: we must still ask whether it is reasonable to see punishment as the only or best way to prevent impunity.

However important we think it that those guilty of public wrongs should not enjoy impunity, this does not by itself mandate the creation of a system of criminal punishment, since impunity could, in a significant way, be prevented by a system of criminal trials that called wrongdoers to formal, public, censorial account. This is not to say that a polity that takes public wrongdoing seriously has no need of a system of criminal punishment: it is only to emphasize, first, that the formal process of calling public wrongdoers to account has significant value even if it does not lead to punishment; and second, that a justification for adding criminal punishment to that process cannot be grounded purely in the perceived need to prevent impunity, without a further argument that the absence of punishment beyond conviction constitutes impunity.

Nonetheless, the thought that a polity needs something more than a criminal process ending with the formal verdict is a powerful one—powerful partly because it can flow from a variety of sources; so too is the thought that that 'something more' must involve something like a system of criminal punishment. It might reflect the retributivist belief that a merely verbal condemnation of the kind that criminal conviction provides cannot, however emphatic it is, suffice to address the wrong that was done, and that a sufficient address would involve some materially burdensome imposition: we then find a familiar range of accounts of why and how such burdens can 'address' the wrong—for instance that they impose a quantum of deserved penal suffering,[128] or drive the censorial message home,[129] or constitute a secular penance, or an 'apology ritual', through which wrongdoers can pay their reparative debt to those whom they wronged.[130] Or it might reflect an instrumentalist belief that only then will the criminal law have the kind of preventive efficacy that it needs if its costs are to be warranted, and if the polity is to discharge its responsibility to reduce the incidence of wrongful(ly harmful) conduct—whether that efficacy is to be achieved by deterrence or by incapacitation or by rehabilitation, or by some combination of those. Others argue that the 'something more' need not be punishment, at least as traditionally understood: not because we should instead adopt, for instance, a 'therapeutic' approach to crime that no longer treats offenders as responsible agents, but because there are appropriate ways of addressing the wrongdoings of responsible agents that do not involve the condemnatory 'hard treatment' that characterizes criminal punishment as it is normally practised.[131]

For present purposes I want to avoid taking a stand on which, if any, of these kinds of reason for doing 'something more' than formally calling public wrongdoers to account, and for making that 'something more' involve some intentionally burdensome

[128] See e.g. M S Moore, *Placing Blame*, chs 2–4.

[129] See e.g. M M Falls, 'Retribution, Reciprocity, and Respect for Persons'; J Kleinig, 'Punishment and Moral Seriousness'.

[130] See Duff, *Punishment, Communication, and Community*; C J Bennett, *The Apology Ritual: A Philosophical Theory of Punishment.*

[131] Some conceptions of 'restorative justice', those that find a place for it within a system of criminal justice that involves trials and convictions, are of this kind (see A von Hirsch et al (eds), *Restorative Justice and Criminal Justice: Competing or Reconcilable Paradigms?*). For interesting suggestions along these lines, see N Lacey and H Pickard, 'From the Consulting Room to the Court Room? Taking the Clinical Model of Responsibility Without Blame into the Legal Realm', and 'To Blame or to Forgive? Reconciling Punishment and Forgiveness in Criminal Justice'.

imposition, could suffice to justify the addition of a system of criminal punishment to the criminal law as I have so far characterized it. What kind of system, serving what aims, through what kinds of imposition, and at what kinds of further cost (material, psychological, social, moral, political), we decide in the end that we can justifiably sustain will bear crucially on our ultimate decisions about what we are to criminalize: for those decisions must depend in crucial part on the likely costs and effects of criminalization, central to which are the sentences imposed on convicted offenders and their likely further effects. However, as we will see in Chapter 7, consideration of such costs and effects becomes relevant only at a later stage of our deliberations about criminalization, once we have determined that we have good reason even to consider criminalization as an option; our present concern is with that earlier determination. All I need to do here is make two points about criminal punishment—or whatever other response we might make to civil-order-disturbing wrongdoing.

First, our response must itself be consistent with the polity's civil order—with the values by which that order is structured, and with the status in that order of those whom we are to punish. I argued earlier that we should resist the tendency to respond to wrongdoers as if they forfeit their citizenship by committing a crime—as if they thereby become outsiders: we must still treat and address them as citizens.[132] This poses a serious challenge to penal theorists: can they provide an account of criminal punishment as something that citizens could properly impose on each other, and to which they could be expected to submit themselves? Can we imagine a system of criminal punishment (one, no doubt, in various ways very different from our own) that is consistent with, or even expressive of, the equal respect and concern that citizens owe each other? I think that we can, especially if we think about the duties that offenders can be said to acquire by committing a crime,[133] and portray punishment not simply as something imposed on offenders, but as something that they can be required, as a matter of civic as well as of legal duty, to undertake. There will then still be the question of whether such a system would have a role for deterrence as one legitimate aim of criminal punishment; but that is not a task I can take further here.[134]

Second, if our response is to treat and address the wrongdoer—as it must if it is to respect his civic standing—as a responsible member of the political community, it should include something like a criminal process, which must itself depend on something like a substantive criminal law. As I argued in the previous section, this kind of response can be said to take civic wrongdoing seriously as wrongdoing, and thus to do appropriate justice to the polity's values, as well as to both the victims (when there are victims) and the perpetrators of such wrongdoing. What comes after that process, what we should do to or demand of those who are found to have committed such wrongs, is a further question, some of the possible answers to which were noted above: but if we are to treat a person as a wrongdoer, we must first call him to account as someone alleged to have committed a wrong that we have declared to be our business—which is what the criminal trial does. This might seem to beg the question against various kinds of 'abolitionist' who argue that we should eschew criminal law with its focus on (or, as they might say, its obsession with) wrongdoing,[135] but the discussion in this and the

[132] See at nn 36–40 above; see also Chapter 3, section 5 on Jakobs' distinction between *Bürgerstrafrecht* and *Feindstrafrecht*.

[133] See also Tadros, *The Ends of Harm*, and *Wrongs and Crimes*, ch. 4, for an account of criminal punishment (one very different from the account I would give) that appeals to the duties that offenders acquire.

[134] See Duff and Marshall, 'Civic Punishment'; Duff, 'In Response', at 374–5.

[135] See nn 79, 90 above.

previous two sections should have answered that objection. Those who commit public wrongs act as they have, and ought to know that they have, good and normally conclusive reasons not to act—that is what makes their conduct wrongful. An appropriate response to their conduct, one that addresses them as responsible agents, must appeal to the reasons by which they should have been, but were not, guided: that is what is required if the response is to be honest or 'transparent'. The response should thus hold them accountable (call them to account) for their failure to be guided by the right reasons—which must give them the chance to deny the accusation of wrongdoing, and call them to answer for the wrongdoing if they cannot plausibly deny it.

Before ending this chapter, and turning (finally) towards an account of criminalization, there is one further issue that I must address; it has to do again with what a polity, and its criminal law or its criminal courts, can say to the 'recusant' who denies that the law is his law, that the values it declares are his values, and that the polity in whose name the law speaks is a community of which he sees himself as a participating member.

7. Recusants Revisited: Reciprocal Accountability

In explaining the role of the criminal law in constituting and sustaining a polity's civil order, I have talked of how 'we', who recognize ourselves as citizens of the polity, should collectively respond to violations of the values that we recognize as our civic values: the criminal law claims to speak in our collective voice, in condemning conduct that violates the shared values by which we define ourselves as a polity, and in calling to account those who commit such conduct. To put the matter in these terms might imply that all members of the polity, all its citizens, must identify themselves as part of that 'we'—that all citizens must speak, in unison, through the law, of the values to which they are all committed; that all must see themselves as sharing in the goods that the polity defines as their common good, and see the polity's civil order as their order. That kind of agreement, that kind of civic commitment by all its citizens, is indeed a necessary aspiration for a polity; but it is obviously very far from actuality. In any polity, there will be at least some people who are formally classed as citizens, but who do not identify themselves as part of that 'we': they do not identify the polity's common good as any part of their good, or see themselves as bound by the associative civic duties that constitute the normative basis of citizenship; they are 'recusants'.[136]

I argued earlier that the recusant's rejection of the associative bonds of citizenship cannot by itself undermine the claim that she is a citizen, with the responsibilities and duties, as well as the rights and benefits, that go with citizenship: membership of normative associations is not always voluntary; associative obligations can be non-voluntarily acquired. But Edwards and Simester argue that the recusant poses another problem for an account of crimes as public wrongs. Their objection is in part that such an account distorts the reasons that a polity has to criminalize familiar kinds of wrong, by suggesting that we, as citizens, should criminalize such wrongs as murder and rape because this will enable our 'community to live[] up to its defining values', thus enabling us to be 'members of the type of community of which [we] aspire to be a

[136] On recusants, see Edwards and Simester, 'What's Public About Crime?', 119–21; and above, Chapter 3 at nn 117–21, 145–7. Their target is the account that Sandra Marshall and I have been developing in several papers (cited by Edwards and Simester): what I defend here is a more developed version of that account.

part': but this, they argue, involves the sort of self-indulgence that Williams incisively criticized in the context of individual morality—a self-indulgent focus on our own collective good as a particular kind of community, when we should be focused instead on the wrongs that ought to be criminalized. The figure of the recusant, they think, strengthens this objection: if the reasons that those who identify themselves as citizens have to criminalize such wrongs have to do with sustaining a political community in which they find their collective good, a recusant can have no such reason to endorse the polity's criminal law or to accept its authority. She does not identify herself as part of this community, or find her good in its good; so she will not see the fact that by criminalizing these kinds of wrong the community will be true to its own values as giving her any reason for action or acceptance.[137]

The initial answer to the distortion objection is that although the self-identifying members of a polity will indeed see a failure to criminalize such wrongs as murder or rape as a failure to live up to their defining values, and thus (since they understand their common good to consist in part in living up to those values) as deleterious to their common good, this should not and need not be the reason why they criminalize such wrongs: that is, what gives them good normative reason to criminalize such wrongs is not that this will serve their good by enabling them to live up to their declared values; and what motivates them to criminalize such wrongs need not be such a concern for their own good. Given that they ought to respond to such wrongs, failure to do so will indeed constitute a failure to live up to their values, and will thus be deleterious to their common good. Analogously, given that I ought to help my friend, failure to do so will constitute a failure to live up to my avowed commitment to the friendship and might, by damaging the friendship, harm me insofar as I find an important part of my good in that friendship; given that a university ought to respond to plagiarism as an academic wrong, failure to do so will constitute a failure to live up to its professed values, and will thus be injurious to its good as an academic institution—and thus to its members' common good as members of such an institution. Such considerations as these are, however, parasitic on the reasons why they ought to respond in such ways. The justifying reason for treating plagiarism as an academic wrong is precisely that it is a wrong that is the university's business, so that it requires such a response from the university; the justifying reason for helping my friend is that she, who is my friend, needs assistance; the justifying reason for criminalizing murders and rapes that are committed in the polity is that these are wrongs that are our business as members of the polity.[138] That is also the reason that ought to motivate us to act: our actions should manifest our commitment to the values in question (to the academic enterprise, or to this friendship, or to the polity's civil order); but our reason for acting thus is not that we will thereby manifest or sustain that commitment. We might encourage ourselves, if we are not sufficiently motivated by that justifying reason, by referring to such considerations—urging ourselves to live up to our values (not to let ourselves down), by pointing out how damaging it would be to fail to do so; but what makes sense of this kind of encouragement (which marks a concession to our normative frailty) is that it helps to motivate us to do what we already have sufficient normative reason to do.

[137] See Edwards and Simester, 'What's Public About Crime?', 114–18 on 'distortion' (drawing on B Williams, 'Utilitarianism and Moral Self-Indulgence'), and 119–21 on recusants.

[138] The object of our practical attention is the wrong; a condition of directing our attention thus is that the wrong is our business (see at nn 107–10 above). Similarly, the object of my practical attention when I help a friend is her need; a condition of directing my attention thus is that she is my friend.

To fall back on this kind of motivational consideration is self-indulgent in a way; but it marks a pragmatic attempt to overcome our own lack of full commitment.

What then should those who identify themselves as citizens of a polity say to its recusants? One possibility, which Edwards and Simester are too quick to reject, would be to offer them the option of becoming long-term guests, or resident aliens, rather than citizens—the option, that is, of giving up their citizenship without leaving the country:[139] this would not free them from their various obligations under the polity's law; but it would turn those obligations from obligations of citizenship to a guest's or stranger's obligations to respect the laws of the alien polity in which she is living. The more important point, however, is that, as we have seen, the justifying reason for criminalizing murder and rape committed within a polity—whether committed by or against self-identifying citizens, or guests, or recusants—is not that by doing so the polity will serve its members' common good, or will live up to its professed values: rather, it is that, given that such wrongs are its business, they require such a response from it. Citizens should also hope that their fellows will identify themselves as citizens, and find part of their good in the polity's good; they might urge recusants to come to recognize the worth of belonging to this association: but those are not the reasons that justify the claim that recusants, like everyone else in the polity, ought to respect its laws. More precisely, as we have seen already, these are not the reasons that justify the claim that recusants, like everyone else, ought to refrain from such wrongs as murder and rape: for those reasons are the pre-legal moral reasons in virtue of which murder and rape are wrongs.[140] Nor are they the reasons why recusants ought to respect the law, and obey it when it demands obedience—why they should, for instance, refrain from conduct that the law prohibits, and answer in court if they are accused of criminal wrongdoing: for those reasons are grounded in the associative duties that recusants have as members (willing or unwilling) of the polity.

It is worth re-emphasizing three further points here about the demands that a liberal republic should make on its citizens.

First, my comments on what a polity should say to recusants, or indeed to those who object to particular aspects of its laws,[141] should not be taken to suggest that what the polity demands is an unquestioning deference to and acceptance of its demands. It seeks respect for its laws; but that should be a critical respect, which takes the law seriously as the product of a democratic process of legislation, but which is also ready to question it.[142] A good citizen tries to understand the law—the mischief at which particular laws are aimed, the reasons that were meant to justify making them; she is ready to debate whether the law is apt for its purposes (and whether those purposes are apt); she respects the law as aiming to specify norms that the citizens are to recognize as, or to make, their own, but does not take it for granted that it succeeds in its aim. One question that arises, but that we cannot pursue here, is whether and when a good citizen will be ready to break the law (and whether such breaches can themselves manifest respect for the law).[143] A further question concerns the discretion that citizens should exercise in the application of the law, and of the criminal law in particular.

[139] See 'What's Public About Crime?', 120: they put too much weight on the fact that the recusants' 'presence in the jurisdiction is neither voluntary nor temporary'; as I noted earlier, associative duties can be incurred non-voluntarily (see at nn 14–16 above, and Chapter 3 at nn 115–16).

[140] See above, Chapter 1 at nn 50–2.

[141] See above, Chapter 3, section 4.

[142] Compare W Edmundson, 'The Virtue of Law-Abidance'; and see at n. 31 above on 'contestatory' democracy.

[143] For a useful recent discussion, see K Brownlee, *Conscience and Conviction: The Case for Civil Disobedience*.

How far, for instance, should they apply a '*De Minimis*' principle in deciding whether to obey the letter of the law, and be ready to act in ways that fit the formal definition of a crime when it seems clear that the action would not involve or threaten the kind of mischief at which the law is aimed? How should they decide whether to report a crime (or what fits the formal definition of a crime) to the police, or whether to respond to it in some other way (or to ignore it)?[144] Given a decent system of law, they should often, no doubt, treat the law as a Razian authority, which they ought to obey because by doing so they are more likely to comply with the reasons that apply to them:[145] but as active citizens of a democratic republic, who see the law as their law, they will also be ready to recognize when that Razian 'normal justification' does not hold, so that they must decide for themselves what the law properly requires of them.

Second, we must distinguish what the polity can hope for from, or ask of, its members (and what they can hope for from or ask of each other as citizens), from what it can require of them—in particular what it can demand from them as a matter of law.[146] It can hope that its citizens will be committed to its defining values—to the conceptions of civil order and the common good by which its civic life is structured (and its very existence as a functioning polity depends on there being a sufficient proportion of citizens who are thus committed); it can seek to encourage such commitment, and the civic virtues that go with it. But if it is to treat citizens with the respect due to them as rational, responsible members of the polity, and respect the freedom and privacy that are central to its liberal values, it must demand much less than that. In particular, it must demand no more than that they conform their actions, their engagements in the shared civic world, to what the law requires, without making any demands on or inquiries into the motives from which they conform; and it must leave them as much room as possible, if not to violate the law, then at least to make it clear that they are conforming under protest (as well as ensuring that there are fora in which their protests can be heard, and in which they can argue for the law to be reformed). The recusant will still be required, on pain of prosecution, conviction, and punishment, to refrain from what the law defines as crimes, and to submit herself to the criminal process if she is accused of crime. But she will not be required to refrain for the appropriate reason—from respect for the values that the law embodies or for the democratic process from which it emerged; she will not face an inquiry into her motives, or prosecution for failing to act on civically proper motives. Nor will she be required, on pain of conviction and punishment, to play an active part in the criminal process, or to display an acceptance of the law's authority by entering a plea at her trial:[147] it will be possible for her to display her rejection of that authority, without adverse legal consequences, by refusing to take part in her trial.

Third, it must be possible for the recusant or dissident not simply to express her rejection of the law (of a particular law, of the law's authority), but to gain a serious hearing for her claims, and to hold to account those who call her to account for her alleged crimes. Part of the point here is that, as a citizen (as someone whom the polity insists on treating as a citizen when it calls her to answer in a criminal court), she must have a voice in the political deliberations through which the polity determines its civil order and its laws; but the issue also has to do with accountability. In what purports to be a community of equals, and so in what purports to be a democratic polity of free

[144] See above, Chapter 1 at nn 177–82.
[145] See J Raz, 'Authority, Law, and Morality'; above, Chapter 2 at n. 34.
[146] See at nn 49–50 above; also Chapter 3 at nn 140–4.
[147] See above, Chapter 3 at nn 140–4.

and equal citizens, accountability must be reciprocal. If I claim the right to hold you to account, to call you to answer for your conduct, I must not only be prepared to listen seriously to whatever answer you might give—for instance to your justification of your conduct; I must also accept that you have the right to call me to account, and be ready to answer to you. In particular, I must be ready to answer for the accusation I brought against you (to justify both the content of the accusation and my implicit claim that I have the standing to bring it); and I must be ready to respond to any counter-accusations that you bring against me:[148] I cannot insist that you should answer to me, whilst denying that I need answer to you. So too, when a citizen is called to trial on a criminal charge, he is called to answer by, and to, his fellow citizens collectively; but they are then also answerable to him. They are answerable within the structure of the trial, since the prosecutor, who speaks and acts in the name of the 'People' or the 'Commonwealth',[149] can be challenged to justify both the charge, by adducing evidence of the defendant's guilt,[150] and the polity's right thus to call the defendant to answer: she must be ready not only to prove her case, but to meet any challenge to the legitimacy of the trial—for instance the argument that the court lacks jurisdiction over this case, or that the trial should be barred for some other reason. But the defendant's fellow citizens are also collectively answerable (the polity is answerable) to him in a wider political context. They (and it) must be ready to answer, for instance, his argument that he acted for what the polity should recognize (though its laws currently do not recognize) as a good, justifying reason;[151] or that his actions were part of a political protest against the very legitimacy of the laws under which he is to be tried—a protest that therefore also denies the legitimacy of his trial;[152] or that the systematic injustices that his group has suffered and still suffers at the polity's hands undermines the polity's, and so this court's, standing now to call him to account.[153]

These kinds of challenge raise two questions (neither of which we can pursue further here). One concerns the proper design of a republican polity, and how far it should insulate the criminal trial from these kinds of challenge, by providing other political fora in which they can be pursued effectively. Should it enable the court to say to the defendant (and to say honestly) that this is not the forum in which he can pursue his challenge to the law or the polity, but that there is another forum in which he can do so? Or should the courtroom itself be one of the fora in which citizens of a democratic republic help to determine, and if necessary to revise, their civil order?[154] The other question concerns what courts can and should do when such other fora are not available to the defendant: can they save the legitimacy of the trial by allowing the dissident defendant to make his case in court—and have it taken seriously; can they constitute

[148] In particular, accusations of the '*tu quoque*' kind; see G A Cohen, 'Casting the First Stone: Who Can, and Who Can't, Condemn the Terrorists'.

[149] See above, Chapter 1 at n. 61. [150] See above, Chapter 1 at nn 100–3, 112.

[151] See, for instance, cases in which English magistrates acquitted peace demonstrators who damaged American fighter planes in protest at the Iraq war: the demonstrators pleaded necessity (the need to prevent an illegal war), making a kind of argument that the Law Lords had firmly rejected in *Chandler v DPP* [1964] AC 763.

[152] See e.g. E Christodoulidis, 'The Objection that Cannot be Heard: Communication and Legitimacy in the Courtroom'.

[153] This is one way to understand the claim that a polity acts wrongly in convicting and punishing defendants who have suffered systematic kinds of political and social injustice: see J Howard, 'Punishment, Socially Deprived Offenders, and Democratic Community'.

[154] See e.g. A Dzur, *Punishment, Participatory Democracy, and the Jury*.

a forum in which he can find not only a hearing, but some kind of (albeit incomplete and unsatisfactory) answer?[155]

The points made in the last few paragraphs were intended to emphasize the fact that a liberal republic should not simply tolerate, and should not seek to silence, its dissidents and recusants: it should recognize them as citizens whose critical voices must be heard, whose challenges must be answered—and should at least sometimes be welcomed, however uncomfortably, as challenging their fellow citizens to think more critically about their civil order. It will still demand that they conform their conduct to the law's requirements, even if they do not see it as their law, given the (unchosen) civic obligations that they owe to their fellow citizens: but those requirements will be (relatively) modest in their scope and their depth, and will leave room for the expression—even if often not for the effective enactment—of dissent.

8. From Civil Order towards Criminalization

The role of criminal law in a liberal republic is to help to constitute, and to sustain, its civil order. It does this initially by providing, in its substantive part, authoritative definitions (and thus authoritative condemnations) of a set of public wrongs that merit a formal response by the polity; and, in its procedural part, the process through which that formal response is made—a response that involves calling alleged public wrongdoers to answer to the accusation of wrongdoing, and to answer for the wrongdoing if they are proved to have committed it. It also typically provides for further measures to be imposed on or required of those convicted of such wrongs; but such measures must themselves be consistent with, or even expressive of, the respect that is still due to public wrongdoers as citizens.[156]

For at least two reasons, this account will seem (indeed, it is) as yet unhelpful in relation to the question of criminalization with which this book began: it does not yet offer any determinate guidance about what kinds of conduct should be criminalized.

First, it tells us that all and only public wrongs are eligible for criminalization;[157] and it tells us that public wrongs consist in conduct that violates or disturbs the polity's civil order: what it does not offer us, however, is any substantive account of such wrongs, or any substantive criteria for their identification. It offers a formal account of the potential scope of criminal law; but what we will need, if we are to engage effectively with the problems of (over)criminalization is surely a substantive account.

Second, it suggests that we have (some) reason to criminalize any and every public wrong: for a public wrong violates the civil order, and criminalization (a declaration of

[155] See further Duff, 'Discretion and Accountability', s. 5. The issue of jury nullification clearly arises here: see A M Rubenstein, 'Verdicts of Conscience: Nullification and the Modern Jury Trial', and above, Chapter 1 at n. 110; for a libertarian celebration of jury nullification, see J D Tuccille, 'Rebellious Jurors Make the World a Better Place'.

[156] This account of criminal law clearly has some affinities with Kleinfeld's ambitious 'reconstructivist' account of criminal law as functioning to protect, and to reconstruct, the 'embodied ethical life' on which a society depends (J Kleinfeld, 'Reconstructivism: The Place of Criminal Law in Ethical Life', 'Three Principles of Democratic Criminal Justice'; for critical discussion, see V Chiao, 'A Response to Professor Kleinfeld's *Reconstructivism: The Place of Criminal Law in Ethical Life*'): but I cannot discuss the differences between the two accounts (in particular the difference between the idea of 'civil order' sketched in this chapter, and Kleinfeld's Hegelian conception of 'embodied ethical life') here.

[157] It thus combines a positive and a negative legal moralism—but a moralism crucially different from Moore's, since it concerns only wrongs that fall within the public realm: see above, Chapter 2, sections 3, 5, and 6.

wrongfulness, a formal calling to account) is, I have argued, an appropriate response to such wrongs. But even if this does not give the criminal law as radically over-ambitious a scope as I argued Moore's legal moralism does, it still seems over-expansive—not only because it appears to give us reason to criminalize quite trivial public wrongs (such as queue-jumping), but also because it ignores non-criminal responses such as (most obviously) the private law of torts.[158]

These issues will be addressed in the following two chapters, which will together provide a (kind of) theory of criminalization.

[158] See A Y K Lee, 'Public Wrongs and the Criminal Law'.

6

Master Principles of Criminalization?

1. The Search for Master Principles

The discussion of civil order and criminal law in the previous chapter generates what might be called a principle, indeed a master principle, of criminalization, in two parts.

A. *We have reason to criminalize a type of conduct if, and only if, it constitutes a public wrong.*

B. *A type of conduct constitutes a public wrong if, and only if, it violates the polity's civil order.*

For the distinctive function of criminal law, as an institution of the kind described in Chapter 1, is that it helps to sustain the polity's civil order; it does this by defining, and providing for an appropriate response to, public wrongs—wrongs that violate some aspect of that civil order.

Even someone who has been persuaded by my account so far, however, might well find this principle disappointing. One reason for such disappointment might be that it seems to favour a worrying kind of relativism. For polities will develop different conceptions of their civil order—indeed, they will develop different civil orders, some of which might be quite repugnant: but this principle seems to hold that members of any polity, however repugnant its civil order might be, have reason to criminalize conduct that violates it. We *might* be able to rule out the use of the criminal law to sustain, for instance, a slave-owning society, or a society that practises an open kind of apartheid, since we might be able to argue that a civil order ('properly speaking') must be an order that gives a respected status to, or that attends to the interests of, all those who are to be bound by its laws. But even if that argument would succeed,[1] it leaves in play a wide variety of polities, with a wide variety of civil orders or of conceptions of civil order, some of which will be repugnant; yet, this principle seems to hold, a polity has reason to criminalize conduct that violates its civil order, however repugnant that order might be. If homosexual conduct, or the denial of God's existence, or women driving cars or going out unveiled, is inconsistent with the civil order of a polity, as its members have defined and constructed that order, then they have—or so I seem to be committed to saying—reason to criminalize such conduct: but if a normative principle of criminalization (and this principle is certainly meant to be normative) has this kind of implication, that is surely a *reductio ad absurdum* of that principle.

I have already addressed a version of this objection.[2] By linking criminal law to civil order, and insisting (as democrats must) that it is for the polity's members to work out their conception of their civil order, I do open the door to a modest kind of pluralism: we cannot plausibly argue that there is just one right or legitimate conception

[1] And it is not clear that it could succeed, unless we built some more substantive ideas of equality or collective welfare into our account of the very concept of civil order.

[2] See above, Chapter 4 at nn 75–6, 81–3. It should be clear from what I say there, and here, that my account does not commit me to a philosophically problematic kind of relativism or non-objectivism about ethics.

of civil order to which every polity should conform. That is not to say, however, that we must therefore refrain from criticizing a polity's civil order or its criminal law so long as it uses its criminal law to sustain its civil order. A person who holds repugnant moral views has, in one sense, reason to act in accordance with them: for from within his existing moral perspective, he has reason so to act;[3] in so acting, he would be acting in accordance with his conscience—which is something one surely should strive to do. But that does not commit us to saying that that is what he ought to do, or debar us from criticizing his moral views, or from condemning the actions that he undertakes on the basis of those moral views. He is indeed acting, formally speaking, as morality requires: he is seeking to guide his conduct by what he takes to be the dictates of morality—perhaps on the basis of careful moral deliberation: but he is, substantively, acting against the dictates of morality—dictates that he has misheard. Analogously, a polity that operates with a repugnant conception of civil order might be operating, in a formal sense, as it should: it might have developed that conception through a process of public deliberation; it might use its criminal law, as criminal law ought to be used, to sustain that civil order, by defining as crimes types of conduct that violate that civil order and calling to account those who commit such conduct. But that does not debar us from criticizing its conception of civil order, or its use of the criminal law to sustain that order, in substantive terms, or commit us to saying that it is right to criminalize what it criminalizes: we can still argue that, although it is engaged in the right kind of enterprise (that of determining a conception of its civil order and grounding its criminal law in that conception), it is engaging in that enterprise badly.

The other, and for present purposes more pressing, reason for disappointment in the principle defined above is that it is purely formal, and thus devoid of substantive content: it can therefore do no substantive work (work of the kind that a principle of criminalization ought to be able to do) in guiding political deliberations about what kinds of conduct we should criminalize. There are in fact two reasons for disappointment in play here. The first concerns the notion of a public wrong: we are told that conduct constitutes a public wrong if it violates the polity's civil order, but are as yet given no substantive guidance on how we are to determine which kinds of conduct fit that definition. The second concerns the relationship between public wrongs and the criminal law: since (as we will see in detail in the following chapter) criminalization is only one among a range of possible responses to public wrongs, we need to know (but have not yet been told) how we are to decide whether or when criminalization is an appropriate response. This lack of content is not surprising so long as an account of the criminal law's role in a polity is set in general terms that aim to be applicable to a wide range of different types of polity with different conceptions of their civil order. Indeed, such an account *should* be relatively formal: it should be such that it is consistent with any of a range of different kinds of substantive content. However, in the previous chapter I began to flesh out that formal account with a distinctive kind of content, by sketching the substance of a liberal republic's civil order, and the way in which criminal law could partly constitute that order: we can surely expect that this more substantive kind of account, if it is to be of any assistance in our deliberations (as members of such a polity) about criminalization, should be able to generate something more substantive than the purely formal principle offered above.

We might then expect, or hope, that that 'something more substantive' would take the form of a master principle, or a master set of principles, of criminalization: for

[3] He has, we could say, 'internal' reason so to act: see B Williams, 'Internal and External Reasons'.

normative accounts of criminalization have often taken that form.[4] I will argue in what follows that the search for such master principles, if they are to be substantive principles, is doomed to failure. First, however, I should say something about 'master principles' and the different forms they can take.

Master principles can be simple and singular, specifying just one criterion of criminalization. That is true, for instance, of a Millian harm principle, if treated as a principle of criminalization: that criminalizing a type of conduct will prevent harm to others is the only consideration that can justify criminalizing it—the only criterion of criminalization.[5] Or they may be more complex and plural, specifying a set of criteria rather than a single criterion (in which case the criteria must of course be mutually consistent; or, if they can conflict, the principle must also specify how such conflicts are to be resolved). Feinberg's 'Liberal Position' is of this kind: it includes the 'Harm Principle' and the 'Offense Principle', and declares that those two principles, 'duly clarified and qualified, between them exhaust the class of good reasons for criminal prohibitions'.[6] In what follows I will, for simplicity's sake, talk of master principles, as if they were all singular in form; but what I say will also apply to plural principles.

Master principles are foundational principles of criminalization. That is to say, they must be principles of *criminalization*—rather than, for instance more general principles of state coercion or interference, since they must help us to determine when to criminalize; this point will become important later, when we discuss the harm principle(s). But they must be *foundational* principles of criminalization: they will themselves be grounded—in, if the argument of previous chapters is right, an account of the polity and its civil order; but they will specify the most basic reasons or criteria for criminalization as a particular kind of practice. A complete theory of criminalization will include further, derivative or non-foundational, principles through which we can derive determinate conclusions about criminalization from its master principle:[7] but our concern here is with the foundational principles from which deliberations about criminalization are to begin.

Master principles must also claim to be exclusive and exhaustive: they must, that is, claim to specify *all* the fundamental criteria for criminalization. For if there are other criteria that bear on criminalization, but that are not specified in or derivable from a would-be master principle, it is not really a master principle, since it cannot claim that it, and it alone, should govern our initial deliberations about criminalization. Thus neither Feinberg's 'Harm Principle' nor his 'Offense Principle' is a master principle,

[4] On master principles see J Edwards, 'Master Principles of Criminalisation'; see also V Tadros, *Wrongs and Crimes*, chs 6–7.

[5] J S Mill, *On Liberty*, ch. 1, para. 9. Mill's harm principle is not a principle of criminalization, since it concerns the purposes for which any kind of 'power' could be 'rightfully exercised'; but he does also say that '[i]f any one does an act hurtful to others, there is a prima facie case for punishing him, by law' (para. 11).

[6] J Feinberg, *Harmless Wrongdoing*, xix; he distinguishes this from 'the extreme liberal position', according to which 'only the harm principle states a good reason' for criminalization. Feinberg himself could not in the end accept either liberal position without qualification or supplementation: he found it necessary to make a 'small' departure 'from the wholly unsupplemented harm principle', to allow for the criminalization of paternalistically motivated coercive interferences with another's freedom, which might not cause harm (*Harm to Others*, 78; see also *Harm to Self*, chs 18–19); and his discussion of legal moralism concluded that the prevention of inherently immoral conduct or 'free-floating evil' always provides a 'relevant' reason, having 'at least minimal weight', for criminalization, and *might* 'sometimes (but rarely)' provide a good reason (*Harmless Wrongdoing*, 322–4, 331). For a version of the 'liberal position', see A P Simester and A von Hirsch, *Crimes, Harms and Wrongs: On the Principles of Criminalization*.

[7] Compare Simester and von Hirsch, *Crimes, Harms and Wrongs*, ch. 8, on 'mediating principles'.

since each specifies only *a* good reason for criminalization—as distinct from *the only* good reason for criminalization. By contrast, Feinberg's 'Liberal Position' is a master principle: it claims to exhaustively specify the only considerations that can constitute good reasons for criminalization.

We should note that this claim to exclusivity and exhaustiveness applies only to principles of *criminalization*—only to principles that specifically concern what we have reason (in principle) to criminalize or not to criminalize: other principles, other goals and values, will be relevant to our deliberations about whether we should all things considered criminalize what we have good reason in principle to criminalize. Moore, for instance, has just one principle of criminalization: we should (we have reason to) criminalize a type of conduct if and only if it constitutes culpable moral wrongdoing. However, first, other principles from outside the practice of criminalization also bear on whether we should, all things considered, criminalize what we have this good reason to criminalize: thus the 'presumption of liberty', which is not itself a principle of criminalization, generates reasons not to criminalize much of what we have, in principle, reason to criminalize.[8] Second, we must attend not only to principles or values, such as those of liberty and privacy, that may generate reasons not to criminalize what we have principled reason to criminalize: we must also attend to the many costs of criminalization to determine whether on balance it is justifiable.[9] Similarly, in discussing criminalization Ashworth and Horder identify a number of 'principles':[10] some of these are indeed principles of criminalization—for instance 'the harm principle' and the principle that criminalization ought to be a 'last resort'; others, however, such as the principles of 'individual autonomy' and of 'welfare', are instead general principles that concern state action and a polity's governance, and thus come to bear indirectly on questions of criminalization.

I will have more to say about these structural features of deliberations about criminalization in the following chapter. In the remainder of this chapter, I will focus on proposed principles of criminalization that are in this sense master principles—as is the 'public wrongs' principle with which this chapter began.

2. Types of Master Principle (1): Positive v Negative

In Chapter 2 I discussed one would-be master principle of criminalization: the legal moralist principle (or family of principles) that connects criminalization to moral wrongdoing. I also there distinguished 'negative' from 'positive' forms of legal moralism.[11] That distinction, together with some others, must also be drawn in relation to other would-be principles of criminalization.

[8] See above, Chapter 2, section 5.

[9] As Moore does. A 'retributive theory of punishment demands that criminal punishment be imposed on all and only those who deserve it', and thus 'requires that, prima facie, all moral wrongs be prohibited by the criminal law' ('Liberty's Constraints on What Should be Made Criminal', 191–2): an 'all things considered' judgment, however, will need to factor in the costs of criminalization and its enforcement, which might sometimes be 'so heavy that the gains to be achieved (in retributive justice) simply cannot outweigh them' (*Placing Blame*, 663). Compare J Schonsheck, *On Criminalization: An Essay in the Philosophy of the Criminal Law*, ch. 3.III, on the three 'filters' through which criminalization proposals must pass: 'principles', 'presumptions', 'pragmatics'.

[10] A J Ashworth and J Horder, *Principles of Criminal Law*, ch. 2; see also the 'principles and policies' discussed in Chapter 3. See also J Horder, *Ashworth's Principles of Criminal Law*, ch. 4.

[11] See above, Chapter 2, section 3.

A negative principle of criminalization tells us what we should not criminalize, or what must count as a good or conclusive reason against criminalization. It might declare, for instance, that we must not criminalize a type of conduct unless it is wrongful,[12] or unless it is harmful to other people;[13] or that the various harms that criminalization inevitably causes always constitute good reasons against criminalization.[14] Such principles do not tell us what we ought to criminalize, or what counts as a good reason for criminalization: they rather specify barriers to criminalization, or conditions that must be satisfied before we can attend to the reasons for criminalization. By contrast, a positive principle tells us what we ought to criminalize, or what can constitute a good reason to criminalize: it might declare, for instance, that we ought to criminalize any conduct that constitutes culpable moral wrongdoing, in order to ensure that it is punished as it deserves;[15] or that the fact that we could efficiently prevent harm to others by criminalizing a type of conduct always gives us good reason to criminalize it.[16]

The distinction between positive and negative principles is related to that between conditions and objects of liability.[17] A negative principle specifies a condition of criminalization: we must not criminalize unless the specified factor or feature is present. To offer a positive principle is, by contrast, to specify an object of criminalization: it specifies a feature or factor that provides the, or a, focus of criminalization. Negative legal moralism makes moral wrongdoing a condition of criminalization, but not a positive reason for it: moral wrongdoing is an enabling condition that makes it permissible to attend to positive reasons for criminalization. Positive legal moralism, by contrast, makes moral wrongdoing the focus of criminalization, as that to which we must respond in this way: we are to criminalize conduct precisely because it is morally wrong. We could thus combine legal moralism with a version of the harm principle—as theorists are fond of doing—in one of two ways. First, we could make harm the object of criminalization: we have good reason to criminalize a type of conduct if and because it is harmful, or if and because by doing so we can efficiently prevent harm;[18] we could then make wrongfulness a condition of criminalization, by holding that we may criminalize harmful conduct (or conduct whose criminalization would prevent harm) only if it is wrongful. Second, we could make moral wrongdoing the object of criminalization—we have good reason to criminalize a type of conduct if and because it is wrong: but we could add a harm-based condition of criminalization by saying that we may criminalize wrongful conduct only if it is also harmful, or only if by doing so we can prevent future harm (or more modestly, only if doing so will not be, on balance, harmful). These two approaches might produce extensionally similar results: whichever we follow we will see reason to criminalize a type of conduct if and only if it is, for instance, both wrongful and harmful; or if and only if it is both wrongful and a type of conduct whose criminalization will efficiently prevent harm.[19] But the difference between them matters: it matters (to our understanding of the issues, if not to the

[12] See e.g. Feinberg, *Harm to Others*, 36; D N Husak, *Overcriminalization: The Limits of the Criminal Law*, 72; Simester and von Hirsch, *Crimes, Harms, and Wrongs*, 22.

[13] Compare Husak, *Overcriminalization*, 66–72, on the 'nontrivial harm or evil constraint', that 'criminal offenses [must be] designed to prohibit a nontrivial harm or evil' (66); later, this becomes simply 'the harm constraint' ('Polygamy: A Novel Test for a Theory of Criminalization', 220).

[14] See e.g. D N Husak, 'Why Punish the Deserving?'.

[15] Moore, *Placing Blame*, 33–5; above, Chapter 2, section 3.

[16] Feinberg, *Harm to Others*, 26.

[17] See above, Chapter 3 at n. 94, Chapter 5 at n. 107.

[18] The difference between these two formulations will be discussed in the following section.

[19] Feinberg's version of the harm principle, which involves defining 'harm' as wrongful harm (*Harm to Others*, 36) in effect amounts to this kind of view.

final outcome of the deliberation) whether a given consideration constitutes a positive reason to criminalize, or only a negative limit on criminalization.

Master principles of criminalization might include negative principles or criteria: they might, for instance, include a wrongfulness constraint to the effect that the non-wrongfulness of a type of conduct constitutes a (good, or conclusive) reason not to criminalize it, or that nothing could count as a good reason to criminalize non-wrongful types of conduct. But it is clear that if they are to guide (rather than simply constrain) deliberations about criminalization, they must include positive principles or criteria: they must tell us what gives us reason (whether good or conclusive reason) to criminalize a type of conduct. This is clearly true of principles such as those offered by Mill, Feinberg, and Moore: the prevention of harm (or offence) to others, or the attainment of retributive justice, constitute good, positive, reasons to criminalize. It is also true of an account like Husak's: although he presents his principles or criteria as 'constraints' on criminalization, at least one of those constraints specifies what could count as a good reason for criminalization—that 'criminal legislation must aim towards a substantial state interest'.[20] Husak does not go on to specify what could count as 'a substantial state interest'—his account is, in that respect, formal rather than substantive, thin rather than thick:[21] but the serving of a substantial state interest does (subject to the other constraints that he specifies) count as a good reason to criminalize.

3. Types of Master Principle (2): Responsive v Preventive

Some principles of criminalization justify it as a response to certain kinds of conduct. Thus a familiar, the more familiar, version of legal moralism offers a responsive principle: what gives us reason to criminalize (in its positive form), or makes criminalization permissible (in its negative form) is the wrongfulness of the conduct that is to be criminalized; criminalization is portrayed as a justified or permissible response to wrongdoing. Another version is possible, however: that what gives us reason to criminalize a type of conduct, or makes its criminalization permissible, is that by criminalizing it we will (effectively, efficiently) prevent future wrongdoing, or at least reduce its incidence.[22]

I will say more about preventive and responsive versions of legal moralism shortly, but this distinction between responsive and preventive principles is more familiar in relation to different versions of the harm principle.[23] In Mill's canonical formulation of the principle, 'the only purpose for which power can rightfully be exercised over any member of a civilised community against his will is to prevent harm to others'. But Mill goes on, in the same paragraph, to explain the implications of this: 'To justify [any kind of coercion], the conduct from which it is desired to deter him must be calculated to produce evil to some one else.'[24]

[20] Husak, *Overcriminalization*, 132.

[21] See further section 5 below, on 'thin' and 'thick' principles.

[22] Compare Edwards, 'Harm Principles', 263–4, on 'act-centered' and 'instrumental' principles; and 'An Instrumental Legal Moralism' ('preventive' is a better label than 'instrumental' because it makes it explicit that what criminalization is instrumental to, on the kind of account that concerns us here, is the prevention of certain kinds of mischief).

[23] For a more detailed discussion of this issue, see R A Duff and S E Marshall, '"Abstract Endangerment", Two Harm Principles, and Two Routes to Criminalisation'.

[24] Mill, *On Liberty*, ch. 1, para. 9; see also *On Liberty*, ch. 4, para. 3, for a similarly responsive version of the principle.

Feinberg, in his classic modern treatment of the topic, makes a similar move. He gives an official formulation of 'the harm principle': 'It is always a good reason in support of penal legislation that it would be effective in preventing (eliminating, reducing) harm to persons other than the actor ..., *and* there is no other means that is equally effective at no greater cost to other values.'[25] When he then goes on to discuss the implications and application of this principle, however, he focuses on the harmfulness of the conduct that is to be criminalized: *Harm to Others* is about the criminalization of conduct that is, in the relevant sense, harmful to others; later volumes discuss whether we can also have good reason to criminalize conduct that is not harmful to others, but that is, for instance, offensive to others,[26] or harmful to the agent,[27] or simply immoral or evil.[28]

We find the same phenomenon in many discussions of 'the harm principle'.[29] What we actually have, however, are two different principles. One is a responsive principle—

We have reason to criminalize a type of conduct if (only if) it is harmful.

The other is a preventive principle—

We have reason to criminalize a type of conduct if (only if) doing so will prevent harm.

(Positive principles are expressed by 'if', negative principles by 'only if'; an exclusive principle, that harm provides the only reason to criminalize,[30] is expressed by 'if and only if'.)

The failure to distinguish the two principles is a mistake, and a potential source of confusion that can be avoided once we distinguish them. It is a non-trivial mistake only if the principles generate different results: if they do not, if the preventive principle gives us reason to criminalize all and only the types of conduct that the responsive principle gives us reason to criminalize (all and only types of conduct that are harmful to others), we might say that they are not two separate principles, but two versions of what is in substance the same principle. But they do generate different results; the mistake is not trivial.

If a system of criminal law has some preventive efficacy, whatever the responsive principle gives us reason to criminalize is also, in principle, criminalizable under the preventive principle: an effective way of preventing harm is to reduce the incidence of kinds of conduct that cause harm; by criminalizing, and so reducing the incidence of, conduct that falls under the responsive principle, we serve the aims of the preventive principle. But the preventive principle is wider than the responsive principle, since it can, we will see, give us good reason to criminalize types of conduct that are not themselves harmful. It seems plausible that we can efficiently reduce the incidence of various harms caused by road accidents by setting strict limits on driving speeds and on drink-driving and by criminalizing breaches of such limits: but in doing so we will be criminalizing some conduct that is not itself in the relevant sense harmful.[31]

That might suggest that proponents of 'the harm principle' really do need just one principle, the preventive principle: that the responsive principle is not a separate principle, but a specific application of a preventive principle. We should still distinguish the two principles, however, for three reasons. First, although the preventive principle implies a responsive principle, one could espouse a responsive principle for reasons

[25] Feinberg, *Harm to Others*, 26.
[26] Feinberg, *Offense to Others*.
[27] Feinberg, *Harm to Self*.
[28] Feinberg, *Harmless Wrongdoing*.
[29] For another, more recent, example, see Simester and von Hirsch, *Crimes, Harms, and Wrongs*, 35.
[30] See above, Chapter 2 at nn 21–3.
[31] See further below, Chapter 7, section 5.

unrelated to the preventive principle: one could argue that the primary reason for criminalizing harmful conduct is not to prevent the harm it causes, but that it constitutes a kind of wrongdoing that should be censured by the criminal law, and for which its perpetrators should be called to public account. Second, what the preventive principle implies is (given the assumption about the preventive efficacy of criminalization) a permissive, positive responsive principle, that we have reason to criminalize conduct if it is harmful. It does not imply, and in its positive form is indeed inconsistent with, a negative or exclusive responsive principle, according to which we can have reason to criminalize conduct *only* if it is harmful: for it permits the criminalization of non-harmful conduct if that would be efficiently preventive. Third, we will see later that the two principles identify two different routes to criminalization—two different ways in which we can come to see good reason to criminalize a type of conduct.

We could, it is true, combine the two principles. Thus we could, for instance, formulate a responsive principle as a constraint on the preventive principle: we have reason to criminalize conduct if doing so will efficiently prevent harm, but we may do so only if the conduct that we criminalize is itself harmful; we may not criminalize harmless conduct even if doing so would efficiently prevent harm (this seems a natural reading of the way in which theorists who do not explicitly distinguish the two principles actually use them). Or we could treat the preventive principle as a constraint on the responsive principle: we have reason to criminalize conduct that is harmful, but may do so only if criminalizing it would efficiently prevent harm. As I will argue later, however, this is not the best way to understand the principles, and the relationship between them: in particular, the preventive principle should not, I will argue, be understood directly as a principle of criminalization (as a principle specifying directly the kinds of ground on which we may criminalize conduct); it should instead be understood as a principle of regulation.[32]

There has recently been something of a proliferation of distinctions between different harm principles. Tadros distinguishes two principles—

HP1. It is wrong to criminalize some conduct v if ving does not cause or risk harm.

HP2. It is wrong to criminalize some conduct v if criminalizing v does not prevent harm.[33]

These two principles are clearly close relatives of, but also crucially different from, the two that I have identified. In particular, HP1 and HP2 are negative, constraining principles, about when we may not criminalize; by contrast, the responsive and the preventive principle can be read either as negative or as positive—and the preventive principle is typically read as positive. Gardner and Shute also note these two ways of reading 'the harm principle', but think that only one is correct: 'the liberal "harm principle" ... forbids the attaching of legal sanctions to wrongdoing except to the extent that this is necessary to prevent harm'; and it 'is enough to meet the demands of the harm principle that, if the action were not criminalized, that would be harmful'.[34] We need not pause here to inquire into the relationship between 'criminalizing Φ will prevent harm' and 'not to criminalize Φ would be harmful'; but it is clear from the history

[32] And Mill's 'harm principle', so often quoted or cited as a principle of criminalization, was actually a principle concerning any exercise of 'power': see at n. 64 below.

[33] V Tadros, 'Harm, Sovereignty, and Prohibition', at 37 and 49: each principle is then revised, in ways that need not concern us here; see also *Wrongs and Crimes*, 98–104. For rather more ambitious sets of distinctions, which include versions both of this distinction and of others drawn in this chapter, see P Tomlin, 'Retributivists! The Harm Principle is Not for You!', at 279–83 (four principles); and Edwards, 'Harm Principles' (24 principles).

[34] J Gardner and S Shute, 'The Wrongness of Rape', at 195, 216.

of discussions of 'the harm principle' that the responsive principle has as much right to be called a 'harm principle' as does the preventive principle.

The distinction between responsive and preventive principles might be most familiar, though also often ignored, in the context of 'the harm principle'; but it can be drawn whatever value is posited as the, or a, ground of criminalization. Suppose we hold, for instance, that the criminal law should be concerned with *Rechtsgüter*: its function is the protection of *Rechtsgüter*—those goods, individual and collective, that should be recognized by the law as meriting protection.[35] This could generate a responsive principle: we have reason to criminalize conduct that directly violates or threatens a *Rechtsgut*. But it could, as well or instead, generate a preventive principle: we have reason to criminalize conduct when doing so would efficiently prevent violations of *Rechtsgüter*, even if the conduct itself does not itself violate or threaten any *Rechtsgut*. Or it could generate a hybrid principle: we have reason to criminalize a type of conduct if by doing so we can efficiently reduce the incidence of future violations of *Rechtsgüter*, on condition that the conduct itself violates or threatens a *Rechtsgut*; or we have reason to criminalize conduct that violates or threatens a *Rechtsgut*, on condition that by doing so we can efficiently reduce the incidence of future violations of *Rechtsgüter*. The same is true if we take the proper purpose of the criminal law to be to protect dignity, or freedom (understood in terms of sovereignty, or the capacity to choose ends, or republican 'non-domination'), or autonomy:[36] in each case the cited value could be taken to give us reason to criminalize conduct that violates or threatens it; or any conduct whose criminalization would efficiently prevent violations of it; or conduct that violates or threatens it, on condition that by doing so we can efficiently reduce the incidence of future violations; or conduct whose criminalization would efficiently reduce future violations of that value, on condition that the conduct itself violates or threatens that value.

We can thus draw a general distinction between two types, or two modes, of criminal law. In its responsive mode, the criminal law responds to conduct that is in some relevant way disvalued—conduct that, for instance, wrongfully causes or threatens harm;[37] in its preventive mode, the criminal law aims to reduce future disvalue (for instance, harm) through criminalizations that (if enforced) will efficiently prevent such disvalue. One question then is whether a plausible master principle could be either *purely* responsive, or *purely* preventive. Could it be plausibly said that we have reason to criminalize a type of conduct just so long as the conduct violates or threatens the fundamental value (just so long as criminalization is responsively apt), whether or not we can hope by doing so to reduce the incidence of future violations: or will a responsive

[35] On this central idea in German criminal law theory (which has become controversial in much the same way as the harm principle), see M D Dubber, 'Theories of Crime and Punishment in German Criminal Law'; N Persak, *Criminalising Harmful Conduct*, 104–18; W Hassemer, 'The Harm Principle and the Protection of "Legal Goods" (Rechtsgüterschutz)'; K Ambos, 'The Overall Function of International Criminal Law: Striking the Right Balance Between the *Rechtsgut* and the Harm Principles', 304–9.

[36] See e.g. M Dan-Cohen, 'Defending Dignity' (dignity); A Ripstein, 'Beyond the Harm Principle', *Force and Freedom: Kant's Legal and Political Philosophy* (Kantian freedom, or 'sovereignty'); A Brudner, *Punishment and Freedom: A Liberal Theory of Penal Justice* (the capacity to choose ends); J Braithwaite and P Pettit, *Not Just Deserts: A Republican Theory of Criminal Justice*, P Pettit, *On the People's Terms* (republican freedom); M D Dubber, *Victims in the War on Crime* (autonomy). See also Chiao's 'anti-deference principle': what gives us reason, or makes it permissible, to criminalize a type of conduct is that 'doing so is the best available means of promoting universal and effective access to central capability' (*Criminal Law in the Age of the Administrative State*, ch. 5.5).

[37] We will see shortly why a plausible harm principle needs to focus on *wrongfully* harmful conduct.

principle be plausible only if it builds in a preventive condition, so that we can have reason to criminalize only if doing so will have some preventive benefit? Or could it plausibly be argued that we have reason to criminalize a type of conduct just so long as this will be preventively efficient; or will a preventive principle be plausible only if it builds in a responsive condition, so that we can have reason to criminalize only if the conduct to be criminalized itself violates or threatens the basic value?

We can explore the former possibility, of a purely responsive master principle, by returning to legal moralism; the possibility of a purely preventive master principle can then be explored by looking at preventive types of harm principle.

Legal moralist principles are typically expressed as responsive principles: either as negative principles that preclude the criminalization of non-wrongful conduct, or as positive principles according to which the wrongfulness of a type of conduct gives us good reason to criminalize it. Responsive criminalization will typically also have some preventive effect, insofar as effective criminalization reminds people of the moral reasons why they ought to refrain from the conduct that is criminalized, or deters or incapacitates potential offenders; and legal moralists can regard this as a benefit of criminalization, which can be weighed against its costs when we come to ask whether we should, all things considered, criminalize a type of wrongful conduct.[38] They might also treat it as at least a secondary aim of criminalization:[39] one reason for criminalizing a type of wrongful conduct is to reduce its incidence. Indeed, a preventive aim is intrinsic to any version of legal moralism, however robustly responsive it is.[40] If we have reason to respond to a type of wrong by punishing it, or by calling its perpetrators to account; if the wrong is in that way our business: we also have reason to seek to prevent its commission, if legitimate means of doing so are available; and criminalizing it is likely to have some preventive efficacy. There are other ways of reducing the incidence of wrongful conduct,[41] and criminalization might be relatively inefficient. But criminalization has an intrinsically preventive dimension: to declare something to be wrong, which is part of what criminalization does, is to declare it to be something that those to whom the declaration is addressed ought not to do; and to declare to someone that she ought not to act in a certain way is to claim that she has conclusive reason not to act thus, which is to seek to persuade her (if she needs persuading) not to act thus. It is also plausible that if criminalization generally had *no* reductive effect on the incidence of the kinds of conduct that were criminalized, we might have no use for criminal law: but that is because criminal law is a practice that treats citizens as, and must therefore presuppose that they are, rational and responsible agents who can be, and who sometimes are, moved by good reasons for action—a presupposition that would be undermined if criminalization generally had no kind of dissuasive effect.

Should responsively-oriented legal moralists go further than this, to build a more demanding preventive requirement into their principle? Should they recognize, for instance, that the fact that criminalizing a particular type of wrongful conduct would probably have *no* preventive efficacy would give us good reason not to criminalize it; or

[38] See e.g. M S Moore, 'A Tale of Two Theories', 44: 'benefits' of criminalization such as crime prevention can be weighed against its costs, to determine 'whether the goodness of achieving retributive justice is enough to make its achievement worth its *net* cost'.

[39] See e.g. M S Moore, 'Liberty's Constraints on What Should be Made Criminal', at 192 ('Retributivism ... yields ... the "moral wrong principle": criminal legislation must exclusively aim at preventing or punishing moral wrongs').

[40] See J Edwards, 'An Instrumental Legal Moralism', s. II.

[41] See above, Chapter 5 at nn 77–9.

even that it would preclude criminalization?[42] That would be to combine a positive responsive principle with a negative preventive principle: we have good responsive reason to criminalize wrongful conduct (that it deserves punishment, or that we should call such wrongdoers to account), but only on condition that by doing so we will reduce the incidence of such conduct. Such a preventive requirement is, as we have just seen, intrinsic to the general enterprise of criminal law, but is less plausible as a requirement on the criminalization of particular kinds of wrong: if we have a system of criminal law at all, surely we have very good, perhaps compelling, reason to criminalize the most egregious kinds of public wrong, regardless of the preventive efficacy of doing so.[43]

Even if a legal moralist accepted a negative preventive principle of the kind suggested here, this would give prevention only a quite modest role in what would still be a primarily responsive master principle: the criminal law's primary focus would still be on responding appropriately to relevant kinds of wrongdoing. Do legal moralists need to go further than this if they are to offer a plausible master principle? Should they give preventive considerations a more positive role in deliberations about what we have good reason to criminalize, as providing part of the rationale for criminalization, at least in relation to some kinds of wrong? One possibility would be to say that when the wrong in question is relatively minor, and the demand that it be punished or that its perpetrator be held to public account is accordingly less insistent, we still have some responsive reason to criminalize it; but the reason to criminalize becomes a sufficient or good enough reason only if criminalization will also have some preventive efficacy. Another possibility would be to extend the scope of the law's preventive ambitions beyond the specific type of conduct that is to be criminalized. A relatively modest illustration of this kind of extension is provided by the wide range of 'preventive' or 'prophylactic' offences,[44] which criminalize conduct that does not itself perpetrate, but in some way opens or paves the way to, a primary wrong with which the criminal law is concerned. We will discuss such offences in more detail later;[45] one example will suffice to make the relevant point here. Terrorist acts (when suitably defined) clearly constitute public wrongs with which the criminal law is properly concerned. If it is wrong to commit a terrorist act, it is also wrong to prepare to do so—to take steps to carry out an intention to do so. Does it follow that we have good responsive reason to criminalize all such preparatory actions;[46] or do we have good reason to do so only if and because we can expect this to reduce the incidence of acts of terrorism? This extends the law's preventive ambition because what makes our reason to criminalize preparatory conduct a good enough reason is that by doing so we can reduce not, or not only, the incidence of such conduct itself, but also the incidence of actual acts of terrorism. The extension is, however, a modest one, since the conduct to be criminalized must be not only wrongful, but wrongful in a way that connects it to the kind of wrong that we aim to prevent: we are to criminalize acts of terrorist preparation because by doing so we can reduce the incidence of the very kind of wrong at which such acts are themselves wrongfully directed.[47]

[42] An argument of this kind is more familiar in the context of criminal punishment, in response to pure versions of retributivism: if punishment had no preventive efficacy, it would be unjustified.

[43] See e.g. N Jareborg, 'Criminalization as Last Resort (*Ultima Ratio*)', 534; and at n. 74 below.

[44] See e.g. A P Simester, 'Prophylactic Crimes'; A J Ashworth and L Zedner, *Preventive Justice*, ch. 5.

[45] See Chapter 7, section 6 below.

[46] See e.g. Terrorism Act 2006, s. 5 ('Preparation of terrorist acts'); and see S MacDonald, 'Cyberterrorism and Enemy Criminal Law', on 'precursor offences' in this context.

[47] Compare Simester, 'Prophylactic Crimes', 67–9, on the need for a 'nexus'.

Edwards argues that legal moralists should go further than this, to adopt a preventive *rather than* a responsive version of legal moralism: the arguments that are taken to support a responsive version in fact, he argues, favour a preventive principle: 'It is always a good reason in support of criminalisation that it would probably be effective in preventing (eliminating, reducing) moral wrongs, and there is probably no other means that is equally effective at a lesser cost to other values.'[48]

First, he argues, the usual arguments in favour of a responsive legal moralism are actually better understood as arguments for a restricted preventive moralism: we have reason to criminalize a type of conduct if and because doing so will efficiently prevent the commission of certain kinds of secondary wrong that consist in the failure to discharge those secondary duties that flow from the breach of a primary duty. I have a primary duty to refrain from committing such wrongs as murder or theft. For a retributivist like Moore, the breach of that primary duty generates certain secondary duties—a duty on others to ensure that I am punished as I deserve, and a duty on me to accept that punishment. A failure to discharge those secondary duties constitutes a secondary wrong; and we can prevent the commission of such secondary wrongs by criminalizing murder and theft, so as to bring it about that I am punished as I deserve. Similarly, on a theory like mine, which focuses on calling those who commit public wrongs to formal account, criminalization can prevent the commission of such secondary wrongs as failing to call public wrongdoers to account or failing to answer for one's wrongs. However, second, if we have good reason to use criminal law to prevent the commission of such secondary wrongs, we also have good reason to use it to prevent the commission of the primary wrongs from which such secondary wrongs derive—to prevent, that is, the commission of such wrongs as murder and theft in the first place. Finally, we might sometimes be able efficiently to prevent the commission of a wrong by criminalizing some conduct that is not itself wrongful: we might find that we can reduce the incidence of a particular kind of wrongful conduct by, for instance, criminalizing some type of conduct that, although not itself wrongful, makes it easier for others to engage in the wrongful conduct, or that is not easily distinguished from the wrongful conduct by a formal offence-definition.[49] A preventive version of legal moralism should thus not merely supplement, but replace, a responsive legal moralism.

Three points are worth making about this complex argument (which I have presented here in admittedly simplified form).

First, Edwards talks of 'instrumental' rather than 'preventive' legal moralism, and even the most robustly responsive version of legal moralism is 'instrumental' in one sense: we criminalize wrongs not simply for the sake of criminalizing them, but in order to pave the way for (to enable, to legitimize) an appropriate response to them—the imposition of a deserved punishment, or a calling to public account of those who commit such wrongs. Those who espouse a responsive legal moralism would not deny that criminalization is in this way instrumental: what they insist is that the main reason for criminalization is to pave the way for such an intrinsically appropriate response, not to bring about any further, preventive effects.

Second, I will not rehearse here the defence of negative legal moralism (in responsive mode) that I offered in Chapter 2, section 4, save to emphasize that it applies to substantive, rather than only formal, criminalization: that is, we might, as Edwards and others have argued, have good reason to enact criminal statutes whose offence

[48] Edwards, 'An Instrumental Legal Moralism', at n. 10.

[49] And see above, Chapter 2 at nn 47–63, on Edwards' argument (in 'Criminalization without Punishment') against negative (responsive) legal moralism.

definitions capture some conduct that is not (and is not believed by the legislature to be) morally wrong; but such enactments are legitimate only if the officials who apply the law (police, prosecutors, courts) can be relied upon to exercise their discretion not to prosecute or convict those who do not commit the kind of wrong at which the law is aimed. If that defence was sound, we should resist the final step in Edwards' argument, and insist that we ought not to criminalize non-wrongful conduct even if by doing so we could efficiently prevent future wrongdoing. However, this does not rule out a modified version of his 'instrumental legal moralism', which retains his preventive positive principle but subjects it to a negative responsive constraint: what gives us good positive reason to criminalize a type of conduct is that this would be an efficient way of reducing the incidence of wrongdoing, so long as the conduct itself is also wrongful.[50]

Third, however, we need to look more critically at a key move in Edwards' argument: that if we criminalize a type of conduct in order thereby to secure an appropriate response to it (whether that response be punishment, or a formal calling to account), we criminalize it in order to prevent the commission of a particular kind of wrong—a failure, on our part, to discharge our collective secondary duty to punish, or to call to account; and a failure, on the wrongdoer's part, to accept punishment or to respond to that call. The trouble with this move is that it makes it all too easy to portray *every* normative reason for action, even the seemingly non-instrumental, as preventive. If I help a stranger in need, I would naturally say that my reason for action is simply that she needs help (which I can provide): my reason, like my action, is responsive to her need. If I pay Jane the £100 I promised her, I would naturally say that my reason for action is simply that I promised to pay her: my reason, like my action, is responsive to that promissory obligation. We *could* then say that in acting as I do I prevent the commission of a certain wrong: I prevent a failure, on my part, to help someone whom I should help, or to keep a promise. But it is unclear why we should adopt such a circumlocutionary way of describing my action—why we should say that I prevent the commission of a wrong, rather than simply saying that I do what is right; and it would be, at best, misleading to say that my reason for acting thus is to prevent the commission of that wrong. Some kinds of action aim to prevent future wrongdoing, but some are responsive; some reasons for action are preventive, but some are responsive: Edwards' argument for a preventive *rather than* a responsive legal moralism undermines that distinction, without good reason.

The upshot of this discussion is that legal moralism, in both negative and positive forms, is best understood as a primarily responsive principle. We should not criminalize a type of conduct unless it is wrongful; and, for a positive legal moralist, we have good reason to criminalize a type of conduct if it is wrongful (in a relevant way). Wrongful conduct, of the relevant (public) kind, makes a certain kind of response appropriate (for Moore, retributive punishment; for me, a public declaration of its wrongfulness and a formal calling to public account); we therefore have reason to criminalize such conduct in order to secure that kind of response. A plausible legal moralism will also have a preventive dimension: we should aim to reduce the incidence of the wrong that we have reason to criminalize; and criminalization can contribute to that aim. But that kind of preventive concern is secondary to the responsive aims that are appropriate to criminal law as a distinctive kind of legal practice.[51]

[50] To which we might add that it must be wrongful in a way that is connected to the wrongfulness of the conduct that we aim to prevent: see at n. 47 above.

[51] See my discussion of a liberal polity's criminal law in Chapter 5, section 4 above.

Other would-be master principles of criminalization might seem to be more aptly understood as preventive principles. This is most obviously true of the harm principle, which is typically, as we saw above, canonically formulated in preventive terms.[52] However, we must recognize, first, that even the harm principle is not plausible as a *purely* preventive master principle; and second, that as a preventive principle it is not best understood as a principle of *criminalization.*

A preventive harm principle could be formulated, as a principle of criminalization, along the lines of Feinberg's account, as a positive 'harm prevention principle':

We have good reason to criminalize a given type of conduct if doing so will efficiently prevent harm to others.[53]

Such a principle seems to provide a very simple way of justifying the creation of a wide range of so-called *mala prohibita*, including offences that a responsive harm principle might not justify. For instance, if our aim is to reduce the harm caused by traffic accidents, we could gain some preventive benefit by criminalizing various kinds of wrongfully harmful conduct: driving when one's capacities are impaired by alcohol or other kinds of drug, for instance, or at a dangerously high speed.[54] We might also believe, however, that we could achieve more effective, and more efficient, reductions in harmful accidents by stricter criminal laws that prohibit exceeding posted speed limits or driving with more than a specified level of alcohol in one's blood:[55] for such laws will be easier to enforce, and will more effectively deter drivers who are either overconfident of their own abilities or hopeful of getting away with breaking the former kind of law. Such laws do not seem to be justifiable by a responsive harm principle: for although much of the conduct they criminalize will be harmful, or at least dangerous,[56] some will not be; there will be drivers who—given their physical condition and capacities, and the circumstances in which they are driving—can not only drive safely (more safely than many of those who obey the law) in violation of such laws, but know that they can do so. If we may criminalize only harmful or dangerous conduct, we have no reason to create offences that criminalize their conduct: but if we tried to formulate laws that allowed them to avoid liability (for instance by recognizing 'enhanced capacity' as a defence), we would radically decrease the law's harm-preventive efficacy. That is the advantage that a harm-preventive principle has over a harm-responsive principle: it allows us to create more efficiently preventive laws.[57]

However, this seems to make the justification of new criminal offences too easy. It allows us to criminalize conduct that is itself neither harmful nor, for all we know so far, wrongful, simply on the grounds that by doing so we can efficiently prevent future harm: but how could it be just or fair to criminalize—to define, condemn, and punish

[52] See at nn 23–9 above. [53] See Feinberg, *Harm to Others*, 26; at n. 25 above.

[54] See Road Traffic Act 1988, ss 2 ('dangerous driving'), 4 ('driving when under influence of drink or drugs').

[55] See Road Traffic Regulation Act 1984, ss 81–9; Road Traffic Act 1988, s. 5. For an interesting discussion of the introduction of the new-style drink-driving offence in England, showing inter alia that it was not only aimed at increased deterrent efficacy, see A E Bottoms, 'Civil Peace and Criminalization', at 261–4.

[56] As we will see (at nn 135–7 below), any plausible harm principle will allow for the criminalization not only of conduct that actually causes harm, but also of conduct that creates an unreasonable risk of harm.

[57] It is an empirical question whether such stricter laws, such as those enforcing speed limits, are more efficient in preventing harm than laws that simply criminalize driving at a dangerously high speed (see L Alexander and K K Ferzan, *Crime and Culpability: A Theory of Criminal Law*, 302–6); what matters here is simply that, under a harm prevention principle, we would have good reason to enact such laws if they would be more efficient.

as wrongful—non-wrongful, non-harmful conduct on that basis?[58] We cannot avoid this problem by interpreting 'harm' along Feinbergian lines, as 'wrongful harm'.[59] For, first, the fact that criminalizing a type of conduct would prevent wrongful harms still does not make that conduct itself wrongful or harmful. Second, it is unclear what could justify such a limitation on the reach of the harm prevention principle. Some of the harms that we could use the criminal law to prevent will certainly be wrongful harms, and that wrongfulness will be part of what gives us reason to seek to prevent them: it is a state's proper responsibility to protect its citizens against wrongful attacks or endangerments that expose them to unreasonable risks of harm. But if our starting point is harm prevention, as a justification for coercive intervention by the state, we will not attend only to wrongful harms: we will see reason to use the law to protect ourselves against a wide range of harms, including natural or accidental harms, that can be averted or reduced by legal regulation—including, for instance, environmental harms. It is a state's proper task to help protect us against threats to our lives and health, whether those threats arise from natural causes, or from accidents, or from wrongful human conduct; we cannot rule out in advance the possibility that the criminal law can play a role in such protection.

Could we deal with this problem by adding a 'wrongfulness constraint'?[60] This would allow us to criminalize a type of conduct in order to prevent future harm, on condition that the conduct itself is wrongful. But, first, to do so would be to deprive ourselves of at least some of the harm-preventive benefits of creating offences of this kind, since it would render the law less effective. Second, it seems plausible that this constraint should require not merely that the conduct to be criminalized be wrongful in some way, but that it be wrongful in a way connected to the reasons for criminalizing it—to the kind of harm that the law aims to prevent:[61] but if the conduct does not itself threaten that harm, as some of the conduct criminalized in this way does not, it is hard to see how it is relevantly wrongful.

To see how a harm prevention principle could ground a justification for criminalization, we must recall the distinction between criminalization and regulation,[62] and the difference between Mill's harm prevention principle and Feinberg's. Feinberg's principle is a principle specifically of criminalization: the prevention of harm is 'a good reason in support of *penal legislation* ...'.[63] Mill's principle, by contrast, concerns any kind of coercion by the state or one's fellow citizens: it precludes any 'compulsion and control, whether the means used be physical force in the form of legal penalties, or the moral coercion of public opinion', unless the purpose is to prevent harm to others.[64] If we are going to justify criminalization by appeal to a harm prevention principle, we must begin with a Millian version: with a harm prevention principle, that is, as a principle not of criminalization as such, but of regulation. It could be formulated thus—

We have good reason to regulate a given type of conduct if doing so will efficiently prevent harm to others.

To 'regulate' a type of conduct might be to prohibit it altogether, or to subject it to some set of restrictions: we 'regulate' the possession of certain kinds of drug by

[58] See Husak, *Overcriminalization*, 103–19; and '*Malum Prohibitum* and Retributivism'.

[59] See Feinberg, *Harm to Others*, 36: 'only setbacks of interests that are wrongs ... are to count as harms in the appropriate sense'.

[60] See above, Chapter 2 at nn 17–18.

[61] See at n. 47 above.

[62] See above, Chapter 1 at nn 45–8, Chapter 2 at nn 31–5.

[63] Feinberg, *Harm to Others*, 26 (emphasis added).

[64] Mill, *On Liberty*, ch. 1, para. 9.

prohibiting it; we 'regulate' the activity of driving by creating restrictive regulations about who can engage in it, and about how they may engage in it.

The line of argument that leads us from this harm prevention principle to the recognition of good reason to criminalize conduct that is not itself harmful is roughly this. We take it as a collective aim, which the state should pursue, to reduce the incidence of a particular kind of harm. We see that one means towards that end is to regulate certain kinds of human conduct: kinds of conduct that are liable to cause such harm, or kinds of conduct whose regulation can help to prevent it. Such regulations will sometimes prohibit conduct that is itself harmful or dangerous: conduct which is already harmful prior to and independently of the regulation, or conduct which becomes harmful once the regulation is in place (as driving on the right-hand side of the road is typically harmful once we have in place a requirement to drive on the left). But they will also sometimes prohibit conduct that is not itself harmful: regulations aimed at harmful conduct can be over-inclusive in that the type of conduct that they prohibit is known to include many non-harmful tokens; other regulations may be concerned with what is needed to ensure the efficient working of the regulatory system, so that breaches of them are remote from any risk of harm. Such regulations are not yet, as far as the logic of their introduction is concerned, part of criminal law (not all regulatory law is criminal law); but we might see reason to bring criminal law into play, when we ask how we should respond to breaches of the regulations. For, according to a positive legal moralist, we have reason to criminalize such breaches if they are wrongful in a relevant way; but surely they can be thus wrongful. If the regulations were legitimately created, as a means to the legitimate goal of harm prevention, and do not impose unreasonable burdens on those who are required to obey them, they are regulations that we ought to obey, as citizens of the polity whose law this is and whose aims we should share; we thus do wrong in breaching them—a wrong that is a public wrong, as a breach of our public regulations, and that thus merits a formal, public, response. Such breaches are therefore, in principle, candidates for criminalization: which is not to say that we should criminalize them, all things considered, since other ways of dealing with them might be more efficient or appropriate; but it is to say (which is all that the harm prevention principle itself, as a principle of criminalization, said) that we have good reason to criminalize them. Thus a harm prevention principle, as a principle of regulation (or as a more general principle of governmental activity), together with a positive legal moralist principle of criminalization, can generate a principle of criminalization: we have good reason to criminalize a type of conduct if it wrongfully violates a regulation that serves to prevent harm.

The distinction between these two stages, of regulation and of criminalization, is sometimes clearly shown in legislation: a statute first lays down regulations to govern some area of human conduct, and then declares the breach of any of these regulations to be a criminal offence.[65] But even when the distinction is not made so explicitly clear, it can and must be drawn as a matter of legislative logic. Suppose that a Road Traffic Act simply declared it to be an offence to drive at more than 70 mph on any public road: this would combine the creation of a regulation, setting 70 mph as the legal speed

[65] See, for one instance, Road Traffic Regulation Act 1984, ss 81–9: ss 81–8 lay down general regulations about speed limits (speeds at which it is or is not 'lawful' to drive, how regulations about speed limits can be made, etc.); s. 89(1) then declares that '[a] person who drives a motor vehicle on a road at a speed exceeding a limit imposed by or under any enactment to which this section applies shall be guilty of an offence'. Without s. 89(1), speeding would be 'unlawful', but not criminal. See also the examples given above, Chapter 1 at nn 45–8; and ss 5, 11(2) of the Road Traffic Act 1988.

limit, with the criminalization of its breach; but its logical structure would be the same as that of a statute that distinguished the two stages (it would also, of course, make it harder to change the speed limit). That is, to understand how the legislature could be justified in creating this offence, we would need to see how the concern to prevent a particular kind of harm could warrant the creation of a regulation; and how the breach of that regulation could then be a wrong that warrants criminalization.

This pattern of criminalization can be discerned in several areas—for instance in matters to do with health and safety at work, with financial transactions, with systems of taxation and social security, with environmental safety and pollution, as well as with road traffic. I will have more to say about this, and about just how a legislature can be justified both in creating such regulations and in criminalizing their breach, later—since we clearly should not take it for granted either that all such regulations are justified, or that it is always wrongful to break them. The point to notice here is that we need to distinguish principles of criminalization from principles concerning other kinds of legal regulation—and that a preventive harm principle is more plausible as a principle of regulation than as a direct principle of criminalization.

It might now be objected that in talking only of 'preventive' principles of criminalization, as the alternative to responsive principles, I have unduly limited the range of possible justifications of criminalization. If criminalization is to be justified, as according to a preventive principle it is, by its beneficial effect in reducing the incidence of some kind of mischief (of harm, for instance, or of public wrongdoing), why should we only be allowed to attend to that preventive benefit; why should we not also be able to attend, as sources of reasons to criminalize, to other benefits that criminalization might bring? Some of those benefits will depend on the (actual or perceived) preventive efficacy of the criminal law: thus the effective criminalization of kinds of conduct that are seen to threaten freedom or security, for instance, might give citizens the kind of assurance, or reassurance, that they need if their lives are to be secure and free;[66] but it does so only because it is seen to be a way of preventing such conduct. Others depend on the law's perceived efficacy as an instrument of retributive justice: it might be argued, for instance, that the satisfaction that the effective criminalization of some kinds of wrongdoing will bring to their victims (and others) gives us reason to criminalize them;[67] but such satisfaction depends on some version of the idea that those who commit such wrongs deserve to be punished. I will say a little more in section 6 about the kinds of benefit that could, or could not, provide good reasons to criminalize, and need make only two comments here. First, if we are looking for a master principle of criminalization, it is plausible that a consequence-focused master principle will make prevention the central justifying aim of criminalization; other potential benefits will be either benefits that flow from prevention, or considerations that become relevant when we ask whether we should, all things considered, criminalize what we have good reason to criminalize.[68] Second, however, we must ask whether any consequence-oriented principle can stand by itself as *the* master of criminalization; or will it need at least to be supplemented by a negative responsive principle, such as the negative legal moralist principle, which constrains the kinds of conduct that may be criminalized for the sake of the consequential benefits of doing so? We have good reason to criminalize a type of

[66] See e.g. Braithwaite and Pettit, *Not Just Deserts*, for a rigorously consequentialist theory of criminal law as serving the end of republican freedom; and see Chapter 5 at n. 77 above.

[67] See e.g. T Honderich, *Punishment: The Supposed Justifications Revisited*, ch. 3, on 'grievance satisfaction' (which he thinks captures such truth as there is retributivism).

[68] See at n. 38 above.

conduct, such principles tell us, if doing so would efficiently prevent the kind of mischief or promote the kind of benefit with which we are concerned: but if the principle is to be normatively plausible, we might need to add a condition of legitimate criminalization to the effect that the conduct to be criminalized must itself be wrongful, or must itself produce or threaten to produce the kind of mischief with which we are concerned.[69]

4. Types of Master Principle (3): *Pro Tanto* v Categorical

Next, we should distinguish categorical from *pro tanto* principles.[70] A principle is *pro tanto* if it tells us what constitutes a reason, or a good reason, to criminalize (or not to criminalize) a certain type of conduct. Feinberg's principles are of this kind: for they tell us that we have good reason to criminalize a type of conduct if by doing so we can, for instance, efficiently prevent harm to others, which implies that we might sometimes have better reasons not to criminalize. Similarly, we might say, the various costs that flow from criminalizing conduct always give us good reason not to criminalize: if we are to justify criminalizing a type of conduct, we must show not merely that we have good reason to do so, but also that that reason is strong enough to defeat this ever-present reason against criminalization. A principle is categorical if it tells us what we must or must not criminalize, thus leaving no room for a balancing of reasons for and against criminalization.

The most obviously plausible categorical principles are negative, such as the negative legal moralist principle that we must not criminalize conduct that is not wrongful: for this is typically asserted as a strict constraint on criminalization; we may not even consider reasons in favour of criminalization if the conduct is not morally wrongful. A familiar consequentialist riposte to any such assertion of a categorical norm is to imagine some more or less outré example in which the only way to avert catastrophe would be to violate the norm. These examples might be fanciful—suppose the whole world would be destroyed if we did not violate the norm—or more realistic: but they do not threaten the categorical status of categorical principles of criminalization. This is not just because we should espouse 'threshold' deontology,[71] according to which a deontologist's categorical principles give way to instrumental considerations if the stakes are high enough; nor just because, if we do not accept a 'threshold' view, we should recognize the tragic possibility of moral dilemmas in which we cannot avoid committing a categorical wrong:[72] we need not take a stand here on which of these views is plausible. The more relevant point here is that we need to distinguish reasons that operate within the practice of criminal law, from reasons that might require us to abandon that practice (or merely to pretend to engage in it). We might come to believe

[69] This is a familiar issue for any consequentialist theory: compare the familiar argument that even if the positive justifying aim of criminal punishment is to be understood in consequentialist terms, any plausible penal theory would need to include a version of negative retributivism as a side-constraint; we must not permit the deliberate punishment of the innocent, even if by doing so we could promote that justifying aim.

[70] Compare Edwards, 'Master Principles', on 'the argument from reasons' and 'the argument from defeaters' (in its 'cancelling' form). Feinberg's discussion of legal moralism (see n. 6 above) draws a distinction between 'good reasons' and 'relevant reasons' for criminalization; I will not make use of that distinction, but will focus on 'good reasons'—reasons that have enough weight to figure seriously in our deliberations.

[71] See e.g. Moore, *Placing Blame*, ch. 17; L Alexander, 'Deontology at the Threshold'.

[72] For what is still a useful collection, see C W Gowans (ed.), *Moral Dilemmas*.

that we must, in order to avert very serious harm (perhaps to the polity's very survival), 'criminalize' conduct that we do not believe to be morally wrong. If we are legal moralists, we will see this as requiring us to abandon the enterprise of criminal law, decisions within which are constrained by the negative principle that we may not criminalize conduct unless it is morally wrongful; we will now be engaged in a pretence, or simulacrum, of criminal law—just as an examiner who 'awards' a passing grade to a clearly fail-worthy paper in order to avert disastrous consequences is abandoning (perhaps for good reason) the academic practice of examining.[73]

It is unclear whether we could also identify a plausibly categorical positive principle, telling us when we *must* criminalize—except an unhelpful formal principle that we must criminalize if the reasons in favour of this outweigh any reasons against it (or if we have 'undefeated' reason to criminalize). Could we say, perhaps, that we *must* criminalize such serious wrongs as murder and rape? This seems plausible if put in hypothetical terms: *if* we have a system of criminal law, we must criminalize such wrongs; there would be a kind of normative incoherence in a system of criminal law that defined some criminal wrongs, but did not criminalize such wrongs as these.[74] Even here, however, we must ask how such wrongs might be recognized. It might be difficult to imagine a polity that took no formal public notice of them; but could we imagine a polity that, for instance, took formal notice of such wrongs, but through its tort law, rather than its criminal law, reserving criminal law for wrongs that lacked individually identifiable victims?

Moore sometimes seems to assert a categorical positive principle of criminalization, talking not of what we have good reason to do, but of what we must do. Thus, for instance, a 'retributive theory of punishment demands that criminal punishment be imposed on all and only those who deserve it'. Given a principle of legality, this leads to legal moralism as a 'theory of legislation': 'criminal legislation must exclusively aim at preventing or punishing moral wrongs, and this it can do by prohibiting all and only those behaviours that are in fact morally wrong'.[75] This seems to leave no room for the weighing of reasons for and against: legislatures must aim to criminalize all and only culpably wrongful conduct. In fact, however, that is not quite Moore's view, since the demands that flow from legal moralism are only 'prima facie': legal moralism 'requires that, *prima facie*, all moral wrongs be prohibited by the criminal law, for otherwise wrongdoers doing those wrongs could not (under the principle of legality) receive their just deserts'.[76] This is not, or need not be, to revert to the logic of *pro tanto* principles or reasons: for we can still distinguish principles that assert requirements or duties from those that only assert considerations—reasons that take the form of requirements or duties from reasons that amount only to considerations.

A consideration is a factor that favours one course of action over others, but that must then be weighed with, and perhaps against, other considerations that bear on the agent's situation: the fact that an acquaintance who is in hospital would enjoy a visit from me might be a consideration that favours visiting her; but (absent a duty to visit her, perhaps because I promised to do so), it is a consideration that might be outweighed by others, such as the fact that if I visit her I will not be able to complete

[73] See above, Chapter 2 at nn 39–40. [74] See at n. 43 above.

[75] M S Moore, 'Liberty's Constraints on What Should be Made Criminal', 191–2.

[76] 'Liberty's Constraints', 191. We should be clear that 'prima facie' duties or requirements are genuine duties or requirements, though they can be defeated or overridden: the claim that something is a prima facie duty should not be misread as the claim that it seems to be a duty, but might on closer inspection turn out not to be (i.e. as a claim that it is only prima facie a duty). See S Kagan, *The Limits of Morality*, 17.

this chapter. By contrast, a duty or demand speaks in more peremptory tones of what I must do or ought to do: if I promised to visit my acquaintance, that is what I now ought to do, even if that means not doing something else (completing this chapter) that might, taken by itself, be of greater value. However, duties and demands can conflict: I might 'have to' break my promise to my friend, to deal with some emergency or to discharge a more pressing duty. One difference between the two kinds of case is that when a consideration is outweighed, I may regret it (it is a shame that I cannot both visit my acquaintance and complete this chapter today); but if I morally 'cannot' carry out a duty or satisfy a demand there is a more significant loss—a moral remainder.[77] I now have reason not merely to regret that I could not attain all the goods that were in play, as I might when I have to act against a good reason for the sake of even better reasons, but to recognize that I failed to discharge a duty; this might not be serious enough to warrant remorse, but it certainly merits—if there is someone to whom the duty was owed—an apologetic explanation. A Moorean legislator might thus recognize not merely that the prospect of serving retributive justice is a consideration that favours criminalizing culpable moral wrongdoing, but that she has a duty to serve justice, and so a duty to criminalize such conduct; but also, in some situations, that that duty must give way to other duties (such as the duty to respect liberty), or to considerations of cost.

The various distinctions drawn so far between types of criminalization principle enable us to recognize different logical patterns of deliberation about criminalization. Three such patterns are familiar from other contexts of normative thought. First, deliberation might be instrumentalist, about the best, or a satisfactory, means towards a future goal.[78] Such deliberation will involve a normative dimension, since we must be clear about just what the goal involves (what constitutes freedom as non-domination, for instance?), and our account of the various 'costs' and 'benefits' of the available courses of action might include 'costs' and 'benefits' that must be understood in normative terms. But it will also need large-scale empirical inquiries, into the likely effects of the various courses of action under consideration; an obvious question is then how far theorists who appeal to this kind of instrumental reasoning can have confidence in the claims that they make—and a familiar suspicion is that they might believe the empirical claims because they seem to support conclusions that are intuitively, normatively, attractive.

Second, our deliberations might be set in non-instrumental terms: not merely as deliberations of the kind that instrumentalists might also need, about the value of various goals or side-effects, but as deliberations about the intrinsic worth of the actions or policies that we are considering. Such worth might be understood in terms of the good and the bad: one kind of retributivist, for instance, portrays the punishment of the guilty as intrinsically good—good, that is, in virtue not of its further consequences but of its intrinsic character as a response to crime.[79] This kind of view, however, is not in the end sharply different from instrumental patterns of deliberation: in both cases, we begin with an account of some intrinsic good to be pursued (or some intrinsic evil to be averted) and work out how best (or satisfactorily) to achieve it. Indeed, on this retributivist view, the enterprise of criminal law and criminalization is precisely

[77] See B Williams, 'Ethical Consistency', 172–6; R Hursthouse, *On Virtue Ethics*, 44–8.

[78] We need not engage here with the debate about 'satisficing' versus 'maximizing' versions of consequentialism—about whether we should seek the best, or just a satisfactory, way forward: see M Byron (ed.), *Satisficing and Maximizing: Moral Theorists on Practical Reason.*

[79] See M Berman, 'Two Kinds of Retributivism'.

instrumental to the end of securing the punishment of the guilty; what we now have is an instrumentalist view that differs from others in its account of the intrinsic good that is to be pursued.[80] Furthermore, even if we begin by positing just one intrinsic good (retribution, for instance) as the proper target of criminal law, we cannot in the end ignore other goods that might accrue, or the various evils that the pursuit of that good might bring: we might argue that retribution is the only good that is intrinsically proper to criminal law as such; but we cannot plausibly argue either that it is the only good that must be relevant as we continue our deliberations from that starting point, or that it is so important a good that no evil effects can outweigh it. Thus if we are to identify a genuinely non-instrumental mode of deliberation, we must explain the intrinsic worth of criminal law in terms not of goods, but of duties—that we *ought* to criminalize certain kinds of conduct, not because this is an efficient way to achieve some consequential good, but because that it is what is required or demanded of us as a response to some features of the situation we are in or of what has happened in the past. So, for instance, we ought to criminalize certain types of wrong because we ought (as a matter of justice, or what we owe to each other as citizens) to respond to such wrongs by formally declaring them to be (public) wrongs, thus providing for those who commit them to be called to public account; this is not to be understood as saying that such formal declarations and callings to public account are intrinsic goods to be pursued. Beginning in this way with duties, with the right rather than the good, is not a way of avoiding instrumental reasoning altogether. We cannot plausibly posit such calling to account (or retribution) as an absolute duty come what may, if only because this kind of institutional practice requires resources, and no one could plausibly claim that a polity should devote all its resources to identifying the guilty and calling them to account: so we must attend to the costs involved in discharging this duty, and also to other duties we might have which, even if they do not directly conflict with this one, at least compete with it for our limited resources. Furthermore, working out how best to discharge this duty also requires instrumental reasoning about how best to structure and organize the criminal law, which will again bring into play the various costs that criminalization involves. But appealing to duty does give us a distinctive starting point, in a principle that is responsive rather than instrumental.

Third, one familiar way to combine instrumental and non-instrumental modes of reasoning is by portraying some reasons or principles as setting 'side-constraints'. The most usual way to do this is to posit an instrumental aim that we are to pursue, but then to recognize non-instrumental, deontological or duty-based, constraints on the means we may adopt in pursuit of that end; even if a particular means would be instrumentally efficient towards the favoured end, it must be ruled out if it is inconsistent with a side-constraint. So-called mixed theories of punishment, including classically Hart's, are of this form: the justifying aim of punishment is specified instrumentally, for instance as the prevention of certain kinds of harm; but even if we could efficiently pursue that aim by punishing an innocent person, or by punishing the guilty more harshly than they can be said to deserve, we must not do so, since we must recognize non-instrumental side-constraints of justice that forbid the (knowing) punishment of

[80] It is true that it differs from some other instrumentalist views in that the good it posits is a good that is intrinsic to a certain kind of action (punishing the guilty) rather than a state of affairs (unless what is intrinsically good is said to be something like the guilty suffering): but although instrumentalist or consequentialist views are often portrayed as holding that the rightness of every action depends on its consequences, they can quite consistently hold that certain kinds of action are intrinsically good—and that other actions, and these actions themselves, are then right insofar as they increase the incidence of such intrinsically valuable actions.

the innocent and the excessive punishment of even the guilty.[81] The most obvious way to apply this structure to criminalization deliberations is to posit an instrumental aim for the enterprise, such as the prevention of harm to others, but then set a 'wrongfulness constraint' as a side-constraint on our pursuit of that goal. But we could go a different way: we could posit a non-instrumental 'justifying aim' for criminalization, subject to an instrumental side-constraint—for instance, that we have a (responsive) duty to criminalize certain kinds of wrongdoing, but should do so only if this would also have beneficial effects (or, more plausibly, should not do so if this would have seriously harmful overall effects).

One upshot of the discussion in this chapter so far is that theorists who posit 'principles' of criminalization need not only to articulate the content of the principle, or the values by which it is structured and informed, but also to make clear just what kind of principle it is (responsive or instrumental, for instance), and just what role it is supposed to play in our deliberations.

5. Types of Master Principle (4): Thick v Thin

There is one more distinction that we must draw—although it marks differences of degree, rather than of categorical kind. It is the difference between thick and thin principles.[82]

A principle is 'thick' to the extent that it has a rich descriptive content, and thus to the extent that it has a descriptive content that enables us to apply it without having to make further, and debatable, normative judgments (in particular, normative judgments of the very kind that we are trying to ground). A principle is 'thin' to the extent that it lacks such rich descriptive content, and thus to the extent that in order to apply it we must therefore make further, debatable, normative judgments (in particular, normative judgments of the very kind that we are trying to ground). An extreme, limiting case of a thin principle would thus be the principle that we ought to criminalize a type of conduct if and only if it is worth criminalizing: to apply this principle we must decide whether this type of conduct is worth criminalizing—the very kind of judgment the principle is supposed to ground. An extreme case of a thick principle would be a principle that we should criminalize a type of conduct if it is thought to be immoral by a majority of the population:[83] to apply that principle we would simply need to engage in an empirical inquiry into public opinion.

The 'moral wrong' principle is thus a thin principle:[84] it tells us that we should, or have good reason to, criminalize conduct if it is morally wrong, but does not by itself tell us anything about what is morally wrong; it leaves that as a matter for further normative judgment and argument. A 'public wrongs' principle is doubly thin, in what might seem a particularly problematic way: for it leaves for further normative discussion both the question of what is to count as wrong, and that of what is to count as 'public'. Of course the 'public' element could be a (relatively) thick aspect of

[81] See H L A Hart, 'Prolegomenon to the Principles of Punishment'; D Scheid, 'Constructing a Theory of Punishment, Desert, and the Distribution of Punishments'.

[82] Drawing on the idea of 'thick' ethical concepts: B Williams, *Ethics and the Limits of Philosophy*, ch. 8; see D Roberts, 'Thick Concepts'. I have talked before of 'formal' as against 'substantive' principles, which is clearly a cognate distinction: the language of 'thick' and 'thin' is, however, preferable, as making it clearer that this is a distinction of degree rather than of categorical kind.

[83] Compare Devlin's 'positivist' version of legal moralism: see Chapter 2, section 2 above.

[84] See Moore, 'Liberty's Constraints', at 192.

the principle if we could say that what is public is what has an adverse impact on 'the public': but if we say, as I have argued, that 'public' here means 'of proper concern to the public' (to the polity as a whole), there will then be a suspicion that in order to decide what is 'public' we must decide what we have reason to criminalize, and engage in the very kind of normative reasoning that the principle was supposed to help us find our way through.[85] By contrast, a 'sovereignty', or 'dignity', or 'non-domination',[86] principle is relatively thick, because these are relatively thick concepts: we might find normative disagreements about just how we should interpret them, and just how they should be applied in the context of criminal law; but they have far more descriptive content than such descriptively bare concepts as 'right' and 'wrong'. Harm principles are also relatively thick to the extent, but only to the extent, that we can specify what counts as 'harm' in descriptive terms: if we can say, for instance, that harm consists in a setback to interests, and can then identify 'interests' in non-moral terms, 'harm' is a thick concept, and harm principles are thick principles; but insofar as we need to make normative judgments about what constitutes an interest, or as to which interests are to count, the principle becomes thinner.[87] The key elements of Husak's constraints on criminal law are also relatively thin.[88] His four 'internal' constraints—the 'nontrivial harm or evil' constraint, the 'wrongfulness' constraint, the 'desert' constraint, the presumption against criminalization—all leave much normative work to be done in determining what is to count as a non-trivial harm or evil, and so on. Of the three 'external' constraints—the 'substantial state interest' constraint, the 'direct advancement' constraint, and 'the 'minimum necessary extent' constraint—the first is very thin, leaving open the normative question of what we should count as a 'substantial state interest'; and whilst the other two will be thicker, once the first is thickened up, their thickness depends on its thickness. The German *Rechtsgut* theory is also relatively thin,[89] in the same problematic way as a 'public wrong' principle: for even if we can identify a set of *Güter* without further normative work, as Feinbergian harm theorists might hope to identify a set of interests whose setting back constitutes harm, we must still determine which of those *Güter* are to count as *Rechtsgüter*, as *Güter* that should be protected by the law; but this requires us to make the very kinds of normative judgment that we are trying to ground.

A thin principle is not an empty principle that can do *no* serious work in our criminalization debates: even if it does not provide substantive criteria or reasons, it can show us what *kinds* of criterion or reason will be relevant (and thus which will not be relevant or appropriate), and what kinds of argument will be relevant (or irrelevant) in carrying on the debate. Given a responsive 'moral wrong' principle, for instance, we know that what is relevant is the moral wrongness or permissibility of the conduct in question, which will also determine the kinds of reason that it will then be appropriate to offer in the discussion. More generally, thin principles will specify the kind of claim for which we must argue if we are to justify criminalization, which will dictate the kinds of argument that will be relevant: thus thin principles can usefully shape, even if they cannot determine the results of, our debates about criminalization.

However, the distinction between thick(er) and thin(ner) principles does, as we will shortly see, point to the central problem for would-be master principles of

[85] See above, Chapter 2, section 6; the discussion of the public realm in Chapters 4 and 5 provided a partial answer to this objection.

[86] See at n. 36 above.

[87] See Feinberg, *Harm to Others*; also Simester and von Hirsch, *Crimes, Harms, and Wrongs*, ch. 3.

[88] Husak, *Overcriminalization*, chs 2–3.

[89] See at n. 35 above.

criminalization. For either the proposed principle will be relatively thick—in which case it can do the kind of work it is meant to do in providing substantive guidance as to what kinds of conduct we may or may not criminalize; but it will face the objection that it is seriously under-inclusive, since it will not cover some kinds of conduct that, we are sure, we do have good reason to criminalize. Or it will be relatively thin—in which case it might avoid the charge of under-inclusiveness; but it will then face objections either that it is over-inclusive, setting no helpful limits on what we may criminalize, or that it can no longer do the substantive work that it was meant to do, since that substantive work is simply shifted to the kinds of normative debate in which we need to engage to thicken the principle up. I will discuss this problem in section 8.

6. Master Principles and the 'Cheapness' of Reasons?

Before asking what kind of master principle, if any, we could plausibly hope to establish for criminalization, we should note a view that would, if right, show that it is a mistake to search for positive master principles of criminalization—for principles that would exhaustively specify the determinate factors (goals, values, considerations) that give us reason to criminalize conduct. This view, which we can call the 'reasons are cheap' view,[90] is clearly expressed by Brink: if 'a genuine moral good could be achieved ... in a way that was completely costless', that fact would give any agent 'a reason to promote the good', whether the agent 'is an individual agent or the state'. There will usually, or always, in fact be costs, which might often give us decisive reason not to try to promote that good; but that one could promote it is nonetheless always a reason to (try to) do so.[91] If we take this view of reasons for action, we will not be able to say anything principled about what positive reasons there are to criminalize any type of conduct, beyond saying, unhelpfully, that we have reason to criminalize a type of conduct just in case doing so would help us towards attaining some good: it will then be a contingent matter to determine, in different contexts, just what goods we might promote by criminalizing types of conduct.

Such a view has some striking implications. Outside the criminalization context it implies, for instance, that the fact that a good grade would bring pleasure to a student's family constitutes a reason for the examiner to award a good grade to an academically feeble essay, as does the fact that the bribe that the student offers the examiner for a good grade would enable her to make a morally productive donation to a charity. The reasons not to do so, and instead to give the essay the fail grade that accurately marks its academic quality, are no doubt overwhelmingly stronger; and such reasons are, no doubt, generally so obviously so much stronger than any reasons that normally obtain for giving an inaccurate grade that the examiner will have habituated herself (or been habituated) to attend only to the academic quality of essays in determining their grades. Indeed, when she and her colleagues discuss how they should go about determining grades, they might reasonably come to the view that they should generally attend only to the work's academic quality, to avoid being distracted by other relevant

[90] See Edwards, 'Master Principles', 142–3.

[91] D Brink, 'Retributivism and Legal Moralism', 510; quoted by Edwards, 'Master Principles', 142. Compare Dempsey's discussion of the 'normal correspondence thesis'—that 'if a person can realize a value through her action, then normally she will have a reason so to act as to realize that value' (Dempsey, *Prosecuting Domestic Violence*, 83–98); and see above, Chapter 2 at nn 152–8, and Chapter 2, section 9 more generally.

but typically weaker reasons. Nonetheless, it is true that she gives the fail grade *despite* the relevant fact that it will disappoint, or even simply that it will fail to bring pleasure to, the student's family, or despite the relevant fact that this will deprive her of the chance to make that donation. That is surely a bizarre view of the reasons that are relevant to the distinctive activity of grading.

Turning back to criminalization, it is presumably true that if we criminalized a certain type of conduct, mandated prison sentences for those convicted of such conduct, ensured that this new law was enforced with reasonable assiduity by police and prosecutors, and committed ourselves to providing and staffing new prisons to cope with the influx of new prisoners; or did so at a time of falling prison numbers, bringing with it the prospect of prison closures and the loss of jobs for prison staff: this would help to boost employment, or to prevent unemployment. These results are surely goods, which we have reason to promote: on this view we thus have reason to criminalize a randomly chosen type of conduct to promote this good. Again, we no doubt have much better reasons to do no such thing—reasons to do with the costs of such a policy, and the availability of other and less costly means of promoting employment; and no doubt the drawbacks to any such policy are so obvious that it would not in practice be considered as an option. Nonetheless, it is on this view something that we would have reason to do. But this does not merely make reasons too cheap—too readily available; it makes the irrelevant relevant. It might be argued that part of the explanation of our currently high incarceration rates is precisely that the policies that lead to them serve the interests (including the employment interests) of the 'crime control' industry:[92] but whilst that might have plausibility as a diagnostic explanation, it can have no traction as a justification (nor, of course, is it meant to have). The point is not that increasing or maintaining employment is not a good *enough* reason to adopt penal policies that will boost imprisonment; it is that this is not a reason—not a relevant or apposite reason that could carry *any* weight—at all.

This also highlights a problem with unqualified preventive versions of the harm principle. If the proper aim of criminalization policies is stated simply as the prevention of harm to others, without any qualifications as to the source or nature of such harm or the character of the conduct to be criminalized, we will find equally absurd implications. Indeed, since the loss of one's job is normally a harm, a setback to crucial interests, the prevention of increased unemployment among prison staff must constitute, on this version of the harm principle, a reason to criminalize conduct in the way suggested above. We can of course avoid this kind of implication by setting negative side-constraints on a preventive harm principle, for instance by arguing that the type of conduct to be criminalized must itself be related to the kind of harm to be prevented, as a source of such harm, or that the conduct must be wrongful (adding, that is, a negative responsive harm principle or moral wrong principle): but we must surely resist the idea that the mere prospect of preventing some harm can give us any reason to criminalize any type of conduct.

Our conclusion should be, therefore, that reasons to criminalize are not *that* cheap. When we begin to think about criminalization, we should not begin (not even when we are trying to lay the basic theoretical foundations for a theory of criminalization) by surveying the whole wide range of goods to whose realization criminalization might contribute, or the whole wide range of evils to whose prevention it might contribute, as sources of potentially good reasons to criminalize. That would be to treat criminal

[92] See famously N Christie, *Crime Control as Industry: Towards Gulags, Western Style?*.

law as a kind of neutral technique, whose character carries no implications about its proper use; but to see it in those terms would be to fail to take seriously its character as a distinctive kind of practice, whose appropriate goals are internal to it.[93]

We can argue about the proper aims of, for instance, such professions or activities as the law, or medicine, or education; but such arguments are in significant part arguments about what these professions or activities are, since at least their immediate goals are internal to them. Medicine is, and cannot but be, concerned with health and illness as aspects of well-being: this leaves plenty of room for argument about how we should understand the concepts of health and illness, and about how the practice of medicine should relate to them, as well as about the other values and principles that should guide or constrain its practice. Medicine does of course involve a range of techniques that can be used to serve a variety of ends, some of which are clearly not medical, whilst others are arguable: as Plato noted, a doctor's technical skills might equip him to be an effective murderer, but murder is not an exercise of medicine;[94] and it is a matter of controversy whether purely cosmetic surgery is a medical practice.[95] The question of whether and when to mobilize a practice can also depend on considerations extraneous to the practice: whether and when to provide medical care, at both individual and collective levels, will depend on a range of non-medical considerations (including those of cost and resource allocation). But we can ask what counts as good reason to treat, or to administer this or that kind of treatment, from within medicine, and the kinds of consideration that are then relevant are determined by a conception of what medicine is—of what it is for: not anything can now count as a good or relevant reason, but only factors that have to do with health and sickness.

We can thus expect that only some kinds of good will generate reasons for criminalization. It is not part of our role as legislators of criminal law, or as officials (or citizens) whose role it is to administer and apply the law, to ask in general terms 'what good can we do?'—any more than it is appropriate for a doctor deciding what medical treatment to offer, or for an examiner deciding what grade to award, to ask in general terms what goods she could achieve: not because only a limited range of prospective goods is, as a matter of practical fact, likely to generate sufficiently strong reasons for action, but because her role as a doctor or an examiner determines what goods or reasons are relevant. So too with the criminal law: our understanding of the kind of practice it is (which includes our understanding of its role in a polity) will determine its proper aims; and these will determine what can count as a good reason to criminalize. Such reasons might, as we will see, be *quite* cheap; but they will not be as cheap as some have supposed. In particular, if the account developed in previous chapters is viable, we can say that criminal law is concerned with civil order, and with kinds of wrong that impinge on that order (just as we can say that medicine is concerned with health, and with kinds of illness, disease, and injury that impinge on health). That leaves open a range of questions about how we should understand civil order in the context of our polity; about just how criminal law is to relate to it (how it can help to constitute it, and how it can help to sustain it); and about the kinds of wrong that should count as

[93] See above, Chapter 2, section 9.

[94] Plato, Republic, I, 333e. This does not rule out euthanasia as a medical exercise, even if it involves administering a fatal drug, since that would (if legitimate) not count as 'poisoning', and would be done for the patient's benefit: whether euthanasia can count as proper exercise of medical craft (Platonic *techne*) is one familiar controversy within medicine about its proper aims.

[95] Which is why it is only available on the National Health Service if it is necessary for health-related reasons: see www.nhs.uk/Conditions/cosmetic-treatments-guide/Pages/is-cosmetic-surgery-available-on-the-NHS.aspx.

public, and thus in principle criminalizable, wrongs in virtue of their adverse relationship to that order: but it does limit the kinds of reason that could count as reasons to criminalize, and the kinds of argument that could lead us towards the conclusion that we should criminalize a particular kind of conduct.

To say that criminal law is concerned with civil order, and with kinds of wrong that impinge on that order, is not to rule out all the various master principles that theorists have suggested: rather, it is to say that if they are to be candidate master principles of criminalization, they must be grounded in a particular conception of civil order and in an account of the kinds of wrong that impinge on that order. Even when a theorist does not do this explicitly,[96] we can reconstruct a conception of civil order from which their favoured principle could emerge. A dignity principle, for instance, could be grounded in a claim that dignity is or should be the (or a) defining value of the polity's civil order, and that conduct thus constitutes a public wrong if it violates or threatens dignity;[97] a harm principle, by contrast, implies a conception of civil order as being essentially concerned with the prevention or avoidance of harm, and thus of public wrongs as consisting in conduct that wrongfully causes or threatens harm. As we noted earlier,[98] even a Moorean legal moralism can be expressed in terms of the maintenance of civil order, by claiming that attaining retributive justice is or should be a central element of the polity's civil order, so that every kind of moral wrongdoing amounts to a public wrong. How far any such principles are plausible, as master principles of criminalization, when set within such a framework remains to be seen: that will be the topic of section 8. The point here is simply that while a claim that criminal law is concerned with civil order, and with wrongs that count as public in relation to that order, limits the kinds of reason that could count as good reasons to criminalize, those limits do not rule out, in advance, any of a wide range of possible master principles of criminalization.

7. What Kind of Master Principle?

As with any practical endeavour, our deliberative life would be easier if we could appeal to a (set of) master principle(s) to guide us. In the case of criminalization, we cannot plausibly hope that a simple set of principles would take us all the way to a final decision about what we should criminalize, if only because issues about practicalities and the allocation of scarce resources will arise between principle and practice: we might hope, however, to find such principles at the first stage of our deliberations, when we ask what we have good reason, in principle, to criminalize (or not to criminalize). I will argue in the following section that such hopes are doomed to disappointment; but a preliminary task is to get clearer about what kind of principle could fulfil them.

Master principles, as we saw in section 1, must be foundational (as principles of criminalization), exhaustive, and exclusive: they must specify all the considerations

[96] As some indeed do: for just one example, see Pettit's account of criminal law in 'Criminalization in Republican Theory' (see also Pettit, *On the People's Terms*; Braithwaite and Pettit, *Not Just Deserts*).

[97] See Polish Constitution, Art. 30; German *Grundgesetz*, Article 1(1); above, Chapter 4 at nn 50–6 (though dignity in these constitutions is one among other basic values; it is not a master principle). The 'is or should be' in this sentence should remind us that our concern here is with normative claims about how a polity should conceive its civil order, not with descriptive claims about how it does conceive it.

[98] See above, Chapter 2 at nn 175–8, Chapter 5 at n. 9 (though I suggested that a Moorean legal moralism looks implausible when framed in this way, as implying an implausible conception of civil order).

or criteria that should bear on the initial question of what kinds of conduct we can have good reason to criminalize. As we saw in the previous four sections, they might be of various kinds: positive or negative; responsive or preventive; *pro tanto* or categorical; and thick(er) or thin(ner). The task now is to determine what kind of principle a master principle will need to be if it is to be both plausible and useful.

First, a master principle that is to guide our decisions about what to criminalize must be, or include, a positive principle, specifying what can count as a good reason to criminalize. It might also include negative conditions. These might be side-constraints on the reasons to criminalize (we have reason to criminalize a type of conduct if by doing so we can efficiently prevent harm to others, on condition that the conduct is wrongful; or we have reason to criminalize a type of conduct if it is morally wrongful, on condition that by doing so we can reduce the incidence of such conduct); or they could set 'positive constraints',[99] by holding that we have good reason to criminalize a type of conduct if and only if the specified condition is satisfied (if and only if it is morally wrong; if and only if by criminalizing it we can prevent harm to others). But a principle that is to guide decisions about what to criminalize must tell us not merely what gives us reason (perhaps conclusive reason) not to criminalize, but what can give us good reason *to* criminalize.

It is worth noting that once we connect criminalization to the maintenance of civil order, and bear in mind that such maintenance can be constitutive as well as instrumental,[100] we can identify a further kind of negative principle—one that concerns not (directly) the character of the conduct that is (not) to be criminalized, or the further effects of criminalizing it, but the implications of the criminalization itself. For instance, if dignity is one of the defining, constitutional, values of the polity,[101] and so central to its civil order, we will have reason not only to criminalize conduct that violates dignity,[102] but also to reject proposed criminal statutes that would themselves violate the dignity of citizens;[103] so too, if rights to liberty, or to privacy, have a constitutional status as defining elements of the civil order, we will have reason to reject criminal legislation that itself violates such rights.[104] That reason might not be conclusive: it might be possible to argue that the right can legitimately be infringed for the sake of some important civil end; but it still creates a presumption against criminalization that must be defeated by stronger reasons, of an appropriate kind, in favour of criminalization. Thus Article 8 of the European Convention on Human Rights declares 'the right to respect for [one's] ... private and family life'; but it allows that that right may be 'interfere[d]' with by a 'public authority' if this 'is necessary in a democratic society in the interests of national security, public safety or the economic well-being of the country, for the prevention of disorder or crime, for the protection of health or morals or for the protection of the rights and freedoms of others'.[105]

[99] See above, Chapter 2 at nn 21–2. [100] See above, Chapter 5, sections 4–6.

[101] See at n. 97 above.

[102] See e.g. T Hörnle, 'Criminalizing Behaviour to Protect Human Dignity'; T Hörnle and M Kremnitzer, 'Human Dignity as a Protected Interest in Criminal Law'; and below, Chapter 7 at nn 119–25.

[103] See M Gur-Arye and T Weigend, 'Constitutional Review of Criminal Prohibitions Affecting Human Dignity and Liberty: German and Israeli Perspectives'.

[104] See e.g. *Lawrence v Texas* 539 US 558 (2003), *Dudgeon v UK* (1982) 4 EHRR 149, on the criminalization of homosexual activity; *Stübing v Germany* (43547/08) 55 EHRR 24 (2012), on the criminalization of adult incest (see T Hörnle, 'Consensual Adult Incest: A Sex Offense?').

[105] See *Stübing v Germany*; and above, Chapter 4 at n. 97. By contrast, the rights against being tortured or enslaved declared by Articles 3 and 4 of the Convention cannot be legitimately infringed.

This serves both to set a constraint (albeit not an absolute one) on governmental action, including criminalization, and to specify the only kinds of reason that can count as good reasons to breach that constraint. Such constraints as these are general principles of legitimate governmental action rather than principles of *criminalization*: but they help to determine the limits of the criminal law, and the kinds of consideration that can justify varying those limits.

Second, a plausible master principle will have both responsive and preventive dimensions. It might be primarily preventive: what gives us good reason to criminalize a type of conduct is that by doing so we can efficiently reduce the incidence of some mischief. However, as we have seen in relation to preventive versions of the harm principle, an unconstrained preventive principle of this kind is not plausible as a principle of *criminalization*. The simple reason for this is that to criminalize a type of conduct is to portray, and condemn, it as wrongful: but the mere fact that it is of a kind whose criminalization would help to prevent some mischief cannot make it wrong; nor can criminalizing it make it wrong.[106] That is why even a prevention-oriented principle must at least include a wrongfulness constraint: we have preventive reason to criminalize a type of conduct on condition that it itself is wrongful. Even that does not go far enough, however: we need to show that there is some 'nexus' between the conduct, *qua* wrongful, and the mischief that we seek to prevent.[107] For instance, it is an offence under English law to drive without insurance, and we can see why such conduct is normally wrongful: it violates a regulation that aims to make sure that those whose faulty driving causes harm can have the cost of such harm covered.[108] It is a distinct and more serious offence to cause death by driving when uninsured,[109] but this is unwarranted: there is no normative nexus between the wrong of driving without insurance and the causation of death. There is such a nexus between driving dangerously and causing death, since such driving increases the risk of causing death;[110] but lacking insurance does not make one's driving more likely to cause death. It is therefore not sufficient that the conduct to be criminalized is in some way wrong: it must be wrong in virtue of its relationship to the mischief that we aim to prevent, or the value that we are trying to protect. That is why it is plausible for Pettit, who advocates a 'broadly goal-centred way of thinking about criminalization and criminal justice',[111] to argue (via a 'presumption of parsimony') that we should 'limit[] criminalization to acts of interference in people's basic liberties which ... are incapable of being effectively restricted in the absence of criminal penalty and condemnation'.[112] Whilst the central aim of criminal law is on this account preventive, it must be focused on conduct that is itself wrongful in a way connected to the value (republican freedom) that is to be protected. That relationship can, as we will see, be of various kinds,[113] and one question for a preventive theorist is how close it needs to be, or how remote it can be, if it is to give us good reason to criminalize; but some such relationship is necessary.

Master principles might instead be primarily responsive: we have good reason to criminalize a type of conduct if and because, for instance, it constitutes a kind of wrongdoing that deserves retributive punishment, or that makes a formal public response appropriate. But, quite apart from the fact that criminalization itself has an

[106] See above, Chapter 2, section 4, on strong and weak versions of the wrongness constraint.
[107] See at n. 47 above. [108] See Road Traffic Act 1988, s. 143.
[109] Road Safety Act 2006, s. 21. [110] See Road Traffic Act 1988, s. 1.
[111] P Pettit, 'Criminalization in Republican Theory', 147. [112] Ibid., 143.
[113] Thus Pettit, for instance, notes that 'candidates for criminalization' might include not only 'acts of interference in people's basic liberties' but 'secondary acts that facilitate or probabilify criminalized acts of interference, or that jeopardize the system for protecting against such acts' (ibid., 143 and 144).

intrinsic preventive dimension, it would be odd to pay no attention to the likely effects of criminalization on the incidence of such wrongdoing.[114] Rather more precisely, for a retributivist such as Moore, the basic principle of criminalization is purely responsive: our reason to criminalize a type of conduct is simply that it deserves the punishment that criminalization makes possible. Consideration of the preventive or other benefits that might flow from criminalization becomes relevant only at the next stage of deliberation, when we ask whether we should all things considered criminalize the kinds of conduct that we thus have good reason to criminalize, and must attend inter alia to the costs and the benefits of doing so.[115] An account that grounds criminal law in civil order in the way that I suggested in Chapter 5, by contrast, does still give it an essentially responsive character: this is an appropriate way for a polity to respond to wrongful violations of its civil order; and once we have a system of criminal law in place, we might think it necessary to criminalize certain egregious kinds of wrong just because they merit or require such a response—just because their perpetrators should be called to public, censorial account. But the enterprise of criminal law is also essentially preventive, or perhaps we should now say persuasive: by responding in this way to public wrongdoing (by defining it as criminal, by calling to account and punishing those who commit such wrongs), it aims in part to dissuade us from such conduct. Such dissuasion must, however, itself reflect the values that define the civil order; it must treat the citizens with the respect due to them as responsible members of the polity. That is why, on this view, it would be misleading to say that the aim of criminalization is prevention, even if we then set side-constraints on the means by which we may pursue that end: that would imply that illegitimate means, such as the criminalization of non-wrongful conduct, might be effective means to our end, although they are ruled out by the negative legal moralist's side-constraint. We should rather say that the end itself, as an end appropriate to a republican polity whose members are to respect each other as responsible citizens, is respectful dissuasion from public wrongdoing, rather than merely prevention.[116]

Third, a master principle of criminalization might plausibly include a categorical element: it might, for instance, categorically rule out the criminalization of non-wrongful conduct.[117] But its positive elements, specifying what could give us reason to criminalize, will not plausibly be thus categorical. They might specify simply *pro tanto* reasons: the consideration they specify (that the conduct in question constitutes a public wrong, or violates dignity or freedom) gives us reason to criminalize it; but that reason could be outweighed by other reasons against criminalizing it. Or they might specify demands or requirements, for instance that justice 'requires that … all moral wrongs be prohibited by the criminal law' so that wrongdoers can 'receive their just deserts':[118] but such demands or requirements are defeasible. Even if we believe that some wrongs must be criminalized (if we have a system of criminal law at all),[119] it would not be plausible to believe this of all wrongs that we have good reason to criminalize,

[114] Compare Chiao's critique of what he calls the 'purely remedial thesis': *Criminal Law in the Age of the Administrative State*, ch. 7.4. See also at nn 41–7 above.

[115] See at nn 38–9 above.

[116] On this kind of account, which connects ends and means normatively, rather than merely empirically, see Duff, *Punishment, Communication, and Community*, 80–2.

[117] Which would be to say that so long as we are engaged in the enterprise of criminal law, we may not criminalize non-wrongful conduct. This leaves open the possibility that an emergency might force us to abandon or pervert that practice and 'criminalize' some type of non-wrongful conduct: see at n. 73 above.

[118] Moore, 'Liberty's Constraints', 191; see at nn 75–7 above.

[119] See at nn 43, 74 above.

or that we justifiably criminalize: it might be true of the most egregious wrongs (what kind of system of criminal law would fail to criminalize such wrongs as murder and rape?); but a master principle must cover all the kinds of wrong that are criminalizable, most of which are surely not such that they *must* be criminalized. We might think that, once a system of criminal law is in place, we must criminalize murder, but we could not plausibly think this of recklessly damaging another's property: it would not follow from this that we could not be justified in criminalizing such damage.

As we will see in Chapter 7, the claim about *pro tanto* reasons to criminalize that plausible master principles make will require qualification. It will not be enough to say that we have good reason to criminalize conduct that satisfies the specified criterion (for instance, that constitutes a public wrong): we must also ask whether we have good reason to criminalize such conduct *rather than* responding to it in some other way; for criminalization is just one among other possible public responses to such conduct. Preventive theorists can recognize a version of this point by building a qualification into their principle: thus Feinberg's preventive 'liberty-limiting principles' are cast in terms of there being good reason to criminalize if doing so would effectively prevent the specified kind of evil, 'and there is probably no other means that is equally effective at no greater cost to other values'.[120] A responsive principle cannot take that form; but it will need to build in some condition to the effect that criminalization is at least as appropriate a response as any other way of responding to the kind of conduct in question—however 'appropriate' is then specified.

The remaining distinction discussed earlier is that between thick(er) and thin(ner) principles of criminalization, to which we must now turn.

8. Thick or Thin Master Principles?

I have already offered a master principle: we have reason to criminalize a type of conduct if, and only if, it constitutes a public wrong, and a type of conduct constitutes a public wrong if, and only if, it violates the polity's civil order. So I am not going to argue that no master principle can be plausible. I will argue, however, that only a thin master principle will be plausible, and that therefore master principles cannot offer us much substantive guidance in our deliberations about criminalization: for only thick principles can offer such guidance.

The thinness of a principle radically undercuts its substantive utility if its descriptive content is so minimal that, in order to apply it, we must not only make further, and debatable, normative judgments, but must make normative judgments of the very kind about which we are deliberating—about whether a kind of conduct merits criminalization.[121] The principle that we have reason to criminalize public wrongs is thus radically thin, even when it is added that a wrong counts as 'public' if it violates the polity's civil order: for it offers us no substantive criteria by which to determine either what counts as 'public' or what should count as a wrong in that realm. Moore's 'moral wrong' principle,[122] by contrast, is formally thin, since to apply it we need to determine what kinds of conduct are morally wrong; but that thinness does not undermine its substantive utility in criminalization deliberations if we can hope to make determinate judgments about what kinds of conduct are morally wrong in advance of such deliberations.

[120] Feinberg, *Harm to Others*, 26; see Edwards, 'An Instrumental Legal Moralism', at n. 10.
[121] See at nn 83–5 above. [122] See Moore, 'Liberty's Constraints', at 192; n. 39 above.

The problem of radical thinness can also be illustrated by looking at another possible master principle, recently advocated by Wellman: that we have good reason to criminalize all and only those types of conduct that violate others' rights.[123] One problem is that we then need an account of what rights people have; there is an obvious worry that in trying to decide what rights we have we will in effect be asking what kinds of conduct are wrong in a way, or to a degree, that gives us reason to criminalize them.[124] Another problem is that of verbs: should we criminalize a type of conduct only if it violates a right (which is Wellman's view); or should we also criminalize conduct that might violate a right, or that enables, or facilitates, or encourages, or prepares for right-violations? Another problem is that even if we can (given a suitable account of rights, both individual and collective) show how the familiar kinds of *malum in se* crime do violate rights, it will be harder to explain *mala prohibita* in those terms, in particular those laws that criminalize conduct in order to assist the smooth running of state institutions: even if those institutions aim ultimately to protect people's rights, it is problematic to portray conduct that might undermine their operations, or that violates the regulations that govern their operations, as itself violating rights. One answer might be that we should shift such *mala prohibita* out of the criminal law into a separate, non-criminal category of *Ordnungswidrigkeiten*:[125] we would need then to ask what role we should allow to this kind of regulatory system—a point to which I will return in Chapter 7. Wellman's answer is that when laws creating *mala prohibita* are justified, those who break such laws do violate rights, 'because one's fellow citizens have a right that one obey the just laws of a legitimate state'.[126] This answer is appealing for someone who holds, as Wellman does, that only rights-violating conduct can be justifiably criminalized (since he justifies criminal punishment in terms of the offender's forfeiture of his rights, and one can, he argues, forfeit one's own rights only by violating another's right):[127] but it shows that a rights-violation theory of criminalization is not significantly thicker than a theory based on the idea of public wrongs, since it leaves the substantive normative work to be done in working out which kinds of conduct should be seen as violating rights, and what kinds of law have any such claim on our obedience. This is not an argument against such a theory: the point here is simply that a thin master principle cannot by itself do much substantive work in determining the proper scope and limits of the criminal law.

I will turn shortly to two other well-known candidate master principles: the harm principle, and the German '*Rechtsgut*' principle (the purpose of the criminal law is to protect *Rechtsgüter*—legally recognized and protected goods). First, however, we should look briefly at some thick candidate principles, which might be expected to do substantive work in guiding criminalization deliberations. There is no lack of such principles: recent literature offers, for instance, a principle of sovereignty or neo-Kantian

123 See C H Wellman, *Rights Forfeiture and Punishment*, especially chs 4, 7.

124 Compare J S Mill, *Utilitarianism*, ch. 5, para. 14: 'It is a part of the notion of Duty in every one of its forms, that a person may rightfully be compelled to fulfil it. Duty is a thing which may be exacted from a person, as one exacts a debt'. Analogously, there is a danger that we will, in the effort to provide a plausible principle of criminalization, end up in effect defining a right as an interest whose violation merits criminalization.

125 See above, Chapter 1 at nn 23–9; and see e.g. Pettit, 'Criminalization in Republican Theory', 144. See also T Hörnle, 'Theories of Criminalization', 309–10. (Hörnle argues that the 'rights of others' form 'the most important class of objects' to be protected by criminal law, but that this does not exhaust the scope of the criminal law, which must also protect '*genuine collective* interests' that cannot be reduced to individual rights: ibid., 304.)

126 *Rights Forfeiture and Punishment*, 11: he develops this argument in detail in ch. 7.

127 See 'The Rights Forfeiture Theory of Punishment'; *Rights Forfeiture and Punishment*, ch. 1.

freedom; a principle of republican freedom as non-domination; a dignity principle; a principle of autonomy.[128] Each of these offers *a* principle of criminalization, specifying *a* reason for criminalization: but is any of them plausible as a *master* principle?

To pursue this question in detail, we would need to ask further questions about how they are meant to operate. They are offered as positive rather than merely negative principles—as sources of reasons or duties to criminalize: but are they to be understood as responsive, or as preventive, or as responsive-preventive? Are we to say, for instance, that we have good reason to criminalize conduct if and only if that conduct itself impinges in the appropriate way on the master value; or if and only if we can hope by criminalizing it to protect or promote that master value; or if and only if the conduct impinges on the master value *and* criminalizing it will protect or promote that value? Second, what are the appropriate verbs here? If we are to talk in responsive mode, is our concern with conduct that *attacks* the master value; or conduct that *violates* it (if that is distinct from attacking); or conduct that somehow *harms* or *damages* it? If we talk in preventive mode, is it only the prevention of such impacts on the master value that gives us reason to criminalize; or (if this is a wider notion) the protection of the master value or its instantiations; or, rather more ambitiously, the fostering of the master value?[129] Third, what distance can there be between the conduct to be criminalized and the master value that is to be protected? If we talk in responsive mode, do we have reason to criminalize only conduct that directly and immediately (however those notions are to be understood) impinges on the master value? Or do we also have reason to criminalize conduct that is more remotely connected to the value: conduct, for instance, that is intended to injure or violate it, or that endangers it or comes close to injuring or violating it, or that enables others to violate it? If we talk in preventive mode, are we supposed to have reason to criminalize a type of conduct just so long as doing so can be expected to contribute efficiently to the protection or promotion of the master value; or only when doing so would have some more direct bearing on the protection or promotion of that value?

I do not mean to suggest that these questions will baffle advocates of master values such as these: only that they must be answered if we are to see what kinds of principle of criminalization such values might generate. However, as we explore possible answers to these questions, we will also see the main problem that faces such principles as candidate master principles.

The problem is familiar. If we say, for instance, that the criminal law should serve to protect 'dignity', whether we put this in responsive or in preventive terms, we face a familiar dilemma. On the one hand, we can try to give 'dignity' a reasonably determinate meaning, and to specify in equally determinate terms the kind of relationship between a type of conduct and dignity as thus defined that gives us good reason to criminalize that type of conduct—a specification both of the relevant verb, and of the relevant distance between the conduct and dignity. This will then provoke the objection that the principle, if proposed as an exclusive principle that only conduct thus related to dignity may be criminalized, is under-inclusive: there are types of conduct that we surely have

[128] See n. 36 above. On Ripstein's account, see E Yankah, 'Crime, Freedom and Civic Bonds'; on Brudner, see S Garvey, 'Review Article: A Hegelian Criminal Law'.

[129] Verbs do matter here: whether we talk, for instance, of 'defending' dignity (Dan-Cohen, 'Defending Dignity', 150); or of 'secur[ing] for all of us the conditions of freedom as independence' (Thorburn, 'Constitutionalism and the Limits of the Criminal Law', 98); or of 'the maximization' of dominion (Braithwaite and Pettit, *Not Just Deserts*, 54); or of 'violations of equal freedom' as the only 'legitimate basis for criminalization' (Ripstein, 'Beyond the Harm Principle', 216) will make a difference to how the principle is to operate.

reason to criminalize (conduct that is currently criminal and whose criminalization seems unproblematic), but that cannot be shown to be justifiably criminalized by this principle. In response to such examples, a dignity theorist could bite the bullet, and argue that the criminal law's scope should be narrowed to exclude these types of conduct: but that strategy is unlikely to persuade, since such counter-examples seem to tell quite convincingly against the claim that this is the only value that bears directly on criminalization. If instead we accept the counter-examples as sound, we might seek to accommodate them by refining the principle: perhaps by expanding the meaning, and thus the extension, of 'dignity'; or by adding new verbs, so that the kinds of relationship between conduct and dignity that could ground criminalization are extended; or by allowing more distant kinds of connection between conduct and dignity to ground good reasons to criminalize. Then, however, we face the opposite objection: that by thus thinning the principle we make it radically over-inclusive, or too vague and indeterminate to do any real work;[130] that it begins to look as if we first decide what kind of conduct we have reason to criminalize, and then look for some way to connect that to dignity—in which case the principle is doing no substantive work in guiding criminalization deliberations, as distinct from providing a way of expressing the conclusions of such deliberations.[131]

I will not pursue this line of criticism, or the responses available to advocates of such master principles, here, since I think that the real problem for would-be unitary, single-principle theories of this kind lies deeper: why should we think that an institution as complex as the criminal law, in a contemporary, pluralist polity, should exist to serve just one single, substantive value? If we begin with a political theory of the state, or of a polity's common good, that posits just one such value as the aim of all state activity, it will of course follow that the criminal law must also serve, and be theorized in terms of, that one value. Or if we begin with a broader monolithic theory of value, it will of course follow that all political activity, state actions, and criminal law must also serve that one true value. I will not debate those issues here, but the prima facie implausibility of a claim that we can capture all value, or all value that should concern a polity and its civic life, in a single substantive concept places the argumentative onus firmly on anyone who advocates such a view. I will try to show in the following chapter that a plausible account of the kinds of reason we can have to criminalize different types of conduct will appeal to a range of different values, and I will not pursue the further question of whether we could ultimately derive all these values from, or show them to be aspects of, some single master value: they have a formal unity in that they are all aspects or elements of the polity's civil order, and need (in order to do their work in guiding decisions about criminalization) have no deep substantive unity. I am by temperament a pluralist rather than a monist: but this is not the place to pursue the arguments against monistic theories of morality, or of politics. From a pluralist perspective, such values as freedom, dignity, and autonomy can play non-exclusive roles,

[130] Compare this comment on the wording of Article 1 of the Universal Declaration of Human Rights ('All human beings are born free and equal in dignity and rights'): 'the world community chose dignity . . . precisely because the term was open enough to hedge controversial judgments between different cultural values' (N Rao, 'Three Concepts of Dignity in Constitutional Law', 185 n. 6).

[131] See Duff, *Answering for Crime*, ch. 6; Duff et al, 'Introduction', 43–52. Edwards shows (in 'Master Principles') that these critical discussions were over-simplified, since they failed to do justice to the various different forms that master principles can take; the discussion in this section should correct that failing, whilst leaving intact (although more precisely articulated) the central objection to thick master principles.

as sources of good reasons to criminalize; but they cannot play the exclusive role that a master principle needs to play.

A principle of criminalization that appeals to civil order does not face the kind of objection faced by thick, substantive would-be master principles: its formal character makes it possible to identify a range of diverse substantive values as providing reasons to criminalize. This advantage is also its main drawback: that it seems to offer no substantive guidance for deliberations about criminalization. Two other familiar principles, the harm principle (or one of the harm principles) and the *Rechtsgut* principle, might seem to retain this advantage whilst avoiding this drawback: for they seem to appeal to relatively thick concepts, of harm or of *Rechtsgut*; but those concepts can capture a range of more concrete substantive values. If, for instance, we define harm in terms of setbacks to interests, we can recognize a diversity of interests, reflecting a diversity of goods; similarly, a *Rechtsgut* theory can recognize a diversity of concrete goods as *Rechtsgüter*. These theories, however, face a familiar kind of problem.[132]

Focusing initially on the harm principle, we might begin with a relatively narrow, and thick, principle: one that takes harmful conduct as its (responsive) object, or at least requires, as a side-constraint, that the conduct to be criminalized for the sake of harm-prevention be harmful; and that provides a reasonably determinate account of harm, for instance a Feinbergian analysis in terms of setbacks to neutrally identifiable interests.[133] For by now familiar reasons, it should also include a wrongfulness constraint: the conduct to be criminalized must be wrongful, and in a way that connects it to the harm that criminalization is intended to prevent.[134] In one way, however, a plausible harm principle cannot be as narrow as the requirement that the criminalized conduct be 'harmful' might imply: for it should surely allow the criminalization not only of conduct that actually causes harm, but also of conduct that creates a risk of harm, or makes the occurrence of harm more likely. The principle should be extended in this way whether our focus is responsive or preventive: if we have reason to criminalize conduct that actually harms an interest, we surely also have the same kind of reason to criminalize conduct that endangers that interest; if our aim is to prevent future harm, we likewise have good reason to criminalize, and so reduce the incidence of, conduct that creates a risk of such harm. A modest extension of this kind could be made by arguing that conduct can be 'harmful' even if it does not actually cause harm, if it is a matter of chance whether harm actually ensues;[135] or by arguing that being exposed to a risk of harm is itself a harm.[136] Such arguments seem unnecessary, however: it is simpler to say that on any plausible version of the harm principle we have good reason to criminalize conduct that causes or threatens to cause harm.[137] We will need to ask shortly whether we should extend the reach of the principle even further than this, to capture kinds of conduct that neither cause nor directly threaten harm,

[132] The literature on both theories is vast. For general discussions, see J Stanton-Ife, 'The Limits of Law', 'What is the Harm Principle For?'; R Hefendehl et al (eds), *Die Rechtsgutstheorie: Legitimationsbasis des Strafrechts oder dogmatisches Glasperlenspiel?*; Ambos, 'The Overall Function of International Criminal Law'.

[133] Feinberg, *Harm to Others*, chs 1–3; on harm see also Simester and von Hirsch, *Crimes, Harms, and Wrongs*, ch. 3; Tadros, *Wrongs and Crimes*, ch. 10.

[134] See at n. 47 above.

[135] See H Gross, *A Theory of Criminal Justice*, 428–36.

[136] See e.g. C Finkelstein, 'Is Risk a Harm?'; J Oberdiek, *Imposing Risk: A Normative Framework*, esp. ch. 3.

[137] Compare the Model Penal Code's specification of the 'purposes' of the special part of the criminal law—'to forbid and prevent conduct that unjustifiably and inexcusably inflicts or threatens substantial harm to individual or public interests' (§ 1.02(1)(a)).

but that in less direct ways make the occurrence of harm more likely, or its prevention more difficult.

If harm is defined in terms of setbacks to interests, we might wonder whether we really have reason to criminalize a type of conduct just so long as it wrongfully sets back *some* interest (and if doing so will prevent future setbacks): or should we set limits on the kinds of interest that the criminal law should protect?[138] We must ask too why this is a task for criminal law: even given that the polity should protect its members' interests, why is this (the creation and use of criminal law) an appropriate method of doing so?[139] However, the most familiar initial objection to harm principles appears if we make them exclusive, insisting that we may criminalize conduct *only* if it is harmful (and/or *only* if doing so will prevent harm). Many theorists do this,[140] but they must then deal with some familiar counter-examples, of kinds of apparently non-harmful conduct that we surely have good reason to criminalize.

Purported counter-examples of this kind include conduct that is deeply offensive but cannot plausibly be described as harmful;[141] coercive paternalistic conduct that infringes the autonomy of the person coerced precisely in order to prevent him harming himself;[142] conduct that violates the rights of others without causing harm;[143] the kind of 'free-floating evil' (as Feinberg calls it) that is exemplified by commercial gladiatorial combat to the death;[144] and such specific wrongs as the desecration of corpses.[145] Another potentially enormous set of apparent counter-examples includes all

[138] See e.g. Feinberg, *Harm to Others*, 37–8, on 'welfare' as against 'ulterior' interests; and Simester and Hirsch, *Crimes, Harms and Wrongs*, on 'resources'. See also Alexander and Ferzan, *Crime and Culpability*, 269–77: if crime consists (as they argue) in recklessly creating unjustified risks to legally protected interests, 'the criminal law must identify those interests that it will protect'—although they do not themselves identify those interests completely or in detail. A further question is whether only human interests are to be protected; or should the law also protect the interests of non-human animals?

[139] It is worth recalling again that Mill did not take his harm principle to be a principle of criminalization, since it was concerned with the exercise of any kind of legal or political 'power' over citizens (see at n. 5 above, and at nn 64–5 above on the harm prevention principle).

[140] Not Feinberg himself (see n. 6 above), but see e.g. Simester and Hirsch, *Crimes, Harms and Wrongs*, ch. 7: although they argue for an Offence Principle along with the Harm Principle, they also think that only harmful offence should be criminal. See also Persak, *Criminalising Harmful Conduct*; Husak, 'Polygamy', 220.

[141] Hence the addition of the Offence Principle to the Harm Principle: see J Feinberg, *Offense to Others*.

[142] See Feinberg, *Harm to Others*, 78; *Harm to Self*, chs. 18–19.

[143] E.g. Ripstein, 'Beyond the Harm Principle'; Gardner and Shute, 'The Wrongness of Rape'—though they also argue that we must criminalize because not to do so would be harmful (see at n. 34 above); H Stewart, 'The Limits of the Harm Principle'. We could also consider the case of the surgeon who burned his initials onto the livers of two of his patients during transplant operations: this caused no pain, and no damage to the livers' functioning, but he was convicted of assault; https://www.theguardian.com/uk-news/2018/jan/12/surgeon-burned-initials-livers-two-patients-fined-simon-bramhall-assault-transplant.

[144] See Feinberg, *Harmless Wrongdoing*, 318–38; Duff, *Answering for Crime*, 128–35. The gladiatorial combat to the death does cause harm to the participants in any ordinary sense of the word, but not Feinbergian harm: for Feinbergian harm must be a wrongful setback to interests (*Harm to Others*, ch. 3), and given his commitment to the '*volenti non fit iniuria*' doctrine (*Harm to Others*, 115–17), harms to which I consent cannot wrong me.

[145] See e.g. D Scoccia, 'In Defense of "Pure" Legal Moralism'; Moore, *Placing Blame*, 646. Moore also mentions cruelty to animals, which is certainly problematic for any proponent of a harm principle who thinks that such cruelty should be criminal, and that the harm required for criminalization must be harm to other people, since it seems perverse to argue that cruelty to animals should be criminalized only because of the harm that it (or the dispositions of those who commit it) might cause to other human beings; the obvious way to avoid this problem is to argue that harm to any sentient being is relevant as a possible basis for criminalization.

the criminal laws dealing with 'regulatory' offences or *mala prohibita* that could be justified by a preventive version of a harm principle, but that criminalize types of conduct many of whose tokens are not actually harmful: for we can in many contexts prevent harm by creating strict regulations, for instance to do with driving, or with health and safety at work, that prohibit conduct that is often but not always harmful.[146] We must also attend to cases in which no harm to identifiable individual interests seems to be in the offing: are we to talk of collective interests, and of criminalizable harms that set such interests back; or could we reduce collective interests to collections of individual interests?[147]

Advocates of a harm principle need not be silenced by such counter-examples. They can, in some cases, argue that the conduct in question should not be criminal, because it is not harmful: but it is hard to deny that we have reason to criminalize at least some of these types of conduct. They might deal with other cases by extending or refining the concept of harm, in particular by recognizing harms that cannot be identified independently of the wrongful actions that cause them,[148] or interests that must be identified in normative terms: we could say, for instance, that I am harmed if my dignity is violated, even if no setback to any other interests can be identified, since I have an interest in dignity—in being treated with due respect. This would make it easier (for better or worse) to explain why we have reason to criminalize 'hate speech', for instance, or certain kinds of pornography: we need not rely on empirical claims about the harmful effects of such things, but can appeal to their inherently insulting or degrading character.[149] But this kind of move undermines the harm principle as a monolithic, exclusionary principle of criminalization: it now seems that I am harmed simply in virtue of being wronged; but while that might be, in the abstract, a plausible expansion of the idea of harm as a setback to interests (for we have surely an interest in not being wronged or insulted), the identification of such harms now depends on the prior identification of those wrongs—in which case the harm principle is radically thinned, since it now depends for its application on prior determinations of what counts as a wrong; and we have no reason to believe that wrongs, or even all wrongs committed against persons, can be captured by a unitary principle. It also threatens to expand substantially the potential scope of the criminal law, or of what can count as a reason to criminalize: it seems, for instance, plausible to say that I wrong another person if I make her the subject of my sadistic sexual fantasies, even if this has no impact on my overt conduct towards her; on this moralized account of harm I therefore harm her; and we thus have reason to criminalize such conduct. If a harm theorist allows such moralized harms into the picture, she seems to incorporate an expansive positive legal moralism into the harm principle; but then the principle loses the advantage over legal moralism that its advocates often claim for it—that it more effectively constrains the scope of a liberal criminal law.[150]

[146] See at nn 54–65 above; and below, Chapter 7, section 5.

[147] For useful discussion of collective interests, and further references, see P Jones, 'Group Rights', s. 5.

[148] Which they anyway need to do if they are to do justice to the way in which rape, for instance, is harmful: see Feinberg, *Harm to Self*, 298.

[149] On hate speech, see J Waldron, *The Harm in Hate Speech*.

[150] Note that this is not to appeal to the kind of 'moral harm' that Feinberg considers, and rejects (*Harm to Others*, 65–70). Feinberg's concern is with whether being made morally worse can count as harm, if it does not set back any of the person's 'want-regarding' interests; he argues that it should not. Our concern here is with setbacks to interests that are 'want-regarding' in the sense that the person might well recognize and avow them as hers, but that can be identified only in moral or otherwise

As for *mala prohibita* or regulatory offences, advocates of a responsive or partly responsive harm principle might go some way towards justifying them by relaxing the requirement that the conduct to be criminalized be itself 'harmful'—that it actually cause or directly threaten to cause harm; perhaps the principle should also allow the criminalization of conduct that is in some less direct way related to the occurrence of harm. For example, some possession offences might be justified in this way. The mere possession of, for instance, a gun, or an explosive device, neither causes nor threatens directly to cause harm: I might keep it in a cupboard in my home, without any intention of using it to cause harm. Similarly, carrying a knife in my bag as I walk down the street neither causes nor directly threatens to cause harm (so long as I do not intend to use it to cause harm).[151] But given the risks that exist of accidents, or of misuse of the gun, explosive, or knife by others, such mere possession can be said to contribute indirectly to the risk, and to the actual occurrence, of the harms that might eventuate; and we can hope to reduce the incidence of such harms by criminalizing such possession.[152] The trouble with this move, however, is that it threatens to make it all too easy to find reason to criminalize, by allowing for the criminalization of kinds of conduct that are only remotely or tenuously connected to harm, and that it is therefore also hard to portray as wrongful in virtue of their connection to that harm.[153] That threat becomes yet more serious if we recognize that we are now focusing more on the preventive than on the responsive dimensions of the harm principle, and that what matters for harm-prevention is not the (direct or indirect) harmfulness of the conduct in question, but the preventive efficacy of criminalizing it. This might lead us, for instance, towards a 'broken windows' policy:[154] by criminalizing various types of low-level social disorder in vulnerable neighbourhoods, we might inhibit the growth of more serious kinds of crime. The criminalized conduct might not by itself be harmful enough to warrant its criminalization; but the harm-preventive efficacy of its forceful criminalization, or the harmful effects of a perceived failure to forcefully criminalize it, might give us good preventive reason to criminalize it. Whether or not such policies are in fact effective (a question we need not tackle here), they illustrate the radical flexibility of a preventively oriented harm principle.

Such attenuation of the connection between the conduct to be criminalized and the harm that we aim to prevent by criminalizing it becomes even more radical when we turn to various kinds of *mala prohibita* consisting in conduct that violates some

normative terms, and with harms that consist in nothing more than a (perhaps consequentially inert) violation of such interests.

[151] Even possession with intent to commit a harmful crime (see e.g. Firearms Act 1968, ss 16, 18; Terrorism Act 2000, s. 57) is not *directly* dangerous, since the actualization of the harm depends on whether that intention is carried out; but for simplicity's sake we can focus here on offences of simple possession.

[152] See e.g. Prevention of Crime Act 1953, s. 1; the various possession offences defined in the Firearms Act 1968; and Explosive Substances Act 1883, s. 4.

[153] See e.g. M D Dubber, 'Policing Possession: The War on Crime and the End of Criminal Law', 'The Possession Paradigm: The Special Part and the Police Model of the Criminal Process'; A J Ashworth, 'The Unfairness of Risk-Based Possession Offences'. See also Simester and von Hirsch, *Crimes, Harms, and Wrongs*, chs 4–5, on the issue of 'remote harms' (on which see Duff and Marshall, 'Abstract Endangerment', at 142–7); and, more generally on this kind of problem, B Harcourt, 'The Collapse of the Harm Principle'.

[154] See, classically, J Q Wilson and G L Kelling, 'Broken Windows: The Police and Neighborhood Safety', and, in response, B Harcourt, 'Reflecting on the Subject: A Critique of the Social Influence Conception of Deterrence, the Broken Windows Theory, and Order-Maintenance Policing New York Style'. For a helpful summary of the arguments about such policies, see M D Reisig, 'Community and Problem-Oriented Policing', 554–62.

regulation whose ultimate aim is the efficient prevention of harm. Strict drink-driving laws, for instance, criminalize not only driving when one's capacities are actually impaired by alcohol, but driving with more than a specified (fairly low) level of alcohol in one's blood.[155] Such laws might well be a cost-effective way of reducing the incidence of the kinds of harm that are caused by drunken driving—more efficient than those that criminalize only impaired driving: but they probably criminalize some conduct that is not itself either harmful or dangerous, since they criminalize drivers who know that they can drive safely (that their capacities are not impaired) when they are over the limit. Similarly, the efficient operation of a system for regulating road traffic, one of whose primary aims is the prevention or alleviation of harms caused by traffic accidents, might be assisted by regulations requiring drivers to obtain test certificates confirming the safety of their vehicles, and to carry insurance:[156] but a failure to conform to such requirements could often not itself be said to cause, or to risk causing, harm. If we are to see how such laws as these might be justified, we must see the (preventive) harm principle as a principle not of criminalization, but of regulation.[157]

The fact that by criminalizing a type of conduct we could serve the aim of harm prevention cannot by itself give us reason to criminalize it, since it cannot by itself make the conduct wrong. The fact that by regulating it we could serve the aim of harm prevention likewise cannot by itself give us reason to criminalize it, since it cannot make the conduct wrong in advance of its being regulated. But that fact can give us reason to regulate the conduct, so long as this would not lay unreasonable burdens on those whose conduct is constrained by the regulations; and if we can then argue that those to whom the regulations apply ought to obey them, and therefore do wrong in breaking them, we can see good reason to criminalize such breaches as public wrongs. What makes such breaches wrongful, however, is not that they are harmful—for they might not be. We might talk instead of an obligation to obey the just laws of a legitimate state, or of a duty to play one's part in this mutually beneficial collective enterprise, or of the wrong of being a free rider on the obedience of one's fellows, or of a demand of solidarity with fellow citizens:[158] thus while harm still figures in the complete rationale for criminalization, it does not figure as a principle of criminalization, or as a direct reason to criminalize; we must appeal to other values than that of harm avoidance to justify criminalization.

This kind of justification of at least some kinds of *malum prohibitum* offence separates harm from wrongdoing. Harm prevention figures as a reason to regulate, and we need not constrain the idea of harm as Feinberg does, by saying that the aim must be to prevent wrongful harm:[159] that constraint is appropriate for a responsive harm principle, according to which we have reason to criminalize harmful conduct, but is unwarranted for a preventive principle of regulation. Some of the harms that we can use the law to prevent will be wrongful harms, and that wrongfulness will be part of what gives us reason to seek to prevent them: one of a polity's proper responsibilities is to protect its citizens against wrongful actions that expose them to unreasonable risks of harm. But if our starting point is harm prevention as a justification for legal regulation, we should not attend only to wrongful harms. Many regulatory regimes, for instance those that concern matters of health and safety in various kinds of risk-creating

[155] See at nn 54–5 above. [156] See Road Traffic Act 1988, ss 45–8, 143.

[157] See at nn 62–5 above.

[158] See Wellman, *Rights Forfeiture and Punishment*, 11 (at n. 126 above); and above, Chapter 2 at n. 54.

[159] Feinberg, *Harm to Others*, ch. 3; see at n. 59 above.

activity, aim to prevent (or at least radically to reduce the incidence of) harms that flow from non-wrongful accidents, or from natural causes, as well as those that can flow from wrongful human action: wrongfulness comes into the picture only when we think about how we should respond to breaches of these regulations, and see that such breaches may be criminalizable as public wrongs.

A further objection to the harm principle, as a candidate master principle of criminalization, now emerges. Once we have made the connection between criminalization and harm indirect in this way, mediated by the creation of regulations that it is then wrongful to violate, we must ask why harm prevention should be the sole basis for such regulation: why must all the regulations whose breach is in principle criminalizable as a public wrong be aimed at preventing harm? Why not recognize that regulations might serve different aspects of a polity's common good, while making the same kind of claim on citizens' obedience? We might say that the regulations must be efficiently tailored to serve a 'substantial state interest': that they must 'directly' advance that interest, and must be 'no more extensive than necessary to achieve [their] objective'.[160] But why should we think that the only state interests that are 'substantial' enough to warrant the creation of regulations whose breach could then constitute a criminalizable wrong must be interests in the prevention of harm?

Suppose that a polity regards the preservation of its shared artistic heritage, consisting partly in significant works of art that might be in private or in public ownership, as an important aspect of its common good. It will then see reason to take various steps towards that aim, which might include the enactment of regulations to do with the recording and maintenance of such works, and setting formal constraints on their export. If those regulations are justified, breaches of them could constitute public wrongs: for instance, someone who illegally exported a protected artwork would now commit a wrong that properly concerned the polity—his fellow citizens collectively. We would then have good, though not necessarily conclusive, reason to criminalize such conduct as constituting a public wrong.[161] We could bring harm into the picture, by talking of the harm to the national heritage that such regulations aimed to prevent (although it would be a distortion to ground that harm in individual interests in looking at such art works): but how would this help? It would be clearer to say that we have here an aspect of the common good, the civil order, that the law helps to protect. It is true that if we held a monolithic theory of value, we would need to justify all governmental activity, including the enactment of regulations and of criminal laws, in terms of that one value; and if that one value was described as, for instance, happiness or welfare, understood in terms of the satisfaction of interests, we would have to say that all governmental action must be aimed at the prevention of harm (so long as this is understood to include promoting goods whose lack would constitute harm).[162] But if we are not committed to

[160] These are Husak's three 'external constraints' on criminalization (*Overcriminalization*, ch. 3): they are also plausible as constraints on the creation of legal regulations.

[161] Compare the provisions (including criminal provisions) of the Export of Objects of Cultural Interest (Control) Order 2003, and the criminal provisions of the Dealing in Cultural Objects (Offences) Act 2003: 'exporting or importing controlled goods without the right licence is a criminal offence' (www.gov.uk/guidance/export-and-import-licences-for-controlled-goods-and-trading-with-certain-countries; 'controlled goods' include various types of 'artwork'). See also the debate about environmental regulations aimed at preserving natural beauty between L Alexander, 'Plastic Trees and Gladiators: Liberalism and Aesthetic Regulation', and J Peterson, 'Legal Moralism, Interests and Preferences: Alexander on Aesthetic Regulation'.

[162] It is no accident that Mill, classical advocate of the harm principle as specifying 'the only purpose' for which a polity can coerce its citizens, was at least formally an adherent of a monolithic normative theory: if the proper aim of all action is the maximization of happiness (defined as pleasure and the absence of pain), all questions of legislative policy can be settled by careful application of this

such a monolithic, welfare-oriented conception of value, we need see no reason to give harm this exclusive role: we can recognize that a polity can be committed to a range of values, which will generate reasons to criminalize conduct that violates them, and to create regulations that will serve them.

I have briefly discussed four related objections to the harm principle as a master principle of criminalization. First, if 'harm' is given a reasonably determinate, substantive meaning, and the principle has the responsive dimension that advocates typically give it, the principle is thick, but also too narrow: there are kinds of conduct that we have good reason to criminalize, but that are not harmful. Second, if we stretch the notion of 'harm' to cover various kinds of alleged counter-example, the principle becomes much thinner, with the result that either it can now do little substantive work in guiding deliberations about criminalization; or the guidance it gives is over-expansive, making it too easy to find reasons to criminalize. Third, some kind of preventive harm principle is plausible as a principle not of criminalization, but of regulation; harm prevention can give us good reason to enact regulations constraining or prohibiting conduct that might not itself be harmful, or wrongful (in advance of the enactment of the regulations): but this is not then a principle, let alone a master principle, of criminalization. Fourth, when we start to think about the kinds of regulation that a polity could see good reason to enact, whose breach it could then see reason to criminalize, we should realize that it is not helpful to say that all such regulations must aim to prevent harm: rather than trying to squeeze all the reasons for regulation (and thus for criminalization) onto the procrustean bed of the harm principle, we should instead recognize a diversity of substantive values that the law, and the criminal law, serves to protect. Of course harm matters: we often regulate conduct in order to prevent kinds of harm that might otherwise ensue; we often criminalize conduct because it wrongfully causes, or is wrongfully intended to cause, or wrongfully risks causing, harm. But if we attempt to rationalize every kind of justified regulation, or every justified instance of criminalization, in terms of harm we deprive the harm principles (preventive or responsive) of the useful roles they can play as non-exclusive principles of regulation and criminalization—as specifying one, but not the only, important consideration that bears on questions about what (and how) we should regulate or criminalize.

Similar problems face the German *Rechtsgut* theory.[163] One advantage that this doctrine has over the harm principle(s) is that it limits its concern to goods or interests that are (or should be) legally recognized and protected: not every kind of good or interest is to be thus protected. It is also then true that if our interest is simply in analysing existing criminal laws, we can ask which goods or interests the criminal law currently protects, and thus (no doubt through some creative interpretation or reconstruction) produce a complete, finite list of *Rechtsgüter*. However, we are engaged now in normative theory, about what the scope of the criminal law ought to be: thus we cannot just take as given, even if we can reconstruct, the list of currently recognized *Rechtsgüter*. We must ask what goods or interests the law *should* protect, and thus face again the same range of questions that advocates of harm principles face. Should we, for instance, include collective as well as individual *Rechtsgüter*, or ground all criminal laws in the protection of individual goods? What is the range of either kind of *Rechtsgut*? What must the relationship be between a type of conduct and a *Rechtsgut* if the protection of

monolithic theory. But it is also striking that Mill was unable to stay true to his officially monolithic, hedonistic utilitarianism.

[163] See e.g. Hefendehl et al (eds), *Die Rechtsgutstheorie*; Persak, *Criminalising Harmful Conduct*, ch. 5; C C Lauterwein, *The Limits of Criminal Law*, ch. 1.

the *Rechtsgut* is to give us reason to criminalize that type of conduct: must the conduct attack, or injure, or threaten, the *Rechtsgut*, or make injury to it more likely? Or must the conduct be such that criminalizing it will make future violations of or injuries to the *Rechtsgut* less likely? Questions of this kind must, of course, be answered by any theory or account of criminalization: if we posit some good to be protected, or a mischief against which the law is directed, we must ask what kind of relationship between conduct and (violations of) that good or between conduct and that mischief gives us reason to criminalize the conduct. It is also true that, as noted just above, a *Rechtsgut* theory does more than a simple harm theory can do to point us towards the right kinds of question to ask: we need to ask not just whether the type of conduct in question bears on some kind of 'harm', or a setback to some interest, but whether it bears on a kind of good or interest that the law ought to protect, thus reminding us that we should begin with that political question. But what it thus offers is a structure of deliberation rather than a determinate content for that deliberation: it is in that sense a thin theory, or a formal theory that has yet to be given substantive content.

Husak's set of 'constraints' on criminalization similarly amount to a thin theory. Although to call them 'constraints' suggests that we are dealing only with negative principles or reasons, they in fact make clear what could count as a positive reason to criminalize: namely, that by doing so we can efficiently and directly advance some 'substantial state interest',[164] subject to the further constraints that the criminalizing statute be 'designed to prohibit a nontrivial harm or evil', that the conduct to be criminalized be wrongful, and that punishment for such conduct be deserved.[165] The 'nontrivial harm or evil' constraint as canonically expressed does not make clear whether we are to understand the point of criminalization to be responsive or preventive, but Husak's further discussion suggests that both are important: criminalization must constitute, or pave the way for, an efficiently harm-or-evil-preventive punitive response to conduct that deserves such a response because it wrongfully involves some nontrivial harm or evil. This is a radically thin theory, since it tells us nothing about what can count as a 'substantial state interest',[166] or as a 'nontrivial harm or evil': these must be left to be worked out through whatever public or political deliberation the polity favours. But that is just what we should expect if the argument of this chapter is sound: the theory tells us what questions must be asked in deliberations about what we should criminalize, and the terms in which answers to those questions must be set; and that is as much as we should expect from a master principle or master theory. However, I would quarrel (or quibble) with two aspects of Husak's account of these constraints. First, to require a 'substantial state interest' gives the state the wrong kind of role: what is relevant here is the public interest, the interests of the polity (to be worked out through a deliberative determination of the scope and contents of its civil order); the function of 'the state' is to provide the institutional mechanisms through which that public interest can be determined and served. Second, I noted earlier that Husak appears to have abandoned the 'or evil' dimension of the 'nontrivial harm or evil' constraint, in favour of a simple 'harm constraint':[167] in light of the discussion above on harm principles, this seems an unfortunate move; we would do better to talk of a 'non-trivial mischief', thus leaving open the possibility that some relevant mischiefs will not be

[164] Husak, *Overcriminalization*, ch. 3, discussing the 'external constraints' on criminalization.

[165] *Overcriminalization*, ch. 2, on 'internal constraints'; the quoted phrases are at 66. The fourth internal constraint, which places the burden of persuasion on those who would criminalize, need not concern us here.

[166] See *Overcriminalization*, 132–44.

[167] See n. 13 above; Husak, 'Polygamy', 220.

plausibly describable as harms, and making clearer the essentially normative character of the deliberations through which we can identify the kinds of mischief with which the law is properly concerned.

The principles discussed in this section can, I have argued, be plausible as master principles only insofar as they are, or become, thin principles. I have proposed an alternative thin—very thin—master principle: we have good reason to criminalize conduct if and only if it constitutes a public wrong; and conduct constitutes a public wrong if and only if it violates the polity's civil order. The advantage of this principle over other thin, or thinned, principles is not that it answers questions that they fail to answer: for it leaves open, as questions to be answered only through an ongoing process of public deliberation, the questions of how a polity should define its civil order, and of what should count as wrongful violations of that order. Its advantage is that it makes clear what kinds of question need to be asked and answered if we are to work out what we have reason to criminalize, let alone what we should all things considered criminalize: the questions we must ask concern the scope and contents of our civil order, and the kinds of wrong that it requires us to recognize and condemn. In appealing to civil order in this way, I ally myself with other 'public law' theorists, such as Thorburn and Chiao:[168] without discussing in detail here the differences between our accounts, I would simply note three points.

First, both Thorburn and Chiao take punishment to be central to criminal law—in which case it must also be central to deliberations about what we should criminalize, since to criminalize is, essentially, to render liable to punishment. As I have argued already, however,[169] we should not understand criminal law in such punishment-focused terms: reasons to criminalize are reasons to censure and to call to public account, whether or not such calling to account leads to punishment. Second, Thorburn's account appeals to freedom as a master value: the proper purpose of criminal law is to protect 'the system of equal freedom itself' against 'efforts to undermine' it:[170] for the reasons given earlier in this section, I think it is neither necessary nor fruitful to try to ground all criminal law, and all reasons for criminalization, in a single, substantive master value. Third, as I noted earlier, Chiao's account of criminal law's role in the polity is instrumentalist: it functions essentially as 'a coercive rule-enforcing institution providing an assurance of general cooperation with legal rules'.[171] I have argued that we should rather see criminal law as partly constitutive of the civil order that it also helps to sustain; and that what justifies criminal law as an institution of the polity is that this is an appropriate way for the citizens of a liberal republic to respond to each other's wrongdoing.[172] Criminal law has a preventive dimension: one of its purposes is to reduce the incidence of the kinds of conduct that it criminalizes. But the character of that prevention is crucial, since the law's preventive efforts must be consistent with the respect that citizens owe to each other as responsible members of the polity; and it is the responsive character of the criminal law that makes it distinctively appropriate as a way of dealing with public wrongs.

One final point is worth emphasizing before I turn, in the following chapter, to the question of how a master principle grounded in the idea of civil order can help

[168] See Chapter 4, section 2 above.

[169] See above, Chapter 1 at nn 16–21, Chapter 4 at nn 25–9.

[170] 'Constitutionalism and the Limits of the Criminal Law', 100.

[171] V Chiao, 'What is the Criminal Law For?', 139 (see above, Chapter 5 at nn 62–6). See also his 'anti-deference principle' of criminalization (n. 36 above).

[172] See above, Chapter 5, section 4.

to structure deliberations about criminalization. The other kinds of responsive master principle discussed in this chapter have typically focused on the legitimate objects of criminal liability, and thus of criminalization: we are to criminalize wrongfully harmful conduct, or violations of *Rechtsgüter*, or attacks on the freedom or dignity or autonomy of others, because it is those kinds of wrong for which agents are to be held liable and punished; an offender is convicted and censured for wrongfully harming another, or for violating a *Rechtsgut*, or for invading another's freedom, dignity, or autonomy. If we read the civil order principle in the same way, it would imply that what agents are to be held criminally liable for is a violation of the civil order: but while the criminalizable wrongfulness of some kinds of conduct does consist in a violation of the civil order,[173] that is not how we should understand the criminalizable wrongfulness of such familiar *mala in se* as murder, or criminal damage. What the agent is liable for in such cases is the substantive wrong he commits against his victim: that that wrong violates the polity's civil order is a condition of such liability, because it brings the wrong within the ambit of this polity's law and the jurisdiction of its courts.[174]

I have argued in this chapter that a master principle of criminalization must be foundational, exhaustive, and exclusive; that it must be positive (even if it includes some negative conditions or side-constraints); that it should be primarily responsive, but should also include a preventive dimension; that in its positive dimension it will be *pro tanto* rather than categorical (or, insofar as it talks of what demands criminalization, those demands will be defeasible); and that it must be thin rather than thick—which means that it will leave a substantial amount of normative work to be done in applying it. Such a principle must also be politically grounded—grounded, that is, in an account of the role of criminal law as part of the polity's political structure. I have, therefore, suggested a two-part master principle focused on public wrongs and civil order—

A. *We have reason to criminalize a type of conduct if, and only if, it constitutes a public wrong.*

B. *A type of conduct constitutes a public wrong if, and only if, it violates the polity's civil order.*

This satisfies the conditions and desiderata noted above. It is foundational, in the sense that it provides the starting point for criminalization deliberations (although it is itself grounded in the political account of criminal law offered in previous chapters). It is exhaustive and exclusive, in the sense that it specifies the only kinds of consideration that can give us reason to criminalize. It is positive—although it has a negative dimension in its 'and only if' clauses. It is responsive, but also has a preventive dimension—at least implicitly, insofar as criminalizing public wrongs is an appropriate way of trying to dissuade their commission. It is *pro tanto*, in the sense that it talks of what we have reason to criminalize, not of what we must criminalize. And it is a thin principle, whose application will require a normative account of the civil order of the polity, and of what kinds of conduct constitute wrongful violations of that order.

I must now turn finally to the question of how we can begin to develop an account (if not a 'theory') of criminalization on the basis of this principle. This account will be partly procedural, and thus compatible with at least a limited range of conceptions of civil order; but I will illustrate it by some more substantive examples, of how

[173] See above, Chapter 4 at nn 4–9; other examples include treason, and the 'Offenses against Public Administration' defined in Articles 230–43 of the Model Penal Code.

[174] See above, Chapter 5 at nn 106–8; and Chapter 7 at nn 81–4 below.

deliberation about the criminalization of specific types of conduct should proceed. What emerges from this will not be a structured account of the proper scope of the, or 'our', criminal law. Such an account might be possible if we could posit a suitably thick master principle—which I have argued is implausible. But once we recognize that a plausible principle will be very thin, and that we should resist the lure of monolithic accounts of the values that bear on criminal law, we will also recognize that the process of working out the proper content, scope, and bounds of the criminal law will be an untidy and piecemeal one, which resists any neat systematization: the most that a general 'theory' can hope to do, as we will see, is to show what kinds of argument will be relevant to that process—what its normative logic must be. Such a 'theory' will disappoint those who want a theory that will itself generate determinate substantive answers: but such disappointment is unavoidable.[175]

[175] I do not mean to imply that such disappointment is peculiar to attempts to find a principled basis for decisions about criminalization: it is, rather, a feature of moral and political theorizing in general.

7

Criminalization and Civil Order

1. A Thin Theory of Criminalization

I argued in the previous chapter that we should not hope to develop a thick master principle, or theory, of criminalization: one that specifies a coherent set of substantive criteria by reference to which we can determine what we have good reason, in principle, to criminalize (let alone what we should criminalize all things considered). But I suggested a thin master principle: a 'civil order', or 'public wrongs' principle—

A. *We have reason to criminalize a type of conduct if, and only if, it constitutes a public wrong.*

B. *A type of conduct constitutes a public wrong if, and only if, it violates the polity's civil order.*

This principle is doubly thin, since it leaves for further normative deliberation both the question of what impinges on the civil order, and the question of what we should count as a wrong in that context: but it can still be useful if it makes clear what kinds of reason are relevant to issues of criminalization, what kinds of claim must be made to support a proposal to criminalize a type of conduct, and what kinds of argument are appropriate on either side of such debates.

This principle is positive rather than (merely) negative: it is the publicly wrongful character of the conduct that gives us reason to criminalize it. It is exclusive rather than non-exclusive: the *only* good reason to criminalize a type of conduct is that it constitutes a public wrong. It is *pro tanto* rather than categorical: even if there are some egregious wrongs that we *must* criminalize, that 'must' holds good only if we assume that we have a system of criminal law, and applies only to a small set of wrongs.[1] It is primarily responsive rather than preventive: in deciding whether to criminalize all things considered, we must attend to the consequences of doing so; but our initial question should be whether criminalization is an appropriate response to this kind of conduct. This fits with the nature of criminal law as described in Chapter 1: criminalization paves the way to a criminal trial, as a process through which citizens are called to account for alleged criminal wrongdoings; its focus is therefore, inevitably, backward-looking. This feature of criminal law (like the fact that punishment must be imposed 'for an offence', and is thus inevitably backward-looking) does not show, however, that our reasons to criminalize must be responsive rather than preventive: our reasons for maintaining an essentially responsive institution could themselves be, as consequentialist accounts of criminal punishment show, preventive. But, although even on a responsive account criminal law still has an integral preventive dimension,[2] a 'public wrongs' principle of criminalization is best understood in primarily responsive terms, in view of the part-constitutive relationship between criminal law and civil order for which I argued earlier.[3] A legal institution that defines a set of public wrongs,

[1] See above, Chapter 6 at n. 119.

[2] See above, Chapter 6 at nn 41–7, 114–16.

[3] See above, Chapter 5, section 4.

and provides a process through which citizens are called to account for their alleged commissions of such wrongs, is appropriate to a republican polity because it helps to constitute a suitable—mutually respectful and mutually demanding—relationship between its citizens: we treat each other as responsible members of the polity, we display our respectful concern for each other and for the values by which we collectively define ourselves as a political community, by taking such formal notice of public wrongs. To say that something constitutes a public wrong is to say that it is our collective business as a polity: it is something to which we have the standing, and might have a responsibility, to respond; and an appropriate response to a wrong is to mark it as a wrong and to call its perpetrator to account.

However, this is so far to say only that criminalization is *an* appropriate response to a public wrong, not that it is *the* appropriate response. We might have *some* reason to criminalize every kind of public wrong, in that criminalization constitutes one possible appropriate response. But it is not the only possible response—as we will see in detail in section 2: our question must therefore be not simply whether we have reason to criminalize, as if the choice was between criminalization and doing nothing, but whether we have reason to criminalize *rather than* responding in some other way.[4] If we are to answer that question, we must attend to the costs and benefits (non-material as well as material) of the various possible responses, but the answer will not depend solely on a comparative balancing of costs against benefits. It could depend on such a comparative balancing if all the responses were different ways of pursuing the same end, since we could then ask which of them constituted the most efficient, or an efficient, means to that end:[5] but that is not the case. Rather, as we will see, the various responses have different ends; so we will need to ask which of those ends (when we must choose between them) it is more appropriate, or important, to pursue.[6]

Before we turn to consider some of these alternative responses to public wrongs, it is worth re-emphasizing two points that emerged from the earlier discussions of the idea of public wrongs as the proper objects of criminalization.

First, on the account offered here, a proposal that we should criminalize some type of conduct must begin with the claim that it constitutes a public wrong: but such a claim has two logically distinct elements—that the conduct in question falls within the public realm, as defined by the polity's conception of its civil order; and that the conduct is, within that context, wrongful. There are thus two distinct ways to rebut a claim that we have (even in principle) reason to criminalize that type of conduct: to argue that it falls within the private, rather than the public, realm; or to argue that it is not wrongful. A critic of the Law Lords' decision in *R v Brown* that consensual sadomasochistic conduct was criminal, if it involved the infliction of actual bodily harm,[7] could thus argue that so long as the consent is free and informed, such conduct is not wrongful—for instance because the satisfaction of the participants' sexual desires constituted a 'good reason' for the conduct, which should be recognized alongside such

[4] Compare V Tadros, *Wrongs and Harms*, 112–14.

[5] That is why Feinberg properly qualifies those of his 'liberty-limiting principles' that take a preventive form by adding that there must 'probably [be] no other means' of achieving the preventive aim 'that is equally effective at no greater cost to other values': *Harm to Others*, 26; see Edwards, 'An Instrumental Legal Moralism', n. 10.

[6] This question arises both in the context of formal law-creation, when a legislature must decide what it should formally criminalize, and in the context of law-application, when officials and lay citizens must decide which formally criminal types or tokens of conduct they should treat as substantively criminal: see Chapter 1, section 7 above.

[7] [1994] 1 AC 212; see above, Chapter 4 at nn 93–7.

already recognized good reasons for inflicting actual bodily harm as 'organised sporting contests and games, parental chastisement or reasonable surgery';[8] or that so long as the consent is free and informed, the conduct falls within the private sphere, and it is not for the law or the polity to judge the quality of the participants' reasons for engaging in it. She could argue, that is, either that consent can justify conduct that is a prima facie public wrong (conduct that counts as public, and that is prima facie wrong); or that consent transfers conduct that would otherwise count as public into the private realm. The latter kind of argument looks more appropriate: surely people should not be required, in order to avoid criminal liability, to justify their consensual sexual practices to their fellow citizens—to argue, for instance, that their sexual desires are not 'perverted and depraved', or that their activities are in fact 'conducive to the enhancement or enjoyment of family life or conducive to the welfare of society', or constitute a 'manly diversion';[9] all they should have to argue is that this is a private matter.[10]

On the other hand (and this leads into the second point to be re-emphasized), it might seem that it is important to resist, in the public realm, the moral views purveyed by the majority in *R v Brown*: to argue that consensual sado-masochistic activity, even when it causes actual bodily harm, is a proper expression of sexual desires that might be unusual but are not 'perverted and depraved', and of the participants' mutual concern; and that even if it is not a 'manly diversion' (as boxing was clearly taken to be by the majority in *R v Brown*), or conducive to family life, it is a morally legitimate mode of sexual self-expression. Analogously, the simplest way to oppose the criminalization of homosexual conduct is to argue that, if it is consensual, it falls within the private realm: legislators therefore need not, and should not, debate its morality or immorality; that is not their business, *qua* legislators. On the other hand, it is important to resist the moral view of homosexuality as a perversion, and to argue that homosexual relationships should be publicly recognized, and indeed celebrated, alongside heterosexual relationships as valuable modes of human relationship: campaigns for social and legal recognition of these relationships, including most obviously the campaign for gay marriage, precisely involve making them a public rather than a private matter.

However, the apparent tension here, between arguing that such sexual relationships should be seen as a private matter and arguing that they should be publicly accepted or celebrated, is only apparent, as we can see once we distinguish the different modalities of the 'public' and the 'private'.[11] The relevant notion of the public for the purposes of criminal law is that of what makes intervention by the polity permissible—with or without the consent of those involved: a public matter is one in which we, as citizens, can insist on taking an interest and claim the right to intervene, whether or not those engaged in the activity want such intervention. But when it comes to the question of enabling gay marriage, or of welcoming and celebrating sexual diversity, the modality is that of what should receive public recognition and support *if* that is what the people

[8] [1994] 1 AC 212, at 245 (Lord Jauncey).

[9] See [1994] 1 AC 212, at 255 (Lord Lowry).

[10] Compare Lord Mustill's dissenting comments in *R v Brown*: 'When proposing that the conduct is not rightly so charged [as criminal] I do not invite your Lordships' House to endorse it as morally acceptable. .... What I do say is that [questions about its morality] are questions of private morality; that the standards by which they fall to be judged are not those of the criminal law; and that if these standards are to be upheld the individual must enforce them upon himself according to his own moral standards, or have them enforced against him by moral pressures exerted by whatever religious or other community to whose ethical ideals he responds' ([1994] 1 AC 212, at 273). This nicely makes the point that conduct that is not the business of the criminal law might be the business of other communities to which the agent belongs.

[11] See above, Chapter 4 at nn 68–74.

involved want: the public character of their conduct is optional. Someone who commits what has been justifiably defined as a crime cannot object to being called to public account on the grounds that his conduct is private; by contrast, someone whose noncriminal sexual habits are made public without her consent can properly complain that this constitutes an invasion of her privacy.[12]

(A third modality of the public is also relevant to matters of sexual conduct, and to issues of criminalization: what it is right or wrong to *make* public voluntarily. My sexual orientation ought to be private as far as the criminal law is concerned, and optionally public when it comes to such matters as marriage. Some kinds of sexual conduct, however (such as full sexual intercourse), *should* be kept private—they should not be foisted on the attention of others by being performed in public places; it will then constitute a public, and in principle criminalizable, wrong to violate such a norm.[13])

2. Responding to Public Wrongs

It is time to turn now to the further complication, noted above, in deliberations about what we could have good reason to criminalize: that criminalization is only one among a number of possible ways of responding to public wrongs.

(a) Do nothing

The simplest response to a public wrong is no response: more precisely, no formal or legal response. For instance, in polities that have an institution of queuing, queue-jumping constitutes a public wrong:[14] there are well-established conventions about how to behave in queues, which enable one kind of cooperative activity for the mutual convenience of those concerned; someone who jumps a queue might not cause significant disruption or inconvenience, but at least behaves uncivilly, and merits (modest) social criticism—which she is likely to receive from others in the queue. Queuing can become a more formal matter, without being regulated by law: businesses of various kinds might operate systems of queuing, and enforce them by refusing to serve queue-jumpers. It would be odd, however, to suggest that we might criminalize queue-jumping: apart from questions about just how the offence would be defined, it is not a serious enough wrong to merit that kind of formal attention. We should note three further points here.

First, suppose that queue-jumping became more problematic: perhaps, given changing social attitudes and expectations, it regularly led to moderate violence. We might then see good (which is not to say conclusive) reason to resort to criminal law: but what form should that resort take? Should we now criminalize queue-jumping itself, as being likely to lead to such violence (likely to cause 'a breach of the peace')? Or should we instead use criminal law only against those who actually engage in the violence (which is probably already criminal)? To answer this question we would need to consider not

[12] This clearly connects to the issue of 'outing' those who have not declared their sexual orientation. This can be legitimate only if the person concerned publicly advocates, or is publicly complicit in, kinds of discrimination (most obviously through criminalization) against sexual conduct in which he himself engages wholeheartedly.

[13] Compare J Feinberg, *Offense to Others*, 12 (stories 14–23) and 17–20 on public sexual conduct; A P Simester and A von Hirsch, *Crimes, Harms, and Wrongs: On the Principles of Criminalisation*, 98; above, Chapter 4 at n. 70.

[14] See above, Chapter 4 at n. 57.

only the pragmatic issue of how we could most efficiently prevent such violence, but normative questions about the conduct of the people involved: should queue-jumpers be held responsible for provoking such violence (which would imply that the violence, even if not justified, was a not-unreasonable response); or should those who resort to violence be held solely responsible for such an unwarranted reaction?[15]

Second, to say that the wrong is not serious enough to warrant criminalization presupposes a conception of how serious a matter criminalization is. If it involves such things as appearing in a criminal court and acquiring a criminal record, it is a serious matter, whatever the punishment; it would be a disproportionate response to such minor wrongs as queue-jumping. Criminalization need not, however, be as serious as that: it could involve quite modest punishments, imposed by a relatively unburdensome process, and not leading to a formal criminal record. One question we must then ask is whether we should extend the spectrum of criminalizing responses, to include much more modest, less onerous, responses to relatively minor wrongs; or whether we should reserve *criminal* law for wrongs lying above a certain (indeterminate) threshold of seriousness—though I do not suggest that we should in this way make queue-jumping criminalizable.[16]

Third, since queue-jumping is a public wrong, on my account we have reason to criminalize it. That reason is clearly not a good enough reason, or even a strong reason; but it is a reason to criminalize. Tadros argues that this is a mistake: for if I admit that 'there are some public wrongs that are too trivial to merit any kind of formal legal response', and thus that 'the reasons for the state to hold [those who commit such wrongs] to account for them will always be defeated', I must also admit that we have no reason to criminalize them.[17] We should criminalize conduct in order (and only in order) to make possible an appropriate response to the conduct we criminalize (punishment, for a Moorean retributivist; or a formal calling to public account): so if that response would *never* be justified in relation to a particular type of conduct, we can have no reason to criminalize it. To assess the force of this objection, we need to specify the relevant reasons that we might have more carefully, and attend to a point noted above—that what matters is not (merely) whether we have reason to criminalize a particular type of conduct, but whether we have reason to criminalize it *rather than* responding in some other way.

If queue-jumping is a public wrong, we have reason to ensure that it receives an appropriate public response—that those who engage in it are suitably (proportionately) held to account for it. Criminalization seems to be one way in which we can provide for such a response: we therefore, we could say, have reason to consider criminalizing queue-jumping. However, first, if we realize that the kind of holding to account for which the criminal law provides would always, inevitably, be disproportionately severe, we might indeed say that we have no reason to criminalize queue-jumping, since we have found that criminalization could not provide for an appropriate kind of response. Second, even if we might be able (as suggested above) to make criminalization a less onerous, less serious, matter, we still need to ask whether we should criminalize

[15] Compare *Beatty v Gillbanks* [1882] 9 QBD 308: members of the Salvation Army were not guilty of 'unlawful assembly' for holding a parade in the knowledge that the 'Skeleton Army' would violently oppose the parade; they could not be held responsible for the ensuing breach of the peace. Compare also *Masterton v Holden* (Chapter 4, n. 70 above): the defendants' conduct should count as 'insulting' only if others were reasonably (with good reason) offended by it; it should not be enough that others in fact felt insulted or offended.

[16] See at n. 29 below.

[17] Tadros, *Wrongs and Harms*, 120 (see 115–20 for the general argument for this conclusion).

rather than (in this case) doing nothing formal; and if we can be confident that queue-jumpers will still be held informally to appropriate account by their fellow queuers, on the basis not of criminal law but of informal social norms, we might decide that queue-jumping will still receive a suitable response even if it is not criminalized. In that case, we would have no reason to criminalize rather than doing nothing formal, because criminalization would be unnecessary. It is, however, important to notice that this is true only because if we do nothing formal wrongdoers will still be called to public account: we have no reason to criminalize, rather than doing nothing formal, because we can, without criminalizing, achieve the good for whose sake we would criminalize. (It matters, of course, that we are confident that the informal response to queue-jumping will be *appropriate*—that it will be fair, proportionate, reliable, and non-discriminatory.)

(b) 'Restorative justice'

Another possible collective response to public wrongs is to avoid any formal legal process, in favour of a publicly organized (and funded) system of mediation, negotiation, or 'restorative justice': that is, to treat (alleged) public wrongs, which could be defined and treated as crimes, as 'conflicts', or 'troubles' that need to be resolved by those involved in them, rather than as crimes whose perpetrators should be called to formal, public, censorial account.[18] There are, of course, many different versions of 'restorative justice', which I cannot explore here:[19] our concern here is with versions that offer not new ways of dealing with crimes as crimes, but ways of avoiding the perspective and structure of criminal law altogether. The adoption of such an approach could be a matter for the legislature, which might decide not to define certain kinds of public wrong as crimes; or for the discretion of officials and citizens who must decide whether to treat as criminal something that fits the formal definition of a criminal offence.

Some of the differences between a formal criminal law response and a 'restorative' response were briefly discussed earlier.[20] 'Restorative' processes are typically informal rather than formal, controlled by those most closely involved in the 'conflict'; they are 'private' rather than 'public'; the discussion is the business of those directly involved, not of the whole polity. They might be focused on harms suffered and how to repair them, rather than on wrongs done and who is to be called to account for them; when they do attend to wrongs rather than only to harms, they might avoid the kinds of categorical judgment of wrongdoing in which criminal law deals, in favour of more nuanced, negotiated understandings of what happened, which might share responsibility between 'victim' and 'offender'. They are intended to lead, not to punishment, but to negotiated agreements about the best way to repair harms and restore relationships.

These differences also point to the kinds of reason we may have—as legislators, as officials, or as lay citizens—to prefer a 'restorative', or a 'criminal', response to a type of public wrong. We need to ask, in particular, whether it is important, and how important it is, to mark the wrong as a wrong: to condemn it categorically as a wrong, to censure its perpetrator as a wrongdoer, by publicly established norms, rather than

[18] See N Christie, 'Conflicts as Property'; L Hulsman, 'Critical Criminology and the Concept of Crime'.

[19] See G Johnstone, *Restorative Justice: Ideas, Values, Debates*; G Johnstone (ed.), *A Restorative Justice Reader*.

[20] See above, Chapter 5 at nn 96–100; also R A Duff, 'Responsibility, Restoration and Retribution'. These are features of some, even many, but by no means all, programmes of 'restorative justice'.

just leaving it to those most closely involved to negotiate their own way of responding to it. We must ask whether it is important, and how important it is, that the process is a public one, conducted in the name of the polity, rather than a private one that involves only the immediate participants. The answers to such questions might not be obvious—especially when the wrongs involved are relatively non-serious wrongs committed among people who must live together not only as citizens, but as neighbours. There will no doubt be situations in which it is more sensible not to treat as criminal kinds of wrongdoing that are formally defined as criminal: situations, for instance, in which it is more important to negotiate a way of living together as neighbours, and of dealing with whatever harm has been caused without trying to apportion blame, than to call the alleged wrongdoers to account and hold them formally liable for their wrongdoing. This might be true of some disputes between neighbours, which involve some formally criminal conduct (minor criminal damage, perhaps) on both sides, but which may be more appropriately dealt with informally as 'conflicts' rather than formally as crimes. However, first, the enterprise of criminal law presupposes that some kinds of wrongs should be formally marked and condemned as such by a public criminal process that calls the perpetrator to account: they should not be left to be negotiated informally by those directly involved, and there is reason for the polity to insist on such a response even if the direct victim of the wrong would prefer to let it drop, or to deal with it informally. Some examples of such wrongs will be discussed later in this chapter, when we will see how their impact on civil order is relevant to their criminalization; one obvious (controversial) example is domestic violence, which prosecutors might insist on prosecuting even against the victim's wishes, on the grounds that 'we', the polity's citizens, have a responsibility to call those who commit such wrongs to public account.[21] Second, even when it is more sensible or appropriate to respond to a criminalizable wrong through a restorative rather than a criminal process, something is lost. We still have reason to criminalize the conduct in question, to call to formal account those who commit such public wrongs; nor is a restorative response simply an alternative means to the same end. We therefore still have reason to criminalize the conduct *rather than* to take a restorative approach: but that reason might not be a good enough reason.

(c) Non-governmental codes

A third possibility is, again, to do nothing directly through the criminal law, but to leave jurisdiction over the wrong to another, non-governmental body. The obvious example of this kind of response is that of professions and their disciplinary procedures.[22] While such bodies act under the aegis of the law, and are constrained by legal requirements, they have substantial autonomy in deciding what to define as 'professional misconduct' and how to deal with it; and sometimes conduct that could properly be defined as criminal, as constituting a public wrong, is left to be dealt with by the relevant profession rather than being brought into the criminal law.[23] Sometimes this can be seen as a matter of delegation: the professional body is better placed to determine

[21] See M M Dempsey, *Prosecuting Domestic Violence: A Philosophical Analysis*. I do not mean to imply that the victim's wishes should be ignored, or should never prevail; only that they should not be dispositive.

[22] See Chapter 2, sections 7 and 8 above.

[23] Or conduct that is formally criminal is in fact left to the profession to deal with: see above, Chapter 2 at nn 131–8.

both whether the accused person did commit the relevant wrong, and what response is appropriate. Sometimes it can instead be seen as reflecting a recognition that the wrong is better understood as a professional wrong, because what is most salient is its character as a violation of the profession's values. I do not suggest that the difference between these two grounds for leaving certain kinds of wrong to the jurisdiction of a profession is clear-cut, nor that it is always a straightforward matter to decide whether the criminal law should claim jurisdiction or leave it to the profession: indeed, part of the message of this section should be that decisions on whether to criminalize a type of publicly wrongful conduct rather than responding to it in some other way are often neither straightforward nor clear-cut.

To take just one instance, sexual relations between psychotherapists and their patients clearly raise ethical issues, and would be indubitably criminal if they were non-consensual, or if they involved the exploitation of vulnerable people.[24] Some American states also criminalize any kind of sexual relationship between a psychotherapist and a patient, whether consensual or not; in other states, such relationships are not criminal unless they involve coercion or exploitation, but are likely to constitute disciplinary offences that can lead to the loss of a licence to practise.[25] How then should we set about deciding whether consensual therapist-patient sexual relationships ought to be treated as potential criminal wrongs, or as a matter of professional discipline? If what is (potentially) wrong with such relationships is that they might be exploitative, and not properly consensual, then the wrong looks like a potential public wrong, of the same kind as that involved in sex with those who might not be competent to consent: it involves the risk, for the patient, of sexual intercourse that is non-consensual. Such crimes are controversial, since it is not clear just how they should be defined, how far-reaching they should be, or how the potential victims are to be identified:[26] but if this is their rationale, it does appropriately portray the conduct in question as a public rather than a professional wrong—as a kind of endangerment from which any citizen should be able to expect to be safe. If, on the other hand, the wrong is seen as consisting rather in the 'unprofessional' character of such conduct, as being inconsistent with or a corruption of the therapist-patient relationship, it begins to look more like a professional than a criminal wrong: a wrong that implicates the particular values of the profession, and is of particular concern to its members, rather than one that implicates the values that structure our civic life.

(d) Non-criminal regulation

A fourth possibility is non-criminal regulation, whether by the primary legislature or by a formal body (such as an inspectorate) to whom the authority to make and enforce regulations on certain matters is delegated by the legislature. This is, of course, one route to criminalization, since a familiar kind of criminal offence (a '*malum prohibitum*') consists precisely in the breach of a regulation enacted by such an authority; but, as we saw earlier, we could also operate a non-criminal kind of regulation, perhaps like the German *Ordnungswidrigkeitenrecht*.[27]

[24] See e.g. Sexual Offences Act 2003, ss 30, 38.

[25] See e.g. P M L Illingworth, 'Patient-Therapist Sex: Criminalization and Its Discontents'.

[26] Should we really see everyone who seeks psychotherapy as vulnerable in this way?

[27] See above, Chapter 1 at nn 23–40. I say 'perhaps' because it is not clear whether *Ordnungswidrigkeitenrecht* should be understood as categorically distinct from the criminal law, or rather as a milder species of criminal law. See generally D Ohana, 'Regulatory Offenses and Administrative Sanctions: Between Criminal and Administrative Law'; F Picinali, 'The Denial of Procedural Safeguards in Trials for Regulatory Offences: A Justification'.

If this is to be a truly non-criminal mode of regulation, then a finding that a person violated a regulation, and is therefore liable to a penalty, must be quite distinct from a criminal conviction: not only must it lead to a less drastic kind of penalty than criminal punishment can be; it must lack the censorial meaning of a conviction. Other differences may follow from this: we might be readier to make regulatory liability in some ways strict, since it does not imply censure-worthy fault; we might see less need for some of the procedural protections to which criminal defendants are entitled, since what is at stake is of less normative moment. Such a regulatory system might seem an attractive possibility, especially if our focus is on cost-effective techniques for reducing the incidence of certain kinds of undesirable conduct, but there are questions to be asked about its appropriateness (as distinct from its cost-effectiveness).[28] One question concerns the way such regulatory systems treat those who are penalized or threatened with penalties: if the aim is simply to deter regulation-violating conduct, we must ask whether it is appropriate to address them in such deterrent terms, even if the threatened penalties are less oppressive than those the criminal law can impose. Another question concerns the way in which such regulatory schemes portray the conduct that is penalized: do they portray as merely 'technical violations' conduct that should instead be marked and censured (perhaps mildly) as wrong? There seems to be a dilemma here: either the regulations have a proper, civic claim on the obedience of those subject to them, in which case breaking them should be marked as wrong (and those accused of breaches should be entitled to the protections that the criminal law offers); or they have no such claim, in which case we have no right to seek to secure obedience to them by the threat of penalties.

That might seem to imply a less modest version of legal moralism than I am supposed to be espousing—as if the wrongfulness of the conduct in question, as the breach of a regulation that we ought to obey, gives us not just a good, but a conclusive reason to criminalize it. For if I agree (as I do) that there is a large gap between 'good reasons' and 'conclusive reasons' to criminalize; and that questions of resources and costs (material and moral) must arise within that gap: surely I must agree that we could have good reason to prefer a non-criminal regulatory approach to some kinds of wrong, as being less costly both materially (because it involves simpler procedures) and morally (because it does not bring the stigma of criminal conviction). This objection, however, draws a false contrast between a necessarily expensive criminal process and an always cheaper non-criminal process. We could instead, as suggested earlier, draw a distinction *within* criminal law between 'mere' violations and crimes,[29] and a distinction between different kinds of criminal procedure appropriate to each kind of offence; we could also limit both the kinds of punishment available for violations, and the further consequences (such as criminal record) that can attach to conviction for a violation.

[28] See R A Duff et al, *The Trial on Trial (3): Towards a Normative Theory of the Criminal Trial*, 189–98 (but contrast V Tadros, 'Criminalization and Regulation'); see also J Horder, 'Bureaucratic "Criminal" Law: Too Much of a Bad Thing?'.

[29] Compare Model Penal Code § 1.04, distinguishing 'crimes' from 'violations'. Violations cannot attract a prison sentence, or 'any disability or legal disadvantage based on conviction of a criminal offense'. The Explanatory Note describes violations as 'a noncriminal class of offenses', which will 'primarily include regulatory offenses based on strict liability and certain minor offenses such as traffic violations': they are portrayed as being similar to German *Ordnungswidrigkeiten*. However, they still count as 'offenses', for which people are 'convicted'; so one could just as well portray them as criminal offences of a categorically minor kind, for which neither some of the formal consequences of more serious kinds of conviction (a criminal record, for instance), nor some of the procedural protections that attach to more serious criminal accusations, are warranted.

Something of this kind already exists, in provisions such as those for 'prosecutor fines' and other kinds of sanction that can be applied without trial.[30]

There are two main considerations in favour of thus distinguishing 'violations' from 'crimes' within criminal law, rather than criminal law from non-criminal regulation. First, it is then easier to include (as we should) provisions for appeal to a criminal court by those who want to contest their guilt;[31] and also easier to avoid concerns about strict liability (which should not be accepted lightly even for non-criminal violations), by making responsibility rather than liability strict for some violations: fault should still be necessary for conviction, but in some regulatory contexts it could be appropriate to shift the evidential burden onto the defendant, through a 'due diligence' defence.[32] Second, it is more transparent: it makes it clear that what justifies the sanction is that the defendant committed a wrong by breaking a regulation that she ought to have obeyed.

This is not to deny that those who enforce such regulations—criminal prosecutors, officials working in government inspectorates—must exercise discretion in deciding whether and when to prosecute, and whether and when to look instead for disposals that avoid prosecution. There are many such possibilities, including the settlements made by tax officials that allow tax evaders to avoid prosecution by paying the tax due and a penalty; 'deferred prosecution agreements' that enable corporations to avoid prosecution if they carry out the terms of a remedial agreement; and other ways in which regulatory agencies can avoid prosecutions whilst still using the prospect of prosecution to encourage those with whom they are dealing to cooperate.[33] These raise difficult normative questions about the factors that should guide such decisions: for instance, about how much weight should be attached to the prospects of reducing future harm (or securing payment of taxes), and how much to the responsive concern to call to formal account those who are guilty of public wrongdoing; and about whether thus enabling some wrongdoers to avoid prosecution is unfair to others who are not offered that chance, or promotes inequality between different kinds of offender (compare the ways in which tax evasion by the wealthy and welfare fraud by the poor are dealt with). All I can say here is that the responsive concern is important, and should not be simply discarded in favour of an instrumental approach that focuses solely on efficient ways of securing future compliance; that here again, as with 'restorative' approaches, the choice is not between different means to the same end, but between different ends; and, accordingly, that even if a prosecution-avoiding approach that seeks a negotiated agreement rather than a conviction is sometimes appropriate, something is lost—public wrongdoers are not called to public account.

(e) Private law

A fifth possibility is to bring the wrong within the reach of the law, but as a matter of private rather than of public law. Tort law is the obvious candidate here, although contract law is also clearly relevant (and it is worth asking why breach of contract should not be a criminal offence even when it does not involve fraud, so long as it involves fault of some kind). Insofar as tort law is concerned with the just or efficient allocation

[30] See above, Chapter 1 at n. 14.

[31] But it would be important to ensure that appeals were not deterred by the prospect of a harsher sentence if they failed (compare R L Lippke, *The Ethics of Plea Bargaining*, chs 1–2, on 'trial penalties' in plea bargaining).

[32] See R A Duff, *Answering for Crime*, ch. 10.2–3.

[33] See above, Chapter 1 at nn 87–90.

of the costs of harm that has been caused, its role is clearly quite different from that of criminal law; nor need it be an alternative to criminal law, since the public prosecution of a criminal charge does not preclude a private tort suit brought by an injured party. More generally, we could allow the same type of wrongfully harmful conduct to be the basis both of a criminal charge and of a tort suit, or we could blur the distinction between the two kinds of response: modestly, by allowing or requiring criminal courts to make compensation orders against those convicted of victimizing crimes; or rather more ambitiously, by allowing the (purported) victim to attach a civil claim to the criminal charge, to have the cases decided by the same court through a single trial.[34] If a type of properly criminalized conduct has an identifiable victim who can claim to have been wrongfully harmed by it, it must also count as tortious, and be a possible ground for a tort suit. If that is so, the question is not how we are to decide *between* criminal law and tort law as possible responses to wrongs that count as 'public' in the sense that they are properly of interest to the polity and its law;[35] it is rather whether we should make either kind, or both kinds, of response available.

That might seem too hasty, if we recognize that tort law can be a matter of seeking recourse or vindication for a wrong, rather than simply damages to compensate for harm:[36] if the focus is on a wrong, that should surely be *either* a criminal *or* a tort matter. But matters are not quite that simple: for a criminal case focuses on the defendant, and on whether he culpably wronged the alleged victim, while a tort case focuses on whether the plaintiff was wronged by the defendant; and the answers to these questions can differ. Under English law, a police officer who shot and killed an actually unarmed man during a botched raid must be acquitted on a criminal charge of murder if he believed (reasonably or not) that what he did was a necessary act of self-defence; but a tort case (brought by the victim's family) for assault and battery should succeed unless the defendant offers plausible evidence that his belief was at least reasonable—or perhaps unless the belief was actually true.[37] We can argue about whether a criminal defence of self-defence should require a reasonable, rather than just an 'honest', belief; but as the judges' toying with the idea that a tort defence should require a true belief (an idea that has no purchase in a criminal case) shows, the focus differs as between the criminal and the tort case. The criminal court must acquit the defendant unless it is proved that he culpably wronged the victim; the civil court must find for the plaintiff if she proves that she was wronged, or wrongfully harmed, by the defendant; and it could be true both that the victim was wronged by the defendant and that the defendant did not culpably wrong her.[38] The defendant in the tort case answers to the plaintiff for a wrong that, she alleges, he did her; the defendant in the criminal case answers to the polity for a wrong that, the prosecution alleges, he committed: the legal implications of the defendant's failure to offer an exculpatory answer, and the possible grounds of exculpation, differ in the two kinds of case.

When we identify a victimizing public wrong, one that is serious enough in its wrongfulness or its harmful effects to warrant a formal legal response, we could thus

[34] See above, Chapter 1 at n. 55, and Chapter 1, section 4 more generally.

[35] See A Y K Lee, 'Public Wrongs and the Criminal Law'.

[36] See above, Chapter 1 at n. 54.

[37] See *Ashley v Chief Constable of Sussex Police* [2008] 1 AC 962; above, Chapter 1 at n. 72.

[38] I leave aside here the further point that if the standard of proof for a conviction in a criminal trial is stricter than the standard of proof for a verdict for the plaintiff in a civil case, as it usually is, tort law can provide a recourse for victims if 'their' perpetrator secures a criminal acquittal (as in the O J Simpson case, when his controversial acquittal on a murder charge was followed by a successful tort suit brought by the family of one of the victims).

decide to make it purely a matter for tort law; or to bring it within the reach of the criminal law as well as of tort law; or, perhaps, to make it purely a matter for the criminal law. The third suggestion is unattractive as it stands, since it denies the victim the chance to seek legal vindication for herself; but it would be more plausible if the criminal process allowed the victim a formal voice, as it sometimes does.[39]

Other questions in this area concern such matters as libel and breach of contract. Libel can be criminal in some countries—although the focus might be less on the wrong done to the person libelled than on the implications for public order;[40] but in England it is a matter of private rather than criminal law.[41] Breaches of contract that involve fraud or deception are typically criminal,[42] but breach of an honestly made contract is not criminal, even if wilful. Once again, we must ask what kinds of factor should be relevant to such decisions about the allocation of wrongs to civil rather than to criminal law. Why, for instance, should minor physical assaults be criminal, when what may be much more damaging libels are civil matters: does our criminal law still reflect the old saw that 'sticks and stones may break my bones, but words can never hurt me'? Why should a minor theft, from someone who does not even notice the loss,[43] be criminal, whilst a harmful, maybe deliberate, breach of contract remains a civil matter: does the law reflect an (implausible) assumption that contracts are not an unavoidable part of everyday life—that they are something on which people choose to embark for the sake of expected profit, and as to which they can be expected to bear the risk of breach, or the burden of seeking a remedy; or the thought that it is more important to enable injured parties to secure compensation for losses they suffer than to call wrongdoers to account; or a concern that criminalization might have a chilling effect?

The features that differentiate tort law from criminal law do not themselves answer questions about when we should resort to criminal law rather than, or as well as, tort law in response to this or that kind of public wrong: but they do indicate the factors to which we should attend in trying to answer those questions.[44] Once we have determined that the kind of conduct in question does constitute a public wrong that merits a formal legal response, we must ask whether it should be left to the victim to decide whether and how far to pursue it (whether to sue, whether to settle the case without securing an admission of liability, whether to enforce a judgment in her favour); or is it a kind of wrong that the polity should make its own, thus both sparing the victim the burden of pursuing the case herself, and (potentially) depriving her of the power to drop it? Should the law's focus be only on whether the complainant was wrongfully harmed by the defendant; or on whether the defendant culpably wronged the complainant? Should a verdict against the defendant lead only to victim-focused damages or reparations; or should it lead to a punishment that marks (as is often said) the 'debt' that the defendant owes to 'society'?

(f) Preventive measures

Finally, we should attend to the range of preventive measures that may be used against those accused or suspected of engaging in harmfully wrongful conduct—in

[39] See above, Chapter 1 at nn 64–7.

[40] See e.g. the German *Strafgesetzbuch* s. 130(1) on 'Incitement to Hatred'; for American criminal libel statutes see http://www.firstamendmentcenter.org/criminal-libel-statutes-state-by-state.

[41] Since the abolition of 'criminal', 'seditious', 'obscene', and 'blasphemous' libel: see Coroners and Justice Act 2009, s. 73; J Heawood, 'Let's Cheer the Demise of Criminal Libel'.

[42] See e.g. Fraud Act 2006.

[43] See A P Simester and G R Sullivan, 'On the Nature and Rationale of Property Offences'.

[44] See above, Chapter 1 at nn 70–83.

particular kinds of measure that are connected to the criminal law in one or both of two ways: they can be imposed on those who are suspected (but have not been convicted) of responsible involvement in criminal activity; and they impose requirements whose violation is a criminal offence.[45] There is a wide variety of such 'civil preventive orders':[46] the two most familiar are perhaps the (now replaced) Anti-Social Behaviour Order (ASBO),[47] and the Terrorism Prevention and Investigation Measures (TPIM).[48] In both cases, there are three stages to the process. First, an official person or body is persuaded that a person has been engaged in criminal conduct—in anti-social behaviour, or in 'terrorism-related activity'; second, an order is made imposing various kinds of restriction or requirement on the person in order to prevent him engaging (or, more realistically, to reduce the chances that he will engage) in such activity in the future; third, violation of those restrictions or requirements is made a criminal offence, rendering the person liable to criminal conviction and punishment.[49] ASBOs have now been replaced by two different kinds of order: a 'criminal behaviour order', which can be made only on someone who has been convicted of an offence, and which therefore will not concern us further here; and a 'civil injunction', which a court can make if it 'is satisfied, on the balance of probabilities, that [a person] has engaged or threatens to engage in anti-social behaviour', and the court 'considers it just and convenient to grant the injunction for the purpose of preventing the [person] from engaging in anti-social behaviour'.[50] The injunction can include both prohibitions and requirements—not merely to refrain from anti-social behaviour, but to act in ways that can be expected to prevent future anti-social behaviour, or to refrain from kinds of conduct (for instance from going to certain locations) that might enable such behaviour. Breach of an injunction is not a criminal offence: but if a breach is proved to the criminal standard (i.e. beyond reasonable doubt) it renders the person liable for 'civil contempt of court', which can attract an unlimited fine or up to two years in prison.

We need not engage here in detail with the familiar criticisms that have been brought against these kinds of measure, when imposed not as punishments for crimes of which those on whom they were imposed had been convicted (we would need to ask then whether they could be apt or proportionate sentences for such crimes), but as preventive measures imposed on those who have not been convicted of a crime.[51] There are three familiar objections to any such imposition.[52]

[45] I thus leave aside for present purposes the kinds of 'criminal preventive order' that may be imposed following a criminal conviction (see A J Ashworth and L Zedner, *Preventive Justice*, 76–7): not because such measures do not raise important normative questions, but because they do not directly concern the question of criminalization. I also leave aside here the ways in which mentally disordered (suspected) offenders can be diverted from the criminal process—from being prosecuted at all, or from being tried, or from criminal punishment (for instance under the various provisions of the Mental Health Act 1983, Parts II and III).

[46] See Ashworth and Zedner, *Preventive Justice*, ch. 4: they list examples of such orders on p. 75.

[47] See Crime and Disorder Act 1998, ss 1–4.

[48] Terrorism Prevention and Investigation Measures Act 2011.

[49] I leave aside a few complications here, for instance concerning the fit between the specification of the conduct that justifies an order and the legal definition of the relevant kind of crime, and the standard of proof required.

[50] Anti-social Behaviour, Crime and Policing Act 2014, s. 1.

[51] See e.g. Ashworth and Zedner, *Preventive Justice*, ch. 4; Simester and von Hirsch, *Crimes, Harms, and Wrongs*, ch. 12; A J Ashworth et al (eds), *Prevention and the Limits of the Criminal Law*; R A Duff, 'Perversions and Subversions of Criminal Law'. But see also P Ramsay, *The Insecurity State: Vulnerable Autonomy and the Right to Security in the Criminal Law*; H Carvalho, *The Preventive Turn in Criminal Law*.

[52] See R A Duff, 'Perversions and Subversions of Criminal Law'.

First, such measures are predicated on the person's alleged involvement in criminal conduct, but do not require his conviction for that conduct at a fair criminal trial. Second, the restrictions are to be justified not as proportionate punishments for his alleged criminal conduct, but purely as means of preventing future crimes; in imposing those restrictions, the court is saying that the person is not to be trusted to refrain from such crime for himself: but whilst we *might* be able to justify some distrust-displaying impositions on someone who has been convicted of a crime,[53] it is inconsistent with the respect that is due to the person as a responsible citizen to impose such measures without a conviction. Third, it is at best dubiously legitimate to criminalize the breach of such individualized orders, especially when it is unclear whether the punishment is simply for breaching the order or in fact and in part for the (alleged) criminal conduct that the order aims to prevent. In the case of civil injunctions, a violation of the injunction is admittedly not technically criminal, and the sanction is for 'contempt of court'. But that is a terminological evasion: if we are to justify such a sanction at all, it must be on the grounds that the person disobeyed a judicial requirement (itself justified by his criminal wrongdoing) that he ought to have obeyed.

There is, however, a different kind of order or injunction that need not face the same kinds of criticism. Suppose we identify (roughly) a kind of conduct that we think is a public wrong that at least in principle merits criminalization: we might talk, for instance, of breach of the peace; or of 'anti-social behaviour'; or of making excessive noise, or of other kinds of 'public nuisance'. But we also realize that it would be very difficult to create a justifiable criminal offence to cover such conduct, since it would be very difficult to define such an offence with sufficient precision and clarity to satisfy the requirements of the rule of law. Thus to define a 'public nuisance' simply as any 'nuisance' that 'materially affects the reasonable comfort and convenience of a class of her Majesty's subjects',[54] or to criminalize 'anti-social behaviour' as such, without further definition or explanation, might leave citizens in serious doubt about what kinds of conduct will or will not constitute an offence—as well as leaving courts and officials with a worryingly broad discretion in interpreting the law *ex post*. One way to address this problem is to provide a two-step process of criminalization that avoids the objections to the kinds of civil preventive order noted above.

A local authority can issue an 'abatement notice' to deal with a 'statutory nuisance': it warns the person that what he is doing constitutes such a nuisance, and that he will commit an offence if he disobeys the notice.[55] Such notices are not themselves criminal laws—any more than is an ASBO or a TPIM, or the regulations whose breach constitutes a criminal *malum prohibitum*; but, like those other kinds of order or regulation, they open the way to criminal law when breaches of them are criminalized. They are, however, crucially different from ASBOs and TPIMs. ASBOs and TPIMs may prohibit conduct that could not be portrayed as wrongful, independently of the

[53] See e.g. A von Hirsch and M Wasik, 'Civil Disqualifications Attending Conviction'; R A Duff, 'Who Must Presume Whom to be Innocent of What?', 185–92; Z Hoskins, *Beyond Punishment? A Normative Account of Collateral Restrictions on Offenders*, ch. 5.

[54] Romer LJ, in *Attorney-General v PYA Quarries Ltd* [1957] QB 169, at 184; quoted as authoritative by Lord Schiemann, in *Nottingham City Council v Zain* 2001 WL 825283, para. 8. See also the useful critical discussion of 'breach of the peace' in Scotland in P Ferguson, *Breach of the Peace*.

[55] See Environmental Protection Act 1990, ss 79–80. See also the provisions for 'warning notices' under the Noise Act 1996, ss 1–4; and the provisions in the Anti-social Behaviour Act 2003, ss 40–2.

order: they prohibit such conduct not because it constitutes the mischief against which the law is aimed, but because it might enable or make more likely future commissions of such mischief. Thus when an ASBO forbids a person to enter a certain part of the town, this is not because the court supposes that entering that part of town is itself a public wrong; it is because by barring the person from that area we reduce the chance that he will engage in anti-social behaviour there. By contrast, the kinds of order noted in this paragraph prohibit conduct that constitutes the very kind of mischief at which the law is aimed (public nuisance, for instance)—conduct that is, albeit not already criminal, at least criminalizably wrong. They provide a clearer specification of the kind of conduct that is to count as criminally wrongful, and a warning that to persist with it will attract criminal conviction; they provide a more precise determination of the law, when those on whom it impinges might be uncertain about its precise scope, and a fair warning of the law's demands to those who might infringe them. Those who breach such orders are not convicted, *ex post*, for conduct that they might not have realized was criminal; they are warned *ex ante* that the specified kinds of conduct are, and will be treated as, criminal.

Such orders could also, of course, be used in relation to existing criminal laws whose precise scope might be uncertain or unclear: prosecutors could seek straightforward convictions in cases that clearly involve the mischief at which the law is aimed;[56] and these kinds of order in cases in which it is not clear, or might not have been clear to the accused, whether the conduct involved the mischief. One could envisage a different kind of 'Anti-Social Behaviour Order' being used in this way: in cases in which it might have been unclear, or unclear to the accused person, whether his conduct really constituted the relevant kind of mischief,[57] the court could make an order that would specify the kinds of conduct from which he must refrain—kinds of conduct that are thus authoritatively judged to constitute the relevant mischief. Such an order would not face the kinds of objection faced by the original ASBOs: for its function would be to make clear to the person concerned just what kinds of conduct would constitute a kind of public mischief that was already criminal, thus giving him fair warning before he faced a criminal conviction.[58]

Various other kinds of existing order have something of this character, though their scope is not always limited, in the way that I have suggested they should be limited, to the prohibition of conduct that itself constitutes the mischief against which the law is aimed. We could consider, for instance, the provisions enabling landlords to seek injunctions prohibiting specified kinds of anti-social conduct by tenants;[59] or enabling someone who fears (further) harassment to obtain an injunction that prohibits the injunctee from engaging in conduct that constitutes harassment.[60] We should be

[56] And, of course, take no action when the conduct does not involve that mischief: see above, Chapter 2 at nn 57–9 on the '*De Minimis*' principle.

[57] For instance, the offence of unreasonably causing 'harassment, alarm or distress' (Public Order Act 1986, s. 5): courts could impose an order only if it had been proved that the person concerned had 'acted in an anti-social manner, that is to say, in a manner that caused or was likely to cause harassment, alarm or distress' (Crime and Disorder Act 1998, s. 1(1)).

[58] Compare also 'Acceptable Behaviour Contracts': Home Office, *A Guide to Anti-Social Behaviour Orders and Acceptable Behaviour Contracts*; see R A Duff and S E Marshall, 'How Offensive Can You Get?', 85–7.

[59] Housing Act 1996, s. 153A.

[60] Protection from Harassment Act 1997: s. 3(3)(a) provides for injunctions 'for the purpose of restraining the defendant from pursuing any conduct which amounts to harassment'; harassment is defined as criminal by s. 2, and s. 3(6) makes it a criminal offence to breach such an injunction.

cautious about providing for injunctions to serve such purposes: their availability should not become an excuse for legislatures to define offences in unreasonably broad and vague terms, leaving the courts an inadequately constrained discretion to decide what types of conduct should count as 'anti-social' or as 'offensive', or to leave the effective definition of offences to the officials who formulate the orders. We should ensure that the scope of the orders is limited to kinds of conduct that really do constitute the relevant mischief, and that both their scope and the reasons for them are made clear to the person against whom they are made. A model here might be the requirements for 'binding over orders'—the modern version of 'binding over to keep the peace': 'rather than binding over to "keep the peace" in general terms the court should identify [in writing] the specific conduct or activity from which the individual must refrain', and it must give its reasons for making the order.[61] We should also make sure that suitably robust procedures for challenging such injunctions or orders are available. With these provisos, however, and with the emphatic proviso that such orders should be considered only when it is not feasible to define the relevant wrong with sufficient clarity and precision in a practicable statutory form, we should be ready to consider such orders as another alternative to straightforward criminalization.

This completes my partial, sketchy survey of some of the alternatives to criminalization that legislators and officials (and lay citizens) may have to consider when deciding how to respond to public wrongs; their availability clearly complicates decisions about both formal and substantive criminalization, in ways to which we must now briefly attend.

3. Criminalization 'in the Public Interest'

Public wrongs are wrongs to which we have, collectively, reason to respond. They consist in kinds of conduct that violate the values by which we define ourselves as a polity, and so violate our civil order: if we are committed, as citizens of the polity, to those values and to that order, we will see reason to respond to their violation. On simple versions of legal moralism, to say that we have reason to respond is to say that we have reason to criminalize such conduct: criminal law is focused on wrongdoing, or on public wrongdoing; so any (public) wrongdoing gives us reason to criminalize. As we have now seen, however, to put the matter in those terms is to oversimplify it. We do have reason to respond to any public wrong, and criminalization is one possible response: but it is one among other possible responses (including the response of doing nothing formal); our question must therefore become the question whether we have reason to criminalize *rather than* responding in one of these other ways.[62] We have, so far, reason to criminalize or to Φ, or to Ψ, or to ... (where Φ, Ψ, and so on are alternative, non-criminalizing, responses); but we must then ask what can give us reason to criminalize in particular, as the appropriate mode of response.

Compare also the provisions for family members to obtain 'Non-molestation Orders': Family Law Act 1996, ss 42–42A.

[61] Crown Prosecution Service, *Binding Over Orders*. These do not involve the kind of two-stage criminalization that I have suggested could be, in principle, legitimate, since the breach of a binding over order is not a criminal offence: it simply renders the breacher liable to forfeit the 'recognizance' specified when the order was made.

[62] Or sometimes whether we have reason to criminalize *as well as* responding in one of these other ways.

That question faces legislators, in deciding what criminal statutes to enact—what to formally criminalize: they must decide what kinds of response to provide, as available or as mandatory, to different kinds of public wrong. But a version of it also faces officials involved in the processes of substantive criminalization, and lay citizens in deciding whether to treat as criminal formally criminal conduct that they might witness or suffer.[63] Officials must ask not just whether there is evidence of the commission of what is formally defined as a crime, but also whether they should respond to it as a crime: whether they should bring it within the criminal process of investigation, accusation, and prosecution. To answer that question they should ask whether it is in the public interest to treat it as a criminal matter: for their responsibility is to serve the public interest, in the ways that their roles define. Lay citizens who must decide whether to report a crime should also base their decisions on the public interest: although it will no doubt be tempting to be guided by more personal considerations, if I witness or suffer what is justifiably defined as criminal by the law, I should ask myself not whether it is in my interest, or in the interests of those most directly involved (including perhaps the perpetrator), to report it, but whether it is in the public interest to do so; I should think, that is, not just as a private person, but as a citizen.

That is one reason why prosecutorial codes distinguish the two kinds of condition that must be satisfied before a prosecution goes ahead. A prosecutor must determine first whether there is sufficient evidence of the suspected person's guilt to justify bringing the case to court,[64] but then whether it is 'in the public interest' to do so; one question that bears on the latter determination is whether some kind of disposal other than prosecution would better serve the public interest.[65]

But what is 'the public interest' in this context: what could make it in the public interest to prosecute an alleged offender, or to opt instead for one of the other available possibilities? Any answer to this question will need to focus on the features that distinguish criminalization (both formal and substantive) from other kinds of response to public wrongs: what could make it in the public interest to favour this particular, distinctive, kind of response? Those features have been identified already in Chapter 1, and so need only be briefly rehearsed here.

First, criminal law deals with wrongs as wrongs. That is to say, the wrongfulness of the type of conduct that is criminalized is not merely a condition of its legitimate criminalization, but the object or focus of criminalization:[66] to criminalize it is to portray it, and censure it, as a wrong. It is also therefore to provide for a particular, wrong-focused process in response to such conduct: the alleged perpetrator is liable to be formally accused as a wrongdoer, and to be called to answer to that accusation, and to answer for the wrong, through a criminal trial. Thus we have good reason to criminalize a type of conduct that constitutes a public wrong, rather than opting for some other kind of response that does not make wrongfulness salient in this way, if and when it is important thus to focus on the conduct's wrongfulness.

Second, criminal law portrays, or constitutes, the wrongs with which it deals as 'public', not only in the sense that they are wrongs of which the polity takes formal,

[63] See above, Chapter 1 at nn 154–82.

[64] See Crown Prosecution Service, *Code for Crown Prosecutors*, para. 4.4; also, for Scottish prosecutors, see Crown Office and Procurator Fiscal Service, *Prosecution Code*, 04. I suggested earlier (above, Chapter 1, n. 167) that the appropriate question at this stage is whether there is sufficient evidence not merely of something that fits the formal definition of a crime, but of the perpetration of the kind of mischief at which the law is aimed.

[65] See *Code for Crown Prosecutors*, paras 4.8, 7.2; *Prosecution Code*, 08–10.

[66] On objects as against conditions, see above, Chapter 3 at n. 94, Chapter 5 at n. 107.

legal notice, but also in the sense that even when there is an individual victim of the wrong, the wrong belongs to all of us collectively, to the polity, rather than to the individual victim. It is we, through the police, the prosecutor, and the court, who call the alleged perpetrator to answer—not the victim; and it is up to us, rather than to the victim, whether and how the case proceeds. The victim might have some informal say in whether the case proceeds, and we noted earlier the possibility of blurring the lines between criminal and civil law by giving the complainant a more formal role—for instance by providing that a case will be brought only if the complainant requests it, or consents to it, or does not object it:[67] but for more serious crimes it is the polity that formally, and in fact, decides whether and on what charge the alleged wrongdoer is to be prosecuted. One question then is whether we should embrace a degree of boundary-blurring between tort law and criminal law. Perhaps instead of trying to draw a clear-cut distinction between crimes, which belong wholly to the polity, and torts, which belong wholly to the victim, we should work with a more nuanced spectrum, from 'pure' crimes at one end, in which the process is controlled fully by the polity, to 'pure' torts at the other, in which the plaintiff has sole control (within the limits set by the legal procedures) over 'her' case; along that spectrum, towards the plaintiff-complainant's end, there would be room for some degree of complainant control or formal participation. For the time being, however, we can take the public ownership of a case as a hallmark of criminal as distinct from tort (public as distinct from private) law: we will then see reason to criminalize a type of wrong, rather than making it a matter of tort law, to the extent that we think it important that the case be owned by the polity in this way—and that the defendant answer to the polity.

Third, criminal law seeks categorical, defendant-focused judgments. That is to say, criminal trials are trials of the defendant, and end either with the categorical verdict that the defendant has been proved guilty of the criminal wrong specified in the charge, or with the categorical verdict that, since his guilt has not been proved, the presumption of his innocence remains undefeated.[68] The trial cannot formally end with a judgment that responsibility is shared between the defendant and the complainant, in the way that a tort verdict can hold the plaintiff partly responsible for the harm in respect of which she sued; or with a verdict that ascribes 'contributory negligence' to the complainant with the effect that the defendant's liability is thereby reduced.[69] Some defences (most obviously, self-defence and provocation) might in effect argue that the victim was partly or wholly to blame for what the defendant did, and might thus be said to put the victim as well as the defendant 'on trial' (often without the kinds of protection that the trial affords the defendant); in other kinds of case, notably rape cases, complainants who give evidence and are subjected to cross-examination (or about whom allegations are made by the defendant) can feel—with justice—that they are also on trial. But these are problematic aspects of a trial, since the complainant is not meant to be on trial: the focus is on whether the defendant is guilty; strictly speaking, even when the defendant's answer to the charge involved claims about wrongdoing on the part of the complainant, an acquittal does not express a formal acceptance of those claims. We thus have reason to criminalize a public wrong insofar as it matters that we seek this kind of categorical judgment on the defendant's conduct—a judgment that either categorically censures him for committing a public wrong, or categorically acquits him.

[67] See above, Chapter 1 at nn 63–7.
[68] On this reading of the 'Not Guilty' verdict, see Duff et al, *The Trial on Trial (3)*, at 83–4.
[69] See above, Chapter 5 at nn 98–100.

Fourth, criminal law typically involves punishment, and further collateral consequences that often attach to punishment. I have argued that we should not take punishment to be the focus of criminal law, or the main point of criminalization, and the legitimacy of many kinds of collateral consequence is controversial—although we cannot engage in that controversy here.[70] However, insofar as we can justifiably attach such consequences, whether penal or non-penal, to conviction for a criminal offence, they can generate reasons for criminalization: one reason for criminalizing a type of public wrong, rather than opting for some other kind of response, is that this will make such consequences available.[71] Criminal law might, as I have argued, have purposes and values independent of criminal punishment; but so long as it includes punishment, and other collateral consequences, they must bear on whether and when we have good reason to criminalize.

What then could make it in the public interest to favour this distinctive kind of response to a kind of public wrong? One obvious answer is that the central public interest is in the prevention of the kinds of public wrong that are candidates for criminalization: the first and central question, for legislators in deciding what to criminalize, and for officials in deciding when to prosecute, is therefore whether doing so will efficiently serve that preventive goal. As I have noted already,[72] a kind of preventive concern is intrinsic to criminalization, since to criminalize a type of conduct is to mark it as something that we ought not to do; and it would be absurd to deny that one reason for making and enforcing criminal laws is that we will thereby reduce the incidence of the kinds of conduct that we criminalize. However, first, even in relation to prevention the question should not be simply whether criminalization is an efficient method of reducing crime, but whether this mode of prevention is an appropriate way for a polity to deal with its citizens. Second, there are also non-preventive reasons for criminalization—reasons that have to do with the importance of taking formal public notice of public wrongs by calling their perpetrators to account. If we focus on punishment as the key identifying feature of criminal law, and are not tempted by the simple retributivist thought that the aim of criminal law is to impose deserved suffering on wrongdoers, we might think that what justifies criminal punishment can only be its efficiency as a means of preventing the kinds of conduct that are criminalized: the public interest in criminalization must therefore be in its preventive efficiency (by acceptable means). But once we take seriously the other distinguishing features of criminal law, as something more than mere preludes or pathways to punishment, we can see how criminal law, as a distinctive kind of response to public wrongs, helps to constitute a distinctive kind of civil order (a civil order that, in its preventive modes, it also protects): it helps to constitute a civil order that takes (whose citizens take) its defining values seriously, and that will therefore respond publicly to violations of those values; and that takes its members seriously as responsible members of the normative political community who can be expected to answer to each other for the public wrongs that they commit.[73]

[70] See above, Chapter 1 n. 21; Hoskins, *Beyond Punishment?*, 'Criminalization and the Collateral Consequences of Conviction'.

[71] Insofar as some such consequences are an inevitable result of criminalization, they can also generate reasons *against* criminalization. Whether they do so depends on whether we count them as costs of criminalization: for instance, whereas for many theorists the burdens that criminal punishment imposes must be counted as costs of criminalization, for some kinds of retributivist they count as part of the very justifying aim of criminalization.

[72] See above, Chapter 6 at nn 41–7, 114–16.

[73] See above, Chapter 5, sections 4–6.

None of this tells us what we should criminalize, either formally or substantively. For, first, the idea of a public wrong has not yet been given determinate, substantive content: I have said a bit about what makes a wrong a public wrong (its relationship to or its impact on some aspect of the polity's civil order), but very little about which wrongs could plausibly be regarded as public wrongs. Second, even if we attend only to the question of what we have good reason in principle to criminalize, leaving aside questions about what we should criminalize all things (including the practical costs and difficulties of criminalization) considered, the most we can say so far is that we have good reason to consider criminalization as one among a range of possible responses to public wrongs: though I have indicated the kinds of question (related to the distinctive features of criminal law) that we must ask in deciding whether to criminalize rather than responding in some other way, I have said almost nothing about how we are to answer those questions.

Here, it might now seem, is where we need a theory of criminalization, which would provide substantive principles or criteria by reference to which we could determine both what we should count as a public wrong at all, and when we have good reason to criminalize such wrongs rather than responding in some other way. But I argued in Chapter 6 that we should not expect to be able to establish such a theory—such a master principle, or master set of principles, of criminalization. It will not help us to say, for instance, that we have good reason to criminalize a type of conduct if and only if it causes or creates a risk of wrongful harm, or if and only if by criminalizing it we can reduce the incidence of (wrongful) harms: for apart from the question of what is to count as a (wrongful) harm, we must ask which kinds of harm concern the law at all, and how close the relationship must be between a type of conduct and a relevant harm if we are to have reason to criminalize that type of conduct; when we have reason to criminalize rather than responding in another way; and whether there are kinds of wrongful mischief that should concern us, as public wrongs, but that cannot be described as harms without stretching the concept of harm so far that it ceases to do any useful work.[74] We can avoid some of these questions if we posit a non-exclusive harm principle, and say only that the (wrongful) harmfulness of a type of conduct gives us *a* good reason to criminalize it, without adding that this is *the only* good reason we can have: but we would then no longer be offering a complete guide to criminalization, and would still face the question of which kinds of harm, or of wrongful harm, are to count as public matters. Something similar is true, I argued, of other would-be thick principles of criminalization: they cannot give us all the guidance we need in trying to decide what kinds of conduct we have good reason to criminalize.

Can a thin principle offer us any useful guidance? The principle that I have proposed is, as we have seen, a thin or formal principle, which can therefore give us no substantive guidance—

A. *We have reason to criminalize a type of conduct if, and only if, it constitutes a public wrong.*

B. *A type of conduct constitutes a public wrong if, and only if, it violates the polity's civil order.*

As we can now see, it also gives us no indication of when we have reason to criminalize a public wrong, rather than responding in some other way. However, we can now add to the principle, in the light of the present discussion: not to specify the kinds of

[74] See above, Chapter 6 at nn 133–62.

substantive consideration that can give us reason to criminalize rather than responding in some other way, but to indicate the kinds of question that we must ask in deciding whether we should, in principle, criminalize rather than responding in another way. We must ask whether it is important, and how important it is, to mark and respond to the wrong as a wrong, by seeking to call its perpetrator to account; whether it is important, and how important it is, that the calling to account be collective—that the perpetrator be called to answer by and to the polity as a whole (and whether or how far the direct victim, if there is one, should have control of the case); whether it is important, and how important it is, to seek an authoritative, categorical judgment of the alleged wrongdoer's guilt or innocence; and whether it is important, and how important it is, to provide for punishment to be imposed on the wrongdoer (as something distinct from the kind of compensation that can result from a tort case or be agreed through a process of mediation or negotiation).[75]

Once we begin to ask such questions as these, however, the distinction I have been drawing between the question whether we have good reason in principle to criminalize a type of conduct, and the question whether we should criminalize it all things considered, begins to blur. The 'in principle' question was supposed to be settled prior to more pragmatic questions of practicable offence definition, of enforcement, and of the various kinds of cost that attach to criminalization. Once we have decided that we have good reason in principle to criminalize Φ, as a public wrong that merits a formal public response, we can go on to ask such further questions as whether we can formulate an offence definition that can be clearly understood by citizens, and applied with reasonable consistency by the courts; whether the effective enforcement of the offence would threaten other important values (of liberty and privacy, for instance); whether the material costs of effective enforcement would be worth incurring, given the significance of the wrong; and, of course, what effect criminalization could be expected to have on the incidence of Φ. But if our question is, as it must be, whether we have good reason to criminalize Φ rather than responding in some other way, such pragmatic questions become relevant more quickly: for a comparison of criminalization with other ways of responding to a public wrong must pay some attention to the practicalities and costs (normative and material) of each kind of response. Nonetheless, in order to keep the discussion within manageable limits, I will focus here on the 'in principle' questions: that is, on the principled reasons we might have, to do with the distinctive character of criminal law, for thinking that criminalization is an appropriate response to a type of public wrong.

A further complication is that the costs of criminalization depend in crucial part on the kind of criminal process we have and on the consequences of a conviction. If our system of criminal law imposes severe burdens on those accused of criminal offences (through an onerous process of investigation and trial), and on those convicted of criminal offences (through the punishments that they then suffer, and the further

[75] Though to answer this last question we will of course need to take a view on the justifying aims of punishment. It is worth remembering, however, that even if we justify punishment in primarily preventive terms, this should not be taken to imply that we have good reason to criminalize only if criminalization can be expected to be an efficient means of reducing the incidence of Φ. It might be important to make the kind of formal declaration that enacting a criminal statute involves, that we take Φ seriously as a public wrong, and the perceived non-enforcement of such a law could undermine that claim that we take Φ seriously: but enforcement—for instance police intervention and prosecutions in obvious cases of Φ—might have no significant effect on the incidence of Φ. The likelihood that criminalization would be in this respect ineffective is relevant to the decision about whether to criminalize, but it need not be decisive.

consequences of conviction such as criminal record), we should reserve criminalization for those kinds of wrong to which it is really important to respond in this way. If, on the other hand, we can construct a system of criminal law that can provide suitably modest and moderate ways of dealing with relatively minor wrongs, we might be able to justify a wider criminal law that makes it possible to prosecute a wider range of public wrongs.[76]

The account that I have suggested here—the public wrongs principle, the considerations that should guide our decisions about whether to criminalize a type of public wrong in preference to some other kind of response—is meant to illuminate the logical structure of deliberations about criminalization: more precisely, as a normative account, it is intended to illuminate the structure that such deliberations ought to have. Those deliberations do not, and on this account should not, display a single systematic structure, of the kind we would find if we could formulate a plausible substantive master principle of criminalization: we cannot, that is, say that we have good reason to criminalize a type of conduct (rather than responding in some other way) if and only if it has a specified substantive feature; we cannot derive conclusions about what we have good reason to criminalize from a single substantive master principle or integrated set of such principles. Our deliberations will inevitably be messier than that, since we will need to appeal to a range of different values in identifying a range of public wrongs—values unified only by the fact that they all play a part in defining the polity's civil order; and we will, as we have seen, need to appeal to a range of considerations in deciding whether we have reason to criminalize a type of public wrong rather than responding in some other way (or providing no formal response at all).

I cannot embark here on a detailed account of the kind of substantive criminal law (its scope and its internal structure) that might result from deliberations structured in the way that I have suggested—deliberations that identify public wrongs in the light of a clear understanding of the polity's civil order and of its defining values, and then ask whether we also have good reason, in light of the distinctive features of criminal law, to respond to such wrongs by criminalizing them. That would be a task for another volume, not for the final part of the final chapter of an already long book. However, I should at least provide some examples of how we should, given the account suggested here, rationally reconstruct decisions to criminalize or not to criminalize various types of conduct: this will help to show how this account can explain some easy cases (cases in which it seems obvious that we should, or that we should not, resort to criminalization) as easy cases, and also explain why some hard cases are indeed hard.

This is what I will do in the remainder of this chapter. As we will see, there are two primary deliberative routes towards criminalization, with different kinds of starting point: the distinction between them roughly matches that between '*mala in se*' and '*mala prohibita*'—between crimes consisting in conduct whose wrongfulness is prior to and independent of its legal regulation, and crimes consisting in conduct that is wrongful only because it violates a legal regulation. (As we will also see, the two routes cannot be kept entirely separate; and the claim that the wrongfulness of *mala in se* is pre-legal will need some modest qualification.) One route, which has the simpler logical structure, begins with wrongs—with the recognition of a public wrong to which we realize that we have reason to respond; criminalization is then at once on the table as a possible response (among others). The other route begins not with wrongs but with harms (or, less frequently, with goods). We recognize a kind of harm that the polity

[76] See at nn 16, 29–30 above.

should seek to prevent or alleviate, or a kind of good that the polity should promote; we then realize that we can efficiently and appropriately alleviate such harm, or promote such good, by a system of legal regulation; and criminalization then appears on the table as a possible response to breaches of such regulations.[77]

4. Varieties of Public Wrong (a): *Mala in Se* and the Construction of Public Wrongs

The most obvious examples of criminalizable wrongs, from a perspective focused on public wrongs and civil order, are those whose only direct victim is the polity as a whole, or its citizens collectively. When a wrong has an identifiable individual victim, it might not be at once obvious how it violates the polity's civil order (unless it is also likely to cause wider fear and anxiety, for instance); we might wonder why it should count as the polity's public wrong, rather than as the victim's wrong—a wrong for the victim to choose to pursue, or not, through the civil courts. By contrast, it is easy to see why wrongs directed against or impacting on some aspect of the polity's collective life count as public wrongs, which concern all citizens as citizens, and to which they must therefore respond collectively. We can mention here such wrongs as tax evasion and other kinds of fraud against the public purse; bribery of public officials; electoral malpractice; damage to public property; and various kinds of public disorder that disturb the peace without injuring or threatening particular individuals.[78] I will say a little more about public order offences, and about tax evasion, below,[79] but will spend no more time here on these kinds of obviously public wrong: I can more fruitfully illustrate the character and implications of an account of crimes as public wrongs by looking at wrongs whose direct victims are individuals rather than 'the public'. Some of these wrongs seem so obviously criminalizable that it is hard to imagine a system of criminal law that did not define them as crimes; murder and rape are the two obvious examples here. We can usefully begin with these, since they are indeed, in one way, the simplest examples: that is, their criminalization is simple both structurally, in that the argument for criminalizing them is direct, and normatively, in that their criminalization seems incontrovertibly justified. As we will also see, however, their criminalization is in other ways not so simple.

Why is it so obvious that murder and rape should be criminal? Any theory of criminalization will have an answer to this question: a simple legal moralist will point out that they are obvious and serious moral wrongs, and a *Rechtsgut* theorist that they violate individual goods that the law of a *Rechtsstaat* must surely protect, while advocates of a harm principle will point out that such conduct is almost always seriously harmful,[80] and that criminalizing it will help to prevent such harms. But what can a

[77] On the distinction between *mala in se* and *mala prohibita*, see above, Chapter 1 at n. 45; and at nn 136–40 below.

[78] See above, Chapter 4 at nn 4–9. There is also treason, which includes the wrong of 'adhering to the King's enemies' (see Treason Act 1351; *Joyce v DPP* [1946] AC 347); but this is not the place to explore the murky history of treason in English law (see J Horder, *Ashworth's Principles of Criminal Law*, 24–6).

[79] See at nn 129–30, 154–5 below: some of these wrongs are not, we should note, 'pure' *mala in se*: not only do they presuppose particular kinds of legal institution (for instance of taxation and of elections); they also involve the violation of legal regulations, so that their wrongfulness cannot be said to be pre-legal. But, as we will see (at nn 135–40 below), the distinction between *mala in se* and *mala prohibita* is not and need not be a sharp one.

[80] We need not ask here whether deliberate killings and rapes are *always* harmful: whether, for instance, death can be a benefit, as in cases of requested euthanasia; or whether we can imagine a case of

public wrongs theorist who appeals to the idea of civil order say? We can say that such wrongs count as public wrongs because they are clearly inconsistent with, manifest violations of, any remotely plausible conception of civil order—any conception, that is, of how the members of a polity can live together as citizens. Some kinds of interpersonal wrong belong, from the polity's perspective, to a private realm: they violate the bonds of intimate relationships, of friendship, or of professional collegiality, but not those of our civic life. If I betray my lover's or my friend's trust, or let down my colleagues, this might be a serious wrong—so serious that it threatens or destroys our relationship; but it does not deny or negate the conditions under which we can live as citizens who share a civic life. Murder and rape, however, flagrantly negate those conditions: how could we imagine a polity in which it was permissible (as far as the polity was concerned) for citizens to murder or rape each other at will? We need not distinguish different conceptions of civil order, reflecting different political theories of state and society, here: for any viable conception of civil order must count these as serious wrongs.[81] Before turning to the ways in which these cases are not so simple, however, we must note two points about their simplicity.

First, they are intrinsically, rather than consequentially, inconsistent with civil order. That is to say, they do not violate that order in virtue of their consequences—for instance in virtue of the fear and insecurity, or further violence, that they might cause; they violate it in themselves, since they are utterly inconsistent with the terms on which citizens could live together. But, second, to say that they count as public wrongs because they violate the civil order is not to say that that is what makes them wrongs. Rape committed in England is a crime under English law, triable in an English court (regardless of whether the victim or the offender is an English citizen),[82] whereas a rape committed in Poland is not; this is because the rape committed in England violates the civil order of that polity, whereas a rape committed in Poland does not. But the wrong is the same in both England and Poland: it is, we might say, a wrong that violates what we owe to each other simply as human beings,[83] and in limiting its attention to murders or rapes committed in England English law does not imply that murders or rapes committed elsewhere are not wrongs, or are not the same, and as serious, kinds of wrong. The violation of the civil order of England involved in the commission of a murder or rape in England is not the object of the criminal law or criminal liability—it is not what the murderer or rapist is convicted of and punished for: he is convicted and punished for the wrong that he did to his victim—just the same wrong as that committed by a murderer or rapist in Poland. That he committed the wrong in England, and thus violated the civil order of England, is a condition of his liability under English law:[84] it is what makes that wrong the business of the English polity and its laws, thus bringing it within the ambit of English criminal law and bringing him

'pure' rape in which the victim is grievously wronged without being harmed (J Gardner and S Shute, 'The Wrongness of Rape').

[81] Compare Hart's discussion of the 'minimum content of natural law': H L A Hart, *The Concept of Law*, ch. 9.

[82] Or a guest, since any decent polity will take wrongs committed against (or by) its guests as seriously as it takes those committed against (or by) its citizens: see above, Chapter 3 at nn 88–94.

[83] Compare M Renzo, 'Responsibility and Answerability in the Criminal Law'; and see above, Chapter 3 at nn 93–4.

[84] See above, Chapter 3 at n. 94, Chapter 5 at n. 107. I leave aside the principles of 'nationality' and of 'passive personality' (see above, Chapter 3 at n. 14, Chapter 5 at n. 115), though the English law of murder applies a nationality principle (Offences Against the Person Act 1861, s. 9). To adopt one of these principles is to extend the polity's civil order beyond its territorial boundaries, to include its citizens wherever they might be.

within the jurisdiction of an English court; but the wrong that is thus made the business of English law is the wrong of murdering or raping a human being.

To say that murder and rape are obvious public wrongs is not yet to say that we have reason to criminalize them, rather than responding in some other way: but it is equally obvious that we have very good reason to criminalize them.[85] Given the seriousness of such wrongs, and the way in which they violate basic conditions of civic life, it is important that we take formal notice of them as wrongs, and seek to call their perpetrators to account: if we allowed such wrongs to be committed with impunity,[86] we would be betraying the basic values to which we purport, as a polity, to be committed. It is important that we collectively call them to public account: it should not be left to the victims (or their families) to pursue the perpetrators.[87] Nor indeed should it be simply up to them whether the perpetrator is pursued: even if the victim or the victim's family is ready to forgive the wrongdoer (as a matter of their personal relationship with him), and would prefer not to see him prosecuted, it is in the public interest that he is called to account, given the centrality of the values that he has violated. It is important too that we make (that a court pass, in our name) an authoritative and categorical condemnation of the wrong, if it is proved against the defendant: these are wrongs from which we should be able to expect to be categorically safe as we go about our ordinary lives (an expectation that is as much normative as empirical); wrongs whose seriousness is not qualified, and whose perpetrator's culpability is not mitigated, by their victim's 'contributory negligence', even if the victim did knowingly act in a way that made her vulnerable.[88] Finally, whether punishment is seen as a preventive matter, or as retribution, or as a communicative enterprise, we can see that so long as we have a system of criminal punishment at all, punishment must be available for such wrongs as these.

Murder and rape are simple (so far) cases of justified criminalization, and it was worth making clear why they are simple cases—before showing why they are not altogether simple. There are equally simple cases on the other side: examples of wrongs that, serious though they may be, it is clear that liberal polities have no reason to criminalize. Some of these have been noted already at various points in this book—most obviously, the kinds of essentially personal wrong we commit against those with whom we have more particular, and intimate, relationships than that of fellow citizens. When I act in a way that violates the bonds of friendship, or of an intimate partnership, I commit what might be a serious wrong, meriting criticism from those whose business it is—from my friends, from my lover: but these are not wrongs that concern my fellow citizens in virtue of our shared membership in the polity; nor, accordingly, can they be the business of the criminal law. However, a common example of a wrong that liberal polities will obviously not criminalize—adultery—is not quite such a simple case, at least in polities that recognize it as a ground for divorce:[89] for to specify adultery as a ground for divorce is to specify it as a public wrong—a wrong that violates the norms

[85] See text preceding n. 75 above for the questions that we must ask in this context.

[86] On 'impunity', see above, Chapter 5 at nn 123–8.

[87] Rape victims might think it better to pursue tort cases against their attackers, rather than relying on the criminal law: but that is a mark of the failure of the criminal justice system, and thus of the polity whose system it is, to call the perpetrators to account as it should.

[88] See above, Chapter 5 at nn 98–9; hence the justified criticism of judges who suggest that a rapist's guilt is mitigated by his victim's careless or even reckless behaviour. Sometimes the wrongness of a homicide can be negated, or qualified, by the victim's role in the matter—most obviously in cases of defence (of self or of others), and more controversially in cases of provocation: but killings whose wrongness is thus negated or qualified are for that reason not murders; and no negligence on the victim's part can mitigate the wrong committed by a wilful killer.

[89] See https://www.gov.uk/divorce/grounds-for-divorce; and Chapter 4 at nn 108–15 above.

of a public institution, of which the polity therefore takes formal notice. It is true that so long as adultery is not also a criminal offence, the polity does not *insist* on taking such formal censorial notice of it: it leaves married couples free to agree that sexual fidelity is not important to their marriage, or to forgive each other's infidelities.[90] But a more consistent view of adultery as a private rather than a public wrong would remove it as a possible ground for divorce (unless, perhaps, a commitment to marital fidelity became an optional clause in a marital contract, whose breach could then be grounds for dissolving the contract).

Although it is thus obvious that any polity must criminalize such wrongs as murder and rape, their criminalization is not an entirely simple matter, as we will see if we ask not just whether, but how they should be criminalized: how should these crimes be defined? Matters would still be relatively simple if we could refer to reasonably clear extra-legal conceptions of such wrongs: for we could then say that, although for practical reasons to do with the requirements of the criminal process the law might need to adopt technical legal definitions of murder and rape, it should as far as possible define them in terms that match those extra-legal conceptions; if the hallmark of a *malum in se* is that it is wrong independently of the law, and if the criminal law should function as a formal declaration and condemnation of such pre-legal wrongs, surely its offence definitions should aim to capture those pre-legal wrongs. There is some truth in this, since we do have some conception of murder and rape as moral wrongs independently of the criminal law's definitions: but we do not, as citizens, share a clear or precise enough collective conception of those wrongs to be able to say that that is what the criminal law should try to capture; the law's task is to construct, not simply to try to mirror, a conception of these wrongs as criminal wrongs.[91]

(The Canadian Supreme Court appeared to take a different view, when it held that Canada's version of the felony murder rule was unconstitutional: for the court appealed to 'the essential elements of certain crimes',[92] as if crimes, or 'true crimes',[93] existed as wrongs independently of any legislative definition, so that legislation could be judged as (un)constitutional in the light of those pre-legal 'essential elements'. There is certainly room for principled argument about the felony murder rule, and about whether subjective recklessness, involving foresight of the risk of the relevant result, should be a condition of liability for any serious crime: but such arguments are about how we, and our criminal law, should construct murder as a criminal wrong, not about the precise contours and structure of a pre-legal essence.)

Once we ask how we should define such wrongs as murder and rape as crimes, we must ask further, more difficult questions, about how we should understand the character of these wrongs, and about their scope. Should we, for instance, see the core wrong of murder as consisting in the knowing, unjustified, causing of death; or in an attack on another person's life? Should rape be defined as paradigmatically a crime of violence, or in terms of lack of consent;[94] should sexual intercourse secured by

[90] And see https://www.gov.uk/divorce/grounds-for-divorce: 'You can't give adultery as a reason [for divorce] if you lived together as a couple for 6 months after you found out about it'.

[91] See more generally L Farmer, 'Criminal Wrongs in Historical Perspective', *Making the Modern Criminal Law: Criminalization and Civil Order* especially chs 8 and 9.

[92] See *R v Vaillancourt* [1987] 2 SCR 636, at 651; *R v Martineau* [1990] 2 SCR 633, at 644.

[93] See *R v Martineau*, at 634.

[94] See V Tadros, 'Rape Without Consent'. Should we indeed define rape as a distinct crime, rather than following Canada's example and defining a broader offence of 'sexual assault' as one kind of assault within the category of 'offences against the person' (see Canadian Criminal Code (RSC, 1985, c. C-46), ss 271–3)?

deception count as rape, or as a different kind of wrong—and what kinds of deception should be taken to negate consent?[95] How should we mark out murder and rape, as the most serious crimes of their type, from other lesser crimes of homicide or sexual assault? We must also ask, in various contexts, what kind of care we should be required to take of or for each other. This question arises immediately in the context of rape, since we need to decide when a mistaken belief in consent should negate liability: should rape be so defined as to require, if not knowledge that the victim does not consent, at least a concurrent awareness that the victim might not be consenting;[96] or should it be enough that the defendant did not 'reasonably believe' that the victim consented?[97] On the latter view, we owe it to a prospective sexual partner not merely not to persist if aware of a risk that there is no consent, but to take 'reasonable' care to make sure that there is consent; we commit the serious wrong of rape if we fail to do so when consent is in fact lacking. In taking this authoritative stand, the law is not—it could not be—trying to capture a shared pre-existing, pre-legal moral conception of rape: it is (those involved in creating the new law are) constructing a conception of rape as a civic, and therefore criminal, wrong.

Analogous issues about the care we owe to each other, and other questions, arise in relation to murder and other kinds of homicide. There are familiar questions, which I cannot pursue here, about defences to murder—about the proper definitions of such complete or partial defences as self-defence and provocation, about whether duress or necessity should be available as defences. There are also questions, revealing for present purposes, about whether euthanasia, or assisting a suicide, should be non-criminal under certain circumstances—non-criminal either as a matter of the formal law, or as a matter of official policy in applying the law.[98] The decriminalization of suicide itself can be seen to reflect a judgment not that suicide is morally permissible, but that it is (assuming a rationally competent agent) a private matter as far as the law is concerned: whilst a polity should, as part of its health and welfare provisions, offer help for those who seek it, it is not for the polity to take a formal view on the ethics of suicide. Given that view, and a respect for the autonomy of citizens who should be able to pursue their legitimate projects, it might seem rational for the polity then to decriminalize both assisting suicide and euthanasia, if (but only if) it could be certain that the assistance or the euthanasia was genuinely requested by a competent agent: for if suicide is in the law's eyes a private matter, so too should a request for assistance be a private matter, and so too should be a helpful response to such a request.[99] That is,

[95] Compare recent, controversial cases in which people have been convicted of sexual assault by penetration when they had deceived their sexual partners about their gender—such deception was held to vitiate consent (Sexual Offences Act 2003, ss 2, 76; the charge could not be rape, which by s. 1 of the Act requires penile penetration, which raises further questions). See A Sharpe, 'Criminalising Sexual Intimacy: Transgender Defendants and the Legal Construction of Non-Consent'; 'There's More than Meets the Eye in the Case of Gayle Newland'. There used to be a distinct offence in Scotland of procuring a woman to have sexual intercourse 'by false pretences or false representations' (Criminal Law (Consolidation) (Scotland) Act 1995 s. 7(2)): this was abolished in the Sexual Offences (Scotland) Act 2009.

[96] See, notoriously, *Morgan* [1976] AC 182.

[97] See Sexual Offences Act 2003, s. 1(1)(c).

[98] On assisting a suicide, see Chapter 1 at nn 168–76 above. I mention this here, since one could read the offence as a relic of the time when suicide was a crime, so that the assister was complicit in a criminal homicide. Suicide was decriminalized in England by the Suicide Act 1961, s. 1 (s. 2 defines the crime of 'complicity in another's suicide'); it was not criminal in Scotland (G H Gordon, *The Criminal Law of Scotland* (2nd edn), 727).

[99] It is important to talk here of requests rather than of consent: consent could be given (gladly or reluctantly) to a proposal or suggestion by another person; a request is a surer expression of the person's own will.

of course, an oversimplified way of putting the argument for the decriminalization of assisting suicide and of genuinely voluntary (competently requested) euthanasia: but it points up two relevant features of the current law and the debates around it.

First, we need to get clear about the mischief at which the law is aimed. In particular, should we take it that the relevant mischief is (as the letter of the law implies) intentional killing, or the intentional assistance of a self-killing, even if it is earnestly requested by a rationally competent 'victim'? Or should we instead understand the mischief as the killing, or 'assistance' in the self-killing, of someone who does not truly want to die; and explain the absence of a formal defence for genuinely voluntary euthanasia, or requested assistance to suicide, in terms of the difficulty of establishing the necessary facts about the request and the requester's rational competence, and the dangers of various kinds of coercion, pressure, or slippery slope if the law formally allowed such a defence? Insofar as the latter interpretation is plausible, it opens the way to the exercise of discretion by officials (and lay citizens) involved in applying the law, to avoid prosecuting cases in which that mischief is clearly not involved.[100]

Second, even those who advocate the decriminalization of requested euthanasia or assisting suicide do not usually propose that the law should treat these as private matters. To treat them as private matters would involve requiring nothing more than a competent request to negate or rebut a criminal charge: the act would be non-criminal just so long as its 'victim' freely requested it.[101] To take this view would not be to judge that such actions are morally justified or permissible just so long as they are competently requested: it would be to judge that it is not for the polity to pass a collective judgment on their morality. However, legal provisions for euthanasia and assisting suicide, both actual and proposed, typically specify more substantive conditions than that: the person requesting assistance in dying must be suffering from a terminal illness, or some other gravely harmful condition.[102] To legislate in such terms as these is to claim that assisted dying is the polity's business, even when done at the competent request of the person concerned: it is for the polity to determine the substantive conditions that give such a request normative authority. Here again we see the importance of distinguishing questions about what falls within the public realm from questions about what should be permissible within that realm.

Further questions about the kind of care that we owe each other, analogous to the question noted above in relation to rape, arise when we turn from murder to other forms of homicide, such as reckless or negligent homicide.[103] For reckless homicide must involve taking or creating a risk of causing death that it is unreasonable to take,[104] while negligent homicide must involve 'a gross deviation from the standard of care

[100] See above, Chapter 1 at nn 173–5, on assisting suicide and the *De Minimis* principle. English courts have been carefully non-committal (or eclectic) in identifying the mischief: thus in *Conway* ([2017] EWHC 2447) the court mentioned 'protection of the weak and vulnerable', 'protection of the sanctity of life', and 'promotion of trust and confidence between doctor and patient'.

[101] I leave aside here the question whether lack of such a competent request would be an element of the offence, to be proved by the prosecution; or whether such a competent request should constitute a defence, for which the defendant would need to adduce evidence. The latter seems more plausible, since it would mark the conduct as a presumptive public wrong, which the defendant must either justify or show to be a private matter.

[102] See above, Chapter 4 at n. 98; see also at n. 135 below on the requirement that the person's condition be verified by doctors.

[103] See Model Penal Code §§ 210.3(1)(a), 210.4; D Ormerod and K Laird, *Smith and Hogan's Criminal Law*, 636–45.

[104] See the Model Penal Code definition of recklessness (§ 2.02(2)(c)); Ormerod and Laird, *Smith and Hogan's Criminal Law*, 129–41.

that a reasonable person would observe',[105] or a gross breach of a duty of care:[106] in determining whether someone who caused death is guilty of one of these offences, the court must therefore judge what kinds of risk it is reasonable or unreasonable to take, or what standard of care is appropriate; which is to judge what kind of care we owe each other. The task of defining criminal homicide thus includes that of deciding what kind of care we should be required to take in our potentially dangerous dealings with each other, on pain of being formally censured as wrongdoers if we fail to take it. This is not a matter of attempting to capture some pre-legal moral conception of due care; it is a matter of constructing a civic understanding of this dimension of the polity's civil order. That constructive task must be discharged, at least in large part, not by the legislature, but by those who apply the law—including juries and lay judges who decide particular cases:[107] it is they who must fill out the criminal law's substantive content.

One further point is worth noting about 'gross negligence manslaughter'. In explaining what kind of negligence should be required for a criminal conviction, Lord Hewart CJ declared that it must be proved that the defendant's negligence 'went beyond a mere matter of compensation between subjects and showed such disregard for the life and safety of others as to amount to a crime against the State and conduct deserving punishment'.[108] I would replace 'crime against the State' by 'wrong that properly concerns the whole polity', and 'conduct deserving punishment' by 'conduct for which its perpetrator should be called to public, censorial account'; and we should not see tort law as 'a mere matter of compensation between subjects', since tort law can also be focused on wrongs:[109] but the key point to notice is that even with culpably wrongful harms as serious as death, we have to decide not just whether we should take formal public, legal notice of the wrong, but whether we should do so through the criminal law or in some other way—such as tort law.[110]

Similar questions, as well as new ones, face us when we ask how, and how far, the criminal law should extend beyond homicide to cover other kinds of wrongful injury to the person. I will simply note some of these questions here, to illustrate the logic of deliberations about criminalization as I am suggesting they should proceed.

It might seem obvious that injuries to the person must be a public matter, in which the polity takes a proper interest (for instance in its provisions to ensure safety, and in its health services); and that wrongfully caused injuries must therefore constitute public wrongs that are, in principle, candidates for criminalization: for we should be able to expect to go about our ordinary business not just without being killed, but without being (culpably, wrongfully) injured. But matters are of course not that simple, since we must ask more carefully both what kinds of injury should count as a public matter, and as wrongful; and when criminalization (rather than some other kind of response) is in principle an appropriate way to respond to them. Two examples will illustrate the need to ask what kinds of injury are to count as public, in the law's eyes.

[105] Model Penal Code § 2.02(2)(d).

[106] See Ormerod and Laird, *Smith and Hogan's Criminal Law*, 637–41.

[107] Thus in English law the question of whether the defendant had a 'duty of care' towards the person who died is a question of 'fact' for the jury (i.e. not a question of law for the judge to decide): see *Evans* [2009] EWCA Crim 650; Ormerod and Laird, *Smith and Hogan's Criminal Law*, 641.

[108] *Bateman* (1927) 19 Cr App R 8, at 11–12; see Ormerod and Laird, *Smith and Hogan's Criminal Law*, 636.

[109] See above, Chapter 1 at nn 53–6.

[110] I assume here, without further argument, that negligence (if properly defined, as a matter of failing to take care that one could and should have taken) is indeed culpable: for apposite argument, see e.g. A P Simester, 'Can Negligence be Culpable?'.

First, we can look again briefly at *R v Brown*—and at other cases involving the consensual causing of physical injury.[111] One question, which exercised the court in *Brown*, is whether those who cause consensual injury have good, or good enough, reason to do so: if they cause it 'for no good reason',[112] their conduct is properly criminalized. But to take that to be a question that the court must ask is to beg a prior question—whether such consensual injuring is a public matter, whose permissibility it is for the polity to decide: one could argue that the *Brown* defendants' conduct should not count as criminal, not on the grounds that such sadomasochistic practices are morally permissible, or that the sadomasochists' reasons for inflicting and accepting the kinds of injury involved are good enough reasons, but on the grounds that it is not for the polity to judge their conduct or their reasons, since the free consent of all participants turns what would indeed have been, absent that consent, a public matter into a private matter. The court in *Brown* seemed to agree that consent could block criminal liability for minor kinds of physical harm, without any need to inquire into the reasons for inflicting it or consenting to it, which would be to accept that consent makes such harms a private matter; but it clearly held that when the harm amounted to 'actual bodily harm', it became a public matter. Once again, therefore, we must distinguish two different questions that must be answered on the way towards criminalization: first, whether the conduct in question is a public matter at all; second, if (and only if) it is a public matter, whether it should be condemned as wrongful. We might have very different views about the morality of various kinds of sexual practice, including sadomasochism: but those views are irrelevant to the question of whether this or that kind of practice should be criminal unless and until we have first determined that it is a public matter—which would be to determine that our civil order includes a conception of the permissible forms and boundaries of consensual sexual conduct. I do not mean to beg the question of whether the civil order of a liberal republic could plausibly include such a conception: perhaps, for instance, it could be partly structured by a conception of dignity, which would open the way to a discussion of whether certain kinds of sexual practice, even when fully consensual, still violate the dignity of those involved.[113] My point here is only that we need to distinguish the different questions—about what is a public matter and about its wrongfulness—that must be answered on the way towards criminalization.

Second, 'offences against the person' certainly include, as paradigm examples, offences of physical injury up to and including death: but there has also been a growing recognition, among theorists and in the law, that other kinds of injury can also constitute public wrongs 'against the person'. One example of this was the extension of the idea of 'actual bodily harm' in English law to cover psychological as well as physical harm: a rather uncomfortable device to fill a perceived gap in the criminal law by extending the scope of an existing offence that had traditionally been understood to involve the causing of physical injury.[114] This was followed, three years later, by the Protection from Harassment Act 1997, which was amended by ss 111–12 of the

[111] [1994] 1 AC 212; see above at nn 7–10, Chapter 4 at nn 93–7. For other cases of consensual injury see V Bergelson, 'The Right to Be Hurt: Testing the Boundaries of Consent'.

[112] That the defendants inflicted injury 'for no good reason' was a constant refrain in *Brown*.

[113] On the protection of dignity as ground for criminalization see e.g. T Hörnle, 'Criminalizing Behaviour to Protect Human Dignity'; T Hörnle and M Kremnitzer, 'Human Dignity as a Protected Interest in Criminal Law'. See also Bergelson, 'The Right to Be Hurt'; and above, Chapter 4 at nn 96–7. However, whilst we can privately debate the moral character of different kinds of sexual practice (insofar as we actually understand them), and might think that some are degrading (violations of dignity), it can be plausibly argued that such debates do not belong in the public realm: as far as the polity is concerned, consent should decisively constitute such conduct as private (see n. 10 above).

[114] See *Chan Fook* [1994] 2 All ER 552; Ormerod and Laird, *Smith and Hogan's Criminal Law*, 738–9.

Protection of Freedom Act 2012 to formally define 'stalking' as a criminal offence.[115] A further extension of the law, focused on domestic abuse, was marked in the Serious Crime Act 2015: s. 76 defined the offence of 'Controlling or coercive behaviour in an intimate or family relationship'; although the offence can involve the fear of physical violence in one of its forms, it can also consist in a pattern of behaviour that 'causes [the victim] serious alarm or distress which has a substantial adverse effect on [the victim's] usual day-to-day activities'.[116] In explicating the character of this kind of wrong, as a public wrong, we could plausibly appeal not simply to some idea of physical or psychological harm, but to the value of autonomy or freedom:[117] central to this wrong is the undermining of the victim's ability to control and guide her or his own life in the way that any person should be able to expect to be allowed to do. To define it as a crime is also to declare that it is a public, not a private, matter: as with other public wrongs that are committed in a domestic context,[118] it is a kind of wrong that violates a central dimension of our civic life and our civil order—the freedom we should have, as responsible agents, to determine our own lives.

Once we break free of the grip of the harm principle(s), we can also more easily recognize other kinds of wrong against the person that should be recognized as public, and potentially criminalizable, wrongs even when they do not involve anything that can be straightforwardly described as physical or psychological harm: we can, for instance, recognize dignity and privacy as values that help to structure our civil order—that help to define what we owe to each other as fellow citizens; and we can recognize violations of those values as candidates for criminalization, as a possible response that will sometimes be the appropriate response. Thus we can explain the distinctive wrong involved in crimes of racial hatred by appealing to the kind of civic dignity, the recognition of their status as citizens, that is due to all citizens—a recognition that the enactment of racial hatred (understood as 'civic hatred') in speech or in action denies to them.[119] This is not yet to say that we should criminalize such enactments. It suggests that we have reason to do so, at least when the hatred is enacted against a vulnerable group, whose sense of their civic standing as recognized members of the polity might thereby be undermined: such enactments constitute a clear civic wrong, which we have good reason to mark and condemn as such; and it is a wrong that we should make our own, as a criminal wrong, as a matter of manifesting solidarity with its targets, rather than leaving it to the victims to pursue for themselves as a civil wrong. However, we must also consider other civic values that might militate against criminalization, most obviously that of freedom of speech:[120] even if we deny that speech enacting civic hatred merits protection, we should obviously worry about over-expansive offence definitions and the chilling effects they can have. Some would also worry about privacy, on the grounds that to create 'hate crimes' is to criminalize people's emotions—which

[115] See Ormerod and Laird, *Smith and Hogan's Criminal Law*, 792–806. See also Criminal Justice and Courts Act 2015, s. 33, Abusive Behaviour and Sexual Harm (Scotland) Act 2016, ss 2–4, on 'revenge porn'.

[116] Serious Crime Act 2015, s. 76(4)(b): see the guidance published by the Crown Prosecution Service in *Domestic Abuse Guidelines for Prosecutors; Controlling or Coercive Behaviour in an Intimate or Family Relationship*; and see the Domestic Abuse (Scotland) Act 2018.

[117] Compare V Tadros, 'The Distinctiveness of Domestic Abuse: A Freedom Based Account'.

[118] Including intra-marital rape: see above, Chapter 1 at nn 143–9.

[119] See above, Chapter 5 at nn 53–7; J Waldron, *The Harm in Hate Speech*; R A Duff and S E Marshall, 'Criminalizing Hate'; Hörnle, 'Criminalizing Behaviour to Protect Human Dignity', 317–19.

[120] See E Heinze, *Hate Speech and Democratic Citizenship*.

is not something that a liberal polity should do.[121] That kind of objection is misguided if what is to be criminalized is the wrong of enacting hatred, since what matters is the manifested meaning of what the hater says or does: actually feeling hatred is neither a necessary nor a sufficient condition for enacting hatred (I can enact an emotion that I do not feel, or conceal an emotion that I do feel). However, when we think about the difficulties of defining, and enforcing, an offence consisting merely in the enactment of civic hatred; and when we think about the other ways in which we could respond to such enactments (including kinds of civil recourse for their victims,[122] and informal social responses), we might end by criminalizing enactments of civic hatred only when they are intended (or likely) to stir up hatred in others, in the case of speech; or when the hatred is enacted in conduct that is independently criminal, whose criminal wrongfulness it can be seen as aggravating.[123] It might be said that this amounts to criminalizing hatred only when it is related to some further kind of harm, thus bringing the (or a) harm principle into the picture: but even if it is helpful to talk of harm in this context, harm now figures not as the primary object of criminalization, but as a condition on the criminalization of the civic wrong of enacting such hatred.

We can also appeal to human dignity to explain why the gladiatorial combats that exercised Feinberg should be recognized as a public wrong even if they are fully consensual: if the aim of the exercise is not, for instance, to display the participants' martial arts or courage, but to provide the spectators with the 'brutal bloodshed' that they have paid for and encourage by 'their bloodthirsty screams',[124] we could argue that this is an essentially degrading activity that is inconsistent with a recognition of the participants' humanity (by the spectators and by each other). Analogously, we can explain the distinctive wrong of voyeurism in terms of the radical invasion of privacy that it involves.[125] This might make it seem that criminalization is all too easy to justify: we need simply appeal to some (vaguely defined) value that we can claim to be an aspect of our civil order, and then argue that we have good reason to criminalize any conduct that can be said to violate that value. But the route towards criminalization is not that easy or swift. First, we need to argue (not just assert) that the value to which we appeal is indeed integral to the polity's civil order—and to provide a reasonably clear account of that value.[126] Second, we need to show how (not just assert that) the conduct we

[121] See e.g. H Hurd, 'Why Liberals Should Hate "Hate Crime Legislation"'; in response see M Al-Hakim, 'Making Room for Hate Crime Legislation in Liberal Societies'.

[122] See e.g. the English Equality Act 2010, and its range of 'enforcement' provisions and remedies (in Part 9).

[123] For speech, see e.g. the English Public Order Act 1986, ss. 17–20 (also the German *Strafgesetzbuch*, § 130; the defamation of the protected group must be done 'in a manner capable of disturbing the public peace'). For hate as an aggravating factor, see e.g. the English Crime and Disorder Act 1998, ss. 28–32; from the US, 18 USCA § 249; California Penal Code §§ 422.55, 422.75; New York Penal Law §§ 240.30, 485.10.

[124] See J Feinberg, *Harmless Wrongdoing*, 128–33, 328–31 (the quoted phrases are from 129–30), responding to I Kristol, 'Pornography, Obscenity, and the Case for Censorship'; see R A Duff, 'Harms and Wrongs', 32–44. I leave aside here the question of whether other kinds of public, commercial fighting are open to the same kind of objection. See also Chapter 4 at nn 54–6 above, on 'dwarf-tossing'. We should bear in mind, however, that dignity (like other values that can generate reasons to criminalize) can also generate constraints on criminalization: if criminalizing a type of conduct, or criminalizing it in a particular way, would violate the dignity of those who engage in such conduct, that is a normative barrier to criminalization (see M Gur-Arye, 'Human Dignity of "Offenders": a Limitation on Substantive Criminal Law').

[125] See Sexual Offences Act 2003, ss 67–8; Ormerod and Laird, *Smith and Hogan's Criminal Law*, 882–4.

[126] This might involve appeal to a written constitution; or a rational reconstruction of the polity's defining values.

propose to criminalize does indeed violate that value. Third, we need to argue that our response to such a violation should involve criminalization rather than one of the other available kinds of response: that such a violation requires a formal, collective, wrong-focused response that depends not on the wishes or will of its direct victim, but on the public judgment of the polity's officials.

The last few paragraphs have been concerned with various wrongs against the person that do not consist in or necessarily involve physical harm. We also need to consider cases in which the physical harm is relatively minor, and ask how far the criminal law should extend its reach. Here the distinction between attacks and endangerments becomes significant.[127] If conduct is intended to injure another person, it is more clearly presumptively wrongful (wrong unless a justification is available), and therefore more obviously a candidate for criminalization, than if it only creates a risk—even a significant or near-certain risk—of injury: for in the context of endangerment we must ask what kinds of risk it is reasonable or unreasonable to take with another's safety, which will also involve judging the worth of the activity in the course of which the risk is created. This is again a matter of constructing a civic understanding of this aspect of our civil order, rather than of mirroring a pre-legal understanding. What kinds of physical contact should we expect each other (and ourselves) to accept as part of ordinary social life in public places?[128] What kinds of risk should we accept as part of the cost of engagement in valuable (or permissible) activities (subject to the availability of compensation if a risk is actualized)? Once we have identified a type of wrongful endangerment, we must then ask again whether criminalization is an, or the, appropriate response to it: how important is it that we collectively insist on marking it as a wrong, and on calling its perpetrators to formal public (and potentially punitive) account—rather than providing no formal response, or making it a civil matter for injured parties to pursue if they wish to do so?

Similar questions arise in relation to the wide range of 'public order' offences: offences that consist not so much in attacks on or threats to individual victims as in threats to the more general 'orderly' peace of the polity.[129] The more serious offences defined by the Public Order Act 1986, such as 'riot' (s. 1), 'violent disorder' (s. 2), and 'affray' (s. 3), are clearly public wrongs that can merit criminalization, since they disrupt the conditions of civic life: but as we move towards the less serious offences defined by the Act, such as 'threatening or abusive words or behaviour, or disorderly behaviour ... within the hearing or sight of a person likely to be caused harassment, alarm or distress thereby' (s. 5.1), we need to ask more difficult questions about how we should react to others' behaviour that we might find disturbing or distressing. In particular, we must ask whether or when it is reasonable to feel 'harassment, alarm or distress' when faced by conduct that we find abusive or disorderly: should we be more ready to tolerate behaviour that we dislike, or even to accept it in a spirit of cultural pluralism?[130] I cannot pursue these questions here, and do not mean to deny the (often

[127] See Duff, *Answering for Crime*, ch. 7.1.

[128] See Ormerod and Laird, *Smith and Hogan's Criminal Law*, 717–18, on the 'exigencies of everyday life'.

[129] See C Wells and O Quick, *Lacey, Wells and Quick Reconstructing Criminal Law: Text and Materials*, chs 4–7; Ormerod and Laird, *Smith and Hogan's Criminal Law*, ch. 32; Public Order Act 1986. See also the striking provisions concerning 'persons attending or preparing for a rave' in ss 63–6 of the Criminal Justice and Public Order Act 1994.

[130] Similar questions arise even more forcefully in relation to 'offensive' conduct: we need to ask not just whether a type of conduct in fact offends others, but whether it is reasonable for others to find it offensive; and, even if offence is reasonable, whether they should be willing to tolerate it (see A von Hirsch and A P Simester (eds), *Incivilities: Regulating Offensive Behaviour*; R A Duff and S E Marshall, 'How Offensive Can You Get?').

cumulative) seriousness of various kinds of 'disorderly' conduct in undermining the conditions of civic life: my point is only that these questions must be asked if we are to justify criminalization; and that to answer them we must engage in a public, political deliberation about how we are to define our civil order.

I have focused in this section on offences against the person as paradigmatic *mala in se*, to illustrate the way in which deliberations about criminalization can be structured by an account of crimes as public wrongs that violate the polity's civil order. Deliberation about property offences will (or should) display the same kind of structure, though I cannot discuss them here: we need to ask what role property (public and private) should play in our civil order; what kinds of property-related conduct belong in the public realm that concerns the law rather than in the private realm (whether, for instance, owners should have an unqualified right to do as they please with their own property, so long as they do not injure or endanger others); what kinds of public conduct in relation to property should count as public wrongs; and whether criminal law is an appropriate, or the most appropriate, response to such wrongs—or are they better dealt with, for instance, as 'a mere matter of compensation between subjects'?[131]

We can also see, in the light of this account, why hard or difficult cases are hard: why we may be unsure or in disagreement about whether we have good reason in principle to criminalize certain types of conduct. We might disagree or be unsure about whether the conduct does belong within the public realm that can concern the law at all: this is, as we have seen, a key question for cases of consensual sexual conduct such as *Brown*, for instance, and for cases of discrimination in the provision of services such as bed and breakfast accommodation.[132] We might disagree or be unsure about whether the conduct, which does fall within the public realm, is wrongful: this is, for instance, part of the disagreement about the criminalization of certain modes of hunting.[133] Or we might disagree about whether criminalization is an, or the, appropriate response to what we might agree is a public wrong: or would it be more appropriate to leave it to private law, as a matter for the victim to pursue (with the polity's help) if he wishes, or to respond to it, formally or informally, in ways that do not focus on calling the wrongdoer to public account? For a final illustration of how these questions bear on deliberations about criminalization (and why it is important to distinguish them), we can look briefly at the question of whether we are right to criminalize the possession and use of certain kinds of drug.[134]

Certain types of drug are dangerous to health (we need not here ask which are dangerous in what ways): what kind of interest, if any, should the polity take in their possession and use? That they endanger health makes them in one way a public matter for any polity that takes it to be part of its responsibility to attend to its citizens' health: it gives us good reason to make provision for treatment for those whose health is affected by drugs; to provide information about which drugs are dangerous in what ways; perhaps also to create a licensing regime to control the manufacture and supply of such

[131] *Bateman* (1927) 19 Cr App R 8, at 11–12; see at n. 108 above.

[132] See above, Chapter 4 at nn 99–101. This was a civil case: but the question of whether conduct falls within the public realm is prior to the question of whether, if it is cognizably wrong, it should be dealt with as a criminal or a civil matter.

[133] See above, Chapter 3 at nn 112, 133. In relation to the mistreatment of animals, it is worth noting that to criminalize such conduct is to insist both that it is a public matter and that it is wrong: which is to insist that the welfare of the animals concerned is a public matter, and that ownership of an animal does not bring with it the right to treat the animal as I see fit—as my property.

[134] See D N Husak, *Drugs and Rights; Overcriminalization*, 164–70. For brevity's sake, I largely leave aside here the manufacture and supply of drugs, which raise different questions.

drugs. Insofar as the use of such drugs endangers health, it might be judged imprudent, and thus a proper object of educational programmes and of public exhortation: but is it properly judged to be wrong, in virtue of its impact on drug-users, given a paternalist concern that citizens not seriously injure or endanger themselves; or in virtue of its indirect impact on others; or in virtue of its implications for our conception of our civil order (is it a kind of activity that we should make publicly, commercially available to ourselves)? But even if it is justifiably judged to be wrong (a very large 'if'), that does not yet give us reason to criminalize it rather than responding in some other way: we might still rightly decide (as advocates of decriminalization often argue) that it is more appropriate to treat it as a public health issue than to focus on its supposed wrongfulness by insisting on calling those who use such drugs to public, censorial, and punitive account.

My discussion so far has been concerned with criminal offences that can count as *mala in se*: although, as I have emphasized, the creation and definition of such offences as crimes involves a process of constructing a civic conception of the relevant wrongs, rather than of trying to capture and reproduce a pre-legal moral conception, the law is dealing with wrongs that have a pre-legal grounding; we are transforming such pre-legal wrongs into legal wrongs, not creating new wrongs *ex nihilo*. My account is thus still a version of legal moralism, since it still portrays the criminal law as being essentially focused on a set of moral wrongs that are taken to merit public recognition and condemnation as wrongs: but it might be more precisely, if less concisely, described as a legal-political moralism, to make clear that the morality in question, in whose light crimes are defined as wrongs, is a political morality. It is a 'political' morality in the sense that it is a morality that is developed and articulated as a collective enterprise by the polity and its members (in a well functioning democratic polity): it is the morality under which they are to live together as citizens. Thus its deliberations about the wrongs that are to be candidates for criminalization must be collective deliberations: as a citizen engaging in such deliberation I must ask myself not, in the first person singular, what values *I* am to take as guides for my own life, but what values *we* can and should take as guides to our civic lives.

I began this discussion of criminalizable public wrongs with *mala in se* because they provide the logically simplest examples of how we can reason towards criminalization: we first recognize a type of conduct as a public wrong, and then ask whether we have good reason to criminalize it rather than responding in some other way. However, *mala in se* do not make up the bulk of our criminal law: the majority of offences are *mala prohibita*; they consist in conduct that is not, or might not be, wrongful independently of its legal proscription. Indeed, if the mark of a *malum prohibitum* is that the conduct it criminalizes might not be pre-legally wrongful, many *mala in se* have a '*prohibitum*' dimension. Sometimes they depend on a prior structure of legal regulation: property offences, for instance, presuppose the regime of property law that defines such matters as ownership. Sometimes the offence definition has an element of regulation that looks more like prohibition than wrong-declaration. For example, abortion is non-criminal in England under specified conditions: these include substantive conditions to do with the risks to the woman's health that the continuance of the pregnancy would pose, but also a requirement that those risks, and the need for an abortion, be assessed by two registered medical practitioners, and that the abortion be performed by a registered practitioner, in a specified kind of medical location.[135]

[135] Abortion Act 1967, s. 1. Something similar is often true of legislation that decriminalizes 'assisted dying' (see above, Chapter 4 at n. 98): there is often a requirement that the person's condition be formally verified by a doctor.

A doctor might carry out an abortion in the knowledge that the substantive conditions are satisfied, to save the woman from the specified kind of harm, but without involving another practitioner: she would then formally commit a criminal offence,[136] but arguably would not be committing the kind of substantive wrong at which the law is aimed; in which case she commits what looks like a *malum prohibitum* (if it is *malum* at all) rather than a *malum in se*.

I will say more about such *mala prohibita* in the following section. All we need note here is, first, that the rationale for such provisions is clear: the aim is not just to require those who would perform abortions to ensure that the substantive conditions laid down in the law are met, but to specify formally what counts as ensuring that they are met; this will also make it easier to prove after the event that they were met. Second, the fact that a *malum in se* offence can have a *prohibitum* dimension would be problematic if the distinction between *mala in se* and *mala prohibita* was required to do any substantive normative work, or to capture something deep about the structure of criminal law: but the distinction does not have such significance; its role, rather like that of the distinction between *actus reus* and *mens rea*,[137] is that of a useful expository device. As I argued earlier,[138] both *mala in se* and *mala prohibita* must, if they are justifiably criminalized, consist in conduct that is wrongful prior to its criminalization—although, as we have seen in this section, its criminal wrongfulness may be partly constructed in the very process of criminalization. The difference between them is a difference in the character or source of that wrongfulness: a crime is *malum in se* insofar as the wrongfulness of the criminalized conduct does not depend on the fact that it violates a legal regulation; a crime is *malum prohibitum* insofar as the wrongfulness of the conduct that is criminalized does depend on such a fact. The offence of 'administering drugs or using instruments to procure abortion' can, in light of the Abortion Act 1967, s. 1, be analysed into an authoritative definition of the central *malum in se*, of trying to procure an abortion that is not necessary for any of the reasons specified in the Act;[139] and a regulation concerning the way in which the existence of such a reason is to be established—by the judgment of two registered medical practitioners. Assuming that this regulation can be justified, someone who performs an abortion without such an assessment by two registered medical practitioners might commit one or both of two connected wrongs: that of performing a substantively unjustified abortion; or that of performing it without having made sure, in the way specified by the law, that it was justified.

I will comment in the following section on what we, or the law, should say to someone who claims to have known that the abortion she performed was justified without consulting another medical practitioner. The point to notice here is simply that what this example shows (as other examples in the following section will also show) is that the distinction between *mala in se* and *mala prohibita* is better understood in terms of a spectrum, rather than as a sharp distinction between two categories of offence. At one end of the spectrum lie (relatively) 'pure' *mala in se*: offences involving conduct whose wrongfulness does not depend on or consist in the breach of a legal

[136] Of 'Administering drugs or using instruments to procure abortion' (Offences Against the Person Act 1861, s. 58)—unless it was an emergency of the kind provided for by s. 1(4) of the Abortion Act 1967.

[137] See Duff, *Answering for Crime*, 202–3.

[138] See above, Chapter 2, section 4.

[139] I leave aside here questions about whether this really is a criminalizable *malum*; our concern here is with the logical structure of the offence, not with its substantive justification.

regulation. At the other end lie relatively 'pure' *mala prohibita*, consisting in conduct whose wrongfulness consists in the breach of a legal regulation that one ought to have obeyed. In between these two ends, we find a range of offences that are neither pure *mala in se* nor pure *mala prohibita*: this should neither surprise nor disturb us. Nor does it mark a deficiency in our criminal law: we live in a complicated, untidy normative world of conflicting and incommensurable values; our ways of dealing with that world—in our extra-legal moral practices and in our legal practices—will therefore also be complicated, resistant to any neat systematization.

I will not provide a detailed discussion of the various, diverse kinds of *mala prohibita*, pure and impure, here: both for reasons of space, and because I have discussed them elsewhere.[140] However, I should say something about them here, to show how an account of crimes as public wrongs can deal with them, and how a legal moralist can find room for them.[141]

5. Varieties of Public Wrong (b): *Mala Prohibita*, Pure and Impure

We have already seen how a legal moralist can find room for *mala prohibita*, without giving up her claim that we can justifiably criminalize a type of conduct only if it is wrongful prior to its criminalization.[142] The first step in the argument is to show that we have good reason to create a legal regulation that prohibits or requires a type of conduct; the second step is to show that, once such a regulation has been enacted, we ought to obey it; the conclusion is that the breach of such a regulation then constitutes a public wrong, which we have reason to criminalize—or, given the discussion in section 1 above, to which criminalization is a potentially appropriate response. My task in this section is to say a little more about the kinds of reason we could have to create such legal regulations, and about why it might be wrong to violate them. If it is wrong to violate them, that wrong is a public wrong: for such legal regulations must be justified by showing that they serve some aspect of the polity's common good; they thus help to construct and protect its civil order, and their breach is a violation of that order.

A polity can have different reasons to create systems of regulation, many of which could be described, abstractly, as concerned with various kinds of coordination problem that people face in trying to live together. One typical starting point is a recognition of some kind of mischief or harm that is liable to arise from a valuable human activity, and that the polity can and should try to minimize. Whilst driving, for instance, and the manufacture of a wide variety of goods, and the production and supply of food and drink, are valuable activities, they create distinctive dangers of serious kinds of harm; it is a proper task for the polity not to outlaw such activities (given their positive

[140] See Duff, *Answering for Crime*, chs 4.4, 7.3, and 'Relational Reasons and the Criminal Law', 191–4; R A Duff and S E Marshall, '"Abstract Endangerment", Two Harm Principles, and Two Routes to Criminalisation'.

[141] For useful discussions of *mala prohibita*, critical and constructive, see D N Husak, '*Malum Prohibitum* and Retributivism', *Overcriminalization*, 103–19, *Ignorance of Law: A Philosophical Analysis*, ch. 4C; S P Green, 'Why it's a Crime to Tear the Tag off a Mattress: Over-Criminalization and the Moral Content of Regulatory Offenses', and 'The Conceptual Utility of *Malum Prohibitum*'; S Dimock, 'Contractarian Criminal Law Theory and *Mala Prohibita* Offences', and 'The *Malum Prohibitum–Malum in Se* Distinction and the Wrongfulness Constraint on Criminalization'; C H Wellman, *Rights Forfeiture and Punishment*, ch. 7.

[142] See above, Chapter 1 at nn 44–8, Chapter 2, section 4.

value), but to find ways of minimizing those harms. One way to reduce the incidence of such harms is to give formal expression to the duty of care that those who engage in the activity incur—to make it a formal legal requirement that they take due care to guard against the dangers that the activity involves. Thus the law might define a criminal offence of driving dangerously,[143] or declare it to 'be the duty of every employer to ensure, so far as is reasonably practicable, the health, safety and welfare at work of all his employees'.[144] The law might also be more specific, identifying particular ways in which an activity can be dangerous: it might, for instance, define offences of driving when unfit to drive through drink or drugs, or of using a vehicle in a dangerous condition.[145] Such laws construct genuine *mala in se*: they provide a formal determination, in the particular context of driving, of the duty of care that we anyway owe each other (especially when engaged in such dangerous activities). Someone who commits such an offence commits a wrong: she unreasonably endangers others, even if she in fact causes no material harm; that wrong is not a creation of the law, in the way that *mala prohibita* are, although it is formally constructed by the law.

However, we may also see reason to create a more complex regulatory regime, one that will include regulations that go beyond authoritative specifications of kinds of pre-legally wrongful conduct. For such specifications will still leave too much room for uncertainties or disagreements about what should count as reasonably safe conduct: drivers who are both well-intentioned and reasonably competent might still be unsure about how they should behave, whilst those who are incompetent, or not well-intentioned, will behave dangerously (encouraged, in the latter case, by the thought that it might be hard to prove what would need to be proved to convict them of one of these *mala in se*). We can avoid such uncertainties by creating more precise regulations about, for instance, how fast it is permissible to drive, or how much alcohol one can have in one's blood when driving, or what depth of tread a car's tyres must have.[146] Similarly, if our concern is with health and safety at work, we might see good reason to go beyond the formal declaration of an employer's duty of care, to provide for the creation of more specific regulations about the kinds of precaution that employers must take.[147] Now a significant feature of many such regulations is, we have seen,[148] that if they are to serve their harm-preventive aims efficiently, they will prohibit types of conduct some of whose tokens will not involve the mischief that the regulations aim to prevent: if we specify a speed limit or a drink-driving limit strict enough to reduce the risks of speed-related or alcohol-related harm to acceptable levels, there will be some drivers who know that they can drive safely while exceeding the limits. Regulations of these kinds provide certainty and clarity, and are more easily enforced; but they do so at the cost of over-breadth. If we are to justify such regulations, we must show that the burdens they impose, especially on drivers who know that they could safely violate them, are reasonable: this will involve showing that they are tailored as narrowly as is

[143] See e.g. Road Traffic Act 1988, s. 2 (also s. 3 on 'careless, and inconsiderate, driving').

[144] See Health and Safety at Work etc. Act 1974, s. 1(1); s. 33 makes the breach of that duty a criminal offence.

[145] See Road Traffic Act 1988, ss 4, 40A.

[146] See Road Traffic Regulation Act 1984, ss 81–9; Road Traffic Act 1988, s. 5; Road Vehicles (Construction and Use) Regulations 1986, s. 27 (and other sections enacting a host of other such regulations).

[147] Thus the Health and Safety at Work etc. Act does not simply declare the general duties of care that employers have (s. 2; see at n. 144 above): it provides for the creation and operations of the Health and Safety Executive (ss 10–14), and for the enactment of binding regulations and codes of practice (ss 15–17).

[148] See above, Chapter 2 at nn 44–53, Chapter 6 at nn 54–7.

practicable to the harm-preventive goals at which they are aimed—for instance, that a regulation allowing such drivers to claim exemptions would be unacceptably ineffective.[149] Even this will not yet justify criminalizing breaches of the regulations, since we have yet to show that drivers commit wrongs in breaking them. We are in the realm of a harm prevention principle here; but that is a principle of regulation rather than of criminalization, and does not yet give us reason to criminalize breaches of the regulations that it rationalizes.[150] However, before turning to that issue, we must note two other kinds of regulation that we might see good reason to create to serve the ends of road safety (analogous types of regulation are also a feature of other regulatory regimes, but for simplicity's sake I will focus on driving).

First, we might see reason not just to require drivers to make sure that they are fit to drive, and that their vehicles are safe to drive, but to enact regulations specifying how they are to do so: for instance to require drivers to hold a driving licence, which they can obtain only by passing an official test, and to have their car formally inspected for its safety at regular intervals.[151] Second, we might see reason to enact regulations aimed at making it easier for officials to check that the primary regulations have been complied with: for instance, requiring drivers to have and to be able to produce a driving licence, or a safety test certificate.[152] Breaches of such regulations are not themselves harmful, and may not be dangerous: someone could know that she is competent to drive, and that her car is in safe condition, without any formal test, while the requirements to hold licences and certificates have to do with administrative convenience, not with conduct that is itself dangerous. Nonetheless, we could surely be justified in enacting such regulations. Some of them, like the requirement to pass a test, make formally clear what is to count as competence or safety; provide a publicly available method both of ensuring at least minimal competence and safety and of assuring others that they have been ensured; and guard against the danger of drivers misleading themselves by overconfidence in their own abilities.[153] Other regulations help make the regulatory system more practicably and economically operational. However, none of this yet shows that we have reason to criminalize breaches of such regulations. Such breaches, if they are *mala* at all, lie towards the pure *mala prohibita* end of the *mala in se–mala prohibita* spectrum: the conduct that they prohibit is clearly not wrongful prior to its legal prohibition. But we have not yet shown that or why such breaches are wrongs at all—especially when they are committed by someone who knows that she can safely break the regulation.

Other routes to the creation of regulations, and thus of offences with a significant *prohibitum* dimension, raise similar questions. Here are two further examples.

First, we might begin not with some harm or mischief to be avoided, but with some good to be achieved, such as the provision of financial resources that will enable the polity to discharge its many responsibilities (though the extent and character of those responsibilities will of course need to be determined by public deliberation). We can quickly recognize that such resources can be provided only if citizens make financial

[149] Compare Husak, *Overcriminalization*, 132–59 on the 'external constraints' on criminalization: a criminal law must 'directly advance' a 'substantial state interest', and its scope must be 'no more extensive than necessary to achieve its objective'. We could apply similar requirements to the creation of regulations of the kind discussed here—although we will see shortly that some kinds of justifiable regulation advance the interest that ultimately justifies them somewhat indirectly.

[150] See above, Chapter 6 at nn 62–5.

[151] See Road Traffic Act 1988, ss 87, 45–8.

[152] See Road Traffic Act 1988, ss 164–5.

[153] Compare also the requirements for medical validation in cases of abortion or of assisted dying; above, n. 135.

contributions, and that those contributions ought to be proportional to the citizens' means (though here again there is plenty of room for political debate about what that proportionality should amount to); we can say that citizens have a responsibility to make a proportionate contribution to the public purse. It will clearly not be enough, however, to issue a general injunction to make a fair or reasonable contribution to the public purse. Even if we also specified how such contributions were to be made, people would have no idea how much they should contribute: the well-meaning would lack the guidance they need, while the unwilling would find it all too easy not to pay their share. So we need a system of taxation, which involves a complex set of regulations: these will determine how our 'fair share' is to be determined, how we are to calculate our tax liability (or have it calculated), how we are to pay our taxes, and how our conformity with the regulations can be checked and verified. Given such a regulatory regime, we can see that some violations of its requirements have a significant *malum in se* dimension: to evade my taxes, or to make a dishonest tax return, is to fail in my civic responsibility to make a fair contribution to the public purse (assuming that the tax system is tolerably fair).[154] Even here, however, the *malum* concerned is far from purely *in se*: for what counts as my 'fair contribution', in the law's eyes, can be determined only through the tax system's regulations. Other breaches of tax regulations lie further towards the *mala prohibita* end of the spectrum: someone who fails to complete and submit a legally required tax return, for instance, might in fact have paid all the tax she ought to pay, and have made sure for herself that that was true; but she breaks a regulation that is designed to make the system of calculating and checking tax work efficiently. Once again we need to ask whether such a person commits an in principle criminalizable public wrong.[155]

Second, we might begin not with some harm to be avoided, but with a genuine *malum in se*: for instance with the wrong involved in the sexual exploitation of young people who are not yet mature enough to make competent decisions in such matters. This is surely a public wrong, since a polity has a responsibility to protect its younger members, and we might think of criminalizing it directly, by enacting a criminal offence of sexual exploitation of an immature person. But there are obvious problems with that approach. Some concern the difficulty of defining the key notions of exploitation and immaturity; some concern the process of proving, in court, that the (alleged) victim was both immature and exploited. Others concern the danger that, if the offence is defined in such terms, whose application involves what might be quite demanding normative judgments, it will not be effective in guiding conduct: those who are not well-intentioned might hope to get away with committing the wrong, given the difficulties of proving guilt; even those who are not radically ill-intentioned might be too quick to form, and act on, the self-serving belief that their intended sexual partner is mature.[156] So instead we might take, as many legislatures have taken, a different approach, which (in its logic if not in its statutory formulation) involves regulation as a prelude to criminalization: we define an age below which a person will, in effect, be deemed to be immature, such that sexual activity with him or her (by a significantly older person) will, in effect, be deemed to be exploitative; we then make it a

[154] Compare the common law offence of 'cheating the public revenue': Ormerod and Laird, *Smith and Hogan's Criminal Law*, 1062–5; Theft Act 1968, s. 32(1)(a).

[155] We should also bear in mind that breaches of tax regulations, even when they are formally criminalized, are in fact very often dealt with non-criminally: see Chapter 1 at nn 87–90 above.

[156] See further A Cornford, 'Rethinking the Wrongness Constraint on Criminalisation', s. IV.B; above, Chapter 2 at nn 44–6.

criminal offence to engage in sexual activity with a person who is below that age.[157] We know, however, that such laws will be both over- and under-inclusive: there will, that is, be people whose conduct formally violates the law, but who know that their sexual partners are mature enough to make competent decisions in such matters; and there will be people whose conduct does not violate the law because their sexual partners are over the specified age, but who do perpetrate the mischief at which the law is aimed, since those sexual partners are not in fact mature enough to make competent decisions (as they might indeed know). Here again, although we began with a genuine *malum in se*, we end with an offence that has a significant *prohibitum* dimension; and we need to ask whether and why we can legitimately criminalize the breach of such regulatory specifications of the 'age of consent', when we know that at least some such breaches will not perpetrate the mischief at which the law is aimed.

If we are to justify the creation of criminal offences of these kinds,[158] offences that involve at least a significant *prohibitum* dimension, we must be able to show that and why the conduct that constitutes the offence is wrongful—wrongful not necessarily prior to its legal prohibition, but prior to its criminalization. The offence involves the violation of a legal regulation: but why is it wrong to violate such regulations? It will not do simply to say that citizens ought to obey laws that have been duly enacted by a democratic procedure, and commit wrongs if they violate them. Quite apart from the question, which we need not pursue here, of whether it is plausible to assert such a general obligation, the citizens of a democratic republic are owed an explanation of *why* they should obey *this* law: 'because it is the [democratically enacted] law' cannot be a complete explanation if they are to be able to recognize the law as their law or make it their own; they need to know what legitimate aims it is intended to serve. The explanations that can be given will be of the kinds outlined above: they will appeal to some significant aspect of the polity's common good (the need to guard against the dangers created by driving, or by industrial manufacturing; or to raise revenue for the public purse; or to protect the immature against sexual exploitation); they will appeal to our civic responsibility to contribute appropriately to the (our) common good; and they will show how the regulations are well-designed to serve that aspect of the common good.

Such explanations can of course be challenged; one reason for publicly spelling them out is indeed to enable them to be challenged. Even if we agree on the aspect of the common good that the regulations are designed to serve, we must ask whether we need such regulations, rather than relying on criminal laws that delineate the relevant *mala in se*—whether it would not be enough, for instance, to criminalize driving at dangerous speeds rather than stipulating speed limits,[159] or to criminalize the sexual exploitation of vulnerable young people rather than stipulating an 'age of consent'. Even if such stipulation is warranted, we must ask whether the stipulated limits are

[157] See e.g. Sexual Offences Act 2003, ss 5–15A (sexual activity with children under 13 is treated differently from sexual activity with those under 16). I leave aside here the question of whether the law should also specify that the offence is only committed by someone who is above a certain age, or a certain number of years older than the child: see e.g. Model Penal Code § 213.3(1)(a). I do not aim here to defend the particular legislation passed by the UK Parliament (for some stringent criticism, see J R Spencer, 'The Sexual Offences Act 2003: (2) Child and Family Offences'; and see above, Chapter 1 at nn 166–7); my aim is only to show how legislation of (roughly) this kind could be justified.

[158] I leave aside here further important questions about just how such offences should be defined: in particular, about whether it is legitimate to make liability strict—as to, for instance, the speed at which I am driving, or as to whether I am over the drink-driving limit, or as to the age of my intended sexual partner. See further Duff, *Answering for Crime*, ch. 10.

[159] See above, Chapter 6 at n. 57.

themselves reasonable—and what should count as reasonable: should we, for instance, impose a 'majoritarian condition', that a stipulated regulatory limit is reasonable only if most of those who violate it would be committing the substantive mischief at which the regulation is aimed;[160] or, if the mischief is serious enough, and the burden of obeying the regulation modest enough, would it be enough that many who break the regulation would be committing that substantive mischief? I will comment later on how we should respond to ill-designed or misdirected regulations: let us assume for the moment, however, that the regulations are adequately justified.

Can we now simply say that any breach of such regulations is wrongful if and because they serve some aspect of the common good—a good that we have a responsibility to play our part in promoting? On the one hand, we can say something more precise than that, about the particular kind of substantive wrongs that are committed by many who break such regulations; but on the other hand, it is not clear that it is enough to say that to someone who claims to know that he can break such a regulation without bringing about the mischief at which it is aimed. We should deal (briefly) with these two points in turn.

Different substantive wrongs may be committed by different breakers of the same regulation. If we look, for instance, at the regulations specifying speed limits or alcohol limits for drivers, or age requirements for sexual consent, we can say that if the regulations are well formulated, many of those who break them will have committed the substantive mischief at which they are aimed: they will in fact have driven dangerously fast, or while impaired through alcohol; or they will in fact have engaged in exploitative sexual activity with someone who was too immature to consent to it competently. Some who do not in fact commit the substantive mischief will have taken an unjustified risk of doing so: rather than obeying the regulation, they will have trusted their own, unreliable, judgment about how fast they could safely drive, or about how much they can drink without impairing their competence, or about the maturity of their sexual partner; even if they were, luckily, right on this occasion, they might well have been wrong, and took an unjustified risk of being wrong. Some who know that they can safely break the regulation might adversely affect the conduct of others in doing so: if for instance, they are seen to be speeding, they might provoke or encourage others to follow suit; and, we might argue, so long as obeying the speed limit is only modestly burdensome, they ought not to take the risk of producing such harmful effects. In the case of other regulations, to do with ensuring that the substantive requirements of safe conduct are met (that one is competent to drive, that one's car is in a safe condition, and so on), we could again say that many of those who break the regulation might in fact be behaving dangerously (driving when not competent enough to do so, driving an unsafe car), while others who trust their own unreliable judgment take an unreasonable risk that their conduct is actually dangerous (that their judgment is wrong). In the case of regulations concerned with the efficient functioning of the system (such as regulations about the possession and production of licences), we can say that even if one who breaks the regulation does not in fact hinder the functioning of the system, he is a free rider on the backs of those who do obey; and so on. I will not go into the details of such accounts of the wrongs committed by breaking such regulations here: the point to note is that various such accounts can be offered, which (if the regulations are well designed) can probably between them explain why in most cases it is wrong to break the regulation.

[160] See Husak, *Overcriminalization*, 110–11: he argues that even a majoritarian condition is inadequate if breaches of the regulation are to be criminalized.

How serious that wrong is depends on the seriousness of the mischief at which the regulatory scheme is aimed, and on the closeness or remoteness of the relationship between the criminalized conduct and that mischief: it is important to notice, however, that what a defendant is convicted, and punished, for is precisely the breach of a regulation.[161] One driver who breaks the speed limit might in fact be driving dangerously, whereas another speeder might not be driving dangerously; one person having sexual relations with an under-age partner might in fact be exploiting a person who is not mature enough to make competent choices in such matters, another might not be: but in each case, both are convicted of the same offence, although they commit different wrongs. So unless provision is made for aggravating factors to be proved at the sentencing stage, both should receive the same kind of (relatively modest) punishment—a punishment that does not reflect an assumption that they committed the substantive mischief.[162]

If a regulation is well designed, I have argued so far, most of those who break it will commit a wrong; that wrong is a public wrong, as breaking a regulation that serves a significant aspect of the common good; it is therefore a candidate for criminalization.[163] But however well designed the regulations are, they will also probably (if they are not under-inclusive) be to some degree over-inclusive: when we stipulate speed or alcohol limits for drivers, or an 'age of consent' for sexual relations, we can expect that some people will in fact be able, and will know that they are able, to break those limits without committing, or taking an unreasonable risk of committing, the substantive mischief at which the regulation is aimed. What can we, and the law, say to a person who admits that he broke the speed limit, or drove with more than the permitted level of alcohol in his blood, but insists that he knew that he could (given his skill, his vehicle, or his physical constitution) do so safely; or who admits that his willing sexual partner was under the specified age, but insists that he and she knew that she was fully mature enough to consent competently? Such claims might be ill-founded: but they might not be; and if they are not, it is not clear why this person ought to obey the regulation, or how he commits a wrong when he breaks it. We can hope that, if regulations are well designed, such cases will be infrequent: but they will still occur.

One question is whether the regulation could be revised so as to exempt such people: but the answer might be that to do so would unduly weaken its efficacy by leaving loopholes for the ill-meaning or incompetent. Another question is whether, if breaches of the regulation are to be criminalized, we could build in a defence that such people could then offer, thus laying on them the burden of at least adducing evidence that they knew they could safely break the regulation:[164] but, apart from similar worries

[161] On the problems raised by this point, see Husak, *Overcriminalization*, 112; Wellman, *Rights Forfeiture and Punishment*, 162–8.

[162] Sometimes the law can include a genuine *malum in se* offence alongside the regulatory offence to capture those who can be proved to have committed the relevant mischief: see e.g. Road Traffic Act 1988, ss 2 (dangerous driving) and 4 (driving when 'unfit to drive through drink or drugs'). It is worth asking whether we could do the same for the wrong of sexually exploiting a young person—or why we should not; see at n. 156 above.

[163] But only for criminalization as one among other possible responses. See, again, the ways in which breaches of tax regulations are dealt with (Chapter 1 at nn 87–90 above), including non-criminal penalties for late submission of tax returns, and penalties for unpaid or underpaid taxes which are based partly on a tax official's judgment on whether the non-payment was deliberate or careless: https://www.gov.uk/self-assessment-tax-returns/penalties; https://www.gov.uk/government/uploads/system/uploads/attachment_data/file/646737/CC-FS7a_09_17.pdf.

[164] Compare Wellman, *Rights Forfeiture and Punishment*, 166–8 (and see 167 on the suggestion that people should be able to obtain advance licences to exempt themselves from the regulation: one problem with such an idea is that it would either require substantial resources, or be another way in which the rich could gain an advantage).

about opening loopholes, we must ask why we should expend the resources that such a provision would require (it would make prosecutions more costly, if such defences had to be disproved, taking up quite significant police, prosecutorial, and court time and resources). It might seem that we should be prepared to expend such resources in order to avoid the unjust conviction of someone who has done no wrong: but the prior question is whether such a person has really done no wrong. Suppose that the burden involved in obeying the regulation (in limiting one's speed, for instance, or not driving after drinking) is relatively light, involving no serious inconvenience; that a strict regulation is significantly more effective in limiting the incidence of the relevant mischief than a less strict regulation that exempted such people would be; and that the costs of allowing such people a formal defence would be considerable. Can we not then say that such people ought to obey the regulation, accepting that relatively mild burden for the sake of the common good, rather than seeking to exempt themselves from it? This would be to appeal to an idea of solidarity with one's fellow citizens: I accept this modest burden that most citizens must accept, because it serves the common good, even though my obedience is not strictly necessary to that end; I do not seek to make an exception for myself. Those with more individualist leanings will find such an appeal implausible; but it fits neatly with the modestly communitarian conception of citizenship sketched in earlier chapters. However, we can resolve such questions about the scope of the criminal law, and about what we can demand of each other by way of obedience to legal regulations, only by determining how we should structure our civil order: what should we owe each other, as fellow members of the polity, as a matter of solidarity?

A final possibility is to rely on a '*De Minimis*' principle, to be applied either by the police or prosecutors in deciding whether to pursue a case, or by courts in deciding whether to convict: a prosecution should not proceed, or the defendant should be acquitted, if his 'conduct did not actually cause or threaten the harm or evil sought to be prevented by the law defining the offense or did so only to an extent too trivial to warrant the condemnation of conviction'.[165] Such a principle, and the discretion that its application requires us to leave to the law's officials, are important to the functioning of a contemporary system of criminal law: although legislatures should not use this as an excuse for sloppily drafted criminal statutes, and although we need to find ways of making the exercise of that discretion accountable,[166] we cannot hope to formulate criminal statutes that will always capture precisely the wrongs that we aim to criminalize; thus discretion will always be needed in applying the law.[167] I do not suggest that such a principle should be used often (although to the extent that regulations and criminal laws are badly drafted, it provides an important safety net); but it can properly be used in what should be relatively rare cases in which a person really does no wrong, in any of the ways discussed above, in violating a regulation or in committing what is formally defined as a criminal offence.

I have been supposing so far that the regulations whose breach is potentially criminalizable are all well designed: that they are narrowly tailored towards a significant

[165] Model Penal Code § 2.12; see above, Chapter 1 at nn 166–76; Chapter 2 at nn 56–64.

[166] See e.g. A P Simester et al, *Simester and Sullivan's Criminal Law*, 496–8, on cases in which formally criminal sexual activity between young people, which should perhaps have been spared prosecution on '*De Minimis*' grounds, were in fact prosecuted; see also Crown Prosecution Service, *Rape and Sexual Offences*, ch. 11.

[167] See also L Zedner, *Criminal Justice*, 129–32; and for a useful general discussion of the respective merits and faults of legislating inevitably vague normative standards (*mala in se*), or inevitably artificial stipulative rules (*mala prohibita*), see T Endicott, 'The Value of Vagueness'.

aspect of the common good, and impose only reasonable burdens on those whose conduct they constrain. As we know all too well, however, this is by no means always the case: so how should citizens respond when faced by regulations that are not well designed, and that therefore make unjustifiable demands on their obedience; and how should prosecutors and courts deal with citizens who then break such regulations? This question raises larger issues in political theory, about what kind of obligation (if any) we have to obey misguided or unjustified laws, and about the conditions under which we may or should (civilly) disobey such laws, that I cannot pursue here. All I would say here is that we must recognize that we are fallible both as law followers and as law makers; that we should therefore be ready to accept, to defer to, laws that emerge from a democratic deliberation aimed in good faith at serving the polity's common good; and that we should therefore be ready to obey even laws that we (perhaps correctly) judge to be to some degree misguided or ill designed—at least so long as they do not require us to act against our consciences.[168] Beyond that, we face a range of questions about the justifiability of civic or conscientious disobedience, and about how the criminal law and its courts should respond to such disobedience, that lie beyond the scope of this book.[169]

In this section I have briefly discussed a small sample of offences that are, to some degree, *mala prohibita* rather than *mala in se*: offences, that is, that consist at least in part in the breach of a legal regulation—in conduct whose wrongfulness consists in part in its prohibited character. My aim has not been to assess the wide range of *mala prohibita* that form such a large part of our existing criminal law, nor indeed to justify the laws that I have discussed: for just one example, an adequate appraisal of laws that criminalize sexual activity with people below a specified age would involve a detailed discussion of the role and significance of sexual relations; of why a mature competence to consent matters, of what should count as competence, and of how heavy the burden of obeying the regulations might be; of how far we can specify, even approximately, an age below which people are very unlikely to have such mature competence; and of whether it really is impracticable to define a suitable *malum in se* offence that does not involve stipulating problematic age limits.[170] What I have tried to show is not whether the laws we have are in order as they stand, but how a legal moralist who holds that the criminal law must take public wrongs as its target can still find room for *mala prohibita* as well as *mala in se*, and can argue that the kinds of conduct that are legitimately criminalized as *mala prohibita* are indeed wrongful prior to their criminalization—albeit not prior to their legal prohibition.

I have also argued that, here as elsewhere in criminalization debates, we cannot hope to find neatly systematic answers. The distinction between *mala in se* and *mala prohibita* is itself far from sharp—which is why we would do better to talk of a spectrum, rather than of two sharply distinct categories; and when we discuss possible justifications for laws creating offences that are to a significant degree *mala prohibita*, we must realize that we can have different kinds of reason for different laws—from which it follows that those who commit such offences commit different kinds of wrong. Laws creating *mala prohibita* are justified insofar as the regulations they enforce are well-designed to serve a significant aspect of the polity's common good; those who commit such offences therefore commit a wrong of failing to play their proper part in

[168] Compare D Markel, 'Retributive Justice and the Demands of Democratic Citizenship', 81–102, on 'dumb but not illiberal' laws.

[169] See above, Chapter 3, section 4.

[170] See Home Office, *Setting the Boundaries: Reforming the Law on Sex Offences*.

serving that good, or refusing to accept their fair share of the burdens that its pursuit involves: but such an abstract account then needs to be given substantive content in what is inevitably a piecemeal way; here again, we should not hope to find thick master principles.

It is not my aim in this chapter to offer anything close to a complete survey of the different types of criminal offence that can be justified through a 'public wrongs' account of crimes: it is rather to illustrate, selectively, how such an account can illuminate questions of criminalization by showing what kinds of factor should bear on such questions and what kinds of argument are relevant to answering them. But we should attend briefly to one other type of crime, which plays a large part in the expansion of our modern criminal law to cover ever-wider realms of conduct.

6. Varieties of Public Wrong (c): Pre-emptive Offences

The focus of this section is on one aspect of 'preventive justice':[171] on the criminalization of conduct that does not itself cause or commit the kind of substantive mischief at which the law is ultimately aimed, but that in some way prepares for that mischief, or enables it, or makes it more likely; or conduct whose criminalization will help to prevent that mischief.[172] We noted one kind of preventive use of the criminal law in section 2(f) above: courts make preventive orders that impose restrictions on a person's conduct, and it is then a criminal offence to violate that order. Our concern here is with a more direct use of the criminal law to criminalize conduct that is somehow related, albeit often remotely, to a substantive mischief, in order thereby more effectively to pre-empt the commission of that mischief.[173] Offences of this 'pre-emptive' sort are not new; many familiar (and relatively uncontroversial) *mala prohibita* are of this kind, since they aim to pre-empt, to prevent, certain kinds of mischief by regulating conduct that make their occurrence more likely. Drivers are required to pass a driving test, and to have their cars checked for safety, because such measures will reduce the chances of road accidents; the same is true of many health and safety regulations. But such offences have proliferated in recent years, most obviously in response to the threat of terrorism, in ways that reach ever further into our ordinary lives, and that formally criminalize kinds of conduct whose connection to the substantial mischief (either in fact or in the agent's intention) is at best tenuous: such proliferation provides one reason to worry that our criminal laws have become over-extensive; so it is worth considering, briefly, what an account of crimes as public wrongs can say about them.

Let us assume that the substantive mischiefs that such offences are intended to pre-empt are indeed genuine public wrongs (terrorist attacks, for instance, or the sexual exploitation of young children), or at least a kind mischief that the polity has a responsibility to try to minimize (deaths and injuries caused by firearms, for instance, which might be intentional, reckless, or accidental). What kinds of criminal offence would it be legitimate to enact with a view to pre-empting such mischiefs? I will not discuss the law of attempts here, or other offences (such as solicitation or incitement) that

[171] See Ashworth and Zedner, *Preventive Justice*.

[172] See Chapter 6, section 3 above, on 'responsive' and 'preventive' reasons for criminalization.

[173] See generally Ashworth and Zedner, *Preventive Justice*, ch. 5; D N Husak, 'The Nature and Justifiability of Nonconsummate Offences'; A P Simester, 'Prophylactic Crimes'; P Ramsay, 'Preparation Offences, Security Interests, Political Freedom'; Simester and von Hirsch, *Crimes, Harms, and Wrongs*, chs 4–5; Tadros, *Wrongs and Harms*, chs 15–17; H Carvalho, *The Preventive Turn in Criminal Law*.

are very closely connected to the substantive mischief—although there is much to be said both about the justifying rationale for such offences (about, for instance, how far that rationale is responsive, and how far preventive), and about how they should be defined.[174] I will instead focus on a few illustrative examples of offences criminalizing conduct that is far more remote from the substantive mischief—that does not even amount to a 'substantial step' towards that mischief:[175] it is such offences as these that raise the most acute questions about pre-emptive or preventive criminal justice.

Some pre-emptive offences are crimes of intention: they criminalize conduct that is intended to lead to the commission of the relevant substantive wrong. It is an offence to 'engage in any conduct in preparation for giving effect to [an] intention' to 'commit[] acts of terrorism',[176] or to possess articles 'for terrorist purposes'.[177] It is an offence to communicate with a person who is under sixteen with the intention of encouraging that person 'to make ... a communication that is sexual', if the purpose is to 'obtain[] sexual gratification',[178] or to arrange to meet a person who is under sixteen with the intention of 'doing anything to or in respect of' that person that would constitute a sexual offence.[179] In one way such offences as these are relatively easy to justify, at least in principle, since (if properly defined) they do criminalize genuine public wrongs: for if it is a public wrong (as it clearly is) to engage in terrorist acts, or to sexually exploit a young child, it is also wrong, in a way that properly concerns the public, to prepare to commit such wrongs.[180] We need to be clear, however, about what such wrongs consist in. It is not enough that the agent intends to commit the substantive mischief—I leave aside here questions about the wrongfulness or criminalizability of bare intentions;[181] nor is it enough that the agent engages in the conduct in question *while* intending to commit that mischief. The conduct must amount to preparation for the commission of the mischief: it must be an integral part of a course of action that is intended to lead to the commission of that mischief. It might be odd to say that someone commits a public wrong, or acts wrongfully at all, in getting up early: but if she gets up early in order to further her plan to commit murder, her action is indeed wrongful—wrongful not in itself, but as an integral part of that larger, wrongful, course of action.[182]

[174] See Simester et al, *Simester and Sullivan's Criminal Law*, ch. 9; Horder, *Ashworth's Principles of Criminal Law*, ch. 12.

[175] I.e. that does not amount to a criminal attempt even under the broad definition of attempt in the Model Penal Code, § 5.01.

[176] Terrorism Act 2006, s. 5.

[177] Terrorism Act 2000, s. 57. Although the offence is labelled 'Possession for Terrorist Purposes', the offence is actually defined as 'possess[ing] an article in circumstances which give rise to a reasonable suspicion that [the] possession is for a purpose connected with the commission, preparation or instigation of an act of terrorism'; it is then a defence for the defendant 'to prove that his possession of the article was not for such a purpose': on this problematic feature of the offence, see R A Duff, 'Perversions and Subversions of Criminal Law', 93–7.

[178] Sexual Offences Act 2003, s. 15A (added by Serious Crime Act 2015, s. 67).

[179] Sexual Offences Act 2003, s. 15.

[180] This is an expanded adaptation of Yaffe's 'Transfer Principle': 'if a particular form of conduct is legitimately criminalized, then the attempt to engage in that form of conduct is also legitimately criminalized' (see G Yaffe, *Attempts in the Philosophy of Action and the Criminal Law*, ch. 1); see Tadros, *Wrongs and Harms*, ch. 16.

[181] For an interesting recent discussion, see G S Mendlow, 'Why is it Wrong to Punish Thought?'. A further question that I cannot pursue here is whether it is ever legitimate to criminalize the mere expression of a criminal intention: see e.g. A Walen, 'Criminalizing Statements Of Terrorist Intent', on American law (18 USC § 2332b(a)(2) (2006)).

[182] See Tadros' response to Scanlon on this kind of case: Tadros, *Wrongs and Harms*, 303–18; T M Scanlon, *Moral Dimensions: Permissibility, Meaning, Blame*, 41–6.

The question about such preparatory offences is therefore not whether we have good reason to criminalize such conduct: we do, since it constitutes a public wrong in virtue of its orientation towards a substantive, criminalizable, public wrong. The question is whether that reason is good enough, and particularly whether any other values to which the polity is also committed militate against criminalizing conduct that is so remote from the substantive mischief towards which it is directed. These might include values that are implicated in the very enactment of a pre-emptive offence of preparation: for instance the value of autonomy, which implies that citizens should be left free to determine their own conduct until it impinges directly on the rights of others, and in particular that even intending criminals should have a *locus poenitentiae*—a chance to abandon their criminal enterprises voluntarily. Other values that militate against criminalizing preparatory conduct during the very early stages of a criminal enterprise have rather to do with what would be involved in enforcing such a law. There might be problems in proving the requisite intent; indeed, the intention to commit the mischief might not even be a determinate intention (as distinct from a possible scheme to which the agent is not yet fully committed). The investigations that enforcement would involve might be highly intrusive—and since they would inevitably be targeted against those who are *suspected* of being engaged in a criminal enterprise, they would intrude on the innocent as well as on the guilty: they would thus threaten our security—security from coercive interventions by the state.[183] I will not pursue these issues here, since it is not my purpose either to argue for a particular account of the proper scope of preparatory offences, or to explore all the considerations that bear on them. My aim is rather to illustrate again the general point that in deciding what to criminalize, we are inevitably deciding how we are to understand and structure our civil order: what role, and weight, should we allow to such values as individual liberty, privacy, and security against state intrusion; or how far should we be ready to sacrifice or compromise such values for the sake of security against such serious mischiefs as terrorism? These are not questions that can be answered through individual reflection on morality. They can be adequately tackled only through a public deliberation about the kind of polity that we are to construct for ourselves: about what we should be able to expect from each other, and from the state (as the polity's institutional manifestation) by way of respect for our autonomous activities, and by way of protection from others' wrongful enterprises; about how ready we should be to accept the risks that others will carry through their un-pre-empted criminal enterprises.

Other, inherently more problematic, pre-emptive offences require no intention directed to the substantive mischief at which the law is aimed: they involve conduct that might somehow assist, or make more likely, the commission of that mischief, even if the agent herself has no intention to bring it about or assist it. The most problematic of these are offences consisting in conduct that would result in the commission of the substantive mischief only through the wrongful conduct of other responsible agents.[184] For instance, it is an offence to 'do[] an act capable of encouraging or assisting the

[183] It is worth putting this point in terms of security, to guard against the temptation to suppose that 'security' must be security against the substantive mischief in question, and thus will always favour the creation of expansive preparatory offences, so that in deciding whether to create such offences we must weigh security against other values: security is actually involved on both sides of such weighing. See L Zedner, 'Securing Liberty in the Face of Terror: Reflections from Criminal Justice'; also, more generally, Simester, 'Prophylactic Crimes', on the 'constraints' that should be put on the creation of such offences.

[184] For a useful discussion, see A Cornford, 'Indirect Crimes'; also Simester and von Hirsch, *Crimes, Harms, and Wrongs*, 58–61, 79–85.

commission of an offence' in the belief 'that the offence will be committed' and that one's 'act will encourage or assist its commission': it need not be my purpose to assist the commission of the offence; the belief that my act will assist it is enough.[185] It is also an offence to collect, or record, or possess 'information of a kind likely to be useful to a person committing or preparing an act of terrorism' (although it is a defence to 'prove that [one] had a reasonable excuse' for such possession);[186] such possession would be connected to the substantive mischief of terrorist acts only via the potential intervening agency of those who would use the information for such purposes.

A robust individualist might reject all such offences, taking a firm stand on the principle of *novus actus interveniens*:[187] if the voluntary act of another rationally competent agent intervenes between my action and the substantive offence (and I did not intend that act or the offence), that not only precludes holding me responsible for the substantive offence; it also frees me from any responsibility for assisting its commission. If someone else chooses to take advantage of some action of mine to commit an offence, that is entirely her responsibility: it is not up to me to attend to such outcomes of my actions, even if they are entirely predictable, as reasons against acting as I do. It is (or should be) hard to maintain a strict version of this stance: if an acquaintance asks to borrow my chain saw, and I know that he intends to use it to destroy another person's property (or even to kill someone), are we really to say that I do no wrong, or at least nothing that should count as a civic wrong, in lending it to him; should the law remain silent about my action? In other cases there is at least more room for argument: if a guest asks me for another drink, and I believe both that this will put him over the limit for driving and that he will nonetheless drive home, should I be said to 'encourage or assist' his commission of the offence of drink driving if I give him the drink; whatever the ethics of hospitality, is this a kind of conduct in which the law should take an interest? In other cases, especially offences of simple possession (as distinct from possession with intent to commit a substantive offence), and especially when what is possessed is not manifestly or inherently dangerous, it is very difficult to justify the law.[188] Thus to criminalize the mere possession of information that might be useful to someone planning an act of terrorism is to declare that we each have a civic responsibility not merely to refrain from providing such a person with information that will help him, but to make sure that he cannot obtain such information through us (or to make sure that if we do possess such information we can offer evidence that we have a 'reasonable excuse' for doing so)—on pain of being convicted of a terrorism-related offence if we cannot do so: but that is not a plausible view of our civic responsibilities. (Nor is it a plausible interpretation of the law's real aim, which is presumably to enable

[185] Serious Crime Act 2007, s. 45; it is a distinct offence, under s. 44 of the Act, to do such an act 'intend[ing] to encourage or assist' the commission of the offence. See also s. 46, covering cases in which I believe my act will encourage or assist the commission of 'one or more of a number of offences', but don't know which. Encouraging or assisting a crime that is actually committed can of course bring the agent within reach of doctrines of complicity, depending on the intentions with which she acts and the relationship of her action to the completed crime (for different versions of such doctrines, see Accessories and Abettors Act 1861, s. 8; Model Penal Code § 2.06; *Strafgesetzbuch* §§ 26–7); but my concern here is with actions that are less closely connected, in intention or in fact, to a completed crime.

[186] Terrorism Act 2000, s. 58; see *R v G* [2009] UKHL 13: for an incisive critique, see J Hodgson and V Tadros, 'How to Make a Terrorist out of Nothing'.

[187] On which see Simester et al, *Simester and Sullivan's Criminal Law*, 96–110.

[188] See M D Dubber, 'Policing Possession: The War on Crime and the End of Criminal Law', and 'The Possession Paradigm: The Special Part and the Police Model of the Criminal Process'; A J Ashworth, 'The Unfairness of Risk-Based Possession Offences'. See also Husak, *Overcriminalization*, 43–4, on possession as an 'ancillary' offence.

the prosecution of those whom the police or security services believe to be actively supporting terrorist activities without the need to prove any such intention.) However, these types of crime highlight an important set of questions about our civic responsibilities in relation to the criminal, or the potentially criminal, conduct of our fellows: how far, in what ways and what contexts, should we expect each other not just to refrain from purposely assisting others in their criminal enterprises, but to make sure that we do not assist those enterprises?

I do not propose to answer these questions here: my aim is rather to make clear what kind of question they are, and how we should set about answering them.[189] They are not questions about the metaphysics of causation: about whether such intervening acts 'really' break the causal chain between my action and the ultimate mischief. Nor are they questions of individual morality: I am not trying to decide whether I should see myself as morally responsible for such outcomes of my actions, or what attention I should pay to what others might do as a result of what I do. They are questions of political morality, about how we should structure our civil order, and understand our relationships with each other as citizens of that order. How far should we adopt an individualist perspective, according to which our civic responsibilities include, of course, our own actions and their unmediated effects, but do not generally include the actions of others—and in particular the ways in which our actions might make it easier for others to commit crimes? How far should we rather take a more communitarian stance, according to which we should attend to such effects of our actions? No simple or general answers are available to these questions: they can be answered only through a series of specific deliberations about the kinds of responsibility that we should accept in relation to different kinds of activity. Should shopkeepers be responsible for the use they know their customers will make of the legal goods that they sell them?[190] Should a doctor be said to 'encourage or assist' the commission of an offence that she knows her treatment will enable her patient to commit more safely?[191] Should a host recognize a civic responsibility not to facilitate his guests' commission of drink-driving offences? These are all questions about how we are to structure important dimensions of our civil order, concerning our civic responsibilities to each other and for each other.

Similar questions arise about reporting actual or suspected criminal activity—either in advance of the substantive crime, to help prevent it,[192] or after the event, to assist the detection of the perpetrator. Should we recognize a general civic responsibility to report such things; and if so, should this be made a legal responsibility, whose violation is criminalized? Should we instead create only more limited duties to report, for instance when the actual or suspected crime is very serious,[193] or the agent holds a position of particular responsibility?[194] On the one hand, if we are to see the criminal law

[189] See Cornford, 'Indirect Crimes'.

[190] For a nice illustration, see *Ulhaq v H M Advocate* 1991 SLT 614 (also *Khaliq v H M Advocate* 1984 SLT 137): a shopkeeper who sold 'containers of solvents and gas lighter fuel' to customers who would, as he knew, use them to sniff glue, and thus to endanger their own health, was convicted of a crime of reckless endangerment, although the customers were adults, and he did not actively encourage their glue sniffing (above, Chapter 1 at n. 137).

[191] See *Gillick v West Norfolk and Wisbech Area Health Authority* [1986] AC 112: does a doctor who prescribes contraceptives for a patient aged 15 aid and abet the offence of unlawful sexual intercourse?

[192] See M Gur-Arye, 'A Failure to Prevent Crime—Should it be Criminal?'.

[193] See e.g. Terrorism Act 2000, s. 38B.

[194] See e.g. the reporting requirements in relation to (suspected) money laundering laid on those acting 'in the course of a business in the regulated sector', by Proceeds of Crime Act 2002, s. 330; and the mass of detailed requirements laid down in the Money Laundering, Terrorist Financing and Transfer of Funds (Information on the Payer) Regulations 2017. See also the American examples given in Husak, *Overcriminalization*, 41–2, and N Abrams, 'The New Ancillary Offenses', 17–21.

as a common law, as a law in whose enterprise we are to be involved as active citizens, we surely should recognize such a civic responsibility—whilst also realizing that it must be exercised with discretion:[195] if crimes are our collective business, as public wrongs, it must in principle be our business to report them. On the other hand, as we have noted before, not all civic responsibilities should be turned into legal duties,[196] and to the extent that discretion is required in exercising a civic responsibility we should also be especially cautious about turning it into a legal duty, given the discretion-chilling effect that this can have. Here again, my aim is not to answer such questions as these. It is to note the ways in which they arise, and to emphasize a point that has been central to this chapter: that to answer such questions we must (in answering them we will) work out an important dimension of our civil order, concerning the kinds of civic responsibility we should have, as citizens, to pay practical attention not just to the effects of our own actions (including their effects on the actions of others), but also to the actions of our fellow citizens—and the ways in which such responsibilities should be qualified or limited by the regard we should also have for the privacy and freedom of those fellow citizens (lest a responsibility to report actual or suspected crime becomes an intrusive busybody's charter).

Several of the issues raised in this section can be illustrated, finally, by looking briefly at the issue of gun possession, which Tadros has used to mount a further attack on the legal moralist's claim (which has been central to my account) that we may legitimately criminalize conduct only if it is wrongful independently of or prior to its criminalization.[197] Guns are dangerous (like so many aspects of our lives): they can be deliberately used to commit serious wrongs; they can be carelessly or incompetently used in ways that can cause serious harm; even when their owners and users take competent care, accidents can happen (or other people can intervene), and cause serious harm. A polity therefore clearly has a proper interest in guns, given their potential impact on important aspects of its common good. How should it treat them?

One possibility is simply to make it clear to citizens that they should take care in dealing with guns: they should not misuse them for wrongful purposes; they should take due care in using or owning them. We could even, to highlight the importance of such care, create an offence of dangerous gun use, analogous to offences such as dangerous driving, and also offer official advice about safe use (perhaps analogous to the British *Highway Code* for drivers).[198] We might well think that that is not enough, however: the ill-intentioned will be unimpressed by such advice, and might hope to get away with ignoring it (given difficulties of proof); the careless and the incompetent will be all too likely to violate it inadvertently. A radical alternative would be to ban all guns (for all except the military, and perhaps specially trained police officers): to justify this, we would need to be able to claim that there are no good enough reasons for wanting to own guns, no legitimate uses for guns, that could make it reasonable to expect us all to accept the risks that gun ownership inevitably creates. (Such a ban need not be criminal: we could enact a regulation banning the possession of guns, and simply provide for the confiscation of any guns held in breach of that regulation.)

[195] See above, Chapter 1 at nn 181–2.

[196] See above, Chapter 3 at n. 140.

[197] See Tadros, *Wrongs and Crimes*, ch. 17. For a careful, sceptical, discussion of the use of criminal law in this context, see D N Husak, 'Guns and Drugs: Case Studies on the Principled Limits of the Criminal Sanction' (see also *Overcriminalization*, 170–3).

[198] Some of the 'rules' in the *Highway Code* are 'legal requirements', whose violation is criminal. Other 'rules' are 'advisory' rather than mandatory, but failure to comply with them 'may be used in evidence' in a criminal case. See https://www.gov.uk/guidance/the-highway-code/introduction (Department of Transport guidance on the Code).

We might think, however, that a complete ban would be unwarranted: that people could have good reasons for wanting to own guns, since guns have legitimate uses (even outside their use as weapons of defensive war or of emergency law enforcement); and that we should therefore be collectively willing to accept the risks of wrongs and of harms that allowing gun ownership will always involve—just as we accept the risks involved in other human activities, such as driving. We might then look for ways of controlling gun use, in order to minimize those risks without banning guns altogether. One kind of restriction would involve banning particular types of gun—types that are especially dangerous, or unlikely to be used for any legitimate purpose;[199] another would involve enacting regulations concerning where and how guns may be held or used.[200] A third kind of restriction would be on gun ownership: we could ban some (categories of) people from owning guns, or allow only some (categories of) people to own guns.

One way to restrict ownership is to start with a defeasible presumption that anyone who wants to own a gun may do so, but then to introduce regulations prohibiting gun ownership to those who satisfy certain conditions: under this kind of regime 'you may own a gun unless . . .'.[201] The other way is to start with a defeasible presumption against gun ownership, but to make it possible to own a gun if one obtains a licence or certificate: under this kind of regime, 'you may not own a gun unless you apply for and are granted a licence'.[202] Whichever approach we take, we will need to ask what kinds of condition should make a person eligible or ineligible for gun ownership: what kinds of condition should be taken to give us good enough reason to believe that a person cannot be trusted to own and use a gun safely; what kinds of condition should a person have to meet to persuade her fellow citizens that she can be trusted to own and use a gun safely? These questions are not, or not simply, epistemic, about the kinds of evidence that could ground epistemically secure predictions of the person's likely behaviour: they are about the kinds and levels of risk that we should be willing to accept in relation to our fellow citizens' conduct, and about the kinds of evidence that we should use in deciding whether and how far to trust them. But I will not pursue these questions here, important though they are. For present purposes, let us suppose that we have enacted a set of regulations that are justified as efficient means to the goal of minimizing the dangers of gun ownership and use: the regulations reliably identify types of people whose trustworthiness as gun owners and users we have good reason to suspect (in the case of prohibitory regulations), or conditions that should assure us of a person's trustworthiness (in the case of licensing regulations).[203]

I have been talking so far of the kinds of regulation that we might enact to serve the aims of gun safety, but not of the role that the criminal law might play in relation to such regulations: in particular, I have yet to show that or why we could be justified in criminalizing breaches of such regulations. I will focus here, for simplicity's sake, on breaches of a complete prohibition on gun ownership, and breaches of licensing

[199] See e.g. Firearms Act 1968, s. 5; Firearms (Amendment) Act 1988, s. 1; Firearms (Amendment) Act 1997, ss 1–7. See also America's Public Safety and Recreational Firearms Use Protection Act (HR 4296, 1994), banning 'the manufacture, transfer, or possession of a semiautomatic assault weapon' (the Act lapsed in 2004, thanks to its 'sunset clause').

[200] See e.g. Firearms Rules 1998 (Statutory Instrument No. 1941, 1998) created by the Secretary of State under the Firearms Act 1968 and the Firearms (Amendment) Act 1988; Home Office, *Firearms Security: A Brief Guide*.

[201] See e.g. Husak, 'Guns and Drugs', 447–9.

[202] See e.g. Firearms Act 1968, ss 1–3.

[203] Further questions arise if the regulations are themselves defective, for instance if they preclude certain types of people from gun ownership for no good reason: but since Tadros' concern is with the enforcement of justified regulations, we need not pursue these questions here (see at nn 168–9 above).

requirements—possessing a gun although one has not even applied for, or has been refused, a licence to do so: for these kinds of case raise the questions that I want to discuss here. Given my commitment to legal moralism, if I am to justify criminalizing breaches of such regulations, I must be able to show that, if the regulations are justified, a breach of them constitutes a public wrong; but, Tadros argues, this is not true, since we can be justified in enacting a prohibition on gun ownership, and criminalizing its violation, and punishing anyone who is proved to have violated it, although some of those who violate it might commit no wrong in doing so. In what follows I will explain why this argument fails. (I will not appeal here to the possibility of justifiably enacting an overbroad regulation, formally criminalizing breaches of it, and then looking to police and prosecutors to avoid the conviction of those who do no wrong in violating it by the discretionary application of a '*De Minimis*' principle:[204] for Tadros asks us to imagine a case in which our preventive aims can be achieved only if the regulations are strictly enforced.)

It is easy enough to show that we have good reason to criminalize at least most breaches of these kinds of regulation: in enacting them, the polity is properly discharging its responsibility to protect its citizens from the kinds of wrong and harm to which gun ownership can lead; and if the regulations are (as we are assuming) well-suited to their protective aims, those who break them will usually be committing a public wrong. If the regulation bans gun ownership completely, one who still owns a gun might keep it for wrongful purposes; or keep it carelessly, thus creating a serious risk of accidental harm, or of its misuse by others; or he might be someone who should not trust himself with a gun, since he is, for instance, liable to resort to violence when angered.[205] Such wrongs have a *malum in se* dimension: independently of any legal regulation of guns, we ought not to keep guns carelessly, or for wrongful purposes, or in contexts that make it likely that they will be misused (including misuse by ourselves). But the legal regulation gives firmer, more determinate (though also to some degree stipulative) shape to those pre-legal norms—as do the regulations that structure a regime of gun licensing; they thus also have a significant dimension of *malum prohibitum*.[206] A breach of such licensing regulations, keeping a gun without a licence, will also often be wrong in one of the same ways as breach of a complete ban on gun ownership: it will involve ill-intentioned, careless, or unreliable ownership. But it will also typically involve other wrongs, even when the ownership is not ill-intentioned, careless, or unreliable. This kind of regulatory regime serves not just to exclude from gun ownership those whom we have reason not to trust as gun owners, but also to specify the formal methods by which we can assure each other that those who own guns can be trusted to do so safely, thus providing not just (objective) security, but the assurance of security; they also make the enforcement of the regime of controlled gun ownership more efficient, since they specify the way in which gun-owners can prove that their ownership is legitimate. One who keeps a gun without applying for a licence or after being refused a licence thus typically commits a wrong even if he in fact meets the substantive qualifying conditions for obtaining a licence: for he fails to provide the assurance of his trustworthiness that his fellow citizens are entitled to require. This is, admittedly, a lesser wrong than that committed by one whose ownership of a gun is substantively dangerous; but it is a public wrong nonetheless, which therefore makes its criminalization in principle appropriate.[207]

[204] See at nn 165–7 above. [205] See Tadros, *Wrongs and Harms*, 320–9.

[206] See at nn 143–7 above.

[207] And perhaps unlicensed gun ownership could be taken to create a presumption that the ownership is dangerous, and thus a more serious wrong; the defendant could then secure a mitigation of

Many, perhaps most, of those who violate either a complete prohibition on gun ownership, or the licensing requirements of a regulatory regime of gun ownership, will thus commit a public wrong in doing so. But can we plausibly claim that *everyone* who violates such regulations commits a wrong? In the case of the absolute prohibition, there will be people who could be trusted, and who know of themselves that they could be trusted, to possess guns safely and discreetly, but who are still prohibited from owning them; at least, there will be such people if we agree (if only for the sake of the argument with Tadros) that there can be good enough reason to possess a gun, legitimate activities in which guns could be used, despite the risks that gun ownership inevitably involves (for no one can offer a cast-iron guarantee that nothing will go wrong). Such people, we can say, should have been allowed to own guns, if only we had a way of reliably distinguishing them from those who should not be allowed to own guns: but we have no such way; so the only secure way to minimize the harms and wrongs that flow from improper gun ownership and use is to prohibit all guns. Something similar could be said about licensing regimes. It seems plausible that a regime of licensing gun ownership will be tolerably effective in its preventive aims only if the conditions for being granted a licence are moderately strict, and that the regulations will as a result deny licences to some who could in fact be trusted, and know that they could be trusted, to own guns safely: such people should have been allowed licences *if* we could reliably distinguish them from those who should not get licences; since we cannot thus distinguish them, our only safe course is to deny licences to them all.[208] In both cases, however, it is not clear that someone who knows that she could be trusted to own a gun, but who is not legally entitled to own one, commits any wrong if she (secretly, discreetly) owns one in contravention of the law. She knows that her conduct does not cause or threaten to cause the mischief against which the law is aimed; she knows that the law is not really aimed at her: why should she obey it?

In such cases, Tadros argues, we may still be justified in criminalizing the person's breach of the gun regulations, and punishing her for it, although she does no wrong: or more precisely, she does no wrong in keeping a gun, *so long as she does not demand that the polity not punish her*; and the polity commits no injustice in convicting and punishing her. For she must realize, as the polity realizes, that given the impossibility of reliably distinguishing her from those who should not possess guns, the polity can achieve its legitimate preventive goals only by criminalizing her conduct along with that of those who should indeed not possess guns, and being ready to convict and punish her along with them. Furthermore, she could avoid conviction and punishment by not owning a gun: assuming that not owning a gun does not unreasonably hinder her legitimate life projects, she therefore cannot complain of injustice if she is convicted and punished. The polity is therefore justified in criminalizing some conduct that is not wrongful—which shows that legal moralism, even in its modest, negative form, is untenable.[209]

I have simplified, but I hope not seriously distorted, Tadros' complicated argument: it needs to be answered not just to defend the version of legal moralism that I have espoused, but to get clear about the normative logic of such offences as these, and about the kind of wrongs that their commission can involve. But the answer has

sentence by offering evidence to rebut that presumption (compare Wellman, *Rights Forfeiture and Punishment*, 162–7, on 'statutory rape').

[208] A proper evaluation of such claims would depend on an assessment of complex types of empirical evidence; but let us assume, for the sake of argument, that the claims can be justified.

[209] See above, Chapter 2, section 4.

in fact already been given, in the account given of the kind of wrong committed by one who violates licensing regulations, and keeps a gun without a licence. Those regulations, I argued, serve not only to forbid gun ownership to those who cannot be trusted to own guns safely, but also to lay down the ways in which we can assure each other that guns are owned only by appropriate people, and reassure each other that we will therefore be (relatively) safe from the wrongs and harms that flow from the misuse of guns; they also lay down the procedures through which gun owners are to be able to prove that they are indeed entitled to own guns. One who violates such regulations might not be creating a risk of the substantive mischief against which they are aimed: but he commits a wrong of failing to provide the assurance of trustworthiness that his fellow citizens are entitled to demand, by the formal procedure that they have specified (as they are entitled to do). Now to enact an absolute ban on gun ownership is not to specify a procedure through which we can assure each other that guns are only owned by trustworthy people: rather, it is to say that there is no such procedure—no procedure through which we could be assured, to an acceptable degree, that those who own guns can be trusted to do so; the (re)assurance that we are entitled to demand, as citizens, can be provided only by not owning guns at all. One who keeps a gun in that regulatory context thus also commits a wrong, of failing to provide the assurance that his fellow citizens demand (as they are entitled to do). Once we turn our eyes from the simple wrong of—to put it crudely—dangerous gun ownership, and look at other kinds of demand that a polity can properly make on its citizens (and that citizens can make on each other), we can see what wrong is committed by someone who keeps a gun in breach of a regulation that justifiably prohibits his ownership, even if he is safe and careful in his ownership and use of the gun.

Much more would need to be said to fill this argument out: much more in particular about the role that security, understood both as a matter of actual freedom from danger and as a matter of perceived safety (of assurance and reassurance),[210] properly plays in the life and governance of a polity.[211] All I have suggested here is, first, that it is a proper aim for a democratic republic to find ways in which its citizens can be assured, and can reassure each other, that they can be trusted not to engage in unreasonably dangerous or threatening kinds of conduct. Second, these ways can include the enactment of regulations concerning, inter alia, the possession and use of dangerous items or instruments: one function of such regulations is to specify formal procedures (such as acquiring a licence) through which the necessary assurance can be provided. Third, one who breaks such regulations therefore commits an in principle criminalizable wrong even if she does not create, and knows that she does not create, a danger of the kind of substantive mischief against which the regulations are aimed. Although we need to be careful in specifying the kinds, and degree, of security that we should be entitled to expect from the polity and from each other, and the kinds of insecurity or risk that we should be ready to accept as part of a decently pluralist civic life, it is hard to deny that security as thus understood is an important value that the polity should protect. It is also hard to deny that, given the size and diversity of contemporary polities, and the relative lack of widely shared informal understandings, prescribed formal procedures will play an important role in providing the formal assurances that we need: they cannot suffice on their own, but they can help to structure a shared civic understanding

[210] Security against the state, as well as against each other: see n. 183 above.

[211] For two very useful discussions of some of the issues here, see I Loader and N Walker, *Civilizing Security*, and Ramsay, *The Insecurity State*. Also relevant here is Pettit's republican conception of non-domination as involving an assurance of non-interference: see above, Chapter 5 at n. 41.

of how security can be assured. Thus here again, deliberations about criminalization, and about the kinds of regulation that the polity can legitimately enforce through the criminal law, must depend on deliberations about the polity's civil order; the law, both regulatory and criminal, helps to structure the civil order that it also then protects.

7. In Brief Conclusion

I have not tried, in the final three sections of this final chapter, to offer a complete survey of the kinds of criminal offence that might be justified under a theory of crimes as public wrongs: that would be an impossible task for one chapter. Instead, I have tried to show how such a theory can help us to understand the normative logic of criminalization deliberations, by discussing a few examples of different kinds of crime. The picture is not a neat and tidy one, of the kind that we might have hoped to build by applying a thick, substantive master principle. Even if we look, as we have been looking, only at the initial questions concerning what kinds of conduct we have good reason, in principle, to criminalize, we must realize that those questions are themselves not straightforward: we must ask whether we have good reason to criminalize a type of public wrong rather than responding in one of the other available ways; what we have reason to criminalize depends in part on what criminalization entails—on whether we can develop a relatively modest, not overly burdensome type of criminal process that could be apt for relatively minor kinds of wrong; in identifying public wrongs we must appeal to a range of different goods and values that structure the polity's civil order; in formulating criminal laws we are not simply trying to reflect, but are in part constructing, those civic values; and although we do need to draw some distinction between '*mala in se*', which involve the relatively direct criminalization of wrongs that have an extra- or pre-legal grounding, and '*mala prohibita*', which involve the violation of a legal regulation, that is a distinction of degree rather than a simple, categorical distinction of kind. But, as I have said before, we should not expect to develop a neat and tidy theory for a normatively untidy world.

Can this kind of theory of criminal law help us address the perceived crises with which this book began—the crisis of 'overcriminalization', the fear that our criminal law is now, 'from the point of view of principle', a lost cause?[212] In part, it should help us to see more clearly just why it is appropriate to talk of crises in this context. It offers a conception of what criminal law ought to be, of what role it should play in a democratic republic—a conception that is based in part on a rational reconstruction of our existing institutions: if that conception is plausible, it also shows us (when we appraise our existing practices in its light) just how far short of it we fall, and just how radically flawed those existing practices are. It does not provide a road map to show us how we might transform our criminal law into something closer to what it ought to be (which would also involve transforming our polities into something more like inclusionary democratic republics of free and equal citizens), but it does offer a sketch of the (distant, ideal) destination towards which we should be trying to travel. Nor does it offer a determinate account of the scope or content of the substantive criminal law of such a polity, or a set of substantive principles whose application could determine that scope and content. It does offer a master principle of criminalization, the public wrongs principle: but that is, as I have argued it needs to be, a thin, formal principle, which leaves

[212] A J Ashworth, 'Is the Criminal Law a Lost Cause?', 253; see above, Introduction at nn 1–3.

most of the substantive work to be done through what should be a process of public deliberation about the construction of the polity's civil order, about what kinds of conduct should be counted as public wrongs within that order, and about appropriate ways of responding to such wrongs. Nonetheless, such a formal principle can make a significant difference to deliberations about criminalization: for it shows what kinds of argument must be offered by those who would criminalize a type of conduct, and what kinds of consideration are relevant to such deliberations; in that way it can guide, and constrain, our criminalization decisions.

As Husak argued, in setting out his 'internal constraints' on criminalization, 'the burden of proof should be placed on those who favor criminal legislation':[213] for to criminalize conduct is to mark it, to condemn it, as wrongful, and to render those who engage in it liable to prosecution, to a conviction that censures them as wrongdoers, and to punishment; we must make sure that we have good enough reason to take such a potentially serious step. The public wrongs principle can show how we should set about making sure that we have good enough reason—not by specifying in substantive terms what can count as a good reason, as thick principles of criminalization seek to do, but by specifying what kinds of substantive claim we must be able to make, and justify.

To justify a claim that we should criminalize a type of conduct, or that it is legitimately and appropriately criminalized, we must argue that it is a public rather than a private matter: that it is a matter that implicates some aspect of the polity's civil order, in which the polity therefore has in principle the standing to intervene. We must argue that such conduct is, when seen in the context of the polity's civil order, wrongful, which is also to argue that we have reason to call those who engage in it to formal, public, censorial (and potentially punitive) account. That argument might, in the case of *mala in se*, be direct: that the conduct can properly be defined, or constructed, as a public wrong in virtue of its pre- or extra-legal character. In the case of offences that are wholly or partly *mala prohibita*, involving conduct that is wrongful only or partly because it violates a legal regulation, the argument must be less direct: we must first justify the regulation in question, by showing that it efficiently serves some aspect of the common good, or averts some mischief that properly concerns the polity, and does so without laying unreasonable burdens on those who are required to obey it; we must then argue on that basis that those who breach the regulation thereby commit a censure-worthy public wrong. Having got this far, having identified a public wrong, we can bring criminalization into the picture as one possible response to such conduct: but we have not yet shown that we have good reason to criminalize it, since we must now argue that we have good reason to criminalize it rather than responding (only) in one of the other ways identified and discussed earlier in this chapter. Only then can we say that we have good reason to criminalize such conduct—and then embark on the further task of examining the practicalities of doing so; that examination might show us that we should not, all things considered, criminalize a type of conduct that we had good reason, in principle, to criminalize.

Would this approach, if adopted by those involved in the processes of criminalization, result in a less expansive criminal law than we now have: would it in that way help to address the crisis of over-criminalization? It is hard to answer that question—partly because, as I have suggested, a lot depends on just what the implications and effects of

[213] Husak, *Overcriminalization*, 100. Husak grounds this constraint in a right not to be punished that is infringed even by deserved punishment: I doubt this right; but a burden of proof constraint need not depend on it.

criminalization are to be. If we assume a system of criminal justice not very different from our own, this approach would result in a much narrower criminal law: given the often oppressive, exclusionary effects of a criminal conviction, we would have good reason to decide that many kinds of currently criminal conduct do not merit *that* kind of response. But if instead we envisage radical reforms to our criminal justice system (reforms of a kind that we anyway have overwhelmingly good reason to seek), so that it becomes a kind of system to which citizens of a liberal republic could submit themselves without thereby losing their civic dignity; and if we imagine a system sufficiently flexible to be able to respond in a modest, non-oppressive, appropriate way to minor wrongdoings:[214] we might expect to end up with what would still be a fairly expansive criminal law. In particular, insofar as pressure to shift some kinds of regulatory breach out of the criminal law into a system of non-criminal regulation reflects a concern that the criminal law is too heavy-handed, too expensive, too oppressive, as a response to such breaches;[215] and insofar as the doubts I expressed about such a system in section 2(d) above are sound: we might expect to end up with a still expansive set of regulatory offences. On the other hand, we might also expect to end up with a much smaller set of pre-emptive offences, for reasons indicated in the previous section: although the mischiefs that such laws aim to pre-empt are, typically, genuine and serious public wrongs, it will be hard to argue that much of the conduct that is currently (formally) criminalized is wrongful either in virtue of its often remote relationship to that mischief, or as violating a justified regulation.

However, as I suggested in the Introduction, the deeper problem with our existing criminal law concerns not its scope, but its lack of principle: that its 'construction' has become 'unprincipled and chaotic',[216] and reflects no 'plausible normative theory'.[217] The approach to criminalization that I have suggested in this book would at least, if seriously followed, give us a more principled, less chaotic, criminal law, whatever its scope: a criminal law structured by the defining values of a liberal republic, and the civic respect that members of such a polity owe each other; a criminal law that we could respect as citizens of such a polity, and make our own, as constituting a good faith attempt to respond appropriately to public wrongs that violate our civil order.

[214] See at n. 29 above. [215] See above, Chapter 1 at nn 23–39.
[216] Ashworth, 'Is the Criminal Law a Lost Cause?', 225.
[217] W Stuntz, 'The Pathological Politics of Criminal Law', 508; see above, Introduction at n. 14.

Bibliography

Abrams, N. 'The New Ancillary Offenses'. *Criminal Law Forum* 1 (1989): 1

Adams, N P. 'In Defense of Content-Independence'. *Legal Theory* 23 (2017): 143

Adler, M. 'Expressive Theories of Law: A Skeptical Overview'. *University of Pennsylvania Law Review* 148 (2000): 1363

Al-Hakim, M. 'Making Room for Hate Crime Legislation in Liberal Societies'. *Criminal Law and Philosophy* 4 (2010): 341

Alegre, S, and M Leaf. 'Mutual Recognition in European Judicial Cooperation: A Step Too Far Too Soon? Case Study—the European Arrest Warrant'. *European Law Journal* 10 (2004): 200

Alexander, L. 'Deontology at the Threshold'. *San Diego Law Review* 37 (2000): 893

Alexander, L. 'Plastic Trees and Gladiators: Liberalism and Aesthetic Regulation'. *Legal Theory* 16 (2010): 77

Alexander, L, and K K Ferzan. *Crime and Culpability: A Theory of Criminal Law* (Cambridge University Press, 2009)

Alexander, M. *The New Jim Crow: Mass Incarceration in the Age of Colorblindness* (The New Press, 2010)

Aliverti, A. 'The Wrongs of Unlawful Immigration'. *Criminal Law and Philosophy* 11 (2017): 375

Alldridge, P. 'Rules for Courts and Rules for Citizens'. *Oxford Journal of Legal Studies* 10 (1990): 487

Allen, C. 'The Nature of a Crime'. In Allen, *Legal Duties and Other Essays in Jurisprudence* (Oxford University Press, 1932)

Allen, C. *The Queen's Peace* (Stevens and Sons, 1953)

Allen, R. 'Alternatives to Prosecution'. In *The Handbook of the Criminal Justice Process*, edited by M McConville and G Wilson (Oxford University Press, 2002): 167

Alschuler, A W. 'A Nearly Perfect System for Convicting the Innocent'. *Albany Law Review* 79 (2016): 919

Altman, A, and C Wellman. *A Liberal Theory of International Justice* (Oxford University Press, 2009)

Alvarez, M. 'Reasons for Action: Justification, Motivation, Explanation'. In *The Stanford Encyclopedia of Philosophy* (Winter 2017 edn), edited by E N Zalta. https://plato.stanford.edu/archives/win2017/entries/reasons-just-vs-expl/

Ambos, K. 'The Overall Function of International Criminal Law: Striking the Right Balance Between the *Rechtsgut* and the Harm Principles'. *Criminal Law and Philosophy* 9 (2015): 301

Anderson, E, and R Pildes. 'Expressive Theories of Law: A General Restatement'. *University of Pennsylvania Law Review* 148 (2000): 1503

Aquinas, T. *Summa Theologiae*; available online through the Aquinas Institute. http://aquinas.cc

Archard, D. 'Political Reasonableness'. *Canadian Journal of Philosophy* 35 (2005): 1

Archbold. *Criminal Pleading, Evidence and Practice* (edited by P Richardson; Sweet and Maxwell, 2016)

Archer, A. 'The Problem with Moralism'. *Ratio* 2017; DOI: 10.1111/rati.12168

Aristotle. *Nicomachean Ethics* (trans. R Crisp; Cambridge University Press, 2000)

Ashworth, A J. 'Victim Impact Statements and Sentencing'. *Criminal Law Review* (1993): 498

Ashworth, A J. 'Is the Criminal Law a Lost Cause?' *Law Quarterly Review* 116 (2000): 225

Ashworth, A J. 'The Unfairness of Risk-Based Possession Offences'. *Criminal Law and Philosophy* 5 (2011): 237

Ashworth, A J. *What if Imprisonment were Abolished for Property Offences?* (Howard League, 2013)

Ashworth, A J, and M Blake. 'The Presumption of Innocence in English Criminal Law'. *Criminal Law Review* (1996): 306

Ashworth, A J, and J Horder. *Principles of Criminal Law* (7th edn; Oxford University Press, 2013)

Ashworth, A J, and M Redmayne. *The Criminal Process* (4th edn; Oxford University Press, 2010)

Ashworth, A J, and L Zedner. 'Preventive Orders: A Problem of Under-criminalization?' In *The Boundaries of the Criminal Law*, edited by R A Duff et al (Oxford University Press, 2010): 59

Ashworth, A J, and L Zedner. *Preventive Justice* (Oxford University Press, 2014)

Ashworth, A J, L Zedner, and P Tomlin (eds), *Prevention and the Limits of the Criminal Law* (Oxford University Press, 2013)

Asp, P. 'The Prosecutor in Swedish Law'. *Crime and Justice* 41 (2012): 141

Avineri, S, and A de-Shalit (eds). *Communitarianism and Individualism* (Oxford University Press, 1992)

Ayres, I, and J Braithwaite. *Responsive Regulation: Transcending the Deregulation Debate* (Oxford University Press, 1992)

Bagaric, M. *Punishment and Sentencing: A Rational Approach* (Cavendish Publishing, 2001)

Baker, E. 'A Case of "Nested Enforcement": Article 83(2) TFEU, Compliance and the Area of Freedom, Security and Justice Post-Lisbon'. In *New Directions in Effective Enforcement of EU Law*, edited by S Drake and M Smith (Edward Elgar, 2016): 256

Baker, G. *Politicizing Ethics in International Relations: Cosmopolitanism as Hospitality* (Routledge, 2011)

Bassiouni, M C. *International Extradition: United States Law and Practice* (4th edn; Oceana Publications, 2002)

Bassiouni, M C, and E M Wise, *Aut Dedere Aut Judicare: The Duty to Extradite or Prosecute in International Law* (Dordrecht: Nijhoff, 1995)

Beccaria, C. *An Essay on Crimes and Punishments* (trans. E D Ingraham; W.C. Little, 1872). http://oll.libertyfund.org/titles/beccaria-an-essay-on-crimes-and-punishments

Becker, L C. 'Criminal Attempts and the Theory of the Law of Crimes'. *Philosophy and Public Affairs* 3 (1974): 262

Bell, D. 'Communitarianism', Stanford Encyclopedia of Philosophy (Summer 2016 Edition), edited by E N Zalta. http://plato.stanford.edu/archives/sum2016/entries/communitarianism/

Benhabib, S. *The Rights of Others. Aliens, Citizens and Residents* (Cambridge University Press, 2004)

Bennett, C J. *The Apology Ritual: A Philosophical Theory of Punishment* (Cambridge University Press, 2008)

Bentham, J. *A Comment on the Commentaries* (1776; in *Collected works of Jeremy Bentham*, edited by J H Burns and H L A Hart; Athlone Press, 1977)

Bentham, J. *An Introduction to the Principles of Morals and Legislation* (1789; edited by J H Burns and H L A Hart; Oxford University Press, 1996)

Bergelson, V. 'The Right to Be Hurt: Testing the Boundaries of Consent'. *George Washington Law Review* 75 (2007): 165

Bergelson, V. *Victims' Rights and Victims' Wrongs: Comparative Liability in Criminal Law* (Stanford University Press, 2009)

Berger, P L. *A Rumour of Angels* (Penguin, 1970)

Berman, M. 'Two Kinds of Retributivism'. In *Philosophical Foundations of Criminal Law*, edited by R A Duff and S P Green (Oxford University Press, 2011): 433

Besson, S, and J L Martí (eds). *Legal Republicanism: National and International Perspectives* (Oxford University Press, 2009)

Besson, S, and J L Martí. 'Law and Republicanism: Mapping the Issues'. In *Legal Republicanism: National and International Perspectives*, edited by S Besson and J L Martí (Oxford University Press, 2009): 3

Bibas, S. *The Machinery of Criminal Justice* (Oxford University Press, 2012)

Biggar, N. *In Defence of War* (Oxford University Press, 2013)

Blackstone, W. *Commentaries on the Laws of England* (4 vols; Clarendon Press 1765–9; available at www.yale.edu/lawweb/avalon/blackstone/blacksto.htm)

Bohlander, M. *Principles of German Criminal Procedure* (Hart Publishing, 2012)

Boonin, D. *The Problem of Punishment* (Cambridge University Press, 2008)

Bottoms, A E. 'Civil Peace and Criminalization'. In *Criminalization: The Political Morality of the Criminal Law*, edited by R A Duff et al (Oxford University Press, 2014): 232

Bowers, J. 'Punishing the Innocent'. *University of Pennsylvania Law Review* 156 (2008): 1117

Boycott, O. 'Rising Nationalism Leaves International Criminal Court at Risk'. *The Guardian* 29 December 2016. https://www.theguardian.com/news/2016/dec/29/rising-nationalism-leaves-international-criminal-court-at-risk

Boyne, S. 'German Prosecutors and the Rechtsstaat'. In *Prosecutors and Democracy*, edited by M Langer and D Sklansky (Cambridge University Press, 2017): 138

Bradley, F H. 'My Station and its Duties'. In Bradley, *Ethical Studies* (Oxford University Press, 1988; originally published 1876): 160

Braithwaite, J, and P Pettit. *Not Just Deserts: A Republican Theory of Criminal Justice* (Oxford University Press, 1990)

Brake, E (ed.). *After Marriage: Rethinking Marital Relationships* (Oxford University Press, 2016)

Brink, D. 'Retributivism and Legal Moralism'. *Ratio Juris* 25 (2012): 496

British Medical Association. *The Law and Ethics of Abortion* (2014). www.bma.org.uk/-/media/.../law_and_ethics_of_abortion_nov2014.pdf

Brown, D. 'Democracy and Decriminalization'. *Texas Law Review* 86 (2007): 223

Brown, G. 'The Laws of Hospitality, Asylum Seekers and Cosmopolitan Right: A Kantian Response to Jacques Derrida'. *European Journal of Political Theory* 9 (2010): 308

Brownlee, K. *Conscience and Conviction: The Case for Civil Disobedience* (Oxford University Press, 2012)

Brudholm, T. 'Hatred as an Attitude'. *Philosophical Papers* 39 (2010): 89

Brudner, A. *Punishment and Freedom: A Liberal Theory of Penal Justice* (Oxford University Press, 2009)

Butler, H. 'Supermax Prisons: Another Chapter in the Constitutionality of the Incarceration Conundrum'. *Rutgers Journal of Law and Public Policy* 9 (2012): 1

Byron, M (ed.). *Satisficing and Maximizing: Moral Theorists on Practical Reason* (Cambridge University Press, 2004)

Cameron, I. *The Protective Principle of International Criminal Jurisdiction* (Dartmouth, 1994)

Camus, A. *The Rebel* (*L'Homme Révolté*; trans. A Bower; Penguin Books, 2000)

Carroll, A, and L Itaborahy. *State Sponsored Homophobia 2015: A World Survey of Laws: Criminalisation, Protection and Recognition of Same-sex Love* (ILGA, 2015)

Carvalho, H. *The Preventive Turn in Criminal Law* (Oxford University Press, 2017)

Cassese, A. *Cassese's International Criminal Law* (3rd edn, revised by A Cassese, L Baig, M Fan, P Gaeta, C Gosnell, A Whiting, Oxford University Press, 2013)

Chalmers, J. '"Frenzied Law Making": Overcriminalization by Numbers'. *Current Legal Problems* 67 (2014): 483

Chalmers, J, and F Leverick. 'Fair Labelling in Criminal Law'. *Modern Law Review* 71 (2008): 217

Chalmers, J, and F Leverick. 'Tracking the Creation of Criminal Offences'. *Criminal Law Review* (2013): 543

Chalmers, J, and F Leverick. 'Quantifying Criminalization'. In *Criminalization: The Political Morality of the Criminal Law*, edited by R A Duff et al (Oxford University Press, 2014): 54

Chalmers, J, F Leverick, and A Shaw. 'Is Formal Criminalisation Really on the Rise? Evidence from the 1950s'. *Criminal Law Review* (2015): 177

Chambers, C. *Against Marriage: An Egalitarian Defence of the Marriage-Free State* (Oxford University Press, 2017)

Chehtman, A. 'The Extraterritorial Scope of the Right to Punish'. *Law and Philosophy* 29 (2010): 127

Chehtman, A. *The Philosophical Foundations of Extraterritorial Punishment* (Oxford University Press, 2010)

Chiao, V. 'Discretion and Domination in Criminal Procedure: Reflections on Pettit'. *Politics, Philosophy & Economics* 15 (2016): 92

Chiao, V. 'What is the Criminal Law For?' *Law and Philosophy* 35 (2016): 137

Chiao, V. 'Two Conceptions of the Criminal Law'. In *The New Philosophy of Criminal Law*, edited by C Flanders and Z Hoskins (Rowman & Littlefield, 2016): 19

Chiao, V. 'A Response to Professor Kleinfeld's *Reconstructivism: The Place of Criminal Law in Ethical Life*'. *Harvard Law Review Forum* 129 (2016): 258

Chiao, V. *Criminal Law in the Age of the Administrative State* (Oxford University Press, 2018)

Chin, G. 'The New Civil Death: Rethinking Punishment in the Era of Mass Conviction'. *University of Pennsylvania Law Review* 160 (2012): 1789

Christiano, T. 'Authority'. *Stanford Encyclopedia of Philosophy* (Spring 2013 Edition), edited by E N Zalta. https://plato.stanford.edu/archives/spr2013/entries/authority/

Christodoulidis, E. 'The Objection that Cannot be Heard: Communication and Legitimacy in the Courtroom'. In *The Trial on Trial (1): Truth and Due Process*, edited by R A Duff et al (Hart Publishing, 2004): 179

Christie, N. 'Conflicts as Property'. *British Journal of Criminology* 17 (1977): 1

Christie, N. *Limits to Pain* (Martin Robertson, 1981)

Christie, N. *Crime Control as Industry: Towards Gulags, Western Style?* (3rd edn; Routledge, 2000)

Cohen, G A. 'Casting the First Stone: Who Can, and Who Can't, Condemn the Terrorists'. *Royal Institute of Philosophy Supplements* 81 (2006): 113

Cornford, A. 'Criminalising Anti-Social Behaviour'. *Criminal Law and Philosophy* 6 (2012): 1

Cornford, A. 'Indirect Crimes'. *Law and Philosophy* 32 (2013): 485

Cornford, A. 'Rethinking the Wrongness Constraint'. *Law and Philosophy* 36 (2017): 615

Cotterrell, R. *Law's Community* (Oxford University Press, 1995)

Crown Office and Procurator Fiscal Service. *Prosecution Code*. http://www.copfs.gov.uk/images/Documents/Prosecution_Policy_Guidance/Prosecution20Code20_Final20180412__1.pdf

Crown Prosecution Service. *Binding Over Orders*. http://www.cps.gov.uk/legal/a_to_c/binding_over_orders/#a02

Crown Prosecution Service. *Code for Crown Prosecutors*. https://www.cps.gov.uk/publications/code_for_crown_prosecutors/

Crown Prosecution Service. *Controlling or Coercive Behaviour in an Intimate or Family Relationship*. http://www.cps.gov.uk/legal/a_to_c/controlling_or_coercive_behaviour/

Crown Prosecution Service. *Domestic Abuse Guidelines for Prosecutors*. http://www.cps.gov.uk/legal/d_to_g/domestic_abuse_guidelines_for_prosecutors/#a02

Crown Prosecution Service. *Election Offences*. http://www.cps.gov.uk/legal/d_to_g/election_offences/

Crown Prosecution Service. *Policy for Prosecutors in Respect of Cases of Encouraging or Assisting Suicide*. http://www.cps.gov.uk/publications/prosecution/assisted_suicide_policy.html

Crown Prosecution Service. *Rape and Sexual Offences*. http://www.cps.gov.uk/legal/p_to_r/rape_and_sexual_offences/

Crown Prosecution Service. *Reduction in Sentence for a Guilty Plea.* http://www.cps.gov.uk/legal/s_to_u/sentencing_-_general_principles/#a17

Crown Prosecution Service. *Victims' Right to Review Scheme.* http://www.cps.gov.uk/victims_witnesses/victims_right_to_review/index.html

Dagger, R. *Civic Virtues: Rights, Citizenship, and Republican Liberalism* (Oxford University Press, 1997)

Dagger, R. 'Republicanism and the Foundations of Criminal Law'. In *Philosophical Foundations of Criminal Law*, edited by R A Duff and S P Green (Oxford University Press, 2011): 44

Dagger, R. *Playing Fair: Political Obligation and the Problems of Punishment* (Oxford University Press, 2018)

Dagger, R, and D Lefkowitz. 'Political Obligation'. *Stanford Encyclopedia of Philosophy* (Fall 2014 Edition), edited by E N Zalta. https://plato.stanford.edu/archives/fall2014/entries/political-obligation/

Damaška, M. 'Evidentiary Barriers to Conviction and Two Models of Criminal Procedure'. *University of Pennsylvania Law Review* 21 (1973): 506

Damaška, M. 'The Reality of Prosecutorial Discretion: Comments on a German Monograph'. *American Journal of Comparative Law* 29 (1981): 119

Damaška, M. *The Faces of Justice and State Authority: A Comparative Approach to the Legal Process* (Yale University Press, 1986)

Dan-Cohen, M. 'Decision Rules and Conduct Rules: On Acoustic Separation in Criminal Law'. *Harvard Law Review* 97 (1984): 625

Dan-Cohen, M. 'Defending Dignity'. In Dan-Cohen, *Harmful Thoughts: Essays on Law, Self and Morality* (Princeton University Press, 2002): 150

Dancy, J. *Practical Reality* (Oxford University Press, 2000)

Dancy, J. *Ethics Without Principles* (Oxford University Press, 2004)

De Búrca, G, and S Gardner. 'The Codification of the Criminal Law'. *Oxford Journal of Legal Studies* 10 (1990): 559

DeGirolami, M O. 'James Fitzjames Stephen: The Punishment Jurist'. In *Foundational Texts in Modern Criminal Law*, edited by M D Dubber (Oxford University Press, 2014): 183

Del Mar, M, and Z Bankowski (eds). *Law as Institutional Normative Order* (Ashgate, 2009)

Dempsey, M M. *Prosecuting Domestic Violence: A Philosophical Analysis* (Oxford University Press, 2009)

Dempsey, M M. 'Public Wrongs and the "Criminal Law's Business": When Victims Won't Share'. In *Crime, Punishment, and Responsibility*, edited by R Cruft et al (Oxford University Press, 2011): 254

Derrida, J. *Of Hospitality* (Stanford University Press, 2000)

Devlin, P. *The Enforcement of Morals* (Oxford University Press, 1965)

Diamond, C. 'Eating Meat and Eating People'. *Philosophy* 53 (1978): 465

Díez, C G-J. 'Enemy Combatants Versus Enemy Criminal Law'. *New Criminal Law Review* 11 (2008): 529

Dimock, S. 'Retributivism and Trust'. *Law and Philosophy* 16 (1997): 37

Dimock, S. 'Contractarian Criminal Law Theory and *Mala Prohibita* Offences'. In *Criminalization: The Political Morality of the Criminal Law*, edited by R A Duff et al (Oxford University Press, 2014): 151

Dimock, S. 'The *Malum Prohibitum–Malum in Se* Distinction and the Wrongfulness Constraint on Criminalization'. *Dialogue* 55 (2016): 9

Dobash, R E, and R P Dobash. *Women, Violence and Social Change* (Routledge, 1992)

Dolinko, D. 'Some Thoughts about Retributivism'. *Ethics* 101 (1991): 537

Dubber, M D. 'Policing Possession: The War on Crime and the End of Criminal Law'. *Journal of Criminal Law and Criminology* 91 (2001): 829

Dubber, M D. *Victims in the War on Crime: The Use and Abuse of Victims' Rights* (New York University Press, 2002)

Dubber, M D. 'The Promise of German Criminal Law'. *German Law Journal* 6 (2005): 1049

Dubber, M D. 'The Possession Paradigm: The Special Part and the Police Model of the Criminal Process'. In *Defining Crimes: Essays on the Special Part of the Criminal Law*, edited by R A Duff and S P Green (Oxford University Press, 2005): 91

Dubber, M D. 'Theories of Crime and Punishment in German Criminal Law'. *American Journal of Comparative Law* 53 (2006): 679

Dubber, M D. 'Paradigms of Penal Law'. In *The Oxford Handbook of Criminal Law*, edited by M D Dubber and T Hörnle (Oxford University Press, 2014): 1017

Dubber, M D, and T Hörnle. *Criminal Law: A Comparative Approach* (Oxford University Press, 2014)

Dubber, M D, and S Stern (eds). 'Symposium: Corporate Personhood and Criminal Liability'. *New Criminal Law Review* 16 (2013): 203

Duff, P. 'The Prosecutor Fine'. *Oxford Journal of Legal Studies* 14 (1994): 565

Duff, R A. *Trials and Punishments* (Cambridge University Press, 1986)

Duff, R A. 'Principle and Contradiction in the Criminal Law: Motives and Criminal Liability'. In *Philosophy and the Criminal Law. Principle and Critique*, edited by R A Duff (Cambridge University Press, 1998): 156

Duff, R A. *Punishment, Communication, and Community* (Oxford University Press, 2001)

Duff, R A. 'Harms and Wrongs'. *Buffalo Criminal Law Review* 5 (2001): 13

Duff, R A. 'Theorizing Criminal Law'. *Oxford Journal of Legal Studies* 25 (2005): 353

Duff, R A. *Answering for Crime: Responsibility and Liability in the Criminal Law* (Hart Publishing, 2007)

Duff, R A. 'Can We Punish the Perpetrators of Atrocities?' In *The Religious in Responses to Mass Atrocities*, edited by T Brudholm and T Cushman (Cambridge University Press, 2009): 79

Duff, R A. 'Perversions and Subversions of Criminal Law'. In *The Boundaries of the Criminal Law*, edited by R A Duff et al (Oxford University Press, 2010): 88

Duff, R A. 'In Response'. In *Crime, Punishment, and Responsibility*, edited by R Cruft et al (Oxford University Press, 2011): 351

Duff, R A. 'Mercy'. In *Oxford Handbook of Philosophy of Criminal Law*, edited by J Deigh and D Dolinko (Oxford University Press, 2011): 467

Duff, R A. 'Responsibility, Citizenship and Criminal Law'. In *Philosophical Foundations of Criminal Law*, edited by R A Duff and S P Green (Oxford University Press, 2011): 125

Duff, R A. 'Responsibility, Restoration and Retribution'. In *Retributivism Has a Past: Has it a Future?*, edited by M Tonry (Oxford University Press, 2012): 63

Duff, R A. 'Relational Reasons and the Criminal Law'. *Oxford Studies in Legal Philosophy* 2 (2013): 175

Duff, R A. 'Who Must Presume Whom to be Innocent of What?' *Netherlands Journal of Legal Philosophy* 42 (2013): 170

Duff, R A. 'Towards a Modest Legal Moralism'. *Criminal Law and Philosophy* 8 (2014): 217

Duff, R A. 'Criminal Responsibility and the Emotions'. *Inquiry* 58 (2015): 189

Duff, R A. 'Legal Moralism and Public Wrongs'. In *Legal, Moral and Metaphysical Truths: The Philosophy of Michael S Moore*, edited by K K Ferzan and S J Morse (Oxford University Press, 2016): 95

Duff, R A. 'Discretion and Accountability in a Democratic Criminal Law'. In *Prosecutors and Democracy*, edited by M Langer and D Sklansky (Cambridge University Press, 2017): 9

Duff, R A, and S P Green (eds). *Philosophical Foundations of Criminal Law* (Oxford University Press, 2011)

Duff, R A, and S E Marshall. 'How Offensive Can You Get?' In *Incivilities: Regulating Offensive Behaviour*, edited by A von Hirsch and A P Simester (Hart Publishing, 2006): 57

Duff, R A, and S E Marshall. '"Abstract Endangerment", Two Harm Principles, and Two Routes to Criminalisation'. *Bergen Journal of Criminal Law and Criminal Justice* 3 (2015): 131

Duff, R A, and S E Marshall. 'Civic Punishment'. In *Democratic Theory and Mass Incarceration*, edited by A Dzur et al (Oxford University Press, 2016): 33

Duff, R A, and S E Marshall. 'Criminalizing Hate'. In *Hate, Politics, Law*, edited by T Brudholm and B S Johansen (Oxford University Press, 2018): 115

Duff, R A, L Farmer, S E Marshall, and V Tadros. *The Trial on Trial (3): Towards a Normative Theory of the Criminal Trial* (Hart Publishing, 2007)

Duff, R A, L Farmer, S E Marshall, M Renzo, and V Tadros (eds). *Criminalization: The Political Morality of the Criminal Law* (Oxford University Press, 2014)

Duff, R A, L Farmer, S E Marshall, M Renzo, and V Tadros. 'Introduction: Towards a Theory of Criminalization'. In *Criminalization: The Political Morality of the Criminal Law* (Oxford University Press, 2014): 1

du Plessis, M, T Maluwa, and A O'Reilly. *Africa and the International Criminal Court* (Chatham House, 2013)

Dworkin, G. *The Theory and Practice of Autonomy* (Cambridge University Press, 1988)

Dworkin, G. 'Devlin Was Right: Law and the Enforcement of Morality'. *William and Mary Law Review* 40 (1999): 927

Dworkin, R M. *Taking Rights Seriously* (2nd imp.; Duckworth, 1978)

Dworkin, R M. *Law's Empire* (Fontana, 1986)

Dworkin, R M. *A Matter of Principle* (Oxford University Press, 1986)

Dyson, M (ed.). *Unravelling Tort and Crime* (Cambridge University Press, 2014)

Dzur, A. *Punishment, Participatory Democracy, and the Jury* (Oxford University Press, 2012)

Edmundson, W. 'The Duty to Obey the Law'. *Legal Theory* 10 (2005): 215

Edmundson, W. 'The Virtue of Law Abidance'. *Philosopher's Imprint* 6 (2006): 1

Edwards, J. 'Harm Principles'. *Legal Theory* 20 (2014): 253

Edwards, J. 'Master Principles of Criminalisation'. *Jurisprudence* 7 (2016): 138

Edwards, J. 'Criminalization without Punishment'. *Legal Theory* 23 (2017): 69

Edwards, J. 'An Instrumental Legal Moralism'. *Oxford Studies in Philosophy of Law* 3 (2018)

Edwards, J, and A P Simester. 'What's Public About Crime?' *Oxford Journal of Legal Studies* 37 (2017): 105

Eldar, S. 'Criminal Law, Parental Authority, and the State'. *Criminal Law and Philosophy* (2017). https://doi.org/10.1007/s11572-017-9452-7

Endicott, T. 'The Value of Vagueness'. In *Philosophical Foundations of Language in the Law*, edited by A Marmor and S Soames (Oxford University Press, 2011): 14

Enoch, D. 'The Disorder of Public Reason'. *Ethics* 124 (2013): 141

Enoch, D. 'Against Public Reason'. *Oxford Studies in Political Philosophy* 1 (2015): 1

Enoch, D. 'Political Philosophy and Epistemology: The Case of Public Reason'. *Oxford Studies in Political Philosophy* 3 (2017): 132

Erez, E. 'Who's Afraid of the Big Bad Victim? Victim Impact Statements as Victim Empowerment and Enhancement of Justice'. *Criminal Law Review* (1999): 545

European Commission, *European Arrest Warrant*. http://ec.europa.eu/justice/criminal/recognition-decision/european-arrest-warrant/index_en.htm

Evans, M. 'Police are "Turning a Blind Eye" to Cannabis across the Country, Experts Claim'. *Daily Telegraph* 22 July 2015. http://www.telegraph.co.uk/news/uknews/law-and-order/11755995/Police-are-turning-a-blind-eye-to-cannabis-across-the-country-experts-claim.html

Falls, M M. 'Retribution, Reciprocity, and Respect for Persons'. *Law and Philosophy* 6 (1987): 25

Farmer, L. 'Criminal Wrongs in Historical Perspective'. In *The Boundaries of the Criminal Law*, edited by R A Duff et al (Oxford University Press, 2010): 214

Farmer, L. 'Territorial Jurisdiction and Criminalization'. *University of Toronto Law Journal* 63 (2013): 225

Farmer, L. *Making the Modern Criminal Law: Criminalization and Civil Order* (Oxford University Press, 2016)

Feeley, M. *The Process is the Punishment: Handling Cases in a Lower Criminal Court* (Russell Sage Foundation, 1979)

Feeley, M, and J Simon. 'The New Penology: Notes on the Emerging Strategy of Corrections and its Implications'. *Criminology* 30 (1992): 449

Feinberg, J. 'The Expressive Function of Punishment'. In Feinberg, *Doing and Deserving* (Princeton University Press, 1970): 95

Feinberg, J. *Harm to Others* (Oxford University Press, 1984)

Feinberg, J. *Offense to Others* (Oxford University Press, 1985)

Feinberg, J. *Harm to Self* (Oxford University Press, 1986)

Feinberg, J. *Harmless Wrongdoing* (Oxford University Press, 1988)

Ferguson, A. *Principles of Moral and Political Science* (W Creech, 1792)

Ferguson, P. *Breach of the Peace* (Dundee University Press, 2013)

Ferguson, P, and C McDiarmid. *Scots Criminal Law: A Critical Analysis* (2nd edn; Edinburgh University Press, 2014)

Finkelstein, C. 'Is Risk a Harm?' *University of Pennsylvania Law Review* 151 (2003): 963

Finlay, S, and M Schroeder. 'Reasons for Action: Internal vs. External'. *The Stanford Encyclopedia of Philosophy* (Fall 2017 Edition), edited by E N Zalta. https://plato.stanford.edu/archives/fall2017/entries/reasons-internal-external/

Finnis, J. 'On "The Critical Legal Studies Movement"'. In *Oxford Essays in Jurisprudence*, 3rd Series, edited by J Eekelaar and J Bell (Oxford University Press, 1987): 145

Fuller, L. *The Morality of Law* (rev. edn; Yale University Press, 1969)

Gaita, R. *Good and Evil: An Absolute Conception* (2nd edn; Routledge, 2004)

Gaita, R. 'Literature, Genocide and the Philosophy of International Law'. In *Crime, Punishment, and Responsibility*, edited by R Cruft et al (Oxford University Press, 2011): 122

Gardner, J. 'Complicity and Causality'. In Gardner, *Offences and Defences* (Oxford University Press, 2007): 57

Gardner, J. 'Reply to Critics'. In Gardner, *Offences and Defences* (Oxford University Press, 2007): 239

Gardner, J. 'Relations of Responsibility'. In *Crime, Punishment, and Responsibility*, edited by R Cruft et al (Oxford University Press, 2011): 87

Gardner, J, and T Macklem. 'Reasons'. In *Oxford Handbook of Jurisprudence and Philosophy of Law*, edited by J Coleman and S Shapiro (Oxford University Press, 2002): 440

Gardner, J, and S Shute. 'The Wrongness of Rape'. In *Oxford Essays in Jurisprudence*, 4th Series, edited by J Horder (Oxford University Press, 2000): 193

Garvey, S. 'Review Article: A Hegelian Criminal Law'. *University of Toronto Law Journal* 61 (2011): 147

Garvey, S. 'Was Ellen Wronged?' *Criminal Law and Philosophy* 7 (2013): 185

Gaus, G. *The Order of Public Reason: A Theory of Freedom and Morality in a Diverse and Bounded World* (Cambridge University Press, 2010)

Gauthier, D. 'Levinas and the Politics of Hospitality'. *History of Political Thought* 28 (2007): 158

General Medical Council. *Professional Conduct and Discipline: Fitness to Practise* (General Medical Council, 1993)

General Medical Council. *To Consider: Introduction of the Civil Standard of Proof* (General Medical Council, 2007)

General Medical Council. *Good Medical Practice* (General Medical Council, 2013)

George, R P. *Making Men Moral: Civil Liberties and Public Morality* (Oxford University Press, 1995)

Goldberg, J, and B Zipursky. 'Torts as Wrongs'. *Texas Law Review* 88 (2010): 917

Goldberg, J, and B Zipursky. *Torts* (Oxford University Press, 2010)

Goldman, A. 'Toward a New Theory of Punishment'. *Law and Philosophy* 1 (1982): 57

Gordon, G H. *The Criminal Law of Scotland* (2nd edn; W Green, 1978)
Gordon, G H. *The Criminal Law of Scotland* (3rd edn, by M G Christie; W Green, 2000)
Goudkamp, J. *Tort Law Defences* (Hart Publishing, 2013)
Gowans, C W (ed.). *Moral Dilemmas* (Oxford University Press, 1987)
Gowans, C W. 'Moral Relativism'. In *The Stanford Encyclopedia of Philosophy* (Winter 2016 Edition), edited by E N Zalta. https://plato.stanford.edu/archives/win2016/entries/moral-relativism/
Green, S P. 'Why it's a Crime to Tear the Tag off a Mattress: Over-Criminalization and the Moral Content of Regulatory Offenses'. *Emory Law Journal* 46 (1997): 1533
Green, S P. 'The Conceptual Utility of *Malum Prohibitum*'. *Dialogue* 55 (2016): 33
Greenawalt, K. 'The Cultural Defense'. *Ohio State Journal of Criminal Law* 6 (2008): 299
Gross, H. *A Theory of Criminal Justice* (Oxford University Press, 1979)
Gross, H. *Crime and Punishment: A Concise Moral Critique* (Oxford University Press, 2012)
Grotius, H. *De Jure Belli ac Pacis* (1625; edited by R Tuck; Liberty Fund, 2005. http://oll.libertyfund.org/title/1947)
Gur-Arye, M. 'A Failure to Prevent Crime—Should it be Criminal?' *Criminal Justice Ethics* 20 (2001): 4
Gur-Arye, M. 'Human Dignity of "Offenders": a Limitation on Substantive Criminal Law'. *Criminal Law and Philosophy* 6 (2012): 187
Gur-Arye, M, and T Weigend. 'Constitutional Review of Criminal Prohibitions Affecting Human Dignity and Liberty: German and Israeli Perspectives'. *Israel Law Review* 44 (2011): 63
Hale, M. *History of the Pleas of the Crown* (1736; reprinted Professional Books, 1971)
Hanna, N. 'Facing the Consequences'. *Criminal Law and Philosophy* 8 (2014): 589
Harcourt, B. 'Reflecting on the Subject: A Critique of the Social Influence Conception of Deterrence, the Broken Windows Theory, and Order-Maintenance Policing New York Style'. *Michigan Law Review* 97 (1998): 291
Harcourt, B. 'The Collapse of the Harm Principle'. *Journal of Criminal Law and Criminology* 90 (1999): 109
Harcourt, B. 'Mill's On Liberty and the Modern "Harm to Others" Principle'. In *Foundational Texts in Modern Criminal Law*, edited by M D Dubber (Oxford University Press, 2014): 163
Harel, A. 'The Triadic Relational Structure of Responsibility: A Defence'. In *Crime, Punishment, and Responsibility*, edited by R Cruft et al (Oxford University Press, 2011): 103
Harel, A. *Why Law Matters* (Oxford University Press, 2014)
Hart, H L A. *Law, Liberty, and Morality* (Stanford University Press, 1963)
Hart, H L A. 'Prolegomenon to the Principles of Punishment'. In Hart, *Punishment and Responsibility* (2nd edn; Oxford University Press, 2008): 1
Hart, H L A. 'Legal Responsibility and Excuses'. In Hart, *Punishment and Responsibility* (2nd edn; Oxford University Press, 2008): 28
Hart, H L A. *The Concept of Law* (3rd edn; Oxford University Press, 2012)
Hassemer, W. 'The Harm Principle and the Protection of "Legal Goods" (Rechtsgüterschutz)'. In *Liberal Criminal Theory: Essays for Andreas von Hirsch*, edited by A P Simester et al (Hart Publishing, 2014): 187
Hawkins, K. *Law as Last Resort: Prosecution Decision-Making in a Regulatory Agency* (Oxford University Press, 2003)
Heawood, J. 'Let's Cheer the Demise of Criminal Libel'. *The Guardian* 27 October 2009. http://www.theguardian.com/commentisfree/libertycentral/2009/oct/27/criminal-libel-free-speech
Hefendehl, R et al (eds). *Die Rechtsgutstheorie: Legitimationsbasis des Strafrechts oder dogmatisches Glasperlenspiel?* (Nomos Verlag, 2003)
Heffernan, W, and J Kleinig (eds). *From Social Justice to Criminal Justice: Poverty and the Administration of Criminal Law* (Oxford University Press, 2000)

Heinze, E. *Hate Speech and Democratic Citizenship* (Oxford University Press, 2016)

Hillsman, S T. 'Fines and Day Fines'. *Crime and Justice: A Review of Research* 12 (1990): 49

Hindelang Criminal Justice Research Center, *Sourcebook of Criminal Justice Statistics*. http://www.albany.edu/sourcebook/tost_5.html

Hirst, M. *Jurisdiction and the Ambit of the Criminal Law* (Oxford University Press, 2003)

HM Revenue and Customs. *Closing in on Tax Evasion* (London: HMRC, 2012). http://www.hmrc.gov.uk/budget-updates/march2012/tax-evasion-report.pdf

HM Revenue and Customs. *HMRC Code of Practice* 9. http://webarchive.nationalarchives.gov.uk/20140206175358/http://www.hmrc.gov.uk/leaflets/cop9-2011.htm

HM Revenue and Customs. *HMRC Criminal Investigation Policy*. http://www.hmrc.gov.uk/prosecutions/crim-inv-policy.htm

Hodgson, J, and V Tadros. 'How to Make a Terrorist out of Nothing'. *Modern Law Review* 72 (2009): 984

Home Office. *Setting the Boundaries: Reforming the Law on Sex Offences* (Home Office, 2000). http://webarchive.nationalarchives.gov.uk/+/http://www.homeoffice.gov.uk/documents/vol1main.pdf

Home Office. *A Guide to Anti-Social Behaviour Orders and Acceptable Behaviour Contracts* (Stationery Office, 2002)

Home Office. *Firearms Security: A Brief Guide*. https://www.gov.uk/government/uploads/system/uploads/attachment_data/file/117794/security_leaflet.pdf

Honderich, T. *Punishment: The Supposed Justifications Revisited* (Pluto Press, 2006)

Hoogenboom, A. 'In Search of a Rationale for the EU Citizenship Jurisprudence'. *Oxford Journal of Legal Studies* 35 (2015): 301

Horder, J. 'Bureaucratic "Criminal" Law: Too Much of a Bad Thing?' In *Criminalization: The Political Morality of the Criminal Law*, edited by R A Duff et al (Oxford University Press, 2014): 101

Horder, J. *Homicide and the Politics of Law Reform* (Oxford University Press, 2012)

Horder, J. *Ashworth's Principles of Criminal Law* (8th edn; Oxford University Press, 2016)

Hörnle, T. 'Hijacked Airplanes: May They be Shot Down?' *New Criminal Law Review* 10 (2007): 582

Hörnle, T. 'Criminalizing Behaviour to Protect Human Dignity'. *Criminal Law and Philosophy* 6 (2012): 307

Hörnle, T. 'Consensual Adult Incest: A Sex Offense?' *New Criminal Law Review* 17 (2014): 76

Hörnle, T. 'Theories of Criminalization'. *Criminal Law and Philosophy* 10 (2016): 301

Hörnle, T, and M Kremnitzer. 'Human Dignity as a Protected Interest in Criminal Law'. *Israel Law Review* 44 (2011): 143

Horton, J. 'In Defense of Associative Political Obligations—I'. *Political Studies* 54 (2006): 427

Horton, J. 'In Defense of Associative Political Obligations—II'. *Political Studies* 55 (2007): 19

Horton, J. *Political Obligation* (2nd edn; Palgrave Macmillan, 2010)

Hoskins, Z. 'Criminalization and the Collateral Consequences of Conviction'. *Criminal Law and Philosophy* (2017); DOI 10.1007/s11572-017-9449-2

Hoskins, Z. *Beyond Punishment? A Normative Account of Collateral Restrictions on Offenders* (Oxford University Press, 2018)

Howard, J. 'Punishment, Socially Deprived Offenders, and Democratic Community'. *Criminal Law and Philosophy* 7 (2013): 121

Hoyle, C, and R Young. 'Restorative Justice: Assessing the Prospects and Pitfalls'. In *The Handbook of the Criminal Justice Process* edited by M McConville and G Wilson (Oxford University Press, 2002)

Hulsman, L. 'Critical Criminology and the Concept of Crime'. *Contemporary Crises* 10 (1986): 63

Hurd, H. 'Why Liberals Should Hate "Hate Crime Legislation"'. *Law and Philosophy* 20 (2001): 215

Hurd, H, and M S Moore. 'Punishing Hatred and Prejudice'. *Stanford Law Review* 56 (2003–4): 1081
Hursthouse, R. *Virtue Ethics* (Oxford University Press, 1999)
Husak, D N. *Philosophy of Criminal Law* (Rowman & Littlefield, 1987)
Husak, D N. *Drugs and Rights* (Cambridge University Press, 1992)
Husak, D N. 'Why Punish the Deserving?' *Noûs* 26 (1992): 447
Husak, D N. 'Guns and Drugs: Case Studies on the Principled Limits of the Criminal Sanction'. *Law and Philosophy* 23 (2004): 437
Husak, D N. 'Applying *Ultima Ratio*: A Skeptical Assessment'. *Ohio State Journal of Criminal Law* 2 (2005): 535
Husak, D N. *Overcriminalization: The Limits of the Criminal Law* (Oxford University Press, 2007)
Husak, D N. 'The Nature and Justifiability of Nonconsummate Offences'. In Husak, *The Philosophy of Criminal Law: Selected Essays* (Oxford University Press, 2010): 117
Husak, D N. 'Strict Liability, Justice, and Proportionality'. In Husak, *The Philosophy of Criminal Law: Selected Essays* (Oxford University Press, 2010): 152
Husak, D N. 'The *De Minimis* "Defense" to Criminal Liability'. In Husak, *The Philosophy of Criminal Law: Selected Essays* (Oxford University Press, 2010): 362
Husak, D N. '*Malum Prohibitum* and Retributivism'. In Husak, *The Philosophy of Criminal Law: Selected Essays* (Oxford University Press, 2010): 410
Husak, D N. 'Polygamy: A Novel Test for a Theory of Criminalization'. In *Criminalization: The Political Morality of the Criminal Law*, edited by R A Duff et al (Oxford University Press, 2014): 213
Husak, D N. 'Social Engineering as an Infringement of the Presumption of Innocence: The Case of Corporate Criminality'. *Criminal Law and Philosophy* 8 (2014): 353
Husak, D N. *Ignorance of Law: A Philosophical Analysis* (Oxford University Press, 2016)
Husak, D N. 'Drug Proscriptions as Proxy Crimes'. *Law and Philosophy* 36 (2017): 345
Illingworth, P M L. 'Patient-Therapist Sex: Criminalization and Its Discontents'. *Journal of Contemporary Health Law & Policy* 11 (1995): 389
Jackson, J. 'Re-Conceptualizing the Right of Silence as an Effective Fair Trial Standard'. *International and Comparative Law Quarterly* 58 (2009): 835
Jacobs, J B. *The Eternal Criminal Record* (Harvard University Press, 2015)
Jakobs, G. 'Kriminalisierung im Vorfeld einer Rechtsgutsverletzung'. *Zeitschrift für die gesamte Strafrechtswissenschaft* 797 (1985): 51
Jakobs, G. 'Selbstverständnis der Strafrechtswissenschaft vor den Herausforderungen der Gegenwart (Kommentar)'. In *Die deutsche Strafrechtswissenschaft vor der Jahrtausendwende*, edited by A Eser et al (C H Beck, 2000): 47
Jakobs, G. 'Bürgerstrafrecht und Feindstrafrecht'. *Höchstrichterliche Rechtsprechung Strafrecht* 5 (2004): 88
Jakobs, G. *Staatliche Strafe: Bedeutung und Zweck* (Ferdinand Schöningh, 2004)
Jareborg, N. 'Criminalization as Last Resort (*Ultima Ratio*)'. *Ohio State Journal of Criminal Law* 2 (2005): 521
Jareborg, N. 'A Comment on Personality and Corporate Crime'. In *Law as Institutional Normative Order*, edited by M Del Mar and Z Bankowski (Ashgate, 2009): 125
Jessberger, F. 'International v. National Prosecution of International Crimes'. In *Oxford Companion to International Criminal Justice*, edited by A Cassese (Oxford University Press, 2009): 208
Johnstone, G. *Restorative Justice: Ideas, Values, Debates* (2nd edn; Routledge, 2011)
Johnstone, G (ed.). *A Restorative Justice Reader* (2nd edn; Routledge, 2013)
Jones, P. 'Group Rights'. In *The Stanford Encyclopedia of Philosophy* (Summer 2016 Edition), edited by E N Zalta. http://plato.stanford.edu/archives/sum2016/entries/rights-group/
Kagan, S. *The Limits of Morality* (Oxford University Press, 1991)

Kahan, D. 'Two Liberal Fallacies in the Hate Crimes Debate'. *Law and Philosophy* 20 (2001): 175

Kauppinen, A. 'Hate and Punishment'. *Journal of Interpersonal Violence* 30 (2015): 1719

Kelly, P (ed.). *Multiculturalism Reconsidered: Culture and Equality and Its Critics* (Polity Press, 2002)

Kelman, M. 'Interpretive Construction in the Substantive Criminal Law'. *Stanford Law Review* 33 (1981): 591

Kelsen, H. *Allgemeine Staatslehre* (1925; translated by A. Wedberg as *General Theory of Law and State*; Harvard University Press, 1945)

Kennedy Institute of Ethics, 'Euthanasia Regulations Around the World'. https://ethicslab.georgetown.edu/euthanasia-map/text.html

Kennedy, C. 'Immanence and Transcendence: History's Role in Normative Legal Theory'. *Jurisprudence* 8 (2017): 557

Kennedy, C. 'Declaring Crimes'. *Oxford Journal of Legal Studies* 37 (2017): 741

Kleinfeld, J. 'Reconstructivism: The Place of Criminal Law in Ethical Life'. *Harvard Law Review* 129 (2016): 1485

Kleinfeld, J. 'Three Principles of Democratic Criminal Justice'. *Northwestern University Law Review* 111 (2017): 1455

Kleingeld, P, and E Brown. 'Cosmopolitanism'. In *The Stanford Encyclopedia of Philosophy* (Fall 2014 Edition), edited by E N Zalta. https://plato.stanford.edu/archives/fall2014/entries/cosmopolitanism/

Kleinig, J. 'Punishment and Moral Seriousness'. *Israel Law Review* 25 (1991): 401

Kleinig, J. *The Ethics of Policing* (Cambridge University Press, 1996)

Kohler-Hausmann, I. 'Managerial Justice and Mass Misdemeanors'. *Stanford Law Review* 66 (2014): 611

Kristol, I. 'Pornography, Obscenity, and the Case for Censorship'. *New York Times Magazine*, 28 March 1971, 1

Kymlicka, W. *Liberalism, Community and Culture* (Oxford University Press, 1989)

Kymlicka, W. *Multicultural Odysseys: Navigating the New International Politics of Diversity* (Oxford University Press, 2007)

Kymlicka, W, et al (eds), *Criminal Law and Cultural Diversity* (Oxford University Press, 2014)

Kyprianou, D. *The Role of the Cyprus Attorney General's Office in Prosecutions: Rhetoric, Ideology and Practice* (Springer, 2009)

Lacey, N. 'In Search of the Responsible Subject: History, Philosophy and the Social Sciences in Criminal Law Theory'. *Modern Law Review* 64 (2001): 350

Lacey, N. 'Historicising Criminalisation: Conceptual and Empirical Issues'. *Modern Law Review* 72 (2009): 936

Lacey, N. 'Community, Culture, and Criminalization'. In *Crime, Punishment, and Responsibility*, edited by R Cruft et al (Oxford University Press, 2011): 292

Lacey, N. *In Search of Criminal Responsibility: Ideas, Interests, and Institutions* (Oxford University Press, 2016)

Lacey, N, and H Pickard. 'From the Consulting Room to the Court Room? Taking the Clinical Model of Responsibility Without Blame into the Legal Realm'. *Oxford Journal of Legal Studies* 33 (2013): 1

Lacey, N, and H Pickard. 'To Blame or to Forgive? Reconciling Punishment and Forgiveness in Criminal Justice'. *Oxford Journal of Legal Studies* 35 (2015): 665

LaFave, W, J Israel, N King, and O Kerr. *Criminal Procedure* (5th edn; West Academic Publishing, 2009)

Lai, H H, and A Amaya (eds). *Law, Virtue and Justice* (Hart Publishing, 2013)

Lamond, G. 'What is a Crime?' *Oxford Journal of Legal Studies* 27 (2007): 609

Langer, M, and D Sklansky (eds). *Prosecutors and Democracy: A Cross-National Study* (Cambridge University Press, 2017)

Lauterwein, C C. *The Limits of Criminal Law* (Ashgate, 2010)
Lavery, J. 'Codification of the Criminal Law: an Attainable Ideal?' *Journal of Criminal Law* 74 (2010): 557
Law Commission. *Rape within Marriage* (No 205, 1992)
Law Commission. *Criminal Liability in Regulatory Contexts* (CP No 195, 2010)
Law Commission. *Simplification of Criminal Law: Public Nuisance and Outraging Public Decency* (No 358, 2015)
Law Commission. *Reforming Misconduct in Public Office* (CP No 229; 2016)
Lee, A Y K. 'Public Wrongs and the Criminal Law'. *Criminal Law and Philosophy* 9 (2015): 155
Lefkowitz, D. 'Should the Law Convict Those Who Act from Conviction? Reflections on a Demands-of-Conscience Criminal Defense'. *Criminal Law and Philosophy* 10 (2016): 657
Lerman, A, and V Weaver. *Arresting Citizenship: The Democratic Consequences of American Crime Control* (University of Chicago Press, 2014)
Lernestedt, C. 'Victim and Society: Sharing Wrongs, but in which Roles?' *Criminal Law and Philosophy* 8 (2014): 187
Lewis, P. 'Informal Legal Change on Assisted Suicide: The Policy for Prosecutors'. *Legal Studies* 31 (2011): 119
Lippke, R L, *The Ethics of Plea Bargaining* (Oxford University Press, 2011)
Loader, I. 'In Search of Civic Policing: Recasting the "Peelian" Principles'. *Criminal Law and Philosophy* 10 (2016): 427
Loader, I, and N Walker. *Civilizing Security* (Cambridge University Press, 2007)
Love, M C, J Roberts, and C M Klingele. *Collateral Consequences of Criminal Convictions: Law, Policy and Practice* (Thomson West, 2016)
Lovett, F. 'Republicanism'. In *The Stanford Encyclopedia of Philosophy* (Spring 2016 Edition), edited by E N Zalta. http://plato.stanford.edu/archives/spr2016/entries/republicanism/
Luban, D. 'A Theory of Crimes against Humanity'. *Yale Journal of International Law* 29 (2004): 85
Luna, E, and M Wade (eds). *The Prosecutor in Transnational Perspective* (Oxford University Press, 2012)
MacCormick, D N. 'Reconstruction after Deconstruction: A Response to CLS'. *Oxford Journal of Legal Studies* 10 (1990): 539
MacCormick, D N. *Institutions of Law: An Essay in Legal Theory* (Oxford University Press, 2007)
MacDonald, S. 'Cyberterrorism and Enemy Criminal Law'. In *Cyberwar: Law and Ethics for Virtual Conflicts*, edited by J D Ohlin et al (Oxford University Press, 2015): 57
MacIntyre, A. *After Virtue: A Study in Moral Theory* (3rd edn; Bloomsbury, 2007)
Mackenzie, M M. *Plato on Punishment* (University of California Press, 1981)
Malatesti, L, and J McMillan (eds). *Responsibility and Psychopathy* (Oxford University Press, 2010)
Markel, D. 'Retributive Justice and the Demands of Democratic Citizenship'. *Virginia Journal of Criminal Law* 1 (2012): 1
Markwick, P. 'Law and Content-Independent Reasons'. *Oxford Journal of Legal Studies* 20 (2000): 579
Marshall, S E. 'The Community of Friends'. In *Communitarianism and Citizenship*, edited by E Christodoulidis (Ashgate, 1998): 208
Marshall, S E, and R A Duff. 'Criminalization and Sharing Wrongs'. *Canadian Journal of Law & Jurisprudence* 11 (1998): 7
Marshall, S E, and R A Duff. 'Public and Private Wrongs'. In *Essays in Criminal Law in Honour of Sir Gerald Gordon*, edited by J Chalmers et al. (Edinburgh University Press, 2010): 70
Marshall, T H. *Citizenship and Social Class* (Pluto Press, 1950; republished in T H Marshall and T Bottomore, *Citizenship and Social Class*, Pluto Press, 1987)

Martí, J L. 'The Republican Democratization of Criminal Law and Justice'. In *Legal Republicanism*, edited by S Besson and J L Martí (Oxford University Press, 2009): 123

Matravers, M. *Justice and Punishment* (Oxford University Press, 2000)

Matravers, M. '"More Than Just Illogical": Truth and Jury Nullification'. In *The Trial on Trial (1): Truth and Due Process*, edited by R A Duff et al (Hart, 2004): 71

McDowell, J. 'Might There Be External Reasons?' In *World, Mind and Ethics: Essays on the Ethical Philosophy of Bernard Williams*, edited by J E J Altham and R Harrison (Cambridge University Press, 1995): 68

Mckenzie, A. '"This Death Some Strong and Stout Hearted Man Doth Choose": The Practice of Peine Fort et Dure in Seventeenth- and Eighteenth-Century England'. *Law and History Review* 23 (2005): 279

McLeod, A. 'The US Criminal–Immigration Convergence and Its Possible Undoing'. *American Criminal Law Review* 49 (2012): 105

Mendlow, G S. 'Why is it Wrong to Punish Thought?' *Yale Law Journal* 127 (2018)

Midgley, M. 'The Objection to Systematic Humbug'. *Philosophy* 53 (1978): 147

Mill, J S. *On Liberty* (Parker, 1859)

Miller, D. *On Nationality* (Oxford University Press, 1995)

Miller, D. *National Responsibility and Global Justice* (Oxford University Press, 2007)

Miller, D. *Strangers in our Midst: The Political Philosophy of Immigration* (Harvard University Press, 2016)

Miller, E J. 'A Fair Cop and a Fair Trial'. In *Obstacles to Fairness in Criminal Proceedings*, edited by J Jackson and S Summers (Hart Publishing, 2018): 239

Mitsilegas, V. *EU Criminal Law After Lisbon: Rights, Trust and the Transformation of Justice in Europe* (Hart Publishing, 2016)

Moore, M S. *Act and Crime: The Philosophy of Action and its Implications for the Criminal Law* (Oxford University Press, 1993)

Moore, M S. *Placing Blame: A Theory of Criminal Law* (Oxford University Press, 1997)

Moore, M S. 'Four Reflections on Law and Morality'. *William & Mary Law Review* 48 (2007): 1523

Moore, M S. 'A Tale of Two Theories'. *Criminal Justice Ethics* 28 (2009): 27

Moore, M S. 'Liberty's Constraints on What Should be Made Criminal'. In *Criminalization: The Political Morality of the Criminal Law*, edited by R A Duff et al (Oxford University Press, 2014): 182

Moore, M S. 'Responses and Appreciations'. In *Legal, Moral and Metaphysical Truths: The Philosophy of Michael S Moore*, edited by K K Ferzan and S J Morse (Oxford University Press, 2016): 343

Morris, C. 'Punishment and Loss of Moral Standing'. *Canadian Journal of Philosophy* 21 (1991): 53

Morris, H. 'Persons and Punishment'. *The Monist* 52 (1968): 475

Mulhall, S, and A Swift. *Liberals and Communitarians* (2nd edn; Blackwell, 1996)

Murphy, J G. 'Marxism and Retribution'. *Philosophy and Public Affairs* 2 (1973): 217

Nagel, T. *The View from Nowhere* (Oxford University Press, 1986)

Nance, D. 'Civility and the Burden of Proof'. *Harvard Journal of Law & Public Policy* 17 (1994): 647

Natapoff, A. 'Misdemeanors'. *Southern California Law Review* 85 (2012): 101

Nathan, C. 'Principles of Policing and Principles of Punishment'. *Legal Theory* 22 (2016): 181

Norrie, A W. '"Simulacra of Morality"? Beyond the Ideal/Actual Antinomies of Criminal Justice'. In *Philosophy and the Criminal Law. Principle and Critique*, edited by R A Duff (Cambridge University Press, 1998): 101

Norrie, A W. *Punishment, Responsibility, and Justice* (Oxford University Press, 2000)

Norrie, A W. *Crime, Reason and History: A Critical Introduction to Criminal Law* (3rd edn; Cambridge University Press, 2014)

Norrie, A W. 'Criminal Law and Ethics: Beyond Normative Assertion and its Critique'. *Modern Law Review* 80 (2017): 955

Oakeshott, M. 'On the Civil Condition'. In Oakeshott, *On Human Conduct* (Oxford University Press, 1975): 108

Oberdiek, J. *Imposing Risk: A Normative Framework* (Oxford University Press, 2017)

Oberdiek, J (ed.). *Philosophical Foundations of the Law of Torts* (Oxford University Press, 2014)

Ogletree, C, and A Sarat (eds). *Life without Parole: America's New Death Penalty?* (New York University Press, 2012)

Ohana, D. 'Trust, Distrust, and Reassurance: Diversion and Preventive Orders through the Prism of *Feindstrafrecht*'. *Modern Law Review* 73 (2010): 721

Ohana, D. 'Günther Jakobs's Feindstrafrecht: A Dispassionate Account'. In *Foundational Texts in Modern Criminal Law*, edited by M D Dubber (Oxford University Press, 2014): 353

Ohana, D. 'Regulatory Offenses and Administrative Sanctions: Between Criminal and Administrative Law'. In *The Oxford Handbook of Criminal Law*, edited by M D Dubber and T Hörnle (Oxford University Press, 2014): 1064

Ormerod, D, and K Laird. *Smith and Hogan's Criminal Law* (14th edn; Oxford University Press, 2015)

O'Sullivan, C. 'Mens Rea, Motive and Assisted Suicide: Does the DPP's Policy Go too Far?' *Legal Studies* 35 (2015): 96

Perrodet, A. 'The Public Prosecutor'. In *European Criminal Procedures*, edited by M Delmas-Marty and J R Spencer (Cambridge University Press, 2002): 415

Persak, N. *Criminalising Harmful Conduct* (Springer, 2007)

Petersen, T. 'New Legal Moralism: Some Strengths and Challenges'. *Criminal Law and Philosophy* 4 (2010): 215

Peterson, J. 'Legal Moralism, Interests and Preferences: Alexander on Aesthetic Regulation'. *Philosophia* 43 (2015): 485

Pettit, P. *Republicanism: A Theory of Freedom and Government* (Oxford University Press, 1997)

Pettit, P. 'Law and Liberty'. In *Legal Republicanism: National and International Perspectives*, edited by S Besson and J L Martí (Oxford University Press, 2009): 39

Pettit, P. *On the People's Terms: A Republican Theory and Model of Democracy* (Cambridge University Press, 2012)

Pettit, P. 'Criminalization in Republican Theory'. In *Criminalization: The Political Morality of the Criminal Law*, edited by R A Duff et al (Oxford University Press, 2014): 132

Pew Trust, *What Crimes are Eligible for Deportation?* http://www.pewtrusts.org/en/research-and-analysis/blogs/stateline/2016/12/21/what-crimes-are-eligible-for-deportation

Picinali, F. 'The Denial of Procedural Safeguards in Trials for Regulatory Offences: A Justification'. *Criminal Law and Philosophy* 11 (2017): 681

Pollock, F. 'The King's Peace'. *Law Quarterly Review* I (1885): 37

Poole, J. *Textbook on Contract Law* (12th edn; Oxford University Press, 2014)

Postema, G. *Bentham and the Common Law Tradition* (Oxford University Press, 1986)

Primoratz, I. 'Terrorism'. In *The Stanford Encyclopedia of Philosophy* (Spring 2015 Edition), edited by E N Zalta. https://plato.stanford.edu/archives/spr2015/entries/terrorism/

Quirk, H. 'The Right of Silence in England and Wales: Sacred Cow, Sacrificial Lamb or Trojan Horse?' In *Obstacles to Fairness in Criminal Proceedings*, edited by J Jackson and S Summers (Hart Publishing, 2018): 75

Quong, J. 'Public Reason'. In *The Stanford Encyclopedia of Philosophy* (Summer 2013 Edition), edited by E N Zalta. https://plato.stanford.edu/archives/sum2013/entries/public-reason/

Rakoff, J S. 'Why Innocent People Plead Guilty'. *The New York Review of Books* 61 (2014) No. 18, 20 November

Ramsay, P. 'Preparation Offences, Security Interests, Political Freedom'. In *The Structures of the Criminal Law*, edited by R A Duff et al (Oxford University Press, 2011): 203

Ramsay, P. *The Insecurity State: Vulnerable Autonomy and the Right to Security in the Criminal Law* (Oxford University Press, 2012)

Ramsay, P. 'A Democratic Theory of Imprisonment'. In *Democratic Theory and Mass Incarceration*, edited by A Dzur et al (Oxford University Press, 2016): 84

Rao, N. 'Three Concepts of Dignity in Constitutional Law'. *Notre Dame Law Review* 86 (2011): 183

Rawls, J. 'The Idea of an Overlapping Consensus'. *Oxford Journal of Legal Studies* 7 (1987): 1

Raz, J. 'Authority, Law, and Morality'. *The Monist* 68 (1985): 295

Raz, J. *The Morality of Freedom* (Oxford University Press, 1986)

Raz, J. 'Can There Be a Theory of Law?' In Raz, *Between Authority and Interpretation: On the Theory of Law and Practical Reason* (Oxford University Press, 2009): 17

Redlich, A D, and A A Özdogru. 'Alford Pleas in the Age of Innocence'. *Behavioral Sciences and the Law* 27 (2009): 467

Redmayne, M. 'Theorizing the Criminal Trial'. *New Criminal Law Review* 12 (2009): 287

Reisig, M D. 'Community and Problem-Oriented Policing'. In *The Oxford Handbook of Crime and Criminal Justice*, edited by M Tonry (Oxford University Press, 2011): 538

Renteln, A D. *The Cultural Defense* (Oxford University Press, 2004)

Renzo, M. 'Associative Responsibilities and Political Obligation'. *Philosophical Quarterly* 62 (2012): 106

Renzo, M. 'Responsibility and Answerability in the Criminal Law'. In *The Constitution of the Criminal Law*, edited by R A Duff et al (Oxford University Press, 2013): 209

Renzo, M (ed.). '"Law, Liberty, and Morality": Fifty Years On'. *Criminal Law and Philosophy* 7 (2013): 417

Reydams, L. *Universal Jurisdiction: International and Municipal Legal Perspectives* (Oxford University Press, 2004)

Richardson, H S. *Democratic Autonomy: Public Reasoning About the Ends of Policy* (Oxford University Press, 2002)

Ridge, M. 'Reasons for Action: Agent-Neutral vs. Agent-Relative'. In *The Stanford Encyclopedia of Philosophy* (Winter 2011 Edition), edited by E N Zalta. https://plato.stanford.edu/archives/win2011/entries/reasons-agent/

Ripstein, A. 'Beyond the Harm Principle'. *Philosophy and Public Affairs* 34 (2006): 215

Ripstein, A. *Force and Freedom: Kant's Legal and Political Philosophy* (Harvard University Press, 2009)

Ristroph, A. 'Conditions of Legitimate Punishment'. In *The New Philosophy of Criminal Law*, edited by C Flanders and Z Hoskins (Rowman & Littlefield, 2016): 79

Roberts, A. 'Dismissals as Justice'. *Alabama Law Review* 69 (2017): 289

Roberts, D. 'Thick Concepts'. *Philosophy Compass* 8 (2013): 677

Roberts, P, and A Zuckerman. *Criminal Evidence* (2nd edn; Oxford University Press, 2010)

Robinson, P H. *Structure and Function in Criminal Law* (Oxford University Press, 1997)

Rogers, J. 'Prosecutorial Policies, Prosecutorial Systems and the Purdy Litigation'. *Criminal Law Review* (2010): 543

Rogers, J. 'The Role of the Public Prosecutor in Applying and Developing the Substantive Criminal Law'. In *The Constitution of the Criminal Law*, edited by R A Duff et al (Oxford University Press, 2013): 53

Rorty, R. *Contingency, Irony, and Solidarity* (Cambridge University Press, 1989)

Ross, J, and S Thaman (eds). *Research Handbook on Comparative Criminal Procedure* (Edward Elgar, 2016)

Rubenstein, A M. 'Verdicts of Conscience: Nullification and the Modern Jury Trial'. *Columbia Law Review* 106 (2006): 959

Sadat, L. 'The International Criminal Court'. In *Cambridge Companion to International Criminal Law*, edited by W A Schabas (Cambridge University Press, 2016): 137

Sanders, A, and R Young. 'The Rule of Law, Due Process and Pre-Trial Criminal Justice'. *Current Legal Problems* 47 (1994): 125

Sanders, A, R Young, and M Burton. *Criminal Justice* (4th edn, Oxford University Press, 2010)

Saunders, H. 'Civil Death—A New Look at an Ancient Doctrine'. *William and Mary Law Review* 11 (1970): 988

Scanlon, T M. *Moral Dimensions: Permissibility, Meaning, Blame* (Harvard University Press, 2008)

Schallmoser, N. 'The European Arrest Warrant and Fundamental Rights'. *European Journal of Crime, Criminal Law and Criminal Justice* 22 (2014): 135

Scheffler, S. 'Is Terrorism Distinctive?' *Journal of Political Philosophy* 14 (2006): 1

Scheid, D. 'Note on Defining "Punishment" '. *Canadian Journal of Philosophy* 10 (1980): 453

Scheid, D. 'Constructing a Theory of Punishment, Desert, and the Distribution of Punishments'. *Canadian Journal of Law and Jurisprudence* 10 (1997): 441

Schonsheck, J. *On Criminalization: An Essay in the Philosophy of the Criminal Law* (Kluwer, 1994)

Schwarzenbach, S A. 'On Civic Friendship'. *Ethics* 107 (1996): 97

Scoccia, D. 'In Defense of "Pure" Legal Moralism'. *Criminal Law and Philosophy* 7 (2013): 513

Sebok, A. 'Normative Theories of Punitive Damages'. In *Philosophical Foundations of the Law of Torts*, edited by J Oberdiek (Oxford University Press, 2014): 312

Seglow, J. *Defending Associative Obligations* (Routledge, 2013)

Serious Fraud Office. *Deferred Prosecution Agreements*. https://www.sfo.gov.uk/publications/guidance-policy-and-protocols/deferred-prosecution-agreements/

Sharpe, A. 'Criminalising Sexual Intimacy: Transgender Defendants and the Legal Construction of Non-Consent'. *Criminal Law Review* (2014): 207

Sharpe, A. 'There's More than Meets the Eye in the Case of Gayle Newland'. *New Statesman* 18 September 2015. https://www.newstatesman.com/politics/feminism/2015/09/theres-more-meets-eye-case-gayle-newland

Sher, G. *Beyond Neutrality* (Cambridge University Press, 1997)

Shiner, R A, and H Ho. 'Deferred Prosecution Agreements and the Presumption of Innocence'. *Criminal Law and Philosophy* (2018) https://doi-org.ezproxy.stir.ac.uk/10.1007/s11572-018-9454-0

Simester, A P. 'Can Negligence be Culpable?' In *Oxford Essays in Jurisprudence*, 4th Series, edited by J Horder (Oxford University Press, 2000): 85

Simester, A P. 'Is Strict Liability Always Wrong?' In *Appraising Strict Liability*, edited by A P Simester (Oxford University Press, 2005): 21

Simester, A P. 'Prophylactic Crimes'. In *Seeking Security: Pre-Empting the Commission of Criminal Harms*, edited by G R Sullivan and I H Dennis (Hart Publishing, 2012): 59

Simester, A P, J R Spencer, F Stark, G R Sullivan, and G J Virgo. *Simester and Sullivan's Criminal Law: Theory and Doctrine* (6th edn; Hart Publishing, 2016)

Simester, A P, and G R Sullivan. 'On the Nature and Rationale of Property Offences'. In *Defining Crimes: Essays on the Special Part of the Criminal Law*, edited by R A Duff and S P Green (Oxford University Press, 2005): 168

Simester, A P, and A von Hirsch. *Crimes, Harms and Wrongs: On the Principles of Criminalization* (Hart Publishing, 2011)

Simon, J. *Governing Through Crime: How the War on Crime Transformed American Democracy and Created a Culture of Fear* (Oxford University Press, 2007)

Singer, R. 'On Classism and Dissonance in the Criminal Law: A Reply to Professor Dan-Cohen'. *Journal of Criminal Law and Criminology* 77 (1986): 69

Sklansky, D. 'Crime, Immigration and Ad Hoc Instrumentalism'. *New Criminal Law Review* 15 (2012): 157

Smith, A T H. 'Codification of the Criminal Law—Part 1: The Case for a Code'. *Criminal Law Review* (1986): 285

Snyder, T. *On Tyranny: Twenty Lessons from the Twentieth Century* (Crown/Archetype, 2017)

Spencer, J R. 'The Sexual Offences Act 2003: (2) Child and Family Offences'. *Criminal Law Review* (2004): 247

Spencer, J R. 'Civil Liability for Crimes'. In *Unravelling Tort and Crime*, edited by M Dyson (Cambridge University Press, 2014): 304

Spena, A. 'Iniuria Migrandi: Criminalization of Immigrants and the Basic Principles of the Criminal Law'. *Criminal Law and Philosophy* 8 (2014): 635

Spena, A. 'A Just Criminalization of Irregular Immigration: Is It Possible?' *Criminal Law and Philosophy* 11 (2017): 351

Sprack, J. *A Practical Approach to Criminal Procedure* (15th edn; Oxford University Press, 2015)

Stanton-Ife, J. 'The Limits of Law'. In *The Stanford Encyclopedia of Philosophy* (Winter 2014 Edition), edited by E N Zalta. http://plato.stanford.edu/archives/win2014/entries/law-limits/

Stanton-Ife, J. 'What is the Harm Principle For?' *Criminal Law and Philosophy* 10 (2016): 329

Steiker, C. 'Punishment and Procedure: Punishment Theory and the Criminal-Civil Procedural Divide'. *Georgetown Law Journal* 85 (1997): 775

Stephen, J F. *Liberty, Equality, Fraternity* (2nd edn; Elder and Co., 1874); http://oll.libertyfund.org/titles/stephen-liberty-equality-fraternity-1874-ed

Stevens, R. 'Private Rights and Public Wrongs'. In *Unravelling Tort and Crime*, edited by M Dyson (Cambridge University Press, 2014): 111

Stewart, H. 'The Limits of the Harm Principle'. *Criminal Law and Philosophy* 4 (2010): 17

Stumpf, J. 'The Crimmigration Crisis: Immigrants, Crime, and Sovereign Power'. *American University Law Review* 56 (2006): 367

Stuntz, W. 'The Pathological Politics of Criminal Law'. *Michigan Law Review* 100 (2001): 505

Stuntz, W. *The Collapse of American Criminal Justice* (Belknap Press, 2011)

Summers, S. *Fair Trials: The European Criminal Procedural Tradition and the European Court of Human Rights* (Hart Publishing, 2007)

Sweeney, J. 'Undead Statutes: The Rise, Fall, and Continuing Use of Adultery and Fornication Criminal Laws'. *Loyola University Chicago Law Journal* 46 (2014): 127

Sypnowich, C. 'The Civility of Law: Between Public and Private'. In *Public and Private: Legal, Political and Philosophical Perspectives*, edited by M d'Entrèves and U Vogel (Routledge, 2001): 84

Szczucki, K. *Proconstitutional Interpretation of Criminal Law* (trans. P Sitnik; Lexington Books, 2016; first published in Polish in 2015 as *Wykladnia prokonstytucyjna prawa karnego*)

Tadros, V. 'The Distinctiveness of Domestic Abuse: A Freedom Based Account'. In *Defining Crimes*, edited by R A Duff and S P Green (Oxford University Press, 2005): 119

Tadros, V. 'Rape Without Consent'. *Oxford Journal of Legal Studies* 26 (2006): 515

Tadros, V. 'Rethinking the Presumption of Innocence'. *Criminal Law and Philosophy* 1 (2007): 193

Tadros, V. 'Criminalization and Regulation'. In *The Boundaries of the Criminal Law*, edited by R A Duff et al (Oxford University Press, 2010): 163

Tadros, V. *The Ends of Harm: The Moral Foundations of Criminal Law* (Oxford University Press, 2011)

Tadros, V. 'Harm, Sovereignty, and Prohibition'. *Legal Theory* 17 (2011): 35

Tadros, V. 'Wrongness and Criminalization'. In *Routledge Companion to Philosophy of Law*, edited by A Marmor (Routledge, 2012): 157

Tadros, V. *Wrongs and Crimes* (Oxford University Press, 2016)

Tadros, V (ed.). Symposium on Political Philosophy and Criminal Justice. *Criminal Law and Philosophy* 7 (2013): 179

Taylor, C. *Moralism: A Study of a Vice* (Routledge, 2011)

Taylor, C M. 'Cross-Purposes: The Liberal-Communitarian Debate'. In *Liberalism and the Moral Life*, edited by N Rosenblum (Harvard University Press, 1989): 159

Taylor, S S. *Marijuana Policy and Presidential Leadership: How to Avoid a Federal-State Train Wreck* (Brookings Institution, 2013)

Thaysen, J D. 'Infidelity and the Possibility of a Liberal Legal Moralism'. *Criminal Law and Philosophy* 11 (2017): 273

Thorburn, M. 'Justification, Powers and Authority'. *Yale Law Journal* 117 (2008): 1070

Thorburn, M. 'Criminal Law as Public Law'. In *Philosophical Foundations of Criminal Law*, edited by R A Duff and S P Green (Oxford University Press, 2010): 21

Thorburn, M. 'Constitutionalism and the Limits of the Criminal Law'. In *The Structures of the Criminal Law*, edited by R A Duff et al (Oxford University Press, 2011): 85

Thorburn, M. 'Punishment and Public Authority'. In *Criminal Law and the Authority of the State*, edited by A du Bois-Pedain et al (Hart Publishing, 2017): 7

Tomlin, P. 'Retributivists! The Harm Principle is Not for You!'. *Ethics* 124 (2014): 272

Tonry, M (ed.). *Prosecutors and Politics: A Comparative Perspective* (*Crime and Justice: A Review of Research*, vol. 41; University of Chicago Press, 2012)

Tripkovic, M. *Punishment and Citizenship: A Theory of Criminal Disenfranchisement* (Oxford University Press, 2018)

Tuccille, J D. 'Rebellious Jurors Make the World a Better Place'. *Reason* 12 December 2017; http://reason.com/archives/2017/12/12/rebellious-jurors-make-the-world-a-bette

Tyler, T. *Why People Obey the Law* (revised edn; Princeton University Press, 2006)

Ulväng, M. 'Criminal Law and Civil Peace'. In *Law as Institutional Normative Order*, edited by M Del Mar and Z Bankowski (Ashgate, 2009): 133

Valentine, M B. 'Defense Categories and the (Category-Defying) De Minimis Defense'. *Criminal Law and Philosophy* 11 (2017): 545

van de Bunt, H, and J-L van Gelder. 'The Dutch Prosecution Service'. *Crime and Justice: A Review of Research* 41 (2012): 117

von Hirsch, A. *Censure and Sanctions* (Oxford University Press, 1993)

von Hirsch, A, and A J Ashworth, *Proportionate Sentencing* (Oxford University Press, 2005)

von Hirsch, A, D Garland, and A Wakefield (eds). *Ethical and Social Perspectives on Situational Crime Prevention* (Hart Publishing, 2000)

von Hirsch, A, J Roberts, A E Bottoms, K Roach, and M Schiff (eds). *Restorative Justice and Criminal Justice: Competing or Reconcilable Paradigms?* (Hart Publishing, 2003)

von Hirsch, A, and A P Simester (eds). *Incivilities: Regulating Offensive Behaviour* (Hart Publishing, 2006)

von Hirsch, A, and M Wasik. 'Civil Disqualifications Attending Conviction'. *Cambridge Law Journal* 56 (1997): 599

Waldron, J. *Law and Disagreement* (Oxford University Press, 1999)

Waldron, J. *The Harm in Hate Speech* (Harvard University Press, 2012)

Waldron, J. *Dignity, Rank, and Rights* (Oxford University Press, 2015)

Walen, A. 'Criminalizing Statements Of Terrorist Intent: How To Understand The Law Governing Terrorist Threats, and Why it Should be Used Instead of Long-Term Preventive Detention'. *Journal of Criminal Law & Criminology* 101 (2011): 803

Walen, A. 'Constitutional Rights For Nonresident Aliens: A Doctrinal and Normative Argument'. *Drexel Law Review* 8 (2015): 53

Walgrave, L. 'Imposing Restoration Instead of Inflicting Pain'. In *Restorative Justice and Criminal Justice: Competing or Reconcilable Paradigms?*, edited by A von Hirsch et al (Hart Publishing, 2003): 61

Weigend, T. 'The Legal and Practical Problems Posed by the Difference between Criminal Law and Administrative Penal Law'. *Revue Internationale de Droit Pénal* 59 (1988): 67

Wellman, C. 'Piercing Sovereignty'. In *Philosophical Foundations of Criminal Law*, edited by R A Duff and S P Green (Oxford University Press, 2010): 461

Wellman, C. 'The Rights Forfeiture Theory of Punishment'. *Ethics* 122 (2012): 371

Wellman, C. *Rights Forfeiture and Punishment* (Oxford University Press, 2017)

Wells, C. *Corporations and Criminal Responsibility* (2nd edn; Oxford University Press, 2001)
Wells, C, and O Quick. *Lacey, Wells and Quick Reconstructing Criminal Law: Text and Materials* (4th edn; Cambridge University Press, 2010)
Williams, B. 'Ethical Consistency'. In Williams, *Problems of the Self* (Cambridge University Press, 1973): 166
Williams, B. 'Utilitarianism and Moral Self-Indulgence'. In Williams, *Moral Luck* (Cambridge University Press, 1981): 40
Williams, B. 'Internal and External Reasons'. In Williams, *Moral Luck* (Cambridge University Press, 1981): 101
Williams, B. *Ethics and the Limits of Philosophy* (Fontana, 1985)
Williams, B. *Descartes: The Project of Pure Enquiry* (Routledge, 2005)
Williams, G. 'The Definition of Crime'. *Current Legal Problems* 8 (1955): 107
Wilson, J Q, and G L Kellin. 'Broken Windows: The Police and Neighborhood Safety'. *Atlantic Monthly* 249(3) (March 1982): 29
Winch, P. 'Ethical Reward and Punishment'. In Winch, *Ethics and Action* (Routledge, 1972): 210
Wittgenstein, L. *Philosophical Investigations* (trans. G E M Anscombe; Blackwell, 1953)
Wolfenden, J. *Report of the Committee on Homosexual Offences and Prostitution* (Cmnd 247; HMSO, 1957)
Wolff, R P. *In Defense of Anarchism* (Harper & Row, 1970)
Yaffe, G. *Attempts in the Philosophy of Action and the Criminal Law* (Oxford University Press, 2010)
Yankah, E N. 'Crime, Freedom and Civic Bonds: Arthur Ripstein's Force and Freedom: Kant's Legal and Political Philosophy'. *Criminal Law and Philosophy* 6 (2012) 255
Yankah, E N. 'Legal Vices and Civic Virtue: Vice Crimes, Republicanism and the Corruption of Lawfulness'. *Criminal Law and Philosophy* 7 (2013): 61
Yankah, E N. 'Republican Responsibility in Criminal Law'. *Criminal Law and Philosophy* 9 (2015): 457
Zedner, L. *Criminal Justice* (Oxford University Press, 2004)
Zedner, L. 'Securing Liberty in the Face of Terror: Reflections from Criminal Justice'. *Journal of Law and Society* 32 (2005): 507
Zedner, L. *Security* (Routledge, 2009)
Zedner, L. 'Security, the State, and the Citizen: The Changing Architecture of Crime Control'. *New Criminal Law Review* 13 (2010): 379
Zedner, L. 'Is the Criminal Law only for Citizens? A Problem at the Borders of Punishment'. In *The Borders of Punishment: Migration, Citizenship, and Social Exclusion*, edited by K F Aas and M Bosworth (Oxford University Press, 2013): 40
Zimmerman, M. *The Immorality of Punishment* (Broadview Press, 2011)
Zipursky, B. 'Rights, Wrongs, and Recourse in the Law of Torts'. *Vanderbilt Law Review* 51 (1998): 1

Index

NB Bare bibliographical references are not indexed.

The manufacturer's authorised representative in the EU for product safety is Oxford University Press España S.A. of el Parque Empresarial San Fernando de Henares, Avenida de Castilla, 2 – 28830 Madrid (www.oup.es/en or product.safety@oup.com). OUP España S.A. also acts as importer into Spain of products made by the manufacturer.

www.ingramcontent.com/pod-product-compliance
Lightning Source LLC
LaVergne TN
LVHW011906200926
848484LV00002B/549
9780199570195